The Cambridge History of Modern France

1   Restoration and Reaction, 1815–1848

Restoration and Reaction, 1815–1848

ANDRE JARDIN

ANDRE-JEAN TUDESQ

Translated by
ELBORG FORSTER

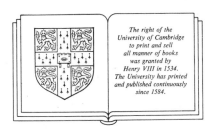

The right of the
University of Cambridge
to print and sell
all manner of books
was granted by
Henry VIII in 1534.
The University has printed
and published continuously
since 1584.

CAMBRIDGE UNIVERSITY PRESS

Cambridge
London   New York   New Rochelle   Melbourne   Sydney

EDITIONS DE
LA MAISON DES SCIENCES DE L'HOMME

Paris

Published by the Press Syndicate of the University of Cambridge
The Pitt Building, Trumpington Street, Cambridge CB2 1RP
32 East 57th Street, New York, NY 10022, USA
296 Beaconsfield Parade, Middle Park, Melbourne 3206, Australia
and Editions de la Maison des Sciences de l'Homme
54 Boulevard Raspail, 75270 Paris Cedex 06

Originally published in French as *La France des Notables*
by Editions du Seuil, Paris 1973 and © Editions du Seuil, 1973
First published in English by Editions de la Maison des Sciences de
l'Homme and Cambridge University Press 1983 as *Restoration and
Reaction, 1815–1848*
English translation © Maison des Sciences de l'Homme and
Cambridge University Press 1983

Printed in Great Britain by the University Press, Cambridge

Library of Congress catalogue card number: 83-5340

British Library Cataloguing in Publication Data

Jardin, André
Restoration and reaction, 1815–1848.—(Cambridge
history of modern France; 1)
1. France—History—Restoration, 1815–1830
2. France—History—Louis Philip, 1830–1848
I. Title   II. Tudesq, André-Jean
III. La France des notables (1815–1848). *English* 944.06   DC256

ISBN 0 521 25241 5

ISBN 2 7351 00383 (France only)

Contents

Chronology

1814

12 March	Royalist uprising of Bordeaux
28 March	The Regency council leaves Paris
31 March	The allied troops enter Paris
1 April	Formation of a provisional government headed by Talleyrand
3 April	End of the Emperor's rule proclaimed by the Senate
6 April	Napoleon abdicates at Fontainebleau; a senatorial Constitution is passed
10 April	Battle of Toulouse
12 April	The comte d'Artois enters Paris
23 April	Armistice is signed
2 May	Proclamation of Saint-Ouen
3 May	Louis XVIII enters Paris
30 May	First Treaty of Paris
4 June	Proclamation of the Charter
5 June	The allied sovereigns leave Paris
30 September	First conversations between Talleyrand and ministers of the allied powers at Vienna

1815

3 January	Talleyrand signs a secret treaty of alliance with England and Austria
1 March	Napoleon lands at Golfe-Juan
20 March	Napoleon arrives at the Tuileries
22 March	Promulgation of the Additional Act to the constitutions of the Empire
30 March	Louis XVIII settles at Ghent
8 and 22 May	Elections to the Chamber of Representatives
9 June	Final act of the Congress of Vienna
18 June	Waterloo
22 June	Second abdication of the Emperor
25–6 June	Royalist disturbances at Marseille
7 July	Formation of Talleyrand–Fouché government
8 July	Return of the king to Paris
15 July	Napoleon leaves France aboard the *Bellerophon*
24 July	Banishment of the accomplices of the Hundred Days
14–22 August	Elections. The 'Incredible Chamber'

24 *September*	Richelieu government
20 *November*	Second Treaty of Paris. Renewal of the alliance of Chaumont
8 *December*	Execution of Ney
27 *December*	Law setting up special courts

1816
12 *January*	Amnesty law excepting 'relapsed' regicides
4 *May*	Attempted uprising at Grenoble
5 *September*	Dissolution of the Incredible Chamber
25 *October*	Election victory of the constitutional monarchists

1817
3–10 *February*	Laîné electoral law
8 *February*	Rural unrest in Brie and Champagne
15 *February*	Conspiracy at Lyon
20 *September*	Elections in which the success of the left permits the formation of an independent party in the Chamber

1818
10 *March*	Gouvion-Saint-Cyr law on the recruitment of the army
September–November	Congress of Aix-la-Chapelle. Occupation of France ended; France readmitted to concert of Europe
30 *November*	Departure of the occupation troops
29 *December*	Formation of the Dessolles–Decazes government

1819
5 *March*	Appointment of a group of Peers who assure a government majority in the Upper House
17–26 *May*	De Serre laws on the press
11 *September*	Election victory of the left
20 *November*	Decazes government

1820
13 *February*	Assassination of the duc de Berry
20 *February*	Second Richelieu government
28 *March*	Law on individual liberty
31 *March*	Law on the press
3–5 *June*	Riots in Paris
12 *June*	Law of the double vote
19 *August*	Foiled insurrections at Paris, Lyon, Colmar
29 *September*	Birth of the duc de Bordeaux
October–December	Congress of Troppau
4 *and* 13 *November*	Election victories for the right

1821
January–February	Congress of Laybach
27 *February*	Ordinance on secondary education curbing the privilege of the University
November–December	First conspiracies of the Carbonari movement (Saumur, Colmar)
15 *December*	Villèle government

1822

24 February	Conspiracy of General Berton
18 and 25 March	Laws on the press
15 June	Conspiracy of Colonel Caron
21 September	Execution of the four sergeants of La Rochelle
19 November	Protocol of the Congress of Verona establishing the conditions in which the powers may intervene in Spain
28 December	Chateaubriand becomes Foreign Minister

1823

28 January	Speech from the throne in which Louis XVIII announces the imminence of war with Spain
4 March	Manuel is ejected from the Chamber
7 April	French troops cross the Bidassoa
28 September	Conquest of fort Trocadero
23 December	Appointment of group of Peers favourable to the right
24 December	Dissolution of the Chamber

1824

26 February–6 March	Election of new Chamber. The 'regained' Chamber
3 June	Withdrawal of the plan for the conversion of government bonds in the face of the hostility of the House of Peers
16 September	Death of Louis XVIII

1825

20 April	Law on sacrilege
27 April	Law on the indemnity for émigrés
1 May	Law on the voluntary conversion of government bonds
24 May	Law on the female congregations
29 May	Solemn coronation of Charles X

1826

7 April	Rejection of the 'right of the eldest' bill

1827

17 April	Failure of a bill for a new press law
29 April	Dissolution of the Parisian National Guard
20 October	Battle of Navarino
6 November	Dissolution of the Chamber
17 and 24 November	Elections yielding a minority for Villèle

1828

5 January	Martignac government
16 June	Ordinances on 'ecclesiastical' schools and seminaries, directed against the Jesuits
18 July	Law on the press
September	French expedition to Morea

1829

8 April	Failure of the bill for administrative reform
8 August	Polignac government
14 September	Treaty of Andrinople

1830

18 March	Address of the 221
16 May	Dissolution of the Chamber
14 June	Landing of the French expeditionary corps at Sidi-Ferruch, Algeria
23 June and 3 July	Legislative elections
5 July	Fall of Algiers
25 July	The four ordinances
27–28–29 July	The Three Glorious Days
31 July	The duc d'Orléans accepts the lieutenant-generalship of the realm. He calls on the Hôtel de Ville
2 August	Abdication of Charles X in favour of his grandson, the duc de Bordeaux
3 August	Meeting of the Chambers
9 August	The duc d'Orléans swears to uphold the revised Charter and takes the title King of the French
11 August	Formation of government combining men of both the resistance and the Movement
25 August	Uprising of Belgium
2 November	Laffitte government
4 November	Opening of the London Conference

1831

20 January	Protocol of London: neutrality of Belgium
2 February	Election of the duc de Nemours as king of the Belgians; he rejects the offer
14 February	Riots at Saint-Germain-l'Auxerrois
13 March	Casimir Périer government
21 March	Law on the municipal councils
22 March	Law on the National Guard
19 April	Law on the election of deputies
5 July	Elections of the Chamber of Deputies
August	French intervention in Belgium after its invasion by the army of the king of the Netherlands
20–2 November	Revolt of the Lyon silk-workers
29 December	Abolition of the hereditary peerage

1832

23 February	Occupation of Ancona by the French
April–May	Legitimist agitation in favour of the duchesse de Berry
16 May	Casimir Périer dies of cholera
5–6 June	Republican riots in Paris
27–8 August	Trial of the Saint-Simonians
3 October	Inauguration of the Rhône–Rhine canal
12 October	Formation of the Soult government, with Broglie, Guizot, and Thiers
22 December	Antwerp falls to the French

1833

March	Occupation of Oran and Mostaganem
21 June	Law on the election of the general councillors
28 June	Guizot law on public education
9 July	Law on expropriation for public purposes

1834

February	Strike of the mutualist workers of Lyon
9–12 April	Republican agitation at Lyon
13 April	Republican riot in Paris
22 April, 18 August	Quadruple alliance among England, Spain, France, and Portugal
21 June	Election of the Chamber of Deputies
July–November	Formation of three different governments

1835

5 May	Beginning of the trial of the accused republican leaders of the April riots
28 June	Abd-el-Kader successfully attacks the French troops in the gorge of Macta
28 July	Fieschi's attempt on the life of **Louis-Philippe**
September	Laws facilitating the repression of the republican opposition

1836

25 January	Clauzel dislodges Abd-el-Kader from the gorges of the Tafna
22 February–September	Thiers government
6 September	Molé government
30 October	Attempted coup of Louis-Napoleon Bonaparte at Strasbourg
6 November	Death of Charles X at Goritz

1837

29 May	Marriage of the duc d'Orléans
30 May	Treaty of Tafna with Abd-el-Kader
16 October	Conquest of Constantinople by General Vallée
November	General elections

1838

February	A project for the construction of railways fails in parliament
November	A French squadron is sent to Mexico
December	A coalition against Molé takes shape

1839

2 March	Elections
8 March	The Molé government resigns; prolonged government crisis
12 May	Insurrection of the *Société des saisons*. Formation of the Soult government

1840

20 February	The rejection of an endowment for the duc de Nemours provokes a government crisis
1 March	Formation of the Thiers government
12 May	Decision to appropriate funds for the return of Napoleon's ashes from Sainte-Hélène

16 May	Speech by François Arago in favour of an electoral reform
16 June	Law guaranteeing the interest payments of the railway companies
15 July	Treaty of London (concluded without France), concerning the question of Egypt
6 August	Attempted coup by Louis-Napoleon Bonaparte at Boulogne
1–3 September	Striking workers assemble in Paris
15 October	Attempt on the king's life by Darmès
29 October	Formation of the Soult–Guizot government
15 December	Ceremonies in connection with the transfer of Napoleon's ashes to the Invalides

1841

22 March	Law limiting child labour in industry
3 May	Law on expropriation for public purposes
13 July	Convention of the Straits and settlement of the Egyptian question
25 July	Election of Ledru-Rollin in Sarthe

1842

11 June	Law concerning the railways
9 July	General elections
13 July	Accidental death of the duc d'Orléans

1843

18 May	Capture of Abd-el-Kader's *smala*
2 July	Sugar law: equal taxation for cane-sugar from the West Indies and beet-sugar from the metropolis
26 August	Beginning of the newspaper *La Réforme*
2 September	Queen Victoria visits France; meeting at Eu

1844

1 August	Bombardment of Tangiers by the squadron of Prince de Joinville
14 August	Victory over the Moroccans at Isly by Bugeaud

1845

27 January	The Chamber votes for an indemnity for Pritchard
February	Villemain replaced by Salvandy as Minister of Public Education
July	Dispersal of the Jesuits throughout France by agreement between the pope and the French government

1846

August	Elections
August–October	Affair of the Spanish marriages

1847

24 January	The Banque de France raises its discount rate
28 January	Law to permit grain imports. Peasant riots at Buzançais
March	Rejection of bills for electoral and parliamentary reforms
May	Teste-Cubières case
5 June	Marshal Bugeaud leaves the governorship of Algeria
9 July	First reformist banquet in Paris
18 August	The duc de Choiseul-Praslin assassinates his wife
23 December	Surrender of Abd-el-Kader
28 December	Speech from the throne indirectly criticising the banquet campaign

1848

14 January	The government prohibits the holding of a reformist banquet in the XIIe *arrondissement* of Paris
21 February	The radicals decide to hold the banquet in defiance of the prohibition; the deputies of the dynastic left succeed in having it moved to a later date
22 February	Popular demonstrations in Paris
23 February	Guizot resigns; shooting incident on the boulevard des Capucins
24 February	Abdication of Louis-Philippe

Preface

After 1815 the life of the French people did not proceed at a uniform pace set by Paris. Slow-moving communications between geographical regions accounted for the persistence of provincial characteristics, which re-appeared all the more forcefully with the Bourbons as they rested on historical traditions at a time when tradition was emphasised as the fore-most monarchical value. The space containing the daily lives of most French people remained very limited and, due to the rather slow and uneven development of communications under the monarchy of limited suffrage (*monarchie censitaire*), its extension was on a regional rather than a national scale.

Historians of the Restoration and the July Monarchy have been pri-marily interested in the activities of the parliament and in the ideological conflicts among the parties; in so doing they placed the State and the government at the very centre of the life of the nation. A variety of reasons accounts for this 'Parisian' point of view: the apparent tranquillity of the provinces, the belief that the country had been rapidly unified through the centralisation of the Napoleonic era, and the anticipation of the homo-genising effects of industrial development, which was assumed to have established a 'bourgeois' class, although so far the sociological analysis of this class remains rather summary.

The provinces had ceased to be administrative entities, but the major cities – not yet as disproportionate in relation to Paris as they were to become – were still the vital centres of the regions under their influence.

Within this diversity the monarchy of limited suffrage appears as a period of both stability and innovation. By comparison with the preceding era, it was indeed a period of stability, favoured by continued peace and the persistence of a social structure that curbed social mobility in response to the leadership of the notables. It was also a stable period because, des-pite the continued or even increased practice of centralisation, it was characterised by a lack of autonomy of the State in relation to the ruling classes. Yet it was also a period of innovation that was reflected in many different areas: in the intellectual ferment that produced liberal or

xvii

traditionalist political theories during the Restoration and, later, various forms of utopian socialism as well as new forms of literary and artistic expression in the different varieties of Romanticism; in the laying of new foundations for political life, produced not so much by the Charter of 1814 as by the manner in which it was implemented, since it led after 1830 to the establishment of the major features of the parliamentary regime; in the formation and development of the political press and the power of public opinion or of a new mentality (at least among a numerically small but active minority), developments that were both cause and effect of economic transformations brought about by the take-off of the 'industrial revolution', although this term is rather inappropriate to the French situation at that time; and finally, in the gap that was opening between the bourgeoisie and the working class, even though these two groups were as yet minorities in a predominantly rural France.

This confrontation between stability and innovation (more complex than the dualism of resistance versus change and movement, or conservation versus progress) can be observed in the evolution of France as a whole, but especially within a more regional framework. The reason is, first of all, that in France a number of regional economies, not all of them evolving at the same pace, existed side by side, and that partial transformations only served to accentuate regional inequalities, given the State's reluctance to interfere, precisely in the name of the underlying liberal principles. This double consideration accounts for the importance we attribute to the life of the French regions; many recent studies make it possible to trace a history of the French regions rather than a history conceived only in terms of Paris. That is why we decided to present, after part 1, written from a national point of view, a part 2 devoted to a study of provincial France in the period that Ernest Labrousse has called 'the end of the economic Ancien Regime'.

The departments of France and their capitals in 1814

PART 1

Historical overview

The establishment of the monarchy
of limited suffrage

How the Bourbons recovered their throne

Public opinion at the fall of the Empire

On 31 March 1814 the allied troops entered Paris; on 6 April Napoleon abdicated at Fontainebleau, and on the same day the conservative Senate appealed to the Bourbons to return.

The rapidity with which the Napoleonic edifice collapsed was due to the concentric march of the coalition armies toward the capital. A strategy was devised on the spur of the moment: General '*Forward!*', the spirited Blücher, had been able to persuade Alexander of Russia, the king of Prussia, and Generalissimo Schwarzenberg to go along, albeit under protest, while the emperor of Austria stayed behind at Langres with the two outstanding diplomats of the coalition, Metternich and Castlereagh. Yet the czar's presence in Paris placed the decision about France's destiny into his hands. He wanted to respect the country's wishes, partly in keeping with his liberal attitudes and partly because he was already planning for a possible Franco-Russian accord. Intrigue prompted him to restore the Bourbons to the throne, but this intrigue responded, at least in part, to a current of opinion that had prepared a country thrown into disarray by the power vacuum and the invasion for their return.

It is not easy, of course, to assess public opinion in a country long accustomed to passive obedience. Yet for three years already, lassitude and disobedience had lamed the Napoleonic regime: military defeats, the increasing burden of conscription and indirect taxes, the conflict with the Church, and the aftermath of the grain shortage of 1811 had led to this disaffection. In 1814 the special commissioners dispatched to the provinces in order to galvanise the country proved pitifully ineffectual by comparison with their models of 1793.

It is true that in eastern France a kind of patriotic frenzy aroused a part of the population against the Prussians or the Cossacks. The czar admitted that guerilla warfare in the Vosges Mountains had cost him 3,000 men; irregular troops harassed convoys and stragglers in Lorraine, Champagne, and Burgundy. But in the Aquitaine Basin Wellington's English troops, who had driven Soult back to Toulouse, were well received. Some of the regions that had not been invaded did not wait for the fall of the regime to express their hostility to it: in Provence rioting against tax-collectors broke out; masses of people gathered along the roads to acclaim Pius VII, who was returning to the Papal States; and in the Vendée the *chouan* leaders openly prepared an insurrection. The western and southern provinces' apparent submission to the Napoleonic regime was in fact a cover for their latent royalism. The vast majority of the French people no doubt did not know who the members of the Bourbon family were at that time. But the different provinces held different images of the society that had been shaken to its foundations twenty years earlier, and the memory of the Ancien Regime was not always detested.

In Paris itself, it was the 'rabble' that remained faithful to the Emperor, and the prefect of police, Pasquier, had been very careful not to call on them for help in defending the city. By contrast, the bourgeoisie – from artisans and hucksters to bankers and great landowners – that served in the legions of the National Guard had greeted the Allies with satisfaction as the token of an early peace. And if the National Guard limited its activities to the defence of persons and property against all social sub-version and failed to chime in with the turbulent demonstrations of some of the impassioned royalists, the municipal council and the general council, as well as the prefects, Pasquier and Chabrol, both members of old noble families, rallied to the Bourbons at the request of a quickly organised royalist committee.

Indeed, the crisis brought to light not only disparities among the various provinces but also the ambiguity of the Napoleonic regime, which had been both a military dictatorship and a social hierarchy that entrusted the nation's leadership to the notables. Even in the army, where the rank and file of the soldiers remained faithful to the 'little short-haired one', high-ranking officers, the marshals and generals who had been showered with wealth, honours, and patents of nobility, abandoned the defeated emperor not only in order to save their property, but also in an attempt to preserve an army.

These great military notables thus fell in with the reaction of the civilian notables. In his efforts to bring about a national reconciliation, to ensure order in the country and the effective working of a centralised regime, Napoleon had made extensive use of the old aristocracy as well as of the parvenus of the Revolution. Generals or prefects issued from the old nobility had in fact served him faithfully as long as things went well for him. But they did not break the ties of family solidarity – or indeed the ties they had formed in their own youth – by which they were connected to the army of Ancien Regime France or Condé's army as well as with the magistrates of the old law courts and the office-holders of former days.

Among the service nobility (*noblesse de fonction*) created under the Empire, the breakdown of the regime raised fears of a neo-Jacobin awakening, and therefore these men were willing to accept a restoration that would tolerate fortunes founded on nationalised property, and overlook the past of ex-monks and former leaders of revolutionary clubs. To be sure, they would have preferred a continuation of the Napoleonic dynasty, but this dynasty did not seem to have firm roots; and furthermore the English example showed that there were constitutional forms that could accommodate both an old dynasty and an elite issued from new classes.

The current of opinion favourable to the king was thus fostered in some regions by popular forces; elsewhere it was more a matter of resignation than of enthusiasm. It was a precarious consensus that was bound to dissolve as soon as the crisis was over.

As long as the campaign in France had wavered between success and failure, royalist sentiments had been rather subdued: it was best to adopt a prudent attitude of 'wait and see'. The comte d'Artois, who had entered France at the Swiss border, had advanced to Vesoul and then to Nancy under the protection of the allied troops, yet had been unable to gather a party about him. Nor had his sons been more successful: Angoulême had spent months of boredom at Saint-Jean-de-Luz since 2 January, and Berry had waited at Jersey for the insurrection of western France to break out. Many civil servants were paralysed by fear of a last-minute accord between the Allies and Napoleon.

Meanwhile, certain secret royalist societies, such as the *Institut philanthropique*, had managed to live through the imperial period. Foremost among them was a new society founded in 1810 at the initiative of Ferdinand de Bertier, called the *Chevaliers de la foi*, which gathered under its banners aristocratic recruits and became a meeting-ground for royalists and unyielding Catholics. The leadership of the society had become convinced that somewhere in French territory it would have to set the example of a highly visible rally to the Bourbons; its choice fell on Bordeaux.

The great port and the region's vineyards were ruined by the blockade, and discontent was rife among all classes of society. It was a Bordelais, the *avocat* Laîné, who in December of the previous year had been the spokesman of the opposition in the Legislative Body. Wellington was persuaded to detach two divisions to occupy the city. They entered on 12 March and Mayor Lynch ordered the National Guard to don the white cockade. A few hours later the duc d'Angoulême received an enthusiastic welcome and formed a kind of provisional government. The impulse spread to some other parts of France, and Toulouse rallied on 10 April.

The Bordeaux affair, though perhaps not decisive, at least served to balance the impression the Allies had received from the resistance of the populations of eastern France.

The strategy of the Allies

While the war was still in progress, the Allies had engaged in extensive negotiations with Napoleon. These were broken off only on 19 March. It is of little importance whether these conversations at Châtillon were conducted by the Allies, wavering and divided as they were, in good or bad faith. Napoleon rejected any treaty that would have left him to govern a France smaller than that of Brumaire. His intransigence was a contributing factor for the signing of the pact of Chaumont, by which the Allies pledged themselves not to make separate peace.

Napoleon thought that if he were to abdicate, the emperor of Austria might impose the regency of his 'beloved daughter'; but Marie-Louise was such a nonentity that the other powers were afraid that she would take all her orders from Austria, while Austria feared that she might fall under the yoke of Napoleon's family, with Napoleon 'listening behind the door', as Talleyrand put it, or even coming through the door once again.

The czar would have preferred, personally, to see a Bernadotte candidacy, but he had to recognise that Bernadotte did not have a firmly committed party, and that his presence at the head of one of the armies of the coalition further reduced his chances. He also realised that the time was not yet ripe for an Orléans candidacy, which was also discouraged by the future Louis-Philippe. In short, everything pointed to the Bourbons, despite Alexander's poor opinion of their abilities.

The British, for their part, thought that this was the best solution. But they did not want to be compromised by restoring the Bourbons, and Castlereagh attempted to convey the impression that he was interested only in unity among the Allies and in the share England would receive after the victory. He let things take their course, and Wellington, a warm supporter of the Bourbons, submitted to his instructions. In the end it was agreed to ascertain the wishes of the French people.

Talleyrand and the provisional government

As soon as the czar arrived in Paris, one man was ready to enter into discussions with him. As a member of the regency council, Talleyrand should have retreated to the Loire, but had managed to have himself confined to his townhouse in the rue Saint-Florentin by making a spurious attempt to cross the barriers at the Champs-Elysées. Alexander accepted his hospitality. The two men knew each other well from their Erfurt negotiations, where Napoleon's former minister had betrayed his master. The power vacuum left by the departure of the regency council gave free rein to Talleyrand. On his initiative the conservative Senate appointed (1 April) a provisional government in which he was joined by his friends Beurnonville, Jaucourt, and Dalberg, and abbé Montesquiou, a former

Constituent and royalist agent. On the next day, the Senate set about preparing a liberally-inspired constitution whose provisions it intended to impose on the new government.

Talleyrand seems to have envisaged the formation of a new regency council with himself as president until very shortly before Alexander's arrival in Paris, but that had not prevented him from getting in touch with the royalists. On 6 March Dalberg, a mere tool in his hands, had sent the royalist Vitrolles to the allied headquarters, albeit without an official message. Vitrolles had claimed that Talleyrand desired the return of the Bourbons 'from the bottom of his heart', and had then proceeded to Nancy, where he reported to the comte d'Artois. On the return from this mission he was taken prisoner. By that time Talleyrand had made up his mind, and he urged the czar to adopt the royalist solution, thereby under-cutting the efforts of Caulaincourt who, on Napoleon's behalf, was making a last effort in favour of the king of Rome.

Caulaincourt's negotiations lost the last chance of achieving their objective when Marmont committed what has been wrongly called his 'treason'. His sixth army corps covered the Emperor between Paris and Fontainebleau. Marmont, who supported the provisional government, concluded an armistice with Schwarzenberg, but the latter promised that its terms would not be implemented during Caulaincourt's parleys with the czar, in which Marmont also took part. In his absence, however, Marmont's lieutenants executed the movement toward Versailles and Normandy stipulated in the armistice that placed Napoleon at the mercy of the Allies.

Talleyrand was thus free to weave his intrigues. From his first floor, to which he had summoned the provisional government, he followed the activities of the czar and the Russian officials on the floor above. He intended, incidentally, to persuade most of the personnel of the Empire to join him in rallying to the Bourbons and to obtain guarantees for the ideas and the men of the Revolution from the new king. The constitution containing these guarantees was unanimously adopted by the Senate in its meeting of 6 April and passed by the vote of the Legislative Body on the next day. It was supposed to be accepted by the sovereign before he ascended the throne.

There was a note of ambiguity in this procedure: on the one hand, it was in the name of legitimacy that the heir of Louis XVI was called back, and yet an attempt was made to bind him beforehand by a contract. On his arrival in Paris on 12 April the comte d'Artois, appointed lieutenant-general of the realm by his brother, had his powers confirmed without swearing to uphold the projected constitution. From the inarticulate, emotional mumblings with which Artois had responded to the welcome of the authorities, Talleyrand culled the statement, 'Nothing is changed in

France, except that one Frenchman has been added', a formula that seemed to promise the expected pledges.

Very soon, however, his little tricks were swept away by the legitimist current: the king's entry into Paris (3 May) unleashed a popular enthusiasm that surprised both friends and foes by its scope. The provinces, by and large, showed their allegiance with equal verve. Only the army was steadfast in its nostalgia for the Emperor; the substitution of the white flag for the tricolour provoked a few instances of mutiny. Already the contrast between the two flags appeared as the symbol of the struggle between two irreconcilable Frances.

Louis XVIII and his entourage

The fact is that the nation's welcome barely disguised the difficulties that lay ahead. It would have taken a vivid and creative imagination to regenerate and unite this divided people; but the Restoration made the strange mistake of claiming Henri IV as its precedent.

Related to the house of Saxony through his mother, whom he resembled, no one looked less like the *Vert Galant* than the obese Louis XVIII, 59 years old at the time, and unable to walk or ride a horse. Very soon people began to call him the 'fat pig'; although those who were able to approach him were struck by his natural dignity. But ministers and courtiers were well aware of his coldness, his lack of naturalness and candour, his attachment to his physical comforts and to good food, and his need for a favourite in whom he could confide and to whom he could send sentimental or clever little notes.

His past was proof that the man had rarely been attractive to others. In the days of Louis XVI, the comte de Provence had been involved in underhanded conspiracies against his brother. Having emigrated at the time of Varennes, he had led the life of an errant prince, driven by the vicissitudes of politics or the war from the successive shelters where he had sought refuge: Verona, various German towns, Mittau; in 1809 he had finally settled in England, where he took up residence at Hartwell, a modest country manor. Upon the death of the 'orphan of the Temple' in June 1795, he had taken the title of king of France. He had met every setback with an impassiveness that had its own grandeur – indeed, when the occasion demanded it, with unexpected physical courage. A sceptic without firm religious convictions, he never had any doubts about the divine right of kings or the pre-eminence of the Capetian race.

From his youth he had posed as an intellectual. His literary taste was that of a pretty wit with a memory crammed full of Latin quotes and with a knack for composing light verses or making the most of a learned or licentious anecdote. But during his exile he had made little effort to keep abreast of the changes and the needs of France. Prematurely old, he was mentally lazy and relied on his ministers to deal with the complexities of government. He instinctively clung to the Ancien Regime and had no conception of the royal function outside the realm of etiquette. Yet at Court and elsewhere he played his role as representative sovereign with consummate skill. An actor and a mime, he knew how to find the proper word with which to seduce or to blame, and he also knew how to deliver in his handsome voice the measured official speeches which he wrote himself in a polished style.

Nor were his merits limited to these areas. He had a feel for the difficulties of the Restoration, and on the occasions when the seriousness of the situation demanded that he rouse himself from his indolence and make a decision, he usually proved to be lucid and prudent. That is why certain historians have made rather too much of his wisdom as an arbiter. Let us retain Guizot's more moderate assessment: 'As a king, he had outstanding negative and latent qualities, and few active and effective ones.'

His junior by two years, the comte d'Artois was unquestionably the more mediocre of the two men. Those who hankered after the old France were passionately devoted to this svelte, white-haired cavalier, this affable, generous, benevolent *gentilhomme* in whom they saw a true royal knight, with all the virtues this title implied in these early days of Romanticism. Sustained by the enthusiasm of faithful followers devoted to his person, the comte d'Artois surrounded himself with intransigent émigrés, thereby arousing his older brother's suspicion that he wanted to be the chief of an ultra-royalist opposition. In fact, Artois wavered between indignation at what he considered excessively liberal measures and an almost fearful respect for his older brother. During the years of exile he had pursued his own policy and had launched his agents into all kinds of irresponsible escapades, although he was always very careful not to appear in person with the army of the princes or in the Vendée. Except for the fact that he had become religious after his dissolute youth, he was still a spoiled, superficial, and stubborn old child, sometimes given to a puerile Machiavellianism. Not as stupid as the liberal tradition would have us believe, he was determined to fight in his haphazard manner against what seemed to him the degradation of royal power. He was capable of making decisions on very minor points and insisting on having his way with the obstinacy that comes with a weak character and a good conscience. All in all, then, an honourable man, though rather unsuited to being a ruler.

A widower like his brother, the comte d'Artois had two sons. The older, the duc d'Angoulême, sickly, impotent, and riddled with tics, looked like a blubbering nonentity. People were sometimes touched by his good will, his simplicity, and his courage; but it was hard to imagine him as a sovereign. He was married to his cousin Marie-Thérèse, Louis XVI's daughter, the other 'orphan of the Temple'. Those who were close to her saw great virtue in her. But this energetic virago, devoid of any feminine charm, had a knack for making herself unpopular by displaying her disdain for everything that recalled the Revolution or the Empire; the bourgeoisie of the time never ceased to call her 'Madame Rancune' [Lady Resentment]. Artois' younger son, the duc de Berry, contrasted with his brother in his solid vulgarity. On him alone rested the future of the Bourbons. It was also hoped that he would make the monarchy popular with the masses and with the army. Unfortunately his lack of judgment, his boasting, and his pointless tantrums very soon made him an embarrassment rather than an asset. Stabbed by Louvel, he was to die with a dignified courage, which was the first major service he had ever rendered the monarchy.

The organisation of the regime: the Charter

The organisation of the regime bore all the marks of haste. Despite the entreaties of the czar, Louis XVIII refused to accept the constitution passed by the Senate. However, in the declaration of Saint-Ouen, promulgated on the eve of his entry into Paris, he did promise to give France a representative system of government.

Meanwhile, he formed a government by adding some 'purer' royalists to the provisional government, ending up with a heterogeneous mixture that included men who were worn out (Malouet for the Navy), mediocre (Blacas, the reigning favourite, for the King's Household), or unpopular (Dupont, the loser of Baylen, for the War Department). There was no prime minister, and no minister was in a position to formulate general directives. For all his experience as a courtier and as a manipulator of expedients, not even Talleyrand, as Minister of Foreign Affairs, would have been able to do so, even if the suspicious king had permitted it, and even if he had not been obliged to leave for the Congress of Vienna; and abbé de Montesquiou, Minister of the Interior, another *grand seigneur* of the Ancien Regime, a man of intelligence and integrity, was fickle and indolent. The ministers soon split into clans and took to considering the council of ministers as a formality, submitting matters relating to their departments directly to the king for his signature. Moreover, Chancellor Dambray tried to revive the structure of the old *conseil royal* in which the council of ministers would have had its place between the *conseil d'en haut* and a *conseil privé* to be created out of the imperial *conseil d'Etat*. But his attempts failed because they were incompatible with both the Napoleonic centralisation and a representative regime.

Meanwhile, the allied sovereigns wished to see France's frontiers and institutions firmly established before their departure.

Talleyrand negotiated the Treaty of Paris of 30 May with the four major

Allies. France was reduced to its frontiers of 1792, which in fact left it with a population greater than that of 1789. The increase in territory after that date had been achieved by an advance of the frontier line toward Belgium (Philippeville, Marienbourg) and in northern Alsace and Lorraine (Saarbrücken). Above all, the frontier had advanced toward the Alps with the annexation of most of Savoy, as well as through the takeover of a number of enclaves, such as the pontifical enclaves of Avignon and the Comtat, the Prussian enclave of Montbéliard, and the annexation of the republic of Mulhouse. On the other hand, the Treaty of Paris permitted England to keep two of the French West Indies, Tobago and Santa Lucia, and Ile de France (the future Mauritius) in the Indian Ocean; moreover, France was made to return to Spain the part of Santo Domingo it had acquired in the Treaty of Basel. France was not required to pay any reparations, was not subjected to military occupation, and was to be represented at the Congress of Vienna, which would meet for the purpose of redrawing the map of Europe.

It would be most unfair to blame Talleyrand for failing to do better. His only weapon was the goodwill of the czar, who wanted to spare France, yet also remained committed to his allies of Chaumont. Having prevailed upon them to soften their claims somewhat, Alexander felt that he had been generous indeed. However, public opinion soon came to see the relinquishment of France's 'natural' frontiers as an infamous deed. Born during the Revolution, this myth was destined for a long career and would provide fuel for nationalist feelings and liberal rhetoric.

Since the allied sovereigns were scheduled to leave Paris on 5 June, the constitution had to be hastily elaborated so that it could be promulgated on the previous day (4 June).

After some hesitation, this act was given the name of 'Charter'. Since the king, upon his return, had been able to safeguard the principle of legitimacy, liberal institutions could only be granted by royal fiat. Two passages in the text of the Charter stressed the continuity in the 'chain of time' with particular clarity. One was the date, given as the nineteenth year of the reign, which seemed to negate the very existence of the Revolution and the Empire; the other was the preamble in which Beugnot's facile pen had taken an 'antique' turn and placed the text into a long line of concessions made by the monarchy since the days of Louis le Gros. The negation of national sovereignty by the Charter was to become a favourite theme of liberal oratory.

The Charter as a whole had been debated in four meetings of a joint committee chosen by the king, made up of members of the Senate and the Legislative Body, plus three royal commissioners, Montesquiou, Ferrand, and Beugnot. Montesquiou had submitted the preliminary draft, which remained unchanged in its major features. Controversial points were above all the relations between Church and State, freedom of the press, the voting rights of the Chambers, and the nationalised properties; these themes were to be sounded again and again throughout the regime. The 79 articles of the definitive text reflect certain English influences, but also some of the ideas of the 'monarchiens' of the Constituent Assembly of 1789:

1 Although it did not solemnly proclaim the rights of man, the Charter recognised the fundamental principles of liberty, equality, and property (including property rights to nationalised property); it called for an independent judiciary, while trial by jury and the abolition of special courts guaranteed the rights of individuals. However, the Charter did provide for the possibility of imposing legal restraints on freedom of the press whenever it became necessary to 'curb its abuses'.

Freedom of religion was assured by the State's protection of the different faiths. But unlike the Concordat of 1801, the Charter proclaimed Catholicism as the State religion.

2 There was no explicit separation of powers; the king as head of the executive also had a large share of legislative power, since legislation was both initiated and promulgated by him.

3 There were to be two chambers: the House of Peers appointed by the king (its members were subsequently recognised as hereditary peers) and the Chamber of the deputies of the departments which, it was finally decided after some hesitation, should be freely elected. The role of the Chambers was essentially to pass legislation, especially the budget, but without the right of amendment. However, the Chambers were also granted the **right** to debate petitions, to make their wishes known and to appeal to the king to introduce legislation.

4 The king, sacred and unaccountable in his person, was to rule with the help of ministers. The latter, who had access to, and indeed could be members of the Chambers, could be prosecuted only under criminal law for treason or peculation; they could only be indicted by the deputies and had to be judged by their peers.

5 The electorate charged with electing the Chamber of Deputies was narrowly defined by property qualifications: in order to vote, a man had to be at least 30 years old and pay 300 francs in taxes; in order to be eligible, he had to be at least 40 years old and pay 1,000 francs in taxes.

In this manner only the notables were able to participate in public life. The principles laid down in the Charter did not always provide a clear direction for the regime. It was obvious, for example, that it pursued the twin aims of protecting the king's power from too much encroachment and of providing for national consultation. Whenever the Chamber disagreed with the executive, it could refuse to pass the budget; in this proviso lay the germ of a parliamentary regime. On the other hand, one paragraph of article 14 authorised the king to 'institute regulations and ordinances necessary for the enforcement of the law and for the security of the State'. The authors of the Charter had simply meant to express the idea that laws could be spelled out in royal ordinances, but the wording provided the king with the possibility of using exceptional powers in crisis situations.

The policies of the first Restoration

Without a well-defined programme and firm direction, the first Restoration amounted to a mixture of liberal goodwill and the resurgence of certain features of the Ancien Regime, although the exact proportions of these ingredients are difficult to assess. The leadership of the State remained largely what it had been under the Empire, but in the absence of clear instructions, ambassadors and prefects had to guess at what the government had in mind. It was a time of 'paternalistic anarchy'.

The organisation of the Chambers showed the regime's desire to leave the personnel of the Empire in place: of the 149 peers appointed, 103 were Senators or Marshals of the Empire and 46 were *grands seigneurs* or ecclesiastical dignitaries; the Legislative Body [of the Empire] formed the first Chamber of Deputies, one-fifth of whose members were to be elected each year.

The purge of the administration was mild indeed: 76 per cent of the personnel was kept on, and while 43 new prefects were appointed, 29 of them came from the Napoleonic administration.

Public affairs were freely discussed in the Chamber of Deputies, and the ministers had to defend their legislative bills in every detail. One of the thorniest problems was the matter of freedom of the press, which had been proclaimed in the Charter. Standing mid-way between those who opposed this freedom and those who demanded an end to all restrictions – men like Benjamin Constant, who was just then writing his sparkling pamphlets – abbé de Montesquiou, advised by Royer-Collard and Guizot, chose a middle way. Censorship, which had never ceased to function, would be maintained for writings of less than 20 printed pages (except for professional works by scholars, churchmen, lawyers, and deputies); newspapers would have to apply for a permit before they published; printers and bookshops would have to obtain a licence. This law barely passed after a very spirited debate, in the course of which the government agreed to limit its enforcement to strictly defined periods of time.

The financial policy of baron Louis

The debate about the budget, or rather the two budgets of 1814 and 1815, had exceptionally far-reaching consequences. The Minister of Finance, baron Louis, left the mark of his forceful personality on these debates. A former ecclesiastical councillor at the parlement of Paris who had emigrated to England during the Revolution, he became a high official of the Treasury Department of the Empire. His approach combined the ideas of the eighteenth century with English practices.

In June 1814 he faced severe difficulties: a deficit whose exact amount was unknown, and which he evaluated at 759 million francs; the disappearance of part of the anticipated revenue for 1814 owing to the loss of territory and the invasion; and the allied princes' promises to abolish the combined taxes (*droits réunis*) levied primarily on tobacco, alcohol, gambling and gold and silver.

Louis postulated from the outset that it was essential to restore the State's credit (5 per cent bonds stood at 65 francs). There was little he could do about the 1814 budget, but for 1815 he brought the deficit figure down to 547 million francs by a drastic reduction of expenses (which fell most heavily on the Navy) and raised the amount of revenue to 618 million francs by augmenting the indirect taxes.

Wishing to repay the public debt without borrowing, Louis earmarked all budget surpluses for its amortisation, along with the revenues from the sale of communal property authorised by a law of 1813, and from the sale of 300,000 hectares of forest (in many cases these forests had belonged to the Church, and their sale was a reassuring sign for the buyers of nationalised property). In anticipation of these sales, the State's creditors received notes at 8 per cent, which was the actual interest rate of public bonds.

Louis' budget was subsequently thrown into disarray by the Hundred Days. Yet he established for years to come the principle that first priority must be given to protecting the State's credit, the price of public bonds being the thermometer of the State's financial health. This policy of fiscal restraint, of honest and frugal management, ensured the State's independence from the banks. But in other than purely fiscal respects, it launched the Restoration on a rather dangerous course, even granted that some of the difficulties to which it gave rise were inevitable. This tight fiscal policy led to an abrupt drop in the number of high positions in the army and in certain administrative agencies, thereby creating a new class of malcontents, such as officers on half pay. It deprived peacetime France of the economic stimulation provided by major public works financed by loans. Moreover, the appropriation of all taxes by the central government left the local authorities without the means to manage their own affairs efficiently, thereby undermining all attempts to bring about decentralisation. Finally, Louis had systematically preserved all the taxes of the Revolution and the Empire. But while the property tax which, incidentally, was unevenly distributed among the departments (the former *pays d'Etat* were still privileged), was heavy, the landowners had the means of contesting it in the Chamber. The regime's failure to make major reforms in the indirect taxes, which were sometimes higher than the value of the item on which they were levied, was a very serious matter, for these taxes affected ordinary food staples, such as wine or salt, and were thus an especial burden for the poor. But the Restoration did not seem to be interested in popularity.

On the other hand, its insensitivity alienated some segments of the upper classes and the army as well.

The king's civil list had been fixed at 25 million francs for the entire reign, to which were added 8 million francs for the princes. This sum, which was lower than the allocations claimed by Napoleon's family and moreover encumbered by heavy outlays for the upkeep of châteaux and royal estates (some of which, such as Versailles, had not been maintained for many years) and of the royal manufactories, was nonetheless sufficient to set up a sumptuous court for the sovereign and his entourage at the Tuileries.

Louis XVIII re-established the services and the etiquette of the years before 1789. Once again there were equerries and chair-pushers, and some of the surviving holders of court offices at Versailles reappeared, white-haired or gout-ridden. But it was impossible to revive the spirit of the old court. The princes, with the exception of the king, whose infirmities reduced his activities, had little interest in wit and whimsy, and the almoners created a pervasive atmosphere of oppressive piety (although a kind of unofficial relief was provided by Father Elysée, an ex-monk turned charlatan to whom the king had entrusted his health). The fusion of two societies which Napoleon had attempted to achieve at his court was in principle continued. But this time the old nobility felt at home and had consciously or unconsciously reactivated the cascade of disdain that fell heavily on the marshals of the Empire or non-noble civil servants. Ney, who had rallied to the king with almost indecent haste, saw his wife, the daughter of one of Marie-Antoinette's chambermaids, weep over the snubs to which she was subjected.

Baron Louis' budget implied the dissolution of part of the imperial army, and Dupont was obliged to send about three-fifths of this army home. Some 12,000 officers were put on half pay, among them old war-horses who no longer knew how to get along in civilian life. As for the Guard, an elite conscious of its valour, it was humiliated when it was re-integrated into the ranks and dispersed throughout the provincial garrisons. As G. de Bertier says: 'The king might have tried to appeal to their pride and to their loyalty by entrusting them with the task of watching over his person.' But this was to take a certain risk, and so the king opted for down-to-earth caution, which can be even more dangerous, especially as other elements were used to rebuild the king's military household of 6,000 men (bodyguards, gate-keepers, honour guards, etc.) in which ordinary soldiers recruited among the nobility received officers' pay and into which five Swiss regiments were incorporated.

Insensitivity of the king and pretension of the émigrés

The anarchy of the first Restoration accounts for the impact of certain words and actions that outraged an already uneasy public opinion.

In presenting a bill providing for the restoration of unsold nationalised properties to their former owners (this law would continue a more discreet practice of the Empire), the minister Ferrand spoke of the royalists who had taken the straight path in following the king into exile, contrasting them with those who had taken the crooked path in serving the different governments France had known since 1789. His words unleashed a storm of indignation inside and outside the Chamber. Ferrand was an old fool, but Louis XVIII must be blamed for demonstrating his esteem for him.

On 7 and 8 June the chief of police, Beugnot, formerly an administrator of the Empire but a courtier by temperament, promulgated police ordinances forbidding all work on Sunday and calling for the decoration of houses along the road of the Corpus Christi procession. These dispositions, which were hardly in keeping with the Concordat, were bound to give rise to the anticlerical polemics in which Paul-Louis Courier was to play an outstanding role a few years later.

To this should be added certain commemorative ceremonies: the transfer to Saint-Denis of Louis XVI's remains was no doubt a moral obligation for the new monarch, but it might have been carried out in a less aggressive manner. Above all, it would have been easy to avoid holding solemn memorial services for Moreau, Cadoudal, or Pichegru.

Yet all these instances of insensitivity were given their full significance by the social climate of this first Restoration.

It was not unusual to see former émigrés attempting to become involved in the administration, trying to check on the regular authorities by means of a kind of supervisory power that was secretly encouraged by the entourage of the comte d'Artois, the 'shadow cabinet' of the pavillon de Marsan. Many nobles claimed honorific privileges in church, such as the front pew, special censing, and the presentation of the consecrated bread; sometimes their pretensions so intimidated the buyers of nationalised property that they willy-nilly sold their purchases back to the original owners.

The clergy was even more virulent. It was composed on the one hand of survivors of the older generation, divided by the rift between constitutional and refractory clergy and often prematurely worn out, and on the other hand of young men trained under the Empire in the seminaries founded by Cardinal Fesch. No intermediary generation existed, since almost no priests had been recruited during the Revolution. In view of the shortage of priests, many of these young 'conscripts of the militant Church', often brought up on ultramontane doctrines and deeply stirred by the persecution of the Church toward the end of the Empire, were entrusted with important responsibilities and seemed intent on purging the nation of its revolutionary sin. They conducted a multitude of missions and collective penitence, made life impossible for married ex-priests, refused to give absolution to buyers of nationalised property, and announced the reinstatement of the tithe. In some provinces, moreover, the local church openly went beyond the limits imposed on the clergy under the terms of the Concordat.

The princes sent on tours of the provinces could not help but notice the disaffection of the local populations; in northern France the duc de Berry was badly received by the army; in the west the duc d'Angoulême saw two posters at the opposite sides of the city gates of Nantes: 'The Vendée began here' and 'The Vendée ended here'. At Angers he had to intervene to prevent the noble or rural cavalry from coming to blows with the National Guard, but at least he spoke words of peace to both sides. By contrast, the comte d'Artois refused to receive the 'constitutional' bishops of Dijon and Besançon when he visited eastern France.

The first Restoration thus ended in 1815 in disappointment and discontent on the part of many of those who had agreed to the return of the king. The opposition newspapers, *Le Censeur* and the Bonapartist *Nain jaune*, which constantly featured caricatures of the begging, ridiculous country bumpkin, had the widest circulation. Soon there was talk of multiple intrigues and military mutinies in favour of an Orleanist or republican regime. But only the Emperor, his popularity rekindled by eight months of absence, could crystallise this discontent. He was kept informed by the emissaries of his brother Joseph, who headed a nucleus of conspirators in Switzerland, and by those of Maret or Fouché.

His situation on the island of Elba was unsettled: the French government had failed to pay him the pension promised by the treaties, and the Congress of Vienna considered sending him to the Azores. He was not the man to let an opportunity slip by.

From the flight of the Eagle to the return of the king

The return of Napoleon

Having escaped from the loosely guarded island of Elba, Napoleon, with a thousand men, landed at Golfe-Juan on 1 April. The fortified town of Antibes closed its gates to him. The people of Provence received him with surprise but without friendliness. The Emperor therefore immediately headed north. On poor country roads he advanced toward Grenoble by way of Digne and Sisteron; crowds of mountain people and artisans of the market towns cheered him along the way. Grenoble could have stopped him, but Colonel de Labedoyère, an admirer of the great man, took his regiment over to him; his example was the signal for the defection of the troops of this fortified place. From 6 March in Grenoble, Napoleon reached Lyon on 10 March, and here the troops of the garrison forced the comte d'Artois and Marshal Macdonald to flee. Finally Ney, who had assembled troops in Franche-Comté and represented the last chance of stopping him before he reached Paris, went over to him at Auxerre on 14 March. Without having fired a shot, the Emperor arrived at the Tuileries on the evening of 20 March and moved back into the palace that had been vacated by the king the night before.

His rapid movement, which sometimes brought him to a place ahead of the news, had once again paralysed his enemies. Everywhere he had retrieved an army that had not been dismantled by the generous peace terms of the Allies, an army that felt that it had not been defeated but rather betrayed the year before. A few rather more cool-headed chiefs were the only ones to stay aloof in the ecstatic reunion between the humiliated soldiers and the Little Corporal.

Sharing the feelings of the army, the populace were caught up in the same excitement; the general discontent had rekindled their Jacobin spirit: 'Down with the nobility!', 'Down with the priests!' they cried, and Napoleon promised to 'lantern' them (hang them from the lanterns) but he was fearful, as he could only conceive of government by the notables.

However, this popular enthusiasm was not shared by the middle classes as a whole, nor even by large sectors of the peasant masses. In Paris the National Guard, the students, and members of the liberal intellectual circles (La Fayette, for example) demonstrated their monarchist loyalty. But this attitude was tempered by the prospect of trouble with the army. As for the king, he resigned himself to leaving for the Netherlands. On 23 March he crossed the frontier and on the 30 March he settled in Ghent.

There was only one way to resist, and that was to foster uprisings in those provinces where the monarchy still had active support. For this purpose the rather dull duc de Bourbon was dispatched to eastern France, but his effort was short-lived. The duc and duchesse d'Angoulême happened to be in Bordeaux to celebrate the first anniversary of the rally of 12 March. The duchess prolonged her stay in that city, which remained favourable to the Bourbons. But when her attempts to win over the garrison failed, she took a ship at Pauillac. The duke had left earlier to assemble his troops, swelled by royalist volunteers, at Nîmes. Setting out for Lyon, he got as far as north of Valence. But, when he was nearly surrounded, he capitulated at La Palud (8 April) and retreated to Spain. Vitrolles, who had tried to make Toulouse the provisional capital of a monarchist administration, was arrested on 3 April.

The Additional Act

For the moment, Napoleon was master of the country, but the country's dominant attitude was a prudent 'wait and see'. Indeed, action groups of *fédérés* sprang up in his favour; these groups were dedicated to safeguarding the conquests of the Revolution and brought together men who had wholeheartedly served the Empire and men who hankered after the Republic. But they aroused more suspicion than patriotic enthusiasm. Moreover, the Emperor intended to share his power only with the notables, who had come to appreciate the liberal principles of the Charter. He had difficulties in forming a cabinet; only Fouché was glad to take back the Ministry of Police, but he almost openly engaged in treason.

This state of public opinion was disconcerting to the Emperor who appeared to be undecided and aged. He realised that the trend toward a representative regime was irresistible and promulgated an 'Act Supplementing the Constitutions of the Empire' which, in fact, replaced the authoritarian principles of the imperial regime with liberal institutions strictly tied to property qualifications. Approved by a plebiscite whose salient feature was the high incidence of abstention, this new constitutional act did nothing to dispel either the disappointment of the populace or the reserve of the notables. Moreover, the imminence of war weighed on everyone's mind. Europe had responded to Napoleon's assurances of peaceful intentions by sending Wellington's British and Blücher's Prussian troops to Belgium as an advance guard of the vast military resources at its disposal. The Emperor tried to disperse them before they were joined by the Russian or Austrian forces. He set out with an army in which the ordinary soldier, once again confident of victory, was led by mediocre or disillusioned officers. He fully realised that even a first victory would do little to daunt the hostile resolve of the Allies. As he set out, he left eastern France in full-fledged revolt and other provinces on the verge of insurrection, while the administration was uneasy and the assemblies (a Chamber of Representatives elected by a tiny minority of voters and an appointed House of Peers) were more interested in paring down his powers than in galvanising the nation. The four-day campaign that ended at Waterloo on 18 June hastened an almost unavoidable collapse.

At Ghent, meanwhile, the king had re-established the daily court routine of the Tuileries. Some of his ministers were there, forming a cabinet that had practically nothing to do (it was here that Chateaubriand, temporarily heading the Ministry of the Interior abandoned by a discouraged Montesquiou, began his political career). News from France and messengers arrived almost unhindered – Guizot, for example, came to enlarge upon the liberal advice submitted by Royer-Collard – and each party tried to use the information that was brought for its own ends. For the comte d'Artois and the duc de Berry were also there, surrounded by their advisers of the pavillon de Marsan. And, of course, intrigue and rivalry were rampant within this group of bored exiles. Two major theses confronted each other: the courtiers explained the return of the Corsican by a conspiracy made possible by the failure to remove the administrators of the Empire from their posts, while the government incriminated the insensitivity of the émigrés and the priests whose arrogance had exasperated the nation. It was therefore necessary to decide which policy should be adopted. A firm decision had not yet been made by the time of the Emperor's second abdication in favour of his son (22 June).

The second Restoration

At this point it was not even certain that the Bourbons would be restored a second time. The matter was discussed at the Congress of Vienna and the czar leaned toward entrusting the monarchy to the duc d'Orléans, who had fled to England. This time, however, it was not the czar who marched on Paris but Wellington, who hoped to bring about a reconciliation between the legitimate king and the new France, and who expressed his preference in much stronger terms than he had done in 1814.

In Paris itself both the Bonapartist and the Orleanist factions in the Chamber of Representatives were strong; the five-man committee on government elected at the time of the Emperor's second abdication included two members from each of these tendencies; but the fifth was Fouché who realised that Louis XVIII was still the competitor most likely to win, and who would soon set about removing the obstacles to his return with Machiavellian cunning and bold intrigues that were to reveal their full scope in the decisive period between 23 June and 6 July.

Having pushed Carnot out of the committee's chairmanship, induced Napoleon to go to Rochefort by giving him to understand that a ship was waiting there to take him to the United States, caused the Chambers to bog down in debates over a new constitution, and dispatched La Fayette to Hagenau, Fouché established contact with Wellington and divided his time equally between official negotiations and secret conversations.

Together with the commander of the British forces he signed a capitulation that called for the retreat of the French forces beyond the Loire. Charged with maintaining order in the capital, the National Guard dealt severely with the *fédérés*. On 6 July the arrival of the Prussians relieved Fouché of the need to keep the Chambers under control and allowed him to show his hand.

After Waterloo, Louis XVIII had hastened to leave Ghent; on 22 June he was joined at Mons by Talleyrand, still basking in the glory of the role he had so recently played at the Congress of Vienna. Considering himself indispensable, he imposed his conditions on the king: the dismissal of

Blacas, a homogeneous government headed by himself, and the establishment of the king and the government in a city not occupied by the Allies. The king agreed to appoint Blacas as ambassador to Naples, but he also would have liked to get rid of Talleyrand, and Wellington had to intervene to avoid a break between them. On 28 June at Cambrai the king issued a proclamation in which he admitted that his government had made mistakes, promised to respect the principles of the Charter, and granted amnesty to his 'subjects who had gone astray', with the exception of the 'instigators of treason'.

Two problems still had to be resolved before he could return to Paris: Fouché and the tricolour flag.

Fouché posed as the indispensable man who alone could rally the capital, and he had convinced Wellington that this was indeed true. This clever operator had rendered so many personal services to the royalists during the Hundred Days that even the purest among them, indeed the comte d'Artois himself, vouched for his worthiness. On 6 July at Arnouville the ex-Oratorian, the regicide member of the Convention, the butcher of the royalists of Lyon, was presented to the sovereign by Talleyrand in a scene that Chateaubriand has made unforgettable, and his appointment as Minister of Police was confirmed. The next day the cabinet was completed and on the following day the king returned to Paris.

If he had reluctantly given in when he agreed to employ Fouché, he could not be persuaded to yield in the matter of the flag, despite the entreaties of those marshals who had remained loyal and especially Macdonald, who had refused to serve during the Hundred Days. Admittedly it was more difficult to change the flag than it had been in 1814, for the restored tricolour had led French troops to Waterloo and royalist France had risen against the Emperor under the white flag. Nonetheless it was humiliating for the army that its latest sacrifices should not even be granted this symbolic reward.

The king's decision reinforced the impression that he had come back 'in the baggage train of foreign powers', a cliché that was soon to become dear to the enemies of the regime. It is true that Louis XVIII had made haste to return to France so as to be one step ahead of the allied sovereigns, who would have liked to take another opinion poll before they decided what kind of regime should be given to France. Nonetheless one cannot help but feel that Talleyrand had given him sound advice when he insisted that he should try to establish himself in a city that the Allies had not yet reached. If on 20 March Napoleon's imagination had carried him beyond reality, Louis XVIII's earthbound prudence once again failed to make him take a step that would have stirred a people's imagination.

The Talleyrand–Fouché government and its problems

The allied occupation

As soon as it was formed, the new government, made up entirely of men who had served the Empire, was faced with the invasion of France. Within two weeks the victors of Waterloo, 150,000 British and Prussian troops, arrived at the gates of Paris, and between July and September the bulk of the allied armies swept into the country in wave after wave. By early September there were more than 1,200,000 foreign soldiers on French soil: Englishmen, Russians, Prussians, Austrians, Bavarians, Wurttembergers, Hessians, Danes, Swiss, etc. Even the Spaniards, though at peace with France, made two brief incursions toward Bayonne and Perpignan.

Legally the coalition powers were allies of the king of France who had abided by the treaty concluded on 25 March against the usurper. And indeed, before crossing the frontiers, the commanding officers always proclaimed that their troops came as friends. In fact, however, all of Europe believed that the mass of the French had rallied to Napoleon and that the time had come to make the defeated people pay the price for this latest alarm that had once again forced the other peoples to go to war. Having failed to appreciate the relative moderation of 1814, the French people would be subjected to the harsh law of conquest. They would also be forced to pay the cost of this new mobilisation by being made to feed, clothe, and house the coalition soldiers.

The first wave struck the frontiers of northern and eastern France on the way to Paris. Already deeply in debt, the eastern departments, which had borne the brunt of the invasions of 1814 and had then been subjected to repeated requisitioning during the Hundred Days, were ruined by demands from all sides. Then, on 24 July, the formal terms of the occupation were announced: the territory to be occupied comprised 61 departments, either in their entirety or in part; north of the Loire, only a part of Brittany and of the Cotentin remained free; and the occupation extended beyond the upper reaches of that river and beyond the lower reaches of the Rhône and all the way to the Mediterranean.

Yet even after it had been stabilised in this manner, the occupation retained its arbitrary character: public funds were seized; contributions in money were levied on the well-to-do; cloth, shirts, and footwear were requisitioned; supplies of bread, meat, wine, and fodder had to be furnished. But the actual practices went even beyond the regulations issued, and the exorbitant table allowances allocated to the officers did not prevent them from requisitioning more. The soldiers consumed as much as 10 bottles of wine or a litre of brandy a day; and the hospitals taken over by the Allies became centres of astounding over-provision. Not only was public property ransacked, private individuals also were subject to exactions of every sort: their harvests were seized, their wives and daughters raped, their homes burned down. From the systematic destruction of works of art to the most mindless waste, everything contributed to the country's impoverishment. Any officials who tried to resist were harshly punished; constables were put in charge of prefects' offices (several prefects were deported to Germany), mayors and tax-collectors were beaten up. The reputation of certain units had become such that the population took to the woods when they approached.

Yet this picture calls for a few additional nuances: the British maintained strict discipline, and while they were unbending in their demands, these were relatively moderate; Wellington, who disapproved of arbitrary acts because he was a gentleman by temperament and also because he feared a desperate revolt on the part of the French, severely reprimanded the Dutch troops under his command. The Russians also were often quite disciplined and free of hatred, except for the Cossacks whose lawless ways and pilfering spread terror wherever they went. As for the Austrians, they tried to make money out of everything, from cut wood to tobacco and stamped paper, which they seized and sold below the legal price. But the most feared and most hated of the occupation troops were the Prussians and the soldiers from the German states previously occupied by Napoleon's forces. Their oppression was systematic. Blücher himself camped out like a trooper at the château of Saint-Cloud and set the example of how to fleece the country.

At the demand of the Allies, the French government had been forced to disband the army of the Loire. It therefore could operate only by persuasion: as early as 9 July, it had created a French commission on requisition, which persuaded the inter-allied commission to centralise all demands. The French commission could do no more than transmit the prefects' complaints to the government. But at least the Allies agreed to let the French administration continue in its function in exchange for a payment of 50 million francs for the upkeep of their troops (and an additional allowance for clothing and equipment of 120 francs per soldier), payable in monthly instalments. In order to meet its most pressing commitments, the government levied an extraordinary loan of 100 million francs on the rich. But the sums already paid to the Allies were not deducted from these payments, and in fact many of the exactions continued to be taken. It was only when they decided to impose a new treaty on France that the Allies, by the middle of September, began to loosen their grip and to evacuate the territory.

The White Terror

Problems of a different order confronted the government with the so-called 'White Terror'. Royalist reactions, initially paralysed by the speed of the flight of the Eagle but later aided by the war, had threatened the imperial regime from within by the end of the Hundred Days: part of the Forez region was in the hands of rebellious conscripts organised in units of 'chasseurs of Henri IV'; the duc d'Aumont had landed in Normandy and openly instigated an uprising. This uprising had rapidly spread throughout the old regions of *chouannerie* [counter-revolutionary activity] from Brittany to Maine, with the Vendée, of course, in the vanguard. Peasant armies had reassembled as early as the middle of April. Yet the movement in these areas no longer had the enthusiasm of its earliest days and was ill-served by dissension among its leaders, some of whom listened to Fouché's advice to wait and see. That is why Generals Lamarque and Travot, though fighting with smaller numbers of troops, had badly beaten the rebels on a number of occasions. After Waterloo the threat of invasion by foreign troops had brought about a rapprochement between the whites and the blues, and, when both sides acknowledged the king's authority, hostilities had ceased.

This did not happen in the Midi. The defeat of the duc d'Angoulême had brought only a truce and the fervently Catholic population of the villages and market towns was restrained only by its fear of the soldiers and the *fédérés*. People were waiting for the return of Angoulême and for help from Spain: 'If the southwest is invaded, the entire region will rise up with a show of unanimity that will astonish the rest of France.' Only the Protestant bourgeoisie of the towns of Languedoc and the block of Protestant peasants in the Cévennes had rallied to the Emperor (at Arpaillargues in the mountains royalist volunteers from Nîmes had been massacred after the capitulation at La Palud). In the large and small towns Catholic nobles, bourgeois, and proletarians banded together in secret societies that were a first step toward the formation of a clandestine army.

The news of Waterloo gave the signal for vengeance. It erupted on 24 June at Marseille, where the British fleet was cruising outside the harbour. The garrison and the compromised families had to leave; but within two days fifty people were killed, two hundred wounded, and eighty houses or shops burnt down. Assassinations and arrests continued under the anarchical rule of a royalist committee, and the first task of the new prefect, Vaublanc, was to empty the prisons. Similar disturbances occurred in the towns of the Rhône valley and at Toulon, where Brune, the commander of the garrison, did not decide to leave until 24 July. As he passed through Avignon, he was murdered and his body thrown into the Rhône.

At Toulouse, the movement brought to light the existence of the '*verdets*', an organisation of volunteers wearing the green cockade of the comte d'Artois. The local secret societies who manipulated them hated moderate royalists as much as the supporters of the imperial regime. There was talk of a 'kingdom of Occitania', loosely tied to northern France. This movement took advantage of the confusion produced by the flight of the officials of the Hundred Days; the duc d'Angoulême had entrusted their functions to local notables, but the government soon appointed other officials to take their place. The royalist societies sided with the former against the latter; General Ramel, a moderate royalist who was chosen by Paris to command the National Guard of Toulouse and had wanted to integrate the individual *verdets* into the Guard, was assassinated in cold blood.

Languedoc experienced a veritable revival of the Religious Wars. At Nîmes, roving bands of lower-class individuals led by the general labourer Trestaillons molested the Protestant bourgeois (Protestant women had their drawers pulled off and were beaten with a nail-studded paddle that marked their buttocks with a bloody fleur-de-lis), and ransacked their homes. Thirty-seven persons were killed; 2,500 fled, among them the most prominent manufacturers. The duc d'Angoulême felt that he had pacified the region and called for a stop to the fighting; but the reopening of a Protestant church on 12 November led to the assassination of General Lagarde who had tried to protect the worshippers.

This explosion of hatred caught the government unprepared. The disbanding of the army, the unexpected outbreaks of popular emotion provoked by roving bands, and the frequent connivance with these elements on the part of nobles and bourgeois, the slowness of communications – all of these factors were invoked as excuses for its lack of control. But even later the government had great difficulties in having some of the perpetrators of this violence condemned. The immediate situation damaged even Fouché's reputation as a clever chief of police. The occupation of the departments of Var, Bouches-du-Rhône, and Gard by the Austrians put an end to the movement.

In a parallel endeavour, the government took steps to deal with the 'accomplices' of the Hundred Days. Ironically, Fouché was called upon to draw up the list of the individuals to be excluded from the amnesty granted by the king at Cambrai. In the end, his very long list ('He didn't forget any of his friends', Talleyrand said) was pared down to 54 names: 17 generals or officers to be tried by military tribunals, and 37 persons, 27 of them civilians, to be placed under house arrest pending the decision of the Chambers. This was the minimum the government had to do, given the pressure of the royalists and the Allies; in fact Fouché and Macdonald, the new commander-in-chief, helped the most endangered of these officials to leave the country. It was their own carelessness that brought about the arrest of Labedoyère, who was condemned and executed on 19 August, and later that of Marshal Ney.

The 'Incredible Chamber' (Chambre Introuvable)

Fouché tried to restore his position of power by engaging in a kind of blackmail: he wrote two reports describing the excesses of the occupation armies and the anti-monarchical attitude of the bulk of Frenchmen and then made these reports public, a strategy that definitively turned the king against him. Among the members of the House of Peers of 1814, 29 had agreed to serve in that of the Hundred Days; they were excluded from the peerage and replaced by 94 new peers. At the same time, the peerage was made hereditary. As for the Chamber of Representatives elected during the Hundred Days, it was dissolved and elections were called to choose a new Chamber of Deputies; the voting age was lowered to 21 years, the age of eligibility to 25, and the number of deputies was increased to 402, although the *collèges électoraux* of the *arrondissements* and the departments that had been instituted during the Empire remained unchanged. Altogether there were 72,000 voters, but only 48,500 of them actually cast their ballots. These elections of 14 and 22 August sent to Paris a Chamber in which 9 out of every 10 deputies were convinced and fervent royalists, the 'Incredible Chamber' as Louis XVIII himself called it.

Whatever might be said in hindsight about the abstentions or the prefects' power to add a certain number of names to the electoral lists, the fact is that the dismay of public opinion at the catastrophic experience of the Hundred Days triggered one of those violent swings of the pendulum to the right that have repeatedly characterised the political crises of recent French history. A Chamber of Deputies of new men, most of them hostile to anything that recalled the Revolution and the Empire, would face a government issued from the personnel of the Empire.

At this point Talleyrand decided that the time had come to throw overboard some ballast in the person of Fouché, for whom the elections had been a personal failure and who agreed to become the French ambassador at Dresden. However, this was not enough to save the rest of the crew, since the captain now laboured under harsh criticism, having partly lost the international prestige that had been the basis of his strength in 1814.

At the Congress of Vienna Talleyrand had been able to restore the role of France as a great European power on an equal footing with the four Allies of Chaumont. Against the threat of Russian hegemony he had signed the secret treaty of 3 January 1815 with England and Austria, and he felt that in doing so he had broken the coalition against France. Unfortunately, the return of the Emperor had re-cemented the alliance among the powers; and when the czar found out about the terms of the treaty, his attitude toward the French minister changed. Yet France desperately needed his goodwill. For Prussia and – though much more hesitantly – Austria made it clear that they wanted to dismember the

French territory by taking away Flanders, the Ardennes, Lorraine, and Alsace. Alexander, though opposed to any annexation of territory, nonetheless could not dismiss his allies' appetites out of hand. He therefore went along with Castlereagh's compromise position of calling for France's return to its frontiers of 1790. France would also have to pay extremely heavy reparations, to be enforced by the occupation of part of its territory over several years. On 20 September the Allies presented the French government with a veritable ultimatum stating these harsh conditions. Talleyrand felt that before he could discuss them, he needed a public display of the king's support. In order to obtain it, he offered his resignation, and Louis XVIII, judging that he no longer needed him, took him at his word.

The Richelieu government

Richelieu and Decazes

On 24 September a new government was formed by the duc de Richelieu, who took the portfolio of Foreign Affairs. His fellow-ministers were, by and large, more right wing than their predecessors. The nomination of Richelieu himself seemed perfectly suited to reassure the new Chamber. Born in 1766, this *grand seigneur* had lost his vast properties during the Revolution. During his emigration he had entered into the service of Russia and was named Governor of Odessa in 1803, later becoming Governor of all of New Russia. Under his administration, settlers were brought in to colonise the vast steppes of southern Russia, and Odessa became the major trading port of the Black Sea. In September 1814, Richelieu had resigned from this great colonising project in order to return to Paris, where he accepted a position at court. His entire past seemed to point to a pure royalist, a mind totally closed to modern France. And indeed, Richelieu did not like the Revolution, detested Bonaparte, and was afraid of freedom of the press. Neither did this excellent administrator have the broad vision of the true statesman. He was at once naive and suspicious, an undistinguished speaker, possessed of an almost pathological sensitivity, and easily thrown off balance by intrigues. But he did have common sense and moderation; above all, he had moral qualities that formed a stark contrast with his predecessor: probity, a demanding sense of honour, and firmness. These qualities would gain him the esteem of the British, who initially viewed this friend of the czar with suspicion; they would also be very helpful to him in the task of reconstruction, an achievement that remains his claim to fame.

Hidden within the cabinet was one crafty collaborator, a man capable of threading his cautious way among the shoals of domestic politics. This was Elie Decazes, the son of a notary of Libourne and the former purchasing agent of *Madame Mère* [Napoleon's mother, Laetitia Bonaparte]. In 1815, when he was thirty-five years old, he had – rather by chance – inherited the prefecture of police. By personally entertaining the king with the scabrous gossip of which the latter was so fond, he so well captured Louis XVIII's senile tenderness that the king soon called him 'my son' and could not get along without his new favourite. And since Decazes had the aggressive and scheming personality of his predecessor in the police department, Fouché, he made sure that his trusty police commissioners spied upon the prefects. Uncultured and without profound ideas, this supple and cautious politician, who for a time had cultivated the extreme royalists, soon convinced himself that the monarchy had to be protected from the excesses of its supporters. Of this he was able to convince Richelieu as well.

But for the moment Richelieu faced the formidable task of negotiating with the Allies. Thanks to the czar he obtained a few concessions. Nonetheless the clauses of the second Treaty of Paris (20 November 1815) were stringent: reduced to its frontiers of 1 January 1790, France ceded Philippeville, Marienbourg, and the duchy of Bouillon to the Netherlands, Saarbrücken and Sarrelouis to Prussia, Landau and the territory north of the Lauter to Hesse and Bavaria, Savoy to Sardinia – altogether 5,000 square kilometres and 300,000 inhabitants. War reparations of 700 million francs, to be acquitted within five years, would be paid to the Allies in fifteen instalments beginning 1 March 1816. A military occupation of northern and eastern France by 150,000 men maintained at French expense would guarantee these payments; the occupation was to last for five years, although provision was made for reducing it to three years. Finally, the debts contracted abroad by previous governments would have to be repaid.

Reaction and purges

On 7 October 1815 the king opened the session of the new Chamber. Its members included more commoners than Ancien Regime nobles, and while the former émigrés, many of whom had served the Empire, accounted for less than one-fifth of the Chamber, the body as a whole was formed of a throng of provincials without a leader, without experience, impassioned and unruly. The *Chevaliers de la foi* therefore took it upon themselves to prepare the legislative agenda by forming core groups of deputies from the majority into caucuses, somewhat after the manner of the *club des Bretons* at the Estates-General. The first formal party, later known as the 'ultra-royalists', came out of these secret caucuses, in which its future leaders first attracted attention. When the liberals became aware of this hidden activity, they credited it to the *Congrégation*, a pious society having links with the Jesuits.

The government felt obliged to pay lip-service to the passions of the majority and proposed repressive measures against the 'accomplices' of the Hundred Days (perhaps with the hidden intention of dealing with the instigators of the troubles in the south as well). A series of laws came to form the core of the 'legalised White **Terror**':

1 The law of public security (29 October), temporarily permitting the arrest of individuals suspected of plotting against the security of the State.
2 The law against seditious speeches and writings (9 November).
3 The law setting up special courts (*cours prévôtales*) (27 December).
4 The amnesty law (12 January 1816), which excluded from the amnesty and punished with exile persons placed under house arrest by the ordinance of 24 July 1815 and the regicides who had rallied to the Hundred Days; in addition, persons indicted for their role during that period before the promulgation of the ordinance would be brought to trial anyway.

During the debate the government constantly had to restrain the escalating rhetoric of the deputies. In one instance it had to throw out an amendment calling for the death penalty for the possession of a tricolour flag! The deputy from Angers, La Bourdonnaye, became famous for calling for 'irons and executioners' and for proposing the dismissal of entire categories of suspects (including, for example, all the prefects in office during the Hundred Days). This system of categories was barely rejected only when Richelieu opposed it in the name of the king.

In fact, the government was divided: Barbé-Marbois, the Keeper of the Seals, and Decazes were moderate in the use of the formidable powers at their disposal, but Clarke, the Minister of War, meted out harsh punishment to military officers who had compromised themselves.

Some of the death sentences that aroused public opinion, like the condemnation of Ney by the House of Peers or that of several other generals, were perhaps difficult to avoid. But the wave of hatred that came to light when Lavalette, the postmaster-general during the Hundred Days, escaped just before his execution and the verbal violence of the extreme royalist party, aimed at unleashing terror against the instigators of conspiracy, served to frighten and alienate public opinion.

As a result, public opinion exaggerated the number of political condemnations made under these special laws: in fact fewer than 6,000 such sentences were rendered (most of them carrying relatively light penalties), and fewer than 250 by special courts – another indication that there was no need to re-establish these special jurisdictions. The purge of the administration, by contrast, was much more severe, affecting perhaps one-fourth or one-third of the civil service.

The government versus the ultras

Subsequently, the debate on the budget became the occasion of open conflict between the government and the Chamber. The finance minister, Corvetto, a former collaborator of baron Louis, was primarily concerned with restoring the State's credit. He had therefore prepared a balanced budget: in order to meet the ordinary expenses, which he reduced to 525 million francs by drastic economy measures, and the extraordinary expenses of 175 million (payments to the Allies and upkeep of the occupation army), he called for increased taxes and licence fees, and for a withholding tax on government salaries.

The Chamber took this budget apart; above all, it strenuously objected to the government's plan for the liquidation of accumulated debts. During the Hundred Days this item had increased from 462 million francs (the figure to which baron Louis had reduced it) to 695 million francs. Corvetto proposed giving the State's creditors promissory notes redeemable within three years through the sale of domain forests. The budget committee of the Chamber, opposed to the alienation of property that had for the most part belonged to the clergy, meant to reimburse the creditors of the Empire with bonds at par value (at this point public bonds stood at 60 francs). Eventually the Chamber decided not to implement this scheme of partial bankruptcy, but this was only after the government agreed to pay the State's creditors in five-year obligations at 5 per cent, without security.

Loss of confidence on the part of public opinion, scepticism about the State's ability to restore its finances among purveyors of capital, fear aroused by the insistent efforts of the majority deputies to recreate the independent wealth of the clergy – such was the result of this first session.

Foreign governments (and especially Wellington as commander of the occupation forces), became concerned about the payments and services owed them under the terms of the treaty, and indeed about the stability of the French monarchy. Wellington tried to gain influence with the comte d'Artois, and also informed Louis XVIII of his concern. Richelieu was deeply humiliated by this interference but he was not in a position to ignore it.

Moreover, it became clear that the elaboration of a voting law in keeping with the dispositions of the Charter was necessary. But on this subject the divergences between the government and the Chamber were such that no vote could ever be taken during this session.

Richelieu had harsh words for the 'madness' of the ultras, despite the bonds of sympathy by which he was attached to them. He had replaced Vaublanc, the Minister of the Interior who was favourable to them, with Lainé. He even considered creating a more docile Chamber by having one-fifth of the membership elected every year. But then he and Laîné were won over by a much more drastic cure proposed by Decazes: dissolution. At the same time, Decazes also succeeded in persuading the king to go along with this idea, and highly secret preparations were made to this effect.

The decree was signed by Louis XVIII on 5 September 1816. The comte d'Artois was informed only after the document was signed: deputies and ambassadors learned about it from the *Moniteur*. An appeal for support was made to the same electorate that had elected this Chamber the year before.

The government's victory was to open a new chapter in the history of the Restoration. Yet the Incredible Chamber was not an empty parenthesis: this assembly had come to interpret the Charter, against the king himself, in the sense of increased independence for the legislative branch: unaccountability of the king, accountability of the ministers, the necessity to obtain the consent of the majority, the Chamber's right to introduce or amend legislation – all of these ideas were being treated in its debates and discussed in a wide variety of pamphlets at the very time when the Chamber was dissolved. The most famous of these pamphlets was Chateaubriand's *De la monarchie selon la Charte*. Thus the ultra-royalist party itself contributed to an evolution that moved the regime issued from the Charter toward a parliamentary regime.

2

The government of the constitutional monarchists

In the period between the dissolution of the Incredible Chamber (5 September 1816) and the assassination of the duc de Berry (13 February 1820), France was ruled by the constitutional party under the governments of Richelieu (until December 1818), Dessolles-Decazes (until November 1819), and Decazes.

In the eyes of liberal historians, this was the best period of the Restoration. They stress, and rightly so, the accomplishment of France's recovery. Yet this recovery was insufficient to mask the political instability or the misery of the masses that marred these years.

Political instability

Called after the dissolution of the Incredible Chamber, the elections of October 1816 took place in a heated atmosphere. The prefects, under instructions from Decazes, pushed for the election of moderate royalists, while the agents of the pavillon de Marsan strongly advocated the re-election of the incumbents. Yet in the end the electorate disavowed most of its previous choices: in August 1815 the king had appeared as the only safeguard of the country's unity, and the enemies of the monarchy had been so discouraged that they abstained; thus the voters had simply elected royalists without giving much thought to the kind of government they were likely to support. Since then, many voters had become concerned about the initiative of the deputies. Now that the king had disowned them, a coalition for the defence of the institutions, ranging from prudent royalists to out-and-out adversaries of the regime, was particularly hostile to the ultra-royalist party. Yet this party retained solid support in western and southern France, but it lost a great deal of ground in other regions. Altogether only 90 of the 238 deputies elected were ultras.

The new majority remained united long enough to pass an electoral law conforming to the dispositions of the Charter. This was the Laîné law (February 1817), which gave the vote to all taxpayers over thirty years old who paid at least 300 francs in taxes and eligibility to men over forty who paid 1,000 francs in taxes. The electors were to meet in a single electoral college at the chief town of the department, and one-fifth of the Chamber of Deputies would be renewed every year.

How representative was an electoral body defined in this manner? The amount of the poll tax (*cens*) was determined essentially by the property tax and the *patente*, a licensing fee levied on merchants and professional men. However, the property tax, which represented a share of all the taxes owed by a department, varied widely from department to department in relation to the taxpayer's income, and the *patente* also varied according to the place and the profession. The right to vote was thus distributed very arbitrarily, and moreover fraud was easily perpetrated.

The electoral body represented a very variable percentage of the population and formed a kind of gerontocracy in a country where young people were in the majority; it was also dominated by the middle classes: within the electoral colleges at the departmental level, taxpayers paying between 300 and 500 francs formed a majority of middling property owners, often including shopkeepers and small-scale manufacturers. This last group, more numerous in the chief towns than in the countryside, was for that very reason less likely to abstain.

In point of fact, the ultra-royalists were probably correct when they pointed out that this well-to-do 'middle class' was most 'infected' with liberal or even anti-monarchical ideas. They themselves pushed for more democratic elections, but advocated voting by stages, anticipating that in the first stage the electors would choose large landowners to be electors in the second stage. To the liberals, by contrast, the Laîné law was the 'holy of holies', and any attempt to change it sacrilegious.

Yet the working of this law was to prove a disappointment to the government. It is true that the ultra opposition lost ground in every election, being reduced to some forty members after the election of 1819. But a new opposition was emerging from the left, and its progress was worrying indeed. To be sure, in 1816 some ten elected deputies were of the extreme liberal persuasion or of doubtful loyalty. But it was after the elections of 1817 that they united with newly elected deputies and formed the independent party, and this party was to gain about twenty seats in the elections of October 1818, when such men as La Fayette, Manuel, and Benjamin Constant were elected. Most importantly, this party received 35 of the 55 seats to be filled in September 1819, while the right lost 12 of its 18, and the centre 12 of its 27. The concern aroused by these results was deepened by the election at Grenoble of the former constitutional bishop Grégoire, elected with the help of votes cast by ultra-royalists who practiced a *politique du pire*. The emotion aroused by the election of this man who had acquiesced in regicide was such that even the liberals dropped him, so that he was unable to take his seat in the Chamber.

The independent party brought together very disparate elements and formed a group in which the most individualistic liberals rubbed shoulders with those who hankered after the despotism of the Empire or the Jacobin era. At that point neither Benjamin Constant, nor the bankers Laffitte or Périer, nor General Foy were ready to work for the fall of the Bourbons. However, the party did contain anti-dynastic elements, but of course they were not in a position to express their true sentiments. It is therefore not easy to assess their importance, especially since they represented a whole gamut of political convictions. Within the group one sees, in 1818 and 1819, a growing adherence to Bonapartist tenets and at the same time the increasingly important role played by secret societies, such as the *Union*, which tended to form the core group of the independent party, just as the *Chevaliers de la foi* formed the core group of the ultras. Even in the provinces, where royalists banded together in such groups as the *Francs régénérés* or the *Bandouliers*, liberal departmental committees in constant contact with Paris were formed. All parties had this clandestine aspect, which accounts for the liberal conspiracies of Grenoble (1816) and then Lyon (1817) (see part 2, ch. 13); the project of kidnapping the king and driving out his government (known as the 'bord de l'eau' plot) attributed to the ultra-royalists in June of 1818 does not seem to have been serious and probably amounted to no more than inconsequential talk. But the police, to some extent aware of this hidden aspect of political life (whose existence a **Benjamin** Constant could deny in perfectly good faith), either exaggerated its importance or used it for its own ends.

By 1817 Richelieu had gradually replaced those of his ministers who had ties with the left with representatives of the centre (Pasquier at Justice, Gouvion-Saint-Cyr at War, Molé at Navy). This 'constitutional party' wanted above all to tie the monarchy firmly to the new France and to found its institutions on the basis of the Charter without leaning towards either democracy or reaction.

But such a party did not constitute a stable base, and the advance of the liberals threatened to dissolve it. Not wishing to engage in a precarious balancing act, the government attempted to enlist the support of both the right and the left, an option that tended to divide the **constitutionalists** into centre-left and centre-right. The former, totally preoccupied with its resentment against the ultras and the memory of the White Terror, felt that the liberalisation of the institutions could be safely accomplished and that most of the opposition of the left could be brought back into the majority. This opinion was for a time held by Decazes and formulated much more dogmatically by the small group of '*doctrinaires*' who wielded great influence by dint of their political skill and their **eloquence**. By contrast, Laîné and Pasquier were inclined to enter into negotiations with the right where, under the influence of Villèle, a 'circumspect' current of opinion seemed to be overcoming the 'exaggerated' wing. The centre-right was especially well-represented in the House of Peers, where it rallied around Cardinal de Beausset; hence its name, the 'cardinal's meeting'.

On his return from the Congress of Aix-la-Chapelle (November 1818), Richelieu found the government in crisis and the majority in disarray. He attempted to form a government oriented toward the right. When these negotiations failed, a new coalition government of all the liberals was formed. Headed by General Dessolles, its most influential ministers were de Serre at Justice and Decazes at Interior (December 1818). This experiment was accompanied by a vigorous purge of the administration and hampered by an offensive on the part of the House of Peers, where the aged Barthélémy directed a coalition of the right and centre-right to pass a resolution calling for the revision of the Lainé law. This resolution was narrowly defeated in the Chamber of Deputies. Decazes had to subdue the belligerent Peers by creating a new batch of 60. But the experiment of a liberal coalition came to an end with the elections of September 1819, the results of which, and the ensuing outrage, have been described above. At that point Decazes made an about-face: forming a centre-right coalition with de Serre, he attempted to negotiate a rapprochement with the ultras. Villèle held talks with him, despite the party's fury against the 'favourite'. De Serre drafted a bill that would give a double vote to the taxpayers in the highest bracket. This bill was to be presented to the two Chambers on 14 February.

The situation changed completely during the night before this vote. The duc de Berry, the only hope of the Bourbon family, was stabbed at the opera by Louvel, a worker in the saddle-making trade, and died a few hours later. The criminal was a loner, but the ultra party blamed liberal ideas, and some of its most radical members wanted to put Decazes on trial. Louis XVIII was unable to stand up to the pressure of his entourage and, much to his chagrin, recalled the duc de Richelieu, naming Decazes ambassador to London and creating him a duke.

The major liberal legislation

The enactment of legislation by the governments of the constitutionalist period was often hesitant and fraught with contradiction. It reached total incoherence in the matter of the Concordat of 1817. After laborious negotiations a concordat designed to replace the Concordat of 1801 was signed with the Holy See and the government even proceeded to nominate new bishops in fulfilment of its provisions; but at that point the government realised that the Concordat of 1801 was a State law that could not be repealed without the consent of the Chambers. Since that consent was not likely to be forthcoming, the treaty had to be abandoned. Instead, the government gradually increased the number of bishoprics to eighty. Nonetheless, some major legislation was enacted, namely, the Gouvion-Saint-Cyr law concerning recruitment and advancement in the army (1818) and the de Serre laws concerning the press (1819).

The military law

The dissolution of the Napoleonic army brought the need for a general reorganisation of the military forces, which marked an important stage in France's recovery. This reorganisation was the principal task of Marshal Gouvion-Saint-Cyr.

The bill he submitted to the vote of the Chambers organised military recruitment in the following manner: every year all the 20-year-old men who had been certified fit for service were to draw a number by lot. Those who drew a 'bad number' were to be incorporated into the contingent of recruits limited to a maximum of 40,000 men, unless they had the means to pay for a substitute. The bill also permitted voluntary enlistment as another source of recruits. The period of active service was to be six years. But thereafter the veterans were to be members of the reserve, although reserve units were never organised.

As for advancement, the bill stipulated that no man could become an officer unless he had served for two years as a non-commissioned officer or unless he had graduated from one of the military schools that admitted students by competitive entrance examination (Saint-Cyr for the infantry, Metz for the artillery). Advancement from one rank to the next was strictly regulated, and two-thirds of all promotions up to the rank of lieutenant-colonel were to be granted on the basis of seniority.

In both Chambers the debate about this **bill** brought one of the liveliest controversies of the Restoration. The ultra opposition even prevailed upon the comte d'Artois to solicit the support of Louis XVIII, who was most displeased at this interference. The objections to the bill centred on its provisions for recruitment, advancement, and the establishment of a reserve army. On the first point, the opponents objected that the law would reinstitute conscription, which the princes on their return had promised to abolish; they strongly advocated a professional army. On the second point, they felt that the rules for advancement would restrict the free choice of the king, which was guaranteed by the Charter. In reality the nobility was defending the 'last refuge' of privilege, believing that the profession of officer had been its exclusive preserve in the old France. Aside from this defence of an old privilege, the ultras were also impelled by a reflex of fear, which became fully manifest on the third point, the matter of a reserve army; for such an army, at least for the time being, would be made up of the veterans of the Empire. If the liberals still had dreadful memories of the White Terror, the royalists were haunted by the thought of an army formed and led by the former 'brigands of the Loire'.

In a speech given on 26 January 1818, the Minister of War 'frankly' dealt with this 'national question that is of concern to all of France, whether civilian or military'. The text of the speech was written by Guizot, but Marshal Gouvion-Saint-Cyr, who in his youth had been an actor, aroused high emotion when he paid vibrant homage to the imperial army:

> We must decide whether there exist in our midst two armies, two nations, one of which will be struck with anathema, declared unfit to serve the king and France. And, to stay within the bounds of what concerns me directly, we must decide whether we will once again call to the defence of the fatherland soldiers who have made its glory, or whether we will declare them once and for all dangerous to its tranquillity. The latter decision would be harsh and unjust, for these soldiers were admirable on the day of battle: they were moved by indefatigable ardour, upheld by heroic patience; they never ceased to believe that they were sacrificing their lives for the glory of France; and when they left their colours, they still had to offer vast treasures of strength and bravery! Will France have to renounce their services? In times of adversity, will it not be able to take pride in these men whom Europe has never ceased to admire?

On this occasion the king and the government gave proof of boldness. The loyalty of the army during the Spanish war was to show that this boldness paid off.

The press laws

Freedom of the press, a principle proclaimed by the Charter, only slowly came into its own. Since the Terror the press had never been free for any length of time and all governments were wary of this power whose influence they were unable to assess. After the restrictive regulations of 1814 and the edict suppressing seditious writings of 1815, the various governments therefore inaugurated a progressive liberalisation only through a series of provisional laws promulgated in 1817 and 1818. Yet all segments of public opinion expressed a very strong desire to be informed – or to be reinforced in their political options – through the reading of newspapers or periodicals.

On the ultra side the great royalist publications were already in existence: the *Quotidienne* directed by Michaud, the historian of the crusades; the *Gazette de France*; the violent *Drapeau blanc*; the Bertin brothers' *Journal des débats*. Not as durable as these publications, the *Conservateur* which, as Chateaubriand proudly claimed, enlisted the collaboration of everyone who counted in the party, attempted to blend ultra tendencies and the pursuit of the great liberties, a goal that was also shared by Fiévée and his *Correspondance politique et administrative*. Liberal papers also were founded during these years, the most important among them being the

Constitutionnel directed by Etienne and Tissot. If the *Nain jaune*, implacably hostile to the regime, was edited in the Netherlands and could only circulate through clandestine channels, more moderate publications such as Comte's *Censeur*, Dunoyer's *Bibliothèque historique*, and the successive organs of the indefatigable Benjamin Constant, *Le Mercure*, *La Minerve*, and *La Renommée*, testified to the importance of liberal thought at that time. In the government's camp could be counted, aside from the *Moniteur* with its political articles, the *doctrinaire* publications, the *Journal général* and Guizot's *Archives philosophiques, politiques et littéraires*.

From time to time, the government or the judiciary would react. The seizing of *La Monarchie selon la Charte* ordered by Decazes, which Chateaubriand tried to oppose in person, stirred up resentment; above all, the condemnation on questionable legal grounds of Comte and Dunoyer, liberal though by no means anti-monarchist writers, to one year of prison underscored the arbitrary nature of this control. A Society of the Friends of Freedom of the Press was founded in 1818, and the ultras were as ardent in the defence of this principle as the liberals.

The Minister of Justice, de Serre, therefore gave the press a liberal statute laid down in three laws, the first dealing with press-related crimes and offences, the second with the procedures of repression, and the third with newspapers and periodical publications. For the first he had sought the advice of the young duc de Broglie, Madame de Staël's son-in-law, who had become an oracle in *doctrinaire* circles; in drafting the third, he had been helped by Guizot, at that time director of departmental and communal administration in the Ministry of Interior. These laws, which were passed by the Chambers in May and June 1819, established several major principles.

The first of these principles was that 'an opinion does not become criminal when it is expressed publicly', meaning that the press cannot commit a crime or offence unless its writing provokes a crime or offence. In applying this major principle, the law defined and limited the categories of actions that could be prosecuted: provocation of a common-law crime or offence, offences against public or religious (this last word was contributed by the right) morality, offences against the king and the constitutional authorities, defamation or libel against private individuals.

The second principle guaranteed that indicted authors would be tried not by professional judges of a criminal court but by a jury. Newspapers were to be published freely, provided they deposited a declaration stating the names of their owners and managers and posted bond.

The de Serre laws established the liberal doctrine in matters concerning the press for several generations to come: freedom of expression derived from freedom of opinion and trial by jury in case of legal proceedings.

The grain crisis of 1816–17

The crisis of 1816–17 was not exclusively a French phenomenon. It also struck Ireland, Germany, and Switzerland, where 1817 is known as 'the year of the beggars' mortality'. But it was exceptionally severe in France because there the climatic causes were compounded by the consequences of the invasion.

The latter came into play first. The arrival of the allied troops in the summer of 1815, shortly before the harvest, attended by the usual trampling over cultivated fields, the flight of the peasants, and plundering, led to a harvest deficit in the most productive grain-growing regions; the Brie region for instance produced only three-fifths of the harvest of 1814. Subsequently, the requisitions that were made until the autumn depleted the grain reserves. Yet by the end of the year the price of bread had risen only slightly, although this does not mean that the population was not suffering, for the invasion had given rise to a crisis in the textile industry in Normandy and Champagne. In any case, it was already clear that in 1816 the period before the new harvest would be difficult.

As it happened, that year's weather conditions were disastrous: long periods of cold rain in the spring, frost in May, repeated hailstorms in August (that of 5 August affected almost the entire French territory); consequently, the grain harvest was mediocre and the wine harvest practically nil. As for the wheat, there was not only a quantitative deficiency but a qualitative one as well.

The rise in the price of grain, and hence of bread, was therefore considerable. M. Chabert, taking 100 as the base index of 1820, calculates that the hectolitre of wheat reached the index of 148 in 1816, and 189 in 1817 (as compared to 102.1 in 1815), while the price of bread reached 131.8 and 167.3 (compared to 89.1 in 1815). Actually, the price rise was very variable even for markets fairly close to each other, although the price curve showed a rising trend everywhere from the first months of 1816 to the middle of 1817, reaching their peak in May, June, or July. Local studies indicate that eastern France experienced the steepest price rise. In the department of Meurthe, the price of wheat almost quadrupled between January 1816 and June 1817, that of rye more than tripled (elsewhere the coefficient indicating the rise in the price of rye, the cereal consumed by the popular classes, often exceeded that of wheat), while the price of barley and oats more than quadrupled. Between July 1816 and July 1817 the price of bread rose from 1 to 3.6 or 1 to 3.4 depending on the quality of the bread. In the wake of these price rises, other foodstuffs as well became more expensive, especially the potato, which experienced a sevenfold price increase between January 1816 and July 1817, while the price of meat, which not everyone could afford, rose from 1 to 1.67 and fat pork to

2.77. The drought of the spring of 1817 brought the additional complication of a deficit in vegetable production.

At Strasbourg the rise in the price of wheat was also considerable. In the Brie region it was somewhat more moderate, for in May 1817 a hectolitre of wheat was worth 49 francs (compared to 20 in January 1816), a hectolitre of rye 36 francs (compared to 11.25 in January 1816). But in this region part of the harvest never reached the market and was sold clandestinely at higher prices by the well-to-do tenant farmers to buyers who came to pick it up after nightfall.

As the harvest of 1817 approached, a slight downward trend appeared in the price curve and continued – though not without some sudden upward jolts – until the good harvest of 1818. But until then the popular classes, whose diet was essentially based on bread, experienced stark hunger.

The administration did its best to keep the cities supplied, and so the suffering was particularly acute in small towns and the countryside. There were regions where for months on end the inhabitants lived on grass, and where poor wretches were found dead of starvation. Once again, scenes from the worst days of the past were relived: starving crowds trying to impose price controls on the foodstuffs in the markets, bands of beggars or brigands attacking convoys of victuals on the roads and rivers. One can follow the route taken by these revolts of desperation, which affected all of the country except the Mediterranean regions, where conditions were somewhat better; surprisingly, they affected the centre of the country more severely than the east.

The first manifestations of unrest can be observed in the department of Nord, in the Croisic region, and at Castres in the spring of 1816. But the first major outbreak of popular excitement took place between November 1816 and January 1817. Almost everywhere, from Ain to Haute-Vienne, from Seine-Inférieure to Lot, markets were attacked, bakeries were looted, and men were sometimes killed in the fighting. Rather more specific in nature were the troubles that shook the Vendée and Mayenne in November and the great riot that held Toulouse in its grip for several days: in these regions where there was no shortage, crowds led by *chouans* or *verdets* attempted to stop the shipping of grain to Bordeaux or Marseille, respectively.

In the second wave of rioting that broke out in May–June 1817, veritable *jacqueries* swept through entire regions. In the Brie region the insurgents started out from Essonnes (3–4 June), took over Château-Thierry, and looted Chauny (10 June), but it was in the departments of Aube and especially Yonne, where the vintners besieged Sens, that the insurrection reached its greatest scope. Some lesser uprisings were nipped in the bud, like that of Bazadais which the prefect of Bordeaux, Tournon, appeased with a promise of amnesty.

In the department of Yonne, Decazes had Sens cleared by 200 hussars and 500 footsoldiers of the guard, and the *prévôtal* [special] court handed down a number of death sentences. In the department of Seine-et-Marne, a screen of four cavalry regiments was deployed from La-Ferté-sous-Jouarre to Voulx as mobile columns of footsoldiers searched the woods. In most places the gendarmerie was unable to cope, and the National Guard was visibly loath to restore order.

The government was slow to realise (or to admit) the extent of the crisis. Unlike the imperial government during the crisis of 1811, Laîné and Decazes made every effort to maintain the free circulation of grain and free trade. However, some attempts at regulation were made by the prefects, who supervised the bakeries, set standards for the composition of flour, prohibited the distilling of grain for the making of spirits, and in some cases even issued rationing cards for bread. In addition, the government spent 70 million francs to import grain from all directions, from Liverpool or Holland as well as from the Levant or the Black Sea. The appearance of Russian wheat at Marseille was a novelty and opened a new trade route along the Rhône.

The prefects, working hand in hand with the notables, followed the example of the government. At Bordeaux, grain was imported from Mogador, and orders were placed in America. But, most importantly, the prefects organised public welfare in the form of public works (*ateliers de charité*) and distributions of bread and rice.

Most of these hunger riots did not extend to political demands, even if a 'proscribed name' was occasionally scrawled on a wall. Certain cases have been seen by historians as evidence of the role played by the popular royalist forces. Yet it should be noted that in Yonne, one of the most troubled departments, it is difficult to decide how much of the agitation was due to the misery of the vintners and how much to loyalty to the Emperor. Similarly, the obscure 'conspiracy' of Lyon (see part 2, ch. 13) certainly had something to do with the food shortage. By and large, however, the political opposition to the regime did not attempt to use these popular outbreaks for its own ends.

Yet this was precisely the fear of the ultra party and especially of the policy-makers of the pavillon de Marsan. These groups feared the departure of the foreign troops. Wellington, no doubt more perspicacious, sensed that the people blamed their suffering on the victors' requisitions, real and imagined. By 1818 he had come to the conclusion that although he might be able to regroup his forces in a defensive position without diminishing their number, the best means of avoiding trouble in France would be, all things considered, to withdraw them. Hatred for the occupier, which might well rally the malcontents around Bonapartist leadership, would thus perish for lack of nourishment.

The duc de Richelieu and the liberation of the French territory

The financial situation and the end of the occupation

For all his doubts and his discouragement, the duc de Richelieu never lost sight of his uppermost concern, which was the liberation of the French soil and the restoration of France to independence and a rightful place in Europe. As far as he was concerned, there was only one way to achieve this goal: the loyal fulfilment, however difficult this might be, of all the obligations the French government had assumed toward foreign states and private individuals. He was aware that this policy was not 'likely to foster love for the family that has been given back to France', but he felt that this goodwill would restore moral prestige to the country and that the government would have better leverage for obtaining more lenient terms from the Allies if it could appeal to their good faith or their good sense.

The duc de Richelieu had been deeply upset by the projects for partial bankruptcy and the demagogical fiscal policies of the Incredible Chamber, which he saw as a threat to public confidence in the French government. 'These gentlemen', he wrote to marquis d'Osmond, 'have attacked the royal prerogative, disregarded the king's ministers, and killed credit, all of this to the cry of "Vive le Roi!".' The Chamber elected in 1816 authorised the drafting of a plan for financial recovery, whose principles were outlined by Corvetto, the Minister of Finance, on 14 November. It called for the exact repayment of all debts, a surplus of receipts over expenditures, an appeal to the confidence of the capitalists by providing safe investment opportunities, and security for all existing fortunes.

The proposed budget was based on these principles and conceived as a first step in a long-term undertaking: it clearly distinguished between ordinary and extraordinary expenditures, and while the weight of the latter, which included the war indemnities and the upkeep of the occupation troops, could not possibly be covered by current receipts, these receipts (774 million francs) were nonetheless much greater than the ordinary expenditures (630 million out of a total of 1,080 million francs). As for the amortisation fund created in April of the previous year, its annual endowment was raised to 40 million francs and in addition received 150,000 hectares of forest and the arrears from repurchased property titles. A clear budget, a tight fiscal policy, and stringent economy measures were to help the government cut back borrowing to the indispensable level. Yet by the end of 1816, French government bonds had fallen to 40 francs, and the government, having been authorised to issue 30 million francs worth of new bonds, was forced to accept very onerous terms in contracting these large loans.

After difficult negotiations, an arrangement was made with Baring of

London and Hope of Amsterdam, at the time the leading international banking houses. After a first agreement concluded on 22 March 1817, two additional loans were granted in the same year in the form of the purchase of bonds valued at a total sum of 26.7 million francs and an advance of 315 million francs. One-third of the third instalment of these loans was taken over by French bankers, like Laffitte and Delessert. The first loan had been contracted in bonds nominally valued at 100 and carrying a 5 per cent interest, but they sold at 55 francs, so that for an interest of 5 francs the bankers only advanced the French treasury 55 francs; on this sum, moreover, they received a commission of 2.5 francs; and finally, interest payments on the loans granted began on the average six months before the drafts were actually issued by Baring and Hope, who here again made a profit of about 2.5 francs. Surely the plentiful money supplies of London could not have found a more advantageous investment opportunity. In addition, the possibility that French government bonds might increase in value opened up a golden perspective. It is true that the very prestige of Baring's gave the capitalists confidence and affected the standing of these bonds in the stock exchange. This is why, despite the massive bond issues, their price rose steadily, so that subsequent loans were contracted at slightly more favourable terms.

The sums to be paid four times a year to the Allies were thus assured, and Richelieu succeeded in persuading the Allies to reduce the occupation troops from 150,000 to 120,000 men starting 1 April 1817, a step that represented an annual saving of 30 million francs for the French State.

But presently a new and unexpected threat arose. The treaties had made France responsible for any sums that France owed to individuals abroad and for any damages it had caused to allied nationals. At the time of the Treaty of Paris these sums were estimated at about 200 million francs. But it turned out that these claims amounted to 1,600 million francs. While the claims filed by the English had been thoroughly examined, the small German States presented totally extravagant claims. The czar was prepared to give in to the demand for a reduction made by Richelieu, who pointed out that France could not possibly raise such a sum; but Prussia opposed the reduction in a violent pamphlet destined for the German public, which had the effect of stifling the goodwill of Austria. Finally, Alexander suggested that Wellington be called upon to arbitrate. The English and Spanish claims were treated separately and evaluated at a capital value corresponding to interest payments of 4 million francs. As for the other claims, Wellington conscientiously carried out his assignment, thanks to Rothschild's reports: he evaluated the total claims at 240 million francs, which was a considerable reduction of the original sum, and authorised the French government to budget 12 million of its revenue from the interest on government bonds for its payment, to take effect on

22 March 1818. Altogether, then, the government had to pay out an additional 16 million in interest on bonds. This time it proceeded differently and placed subscriptions for 14.6 million francs worth of bonds on the open market. The capitalists' demand [for these subscriptions] reached 163 million francs and the government chose those subscribers who offered the best security.

Despite this repeated need for borrowing, Richelieu decided to pay off the indemnity owed to the Allies two years ahead of schedule. Even though the Treaty of Paris had not spelled out a formal relation between the payment of the indemnity and the occupation, Richelieu hoped that once the former was paid off, the latter would be reduced to three years instead of the five years foreseen in the Treaty of Paris. The only objection that could be made to retiring the troops at the end of the third year was the fear that a revolution might break out following the departure of the occupation armies. We have already spoken of the haunting fears of the ultras, especially in the face of the recent popular unrest and the electoral advances of the liberals. The comte d'Artois took the unfortunate step of broaching this question with the Allies, ordering a *note secrète* written by Vitrolles to be handed to Count Orloff, aide-de-camp to the czar (May 1818); it is probable that in doing so the comte d'Artois intended to make the sovereigns pressure Louis XVIII into changing his government, but Decazes published a truncated version of this *note* and the public was convinced that the comte d'Artois had asked for an extension of the occupation. As a result of this ill-considered action, the heir to the throne was relieved of the supreme command of the National Guard.

The Congress of Aix-la-Chapelle and the end of France's isolation

The French problems were examined once again at a congress meeting at Aix-la-Chapelle on 27 September. The three continental sovereigns were present; Castlereagh headed the English and Richelieu the French delegation. An agreement between Metternich and Castlereagh kept the minor powers out of this meeting, despite the wishes of the czar, who was suspected of wanting to use them to establish a Russian hegemony in Europe. Agreement was easily reached concerning the end of the occupation of France and the dissolution of the ambassadors' conference in Paris, which had been an irksome tutelage for the French government. Nor did the financial arrangements for the next two years, well prepared by the present government's negotiations with Baring and Hope, raise any particular difficulties. France owed 280 million francs, a sum that was reduced to 265 million; of this, 100 million were budgeted as interest on bonds in the Great Book of the French Debt under the date of 22 September 1818, and it was decided that the remaining 165 million francs would be paid by Hope and Baring in 9 monthly instalments beginning 6 January 1819.

Prussia proposed that the upkeep of an international force stationed in the Netherlands be substituted for the occupation; this proposal was rejected. Richelieu had hoped that the Treaty of Chaumont, concluded against France for a period of twenty years, would be repealed. This did not happen, and in fact the czar himself, in whom he had placed his hopes, declared to Metternich and Castlereagh that he wished to renew it. But henceforth the treaty was to be secret and would be invoked only in case of a revolution in France.

When it came to the future organisation of Europe, however, two opposing conceptions emerged; that of the czar, who advocated the formation of a body representing all nations, was rejected in favour of the Anglo-Austrian conception calling for occasional meetings of the great powers only. But in order to prevent Alexander, who was isolated within this quadruple alliance, from yielding to the temptation of concluding a parallel bilateral accord with France, as his ambassador to Paris, the Corsican Pozzo di Borgo, urged him to do, it was decided to enlarge this European directory by admitting France as an equal member. On 4 November the Allies therefore asked France to 'participate in its present and future deliberations'. Richelieu, having consulted with the king, responded favourably on 12 November.

Though initially disappointed at the renewal of the quadruple alliance, he was satisfied with the end results of the congress. Having become a secret treaty that would be invoked only in case of a revolution in France, the accord of Chaumont had lost much of its significance. On the other hand, the open and **unrestricted** admission of France as an equal partner in a directory that would debate the major issues of Europe indicated that France had recovered its position as a great nation. Richelieu had accomplished the task he had set for himself.

At the time, virtually no one contested the loyalty and the skill of the duke who, with means very different from those of his predecessors, had been able within three years to accomplish the recovery of a country whose very national unity was in jeopardy. By contrast, the financial recovery he had accomplished with the help of Corvetto, an indispensable precondition for the improvement of France's diplomatic position, gave rise to the most heated criticism.

One of the principal grievances against Corvetto was that, in contracting the major loans, he had dealt with foreign rather than Parisian bankers. This reproach was forcefully stated by both Casimir-Périer and Villèle, who claimed that by calling for competitive bids for these loans, they could have been obtained at rates from par value to 10 per cent. This claim no doubt does not take into consideration the restricted French market (most of the capitalists who subscribed directly to the publicly advertised loan seem to have been speculators rather than lenders) or, above all, the exceptional confidence that Baring gave the foreign powers.

The fact that Baring's was willing to lend money to France, albeit at onerous terms, gave them confidence that France would recover. Moreover, in the final analysis, it was probably wiser to finance these payments with English or Dutch gold than to perform a massive drain of capital that was liable to dry up the internal investments needed to stimulate the French economy.

However that may be, an extremely heavy tax burden was imposed on property owners and above all on ordinary people by means of indirect taxes on consumer goods. This policy was bound to make the regime unpopular.

3

The royalist reaction

The second Richelieu government (20 February 1820–14 December 1821)

The assassination of the duc de Berry stunned public opinion, but did not result in one of those movements for unity that sometimes occur in the wake of a catastrophe. On the contrary, it only served to exacerbate the hostility between ultras and liberals.

Repression

Despite Louvel's confession, the ultras did not believe that he had acted in isolation. All of Europe seemed to them to be shaken by the machinations of a vast conspiracy against all legitimate dynasties: since 1817 student unrest had agitated Germany, and in March of 1819 the writer Kotzebue, suspected of being an agent of the czar, had been assassinated at Mannheim by the student Sand. In January 1820, Riego's uprising at Cadiz had forced Ferdinand VII to accept the constitution of the Cortes of 1812, and in July of the same year the military imposed the same constitution on his old uncle, Ferdinand I, king of Naples. The unrest was soon to spread to Portugal, then to Piedmont (March 1821). Still haunted by the memory of the Hundred Days, the royalists demanded stringent measures of precaution and repression. While some of the 'exaltés' saw Decazes as an enemy of the dynasty, the others felt that he was morally responsible because of his lenient attitude toward the liberals.

The liberals for their part suspected the ultras of making all this noise in order to do away with the Charter. It seemed to them that the defence of the liberties recognised in that document justified the recourse to illegality. La Fayette almost openly said so in the Chamber.

In the aftermath of the duke's death, therefore, when Decazes proposed emergency measures to the Chamber, the left was hostile; and so was the right, because of their author. In replacing Decazes, it was essential to find a man who stood above the parties, and that man could only be Richelieu.

Well aware of his limited ability to solve this internal crisis, the duke nonetheless yielded when the comte d'Artois pledged his support to him.

He formed an administration of constitutional royalists whose mainstay was the comte de Serre as Keeper of the Seals. Thoroughly frightened by now by the advance of the left, de Serre was ready to undo his own work and to fight his former friends, the *doctrinaires*, who had openly passed over to the liberal side. The Chamber became divided into two adamantly hostile camps, and in the course of impassioned debates the governmental faction, together with the right, was able to muster a very narrow majority to pass measures designed to limit public liberties that were scarcely different from those that had been prepared by Decazes before his departure:

1 Suspension of personal liberty, which made it possible to arrest and detain individuals suspected of conspiracy for three months without trial.
2 Modification of the press regulations, including the restoration of advance permits and, temporarily, censorship for newspapers and periodicals. The *Minerve* and the *Bibliothèque historique* succumbed to severe repression, while Chateaubriand himself ceased the publication of the *Conservateur*. Surviving opposition papers such as the *Constitutionnel* led a precarious existence.
3 A new electoral law, the so-called 'law of the double vote'. The Chamber of Deputies consisted of 258 members elected by voters who paid at least 300 francs in direct taxes. Henceforth these deputies were to be elected no longer by their department but by their *arrondissement*, a modification with which the left was willing to go along. In addition, however, a 'high' electoral college, formed by a fourth of the department's electors, namely those who paid the highest amount of taxes, would meet at the departmental *chef-lieu*. In this manner, 172 additional deputies (or two-fifths of the Chamber expanded to 430 members) would be elected by one-fourth of the electorate.

First stirring of the opposition

The debates that filled the session of 1820 were among the most remarkable of the Restoration. In order to compensate for the lack of information in the newspapers, the opposition deputies spoke 'out the window'. And this was barely a metaphor, for crowds of people waiting for news and watching the voting applauded or berated the deputies (when Chauvelin, a deputy of the extreme left, was so ill that he had to be carried to the Chamber, the reception he was given amounted to a veritable triumph). In June fighting broke out among the spectators, and on 3 June the student Lallemand was clubbed to death by the *gardes du corps*; his funeral very nearly turned into a riot.

These first disturbances heralded the adoption of illegal means on the part of one segment of the liberals. By August, there was a veritable conspiracy which, however, was foiled by the government. But neither the violence of the opposition nor its recourse to illegality found much resonance among the masses of provincial Frenchmen. Loyalty to the monarchy was manifested at the birth of the duc de Bordeaux, the posthumous son of the duc de Berry, who was called 'the child of miracle', and the November elections showed a return to favour of the right. Not only did the right do well in the 'high' electoral colleges, the left also suffered heavy losses in those *arrondissements* colleges which elected one-fifth of the Chamber that year. In the Chamber the liberals were left with 80 members out of a total of 430, with the rest divided between government supporters and ultras.

This situation was actually a new danger for Richelieu, who tried to parry it by creating ministerial posts for Villèle and Corbière, the most reasonable leaders of the ultra party, who thus became members of the cabinet in December 1820. Here they always made it a point to voice the demands of the right in order to remain above suspicion from that quarter. In July 1821 they demanded that their party be given the Ministries of Interior and of War; this caused their break with Richelieu, and they went back to the Chamber as ordinary deputies. When the elections of 21 October further strengthened the right, it decided to join the opposition. This step was encouraged by the left, which felt that a government of the right would soon prove its inability to govern.

At that point the government's foreign policy also furnished ample ammunition to its critics. As we have seen, the king of Naples had been constrained to accept the Spanish constitution of 1812 and Metternich had considered restoring the absolutist regime by Austrian troops. He did, however, agree to the calling of a congress at Troppau (October–December 1820) and another at Laybach (January–February 1821). France was torn between the desire not to remain apart from the continental powers and the desire to keep the Austrians out of Naples. The French government hoped to come to an agreement with Russia and to impose a mediated settlement that would reconcile Ferdinand I and his subjects with a more moderate constitutional regime. But Alexander no longer favoured liberal institutions and had become increasingly interested in the Levant. The French foreign minister, Pasquier, was unable to give realistic instructions to the French representatives; moreover, these two men, La Ferronays, ambassador to St Petersburg, and Caraman, ambassador to Vienna, were totally at odds with each other. At Laybach, the arrogant presence of Blacas made the French delegation look a little less pathetic. Yet he was unable to persuade his government to send French troops to Naples to head off the Austrians.

The Austrians thus had a free hand in Italy. Their occupation troops were sent not only to Naples but also to Piedmont after the insurrection of 1821, and to all the States in between that were needed for strategic purposes. The French critics of the right, sensitive to the loss of French prestige, and those of the left, which blamed the government for failing to support the Italian constitutionalists, joined together in one paragraph of an address expressing the wish that peace not be 'purchased at the price of sacrifices incompatible with the honour of the nation and the dignity of the crown'.

In domestic affairs, the two opposition parties also demanded an end to censorship of the press and Richelieu was faced with the choice between his own resignation and the dissolution of the Chamber. The comte d'Artois, despite his promises, did not like him, and King Louis XVIII, increasingly indifferent to politics, withdrew his support. On 15 December an exclusively 'ultra' government was formed.

The second Richelieu administration was thus a transition government between the constitutionals and the right. But it did plant the seeds of the regime's ultimate demise; fear of revolution and the pessimistic awareness of his own weakness caused Richelieu to rely exclusively on repressive measures and on the political support of the upper classes, especially the nobility. His decision not to enlarge the scope of political life, a policy that had hitherto been vocally supported by many of the ultras, placed the regime at the mercy of a tiny and arbitrarily chosen electorate.

Conspiracies and the Carbonari movement (1820–2)

The secret societies

In 1820 and 1821 the liberal revolutionary movements that troubled the Europe of the Holy Alliance also agitated the political life of France. Here as elsewhere they were the work of secret societies. But if the French conspirators had contacts with German émigrés in Alsace and Italian émigrés in the southeast, and if they also occasionally met other exiles in Switzerland, these contacts remained sporadic. An international federation of revolutionaries directed by a central committee with head-quarters in Paris as Metternich claimed, or in Italy as the head of the police Franchet-Despéret believed, was a pure figment of the imagination. To be sure, the pro-Romantic or Romantic current with its propensity for mystery, occultism, and initiation rites provided a European-wide context for these parallel movements, but while imitations did occur, each of these movements had its own autonomy.

In France, moreover, the liberals were neither the first nor the only group to band together in secret societies. We have seen the role of the *Chevaliers de la foi* and of freemasonry which, once it was liberated from the constraints it had suffered under the Empire, accommodated a consider-able diversity of political options and experienced the proliferation of its lodges. For the liberals, on the other hand, the basis of clandestine activity was the discontent of well-defined social classes to whom the regime denied any other means of expression. Above all, this was true for the army and the students.

It is easy to understand the army's longing for the past, and historians have emphasised, not without exaggeration, the case of the retired officer on half pay who lived in straightened circumstances, remembering the glorious days of the past. Yet the army suffered more than just nostalgia. The officer on active duty was poorly paid, had little chance of advancement, and lived in fear of purges, such as the one that was carried out in 1820 by the Minister of War, Latour-Maubourg. Moreover, many noble officers were promoted over the heads of commoners, in disregard of the Gouvion-Saint-Cyr law. The problem of advancement was particularly acute for the non-commissioned officers, whose future was blocked by the absence of military operations. The fact is that in an army that conceived of itself as the most loyal part of the nation, conspiracies had practically never ceased since 1814.

The problem facing the non-commissioned officers assumed even greater scope for the students. The Revolution and the Empire had called upon young leaders to fill the gaps left by the emigration or the war. The Restoration reduced the number of civil servants (to 190,000), yet failed to create employment in the economy. Since the birth rate had remained high in France, large numbers of young bourgeois faced a future in which they would swell the ranks of lawyers without cases and physicians without patients. This conflict of generations involved clerks and shopkeepers' assistants as well as a segment of the professional bourgeoisie that was hard put to make ends meet.

A third, sociologically more varied, element included those who because of their close ties to the Revolution were hostile to all forms of reactionary politics: owners of nationalised property, the Protestant manufacturers of eastern France, and so forth.

That is why secret societies soon began to spread. The first of these were Bonapartist military groups, such as the *Epingle noire* and above all the *Bazar français*, which used the cover of a business venture to call active or retired officers to meetings in a café; many of these officers, from Fabvier to Caron, later became leaders of conspiracies. Simultaneously, and as early as 1815, student associations were founded; some of their members had the prestige of having served as volunteers during the Hundred Days. The *Société diablement philosophique*, for example, whose two founders Bazard and Buchez later wielded considerable influence in revolutionary circles, eventually became a masonic lodge, *Les amis de la Vérité*, and although it took rather unusual liberties in the matter of ritual, it had some 1,000 members in 1820. In western France, one major secret society seems to have been the oldest of all: the *Chevaliers de la liberté*, which had already existed under a different name during the first Restoration.

Founded by an ex-major of the imperial army living at Saumur, and having recruited its first members both at the Cavalry School and in civilian circles, it encountered fertile ground among the bourgeois of the western towns, and it was soon joined by more popular elements, such as bargemen of the Loire and artisans.

In a different style, the *Union*, a society founded in Paris by a lawyer from Grenoble, Rey, seems to have been mainly preoccupied with training the leadership for a future revolutionary movement. Among the members of this society one finds politicians and prominent lawyers such as La Fayette, Corcelle, Merilhou, and others. Some of its membership came from the *Société des amis de la liberté de la presse*.

During the demonstrations of 1820, contact was established between the men of the *Amis de la Verité* and those of the *Bazar français*. Since both groups felt that the law of the double vote violated the spirit of the Charter, it was decided that the time for insurrection had come. On 19 August the military were to issue the call to arms in the barracks and march on the fort of Vincennes, while the students massed across the street from the Pantheon in the building inhabited by one of their leaders, Joubert, would call the outlying districts of Paris to insurrection. Movements in support of their action would break out in the provinces.

As it happened, these preparations were brought to the attention of Marmont, who immediately alerted the government. In view of the precautionary measures that were put into effect, the conspirators decided to call off the uprising at the last moment. The Court of Peers charged with prosecuting the conspiracy did not take it very seriously. Some of the minor figures were condemned, but the ringleaders were not pursued.

The short-lived Carbonari movement

It was in the wake of this failure that the *Charbonnerie*, or Carbonari movement, was organised. The Italian Carbonari was a secret association originally formed in opposition to the regime of King Joseph of Naples, and its vocabulary was borrowed from the woodcutters and charcoal-burners who had always lived on the margins of society, in southern Italy as elsewhere. Since then this secret society had adopted – in addition to its traditional Christian symbolism – a liberal attitude. In France, many Italian émigrés and Corsicans who had returned to their island (one of them, a man named Limperani, was to play a role in the conspiracies) had retained their affiliation with the Carbonari. But the French Carbonari movement really started only after Joubert and his friend Dugied, who had fled to Italy after 19 August, were initiated. Upon their return to France in March 1821, they adapted the Neapolitan statutes to their French milieu. They felt that the rigorously clandestine character and the military organisation of the Carbonari movement would be a guarantee of success.

Every Carbonaro belonged to a 'stand' ('*vente*') of ten members, paid dues and was pledged to have a gun and 25 cartridges in readiness. There was a whole hierarchy of 'stands' on the communal, departmental, and national level. Each higher echelon was formed by delegates from the lower echelons, but the rank and file only knew their comrades in their own stand; this compartmentalisation allowed only limited infiltration by the police. At the top, the high or supreme stand was composed of two elements: young people like Buchez, Bazard, Dugied, and seasoned politicians or great notables, such as La Fayette, Dupont de l'Eure, Voyer d'Argenson, Koechlin, Corcelle, and others.

While the rhetoric was still that of the French Revolution, and while the tricolour remained the venerated emblem of the movement, its political programme was rather vague. Nor could it be otherwise in a society whose membership included military men and civilians, republicans and Bonapartists.

New members were recruited with a rapidity that can only be explained by the vivid memories of the White Terror and the fact that some existing secret societies, such as the *Chevaliers de la liberté*, were incorporated as a body. The stands were organised by delegates sent for the purpose from Paris. Sixty departments were affected by the movement, although membership was largest in Paris and in the western and eastern departments. The total number of affiliates may have reached 30,000.

Without wasting any time, the Carbonari movement began to prepare its conspiracies. The first uprising would begin with an action at Saumur on 24 November 1821, to be followed by an insurrection at Belfort that was to spread throughout Alsace. This latter insurrection was carefully prepared, for Koechlin had used his workshops to shelter the military cadres who had escaped the repression of the insurrection of 19 August, and the garrisons were thoroughly undermined. Yet this uprising ended in double failure: at Saumur the director of the Cavalry School most probably knew about the plot all along, and at Belfort the suspicious zeal of some of the conspirators led the military authorities to discover the secret at the last moment, whereupon the most heavily compromised of the plotters fled. La Fayette, already on his way to Alsace, changed his itinerary. In February an attempt to rekindle the movement in Alsace was made by General Berton who, with 150 men, mostly peasants, marched on Saumur, where he did not elicit any response.

Even though the government had failed to grasp the scope of the first conspiracies, it was now on the alert. That is why in February 1822 it ordered the transfer from Paris to La Rochelle of the 45th regiment of the line whose attitude was considered bad. And indeed, a rather large number of non-commissioned officers had been affiliated with the Carbonari movement in the capital. En route to La Rochelle they committed all kinds of imprudent acts and, once arrived at their destination, they started plotting with the local stands in order to prepare an uprising. At that point some of them lost their nerve and denounced their comrades, who were arrested. They were arraigned before the assize court in Paris, to which the prosecutor-general, Marchangy, presented an outline of the entire organisation. However, the councillors for the defence, themselves Carbonari, were able to prevent the defendants from speaking. Four sergeants were condemned to death and went to the gallows on 21 September. King Louis XVIII would have been well advised to pardon them, for popular sentiment was roused to pity for these young people, who were seen as 'martyrs to the cause of freedom'.

Other conspiracies were foiled all the more easily as they were provoked by the police. At no time was the regime seriously threatened. Severe repression dismantled the network (altogether 12 men were executed) and the Carbonari movement subsided as quickly as it had arisen. Moreover, it was riven by internal dissensions. The enthusiasm of the rank and file contrasted with the excessive personal prudence of the leaders. In fact, it was impossible to form a supreme command in which fervent young students could work effectively with seasoned old warhorses from the Chamber and the Bar.

The Carbonari movement was a training-ground for some of the politicians we shall see in action later; but the Romantic character of its activities condemned it to failure. The last attempts to bring about an uprising of the army during the Spanish war served to underline its impotence.

The Villèle government and its accomplishments

The ultra-royalist government formed on 15 December 1821 included the following members: Villèle, Finances; Corbière, Interior; Montmorency, Foreign Affairs; Marshal Victor, duc de Bellune, War; Clermont-Tonnerre, Navy; Lauriston, King's Household. The liberals, who had acted as midwives to this birth, predicted a short life to this administration chosen by Monsieur [the king's brother]. Yet Villèle remained in power for almost six years, until January 1828, which is almost two-fifths of the entire lifespan of the Restoration.

Mathieu de Montmorency, a *grand seigneur monarchien* of 1789 and close friend of Madame de Staël, had totally identified himself with the *Chevaliers de la foi* and the Congregation, and Louis XVIII was wary of his involvement in coteries; Peyronnet, a public prosecutor from Bordeaux, was solid and mediocre; the erstwhile drummerboy Victor was the most magnificent soldier of fortune to have rallied to the Restoration, but no one credited him with keen intelligence or administrative ability; Corbière, a great landowner from Brittany, had a subtle and cultivated mind concealed under a rustic exterior, but his laziness was incurable. The new team was dominated by his friend Villèle even before the council of ministers was given a president in August of the following year.

Villèle

Born in 1773 into a family of minor but ancient nobility from the Lauraguis [in southwestern France], Villèle began his career in the royal navy, carrying out his father's intentions. He was on a voyage to India at the time of the Revolution; having been temporarily imprisoned as a suspect under the Terror on the Ile de France, he took up a new career as planter on the Ile Bourbon, where he married a Creole, the daughter of a rich landowner. From 1798 to 1802 he served in the Assembly that administered the colony while it was cut off from the motherland and played an important role in that body. In 1807 he returned to France to take possession of the family estate at Morvilles near Toulouse; at that point he seemed to be completely absorbed by his harvests and his account books. But in 1813 he joined the *Chevaliers de la foi*; in 1814 he wrote a pamphlet against the Charter and in favour of decentralisation; in 1815 he became mayor of Toulouse and was suspected of sympathy for the *verdets*. Later, as deputy, he supported parliamentary liberties and more democratic voting procedures. One wonders whether this was the ploy of an ambitious politician or a fleeting moment of exaltation in a well-ordered life. However that may be, by 1819 he returned to his normal pattern and negotiated with Decazes; in opposition to the 'impatient' wing of his party, he was the leader of the 'circumspect' wing.

Villèle's reputation did not emerge unscathed from the claws of Chateaubriand or from the slander of the liberals. Taking an equitable approach, Lamartine suggested that his contemporaries take a second look before they judged this puny little man with his angular, pock-marked face, this orator who spoke with the nasal twang of a strong Toulouse accent.

Let us therefore look at his correspondence and his diaries. A rich variety of the domestic virtues distinguished this landed gentleman, who combined strict probity with a very strong interest in money honestly acquired. This last trait was one he would bring to the service of the State, to which he was unselfishly devoted. A lucid analyst of concrete problems and extremely hardworking, he had the ability to give a clear account of even the most complex situations. How paradoxical that out of the ranks of the ultra party, so given to ranting and living on dreams suffused in metaphysics and mysticism, Villèle, a lukewarm, conventional Christian and a man without humanistic culture, should have risen to the top by dint of a precise, down-to-earth intelligence sharpened in the study of financial and administrative documents. With the denigrating intention one would expect of him, Chateaubriand called him a forerunner of the economist–politicians of the July Monarchy. Though possessed of different passions, he was perhaps closest to the great administrators of the imperial regime.

For him, politics was a matter of skilful manoeuvring, of bending when opposition was too strong and thereby trying to avoid the worst consequences; it was this selective use of compromise that contributed to the longevity of his government. At the very beginning of his tenure in office, Villèle, who had neither the charm nor the verbal facility of a court favourite, sought to secure his position by cultivating the king's latest platonic passion, Madame du Cayla, the elegant 'nymph of the sacristy'. This was a rather risky step to take, for the lady was not only greedy, she was also the tool of the *dévot* party.

There are those, however, who criticise Villèle on more serious grounds: namely for his attempt to tie the regime to a petty accountant's ideal at the very time when the country was regaining its freedom of action. In an era filled with romanticism and enthusiasm, Villèle remained totally untouched by the intellectual ebullience of his time. In this respect the administrator and frequently astute politician was unable to attain the stature of a true statesman. Here the irony of the vicomte [Chateaubriand] hits the mark: '[M. de Villèle] was a great help in all affairs; a cautious sailor, he never went to sea in a storm, and while he always dexterously manoeuvred his ship into a known harbour, he would never have discovered the New World.'

Yet Villèle's accomplishment as Minister of Finance was remarkable indeed: he completed the centralisation of various departments, laid down the rules of book-keeping for public finance, and created a system that made it possible for the *cour des comptes* to oversee all the expenditures of the State. These principles of public finance, which for the first time prohibited the improper shifting and malversation of funds, are in force to this day. He also instituted effective measures with respect to the budget: as early as 1823 he put an end to the hitherto regular practice of allocating a twelfth of the budget to unforeseen expenses, and his estimates were exact and genuine. Moreover, he submitted his budget to the vote item by item, rather than in the customary form of individual ministerial budgets, thereby strengthening parliamentary control, at least in this area. With the exception of that of 1827, all of his budgets left a surplus, so that he was able to perform tax cuts; however, the latter affected not so much the internal tariffs and excise taxes on consumer goods as the property taxes. In lowering them, Villèle achieved a two-fold objective: the elimination of some segments of the middle class from the ranks of those who paid enough taxes to vote and a lighter tax burden for the great estates that were deeply in debt owing to the decline of grain prices since 1820. In his social preoccupations Villèle could see no further than Morvilles.

But as head of the government, Villèle was always the man of his party, and the liberals were highly critical of a 'deplorable system' which, though certainly practised before him and later perfected by Guizot, nonetheless deserves to be linked with his name: this was the purging of the civil service, the drawing up of deliberately skewed electoral lists by the prefects, and the distribution of official favours by the deputies of the government party. One of the most characteristic traits of this system was perhaps the temptation to muzzle the opposition by failing to uphold that great boon to the freedom of opinion, the de Serre laws [of 1819]. It is true that the censorship temporarily established by the Richelieu government was abolished. But the laws of March 1822 subjected the periodical press to preliminary permits and above all allowed for trials to investigate a paper's tendency. Repeated convictions on such vague grounds as insult to the king or to religion could lead to the suppression of a periodical. At the same time, the government took secret steps to buy up troublesome newspapers.

Yet it would be a great mistake to believe that in the years around 1824 the indignation of the opposition and of the intellectual circles of Paris was shared by the provinces. The voting and taxpaying classes rightly or wrongly gave credit for the rebirth of prosperity to the regime; they disapproved of the conspiracies, and liberal leaders like La Fayette and Voyer d'Argenson lost their seats in 1822 in the very first election for the partial renewal of the Chamber. Finally, the conduct of the war with Spain signalled the rallying of the army and the consolidation of a regime whose future had hitherto seemed uncertain.

The debate about public bonds

Villèle used this favourable climate to press for the renewal of the entire Chamber. Elected in 1824 for a seven-year term, the new Chamber counted only 19 members of the liberal opposition out of a total of 430 deputies; in fact, this 'regained Chamber', about three-fifths of whose members were nobles, while more than half were former émigrés, was more 'right wing' than the 'Incredible Chamber' and equally impossible to discipline.

Villèle could now submit to the vote two major bills, which were related to each other. In his opening speech of 23 March 1824 the king alluded to the need for 'closing the last wounds of the Revolution' by paying indemnities to the émigrés. Ever since this issue was first raised by Marshal MacDonald in 1814, it had produced a steady stream of petitions, brochures, and polemics. But Villèle, exhibiting a financial prudence that was no doubt a political mistake, wanted to settle the ways and means of this compensation by proposing that it be converted to government bonds. The matter was complicated by the fact that by 5 March the value of 5 per cent government bonds had reached 104.80 francs, owing not only to the restoration of the State's credit but also to the general drop in the interest rate. It seemed unreasonable to have the *caisse d'amortissement* use taxpayers' money to redeem above their face value bonds purchased at 50 or 60 francs ten years earlier, or even at 7 francs under the Convention. Moreover, this high yield prompted investors to place into State bonds large amounts of capital that could have been invested in commerce and industry. Villèle's bill presented the bondholders with the following dilemma: they could either redeem their 5 per cent bonds at face value or they could exchange them for 3 per cent bonds issued at 75 francs. A syndicate of the Rothschild, Baring, and Laffite banks would carry out these operations and guarantee the value of the bonds. Every year the interest payments to private holders of 5 per cent public bonds took 140 million francs out of the budget. Obligations of 3 per cent issued at 75 francs would lower this figure to 112 million francs, thus saving the State 28 million.

Some of the bondholders had invested very small sums. They were retired shopkeepers and retired servants, almost all of them living in Paris. But almost 100 million francs in State bonds were held by capitalists (22,100 of these received incomes of 1,000 francs, and 1,600 received more than 10,000 francs). Baron Roy, the former Minister of Finance in the second Richelieu government, had an income of 500,000 francs from government bonds and was one of Villèle's most unrelenting adversaries.

The Chamber passed Villèle's bill with a majority of less than 100 votes. Since the connection between the indemnity to the émigrés and the conversion was common knowledge, some of the émigrés formally stated that they had no intention of depriving the bondholders in order to receive their indemnity. In the Chamber of Peers the owners of State bonds found, as the duc de Broglie put it, 'a good pretext and someone to put it to use'; the good pretext was the interest of the small bondholders and the man to put it to use was

> the archbishop of Paris [who] poured out his heart in a doleful and dejected oration whose intended effect was a general outburst of emotion and the formation of a majority which . . . did not wish to discuss the matter any further. Completely bewildered, M. de Villèle offered in vain to except bondholders whose total investment was less than 1,000 francs. The bill was rejected by a majority of 128 to 94 votes.

Chateaubriand, at the time Minister of Foreign Affairs, had participated in the conspiracy; 'because of his rivalry with his chief, he had not been adverse to tripping him up. It was a caper for which he paid dearly, and in cash', for he was dismissed from his ministerial post 'like a lackey', subsequently drawing the *Journal des débats* into relentless opposition to Villèle.

Twenty years later, in writing his *Mémoires*, Villèle confessed that he 'still felt very badly about the 800 million that the rejection of the bill cost France, not to mention the harm that this unfortunate vote inflicted on other interests'. A law passed the following year provided that voluntary conversion could be used to obtain a reduction in taxes. This law resulted in a distinction between 3 per cent, 4.5 per cent, and 5 per cent bonds; but since the operation took place amidst a recession, its effect was rather disappointing.

The 'émigrés' billion'

Meanwhile, the indemnity for the émigrés had only been put off by the failure of the conversion project. Louis XVIII, who died on 16 September 1824 had hoped that the indemnity law would be passed; Charles X fervently wanted it to pass.

It is obvious that this law raised a question of legitimacy that was bound to produce a clash between the supporters and the adversaries of the Revolution and that in order to achieve the victory of this law (it was passed in April 1825), the government had to fight on two fronts. The liberals saw it as a penalty for the Revolution imposed on the country, and Benjamin Constant declared that it amounted to 'heaping opprobrium' on the buyers of nationalised property; opposition from the extreme right used even more violent language and called – despite the Charter – for the restitution of the 'stolen properties'. In fact the problem was compounded by the restitution of about half of the nationalised property that had already been accomplished, albeit in a totally arbitrary manner: the Empire had restored to their owners all the unsold properties, except for certain categories and with special consideration for nobles who had rallied to the regime; a law of 1814 had restituted properties still in the hands of the State, though excepting properties used by certain State agencies. Finally, ever since the first Restoration, some émigrés had obtained the restitution of their properties by dealing directly with the buyers. There was a general decline in the market value of former émigré properties, which could fall to 30 per cent below their real value.

Villèle's indemnity bill was therefore conceived as an appeasement measure, a point of view that was stressed in Martignac's report on the bill. A *bona fide* estimate – which failed, however, to allow for the rise in land values since 1790 – fixed the total sum owed for these properties at 988 million francs. The government decided to pay this money in 3 per cent bonds and asked that annuities in the amount of 30 million be paid over a period of five years, a sum that corresponded to one billion in capital: hence the formula 'the émigrés' billion'. In fact, only 26 million in annuities on 3 per cent bonds were actually paid, corresponding to a nominal capital of 867 million; taking into consideration the cuts in annuities made by the July Monarchy, M. Gain has evaluated the total amount of the indemnity at 630 million francs.

The government approved 25,000 demands for indemnity from 700,000 persons. Certain frontier departments were ahead in the number of indemnities granted (Bas-Rhin had 1,507, but 1,432 of these claimants received annuities of less than 100 francs), but in terms of the total amounts paid, the region of Paris, western France and the Saône basin were the greatest beneficiaries, while southern France received very little. Forty-two claimants received annuities above 30,000 francs, while 842 received more than 6,750 francs in annuities. The Orléans family was able to reconstitute a veritable apanage, and among the other major bene-ficiaries one notes the Montmorency, Talleyrand, Rohan, and La Fayette families. Aside from these *grands seigneurs*, the rank and file of the former émigrés only received sums that were insufficient to acquire rural estates. Altogether, the indemnity seems to have had little impact on the distribu-tion of landed property.

Paradoxically, the principal beneficiaries were probably the new owners of nationalised properties, for whom the indemnity law spelled the end of insecurity and of the depreciation of their property. And this matter con-cerned more than a million Frenchmen. In reading the newspapers, they must have felt that those who spoke for them in the Chambers were rather pessimistic.

But Villèle could not enjoy his victory, for the fight had unleashed too many passions. Moreover, as bad luck would have it, the liquidation of the indemnity coincided with a full-blown recession. In 1825 Villèle considered retiring, a step that would no doubt have left him with a better reputation. Before we look at the decline of his administration, let us look at one of his successes, the Spanish expedition.

The Spanish problem and the French expedition

Spain and the Holy Alliance

The major powers had planned to hold another congress at Verona in September 1822 in order to consider the situation of the Italian States; but the turn of events in Spain placed the spotlight on the Iberian Peninsula. In July, the supporters of the absolute monarchy had attempted a forceful takeover, whose failure had made the king a prisoner of the 'exaltados'; nonetheless the absolutists had set up a regency at Seu d'Urgel and controlled parts of Aragon, Navarra, and Galicia.

What was the major powers' attitude toward the Spanish problem? England, where Canning had replaced Castlereagh, was opposed to intervention of any kind. Ever since 1813, it had considered Spain as a kind of private hunting-ground; moreover, it also wished to safeguard the privileged economic position it had won in Spain's former American colonies.

The czar, by contrast, favoured intervention in the name of solidarity among the sovereigns, which was after all the founding idea of the Holy Alliance. He envisaged an **international** expeditionary force, which would once again have brought Russian troops into western Europe. In any case, he was not opposed to armed intervention and pledged his support.

Metternich's position was a complicated one, and he frequently changed his tack: he was still hoping to bring the English into the Alliance and was alarmed at the thought of an intervention that might lead to Russian hegemony on the Continent, but neither did he wish to see a French involvement in the Peninsula for, if the French by mediation or by intervention imposed a constitutional regime on the pattern of the Charter, the contagion was liable to spread to Italy.

The French intervention

In France Villèle was opposed to a military intervention, despite his concern about the English influence in the Peninsula and his wish to re-establish contact with the American colonies. Originally adopting a defensive posture, he transformed a *cordon sanitaire* designed to keep out yellow fever into a corps of observers as the situation deteriorated. But Montmorency, the French representative at the Vienna meeting and later at the Congress of Verona (September to December 1822), wholeheartedly favoured an intervention on behalf of the Holy Alliance.

Disregarding Villèle's instructions, Montmorency set himself up as the Alliance's 'reporter' for the Spanish situation and asked the Allies how they would view a break in the diplomatic relations between France and Spain and what kind of moral and, if necessary, material support France would receive. Wellington, who represented England, walked out of the congress, but the other Allies assured France of their support in case an attack by Spain or an attempt against Ferdinand VII made a French intervention necessary. The allied powers decided to send notes to the Spanish government, asking it to spell out its intentions toward the king; relations would be broken off in case of its refusal to support him. Metternich, incidentally, did not believe that this step would automatically lead to an armed intervention by France; but if it should come to pass he wanted it to be controlled by the Holy Alliance. Montmorency had been persuaded to go along with this idea, but Villèle and the king felt that if France were obliged to act, it should do so 'on its own terms'; hence the intense clash of opinions that ended with Montmorency's resignation (25 December).

He was replaced by Chateaubriand, who had already acted as his deputy at the Congress of Verona after the essential business had been taken care of. Chateaubriand was no novice in diplomacy; he had served under the Consulate and later, under the Restoration, had proved himself a capable and perspicacious minister to Berlin and London, where he had replaced Decazes. He considered the war inevitable and said so in the Chamber on 28 December 1822; on 25 February he demonstrated that for France it was a matter of regaining its position in Europe.* Chateaubriand succeeded in preserving the French character of the expedition, containing Canning in his neutral stance by stressing the Russian threat and confining Metternich to an observer's role.

As for the expedition led by the duc d'Angoulême under the guidance of generals of the Empire (Molitor, Oudinot, Moncey, and Major General Guilleminot), it was almost a military outing. The duc d'Angoulême crossed the Bidassoa in early April and ended the campaign at Cadiz, where the Cortes had taken the king, on 28 September, shortly after the one military engagement of any significance, the taking of the Trocadero fortress. The major difficulty of the campaign was the initial shortage of supplies. Ouvrard appeared just in time to solve this problem; the terms of his dealings with the duke subsequently caused Villèle to protest. Another difficulty, in Spain itself, was the inability of the French to form an enlightened provisional government that would be obeyed and to put a stop to the vengeful acts of the absolutists, whose adversaries the duc d'Angoulême tried in vain to protect by the ordinance of Andujar.

The most important result of this expedition – aside from the influence exerted in a country that would remain under French occupation until 1828 – was its effect on the domestic front: the baptism of fire of the white flag had taken place without the least breach of discipline on the part of the army, contrary to the expectations of the liberals. It looked as if the throne was consolidated.

The end of the Villèle government

Opposition and dissension

The 'regained' Chamber that had seemed to promise Villèle an easy time in his dealings with the parliament soon experienced the splintering of its majority: the 'hardliners' (*pointus*) like La Bourdonnaye, who dreamed of an aristocratic monarchy that had no basis in the Charter or indeed in their own time, the 'defectors' who, inspired by Chateaubriand,

---

* It was in the course of the ensuing debate that Manuel gave a speech that seemed to be a justification for regicide. Expelled from the Chamber by the police, Manuel was seen as a hero of the liberal cause, along with the braidmaker Mercier who, as a sergeant of the National Guard, refused to lay hands on Manuel. Depicted in the popular iconography, the faces of Manuel and Mercier became known all over France.

wanted to reconcile the monarchy and modern liberties, the clericals or *Chevaliers de la foi* who had schemed against the government ever since the resignation of Montmorency – all of these factions tended to reduce the majority of the 'big bellies' who could be bought with favours from above. Irrelevant polemics, the settling of old scores, bargaining and blackmail to obtain positions, all concurred to show once again the French aristocracy's lack of a sense of politics. In the House of Peers Villèle did not have a majority: here former civil servants of the Empire and peers raised to that dignity during the constitutional period acted as effective advocates of civil liberties. The eloquence of a Pasquier, a Broglie, or a Molé was seconded by the voice of Chateaubriand, while the moderate elements among the pure royalists, the 'cardinalists', could never be counted on. Everywhere the opposition had enlisted the superior talents. This was also true in the press, where the violent anti-government diatribes of the *Constitutionnel* and the *Courrier* chimed in with those of the *Journal des débats*, the *Quotidienne*, or the *Drapeau blanc*. To counteract them, the government press could usually count only on the *Gazette de France* and the *Etoile*. Villèle thus had to deal with permanent dissent from those to his right and with a left that kept the upper classes in a state of permanent anxiety.

Finally, Villèle also had to get along with the court. The late king had had favourites, but too much disdain for his surroundings to be influenced by them. Charles X was fond of and listened to his intimates, shallow *grands seigneurs* who considered Villèle a country bumpkin, and eventually managed to undermine the king's initial confidence in the political genius of his minister. Upon the death of Louis XVIII, when the king's household was ritually dissolved, Villèle

> could not help thinking that it would be a very politic act on the part of his successor to refrain from reconstituting a similar one; that in our days great danger to our kings is inherent in the existence of so large and so costly a court with the endless claims it engenders; that such a court is no longer in keeping with our way of life; and that it is liable to compromise the king in all kinds of ways, especially in a country like ours and in view of the kindness that is a natural attribute of the princes of the House of France.

Yet despite his forebodings, Villèle had to give consideration to the suggestions of the royal entourage.

Throne and altar

The 'regained' Chamber and the court agreed that the Church should have a greater voice in the State, a policy which, when it was unveiled early in 1825, greatly alarmed many segments of the bourgeoisie and the lower classes. Not that the clergy had waited until then to manifest its close ties to the Restoration; it had already, and with varying success, embarked upon a project of re-Christianisation and reconstruction (examples will be given in part 2). But it was only under the reign of Charles X that the Church, with the connivance of the regime, seemed to exercise a domination that was often imputed particularly to the Jesuits.

It is true no doubt that the 'Fathers of the Faith' had managed to insinuate themselves into key posts as confessors (especially to members of the *Congrégation*, a charitable society that included many courtiers and whose purpose was widely considered to be identical with that of the *Chevaliers de la foi*), as educators and missionaries. Yet they did not enjoy the favour of the royal family or, of course, that of Villèle. But their mythical image came to embody all of the occult power wielded by the clergy, the denial of freedom of conscience, hatred for the legacy of the Revolution, and the intervention of a foreign State in the affairs of France. This image served as a tangible target for the hostile reaction against clerical interference of any kind aroused among the masses of Frenchmen as well as among the liberal elites.

On 29 May 1825 Charles X had himself crowned at Reims with a pomp that recalled the great days of the Ancien Regime, although the men of the new France were also asked to participate in the ceremony. What shocked public opinion in this coronation of 'Charles the Simple' was perhaps not so much the fact itself as the sight of the king prostrate before the archbishop, Mgr de la Fare's inept sermon against the Charter and freedom of religion, and the traditional gesture of touching the scrofulous. A year later, when the king followed the jubilee procession on foot, dressed in violet, the colour of mourning, the Parisian people imagined that he had become a bishop and rumour had it that he was saying mass. This was absurd, of course, but symptomatic of popular distaste for the priest-ridden government.

This distaste spread to the provinces when missions and major religious pageants were conducted with the support of the public authorities or the army. Civil servants and students accused the *Congrégation* of keeping a tight hold over advancement in or access to government service; of exerting, in a way, the same kind of secret control that was to be imputed to freemasonry in the heyday of the Third Republic. The Ministry of Public Education and Religious Affairs, headed by Mgr Frayssinous, was able to staff the key posts in the University with ecclesiastics, to create fully accredited secondary schools [*collèges*] that were not controlled by the University, and to restore considerable influence over primary education to the bishops. Yet Frayssinous was largely outdone by an ultramontanist party, brilliantly led at that time by Lamennais, who thundered against the 'atheist State'. In the end, however, this excessive rhetoric served to rekindle the old Gallicanism (a *Memorandum exposing a religious and political system designed to overthrow religion, society, and the throne* in which Montlosier attacked the Jesuits met with considerable success).

Demonstrations of anticlericalism showed no respect for the sacred character of churches, where jeering during the sermon, ink in the holy-water basin, and other pranks eventually gave way to depredation and theft. In response, the ultra party forced Villèle to pass the law concerning sacrilege in churches which, in defiance of the tenets of modern legislation, imposed the death penalty for the theft of holy vessels containing the host and the punishment for parricide (death preceded by the cutting off of one hand) for the profanation of the host.

Villèle's failures

But nothing showed the passionate atmosphere of public life more clearly than the so-called 'right of the eldest' bill. The idea – despite claims to the contrary – seems to have originated with Villèle, who kept working on measures that would lead to the creation of a rural aristocracy in the English manner. In the form submitted to the vote, the bill permitted the 8,000 French families who paid 1,000 francs in taxes to add to the eldest son's share in the inheritance – unless otherwise stated in the will – all assets left over after legal portions were paid to the younger children and also allowed them to entail their estates. The Peers rejected this bill as a betrayal of the great principles of the civil code (even though the peerage itself was entailed to eldest sons!) and the city of Paris, though hardly concerned one way or the other, celebrated with an illumination.

Villèle finally became so exasperated that he decided to take stringent measures to combat this anarchy: as we shall see, the dissolution of the Parisian National Guard (29 April 1827) was a mistake of far-reaching consequences. Another measure that became notorious was the 'justice and love bill', ironically referred to by this title because of an unfortunate expression used by the minister Peyronnet in introducing it on 26 December 1826.

In fact, Villèle felt that the root causes of all his troubles were the press and the leniency of the courts in dealing with 'deviant' writings. As G. de Bertier has put it: 'He attacked the fever rather than the disease.' Moreover, he was incited to do so by the king, who was incensed by the caricatures, the songs, and the articles that ridiculed him or distorted his intentions. Increases in the stamp duties and in the fines for press infractions suggested that his aim was nothing less than the strangulation of the periodical press. This point was made in celebrated speeches by Casimir Périer ('Printing in France is being shut down for the benefit of Belgium') and by Royer-Collard ('As far as the law is concerned . . . a rash act of improvidence was committed on the great day of creation . . . when man was permitted to go out into the universe free and intelligent . . .'). Passed by the Chamber of Deputies, the bill was withdrawn in the face of its reception by the House of Peers. Paris once again celebrated with an illumination, and barricades went up in the Porte Saint-Denis quarter.

At this point Villèle played his last card. On 6 November 1827, he asked the king to nominate 76 new peers and to dissolve the Chamber of Deputies, fixing the elections for the *collèges d'arrondissement* for 17 November and those for the *grands collèges* for 24 November. In 1824 a similar experience had shown that the liberal opposition had only a tenuous hold among the taxpaying bourgeoisie and, moreover, it was felt that since then a part of the liberal clientèle, the owners of former nationalised properties, had been appeased. But in 1827 a new generation of liberals, no longer given to romantic outbursts of violence, was able to instigate throughout the country a current of opposition against the ultras and the aspirations of the clergy. The *Aide-toi et le ciel t'aidera* Society [heaven helps those who help themselves], whose secretary was Guizot, worked long and hard in pursuit of this aim, distributing brochures and appeals, seeing to it that 'forgotten' electors were registered (registration increased by 23 per cent through their efforts), and criticising the pressure applied by the administration. The two oppositions, one on the left and one on the right, finally joined forces; the former obtained some 180 seats and the latter 70; this left only about 180 government supporters. Villèle realised that he had to leave (5 January 1828).

He left behind not only an unruly Chamber but a political situation that had drastically deteriorated since 1824. No doubt more responsibility must be assigned to the ultra party than to its leader; furthermore the economic crisis which we shall examine later added to the atmosphere of discontent.

Already thoughtful people were concerned about the very future of the dynasty, and a brochure by Cauchois-Lemaire advocating an Orléans monarchy met with widespread approval. Yet the great majority of the political class – including the liberals – did not wish for the fall of the throne, only for a change in policy. Would the king understand that the existence of institutions implied constant change or would he ensconce himself in the exercise of his prerogative which the wording of the Charter had seemed to justify?

The Martignac experiment

Charles X and Martignac

The king seemed to be leaning toward conciliation. The new government, made up of members of the centre-right or of men of indistinct political persuasion, was headed by Martignac, a lawyer from Bordeaux. Flexible and eloquent, he came from the segment of the right that had viewed the evolution of the reign with alarm. In terms of his political career, Martignac lacked 'clout', but his endeavours awakened the hopes of public opinion, especially in the provinces. The tour of eastern

France undertaken in 1828 by Charles X accompanied by his prime minister was almost a triumph; liberal notables everywhere came to salute the king, who mistakenly attributed this success to his personal popularity.

A dialogue between the centres of power could have been established if the Martignac experiment had been a sincere effort. The fact is, however, that Martignac was reined in at every turn by the will of the king, who wanted to practice Villélism without Villèle. Martignac was compelled to carry out difficult balancing acts and was unable to reorganise the prefectoral administration, since the king protested that this would force him to dismiss his best servants.

In order to defuse a demand for the indictment of his predecessor, Martignac sought to divert attention toward that favourite target, the Jesuits (June 1828). Two ordinances excluded members of non-certified orders from teaching in ecclesiastical secondary schools (the Jesuits had eight of these at that time, among them the famous school of Saint-Acheul), and placed these schools under the control of the University. These ordinances provoked a short-lived rebellion on the part of the bishops.

With respect to the press, Martignac asked the Chamber to pass a new law (24 June 1827) abolishing preliminary permits and trials to investigate a paper's tendencies, although trial by jury for cases involving the press was not restored.

In the course of the year 1828, Martignac had commissioned a study concerning a reform of the administrative systems on the communal and departmental level, and in February 1829 he presented two bills in this area to the Chamber. They called for replacing the appointed members of the municipal and general [departmental] councils by elected members, although suffrage was to be strictly limited by property qualifications. The Chamber decided to give priority to the second bill, which reserved the right to vote to fewer electors than could vote in the legislative elections. Over Martignac's objections, it amended this bill, whereupon the king withdrew it. The king was triumphant, having demonstrated that it was impossible to deal with the liberals. Leaving Martignac in his post until the end of the session, he set out to prepare a government of his own choice.

Yet despite its weakness in domestic affairs, the Martignac government put the finishing touches to the restoration of France's importance in European affairs.

France and the independence of Greece

Once he had replaced Chateaubriand with the insignificant baron de Damas, Villèle had conducted France's foreign policy himself: there were to be no initiatives, since the continental powers formed too powerful a block and since England dominated the seas. Over the protest of both oppositions, this hands-off policy caused France to remain neutral during the emancipation of the Spanish colonies, to acknowledge England's right to intervene militarily in Portugal, and to take only limited action in defence of its commercial interests in the Levant.

Meanwhile, the Ottoman Empire had become a major preoccupation of the continental powers. Following the uprising of 1821, the Greeks had declared their independence at Epidaurus in 1822 and gained some important victories; but since 1824 they had suffered setbacks, due to internal dissension and especially the fact that Egypt had joined the fray: the sultan had asked Mahomet Ali to come to his aid, and the latter had sent his fleet, commanded by his son Ibrahim, with the intention of reconquering Candia and the base of Navarino in Morea. Also, the fall of Missolonghi (1826), where Byron had died, and the fall of Athens (1827), defended by Colonel Fabvier, formerly Marmont's chief of staff, seemed to spell the end of the Greek independence movement.

On several occasions, Czar Alexander had been tempted to intervene, but he had been checked by Metternich's remonstrances and by the hostility of the English. After his death (December 1825), Nicolas I was much more eager to become involved. But before doing so, he wanted to enforce the clauses of the Treaty of Bucharest (1812) providing for the independence of the Danube provinces and freedom of trade in the Black Sea. Wellington, at that time prime minister of England, decided to back his claims in order to limit the potential damage, and the protocol of 4 April 1826 recognised the czar's right to settle these matters in the northern part of the Ottoman Empire, but designated England as the mediator between the Turks and the Greeks. Once the Convention of Akkerman (October 1826) had given satisfaction to Nicolas I, he urged the British to carry out their task of mediation. At this point Canning decided to associate Villèle with his effort, for he felt that Villèle's lack of enthusiasm for the Greek cause would counterbalance the Russian influence. The Treaty of London (concluded in July 1827) stated that the three powers would compel the sultan to accept their mediation in setting up an autonomous Greek State.

Public opinion forced Villèle to come out of his reserve. A powerful pro-Greek movement had sprung up in France, spawning a rich literature ranging from the preface to Fauriel's *Chants populaires grecs* (1824) and C. Delavigne's *Messéniennes* to Béranger's *Chansons* and later (1829) his *Orientales*. In the name of the principle of nationhood, the liberals had been the first to show their enthusiasm; but the right-wing press (with the exception of the *Gazette*, which remained faithful to Villèle) also protested against the massacres of Christians and evoked the crusades. Delacroix's painting *Les Massacres de Chio* had deeply affected the visitors to the *salon* of 1824. A philhellenic committee headed by Chateaubriand sent help and volunteers to the insurgents. Charles X was personally won over to the Greek cause.

To Villèle all of this meant little more than the epiphenomenon of trouble with the parliament, but in compliance with the Treaty of London, the French Mediterranean squadron did join the British and Russian squadrons. Since the sultan refused to accept a peaceful settlement, a mediation by force became necessary. Incidents occurring on 20 October 1827 at Navarino led to the sinking of the Turko-Egyptian fleet by the allied squadrons. Villèle did not enjoy the news: 'Canon fire is bad for good money', he noted.

But La Ferronays, former ambassador to Saint Petersburg and foreign minister in the Martignac government, was made of sterner stuff. While the czar decided to march on Constantinople over land, and while the British slipped away, La Ferronays secured an agreement stating that France alone would carry out the armed mediation of the conflict between the Turko-Egyptians and the Greeks of Morea. Thereupon General Maison's expeditionary force replaced the Egyptian troops managing, despite the manoeuvring of the English, to remain on good terms with Ibrahim. The Russians compelled the Turks to sign the Treaty of Andrinople (1829), of which more will be said later. It is sufficient to note here that La Ferronays' action, continued to Polignac and ably seconded by Guilleminot, ambassador to the Sublime Porte, succeeded in wresting from a reticent England the complete independence of Greece, thereby restoring France to its former moral leadership in the Near East and laying the foundation for a Franco-Russian accord.

4

Intellectual life during the Restoration

Literary life and scientific activities

The public and the salons

It is notoriously difficult to capture the notion of 'the public'. Under the Restoration it was surely not one and the same public that went to see the paintings of the *salons*, read the papers of the *Académie des Sciences*, and perused the newspapers in the cafés.

The masses of rural dwellers contented themselves with a literature of almanacs, but the influence of this kind of reading is very hard to assess. It was, after all, quite diverse, ranging from pious or moralistic brochures like *Le Juste Châtiment de Dieu envers les enfants qui sont désobéissants à leurs père et mère et la peine qu'ils souffrent dans les enfers avec plusieurs exemples* [God's just punishment of children who are disobedient to their parents and their suffering in hell, with several examples] to corrosive texts like the *Testament du curé Meslier*.

The workers of the journeymen's associations read more, sometimes even literature of quality. Agricol Perdiguier has testified to the admiration that was aroused when Corneille's tragedies were read at gatherings held by the 'housemothers'. The numerous authors of popular poetry, even the wigmaker Jasmin who wrote in the dialect of Toulouse, took their inspiration from classical models. Conversely, bourgeois and aristocrats sometimes read 'novels for chambermaids'. Yet there was a specifically popular literature consisting for the most part of novels. First published in 1799, *Coelina ou l'enfant du mystère* by Ducray-Duminil had sold a million copies by 1830. Publishers of such books had started using travelling salesmen in 1813 and worked hard at expanding their clientèle.

Nonetheless, literature continued to cater above all to a cultivated readership. Often published in very small editions of 300 copies, the number of volumes of poetry published was higher than that of novels. It was not until the end of the Restoration that a relative decline in the publication of poetry became apparent.

Newspapers had limited circulation, since a year's subscription cost 72 or

80 francs. In 1826 the dailies of the capital had only 65,000 subscribers, 50,000 of whom subscribed to the opposition press. This was considerably less than the number of qualified voters, especially since subscriptions from reading clubs or cafés are included in this figure. It is virtually impossible to ascertain the number of readers who did not subscribe to a paper. However that may be, only the *Journal des débats* and the *Constitutionnel* published editions of 20,000 copies.

While it is true that the cultivated public had, by and large, received a classical education, this does not mean that major differences in attitude did not divide the generations. The oldest generation, 45 years old in 1815 and 60 in 1830, remained steeped in the classical tradition. It furnished the last, hairless rearguard at the battle of *Hernani* fought in the pit of the Théâtre français. These were the men at whom Préault shouted from the gallery: 'To the guillotine, baldheads!' The next generation (20 to 45 years old in 1815) had been moulded chiefly by the events in which it had participated and still hankered after the glories of the Empire. The 'children of this century', finally, scarred by defeat and faced with the prospect of limited opportunity, were a generation that questioned all received ideas as well as their elders, a generation that had its aggressive elements in the art students of '*Jeune-France*', but it was fundamentally a serious generation, eager to form its own judgment. All in all, there was a general atmosphere that gave this period its nobility, manifested in ardently held convictions, fervent discussions, and in a pervasive curiosity about intellectual matters that gave rise to a multitude of literary circles and public lectures on even the most arid subjects. A scientist like Ampère aspired to become a philosopher, Delacroix and Berlioz were writers, Hugo and Mérimée were graphic artists, and there were other intellectuals who could never settle down in one discipline. It was as if the spirit of conquest, imprisoned for so long in old frontiers, had broken out into the unlimited field of knowledge. This love of intellectual pursuits characterised the sociability of the period.

Yet the salon was necessarily an 'intellectual clearing house'. Madame Ancelot, an expert judge in this matter, defined a salon as follows: 'An intimate meeting-ground over several years, where people meet and seek each other out and where they have some reason to enjoy those whom they encounter.' These reasons could be a matter of snobbery and love of intrigue or they could involve matrimonial strategies. But the great salons of the provinces and especially Paris attest to the lustre of intellectual life under the Restoration that would be nostalgically remembered by those who had known it.

Some of these salons revived those of the eighteenth century. Every Monday, Madame de Rumford, Lavoisier's widow, gave a dinner in her townhouse for intimate friends of the house or foreign visitors. On Fridays she entertained a larger group of guests, frequently with a concert by renowned musicians. These gatherings included many scholars, such as Laplace, Arago, Berthollet, and Humboldt. At Madame de Condorcet's Parisian home (in the present rue de Penthièvre) or at her 'maisonette' in Meulan, it was possible to encounter survivors of the ideology movement, such as Destutt de Tracy, as well as Benjamin Constant, Fauriel, and Guizot. Madame Vigée-Lebrun in a tiny flat in the rue de Cléry had a salon frequented by *grands seigneurs* steeped in nostalgia for the past. Before her death (1817) Madame de Staël found happiness in reviving the famous Necker salon. Thus the great tradition of Ancien Regime Versailles and Paris was transmitted to the salons of the faubourg Saint-Germain. Among the most famous of these was the salon of the duchesse de Duras, a friend of Chateaubriand's and a novelist herself. There were not many salons kept by the nobility of the Empire, but that of the duchesse d'Abrantès provided a field of observation for Balzac.

Certain salons had a specifically political cast: that of Talleyrand, renowned for its sumptuous dinners, was presided over by his niece, the duchesse de Dino. It was frequented by diplomats, distinguished foreigners, and public figures (including young men eager to make their way, like Thiers) who could watch the casual master of the house at his eternal party of whist. The duchesse de Broglie, Madame de Staël's daughter, received mostly philosophers and *doctrinaire* politicians. The marquise de Castellane dedicated her half-political and half-literary salon to the entertainment of Molé, one of the most brilliant conversationalists of the time. At La Fayette's salon in the rue d'Anjou, the liberal nobility was submerged in a throng of bourgeois, enlivened by Americans and young people who asked to see the great man; in summer the château of La Grange where the entire family clan met together was scarcely less accessible. The other liberal salons, however, were even more exclusive than the aristocratic ones. 'Liberalism under the Restoration', it has been said, 'was not so much a party as a society'; the same people met again and again at the same houses in town and country, at the same dinners.

More open were the salons frequented by the intellectuals, like that of the painter Gérard in the rue Bonaparte, where one could meet Humboldt as well as the princess Belgiojoso, Delacroix as well as Rossini, Mérimée as well as Madame Ancelo. Every evening the guests would informally discuss every conceivable topic, and around midnight tea and pastry was served. Yet there were other salons that played a more important role in the history of literature and the arts.

One of these was kept by the critic Delécluze in the rue de Chabanais. It was frequented by young writers (Mérimée, Stendhal, J.-J. Ampère) whose Romanticism was tempered by their adherence to liberal ideas. Another was the *cénacle*, the famous salon of the bibliothèque de l'Arsenal, whose librarian, the novelist Charles Nodier, received the whole tribe of the Romantics, Hugo, Musset, Lamartine, Soumet; there was dancing and card-playing, but above all there was exchange of ideas about literature and art. Another salon kept by the imaginative and cultivated Madame Swetchine, a great lady of Russian origin, was the seedbed for a renewal of Catholicism. But the most famous salon of all was that of Juliette Récamier who, on the edge of financial ruin, had moved to l'Abbaye-aux-Bois near Saint-Germain-des-Prés in 1819. Sainte-Beuve has left us a good account of the importance of this salon for the society of that time:

> Never was Mme Récamier's position in high society greater than when she lived in that humble abode on the outskirts of Paris. It was there that her gentle genius developed to the benefit of all. Whenever she had friends on opposite sides of a controversy, she brought them together at her house . . . Here was a woman who, without leaving her sphere, accomplished a civilising mission of the highest order.

Most of Madame Récamier's *habitués* belonged to the royalist party, and Chateaubriand was their idol; to be invited was an honour coveted no less by *grands seigneurs* than by writers. To be encountered there, aside from Ballanche, a philosopher from Lyon who was practically a fixture, were men like the duc de Montmorency and the duc de Noailles, Barante, Sainte-Beuve, Lamartine, or the Ampère brothers. In the modest flat the chairs for the ladies were arranged in a circle, while the men moved around. This 'monarchical arrangement' allowed Juliette to bring together guests who had a natural affinity for each other or to show off the talents of one among them. The great days were those when some new work was read to a small group. It was at Madame Récamier's that Chateaubriand made fragments of his *Mémoires d'outre-tombe* known to a select public.

The revolution of 1830 brought a decline in this salon life. The political hatreds between legitimists and Orleanists had heated up to the point where cordial social relations were no longer possible. In addition, the rising status of businessmen made for concepts of social life unlike those of the men of leisure who could spend every evening at social gatherings. The salons of the Restoration aged, and few new ones sprang up to replace them.

Scientific activities

The cultivated public took considerable interest in scientific matters, and the publication of Pancoucke's *Encyclopédie méthodique* between 1778 and 1823 symbolised the continuation of the eighteenth century's effort at popularisation. A more specialised public could read the reports of the Académie des Sciences, which was very active at that time. Unlike Germany, France did not have a network of modern universities; the principal centres of research were the Ecole Polytechnique, the Muséum, the Sorbonne, and the Collège de France, which was being revived.

The Romantic era was as revolutionary in the history of mathematics as in the humanities. The problems posed by Descartes, Newton, and Leibnitz in analytical geometry, the calculation of quadratures and the integration of differential equations were virtually solved. The theory of functions of imaginary variables, which took mathematics out of the realm of the concrete, spelled a fundamental renewal of the discipline. Cauchy (1789–1857), professor at the Polytechnique and later at the Collège de France, an intransigent legitimist who ceased teaching in 1830, laid the foundation of this theory; he left more than 700 papers dealing with all fields of mathematics. In geometry, Poncelet (1788–1867) published in 1822 his *Traité des propriétés projectives*, whose characteristic feature was the generalised use of perspective and plane sections and the systematic introduction of infinite and imaginary elements.

Another characteristic of the time was the close association between mathematics and physics. The physicists were intent upon expressing their findings by means of formulas and some of them were creative thinkers in both disciplines. Among them were Jean-Marie Ampère (1776–1836) and Fourier (1768–1830), who in his *Théorie analytique de la chaleur* defined new series.

In optics, Fresnel (1788–1827) to whom we owe the graduated lens which considerably increases the lighting power of lighthouses, formulated the wave theory of light, thereby overthrowing the Newtonian hypothesis that saw light as the emanation of luminous particles from a luminous body. With the help of François Arago, Fresnel's theory gained general acceptance and still stands today. Moreover, whole new branches of physics were springing up: thermodynamics with Sadi Carnot (1796–1832), the son of the great Carnot, who in 1824 established the equivalence between heat and energy, and electromagnetism, which Ampère created in 1820 by means of some masterful experiments conducted in his flat.

Inorganic chemistry exploited a fruitful hypothesis, namely that all gases contain the same number of molecules in a given volume and under equal conditions of temperature and pressure. This theory was deduced (simultaneously in Italy by Avogrado in 1813 and in France by Ampère in 1814) from Gay-Lussac's (1778–1850) law of the equal dilatation of gases formulated in 1806. In another area, electrolysis enabled Gay-Lussac and Thénard to isolate new elements. Organic chemistry took a step forward with the publication of Chevreul's work on lipids.

In astronomy, finally, Laplace (1749–1827) stated a major hypothesis marked by the evolutionary ideas that were just beginning to take shape. The solar system, he claimed, originated as a nebula turning around a highly concentrated nucleus; the cooling of its outer layers in conjunction with its rotating movement led to the formation of rings which, by a process of condensation, became planets from which satellites eventually detached themselves. Although it is no longer accepted today, his concept played a major role in the history of ideas of the nineteenth century.

At the Muséum d'histoire naturelle (known as the 'Jardin du roi' before its reorganisation in 1793) three masters brought about decisive advances in zoology. The oldest, Lamarck (1744–1829) had worked with Buffon in his youth. In 1793 he was a candidate for the chair of invertebrate zoology at the Muséum and changed his field from botany to zoology. The results of his teaching were incorporated into his *Histoire naturelle des animaux sans vertèbres* (1815–1822). But he was also interested in many other fields of science, from meteorology to geology, and threw out bold, sometimes wild hypotheses in all of them. It was his view that nature had created life by a succession of creations, but that it began with the simplest [forms of life], creating the most complex organisms only in the last stage, both in the vegetal and in the animal kingdom. This transition from simple to complex forms, he held, takes place continually under the impact of circumstances. Circumstances created the webbed feet of birds living in an aquatic environment and the feet capable of grasping a round object of birds living in trees; these acquired characteristics are then transmitted by heredity. Man also is subject to this rule, and Lamarck stripped him of his role as the king of creation. He thus substituted for the concept of a world created with all its attributes fixed in place (as it is imagined in the Bible) a dynamic vision of life on this earth, a vision that Buffon had already dimly perceived, although he had hesitated to pursue it.

At Lamarck's side, Geoffroy Saint-Hilaire (1772–1844), who held the chair of vertebrate zoology at the Muséum, noted that 'nature has indeed formed living beings according to a single pattern but has varied them in a thousand ways in all their accessory parts'. This fundamental concept of the animal world led him to discover the laws underlying these differences and to establish some major principles in this field: these were the principle of balance among the organs, postulating that hypertrophy of one organ goes hand in hand with atrophy of another, and the principle of connectedness, which prevents an organ from changing its position in relation to others. In illustrating these principles, Geoffroy Saint-Hilaire called not only on comparative anatomy but also on embryology and teratology. In this manner he too was led to the idea of the evolution of species.

Georges Cuvier (1769–1832), born into a modest Protestant family at Montbéliard, studied at Stuttgart and soon attracted attention with his studies of molluscs. Geoffroy Saint-Hilaire brought him to the Muséum in 1802. Under the Restoration, Cuvier was an important dignitary of the regime: chancellor of the University, councillor of State, and superintendent of non-Catholic religious affairs. His scientific conceptions remained consistent with a literal interpretation of the Bible and with Aristotelian philosophy. He endeavoured to show the plan of creation and emphasised its harmonious character. Taking his basic data from comparative anatomy, Cuvier set out to classify the species. Thanks to the principle of connectedness among organs, he advanced the field of palaeontology in decisive ways, although he accounted for the extinction of certain species exclusively in terms of the catastrophes that have taken place throughout the history of the world. This static concept of nature brought him into conflict with Geoffroy Saint-Hilaire in the celebrated polemic of 1830. While Cuvier's science gave him a certain advantage, the great question concerning the evolution of the world and of man was in fact stated in terms that were magnificently summarised by Goethe in his conversations with Eckermann: 'Henceforth . . . in the natural sciences the human mind will dominate and become master over matter. Science will be able to look upon the great laws of creation and God's mysterious laboratory.'

Medicine, an applied science

Medical studies could be pursued at the faculties of medicine in Paris, Montpellier, and Strasbourg, to which must be added the military hospital of Val-de-Grace [in Paris], where public health officers were trained. In addition to their courses, medical students were required to take clinical training. Surgeons and physicians followed the same course of study and almost all of them practised all branches of medicine. The primary training of the future physicians remained classical, although the armies of the Revolution and the Empire had brought priests threatened by the guillotine and even simple charlatans into the medical profession.

Most medical theories conceived of disease as a kind of struggle between two antagonistic forces. Some of them believed in a vital principle independent of the soul or the physiological organisation of the body. Seen in this perspective, disease had only one cause: the iatrophysicians saw it as a disruption of the equilibrium between the body's fluids and the elasticity of the tissues, thus reducing medicine to the solution of plumbing problems; the humourists thought that disease was caused by an excess of humours, which had to be evacuated, in particular by emetics; Broussais and his students saw disease as the outcry of an irritated organism, which had to be calmed down with marshmallow tea or by the application of bloodsuckers.

Broussais, a crusty veteran of the imperial armies who had found a niche teaching at the military hospital of Val-de-Grace, thundered against his colleagues at the faculty of medicine, in particular against 'the man with the ear-trumpet', the pious Laënnec with his stethoscope. Yet the future was to vindicate the physicians of the clinical school (Laënnec, Dupuytren, Cruveilhier). Their innovation consisted of the examination of the patient and the search for organic lesions. But this method had not yet won the day.

For the moment, charlatans were a tough competition for the school medicine, even among the educated public. When Casimir Périer was dying of cholera, a practitioner of magnetism was called to his bedside.

Dr Koref, a disciple of Mesmer, was a highly successful charlatan. Indeed the therapeutics of even the most official medicine continued to use some rather astonishing means: physicians prescribed not only herbal potions but also sorcerers' remedies, such as rattlesnake broth or woodlouse wine. Asthenics were doped with alcohol or opium. Récamier used hydrotherapy to treat typhoid fever as well as nymphomania.

Like other disciplines, medicine was undergoing a true mutation, but no fruitful hypothesis had yet emerged, so that its archaic aspects continued to prevail.

History

Not surprisingly, the public at large was interested above all in the history of the Revolution. The success of (frequently prettified) *mémoires* about that period attests to this fact.

A young man from Marseille, Adolphe Thiers, set out to write a general history of that period; in 1823, he published the first volume of a *Histoire de la Révolution* whose tenth and last volume was to appear in 1827. Aside from published sources, he also consulted survivors of the great drama. Continuing the lineage of Voltaire's great historical writings, his account is clear and on the whole unconcerned with moral considerations, although one does sense that the author was partial to the new society. In 1824, his friend Mignet had published in the same vein a much shorter *Histoire de la Révolution française*. But then Madame de Staël, before her death, had also written her *Considérations sur la Révolution française*, a book that amounted to a plea for the 'monarchiens', but nevertheless provided many fruitful insights into the social forces that had confronted each other during the Revolution. The success of Thiers should not make us forget the importance of her work.

Another focus of public interest were the Middle Ages. To some extent this interest had been stimulated by the Musée des monuments français organised by Lenoir under the Convention (it was here that Michelet found his vocation as a historian). In 1824, Barante brought out his *Histoire des Ducs de Bourgogne de la Maison de Valois*, which was a great success: a simple presentation of the chronicles written at the time, it pleased the readers of the Romantic era with their taste for the picturesque. The same emphasis on local colour can be found in the writings of Augustin Thierry (*Lettres sur l'histoire de France*, first published in the form of newspaper articles; *Histoire de la conquête de l'Angleterre par les Normands* [1825]; and *Récit des temps mérovingiens* [1833–40]). Vibrant and colourful, Thierry's account closely followed the sources and the author did not exhibit much critical spirit. He transposed into the past the modern struggles between the nobility and the Third Estate, tracing them back to the struggle between the Franks, seen as the ancestors of the feudal seigneurs, and the Romanised Gauls, seen as the defenders of civilisation.

But the greatest historian of the time was Guizot, who published his 1828–9 Sorbonne lectures as *Histoire de la civilisation en France* and *Histoire de la civilisation en Europe*. For Guizot, the actual story was of minor importance, for 'the connection between events, the relationship that unites them, their causes and their effects are facts just as important as the accounts of battles and visible events'. Within the compass of Europe he showed, allowing for national nuances, a parallel development from the fall of the Roman Empire to the age of the absolute monarchies. While Guizot did not discount the action of great men, he felt that the moving forces of history are the great constituted bodies (such as the Church), the institutions that have grown out of a people's way of life and in turn have their impact on society, and the existence of classes and the struggles among them. According to Guizot, these social forces are manifestations of the human spirit, mainsprings of the material and moral progress of civilisation that makes up history, 'that ocean . . . in which all elements of a people's life come together'. While its documentation is at times a bit hasty, Guizot's work represents an unprecedented effort at interpretation – his indebtedness to Mably notwithstanding. Moreover, Guizot was also interested in expanding the sources available to scholarship and published a set of *Mémoires relatifs à l'histoire de France* and a set of *Documents relatifs à l'histoire d'Angleterre*. Never before had history occupied as important a position in men's thinking. It was a time of decisive advances for this discipline.

Liberalism and its critics

The liberal credo

The philosophy of the time showed little originality. The relative decline of sensualism and materialism in the face of the renewed vogue of spiritualism that had developed during the Empire continued. Maine de Biran, the most original of the philosophers of the time, rehabilitated introspection and found in man both a passive state ruled by external determinants and the capacity for voluntary activity, the sign that his spirit is free. He had recently become interested in mysticism and in the ability of the free human spirit to lose itself in God. Royer-Collard, who had briefly lectured at the Sorbonne at the end of the Empire, had opposed a philosophy of perception inspired by the Scottish thinkers to the reigning sensualist views. At the beginning of the Restoration he became so involved in politics that his chair was given to Victor Cousin (1792–1867). The brilliant lectures of this 22-year-old teacher inaugurated the career of one of the most authoritarian mandarins that ever ruled academic thinking. Yet his eclectic doctrine amounted to little more than a history of ideas.

Metaphysical problems, of course, had not vanished from the consciousness of the men of the Restoration. But since they had just experienced a great upheaval, their thinking was essentially oriented toward the relationship between the individual and society.

Liberalism held out one solution to this problem: the freely consented association of individual endeavours is beneficial to the social body as a whole. The liberals were therefore hostile to privileges held by corporate bodies, classes, or organised religion and left it up to the individual to deal with a State stripped of many of its powers. Heirs to the spirit of 1789, they admired the Declaration of the Rights of Man and the night of 4 August. Freedom of thought, religion, speech, and press and protection against an arbitrary judiciary (in particular through the institution of trial by jury) were the liberal credo's articles of faith. Equality among individuals, it was felt, was a matter of enjoying the same civil rights. The representative regime, that is, the existence of a legislative branch of government elected by voters enlightened enough to choose the representatives of the nation, gives the nation a voice in managing the country's affairs. But of course there were nuances within this common set of principles. Under the Restoration one finds several liberal 'families', differentiated according to party affiliation.

The liberal families

To begin with, liberalism was the reigning ideology of the left, although here it sometimes became impregnated with a Jacobin or nationalist attitude that was foreign to its essence. Often expressed in a rather cursory fashion in the *Constitutionnel*, in Béranger's songs and Paul-Louis Courier's pamphlets, this brand of liberalism was adamantly hostile to the Ancien Regime, to the 'tithes and feudal rights' whose dreaded memory it diligently kept alive, and imbued with a vigorous anticlericalism directed mainly against Rome and the Jesuits. The self-styled guardian of the society issued from the Revolution and the Empire, it exhibited a kind of special tenderness for the small property owner, the hardworking bourgeois, and the old military man.

But the left also included original theoreticians of liberalism, the most remarkable of whom was Benjamin Constant (1767–1830). Born at Lausanne as the son of French Protestant refugees and cosmopolitan in his education, he led an exciting life profoundly marked by a stormy love affair with the effervescent Germaine de Staël. The weakness of his character became manifest during the Hundred Days when, having first published a scathing article against the 'tyrant', he then took part in the elaboration of the Additional Act. His keen intelligence and his steadfast struggle on behalf of freedom make up for his personal shortcomings. His many writings, books, memoranda, articles (published in the *Mercure*, the *Minerve*, etc.) add up to a coherent political system. Benjamin Constant noted that in modern times private life has become the most precious part of existence, the part that must be preserved from arbitrary interference of the powers that be. To this end, a unity of purpose must exist between power and public opinion within the framework of the representative system. Constant recognised the principle of popular sovereignty but restricted the exercise of voting rights to property owners, feeling that they alone were sufficiently independent to exercise it. As for the sovereign, he was a 'neutral' power who only acted as an arbiter in case of conflict between the legislative and the executive. Without holding a brief for heredity or legitimacy, Constant favoured the constitutional monarchy because the Republic had given rise to despotism at the time of the Consulate and also because he was more disposed to evolution than revolution.

The constitutional party also had its liberal thinkers: the *doctrinaires* Broglie, Guizot, Barante, Rémusat, and especially Royer-Collard, every one of whose speeches was an event at the time. Beneath the brilliant rhetoric, his doctrine was simple: the basis of the law is the Charter, the fundamental contract between legitimate power and the nation. It is the fountainhead from which flow all legislative, executive, or electoral functions. The latter function does not imply popular sovereignty, only reason is sovereign. Yet Royer-Collard, a firm defender of royal prerogatives at the beginning of the Restoration, seems to have sensed the need for greater flexibility in a country where 'the tide of democracy was running strong'.

Even on the right, liberalism was not absent. It was represented in the *Conservateur* during its brief lifespan (1818–20) and the *Journal des débats*. The principles of the parliamentary regime, and in particular the responsibility of the ministers, were vigorously supported as early as 1816 by Chateaubriand in *La Monarchie selon la Charte* and freedom of speech and of the press remained basic tenets of the counter-opposition on the right.

Yet the ultra-royalists espoused certain anti-liberal concepts that were most ably advocated in the Chamber by M. de Bonald. These concepts owed a great deal to ideas first expressed abroad by Joseph de Maistre and Edmund Burke. They were traditionalist and theocratic. The individual, they postulated, remains subordinated to society, which evolves as slowly as a growing tree, undergoing an organic development that must not be disturbed by any revolution, for revolution is a crime of revolt for which Protestantism has set the example. The individual exists only through society, which is formed in concentric circles, each one of them subject to one head, and ranging from the family and the community all the way to the State, where the king is but 'God's representative', as in Bossuet. The theocratic aspect of these theories was even more pronounced in Lamennais, who claimed that the only society that was perfect, because based on common consent, was the Church.

Economic liberalism and the beginnings of communism

Liberalism was applied not only to politics but to economic life as well. The physiocrats who in the eighteenth century had proclaimed the need to 'laisser faire, laisser passer' were already liberals. But the true teacher of the early nineteenth-century economists was the Scottish thinker Adam Smith; especially so in the case of Jean-Baptiste Say (1767– 1832). The erstwhile owner of a spinning mill that had gone bankrupt at the end of the Empire, Say taught a course at the Ecole des Arts et Métiers and in 1828–9 published a book in which he expanded the ideas of his *Traité d'économie politique* of 1803. It contained the basic ideas concerning the need for freedom of production and exchange, with special emphasis on the role of the entrepreneur. But Say departed from the English economists with a theory of value based not on production costs but on utility; and finally he formulated the law of markets, stating that 'products are exchanged for products', a law that reduced the role of money to a mere intermediary step in conducting exchanges and denied the possibility of a general crisis of overproduction. Say's work was characteristic of the optimism of the French school of political economy.

However, the benefits of free competition were contested by the Genevan Sismondi and by the first socialists, Saint-Simon and Fourier.

Comte Henri de Saint-Simon (1760–1825), offspring of a younger branch of the old noble family of Picardy that had produced the famous mémoires-writer, had led an adventurous life at the end of the Ancien Regime. During the Revolution he speculated in confiscated national properties, an activity that failed to keep him out of prison during the Terror. Later he devoted himself to a 'scientific career', returning to his studies and entertaining famous scholars. From 1802 to his death he was constantly writing. But by 1806, he was financially ruined and only escaped total destitution through the help of a few friends.

From 1802 to 1816, Saint-Simon's central preoccupation was to create a science of man that would bring moral factors to bear in the field of rational knowledge. He thus returned to the concerns of the *Encyclopédie*, but brought to them the historical orientation of his time. In particular, he analysed the revolutionary crisis brought about by 'the transition from a feudal and theological system to an industrial and scientific system', concluding that 'industry contains all the real forces of society'. On the basis of this idea, Saint-Simon was to propose, beginning in 1816, a reorganisation of the modern world that would bring an end to the anarchical state of production by uniting bankers, merchants, agricultural producers, and industrialists in an 'industrial party'. Capital would be provided to the most capable, and the government would be entrusted to three boards [*Chambres*] respectively responsible for invention (writers, artists, engineers), examination (mathematicians, physicists), and execution (managers). Private property would not be abolished, but inheritances would disappear.

As early as 1819, in his celebrated parable, Saint-Simon had stressed the opposition between the idle classes (nobility, clergy, jurists, large landowners) and the useful classes who participate in production. In his last work, *Le Nouveau Christianisme*, in which he asserted the need for a new religion founded on love and fraternity, he stated that such a religion 'must guide society toward the great goal of achieving as soon as possible an improvement in the lot of the poorest classes'. Indeed he believed that the transformation of society was near and on his deathbed told his disciples: 'The pear is ripe, go and pick it.'

Charles Fourier of Lyon (1772–1837) had led the life of a '*sergent de boutique*' and old bachelor, a 'pillar of *tables d'hôte* and brothels'. A bizarre personality whose mind combined crazy ideas with surprising insights, Fourier formulated a sweeping indictment against the 'civilisation' of his time. The sale of an apple in a Parisian restaurant for a hundred times the price it cost at the place of production was an eye-opener for him: by means of commerce and speculation, he felt, the middlemen create artificial shortages and become rich at the expense of the poor. And poverty was precisely the problem that haunted Fourier.

To 'civilisation' he opposed 'harmony', the society of the future to be founded on the principle of Newtonian attraction. This society would allow all human passions to express themselves, and this would bring about an upheaval in nature itself. At the basis of society, the phalanstery would form an all-inclusive group of men and women animated by complementary passions, and this free association would produce the goods to which all would help themselves according to their needs. Fourier endlessly described this happy society, in which horticulture would occupy a choice position. Even more endlessly he analysed and classified the passions, whose diversity would be the foundation of the future harmony.

Every day at noon, Fourier waited for the capitalist who would help him create the phalanx, the first cell from which this new world would grow. He never appeared.

Romanticism

The rise of Romanticism in literature

Romanticism was the deepest and most universal current of thought and sensibility to sweep Europe since the Renaissance. It first appeared in the literatures of northern Europe. In England it expressed itself in melancholy poetry about nature and ruins, in interest for old popular ballads and in the glorification of the age of Shakespeare over a classicism that had never really taken root. In Germany, where classicism had been pure imitation, the despairing or tumultuous literature of *Sturm und Drang* was born in 1770, to be followed in the years around 1800 by the great period of Romanticism in which philosophy, lyric poetry, and mysticism rehabilitated and glorified the Germanic Middle Ages.

In 1815 France was not yet so profoundly affected. To be sure, a current of sensibility that had existed ever since Rousseau was given to expressing melancholy feelings and the love of nature. Chateaubriand above all sounded new literary themes in his works from *Atala* to *René*, as well as in his *Génie du Christianisme*. But his '*mal du siècle*' [world weariness] did not amount to a negation of the established literary values.

By and large the literary world continued to believe that the ideal of beauty was transmitted from the Greeks to the Romans, from the Romans to the French seventeenth century, and from there to Voltaire. To create a valid work of literary art was thus to imitate and respect the rules arising out of this tradition: preference for classical subject matter, separation between the tragic and the comic genre, adherence to the three unities of the theatre, and a chaste style that forbids the use of coarse language. Lyric poetry was particularly constrained by this approach and could be justified only in terms of its craft: abstract passions, gods with their well-defined attributes, stereotyped metaphors (the thermometer was the 'captive mercury', the worm the 'skilful sapper'), an entire language of conventional ciphers to which a classical education provided the key placed a screen of falsehood between man and the real world. In the writing of prose, a precise narrative clarity inherited from Voltaire was hardly suitable for expressing emotions or for description. In short, classicism had become sclerotic.

Yet the public had changed. To be sure, some people, those who were educated in the *collèges* of the Ancien Regime, still took pleasure in such formalistic games, but certainly there were many readers who, having been formed by events rather than by schools, wanted to find in books the emotions of action or of life itself.

Therefore, the tide that in the heyday of classicism had carried French literature to all of Europe was now changing. The Restoration witnessed the growing favour of Shakespeare, performed on two occasions in Paris by English troupes; Shakespeare, in whose plays the tragic and the comic existed side by side, as they do in real life. Frenchmen read Walter Scott who evoked the chivalric adventures of the past with such poetic vigour that he greatly stimulated the formation of the chivalric and medieval dream world of his era. They were stirred by Byron, whose death at Missolonghi aroused extraordinary emotion. They also loved the German literature, Schiller's theatre, the Goethe of *Werther*, who was better understood than the author of *Faust*, despite Nerval's beautiful translation of the scenes that inspired Berlioz. But the French public was also interested in the Spanish theatre of the Baroque, and there was a veritable Dante revival at the same time as *The Last of the Mohicans* arrived from America. Literary curiosity also turned toward folklore (in 1824 Fauriel published his *Chants populaires grecs* in the original language and in translation).

Emigrés or Swiss citizens frequently served as intermediaries: the émigré Villers, an apologist of the German woman, partly inspired Madame de Staël's *De l'Allemagne*, revealed to the French public only in 1814, and the Genevan Sismondi published his lectures on the literatures of southern Europe with great success.

The public was bound to wish for a similar enrichment of French literary life. Around 1815, Romanticism was a rebellion against the iron rules of the classics. Only gradually did the movement which, like all revolutionary movements, refined its tenets as it went along, come to propose a positive credo.

In the beginning, classicism and a liberal patriotism were closely allied. Shakespeare was described as 'Wellington's aide-de-camp' and fidelity to Voltaire, to ideology, to classicism, and to France formed a single entity. The first Romantics (Soumet, Guiraud, Nodier) attached major importance to legitimacy, which they saw as a liberation from the Napoleonic despotism, and to religious sentiment, which they saw as a means to rescue the individual from sensualism, a philosophy that threatened the integrity of the human person. They therefore adopted the stance of legitimists and Catholics (Nodier wrote regularly in the *Quotidienne*) in opposition to the proponents of a liberal and rationalist classicism.

The latter, in turn, objected to the imitation of foreign models (especially the English 'Gothic novels') in the fiction written in the 'frenetic' style of the new school. Among these works were the novels of the vicomte d'Arlincourt, the novellas of Nodier, and *Han d'Islande* by the young Victor Hugo. But it was impossible to stop the new poetry that had come into its own with Lamartine's *Méditations* (1820), in which the young poet, a Catholic and ultra-royalist though unattached to any party, celebrated love and death, religious sentiment and harmony with nature in simple and moving terms. Equally successful were Victor Hugo's first *Odes* (1822) and Vigny's first *Poèmes* (1822). During the same years, the classical style was paradoxically highly acclaimed in writings concerning current issues, such as Jouy's *Hermite en province*, the admirably incisive pamphlets of the Hellenist and wine-maker Paul-Louis Courier, and the second volume of Béranger's *Chansons* (1821), whose authorship, incidentally, was a matter of considerable controversy.

Meanwhile, after 1820, the young Romantics banded together, first in the *Société des bons livres*, a title that betrayed their inspiration, and in the *Muse française* (1823–4). Directed by Emile Deschamps, the latter group was characteristic of the troubadour fashion of the day: 'Gilded chivalry, the pretty Middle Ages of the Lady of the Manor . . . the Christianity of chapels and hermits, little orphans and little beggars were all the rage', Sainte-Beuve was to write about this group.

The conservative wing of the royalist and Catholic party (this was during the Villèle regime) suspected these unwelcome allies of heresy. The year 1824 brought a violent offensive against them, sponsored by the right wing of the academic establishment in the person of Auger and by the government represented by Mgr Frayssinous. Briefly speaking, two parallel phenomena were involved here: the break between Villèle and Chateaubriand in politics and that between the old right and Romanticism in literature. To be sure, in the following year Lamartine and Victor Hugo celebrated Charles X's coronation, but they insisted on their right to be men of their own time and acknowledged their debt to the French Revolution. 'Is the harvest less beautiful for having ripened on the volcano?' wrote Victor Hugo. This was the beginning of an evolution that eventually led the author to assert that Romanticism was 'a literary form of liberalism'.

The birth of the *Globe* in 1824 contributed in no small measure to the about-face that would detach the Romantics from the doctrines of legitimacy. At the *Globe* Dubois gathered about himself a liberal team ranging from Carbonari to *doctrinaires*, men like Rémusat, Thiers, Duvergier de Hauranne, Sainte-Beuve, and others. They repudiated certain excesses of the Romantic movement but professed that literature had to express society, as Madame de Staël had shown; they therefore rejected the rules of classicism, which they did not see as an immutable expression of French taste. This taste had varied over time and 'the great masters were called thus only because they were creative'. Sainte-Beuve published in the columns of the *Globe* parts of his *Tableau historique et critique de la poésie française et du théâtre français au XVIᵉ siècle*, showing that in some ways Ronsard and the writers of the Pléiade were early precursors of Romanticism. The idea that literature was shaped by history – an idea that was indeed befitting to that time – thus triumphed in the columns of the *Globe*, and on this point Victor Hugo was very much in agreement when he wrote his famous preface to *Cromwell* (1827). Thus was formed a kind of coalition for the defence of free expression and free choice of subject-matter (such as exoticism, which triumphed with the *Orientales*). Despite certain divergences of opinion, this coalition united the moderate Romantics of the Delécluze salon (among others Mérimée who had just published the *Théâtre de Clara Gazul* and Stendhal, the recent author of *Racine et Shakespeare* and of *Armance*) with the more extremist members of the *Cénacle*. All of them agreed to further the cause of the drama and to write historical novels or novels about contemporary life.

The decisive battle was fought in the theatre. The classicists jealously guarded access to the Théâtre français to themselves, even though since 1825 that institution was directed by an administrator who favoured the new art, baron Taylor. To have a Romantic drama performed with rousing success by this company, which at the time enjoyed great prestige but remained hostile to the new art, would amount to a consecration of the new school. The 'battle of *Hernani*' was therefore but the crowning episode of a veritable war. Already in 1828, Alexandre Dumas' *Henri III et sa Cour* had been performed with great success by some of the boulevard theatres, but Victor Hugo's *Marion de Lorme* did not pass the censorship of the Théâtre français. But then Vigny's *Othello*, a drama based on Shakespeare, was accepted there in 1829, and its success opened the way, especially in conjunction with the pitiful failure of a tragedy put together according to the classical recipe by the academician Arnault, *Pertinax* (the Romantics called it '*le père tignasse*' – unkempt old man). Finally, on 25 February 1830, the two camps clashed at the première of *Hernani*,whose triumph marked the triumph of free expression in art.

Romanticism and the visual arts

Romanticism penetrated the visual arts to varying degrees. In painting the rivalry between different styles and schools makes this period, which abounded in talent, one of the most lively and varied eras in all of French art.

The Empire had been the reign of David. In his opinion, the painter should take his inspiration from antiquity, which has provided the models of ideal beauty and civic virtue. David therefore painted large canvases of balanced composition, inspired by Livy and Plutarch (*The Rape of the Sabine Women, The Oath of the Horatios*, etc.), showing strictly outlined, usually nude figures, in which the evenly applied colour serves only to emphasise the design. In these static and severe works the master kept his temperament under strict control and meant to teach his students the same austere discipline. But in 1815 the 67-year-old David, a former regicide member of the Convention, went into exile to Brussels. A new group of painters born around 1770 thus moved to the forefront. And while these men had experienced his influence, all of them now tended to free themselves of it.

David had entrusted his atelier to Gros. The erstwhile illustrator of the imperial epic now set out to record for posterity the *Adieux de Louis XVIII en 1815* and the *Embarquement de la duchesse d'Angoulême à Pauillac*, interspersing such historical scenes with mythological compositions. Torn between an art based on colour and movement and his fidelity to David, Gros disconcerted his pupils and the public and also felt himself to be declining. He was to commit suicide in 1835. Girodet, despite his choice of subjects from the Romantic literature, remained a more academic painter in the execution of his canvases. Gérard had become the official portraitist. Prud'hon, who had always remained at the fringe of the official school, completed his career with a number of religious paintings, among them *L'Assomption de la Vierge* (1819) and *Le Christ expirant sur la croix* (1823). In his lighting, his depiction of emotion, and his graceful style inspired by Corregio, he came close to Romanticism.

Romantic painting burst into full bloom with Géricault (1791–1824), who was passionately interested in horses and in English painting, but also devoted himself to the study of madmen and dead bodies. His famous *Raft of the Medusa* (1819) combined the diagonal composition of the baroque with the pyramid-shaped composition of the classics, bathed the crowded scene in a lugubrious chiaroscuro, and made use of bituminous tones. This great tragic work combined inspired verve with perfect technical mastery. Following the premature death of Géricault, his friend Eugène Delacroix (1798–1863) became the incarnation of Romanticism. His mother, the daughter of the great German cabinet-maker Oeben, had married Charles Delacroix, a member of the Convention and Minister of Foreign Affairs. Talleyrand who had replaced him in this latter post was undoubtedly the painter's real father. Orphaned at the age of 16 and perhaps convinced that a public career was closed to him because of his name, Delacroix chose painting over literature, for which he also had a marked talent. His first major painting, shown at the 1822 salon, was *Dante et Virgile aux enfers*; it was followed in 1824 by *Les Massacres de Chio* and in 1827 by *La Mort de Sardanapale*, inspired by Byron. At this point he had reached the full mastery of his first manner, having spent time in England where he had learned from the water-colourists how to lighten his colours. Delacroix applied his colours in individual touches, but the relations among them made his painting a veritable visual symphony that played off glowing red tones against shadows. For Delacroix, painting was first and foremost 'a celebration', but it was also more, and the public shared the emotion aroused in this cultivated aristocrat by the reading of Byron or Dante. The viewer was carried along by the painter's free creative imagination.

Such creative rapture was not in keeping with the academic rules. Consequently, the Institute threw itself into the arms of Ingres (1780–1867), who in 1824 had just returned from Italy, and appointed him as David's successor. In fact, Ingres was most 'academic' in his shortcomings, that is, in his pontificating manner and his intolerant character, in his inability to depict life, and his unsubtle colour. But his highly praised design makes for wonderful arabesques that have nothing in common with the austere lines of David's design, any more than do his nudes, which can be sensuous to the point of eroticism. The true classic by temperament was no doubt the landscape artist Camille Corot (1796–1875) who in 1825–8 returned to the great tradition of the French landscapists and painted luminous and serene scenes of the Roman countryside in the first mature phase of a career that was to end at the threshold of impressionism.

These men are seen today as the great painters of the Restoration era. But the hierarchy of values was different for the contemporaries who greatly admired Horace Vernet or even Delaroche, whom we today consider competent but mediocre. Of course, all classification is arbitrary. Frequently even painters of a classical temperament succumbed to the vogue of picturesque or Oriental subject-matter. Among the minor masters, one notes an extreme variety of genres, ranging from Boilly's scenes of middle-class life to the *turqueries* of a Decamps, who is totally forgotten today but was a great success in his time. Many of these painters, incidentally, were colourful personalities: for example, the Provençal Granet.

French sculpture was touched by Romanticism later than painting. Canova had very clearly dominated the imperial era. Later the Corsican Bosio, whom Louis XVIII liked for his verbal brilliance, was commissioned to do the Louis XIV for the place des Victoires, the kneeling Louis XVI for the expiatory chapel, and the Henri IV as a child for the king's bedchamber, while the Henri IV for the Pont Neuf was entrusted to Lemot. All of this remained strictly academic.

And so did architecture. As we shall see in the second part of this work, the Restoration continued the building projects begun in Paris under the Empire. The all-purpose, low-slung temple and the church inspired by the old Romanesque basilica preceded by a portico were the prototypes used again and again with varying degrees of success. As under the Empire, Percier and Fontaine dominated the world of architecture by their unsectarian antique inspiration and their elegant ingeniousness. Yet in the long run the evolution of the public's taste was to have an impact on architecture and sculpture. In 1821 the decor displayed at Notre-Dame for the baptism of the duc de Bordeaux was Gothic in inspiration, as were the trappings of Charles X's coronation. The lithographs of Achille Devéria and Johannot created the troubadour fashion; costume balls in medieval dress were all the rage, and the jewels worn by the women evoked a chivalric setting; indeed even cumbersome gargoyles could sometimes be seen to sprout from their bodices. Victor Hugo and other artists lived surrounded by a bric-a-brac of reading desks and carved chests. Happily, this archaeological fashion led to a movement for the preservation of French historical monuments, whose riches were depicted in baron Taylor's magnificent albums. In the period from Hugo's call to arms: 'War to the demolishers!' in 1825 to Mérimée's appointment as inspector of historical monuments in 1831 (a post in which he was to employ the services of Viollet-le-duc) and the creation of the commission on historical monuments by Guizot in 1837, useful protective measures were taken, some mistakes notwithstanding.

But it was not only the medieval fashion that led to the questioning of the accepted academic standards. A better knowledge of antique art showed it to be diverse and quite unaffected by standards of any kind. The Parthenon frieze, brought to England by Lord Elgin, surprised the beholder by its liveliness and its lack of constraint. Shortly thereafter, Hittorf was to publish his *Architecture antique de la Sicile*, which showed the gaudy polychrome decoration of the antique temples.

Hence the salon of 1833 marked the massive inroads of the Romantics: Barye presented a *Lion aux serpents*, Rude a *Pêcheur napolitain jouant avec une tortue*, Moine a realistic and moving portrait of Queen Marie-Amélie, Etex a painting of *Caïn et sa race maudite de Dieu*. But in the very next year the jury set up barriers against such works and only accepted Préault's *Tuerie* 'in order to punish the author and to provide a frightening example to the young'. The hope of obtaining official commissions kept many sculptors within the closed ranks of the eclectics, whose very type was the elegant but mediocre Pradier. It is true, however, that even David d'Anger, who was so highly praised by the Romantic writers and who produced medallions of all the celebrities of the time, was no more than a second-rate talent.

As for architecture, its belated Romanticism amounted to little more than an imitation of the Gothic style. While the Romantic period produced brilliant works in painting, and while the later development of a few artists of genius, like that of Rude, made up for the earlier groping of the sculptors, architecture remained the least original of the visual arts of the time.

Music

The richness of French painting is not found in music, that major art of German Romanticism.

For large segments of the bourgeois public, music was essentially the opera, an art form designed to enhance the drama and the visual splendour of the performances at the Opera House whose new decor was created in 1830 by the Italian Ciceri. This was an exceptionally brilliant period in the history of the Paris Opéra and the Théâtre des Italiens, which attracted peerless singers, from Nourrit to Pasta, to whose voices the composers adapted their scores. The repertory was not always mediocre, for one does find performances of *Don Giovanni* and *Der Freischütz* (which opened triumphantly in Paris in December 1824), albeit in Castil-Blaze's garbled versions, with pieces from other works, continuous ballet accompaniment, and so on, but this bothered neither the critics nor the public. The recital, brought into fashion in 1833 by a young Hungarian, the 13-year-old Franz Liszt, was also a kind of acrobatic feat. Virtuosity and improvisation were especially appreciated in pianists and violinists, all of whom were completely eclipsed in 1833–4 by Paganini, the 'sorcerer' who was also able to create genuine music in his diabolical *capriccios*. To be sure, there were also some chamber music groups; most notably, Habeneck founded the concerts du Conservatoire in 1828, and it was here that Beethoven's symphonies were revealed to the French public, although only to an elite.

This situation can only be understood if it is viewed in a long-term perspective: the disregard for French music goes back to the end of Louis XV's reign, when the French public preferred the light music of the Italians to the learned French school of that time. During the Revolution cultivated patronage disappeared almost irretrievably, for it was not revived by the salons of the Restoration. On the other hand, the Revolution favoured popular and civic music to be performed out of doors, featuring choruses and woodwind and brass instruments. The failure of this programme still remains to be studied. More than the Italians, Belgian musicians had been involved in these endeavours, but the best of them disappeared around 1815: Grétry had just died, Méhul would soon follow him, and Gossec retired. The transalpine vein, by contrast, seemed to be inexhaustible: Spontini, who had settled in Paris during the Empire, was put in charge of the festive music for the wedding of the duc de Berry in 1816, and in the same year Cherubini, the firmly entrenched director of the Conservatory of Music and superintendent of the royal chapel, wrote a *Requiem* for the solemn reburial of Louis XVI's remains. Cherubini incidentally was better than the reputation his narrow-minded and spiteful character has earned him. His severe craftsmanship did not exclude original inspiration. But it would be pointless to enumerate all the minor musicians who came from Italy to exploit the Parisian market.

Rossini was far above them. The opening of the *Barbier de Séville* in the capital was a triumph (1819) and a few years later he agreed to take over the direction of the Théâtre des Italiens, where he was given exorbitant privileges. For several years he dominated the musical life of Paris. His works made use of very plain techniques: the persistent repetition of the theme and an ever-increasing pace made them easy to understand even for the least talented listener. But there is no denying his scenic verve, the graceful flow of his melody, and the elegance of his orchestration. Curiously enough, his serious operas, which are rarely performed today, seduced the contemporaries more than his comic operas. In 1829 Rossini made a remarkable effort to renew his style with *Guillaume Tell*. But the public did not follow him. It now shifted its favour to Fromental Halévy with his laborious pathos and to Meyerbeer, whose *Robert le Diable* of 1831 was a triumph. While Meyerbeer was not the 'absolute zero' that Wagner has called him, it is true that he used a great deal of bombastic pomp and cold, solemn craftsmanship to make up for his lack of inspiration, a deficiency for which this son of a German banker further compensated with his outstanding talent for self-promotion. Meanwhile Bellini, whose graceful melody was upheld only by a meagre array of orchestral pattern, and the effusive Donizetti came to maintain the Italian presence.

Yet there was also a noteworthy group of French composers. One of them was Boieldieu (1775–1854), a musician from Rouen who had lived in Russia during the Empire and whose *Dame blanche* of 1821 was seen as the greatest masterpiece of the troubadour style. The fact is that Boieldieu was better than his success. While he was lacking in craftsmanship, he did have an elegance all his own, and it is perhaps regrettable that he wrote so little aside from his stage music. Ease and clarity also characterised the industrious Auber who for forty years wrote highly successful works for the Parisian stage. Posterity remembers him primarily for his *Muette de Portici* (1828), and Wagner placed him above Rossini. Herold's facile Romanticism brought him a large international following and the esteem this musician was accorded by cultivated circles is surprising to us today.

Such a following was never acquired by Hector Berlioz (1803–69). His *Huit scènes pour Faust* of 1828 and his *Symphonie fantastique* of 1830 already showed him in full possession of his mastery. Whether he commented with his music on Goethe or Byron or whether he wrote about the literature of his own country, he himself was always present as the solitary, embattled hero who bares his innermost heart. Exalted passions, despair, anger, or manly tenderness pervaded an orchestration whose magnificence of sound was all his own. Only east of the Rhine could he (who as a critic had spoken so knowledgeably of Beethoven) find great symphonic composers who were close to him, even though his phrasing was more Latin, descriptive, and luminous under its great cloak of harmonious sound. It was some time before the musicians understood that Berlioz was practising the new genre of the symphonic poem. But the public of 1830 saw only histrionics in his fire, provocation in his liberty.

Thus it rejected the message of the only great French Romantic composer. Yet it accepted some of the outward innovations of Romanticism, such as the close connection between text and music (Scribe and Meyerbeer working together!) and a livelier evocation of dramatic events and everyday life. There were a few scholars and a few organists whose obscure labours prepared the Renaissance of French music. The public of the opera and even the recitals ignored them.

Intellectual life during the Restoration was often bold and passionate. The eighteenth-century undertaking of drawing up the great catalogue of the workings of the universe was continued amidst controversies of all kinds. The thinkers of the Restoration era tended to place renewed emphasis on the role of irrational forces and to substitute the idea of a continuous creation for that of immutable and stable laws. The upheavals of the Revolution had made them aware of the fragility of all social and mental structures and the nineteenth century was from the outset dominated by the idea of evolution. It was to be the century of history in the largest sense. However, within this general widening of man's horizons, all branches of knowledge did not progress at the same pace.

Yet they did raise new questions about man's relationship with nature, with God, and with his fellow man. In this last respect the individual, freed from the constraints that had fixed his place in society, came face to face with a new dimension of freedom: henceforth he wanted to rely on his own judgment and his own taste to decide what is true, or beautiful, or good.

5

The revolution of 1830

From prosperity to crisis

Before turning to the political developments that led directly to the explosion of 1830, we should describe the change in the economic climate that made the years 1821–5 so different from the last years of the Restoration.

The former period had witnessed enormous investments in industry, despite the absorption of a great deal of capital by public bonds and loans for canal-building. The imposition of protective tariffs had opened the way for industrial expansion, yet by the same token overseas trade was unable to regain its former position in the French economy. As a result, the years 1821–5 brought, all at the same time, the first spate of railway construction with the building of the Loire line, the rapid development of steamshipping on the French rivers, the creation of great metallurgical operations in the Massif central and eastern France, the multiplication of spindles in the cotton industry of the departments of Haut-Rhin and Nord, a doubling in the number of looms in the silk industry of Lyon, and the construction of new housing in the northern part of Paris. This spurt of industrial growth prompted the banks and major investors to inflict a dangerous imbalance on the money market by tying up excessive amounts of capital at the expense of circulating capital.

In England, where this imbalance was even more pronounced, it was further aggravated by the scope of foreign investments. In 1825, London was hit by a serious crisis whose repercussions came to be felt at the Paris stock market in November of that year. The Banque de France, whose reserves were threatened, raised its discount rate. This tightening of credit and the ensuing panic at the stock market sent many banks into bankruptcy; many industrial and commercial enterprises also failed. Hard hit by unemployment were Flanders, Normandy, and Alsace (although in the latter province the distress reached such proportions that early in 1828 the Banque de France decided that it would no longer discount Alsatian bills). Certain sections of Paris were beginning to look as they still looked during the July days, like a huge abandoned building-site.

France took a long time to recover from this crisis, which had come about through speculation and overproduction: a kind of languor affected the French economy until well after 1830. As bad luck would have it, this problem coincided with an agricultural crisis. This crisis had been set in motion between 1826 and 1829 by a sudden decline in the production of potatoes, which had become a staple in the diet of the masses. Above all, the years 1827–30 were marked by poor grain harvests. In 1829, the price of a hectolitre of wheat rose by about 50 per cent over the 1826 price and remained at this high level until 1832. The price of rye rose even more sharply.

In small towns and in the countryside the troubles traditionally associated with years of shortage reappeared: fighting in the market squares where a few representatives of the public authorities were assaulted and where the crowds, accusing the king and the Jesuits of wanting to starve the people, set their own prices for foodstuffs; attacks on convoys of cereals; roving bands of agricultural workers or artisans engaging in begging, threatening behaviour, and sometimes arson. An entire zone reaching from the Nivernais to the Vendée and from there to the estuary of the Seine experienced these troubles, which reached their highest pitch between February and July 1829.

For Paris, the statistics of the municipal tolls show that the value of merchandise imported into the capital declined from 30 million francs in 1826 to 24 million in 1830. After 1827 in particular, bankruptcies became more and more frequent in middling as well as major enterprises. Part of the work force left the capital, but even so it became necessary to set up public works schemes. The price of a 4 lb loaf of bread (which at 13 sous reached the danger level, since this sum represented half of the average wage) rose constantly: from 11 or 12 sous at the beginning of 1827 to 18 or 19 sous during the winter of 1828–9 and to 21 sous in May of 1829. It is not difficult to imagine the hardships of the winter of 1829–30 (when the Seine froze over) for the poor classes, who were undernourished and unable to heat their dwellings. The spring of 1830 brought a slight improvement, with the price of bread returning to 15 sous, where it stabilised to some extent.

Yet in the summer of 1830, a climate of anxiety continued to prevail among the workers who were not sure that the next day's wages would be paid, the artisans who had almost no commissions, and the small shopkeepers who had few customers.

The Polignac government and the suicide of the monarchy

Lack of awareness on the part of Charles X caused all these different kinds of discontent to crystallise in an anti-dynastic opposition.

On 8 August the king dismissed Martignac, whom he blamed for having lost his majority in the Chamber, and constituted a government after his own heart. He managed to give the key posts to the most unpopular men: Foreign Affairs to prince Jules de Polignac, Interior to La Bourdonnaye, and the War Department to Bourmont.

Polignac combined in his person the attributes of being the son of one of Marie-Antoinette's favourites (and it was rumoured that he was the offspring of an adulterous liaison with the comte d'Artois), of being a former émigré (at the age of nine!), of having plotted against the Napoleonic regime, of being a member of the *Congrégation*, and of having married an Englishwoman. La Bourdonnaye had in 1815 called for 'irons and executioners!' to deal with the accomplices of the Hundred Days, and Bourmont, a former *chouan* temporarily rallied to Napoleon, had gone over to the enemy on the eve of the engagement of Ligny and it was whispered that he had given away the Emperor's plans. From the *Journal des débats* to the *Globe*, the press erupted in violent protest, and the first of these papers' editorial of 10 August was long remembered:

> Thus it is broken once again, that bond of love and trust that tied the people to the monarch! Here they are again, the court with its old grudges, the emigration with its prejudices, the priesthood with its hatred of freedom, throwing themselves between France and her king . . . Koblenz, Waterloo, 1815! These are the three principles, the three protagonists of our new government!

The public believed that the king was determined to 'climb on his high horse'. In fact, this was not true: the king had also given portfolios to moderates, and the other ministers were not likely to perpetrate a *coup d'état*. It was through a total lack of psychological insight that he had called on the unpopular trio to head the government.

How did they themselves feel about it? Bourmont was a special case, an unpleasant person, a born underling who had known how to win the confidence of the duc d'Angoulême. La Bourdonnaye was a muddled thinker, all verbal violence. The principal character was Polignac, a man of almost mystical piety and anything but a man of action. He had shown diplomatic qualities as ambassador to London (1823–9), but he was blinded by his extravagant presumptuousness. Unfamiliar though he was with the French political scene and with the reactions of his contemporaries, he had no desire to do away with the Charter.

The new government soon showed its inability both to prepare for the sessions of the Chamber and to purge its administrative cadres. In foreign policy Polignac confirmed the new direction outlined by La Ferronays, consisting of a pro-Greek stance and calling for an entente with Russia. He made bold plans for using the prospective division of the Ottoman Empire as the basis for a complete redrawing of the map of Europe that would have restored Belgium and part of the left bank of the Rhine to France.

The czar did not take these fantasies seriously but did indicate his willingness to involve France in any reorganisation of the Near East that might become necessary. He also assured Polignac of his support for the Algerian expedition.

Thereupon, after protracted negotiations with Mahomet Ali, the government decided on 31 January 1830 to intervene directly in the regency of Algeria. The active preparations conducted by d'Haussez, the Minister of the Navy, culminated in the embarkation of an expeditionary force commanded by Bourmont (whose manoeuvrings had eliminated Marmont, who was to head the expedition originally). This force seized Algiers on 5 July. The king and Polignac were able to withstand all attempts at intimidation on the part of the British government, thereby preserving France's future freedom of action in North Africa.

On the domestic front the government hoped to use this expedition not, as has been supposed on the strength of some ill-considered statements by certain military men, for a direct intervention to restore the king's authority, but for the enhancement of his prestige. This was not to be, for on 9 July, when news of the conquest of Algiers reached Paris, the crisis had reached an acute stage and was nearing its denouement.

On 2 March, when the king had opened the session of the Chamber, he had indeed proclaimed his loyalty to the Charter, alluding, however, to 'culpable manoeuvres' which he 'would have the strength to overcome'. In response, a committee charged with drafting an address to the king reminded him that the Charter 'makes concord between the political views of your government and the wishes of your people the condition for the smooth functioning of public affairs. Sire, our loyalty and our devotion condemn us to tell you that this concord does not exist today.'

This address was endorsed by a vote of 221 to 181 and read to the king on 18 March by the president of Chamber, Royer-Collard, who had participated in its writing. The problem at issue was the king's right to choose his ministers as he saw fit, and it is not certain that in a strictly legal sense Charles X was in the wrong. After all, Royer-Collard himself had proclaimed in 1816: 'If ever the day comes when the Chamber can dismiss the king's ministers, it will mean the end not only of the Charter but of the monarchy itself.' Since then the conceptions of the *doctrinaire* had evolved, but the king had not changed.

Rather than dismiss his ministers, Charles X decided to dissolve the Chamber and to appeal to the electorate. It was a legal solution, but looming behind it the parties saw the possibility of a change of regimes. A republican party of young men had recently been formed, with the *Tribune des départements* as its organ; in other circles there was increasing interest in an Orleanist solution advocated in veiled terms by the *National*, a publication for which Thiers and Carrel wrote under the secret patronage of Talleyrand.

The elections themselves (23 June and 3 July), in which the king and the clergy involved themselves in rather unfortunate ways, ended in disaster for the government. Instead of the '221' members of the opposition, there were now 274.

Most of them, however, were convinced that the king would yield and sought to facilitate his retreat. But the king felt that such weakness would spell his ruin. Invoking a paragraph of article 14 of the Charter (cf. above, p. 13), he believed that the circumstances justified his taking exceptional measures and that moreover, since the election procedures were not spelled out in the Charter, he could modify the recruitment of the Chamber of Deputies as he saw fit, a theory that was at the time brilliantly defended by the ultra-royalist Cottu. Charles X therefore decided to reform the recruitment of candidates by royal ordinance.

Prepared in deep secrecy, the four ordinances that precipitated the insurrection were signed by the king and his ministers on 25 July. Their content was as follows:

1 The first suspended freedom of the press, restored censorship, and subjected all periodicals and all brochures of less than 20 pages to preliminary authorisation.
2 The new Chamber was dissolved.
3 The number of deputies was reduced to 258. The deputies were to be elected by the electoral colleges of the departments only; the colleges of the *arrondissements* were reduced to the role of proposing candidates. The *patente* (a fee paid for professional licences) and the tax on doors and windows were no longer to be counted in calculating the amount of taxes that entitled a man to vote. These measures had the effect of further shrinking the segment of society whose confidence might have given support to the monarchy. The electoral colleges were convoked for 6 and 13 September.

The insurrection

From resistance to revolt

Although political tension had been building up for several weeks, the publication of the ordinances on the morning of 26 July stunned the the opposition. Many deputies had stayed in the provinces after the last elections. A sudden drop in the price of public bonds in the stock market was a first sign of trouble; by coincidence the election of judges for the commercial court, planned for this Monday, had brought to the Hôtel de Ville of Paris scores of manufacturers and businessmen who shared their misgivings with each other and considered closing their enterprises in order to be free to protest the royal decision.

First to react on that day were the journalists who, along with the typesetters, were most directly affected. They held a meeting at the offices of the *National*; students and electors joined them to discuss the situation. The former talked of revolt, the latter talked of a tax strike, a procedure used in seventeenth-century England that they wanted to imitate. In the end a statement of protest signed by 44 journalists was drawn up; invoking the Charter, it refused to recognise the dissolution of the Chamber of Deputies and the authority of the government which, it said, 'has today lost the character of legitimacy that commands obedience'. Yet the royal power was not questioned, and although the statement denounced 'a coup d'état', it concluded with these words: 'We, for our part, will resist it; but France itself must decide how far it will carry its resistance.' The principal authors were Adolphe Thiers for the *National*, Cauchois-Lemaire for the *Constitutionnel*, and Chatelain, the director of the *Courrier français*. The editors of the opposition papers obtained permission to publish from the judge of the court of first instance, Debelleyme, despite the prohibition of the prefect of police. But the day as a whole was quiet and brought no spontaneous popular reaction.

On 27 July, the first of what came to be called the 'Three Glorious Days', simple resistance turned to revolt. The government had wanted to make a show of authority; the *National*, the *Globe*, and the *Temps*, which had been published without authorisation, called for open resistance, and the police commissioner had their presses demolished. Marshal Marmont, the military commander of Paris, commanded a force of 12,000 men, and although he had restored order in Paris during the troubles of 1827 with only 1,000 men, his name had become synonymous with treason for the people of Paris. His troops had to intervene in several places; by three o'clock in the afternoon they were dispersing the crowds that had gathered around the first barricades near the rue Saint-Honoré and in the streets adjoining the Bourse, at the Palais-Royal and on the place Vendôme. Toward eleven o'clock that evening, he sent his men back to their barracks, thinking that the agitation had quieted down.

Yet on this first day the resistance had become organised; the liberal deputies who met at Casimir Périer's house still considered only legal means of resistance, even though they were soon overtaken by those whom we would call today the uncontrolled elements. Jacques Laffitte, General La Fayette, and Guizot returned to Paris on the evening of 27 July. The opposition deputies also were only looking for a means to protest the ordinances without envisaging an eventual overthrow of the sovereign.

From revolt to revolution
During the night of 27–8 July, the movement became revolutionary. Everywhere in the eastern part of Paris barricades had been erected, and young republicans had led the poor people of the faubourg Saint-Antoine in pillaging gun shops and in cutting down the trees of the

boulevards (an activity in which *concierges* and owners of nearby houses also participated).

Marmont's troops clashed with at least 8,000 armed men. The army of the line, many of whose lower-ranking officers had served in the armies of the Revolution and the Empire, was favourably disposed toward the nationalist idea espoused by the insurgents and often fraternised with them. The three columns that were to converge on the Hôtel de Ville were blocked.

At this point, the parliamentary opposition offered its arbitration in the form of a delegation headed by Laffitte and Casimir Périer. Generals Lobau and Gérard called on Marshal Marmont to order his men to stop firing but were refused; nonetheless the forces of order informed the king of their *démarche*. But despite the urging of baron de Vitrolles, Charles X rejected all demands for the retraction of the ordinances, since he shared Polignac's illusions about the situation.

By the morning of 29 July, Marmont could count on little more than the Swiss and the guard; these forces retreated from the Louvre to the barrier of the Etoile. The Babylon barracks had been taken in an action led by a young *polytechnicien*, Vaneau, who was killed in the fight, and the Palais-Bourbon was also invaded by the insurgents.

Paris was now in the hands of the revolutionaries, who had suffered casualties of almost 800 killed and almost 4,000 wounded (fewer than 200 of the troops had been killed and 800 were wounded). But was this already a full-fledged revolution?

After long hesitation the deputies, frightened by the street fighting (even if it turned to the disadvantage of the king's forces), had finally on the evening of 28 July drawn up a statement of protest that was published on the next day, signed by 73 deputies (41 of whom were present).

They refused to recognise the dissolution of the newly elected Chamber, without as yet questioning the king's authority. Yet a new authority was already taking shape. The director of the newspaper *Le Temps*, Baude, had become the self-styled prefect of police, and General (?) Dubourg had moved into the Hôtel de Ville. The deputies meeting at Laffitte's house were increasingly eager to direct, or more precisely contain, the revolutionary movement. The street fighters wished to see General La Fayette, who was quite willing to resume the role he had played in 1789, take command of the Parisian National Guard; the liberal deputies, who had no choice but to accept this as given, attempted to counterbalance his position by setting up, also on 29 July, a *municipal committee* (no one as yet dared call it a provisional government) that included Casimir Périer, Laffitte, Lebau, de Schonen, Audry de Puyraveau, and Mauguin. The new power structure was elaborated jointly by the Hôtel de Ville and the Hôtel Laffitte, which remained the hub of the entire Parisian movement.

The Orleanist solution

King Charles X made the decision to change his government too late, on the evening of 29 July; and during the night of 30–31 July rumours of a people's march on Saint-Cloud precipitated the departure of the king and his court for Rambouillet. Too late also came the appointment of the duc d'Orléans as lieutenant-general of the realm and the abdication on the next day, 2 August, of Charles X in favour of the young duc de Bordeaux. Travelling via Dreux and Cherbourg, Charles X was to reach England without major difficulties.

The demise of the older branch of the Bourbon family did not spell the victory of the republicans who, now that they were in control of the streets on 30 July wanted to proclaim the Republic and offer the presidency to General La Fayette; the crowds on the boulevards were singing '*Ça ira*'. On that same 30 July a proclamation written by Thiers and some others was circulated in Paris: 'Charles X can never return to Paris, he has shed the people's blood. The Republic would lead to dreadful divisions, it would bring us into conflict with all of Europe. The duc d'Orléans is a prince devoted to revolution. The duc d'Orléans is a citizen-king.' Talleyrand, Laffitte, and Béranger seem to have played a role – whose respective importance is difficult to assess – in presenting the Orleanist candidacy.

This proposition was all the more readily entertained by the opposition deputies as most of them, deeply concerned about the future, had made great efforts to bring about a conciliation. Thiers was sent to the duc d'Orléans at Neuilly to offer him the lieutenancy-general of the realm, and since the duke was not there, Thiers transmitted the deputies' proposal to his sister, Madame **Adélaïde**. Having returned during the night of 30–31 July, the duc d'Orléans, who had also been solicited by Mortemart on behalf of Charles X, finally responded to the *démarche* of the liberal deputies. On 31 July, Louis-Philippe d'Orléans addressed the people of Paris in a proclamation written with Dupin and Sebastiani; he accepted the functions of lieutenant-general and declared: 'Henceforth the Charter will be a reality.' On the same day he went to the Hôtel de Ville, where he was formally received by La Fayette and the municipal committee. His symbolic presentation from the balcony of the Hôtel de Ville amounted to a popular coronation.

Yet for all that the duc d'Orléans was still only lieutenant-general of the realm and it was in this capacity that he appointed a governmental commission including Dupont de l'Eure (Judicial Affairs), Gérard, Guizot (Interior), and baron Louis. On 3 August the Chambers were called together and a revision of the Charter was decided upon. The choice of a definitive solution was becoming urgent; revolutionary movements were flaring up in different French cities, at Bordeaux, Nantes, Lyon, and elsewhere, while in Paris revolutionary elements were expressing their dissatisfaction in the streets surrounding the Palais-Bourbon. The intervention of General La Fayette appeased them, but the threat remained and made the deputies most uneasy. The discussion was therefore conducted with considerable speed; at the Chamber of Deputies only 252 of the 430 elected deputies were present for the vote; 219 voted for the revision of the Charter that would allow for the formation of a new monarchy, 33 voted against it. In the House of Peers, of 114 of those present (at that time there were 365 voting Peers), 89 voted for the revision, 15 abstained, and 10 voted against it, among them Chateaubriand who publicly expressed his opposition: 'A new Cassandra', he declared, 'I have sufficiently importuned the throne and my fellow Peers with my unheeded warnings. . . . After all that I have done, said, and written on behalf of the Bourbons, it would be altogether despicable for me to turn against them when, for the third and last time, they are on their way to exile.'

Having declared the throne vacant on 7 August, the deputies took themselves to the Palais Royal to inform the duc d'Orléans officially that he had been elected king of the French. The official enthronement took place on 9 August at the Palais-Bourbon; the man who became Louis-Philippe I swore to uphold the revised Charter, and the fleur-de-lis was replaced by the tricolour flag. The government that was officially announced on 11 August included the commissioners appointed a few days earlier, as well as Laffitte (who also served as president of the Chamber of Deputies), Casimir Périer, Dupin, the duc de Broglie, and Sebastiani. Thiers, who had been instrumental in forming the government, became secretary-general of Finance and La Fayette was appointed commander-in-chief of the National Guard.

Significance and interpretation of the July revolution

Since the revolution was primarily a political matter, the change of dynasties provided a political solution.

The new sovereign was born in 1773. His reputation as a liberal was related first and foremost to the memory of his father Philippe-Egalité, Jacobin and regicide member of the Convention before he himself died on the guillotine. Even more important was Louis-Philippe's presence at General Dumouriez's side at the battle of Jemappes. In 1830 these memories had not yet become commonplace for official speeches, and the new king owed to them most of his popularity. After the elimination of the Girondins in 1793, Louis-Philippe had gone into exile to Switzerland, then to the United States, and finally to Naples, where in 1809 he had married Princess Marie-Amélie, the daughter of the king of the Two

Sicilies, who was also in exile. Although the Restoration had restored his immense fortune to him, he had remained aloof from counter-revolutionary politics. His apparently simple habits, his family life (he had five sons and three daughters), the fact that his older sons attended royal *collèges*, and his reputation as a Voltairean and a liberal made Louis-Philippe the very model of a 'citizen-king' as conceived by the Parisian bourgeoisie. This image of the new sovereign was to be brought into sharper focus as his reign progressed, increasingly giving it the character of a 'bourgeois monarchy'.

Immediately following the July days, Louis-Philippe still enjoyed genuine popularity, as even Louis Blanc had to admit when he described the review of the National Guard on 29 August on the Champ de Mars. This is precisely why the new sovereign continued to be seen as the 'king of the barricades' by the other European monarchs. Once again, fear of revolutionary France and of the Parisians was running high in the rest of Europe, for there was concern that the democratic agitation might spread to Belgium, Germany, and Italy. The czar's agent, Pozzo di Borgo, called La Fayette 'the protector and evident fomenter of this crusade of universal perturbation'. The British government under the Duke of Wellington, though not exactly sympathetic to the new sovereign, nonetheless was the first to recognise him on 30 August; other States (last among them Russia) soon followed. Clearly the foreign sovereigns also saw Louis-Philippe as the means of avoiding a republic in France.

The French themselves, at least those who at the time represented public opinion and had accepted the new regime, soon split into two different camps. For some – they were called the party of the Movement, but we must not misunderstand this party label, which by no means corresponded to the kind of structured organisation that this word would imply today – the July revolution was not completed in 1830; it would have to continue and to enlarge the scope of its action. A liberal revolution, it would also have to become a national and social movement (aiding the aspiration of oppressed national groups); moreover it meant that the popular element, at least in Paris, had become conscious of its strength. As far as Dupont de l'Eure, Laffitte, and Armand Carrel (who at that point still supported Louis-Philippe) were concerned, Louis-Philippe had been chosen 'even though he was a Bourbon'. Most of the newly founded newspapers, such as *Le Patriote* or *La Révolution de 1830*, had benefited from the *de facto* suspension of the measures limiting the freedom of the press and were favourable to the Movement; its principal organ was still *Le National*, while the *Tribune des Départements* was openly republican.

A sizeable fraction of the former liberal opposition to the Restoration adopted a very different interpretation of the July revolution; for Casimir Périer, for Salvandy, and especially for Guizot who, together with the *doctrinaires*, became the theoretician of this resistance to the revolutionary movement (only later was this group referred to as the 'party of order'), there had been no revolution, only a reaction to a *coup d'état* perpetrated by Charles X when he promulgated his ordinances. If the duc d'Orléans had been chosen, it was 'because he was a Bourbon'; and the Movement of 1830 was based, they claimed, on the principles of 1789. Liberal newspapers like the *Constitutionnel* and those that had rallied to the new regime like the *Journal des débats* defended this view, whose proponents hoped above all to implement the programme of the liberal left of the Restoration, that is, to guarantee the exercise of civil liberties by limiting the pressure brought to bear by the clergy and the public officials. With respect to the former, an anticlerical agitation fanned by the most revolutionary elements began to develop; as for the latter, they were subjected to a regular policy of dismissals and purges facilitated by the loyalty oath to the new sovereign required of civil servants. This oath led to many resignations in the magistracy and the army. Hastily made appointments gave rise to frantic place-seeking that was criticised even by staunch supporters of the July revolution: the poet and pamphleteer Méry wrote *La Curée*, and Armand Carrel refused a prefectship (to be sure, it was that of Aurillac).

Part of the bourgeoisie thus exploited a revolution it had manipulated for its own ends. This discredited the new regime in the eyes of the popular classes, especially since not all of those who aspired to public employment were able to obtain it, so that they swelled the ranks of the malcontents.

Continuation and failure of the revolutionary agitation

The revolution had precipitated another economic crisis just as the French economy was beginning to recover from that of 1827. The various aspects of this crisis will be dealt with later; here it should be pointed out only that it contributed to the aggravation of popular discontent which benefited the small republican groups in Paris that were unhappy with the outcome of the Three Glorious Days. In Paris the *Société des amis du peuple* founded on 30 July 1830 by Godefroy Cavaignac, Blanqui, Buchez, Trélat, and Raspail, was both republican and concerned with social issues; to a large extent it was composed of students of law and medicine and young clerks. Its name, which recalled the first Revolution, and its style, which involved mass meetings of 1,000 persons at the Pellier riding school, were upsetting to public opinion and caused the neighbourhood merchants to expel it from this location as early as 25 September 1830.

Steeped in the history of the First Republic, this society wished to reenact the first Revolution. The resignations of the duc de Broglie, Guizot, and Molé at the end of September had resulted from dissension within the government; the departure of these most staunchly anti-democratic elements was a success for the democratic movement in appearance more than in reality. Actually the new Laffitte government, which was in power between 2 November 1830 and 12 March 1831, did not include any men of the Movement except Laffitte himself and Dupont de l'Eure, while loyal supporters of Louis-Philippe headed the Ministry of Interior (young comte de Montalivet) and of Foreign Affairs (Sébastiani).

In connection with the trial of Charles X's ministers, the Movement voiced demands for the re-enactment of the trial of Louis XVI under the Convention; but the circumstances were not comparable and the debate on an indictment by the Chamber of Deputies precipitated a first day of rioting in Paris on 17 October. But it was only the hearings in the Court of Peers on 21 December and the announcement that instead of death sentences only prison terms had been imposed that provoked a veritable uprising in the streets of Paris. Young students who opposed the death penalty served to tone down the excitement, which soon subsided.

The other major issue for which the republicans agitated was support for national movements, especially those of Belgium, Italy, and Poland.

The Laffitte government

Faced with severe financial difficulties as shown by a considerably augmented budget, the Laffitte government had to produce a token of its ability to maintain order. A law passed on 14 December 1830 reduced the *cautionnement* [surety bond to be posted by publishers], but this was also a way to remind publishers that there was a press law (the stamp duty remained unchanged) and that it would be enforced.

La Fayette's resignation from the general command of the National Guard (in protest against the budget cuts in this item) on 24 December was a severe blow; as a gesture of solidarity Dupont de l'Eure also resigned his ministerial post, thereby discrediting the Laffitte government with the left. Yet this government had already begun to work on the extension of the representative regime and promulgated several laws even after Dupont's departure. The law of 21 March 1831 concerning the organisation of municipal governments modified one of the essential aspects of French political life by providing for the election of municipal councils. Henceforth more than 2 million Frenchmen voted in municipal elections, but their number was inversely proportional to the demographic size of their commune.

A law of 22 March 1831 gave the members of the National Guard the right to elect their officers, thereby democratising the most characteristic institution of the July Monarchy, the one that was most consistent with the citizen-king.

Finally, the law of 19 April 1831 lowered the tax qualification for eligibility from 1,000 to 500 francs, and the qualification for voting from

300 to 200 francs, a measure that doubled the electorate to about 200,000. Political power remained narrowly circumscribed, however, and the concept of suffrage as a function (requiring some competence warranted by a certain level of fortune) had not yet been overcome by the concept of suffrage as a right.

Laffitte was justified in feeling that he had the support of the Chamber. There had been no further general elections, but the 113 by-elections that had taken place at the end of 1831 to replace the deputies who had resigned or refused to take the loyalty oath had, by and large, supported his policy-line, although, to be sure, that line was as yet rather undefined. The banker Laffitte had nothing of a revolutionary about him; his progressive views – in politics as well as in the matter of credit – went hand in hand with a casual friendliness but also with a rather excessive desire for popularity that entailed a certain irresolution, a flaw that his adversaries did not fail to exploit.

The anticlerical agitation

In the provinces, support for the revolutionary movement primarily took the form of anticlerical agitation: seminaries were sacked (at Saint-Omer, Auxerre, and Metz), mission crosses were torn down (at Poitiers, Niort, Saint-Maixent, Chalon-sur-Saône), and Mgr Forbin-Janson had to flee Nancy. Almost everywhere the clergy was suspected of sympathies for the Carlists, the partisans of Charles X.

A tactless act of the Parisian clergy – a funeral service in memory of the duc de Berry celebrated in the Parisian church of Saint-Germain de l'Auxerrois on 14 February 1831 – gave rise to a popular demonstration. The deeply anticlerical National Guard failed to stop the sacking of the church and that of the archbishop's palace next door on the following day. The government adopted an ambiguous stance: Thiers, under-secretary in the Ministry of Interior, did nothing to stop the rioters, perhaps in order to give a warning to the legitimists and to deflect the revolutionary passions away from the king and the bourgeoisie. On the other hand the dismissal of the prefect of police Odilon Barrot was an (inadequate) token response to those who called for the return of order in the streets. Laffitte, unable to adopt a consistent line of conduct, contradicted by Sébastiani's diplomatic reports, pursuing a peaceful policy that ran counter to all the declarations of the Movement's newspapers as well as his own, and isolated within the council of ministers which wished to avoid renewed outbreaks of rioting, open war, or even the dissolution of the Chamber, was forced to resign on 12 March. It is an open question whether he had discredited the policies of the Movement or whether he had served to catalyse the revolutionary movement by isolating it from the great majority of the nation and even from the Parisian population until the time when a policy of law and order, of open resistance to the revolutionary movement, had become possible. Both roles are fatal to a politician, and Laffitte was no exception to this rule.

The economic crisis

Not only had the Laffitte government experienced serious diffi-culties in foreign politics, which will be analysed later; the still unstable French economy had also been unable to withstand the revolutionary upheaval. As early as August 1830, agitation of a more social than politica. nature had provoked demonstrations in Paris and in several manufacturing towns; their demands had focused on such things as fixed wage scales (as in the case of the carpenters and locksmiths of Paris) or the expulsion o foreign workers. Street demonstrations had taken place in such towns as Nantes, Mulhouse, and Saint-Etienne. There had also been strikes. This agitation was denounced by the men of the July revolution, who supposed or implied that it was provoked by Carlist agents: 'The real workers', the *National* had written on 17 August 1830 '[are not interested] in breaking machines or demanding higher wages.'

But these incidents, along with troubles in the agrarian sector – where there were demonstrations in market squares demanding lower wheat prices, protests against the administration of the indirect taxes (at Arbois and Besançon), or the forestry administration – had above all the effect of paralysing commercial and financial activity. In the countryside a wave of arson was a source of anxiety for the inhabitants during the summer of 1830 and again in 1831. The collapse of the stock market was spectacular: in 1830, public bonds fell from 84.5 francs to 65 francs; a share of stock in the Banque de France fell from 1,890 francs to 1,510. One of the principal victims of this collapse was the banker Laffitte.

Many banking houses had to suspend payment by the end of 1830 and in 1831, both in Paris, where too much capital had been invested in con-struction at the end of the Restoration, and in Le Havre (in connection with the crisis in the textile industry), Lille, Grenoble, and Bordeaux. Baron Louis established a fund of 30 million francs to help commerce and industry and discount banks were set up in the provinces to aid commerce in eleven towns. The gravity of the situation is clearly indicated by the drop in the volume of loans granted by the Banque de France; from 909 million francs in 1830 it fell to 184.3 million in 1832.

Local towns had to support growing numbers of indigents, a fact that constituted a heavy burden on municipal finances and brought discredit to municipal governments that had come to power in the wake of the July revolution, many of them composed of men of the Movement. At the local level these men, just like Laffitte on the national level, had served to catalyse the revolutionary movement. Faced with very severe difficulties, they exhausted their popularity, whereupon the most conservative elements, only too happy to see them worn down by the exercise of power, held them responsible for the crisis.

The great fear of 1832

Hard times for industry and commerce brought stagnation for business and unemployment for the workers with their attendant train of poverty, nervous tension, and malnutrition. It is in this context that cholera appeared in France, rapidly spreading from town to town and bringing fear and death in its wake. While the insalubrious neighbourhoods of Lille and Rouen were hard hit, the epidemic was most murderous in Paris: more than 18,000 persons died, 12,733 of them in the month of April 1832 alone. Not that the wealthier inhabitants were necessarily safer, after all the most illustrious victim was Casimir Périer, the prime minister.

Yet statistically the popular masses were hardest hit, and also the most frightened. The great fear of 1832 was a blend of epidemic, riot, and repression; the bourgeoisie found itself in fortuitous and forced solidarity with the indigents who were liable to spread the disease. The epidemic increased popular exasperation which, in turn, facilitated the spread of the disease. Because everyone was terribly on edge, the slightest incident could turn into a riot; already at the beginning of April 1831 a modification in the street-cleaning service of Paris had precipitated a riot of the rag-pickers. In early June, a riot following the funeral of General Lamarque (to which we will return presently) provided a political outlet for the agitation that gripped the lower-class neighbourhoods. A pervasive climate of violence, later described by Victor Hugo in *Les Misérables*, settled over Paris. In its uneasiness the bourgeoisie increasingly abandoned its liberal principles, taking a more and more distant attitude toward the lower classes, which in many respects had shown themselves to be 'dangerous classes'. The moment for a common revolution, and even for conciliation, had passed.

There will be no revolution

Even before the fall of Laffitte, his successor had been chosen: it was Casimir Périer, the president of the Chamber of Deputies. The other ministers, especially Marshal Soult, and also the king, soon realised that the new prime minister intended to rule. The cabinet was formed on 13 March; on 18 March Casimir Périer announced his programme to the Chamber: 'In domestic affairs, order without sacrifice to our liberty; in foreign affairs, peace without giving up any of our honour.' A man of action, a banker and industrialist, and one of the principal liberal leaders of the Chamber during the Restoration, this scion of one of France's most prominent bourgeois dynasties had inherited from his family tradition the spirit of Vizille* and a deep attachment to the liberal spirit of 1789. A man of precarious health, but authoritarian and hardworking, he presented a stark contrast to his predecessor.

The means he used to conduct a policy of repression were strictly legal. His purge of the administration was directed against mayors, prefects, and especially sub-prefects and State attornies, like Cabet; some units of the National Guard were also dissolved. Court proceedings against the press and confiscations of newspapers became increasingly frequent, even though the juries often acquitted the journalists. A new law passed on 10 April 1831 provided for stronger measures against unlawful assembly; it was used as early as 16 April to deal with the agitation stirred up by the acquittal of some young revolutionaries (Godefroy Cavaignac, Trélat) who had been arrested in December in connection with the rioting provoked by the trial of the former ministers of Charles X.

This policy of repression was directed not only against the republican movement; it also repressed the various social movements. The revolt of the *canuts* of Lyon (which will be treated in part 2) brings out the class-bound character of the policies pursued by the Resistance. To some extent, however, Casimir Périer's action was also motivated by a certain liberalism, the conviction that the State should not intervene in social relations.

This 'liberal' policy was still in keeping with certain aspirations espoused by the opposition under the Restoration; the law instituting a day of national mourning on 21 January, the anniversary of the execution of Louis XVI, for example, was repealed. The hereditary peerage, which had been defended by Thiers and Guizot, was abolished by the law of 29 December 1831. On this occasion Casimir Périer had compromised, but had defended the king's right to nominate the peers against an elective principle. In fact, the abolition of the hereditary peerage caused a weakening of the Upper House, which became too dependent on the executive; this in turn strengthened the elected Chamber. The first elections since the lowering of the property qualifications had taken place in July 1831; the majority of the new deputies had voted against the hereditary peerage, but the results were ambiguous. Was this the influence of the Movement? Or was it that of the Resistance? Above all, these elections had yielded the first crop of deputies of the July Monarchy who always endeavoured to derive the maximum benefit for their constituents or their *arrondissement* from their conditional support of the government. In the election for president of the Chamber, 181 votes went to Girod de l'Ain, the government candidate, against 176 to Laffitte, the candidate of the Movement.

In his relations with the Catholic Church, Casimir Périer continued the anticlerical liberal tradition of the Restoration era. Nonetheless the

---

* It was at his family château of Vizille that the representatives of the different orders of the Estates of Dauphiné demanded the calling of the Estates-General in 1788.

government affirmed freedom of worship and attempted to improve its relations with the bishops, which in Paris were still strained because of Mgr de Quelen. On the whole, the government remained extremely suspicious of the clergy, especially that of western France. The fact that permits for religious processions and municipal subsidies for the clergy were not granted in many towns contributed to bringing numerous Catholics into the legitimist camp.

Yet a new current of thought, represented by abbé de Lamennais, had attempted to reconcile the Church and liberal principles by making a radical break with the age-old alliance between throne and altar. But then Lamennais' journal *L'Avenir*, which was disliked by most of the bishops, the implicit criticism of Pope Gregory XVI whom Lamennais had consulted in Rome, and government proceedings against comte de Montalembert who had wanted to open a Church school in Paris, rue Saint-André-des-Arts, soon ruined this first current of Catholic liberalism.

Even before Casimir Périer died on 16 May 1832, his illness had weakened the government; as a result – and this was particularly true between May and October 1832, when the government continued to function as before, but without a head – Louis-Philippe was able to play a more active role; in fact the king, believing that he was more qualified than anyone else because of his long experience, assumed the role of prime minister: this was an equivocal situation that was viewed with grave misgivings by conservative opinion. The adversaries of the regime seized upon these circumstances to revive their agitation in several areas. The funeral of General Lamarque who had died, also of cholera, on 2 June 1832, provided an occasion for the republican secret societies. On 5 June an attempt to seize the republican leader's body at the Pont d'Austerlitz where the procession was supposed to end and to carry it to the Panthéon failed, but several neighbourhoods were in a state of insurrection. The secret societies felt that they could count on the parliamentary opposition, which had just published the minutes of a parliamentary meeting held on 28 May at Laffitte's house at the prompting of Odilon Barrot. The document was signed by 134 deputies, and in the hope of rallying such republicans as Garnier-Pagès, Cabet, and Voyer d'Argenson the text made use of violent language: 'The Restoration and the revolution are once again in confrontation; the old struggle which we had thought was over is beginning anew.' Yet the leaders of the parliamentary opposition refused to take the leadership of the insurrection and La Fayette, by now an old man, still hesitated on 6 June. Laffitte, Barrot, and Arago went to see Louis-Philippe; they disavowed the riot (which, instigated by the young republicans, had started the night before), but urged a change of policies without proposing any means of achieving it. Order was rapidly restored on 6 June, but there had been murderous fighting during these two days, especially in the cloister of Saint-Merri, where the last of the insurgents were massacred by the army and the National Guard.

The parliamentary opposition objected to the ordinance of 7 June 1832, which declared a state of siege for the city of Paris and imposed court martial for the insurgents who had been arrested. But it would not resurrect the opposition that Charles X's ordinances of June 1830 had aroused. The defeat of the republicans (Louis-Philippe commuted the seven death sentences imposed in the trials of the insurgents to deportation), the death of the duke of Reichstadt in Vienna on 22 July, the failure of the legitimist agitation in support of the duchesse de Berry, all served to reinforce the stability of the July Monarchy. It became clear that the revolution really had ended in 1830. Casimir Périer's actions had inaugurated the policy of the '*juste milieu*' that would be invoked by his successors, although not all of them interpreted it in the same manner. The 'days' of July 1932 put an end once and for all to the hope that the revolutionary movement could be revived. Conservative attitudes henceforth had the upper hand among the voting minority that became more and more identified with the bourgeoisie. No longer was there room for sentiments and illusions in political life, which became a matter of rationality and self-interest.

6

Conservative liberalism

Most of the liberals of the Restoration had been willing to adjust to the evolution of a parliamentary regime, especially since such a regime limited the authority of the State and encouraged individual initiative. But the July regime had barely begun to work out political solutions to the difficulties that were facing it when the sudden emergence of the social question at Lyon gave the signal for the conflict between the proletariat and the bourgeoisie that turned many liberal bourgeois into conservatives.

The July regime takes root

The government's anti-revolutionary policies had also been effective in curbing legitimist agitation. Moreover, the defeat of the duchesse de Berry had consolidated France's diplomatic position. The continued rule of Louis-Philippe became a guarantee of peace in Europe. The government formed in 1832 (12 October) was headed by a great military name, Marshal Soult, duc de Dalmatie, a man without parliamentary obligation or fixed opinions. The actual power was shared by Thiers, Minister of Interior, and the duc de Broglie, who headed the Foreign Office. A liberal aristocrat, Broglie had agreed to serve in the Cabinet only on condition that a post also be given to Guizot, who thus received the portfolio of Public Education. Among the rest of the ministers, Humann at the Ministry of Finance and Barthe, a former Carbonaro, at the Ministry of Justice, were not helpful to the popularity of a government that from the outset aroused the hostility of most of the Parisian press.

Nonetheless, this government brought about a major stabilisation. In foreign policy, its intervention at Antwerp against the Dutch strengthened its position with respect to the parliament, and later the arrest of the duchesse de Berry (7 November 1832) was a success for the policy of Thiers, who wanted to make a point of the open break between the government and the partisans of the fallen dynasty. The violent attacks of the legitimist press and the verbal excesses of a Chateaubriand served to intensify the repression, which involved searches of legitimist homes, police surveillance, and even arrests; all of which opened a gap between the new regime and those who hesitated to rally to it, and also turned away a part of the Catholic notables who were shocked by the sometimes justified but often excessive measures against the clergy.

New legislation and the rise of conservatism

At the bidding of the government, the Chambers set out to implement the programme announced in 1830. The law of 21 June 1833 completed the extension of the representative system by providing for the election of the members of the departmental [or general] councils and those of the councils of the *arrondissements*. Drafted by Guizot, the public education law of 28 June 1833 was part of the search for a rational policy exemplified at the highest level by the reconstitution of the Académie des sciences morales et politiques, another achievement of Guizot's. This academy was to be a body dedicated to reflection; its purpose was to give guidance to the representatives of the nation and to rationalise power. By means of this institution the individuals who elaborated or supported the social thought of the period established close ties of solidarity with the notables of the July regime; the principal bond uniting its members was a shared liberalism.

At the most modest level, the public education law was an expression of the same concept, for it represented education as the necessary preparation for eventual participation in public life, for an improvement in the methods of work and production and hence as a means to reduce poverty. The legislators felt that it was bound to result in a 'moralisation' of the popular classes who, once they were better educated, would no longer think of revolt. Guizot did not separate education from moral and religious instruction. The obligation imposed on every commune to open a school and to pay a teacher for teaching the poorest children free of charge while the others had to pay a monthly fee was not uniformly enforced. Nonetheless the law provided impetus to education. The percentage of illiterate conscripts declined from 50 per cent in 1835 to 39 per cent in 1850. Yet the fact that the teachers were placed under the tutelage of the mayors caused primary education frequently to reflect petty local preoccupations; town councils and parents in most rural communes were primarily interested in keeping down expenses and looked only for immediate utility in education. Guizot's educational legislation was by no means a tool for upward social mobility; such mobility was fostered, at best, only by secondary education, for which the July Monarchy achieved no major reform, perhaps because it was unable to resolve the long-standing issue of freedom of education. The school reform, conceived at a time when France was preparing to make a new beginning and to train future generations in a new manner, was designed to foster a social cohesion that would benefit the new bourgeoisie. 40,000 docile schoolteachers who followed the will of their mayors and prefects would wean the young generations away from the clergy with its suspected legitimist sympathies and also arm them against subversive democratic ideas. It would no doubt be inaccurate to attribute to Guizot's school policy in 1833 the conscious intent to foster the triumph of a narrow conservatism, but in fact the liberal and individualist moralism underlying his reform achieved just that result.

The economic recovery that began at the end of 1833 and was well under way by 1835 facilitated the government's task. For a few years employment was plentiful in metallurgy and mining as well as in home construction and renewal, and transportation.

Yet the maintenance of order remained the outstanding preoccupation of the powers that be. A stable peace and a gradual return to prosperity which, though relative, contrasted with the preceding years, contributed to strengthening their authority, especially since the democratic opposition, in becoming more revolutionary, had also become numerically smaller and more isolated.

New forms of democratic opposition

As it became clear that the conservative evolution of the July regime put an end to the hope of re-enacting the first revolution, the republican opposition reorganised itself on a new basis. Not that it broke entirely with all the partisans of the July regime. The dynastic left, including Laffitte, who was becoming exhausted by his prime ministership, Odilon Barrot, a prominent bourgeois lawyer who served on the *Conseil d'Etat* and on the Supreme Court (*Cour de cassation*), and a certain number of deputies who were more progressive than their constituents, participated with the republicans in the *Association libre pour l'instruction du peuple*, which flourished in Paris in 1833, or in the *Association pour la liberté de la presse*.

But in the face of the repression to which they were subjected the young republicans adopted a more secret style of action. Setting themselves apart from those of their elders who, like Armand Carrel, were deeply attached to liberalism, and more open to social (the word socialist was not yet used) ideas, they returned to the Jacobin tradition. Their movement harked back to the *Société des droits de l'homme et du citoyen*. Issued from the section of the *Amis du peuple* that had been in charge of liaison with the Parisian workers before June 1832, it reconstituted itself during the summer in a more secret form, counting some 170 sections and almost 3,000 members in Paris alone. In the provinces it proliferated mainly in eastern France and in the Lyon area. The publication of the manifesto of the *Société des droits de l'homme* in the newspaper *Tribune* on 22 October 1833 made it quite clear that this society placed itself in the Jacobin tradition, as did its very name; as did the names of *Robespierre, Marat, 21 Janvier*, or *Babeuf* given to some of its sections. The text of the manifesto affirmed the all-powerful and all-embracing character of the republican State to come. It was also sympathetic to socialist ideas, for the dispersal of the Saint-Simonian group had acquainted the republicans with certain of their ideas concerning the organisation of work and the limitation of property rights.

The republican propaganda made use of the press, brochures, and pamphlets, among them the broadsides published by Cormenin, a notable of more liberal than republican persuasions, under the pseudonym of Timon, which seriously impaired Louis-Philippe's already fragile popularity. Press trials made the existence of republican newspapers precarious, especially in the provinces, but they did provide the democrats with a forum to popularise their ideas. As for the prisons, they became, especially after 1832–3, schools of republicanism for labour leaders condemned for instigating strikes.

Yet, as the elections of 1834 were to show, the republican propaganda had little effect on the electorate, which was hostile to republican ideas since it saw them as synonymous with revolution.

On the other hand, the few republican deputies who adopted a revolutionary stance in the Chamber were considered too timid by the advocates of direct action. Repressive measures against the latter, such as the dissolution of the *Société des droits de l'homme* (which continued its activities in secret) or the outlawing of street-vending of newspapers, proved ineffective in 1833. The government therefore prepared a new law concerning associations of fewer than 20 persons. These measures provoked a strong reaction from the republicans, not so much the parliamentary leadership as the militants. This movement erupted in April at Lyon. In Paris the Minister of Interior, Thiers, took preventive measures, suspended the newspaper *Tribune* and had some 150 ringleaders of the *Société des droits de l'homme* arrested. On Sunday morning, 13 April, members of the Parisian sections of the society, deprived of their publication and without responsible leadership, erected barricades in the Saint-Merry quarter, in the rue Beaubourg, in the rue aux Ours, and in the rue Transnonain – and it is possible that the most passionate among them let themselves be influenced by *agents provocateurs*. The government could count on the National Guard and on the troops of several generals. The next morning at dawn the troops cleared the barricades; believing that shots were fired from a window at 12 rue Transnonain, the troops entered the house and killed almost all the men living there, most of them peaceful citizens. It was a deplorable excess of repression; and the republicans immediately seized upon it to divert attention away from the failure of their uprising and later used it against Bugeaud, the commanding general whose troops occupied the street in 1834. Daumier made a tragic drawing of the incident. Two days of rioting in Paris resulted in some ten deaths among the forces of order and about fifteen among the insurgents, not nearly as many casualties as at Lyon. The public authorities used the manner in which the riots had been put down and the trials of the accused participants in April to gain support among the bourgeoisie which, in reading the conservative press, had become thoroughly frightened by the scope of the revolution that had been averted.

The disarray of the republicans was apparent in many areas. They failed, for instance, to exploit the death on 20 May 1834 of General La Fayette, who for the youngest among them had already become nothing more than a vain old man, a has-been. By contrast, the trials of the accused of April, which lasted until January 1836 and was marked in July 1835 by the escape of 28 of the principal ringleaders (among them Godefroy Cavaignac and Marrast), was turned into a veritable republican party congress by the defence. But as the trial went on and on, it accentuated the influence of the more extremist elements and ended by sowing new dissension in the republican ranks. Completely disavowed in the 1834 election of deputies and severely crippled by the demise of the *Tribune*, a staunchly republican newspaper that had folded under the weight of heavy fines, the republicans were isolated. The attempt on the life of Louis-Philippe on 28 July 1835 on the boulevard du Temple where the king had reviewed the National Guard resulted in eighteen dead (among them Marshal Mortier) and twenty-two wounded; the three principal perpetrators were executed. Fieschi, their leader, was nothing but an adventurer who had already been convicted several times, and his accomplices had been active in republican agitation. The government, and Thiers in particular, exploited the strong feelings aroused by Fieschi's attempt to deal with the republicans once and for all. The Chambers, called into emergency session in August 1835, passed what were to be called the September laws; one of these reorganised the assize courts and the terms under which seditious acts were to be judged, another provided for secret voting by juries and reduced the majority needed for condemnation, while others imposed more stringent controls on the press and authorised the prosecution of offences committed by the press and other means of expression, engravings in particular. Henceforth it was forbidden to contest the principle of the regime and it became illegal to profess republicanism.

The laws of September 1835 did not curtail civil liberties as drastically as their adversaries claimed; the virulence of the opposition newspapers in the ensuing years of the July Monarchy would be sufficient to make this point. For the moment, however, these laws did cause the demise of some thirty republican newspapers; and juries, following the general trend of the bourgeoisie, did become more severe. As a party, the republicans were indeed destroyed; when Armand Carrel was killed in a duel by Emile de Girardin, a young republican named Edgar Quinet could write on 6 August 1836: 'The republican party is in the coffin with Carrel; it will rise from the dead, but it will take a long time.'

The political personnel and the elections

The Orleanist party line that had triumphed over the republican danger and the legitimist threat had been elaborated by an ideologically as well as socially homogeneous group rather than as a result of personal policy-making. It was pursued by the successors of Casimir Périer and such eminent politicians as the duc de Broglie, Thiers, Guizot, comte Molé, but also by Dufaure, Duchâtel and erstwhile men of the left like Barthe. Added to these politicians recruited among lawyers and intellectual professional men and also, in the case of the oldest, among former officials of the Napoleonic Empire, were the military who served in the various cabinets. The government was especially willing to make use of the army, a legacy of the Napoleonic era, when it was at peace. This prestige was the reason why Marshal Soult, Marshal Mortier, and Marshal Gérard became prime ministers. With Jacques Laffitte and Casimir Périer the government had seemed to inaugurate the rule of the bankers; yet the business world only rarely furnished a minister, although it certainly did find others to represent it.

The governments (and they changed frequently between 1832 and 1837; there were seven during the legislature elected in 1834 alone) almost always included the same men and the differences between them were more a matter of personal rivalries (aggravated by the likes and dislikes of Louis-Philippe) than of opinions. The increasing number of Peers in these governments made them increasingly unrepresentative of the elected Chamber; the choice of one of them as prime minister (especially in the case of comte Molé) also contributed to holding up the normal evolution toward a parliamentary regime.

The elections gave support to the policy of the *juste milieu* and stabilised the personnel of the parliament. The early elections of 21 June 1834 dealt a severe blow to the left. The government could count on 320 votes, compared to 90 for the opposition and some 40 undecided votes. These elections of 1834 brought to light a shift in public opinion more than a shift in personnel or in categories, for some of the deputies elected in 1831 who had been far to the left moderated their stance, either from conviction (because they were frightened by the republican agitation) or by way of adapting to their constituents, who were more attached to the new regime and to social order than they were. But there were also close to 173 new deputies out of a total of 495 (although some of these men had served in

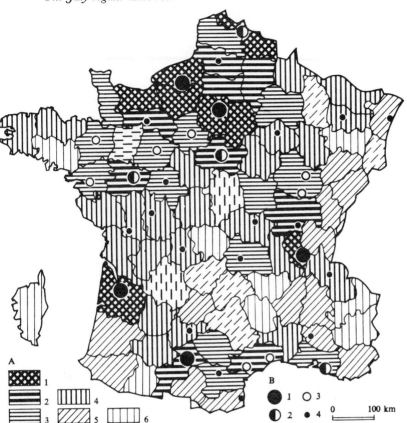

1 Distribution by department of voters paying more than 1,000 francs in taxes,
   c. 1840

   A 1 more than 400   3 between 201 and 300   5 between 50 and 100
     2 between 301 and 400 4 between 101 and 200   6 less than 50

   Note: Broken lines indicate departments for which complete electoral lists for
   the July Monarchy were not available. In these cases we have used the lists of
   eligible voters from the Restoration period, modifying them in light of the
   evolution of neighbouring departments or of extant voters' lists of the July
   Monarchy for certain *arrondissements* (these were available, for example, in
   Aveyron and Dordogne).

   B 1 towns where more than 200 persons paid more than 1,000 francs in taxes
     2 towns where between 100 and 200 persons paid more than 1,000 francs in
       taxes
     3 towns where between 70 and 100 persons paid more than 1,000 francs in
       taxes
     4 towns where between 40 and 70 persons paid more than 1,000 francs in
       taxes

2   Percentage of voters (qualification: 200 francs in taxes) in the total population,
    by department

  1 departments with more than 10 voters per 1,000 inhabitants
  2 departments with between 8 and 10 voters per 1,000 inhabitants
  3 departments with between 6.5 and 8 voters per 1,000 inhabitants
  4 departments with between 5 and 6.5 voters per 1,000 inhabitants
  5 departments with fewer than 5 electors per 1,000 inhabitants

  A boundaries of departments counting more than 3,000 voters in 1840–2
  B boundaries of departments counting fewer than 1,500 voters in 1840–2

  Source: Alfred Legoyt, *La France statistique, 1845*, table H, based on the figures
  published by the electoral lists of 1842

the legislature in earlier periods). The third party with some 100 seats
gained what had been lost by the republican left, which was now represented by a very small minority. But the general renewal of the Chamber
varied greatly from department to department, as can be seen from map 1,
considering that 15 departments (often the poorest ones) re-elected all of
the incumbents, while 15 others chose more than half of their deputies
among newcomers.

These elections were an indication that the anti-revolutionary policies were successful but also running out of steam. The very scope of the victory of the supporters of the July regime made cohesion among them more difficult. Passed by 256 votes, the address [to the government] drafted by deputies who were often rather critical of the persons of the ministers themselves revealed the ambiguity of the majority.

The elections of November 1837, called by Molé in order to widen his majority, and even those of March 1839 to which we will return presently, were remarkable not so much for the political orientation they fostered as for the stability of the parliamentary membership (even if in 1837 there were 152 newcomers among the 459 deputies). The property qualifications needed to stand for election and the expenses of a stay in Paris limited the choice of candidates to a small number. The changeable nature of public opinion and the absence of great debates on great issues made for deputies who saw their parliamentary careers in terms of personal achievements they could use to impress their constituents; deputies were likely to make their support of the government contingent on favours from the central government and on the approval of their demands for funds or positions by the different ministries.

While the scope of political debates in the Chambers became more circumscribed, politics did begin to play a major role in the administration, where it influenced the recruitment and advancement of the prefects, the holders of high government posts (*grands corps*), the magistrates, and the civil servants of the ministries. This was one more bond between the high administration and the world of politics, justifying to some extent the indictment of the Orleanist State as a 'protective syndicate for the ruling class'.

Attempts at political renewal

The Chambers

The success of the policy of resistance [to republican agitation] in 1834 and the political listlessness resulting from the all too frequent collusion between governmental pressure and compliance on the part of the governmental majority that kept the Molé government in office in 1838 made for elections that reflected new cleavages within public opinion in 1834 and 1839. This was not the case, however, in the elections of 1837, which were called with mixed success to strengthen the majority of the Molé government and resulted primarily in strengthening the centre at the expense of the more ideological tendencies (such as the legitimists, the dynastic left, and the *doctrinaires*). Henceforth the issue was not so much the interpretation of the revolution (which was resolved in the most conservative fashion) as the cleavage between supporters and opponents of the government. In 1839 a coalition brought together all those who opposed the Molé government, uniting the republicans led by Arago with legitimists such as Berryer and including all the different dynastic tendencies ranging from Odilon Barrot's left to Thiers' centre-left and Guizot's *doctrinaires*. As we shall see, the success of the opposition was not commensurate with its efforts – although it did bring about the resignation of Molé.

What was at issue was the use of power, rather than its ideology, and in 1839 the opposition to Molé objected most strenuously to what it considered the king's excessive intervention in politics. It was only toward the end of the July Monarchy, in the elections of 1846, that a large conservative and governmental majority emerged. The July Monarchy thus never witnessed the formation of major parliamentary parties after the English manner that several of its leading politicians would have liked to see.

The most tightly organised parties, those that had the most explicit ideology – that is the radicals, the legitimists, and later the dynastic left – were precisely those that had the least impact on the electorate. The electorate and the deputies were more interested in the interpersonal relationship between elector and candidate. Voting on the level of the *arrondissement* contributed to this attitude, and the deputy was seen more as the spokesman for local interests than as representing a part of the nation. This is the reason why so many jurists (barristers, notaries, magistrates) and civil servants were chosen by the electors on the grounds of their real or supposed abilities. The delay and the imprecision with which information reached the provinces made it possible for a deputy to project two different political images to the Chamber and to his constituents. Garnier-Pagès and later Ledru-Rollin were more advanced than their constituents in Sarthe; conversely many former legitimists who had rallied to the July regime were able, sometimes with the support of the prefects, to preserve their legitimist image in their departments, as Lahaye-Jousselin did at Châteaubriant.

Even when political issues were put forward, as they were in 1839, the electorate was more likely to make its choice on the basis of personal issues than in terms of the ideological options presented; that is why the modifications were not as profound as the tone and the scope of the polemics would lead us to believe.

This depoliticisation, which resulted from the quasi-unanimous belief of the electorate in the value of the social system founded on individual property, imparted the character of local and personal rivalry to economic and even political disagreements. The political leadership of the July Monarchy felt that it had found a formula for stable government, a balance between order and freedom. The amnesty for all political convicts on the occasion of the marriage of the duc d'Orléans to the duchess of Mecklenburg-Schwerin in May 1837 had been well received by the conservatives as well as by the dynastic left that had demanded it, and Molé's overtures to the Catholics and the legitimists, some of whom were beginning to rally, had also contributed to this stability.

The development of prosperity

Prosperity, stimulated by technical advances, was one of the aims of the July Monarchy. Leaving aside its economic aspects for the moment, prosperity also had political implications. The liberal principles espoused by the leadership of the regime were applied in a rather pragmatic manner. There was no question, for example, of revoking the protective tariffs that benefited the French producers at the expense of the consumers. The State refused to intervene in social relations yet supported – in the name of 'right to work' – the employers against the striking workers at the very time when the law instituting the work book (which, to be sure, was widely ignored) hampered the workers' right to work.

Nonetheless the State, acting through its government agencies, did pursue an economic policy, not only by its open support for the development of material interests but also by instituting policies designed to develop the means of circulation. Let us look first at the circulation of money. The bankers Laffitte and Odier and one of the government supervisors (*censeurs*) of the Banque de France, Hottinger, wished to see a lowering of the discount rate of the Banque de France, but the majority of that bank's board objected to this policy in the name of the stockholders and also from fear of inflation. The government preferred to establish a number of banks of issue in the provinces (at Lyon, Marseille, Lille); and in fact these creations were so successful that by 1836 the Banque de France decided to open branch offices in Reims and Saint-Etienne and later in other towns as well.

Economic concerns were also involved in the government's public works policy. In a first phase, this policy continued that of the Restoration, which had granted concessions for the building of canals to private companies. A law of 1835 established a permanent fund for State maintenance of a certain number of rivers. The State also stimulated overland transportation; the law of 22 May 1836 concerning local roadways required local communes to maintain the local roads and at the same time granted them the right to collect a toll.

The State assumed a greater role in the construction of new facilities at the port of Le Havre, where the building of the new Vauban basin was completed only after the law of 9 April 1839 had been passed. This law also approved the construction of the Florida basin and was later applied at Saint-Nazaire also.

The construction of railways became a political issue as soon as the first stage of short-distance rails was completed. As early as 1837 the Molé government drafted a first comprehensive project designed to permit

France to catch up in this area. A second project was presented in February 1838; its author Legrand, director of the agency of Bridges and Roads (*Ponts et Chaussées*), deputy from Mortain, and later Under-Secretary of State for Public Works, had drawn up a comprehensive plan calling for seven lines starting out from Paris and two transversal lines. The scope of the project, which required a total outlay of one billion francs, was one of the reasons for the delay. The unfortunate financial experience of the two railways between Paris and Versailles, which had suffered from the crisis begun in 1837, served to show that private capital alone would be insufficient; Legrand's plan now called for construction by the State. In the parliamentary committee the majority vocally supported the recourse to private companies, and the fact that the chairmanship of the committee was given to Arago, a radical but a systematic thinker, was an indication that the fear of strengthening the Molé government was stronger than the desire to find the most effective solution to a practical problem. Arago's recommendations were approved by the majority of the Chamber, which rejected the government's project by 196 to 69 votes, thereby paralysing one of the few attempts to provide a direct political impetus to the economy.

In practice, State support for economic activities primarily took the form of protective tariffs. Also, government contracts for army and navy supplies were eagerly sought by the manufacturers, especially the drapers of southern France who thus had an interest in extending the conquest of Algeria. In fact, France's economic development constantly raised new problems that the government had to resolve. This was the case in the struggle between the two kinds of sugar, which pitted the spokesmen for sugar-beet (mainly in the northern departments) against the defenders of sugar-cane, most of whom were concentrated in the southern ports that traded with the West Indies. On various occasions the issue of free foreign trade was raised more or less openly, although no new decision was ever made. The reasons for raising this issue were many: ideological considerations, the liberal principles of economists like Michel Chevalier (who were often viewed with suspicion by the business community), the search for new markets (by the wine interests, especially at Bordeaux and by the manufacturers of silk and other luxury goods), and even political or diplomatic considerations (in 1834 it would have been helpful to seal the rapprochement with England and in 1840 a closer alliance with Belgium was desirable).

An *enquête* concerning the various customs barriers conducted in 1834 showed that most of the manufacturers interviewed felt that a lowering of the customs barriers would inevitably bring a recession; they also pointed out that it would lead to social unrest, for they saw wage cuts as the only possible means of bringing down their prices to meet international competition. Under these circumstances the government instituted only a few minor changes. Ordinances promulgated in 1834 and 1835 lifted the prohibition against the import of fine cotton thread and certain kinds of wool thread.

Even though these problems were not solved in a manner that appreciably changed the current regulations and the existing situation, they represented a profound change in the subjects debated in the Chambers. In the Chamber elected in 1834 and in the subsequent legislatures, personal memories of the Revolution (which were more alive in the House of Peers, whose members were older) and great ideological debates became increasingly rare. To be sure, both still gave rise to great moments of parliamentary rhetoric; but more concrete issues, issues that were closely linked to economic and material interests, now had greater weight in the formation of majorities and in the fluctuating positions of the deputies. A new generation that had not personally experienced the Revolution and the profound divisions to which it had led had taken its place in the parliament and in the State. In the Chamber elected in 1839, 58 per cent of the members were born after 1789; this was in marked contrast with the House of Peers, where at the same date only 12 per cent of the members were younger than fifty. By 1839, then, the political priorities of the elected Chamber had become clear, and the two Molé governments had done their share to foster this new attitude: henceforth the trends of the economy were uppermost in people's minds and kept them away from political agitation. Yet there were some who wished for a more active political life.

Thiers

One representative of a more wide-ranging political concern had already set an example. This was Adolphe Thiers, a man who was extremely concerned about the image he presented to public opinion and at the same time very sensitive to the vagaries of that opinion. Starting out as a minor journalist, he had come a long way since his arrival from Marseille; and while he no longer wrote for newspapers, he closely watched what they wrote and patronised a number of them, most notably the *Constitutionnel*. Although he was a man of order and an energetic Minister of Interior, his first government, formed on 22 February 1836, was considered liberal. Surrounding himself with self-effacing men, taking charge of foreign affairs and intent upon conducting a forceful national policy without too much concern about the direction it would take, he had practised a policy of 'alternating pledges': taking advantage of the splintering of the Chamber into six factions, he had sought support sometimes from one faction, sometimes from another, and sometimes from the regional interests. What Thiers brought to the government was not so much a new policy as a new style of politician. His foreign policy was rather confused from the outset, and he was preparing to intervene directly in Spain against the Carlists and in support of the liberals. But since the latter were unable to control their most revolutionary wing, Louis-Philippe had refused to play their game.

By resigning, Thiers had salvaged his reputation as a liberal (after all, his fall was caused by his disagreement with the king, not by the Chambers) and as a nationalist: henceforth he was seen as the champion of national independence and the English alliance against the counter-revolutionary forces. These attitudes, superficial though they were, appealed to the *petite bourgeoisie* of Paris, which was always prone to flag-waving. French intervention in Spain would have opened the door to adventurism, which neither the country's voting minority (the so-called *pays légal*) nor the Chambers wanted. The king's intervention to prevent it resolved an equivocal situation, but it is a fact that this role of the king and especially the choice of a prime minister from outside the Chamber was not designed to make the task of the new cabinet headed by comte Molé any easier.

Thiers' retirement was only temporary; he had a very keen sense of the trends of public opinion, meaning the large segments of the lower and middle bourgeoisie who at that time constituted the bulk of the readership of the press and furnished the principal contingents of the National Guard. The social ascent of M. Thiers, a petty scribbler who had become a minister of state and the son-in-law of the receiver-general Dosne, was the dream shared by this entire social category; conversely this background marked him as a parvenu in the eyes of the aristocracy and the old bourgeoisie. As for the peasants, Thiers ignored them, as did most of the politicians of the July regime. Retired from power, Thiers once again took up his historical studies, using them now to prepare his return to political life. In July 1839 the publishing house of Paulin and Cerfbeer negotiated with him for the contract to a *Histoire du Consulat et de l'Empire*, the first volume of which appeared in 1845. In Napoleon Thiers celebrated the soldier of the Revolution.

While it is impossible to measure how much of this was conviction and how much political expediency, Thiers did mobilise the Napoleonic sentiments that lay dormant in the hearts of most of the population. It was he who in 1836 had inaugurated the building of the Arc de Triomphe whose construction had been decreed by Napoleon. Above all he announced during his second prime ministership in May 1840 that he had successfully negotiated the return of Napoleon's ashes. Requested in petitions for ten years, this step was to enhance the 'nationalist' reputation of his government.

And Thiers knew how to bide his time. In the coalition formed to oust Molé, he had played a crucial role by contributing not so much a programme as a formula. This formula: 'The king rules but does not govern' may or may not have actually been pronounced by him, but it was attributed to him and made him the defender of the parliamentary regime.

In February 1839 it was decided to dissolve the Chamber elected in October 1837, even though it had just passed a vote of confidence for the Molé government by a vote of 221 to 208 in its debate about the address. These elections of 2 March marked a turning-point in the July Monarchy, since their outcome (about 200 supporters of the government against 240 opponents) brought the fall of the Molé government, a prolonged inability to form a new government, and a string of governments pursuing constantly changing policies. Most importantly, the elections had taken place in an atmosphere of intrigue, pressure, and even corruption that discredited the regime. The Molé government had dismissed many civil servants suspected of sympathising with the opposition.

The most violent polemic was fought out in the press, and mutual accusations disclosed and even exaggerated the evildoing of the ruling group to the country at large. Economic difficulties spawned by the American recession, the discredit of the regime, and the power vacuum ensuing from the difficulties in forming a new government rekindled the hopes of the small revolutionary minority that dreamt of seizing power in order to change society. On 12 May an attempt to precipitate an uprising plotted by the secret society *Les Saisons* gathered no more than a few hundred affiliates around Auguste Blanqui, Barbès, and Martin Bernard. Within a few hours the forces of order brought the situation in the Saint-Denis and Saint-Martin quarters under control; in the aftermath of the fear aroused by this episode, Marshal Soult was able on that same day to form a government without a real leader, without a coherent majority, and without a well-defined policy. This was to attribute to the king a role that ran directly counter to the results of the last election. It was therefore not surprising that Louis-Philippe's ill-considered attempt to obtain from the Chambers an endowment for his second son, the duc de Nemours (rejected by a margin of 226 to 220) led to the fall of this puppet government on 22 February 1840.

In the face of this renewed disavowal of a major role in government for the king, Thiers' return to government became imperative. The government formed on 1 March included as principal ministers Charles de Rémusat at Interior, Vivien at Justice, Victor Cousin at Public Education, and General de Cubière at War.

Thiers set the tone of this government and the ministers met without the king, although major decisions were discussed between the king and Thiers, joined in August 1840 by Guizot, who served as France's ambassador in London. Thiers, a parliamentary orator of consummate skill, the man whom Sainte-Beuve called 'the great juggling artist' was able to project to public opinion the image of a defender of the parliamentary regime and representative of nationalist and liberal ideas, while the king saw him as a minister with whom he could talk and get along. Accepting him willy-nilly, the conservatives and the legitimists considered Thiers a man of the Revolution.

The government formed on 1 March 1840 attempted to enlarge its majority; the reassignment of thirteen prefects and nineteen sub-prefects was primarily designed to satisfy the dynastic left. But this political opening did not go very far. Since 1839 a whole movement calling for wider suffrage had developed, and more than 188,000 signatures had been collected for petitions demanding the right to vote for every member of the National Guard. Yet the Chamber of Deputies refused to consider these petitions and listened only impatiently to a speech by Arago on 16 May in which he called for both universal suffrage and 'a new organisation of work'. Thiers shared the opinion of the majority, having declared earlier: 'National sovereignty, understood as the unlimited sovereignty of the broad masses, is the most erroneous and the most dangerous principle for society that can be evoked.'

On 1 July 1840 a communist banquet was held in Paris; the government did not object but did prohibit a banquet planned for 14 July in the faubourg Saint-Antoine to celebrate the anniversary of the storming of the Bastille. Other banquets were planned for that same day at Poitiers, Rouen, Marseille, Chagny, and other places.

The fact that radical or reformist demands coincided with the agitation triggered by the Treaty of London, the diplomatic crisis, and labour unrest was upsetting to bourgeois public opinion. Meanwhile economic difficulties, the stagnation of commerce, and the high cost of grain had also provoked real disturbances; in the course of rioting at Foix, government troops had fired on the crowd and killed thirteen demonstrators. Soon the unrest had spread to the workers. Strikes in Paris were tolerated until August, but by the beginning of September they had become very widespread (on 3 September some 10,000 workers assembled at Bondy), and when barricades went up in the faubourg Saint-Antoine on 7 September, the troops were called out and the prefect of police forbade all assemblies. In fact, order was quickly restored; but the conservative press, dismayed by the general patriotic fervour and certain rash statements made by Thiers, lumped together political agitation, labour unrest, and the bellicose stance of the government in its disapproval. A new attempt on the king's life, perpetrated on 15 October by Darmès, a former member of the secret communist society, seemed to justify this concern.

Thiers did not have a well-defined political programme, but his government seemed to favour a dynamic economy and in the course of its only legislative session successfully submitted to the Chamber several laws concerning the major capitalist institutions that were of personal interest to the head of the government. These were the renewal of the government charter of the Banque de France, the first pledge of security granted by the government to a railway line (Paris–Orléans) by the law of 15 July 1840, and the concession for a steamship line between France and the United States by the law of 16 July 1840. Thiers' reputation as a friend of business was sufficiently well established to lead to accusations – probably unfounded – that the government's delay in ratifying or publishing the Treaty of London, which isolated France on the Near-Eastern issue, was a manoeuvre designed to permit his father-in-law Dosne, receiver-general and regent of the Banque de France, to speculate in the stock market. Giarardin's newspaper *La Presse* insidiously spread these rumours, and at the same time orchestrated – initially almost alone in failing to share the general enthusiasm for a bellicose reaction to the Treaty of London – the campaign for peace with the support of Lamartine.

Along with the political poker game that he had lost by betting on the resistance of Mahomet Ali and the military preparations made by the government (increase in the size of the army and the number of naval units, construction of fortifications around Paris), everything now seemed to go wrong for Thiers. He had flattered the nationalist feelings of his compatriots by preparing the return of Napoleon's ashes; now a second attempted *coup* by Louis-Napoleon Bonaparte, which was rapidly aborted on 6 August at Boulogne, was like a distorted counterpart of Thiers' endeavour. The political exploitation of the Napoleonic legend had not reckoned with the diplomatic crisis of the summer of 1840, which aggravated the latent anglophobia of popular attitudes. Thus cast in the role of sorcerer's apprentice, Thiers had to deal with nationalist agitation (which he himself had aroused), liberal and radical agitations (which he had tolerated), and social agitation (which he had indeed sought to curb). Conscious of his failure and threatening to go to war against all of Europe – without quite believing that this was necessary – Thiers did not wait for the Chambers to act. When the king refused to increase the size of the army once again, he resigned on 20 October.

Thiers' failure was not only that of one man and of a diplomacy considered too aggressive by the king and the ruling circles. It was also the failure of the extension of the parliamentary regime. By producing more noise than action, the second Thiers government had reinforced the conviction held by the ruling categories and the overwhelming majority of the deputies that power had to be more stable and more oligarchical. The disruptive character of popular sentiments had been demonstrated by an explosion of nationalist fervour during the summer of 1840 and during the Napoleonic apotheosis of 15 December of that year, when Napoleon's coffin was solemnly placed in the Dôme des Invalides. This was all that was needed to persuade the voting minority to temper its passions for the sake of its interests and to forsake forward movement in favour of conservation.

Guizot and the conservative system

The government formed on 29 October 1840 and nominally headed by Marshal Soult until 1847 illustrated the close connection between one politician, Guizot (who in fact directed the government in addition to his own Ministry of Foreign Affairs and officially became prime minister only in September 1847) and a political system founded on the power of the notables.

The new government faced a difficult situation. Diplomatically, France was isolated on the Near-Eastern issue. Within the parliament there was no clearcut majority; Thiers' warmongering stance had led the opposition to denounce his successor as the embodiment of a 'government of peace at any price' and submission to foreign powers. In domestic affairs the year 1840 was marked by popular unrest brought about by the economic crisis that had gripped France since 1838. In financial matters, finally, the building of fortifications around Paris ordered by Thiers in response to the diplomatic crisis had unbalanced the budget and eventually also exposed his successors to accusations that they meant to turn Paris into a prison. Public opinion, especially in Paris, was unfavourable to the new government. That is why its titular head was not the unpopular Guizot who was disliked in many quarters. The legitimists objected to his past as a Protestant academic, some of the conservatives did not forgive him for his participation in the coalition against Molé, while the radical or the dynastic left saw him as the theoretician and spokesman of the policy of resistance to the democratisation of political life.

Following its rather precarious beginning, this government was nonetheless to be the longest of the reign, and Guizot's eventual fall also spelled the end of the regime with which he had gradually become identified.

The regime of the notables

The term 'notables' was used by contemporaries to define the ruling categories: aristocrats, pseudo-nobles, or upper bourgeoisie. Whenever a new prefect arrived in his department, he would write as soon as possible what Bocher wrote from Auch in May of 1839: 'I have already had the honour of receiving a part of the town's *notables*.'

The power of this milieu of notables was based first and foremost on wealth, for participation in political life was contingent on property qualifications. There were about 250,000 men who met the property qualifications for voting (*électeurs censitaires*) and 56,000 'eligibles' paying at least 500 francs in taxes; the number of taxpayers paying more than 1,000 francs (representing the amount necessary for eligibility before 1830) was about 18,000 in the France of 1840. Among the latter, no more than 16 per cent were businessmen and industrialists, yet their influence was greater than this percentage suggests.

Family traditions also defined the milieu of the notables. In most cases the notable was an inheritor. The long-lasting leadership role of the Orleanist notables contributed to the increased influence of the notables generally and perpetuated the presence of the same families and the same social category among those who wielded power. The notable lived in a social era that gave him a long-term perspective, for he had a past, he had a future, and he had control over time; and since his income was based on as immutable a right as the right of property under the July Monarchy, he was bound to dominate those who could only earn their livelihood day by day, week by week, or month by month. A third factor in achieving notability was personal ability and influence wielded either through public service or through a representative function, although certainly there were parvenus of modest origins who were able to become part of this milieu, and here the example of Thiers comes to mind. It is no coincidence that Balzac depicted the Rastignac type as living in this period. But these parvenus, or at least their descendants, often became the most ardent defenders of the oligarchical system in which they had managed to take their place. They were not about to question the social and political system; such questioning was more likely to be spawned by antagonisms within the world of the notables, as in the case of legitimist opposition to the July regime.

The regime of property qualifications (*régime censitaire*) accentuated interrelations between the different forms of power, whether it be economic, political or administrative. The property qualification for eligibility was fixed at a tax payment of 500 francs, but in the Chamber of Deputies of 1840 almost two-thirds of the members (294 out of 459) paid more than 1,000 francs in taxes; wealth was considered a token of independence, ability, and also solidarity with the system. A considerable proportion of the Peers of France, the deputies, and the members of the departmental councils held government offices. At the end of the July Monarchy the Council of State included 42 deputies and 40 Peers as regular or associate members.

These ruling categories wielded power on a local level, for their dominance originated in the provinces, whether they were great landed proprietors or the heads of industrial enterprises that foreshadowed the large-scale capitalism to come. Control of the local administration implied that the notables could not control their region without also taking part in setting the direction for the country as a whole by playing a leading role in the parliament, in the administration, and in the as yet rather un-developed economic or intellectual institutions, either in person or through proxies.

The accumulation of different powers in the same hands was tempered, however, by regional antagonisms; because of the (relative) weakness of the central power, contradictory pressures were brought to bear, and the interplay of influences had virtually attained the status of a doctrine. The conscious rivalry that had pitted landed property against mobile capital-ism at the end of the Restoration gave way to conflict of interest on the regional, local, and personal level.

Economic growth

Coming to power after a period of crisis (in 1840) and a period of instability (fifteen governments in ten years), the Soult–Guizot govern-ment benefited from the fear felt by the notables and large segments of the bourgeoisie during times of crisis and revolution. It was to play on these feelings by proposing a government programme stressing peace, stability, and prosperity.

Given the improved diplomatic situation resulting from the solution of the Near-Eastern issue and the Franco-British alliance, the preservation of peace became the precondition for economic development.

Sound financial management contributed to this prosperity, even if efforts to increase the tax base made by the Minister of Finance, Humann, gave rise to fiscal protests at the time of the census of 1841. Government spending became a factor of growth, since 534 million francs were put into public works, especially railway construction, but the distribution of these projects aggravated the existing regional inequalities.

The policy of keeping the prefects in their posts instead of removing them at every change of government as before enabled these eminent administrators to give more continuity to the modernisation of their departments, as in the case of Chaper at Nantes. The collaboration between government agents and the local notables also contributed to this development; mayors and prefects encouraged the founding of savings banks (345 existed in 1844) which became symbols of an era that praised saving and profit through saving. The preservation of order that also favoured prosperity was easily accomplished until the crisis of 1846. In Paris, the municipal guard provided police protection with a force num-bering at most 3,000 men.

The established order and the resulting prosperity mainly benefited the owners of the means of production, although it is true that this was a large group, given the substantial number of owners of small property and small artisanal enterprises. We should not be carried away by the myth of the liberal State strictly abstaining from intervening in economic life. To begin with, free competition worked in favour of the strongest and led to increasing concentration of economic power precisely under the Soult–Guizot government, especially in the railways, in metallurgy, mining, and the glass, sugar, and spinning industries, as can be seen from the government permits authorising the formation of stock companies. Moreover, the State distorted this competition by its protective tariffs and also by the close ties that existed between the political authorities, the administrative authorities, and major business companies. Following the enactment of the law of 11 June 1842, which was to become the charter for the construction of a railway network in France under the joint auspices of the State, the local governments, and several private companies, the latter made sure that their boards of directors included Peers of France, deputies, generals, magistrates, or holders of titles of nobility. The State played the role of arbiter in disputes between rival groups that perpetuated local antagonisms, pitting one town or one department against another when it came to tracing the projected routes, or one neighbourhood against another in the competition for the location of a railway station, but its decisions were not always independent of political considerations.

Freedom of work in fact amounted mainly to the employer's freedom to run his enterprise under the protective shield of the legislative and juridical apparatus that permitted him to cut back wages, to modify working hours, and to dismiss his workers at will, while the workers, as we pointed out earlier, were constrained to present their work books wherever they went, although potential employers paid little attention to this regulation.

Liberalism thus did not mean the complete neutrality of the State. By both its non-intervention, and indeed the form of its intervention, it favoured the producers over the consumers, as did the government's protective tariffs and especially its fiscal policy, which derived most of its resources from direct and indirect taxes that weighed most heavily on the consumers of the popular classes.

Yet eventually the State was obliged to intervene in response to new problems with which it was faced; *nolens volens* the July Monarchy submitted to parliament the law of 22 March 1841 regulating child labour in factories (although this law only prohibited the employment of children under eight). This was the result of protracted negotiations begun under previous governments. Of little interest to a good part of the Chamber (only 235 of the 459 deputies were present for the vote), the law was implemented after considerable delay.

There are indications that Guizot and Duchatel were indeed interested in stimulating the French economy, but opposition to a commercial union with Belgium (and perhaps Holland) led them to abandon a project that would have provided a stimulus for French industry. Attempts, notably in 1845, to solicit the advice of the departmental general councils on agricultural problems and the matter of agricultural loans came to nothing. It was difficult indeed to legislate innovation in a conservative system; the economic expansion (to which we will return presently) was threatening the coherence of the traditional society sustained by the notables at the very time when the system of government that was its political expression was beginning to harden.

From stability to political stagnation

The desire to enlarge his **parliamentary** majority came to dominate every aspect of Guizot's policy. His political programme had been disclosed to the Chamber of Deputies on 3 May 1837: 'I want, I seek, I serve with all my strength the political preponderance of France's middle classes.' This was the policy he still defended after 1840, expressing it both to the deputies and to the voters of Lisieux; for example, in August 1841: 'Strengthen your institutions, become enlightened, become rich, improve France's moral and material situation', he declared before the Chamber on 1 March 1841. But the formula: 'Become rich through work and saving' was not made to inspire devotion. Accustomed to unpopularity, more admired than loved even by his partisans, Guizot could always count on the king's support and felt that he was in a better position than anyone to pursue a policy of the *juste milieu* that would ensure order and liberty according to the wishes of the bourgeoisie; but the stability of government that had been so urgently wished for after the crisis of 1840 eventually turned into immobility.

As a matter of parliamentary tactics, Guizot used any potential threats to the July regime to strengthen the government's authority. In this manner the death of the young duc d'Orléans in July 1842 – he was killed in a carriage accident – led to increased solidarity among the political forces favourable to Louis-Philippe's monarchy. It was to be the last of the major displays of sympathy for the king. The newspapers of the dynastic opposition, which the king was said to favour, expressed the most intense emotion; on 14 July the *Constitutionnel* was published with a black border, and the *Siècle* spoke of 'Paris in the throes of true mourning'. The recent legislative elections had produced only a small majority for the government. The addresses sent to the king by the municipalities, the National Guard, the chambers of commerce, the law courts, and the bishops (53 out of 81) bore witness – even if they were to some extent gestures of conformity – to an attachment to the sovereign that was bound to be carried over to his government. The vote on the law providing that in the event a regency should become necessary it should fall to the duc de Nemours, who was known for his conservative attitude, rather than to the duchesse

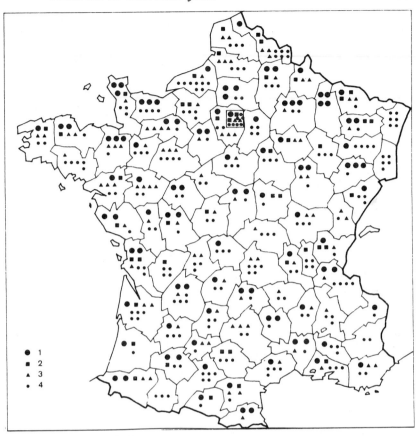

3   Parliamentary stability of the July Monarchy, 1848

   1 deputies serving since 1831
   2 deputies serving since 1834
   3 deputies serving since 1839
   4 varying deputies

Note: Because of the use of the *arrondissement* as a constituency, the greater or lesser degree of continuity of parliamentarians was determined by local circumstances rather than by regional voting trends.

d'Orléans was a success for Guizot and for the king. For once Louis-Philippe had the support of Thiers, who in this instance did not vote with the opposition. The law was passed on 20 August by 310 votes in favour out of a total of 404 votes cast. Louis-Philippe and Guizot concluded from this vast outpouring of sympathy that the Orléans dynasty was more solidly entrenched than they had believed. They misinterpreted the agreement between the sovereign and these expressions of public opinion as a mandate to pursue the same policy and as approval of royal influence in the government. Looking ahead to the future, many members of the dynastic opposition, aware that the duc de Nemours was considered less liberal than his father, lost all hope of seeing the regime evolve in a direction that would satisfy them. The tacit contract between the king and the country was still contingent on the persistence of foreign and domestic peace. During the debate on the regency, Thiers had declared: 'Behind the July government there is the counter-revolution, in front of it is anarchy.'

Given this situation, Guizot made full use of the legitimist agitation that began to stir at the end of 1843, for he was not adverse to exaggerating dangers in order to maintain himself in power. The legitimist opposition had seemed less dangerous when it became a parliamentary faction, especially with Berryer at its head. But now the death of the duc d'Orléans had weakened the new dynasty, thereby rekindling the hopes of the young duc de Bordeaux. Impelled both by the need to consolidate the divergent tendencies of legitimism and by the desire to confirm his role as the pretender (if only to check the growth of Louis-Philippe's support), his partisans made arrangements to have him visit London under the quickly dispelled incognito of comte de Chambord, and in late November and in December 1843 almost a thousand legitimists called on him at his residence in Belgrave Square to salute the man who for them was 'Henri V'. The presence among them of one Peer of France and five deputies gave rise to a debate in the Chamber of Deputies that ended with a 'censure' of the deputies who had visited London and thereby indicated their allegiance to a different form of government. This vote passed narrowly by a margin of 220 to 190 and after many passionate speeches against Guizot. After this incident no one could accuse the July regime of forgetting its origins; but in putting a stop to the legitimist notabilities' rally to the conservative system, the same incident also weakened the system and intensified the tensions within the ruling groups.

For the moment, however, the opposition – reduced as it was by its internal divisions to criticising Guizot and to whipping up anglophobic and chauvinistic sentiments – did not constitute a serious threat. But the representative system was being subverted precisely by this absence of a political alternative within the framework of the institutions themselves. The very stability of the system caused it to become brittle and worn; in the high administration as well as in the municipalities the same men stayed on and on and tended to monopolise the advantages accruing from power. In seeking promotions, sub-prefects, magistrates, and civil servants of every kind counted more on the support of the deputy of their *arrondissement* (especially if he belonged to the government party) than on their superior in the hierarchy. In the towns the prefects' frequent difficulties in finding notables willing to take over the monotonous and time-consuming function of mayor led the government to side with the existing municipalities and with the local notables, even if they were in conflict with its own agents.

The pressure of special interests

The effectiveness of the central power was neutralised by opposing pressure groups representing either material interests (as in the case of the two kinds of sugar, the very symbol of a hopeless predicament) or moral interests. The Guizot government was favourable to the abolition of slavery in the colonies, and so was public opinion. The Chamber of Deputies had adopted the principle of emancipation in May 1844, in 1845, and again in May 1846, but since no agreement about its methods could be reached, the *status quo* continued. It was aided and abetted by the concerted action of the small pro-slavery minority that used money, the press (notably the writings of Adolphe Granier de Cassagnac), and the speaker's platform to defend its cause. The laws of 18 and 19 July 1845 concerning the slaves' right to purchase their freedom and on colonial legislation provided for the end of slavery, but put off its implementation until later.

Nor was the government able to come to grips with the issue of freedom of secondary education. To be sure, the issue of education was complicated by the tensions between the Catholic Church and the State. It should be pointed out, however, that after 1840, owing to the pressure of the papacy, to the meddling of Queen Marie-Amélie who sought to temper Louis-Philippe's Voltairean attitude and even to a spiritual renewal that could not fail to affect a man like Guizot, the solidarity between the Church and the legitimists was no longer as close as it had been during the first years of the July Monarchy. In 1840 the appointment of Mgr Affre to the archbishopric of Paris, where he replaced the outspoken aristocrat Mgr de Quelen, was an act of appeasement. In 1831 the Catholics, and especially the legitimist Catholics, had not followed abbé Lamennais or Montalembert when they demanded freedom of education, which at the time was considered an extension of revolutionary action. After 1836, and especially after 1841, the government elaborated several educational projects designed, it was hoped, to improve the relations between Church and State, for this seemed to be the surest way to rally a part of the legitimists. Spearheaded by Montalembert, who at the time had the support of *L'Univers*, and by Louis Veuillot (in other respects a staunch supporter of the July Monarchy), the formation of a committee for the defence of freedom of education, which in August 1844 became the electoral committee for the defence of religious freedom, served to widen the scope of the movement in favour of freedom of education.

In the end the projects elaborated by the various ministers (Villemain in 1841 and 1844, Salvandy in 1847) were withdrawn in the face of the clergy's hostility and the opposition of those who defended the monopoly of the University. A government report on secondary education in 1843 mentioned the existence of 102 institutions, 40 of them directed by clerics, and 914 boarding-schools with a total enrolment of almost 35,000 pupils who were given some of their courses in State-sponsored *collèges*. Students enrolled in private establishments and preparatory seminaries (*petits séminaires*) represented about half of the student population in secondary education; but this was the *de facto* situation, and the rectors of several universities complained about the competition these religious establishments constituted for the public *collèges*. The government's position had been neatly formulated in the king's speech from the throne at the end of 1843, promising 'freedom of education as well as the preservation of the State's authority and activity in public education'. This compromise position was completely inadequate because it failed to satisfy either the 'Neocatholics' who called for 'freedom as in Belgium' or the defenders of the University, a group that included not only the anticlerical bourgeoisie but also those who, like the *Journal des débats*, were distressed by the exaggerated violence of the anti-University campaign conducted by bishops like Mgr Clausel de Montals. The fruitless debates in the Chamber were a real disservice to the government. Having compromised itself in the eyes of some segments of the Orleanist bourgeoisie by its concessions to the clergy, it also saw a part of Catholic opinion turn against it, while the clergy became less and less interested in upholding the regime. Its half-measures did not satisfy anyone when it negotiated, for example, the departure of the Jesuits with the Vatican and yet closed its eyes to the *de facto* privilege of the preparatory seminaries. Worst of all, the preservation of the *status quo* prevented all progress and all modernisation of secondary education, despite its inability to meet the needs of society. On this point also, the conservative system obstructed any possibility of evolution.

The elections of 1846

Depoliticisation?

The legislative elections of 1846 seemed to spell the definitive triumph of Guizot's conservative system. They took place in the most favourable social and political conditions.

The *Revue des deux mondes*, not exactly an organ of the government, noted on 30 June: 'The general elections are being prepared and will be held at one of the most tranquil moments France has known for many years.' The electorate was more interested in promises favouring the development of local interests than in ideological debates. As early as March 1846, Léon Faucher, at the time a journalist connected with the liberal opposition, complained about the pervasive lack of interest in politics: 'In this country the spirit of politics is dead, and has been dead for several years: no one cares about anything but making money and building railroads.'

During the campaign the government could take credit for maintaining order in domestic affairs and for France's prestige abroad, a point that was reinforced by the impending success of the negotiations in progress in Spain. The government's opponents were therefore frequently obliged to present themselves to their constituents as defenders of order: Abraham Dubois, a deputy of the dynastic opposition from Avranches, asserted his 'love of peace, order, and our liberties'. Aside from the Parisian candidates, few felt that they could stray from the conservative shibboleths.

For all of the opposition's noisy attacks on the 'pritchardists' (candidates for re-election who had supported Guizot's appeasement policy during the Pritchard affair), only two or three of the government party's deputies failed to be re-elected.

Supporters and opponents of the government
The efforts of the different opposition parties to unite had encountered considerable difficulties, since every one of these groups suffered from dissension within its own ranks. The legitimists were divided into those who wanted to bring their propaganda into the popular milieux and were ready to deal with the republicans and those who favoured parliamentary action and therefore were more inclined to come to an understanding with the dynastic opposition. The latter also was divided into multiple factions, such as Odilon Barrot's dynastic left, Thiers' centre-left group, and even smaller groupings led by Tocqueville or Dupin. Yet the strength of the government party was so great that heterogeneous coalitions were an absolute necessity. Accordingly, some of the radicals gave up their anticlericalism; at Cholet in western France, a town that had experienced bitter antagonism between the 'whites' and the 'blues', voters who supported the dynastic opposition did not re-elect the 'governmental' incumbent but replaced him with a legitimist, Quatrebarbes. In several *arrondissements* the Catholic clergy campaigned against the government's candidates, sometimes because they were Protestants (like the deputy-governor of the Banque de France, Vernes, in Doubs) and sometimes because their opponent was a Catholic legitimist. For the most part, it was the opposition candidates who banded together in campaign committees, and in the provinces alliances between the legitimists and the left were usually formed at the behest of the leadership in Paris.

But such rapprochements could also turn the electors against the opposition candidates. Many legitimist notables felt more comfortable with Catholic conservatives, who shared Montalembert's views on freedom of education, than with the radicals.

The conservatives also had a few campaign committees, especially in the major cities, Bordeaux, Rouen, Lille, where they had the support of big business and the press. But their main asset was the pressure brought to bear on their behalf by the administration. This pressure assumed many different forms. Sometimes the electors themselves approached the administration; thus the attorney-general of Montpellier informed the Keeper of the Seals on 24 July of 'a *démarche* by the principal electors of Pézenas, proposing [to the prefect] that they would choose as their deputy whomever he designated, *his horse if he so desired*, provided the railway came through the town'.

Administrative pressure availed itself of a wide variety of means (as we discuss in part 2). Electoral considerations played an important role in the awarding of decorations, in appointments and/or reassignments of magistrates and civil servants. Defeated opposition candidates would hold the administration's interference responsible for their failure and denounce the corruption of electoral practices and the existence of 'rotten boroughs', even though successful opposition candidates sometimes also benefited from this situation. In fact, explicit denunciations of corrupt elections and the outright buying of votes were rare. The election of Drouillard, a wealthy ironmaster at Quimperlé, was invalidated and when his case was tried before the assize court, five defendants were convicted; the two candidates of this *arrondissement* were conservatives, and both of them had engaged in extortion, but it so happened that Drouillard was defended by the legitimist deputy Berryer.

The balloting

The extensive scope of the electoral campaign and the exceptional efforts made by the opposition parties further improved the position of the government, which could now count on 291 deputies.

Abstentions were particularly rare in places where the contest was close. At Libourne, where three well-organised candidates were pitted against each other, participation was 88 per cent; at Forcalquier, where an incumbent of the opposition party was defeated, 94 per cent of the electors cast their ballots; and 90 per cent of the electors took part in the three rounds of balloting that were necessary at Caen. Particularly high in the smaller electoral colleges, participation was also high in some of the larger ones, amounting to 95 per cent at Nîmes and 91 per cent at Montpellier extra-muros (where two incumbent legitimists were defeated). In some cases the minority made its views known by systematic abstention; at Marseille Berryer was re-elected by 385 out of 399 votes, but only 48 per cent of the electors cast their ballots.

This shows that there were several types of campaigns and elections, translating the different forms of the notables' hold over local political life. The traditional campaign was aimed at small electoral colleges, and here the restricted number of electors permitted the candidates (usually few in number) to contact all of them personally; 84 per cent of the deputies were elected by fewer than 400 votes, which meant that they were able to know exactly who would vote, to calculate how individuals would vote, and to exert direct influence. Indeed, 233 deputies were elected by obtaining between 200 and 300 votes; 152 were elected by fewer than 200 votes, and some 10 by fewer than 100 votes.

Only 27 electoral colleges counted more than 1,000 members; these were the eleven *arrondissements* of the department of Seine (where the second *arrondissement* had the largest number of electors in all of France, namely, 2,968), two each in Lyon, Lille, and Rouen and one each in Marseille, Orléans, and Amiens. Most of these were in the major cities, in which a diversified press had politicised the elections to a greater extent.

One can also analyse this election in terms of the degree of competition. Such an analysis reveals that 55 per cent of the deputies (251) were elected in the first round by the absolute majority of the registered voters; in 36 colleges one candidate received all the votes; in 30 others the winner obtained more than three-fourths of the votes cast: Guizot at Lisieux received 523 of the 561 votes cast, and Odilon Barrot was elected by a similar margin at Chauny. 117 deputies (55 per cent of the Chamber) had been elected in the first round by the absolute majority of those who had voted, but only by a relative majority of the registered voters.

Less than 20 per cent of the Chamber was elected in the second round (55 deputies) or even the third round (27 deputies) of the most closely contested but not necessarily the most politicised elections.

In the absence of constituted and well-organised political parties, votes were cast for individuals (or interests, or passions) rather than for (or against) a programme. The electors who voted for Ledru-Rollin in the electoral college of Le Mans-campagne were, to be sure, opposed to the government, but there is little reason to believe that all of them were radicals who shared the advanced ideas of the man they had elected. It was only in the large cities that the distribution of votes between supporters and opponents of the government bore some relationship to the electors' political attitudes; Paris for example cast 8,965 votes for the opposition candidates against 5,483 for the conservatives.

The new Chamber

The Chamber elected in August 1846 was the only one to have given the reign of Louis-Philippe a coherent majority, consisting of 291 out of a total of 459 deputies. It was also the Chamber that witnessed the fall of the regime; and this contrast deserves to be analysed as a paradigm of the regime of restricted suffrage (*régime censitaire restreint*) as a whole.

In political terms the numerical weakness of the opposition was compounded by its internal division. At the extreme right, the legitimists, having lost ten seats, were reduced to sixteen; the extreme radical left consisted of twelve deputies.

The Orleanist opposition, which was dissatisfied with the government but not with the regime, had no homogeneity. Some 100 deputies belonged to the dynastic opposition led by Odilon Barrot; it was recruited among deputies from rural departments wealthy enough to produce independent notabilities (Aisne, Drôme, Indre-et-Loire), from the western departments where distrust of the legitimists made the Orleanist bourgeoisie inclined to vote for anticlerical candidates, and from eastern France where the electors' vivid nationalist sentiments were offended by Guizot's diplomacy. The centre-left led by Thiers only had a few deputies. Finally, there was a small number of liberal moderates who defied the government; they did not work together but among them were such personalities as Tocqueville, Lamartine, and Dufaure.

There was not much difference between this last group and the 'progressive conservatives' who, for their part, remained within the governmental majority, although by dint of their age (they were younger) and in view of the role they were to play later, notably during the Second Empire, they represented an element of renewal within the ruling class. They were more interested in economic policies than in political ideology. Among them one finds representatives of the regime's 'gilded youth', like the future duc de Morny, and a group of 'technocrats', engineers, economists, or business managers. Altogether some 25 to 30 deputies represented this new style; and while they had no doctrine, no programme, and no leader, they were the first to bring a sentiment of dissatisfaction to the governmental majority.

And even that majority was composed of heterogeneous elements. There were liberals of the Restoration who had turned conservative; converted legitimists; local notables always ready to support the government in order to partake of the advantages that accrued to those who held power. There were also civil servants whose vote was frequently tied to hopes of promotion; many voters considered them the best means to obtain favours from the State.

In the Chamber elected in 1846, 188 deputies, or 40 per cent of the membership, were civil servants. While a few of these men sat on the opposition side and even on the extreme left (Arago), most of them were staunch supporters of the government and thus contributed to the depoliticisation of public life in favour of the efficient management of material interests; the presence of many magistrates undoubtedly improved the legislative competence of the Chamber but did not make it amenable to change.

Representatives of the liberal professions were more likely to be found in the ranks of the opposition. Most of the opposition leaders were lawyers, like Ledru-Rollin, Odilon Barrot, Billault, Dufaure, or Berryer. There were sixty-two legal practitioners, seven or eight physicians, eight journalists (mostly from the opposition), and a few writers like Thiers and Lamartine.

In fact such men as Lamartine, Tocqueville, or Rémusat belonged to the category of large property owners; indeed even the two categories mentioned above, the civil servants and the liberal professions, derived their political qualification and the tax payment that gave them eligibility from the ownership of land or real estate. Property owners who did not exercise a profession accounted for two-thirds of the Chamber (about 308 out of 495), but several of these men had exercised a profession in the past, often that of magistrate or military officer.

As for the economic professions, banking, commerce, or manufacturing, they were represented by a minority of some forty deputies, but these were wealthy merchants or bankers who belonged to great economic dynasties, among them Joseph Périer, the Foulds, d'Eichthal, Gouin, and the ironmaster Schneider.

In addition, other deputies had direct connections with commercial, industrial, or financial activities, since about fifty of them served on the boards of directors of major companies.

The elections of 1846 reinforced the stability of the parliamentary membership; 111 new deputies were elected, but many of them had served in earlier legislatures. In 21 departments all the incumbents were re-elected; in the cities change was somewhat more frequent (all three of the incumbents were defeated in Toulouse, two out of three in Marseille, two out of three in Bordeaux, Rouen, etc.), yet Lyon re-elected all of its deputies and in the department of Seine eleven out of fourteen were re-elected.

These elections of 1846, then, appeared to differ from earlier ones only by the fact that they strengthened the government's majority. Still dominated by the notables, they were more indicative of the structure of society (where social and economic power engendered political power) than of an ideology. Yet they brought to light two characteristics which, although not entirely new, had become more pronounced: the disproportionate number of civil servants and the far too powerful attraction of Paris for the members of parliament made for an unrepresentative body; 174 deputies (not counting those from the department of Seine) had taken up residence in Paris but were elected from the provinces. Not unrelated to the rise of capitalism and the increasing collusion between the State and the ruling categories, this reinforcement of the central position of Paris created an ever-widening gap between Paris and the nation's leaders, for although these men exercised their power in Paris, they used it to thwart the most fundamental aspirations of the people of Paris, and of the petty bourgeoisie as well.

7

The foreign and colonial policy of the July Monarchy

France's position in 1830. Foreign policy options after the July revolution

The Restoration had left a much better record in foreign than in domestic affairs. Having recovered its place among the major powers as early as 1818, France once again played an active role in European affairs, rebuilt its army, and constructed a new fleet. The restoration of the navy had been initiated by baron Portal, a shipping magnate of Bordeaux, the city where the memory of the French overseas trade was still very much alive. Portal was appointed director of colonial affairs in the Ministry of the Navy (1815–18) and minister between 1818 and 1821. After his retirement, his efforts were continued by Tupinier, named director of ports and arsenals in 1824. As we have seen, the navy played a role in France's Mediterranean policies: although it did not yet have the capability for enforcing the blockade of Cadiz in 1823, it enabled France to act decisively in Greece and in 1830 to carry out the difficult landing at Algiers. By that date, France had clearly established its presence in the Mediterranean, 'the political sea of our day' (Tocqueville), for it had clearly understood that major economic and political transformations would ensue from the opening of the Near East. Hence France made its influence felt at Constantinople, where the good relations between the sultan and Ancien Regime France were restored, and acted as a friend to the young Greek State, and almost as a tutor to Egypt, where French engineers planned major public works projects, French instructors trained the army, and French dry-docks built ships. In addition, France became deeply involved in the regency of Algiers, a fact which in conjunction with the role played in Spain testified to its power in the western basin of the newly important Mediterranean.

The remains of the old colonial empire that France had been permitted to keep under the treaty of 1815 were modest indeed, and in 1825 Villèle had recognised the independence of Saint-Domingue. The prosperity of the 'sugar islands', Bourbon, Martinique, and Guadeloupe, was threatened by the abolition of the slave trade and by the development of the beet-sugar industry in the mother country. On the other hand, the Restoration had witnessed new naval operations leading to the discovery of remote territories and new colonisation projects: attempts were made to penetrate the African interior along the Sénégal river, to populate Guyana, and to gain a foothold at Sainte-Marie de Madagascar. All of these attempts ended in failure, but they paved the way for the successful ventures of the next regime.

For the moment, however, relations with the major European powers were still France's central preoccupation. Liberal opinion continued to dream of the recovery of the left bank of the Rhine, and Chateaubriand and Polignac would have loved to make this dream come true. Except when it came to the realisation of this chimera, France in 1830 could count on the czar's friendship and Metternich's lenient attitude, two factors that permitted it to defy the British displeasure at the time of the conquest of Algiers.

The revolution of 1830 wrought havoc with this diplomatic chessboard. Though deeply concerned about this new development, the czar and Metternich decided not to act unless France went so far as to intervene in the rest of Europe. As for Wellington, at the time prime minister of England, and the British ambassador to Paris, Lord Stuart of Rothsay, they were not exactly favourable to the event, although they did not mind the departure of Charles X.

French aggression in Europe was indeed a possibility. The country had been gripped by a kind of patriotic fever, brought to an even higher pitch by foreign refugees. Meanwhile, masses of men took up arms in National Guard units that sprang up everywhere in an extraordinary burst of nationalist fervour that lacked a clearly defined goal. The elderly La Fayette was used as the figurehead of this movement. Yet the first government of the new regime declared as early as 3 August: 'France will show the rest of Europe . . . that it cherishes peace as much as its liberties and wishes only for the happiness and the tranquillity of its neighbours.' The new king assured the foreign capitals that his presence was a true guarantee against all bellicose intentions. He succeeded in convincing them and the British government recognised him on 31 August; Prussia and Austria followed suit and so, rather begrudgingly, did the czar.

Foreign policy under the Restoration had been handled largely by the king. Louis-Philippe had no intention of giving up this royal prerogative. To be sure, he had to use a little more guile to achieve it, but his natural cunning, disguised under a spurious affability, served him well. Many 'royal secrets' existed under his reign, and many problems were dealt with in secret between the king and foreign ambassadors. Some of his ministers demurred: Casimir Périer with his usual violence, Broglie with his honest rigidity, and Thiers who argued with the king about 'who should be in the driver's seat'. The others acquiesced.

In carrying out his policies, the king was given to cheap stratagems, to wordy and frequently blustering language, and to bending his course in accordance with dynastic considerations. But his policy had one central idea, which he pursued with courageous obstinacy: the preservation of peace in Europe. Looking with the advantage of hindsight at the war fever that gripped even the coolest heads of the time, who were ready at every minor crisis to launch this fragile State into adventures for which it was not prepared, one cannot help but think that the epithet bestowed on the king, 'the Napoleon of peace', was not undeserved.

The independence of Belgium

On 25 August revolution broke out in Brussels. Taking their inspiration from the 'Three Glorious Days', the insurgents wished above all to free Belgium from the union with Holland, into which it had been forced by the kingdom of the Netherlands in 1814. If their wish for autonomy had been granted, they would no doubt have been willing to keep the Dutch sovereign or to accept a prince of his family as their king. But the devious machinations of the king and especially the failed attempt of the prince of Orange to regain Brussels by force (23–7 September) led the provisional government of Belgium to declare independence (4 October).

However, the kingdom of the Netherlands was founded under an international statute that gave the Allies of 1814 the right to garrison their troops in certain fortresses located in Belgian territory in case of a threat from France and obliged the Allies to guarantee the existence of the kingdom. Under this statute, King William appealed to the Allies as early as 7 September. But if Czar Nicholas I assembled troops in Poland, the king of Prussia, Frederick William IV, the closest neighbour of the Netherlands, was primarily interested in defending Westphalia against the spread of the revolutionary contagion, while the Austrian government was absorbed in its Italian problems.

The prime minister of England, the country most closely concerned because of the unsolved question of Antwerp, was Wellington, who had had a hand in the formation of the kingdom of the Netherlands. In addition to his domestic difficulties, however, Wellington had to reckon with a hostile attitude toward the Dutch, whom the English detested as their rivals in commercial matters.

By contrast with this wavering attitude on the part of the Allies, the French position was clearly stated by Molé, the first Minister of Foreign Affairs of the new monarchy: France would not intervene in Belgium, but if foreign troops were to invade that country, France would come to its aid.

Meanwhile, the decision between war and peace had to be made by the English, and in this situation London became the focal point of European diplomacy. Talleyrand was appointed ambassador to London and upon his arrival at Dover the broken old man ('looking like a dead lion') received from the English crowd, which manifestly hoped to preserve peace, the only popular acclamation of his career. Side-stepping the super-vision of his successive ministers, he corresponded directly with the king.

The first decision that Aberdeen, the British foreign minister, and Talleyrand persuaded the continental powers to make was to submit the Belgian question to a European congress of the five major powers. This 'Conference' met in London on 4 November and remained in session for almost three years. Russia was to see its influence in this body diminished by the Polish revolt that broke out in that same month of November in 1830. While this conference was deliberating in London, the Belgian Congress met at Brussels on 10 November. Elected by suffrage based on property qualifications and empowered to draw up a constitution, it voted for independence on 18 November, and on 23 November decided that Belgium would be a monarchy. In this manner a kind of dialogue between the Conference and the Congress was held across the Channel; it was often quite unfriendly, since the Belgian Congress, unwilling to have the future destiny of its country shaped by an organ of the major powers, was hardly in a position to offer any resistance.

On 19 November, after the English elections, Wellington was replaced by Grey and Aberdeen by Palmerston. Palmerston immediately took charge of the Conference. Suspicious of France but favourable to national aspirations, he wished to create an independent Belgium that would not be subject to interference from France. He therefore joined forces with Talleyrand in order to obtain the emancipation of Belgium but rejected the French government's offer to conclude a defensive alliance, suspecting France of trying to create a rift between England and the other monar-chies.

As early as 20 December the Conference recognised Belgium as an independent country. The new State was pledged to permanent neutrality (20 January), a precaution aimed at tying France's hands and curbing the natural sympathies between the two States; on the same date the boun-daries of Belgium were established. Luxembourg and Limbourg were not included in the territory even though both had participated in the anti-Dutch uprising; also, France was not allowed to regain its boundaries of 1814, which would have restored Philippeville and Marienbourg to France. By contrast, the Prussians retained the right to keep garrisons in Luxem-bourg as a safeguard against any French thrust toward the Rhine. Belgium was charged with 16/31 of the public debt of the kingdom of the Nether-lands; and finally, on 1 February 1831, it was decided that the future sovereign would not be a member of the five ruling families of the major States.

The agreements concerning the frontiers and the debts aroused the indignation of the Belgian Congress (soon the Belgians would accuse Talleyrand of having made too many concessions because his palm had been greased by the king of Holland). A powerful movement favouring the candidacy of the duc de Leuchtenberg, the son of Eugène Beauharnais, for the throne of Belgium emerged in Belgium. This candidacy was also viewed favourably by a part of the liberal opposition in France that still yearned for the Napoleonic Empire. In order to dispel this threat, Louis-Philippe tacitly encouraged his ambassador Bresson to launch the candidacy of his (Louis-Philippe's) second son, the 16-year-old duc de Nemours, and to make it clear to the Congress that the king of France could be persuaded to go along if the young man were elected. As part of the same strategy, France seemed unwilling to ratify the agreement concerning the frontiers.

This intrigue just barely succeeded. Nemours was elected by 97 votes; Leuchtenberg received 74, and the Archduke Charles 21 votes.

On 17 February, Louis-Philippe received the delegation of the Congress that had come to inform him of this result: he refused to accept the offer and seized this opportunity to demonstrate his devotion to peace to all of Europe. Leuchtenberg had become impossible, and the Belgians had been tricked. Eventually the Congress decided to elect Leopold of Saxe-Coburg, the widower of an English princess, who had earlier refused the throne of Greece. His candidacy was supported by both Palmerston and Talleyrand. As a present for his accession to the throne, Palmerston was able to persuade the Conference to sign a treaty in 18 articles promising substantial amendments to the treaty concerning the frontiers. However, this treaty was never implemented. On 21 July the new king swore to uphold the constitution ratified by the Congress and assumed his duties.

Then on 3 August, the king of the Netherlands, who had not recognised the 18 articles and had reassembled an impressive military force, invaded Belgium, which proved unable to put up any resistance. Casimir Périer, the French prime minister, immediately ordered Marshal Gérard to march into Belgium, and it was Gérard who forced the Dutch to turn back to the frontier.

The weakness of their national defence rather discredited the Belgians. Talleyrand hinted that a partition of Belgium among Prussia, Holland, and France might be the best solution, but nothing came of this suggestion. However, the treaty in 24 articles now took precedent over the treaty in 18 articles. While it did give to Belgium the Walloon part of Luxembourg, the rest of that province remained the property of the king of Holland, who also kept a part of the Limbourg province and Maestricht.

The Belgians begrudgingly accepted these terms, but King William [of Holland] refused to consider any modification whatsoever of the first agreement concerning the frontiers. A Franco-British expedition was needed to make him order the evacuation of the fortress of Antwerp: while the British fleet blockaded the Dutch coasts, Marshal Gérard seized Antwerp and took the garrison prisoner (22 December 1832). An armistice was signed at that time, but it was not until 1838 that the king accepted the 24 articles that permitted him to regain possession of the Limbourg province and of Luxembourg, which in effect were still occupied by the Belgians. This time France and England had to put pressure on the Belgians to relinquish these areas.

The territorial advantages obtained by France in all of this were nil, since France had not even recovered its frontiers established by the first Treaty of Paris of 1814; of the thirteen forts located along its frontiers, only five were dismantled, and even these were not the ones France had chosen. But Louis-Philippe and Talleyrand, men of the eighteenth century that they were, thought that the conquest of territory was not what counted. And indeed, the formation of a new State whose friendship was not in doubt and which depended exclusively on France for support was a considerable achievement. It was further strengthened by a dynastic tie when King Leopold married Louis-Philippe's daughter Louise, whose warmth was to make her a queen much beloved by the Belgian people.

The system of alliances designed to guarantee the Netherlands against French intervention had failed to operate. Despite the July days, France had broken out of the isolation which the system of alliances had been intended to preserve. Thanks to its moderation in dealing with London, France was able to achieve a rapprochement with England, a country with which France shared a common political climate, having similar institutions. France and England felt close to each other in the face of the solidarity of the absolutist powers which still yearned for the Holy Alliance. By 1831 Palmerston could pay homage to 'an Entente Cordiale that will contribute to the peace of the world'.

The first Entente Cordiale and its problems

Excellent conditions for a true alliance between France and England seemed to exist in 1833: Franco-English collaboration had compelled the king of Holland to conclude an armistice; in the Near East the treaty of Unkiar-Skelessi between the czar and the sultan seemed to give the czar control over the Ottoman Empire, a situation that threatened both the French and the English position in the area; and, finally, the French and the English had shown the same sympathy for the liberal movements of Germany and Italy in 1832. Indeed, when the Austrians had intervened in the Romagna to quell an uprising against the pope, Casimir Périer had stationed a small French force at Ancona. Warm feelings of mutual respect and affection united the great whig lords of England like Lord Holland and the governing elites of France, especially the *doctrinaires* and the duc de Broglie, Minister of Foreign Affairs.

In the face of this entente, Metternich felt it necessary to reaffirm the unity of the absolute monarchies. During a meeting at Münchengrätz the emperor, the czar, and the king of Prussia signed several agreements: one of these reaffirmed in general terms the principles of the Holy Alliance and proclaimed 'the right of every sovereign to call for help in domestic crises or in the case of a threat from abroad on such other independent sovereigns as seem to him most qualified to provide that help'; if such help had been requested from one of the three courts and if another power raised objections, all three courts were to consider themselves involved. This treaty was intended to intimidate the western powers, especially France. It failed to do so, for when it was communicated to Broglie he responded disdainfully and his note of 6 November 1833 restated the major lines of the French policy of non-intervention: 'There are countries where, as we have declared with respect to Belgium, Switzerland, and Piedmont, France will not under any circumstances tolerate any intervention from foreign countries. Whenever a foreign country occupies the territory of an independent State, we shall feel that it is our right to take such measures as our interests demand.'

In December of the following year he approached Palmerston with a view to discussing a defensive treaty. Palmerston backed off: 'We wish to remain free to appraise each situation as it arises.' This formulation summarises Britain's position from Canning to 1904, but in this instance it also reflects the political and economic problems of the Entente.

In the Iberian peninsula, Portugal and Spain were at the time in similar situations. In Portugal, the young Queen Maria, having come to the throne through the abdication of her father Don Pedro who had chosen to become emperor of Brazil, had been faced since 1827 with a civil war unleashed by her uncle, Don Miguel; in Spain, where Ferdinand II, shortly before his death (September 1833), had rescinded the Salic law at the urging of his fourth wife Maria-Christina and in favour of his 3-year-old daughter Isabella, Isabella's uncle, Don Carlos, contested her right to rule with the support of the clergy and the northern provinces. United by their adherence to absolutist principles, the Miguelists and the Carlists received aid from Austria and also from the legitimists on the other side of the Pyrenees. However, the French and English governments had never agreed to defend the constitutional parties against them. When certain French nationals were molested by Don Miguel, at that point in control of Lisbon, Casimir Périer had sent a squadron that captured the Portuguese fleet in the Tajo and demanded apologies and reparations (July 1831), much to Wellington's annoyance. Don Pedro eventually enlisted the help of England and Spain to force his brother Miguel to capitulate at Evora (May 1834). France did not intervene on this occasion.

At the time of the unsuccessful French initiative for a defensive treaty with England, Palmerston had nonetheless informed Talleyrand of the existence of a treaty between England, Spain, and Portugal and had invited France to join. He proposed a new agreement concerning Portuguese affairs (22 April 1834) stipulating that France would intervene against Don Miguel only if asked to do so; similarly, the further agreement of 18 August that extended the earlier agreement to include Spain, thereby transforming it into a 'quadruple alliance', stipulated that England could help the constitutional governments by means of economic advantages, while France would for the moment limit its intervention to preventing their enemies from receiving help from the north of the peninsula.

In 1835, when Don Carlos became increasingly successful in northern Spain, the government headed by Martinez de la Rosa solicited the help of the French army, since it had become clear that the support of a peacekeeping force was insufficient. If Louis-Philippe, despite the entreaties of Thiers, was firmly opposed to this intervention, the English attitude on this occasion was characteristic, for Palmerston declared that he did 'not wish to do anything that would make him a party to such a measure, which would compromise the tranquillity of Europe'. As a result of France's abstention, the moderate pro-French government of Spain was replaced with a progressive pro-English government (1836); then, between 1840 and 1843, the dictatorship of the 'regent' Espartero turned over the Spanish market to England in return for British support. In Portugal, as might be expected, the British government restored its exclusive quasi-protectorate by arranging the marriage of the young queen to Ferdinand of Saxe-Coburg (1835).

In the Iberian peninsula Franco-British collaboration had thus turned into a rivalry in which France came out second best.

Quarrels also arose in various other parts of the world: in Greece, where the two countries had pledged themselves to guarantee loans contracted in the money markets of London and Paris in order to consolidate the government of the young king Otto of Bavaria; in **Senegal,** where the French had acquired the monopoly of the rubber trade with the Trarza Moors; in Portendick Bay, where a British ship was seized as it was discharging arms for a rebellious tribe and where the ensuing blockade of the coast by the French fleet marked the beginning of a conflict that was to last for twelve years; and finally in Algeria, where Palmerston attempted to involve the Turkish fleet.

In England, moreover, the powerful industrial and commercial circles who sat in the House of Commons since the elections of 1834 complained that the Entente with France did not produce any economic advantages for them. Palmerston let it be known that unless tariff concessions were forthcoming, 'the political understanding between the two countries would be weakened'. And it is a fact that the tariff policy that the July Monarchy had inherited from the Restoration not only called for high tariffs but even prohibited the importation of articles that were crucial to British commerce, such as iron, steel or copper products, cotton and woollen thread, cloth, clothing, etc.

The duc de Broglie, personally a free-trader, fully understood the implications of this problem. Having commissioned a study of these questions that was carried out by a French government agency in collaboration with John Bowring, editor of the *Westminster Review*, he drafted a bill that called for only a moderate tariff on English cotton yarn. But this bill did not pass in the Chamber. Broglie could do no more than issue an executive ordinance permitting the export of unprocessed silk as requested by the English industrialists. Neither this concession nor the subsequent lifting (1836) of the prohibition against the import of cotton yarn and the lowering of the tariffs levied on coal, pig iron, and wool satisfied the English. In granting the concessions for the building of the railways, the French Chamber would place most of its orders with French metallurgical enterprises. The English government retaliated with a tariff on French wines and brandies, knowing full well that this measure was 'absurd'. A movement of vehement protectionism sprang up in France under the pretext of saving the French cottage industry from the dire effects of allegedly inadequate tariffs on linen yarn and cloth. Only the major ports, the wine-producing areas, and Lyon remained favourable to free trade. The goodwill and the liberal concepts of certain members of the government had to yield to the manufacturers' lobby. An attempt to negotiate these issues with England in 1839 once again ended in failure.

By now Palmerston had come to view the Entente with France as no more than a means to forestall a Franco-Russian alliance (and it should be noted that he did not realise the depth of Nicolas I's hatred for the French regime). As for the French statesmen, not only Thiers or Molé but even Talleyrand and Broglie had come to feel by 1835 that France should move away from England and seek closer relations with Austria. Ruled by the party of resistance, France was in fact becoming a bastion of the forces of order in Europe. And while its interests did not always coincide with those of Austria, particularly in Italy, possibilities for collaboration did exist.

One of these was Switzerland. A country where law and order were upheld by the powerless cantonal authorities, Switzerland had become after 1830 an all-important refuge for fugitive or exiled Poles, Germans, and Italians. Very soon it became the centre of plots against neighbouring countries, especially under the influence of Mazzini who while living in Switzerland welded the revolutionary forces of all countries together in his Young Europe. In 1834 he incited his followers to foment two simultaneous insurrections in Savoy and Germany. Piedmont, the German States, and Austria protested vehemently. The French government came to an understanding with Austria after Montebello, the new French ambassador, had arrived in Berne (April 1836) and, interfering in the internal affairs of the Swiss Confederation, demanded that Switzerland take measures against the refugees in coordination with Austria. And while he succeeded in having Mazzini sent to England, he looked rather foolish when he pressed for the expulsion of a man called Conseil, a French *agent provocateur*. After Louis-Napoleon's attempted coup at Strasbourg, he demanded his expulsion, although Louis-Napoleon was a Swiss citizen. In 1838 France stationed an army corps in the department of Jura, while the Swiss militia was mobilised across the border. Under these circumstances Louis-Napoleon did not wish to risk a war and left for London.

In 1836 Thiers had wanted to broaden the agreement with Austria and to take it a decisive step further. He therefore carefully abstained from protesting the intrusion of the three continental powers' troops in the Republic of Crakow. He secretly offered the Austrian ambassador his help in bringing about a marriage between the son of Don Carlos and Queen Isabella. Above all, he tried to obtain the hand of an Austrian princess for the duc d'Orléans. When the latter was sent to Vienna, he completely won over the Archduke Charles and his daughter Theresa, but Metternich could not be persuaded to permit this marriage, especially since Alibaud's assassination attempt occurred just at that time. All kinds of evasive statements notwithstanding, the reason for this refusal was clear to everyone: 'No one will doubt that the House of Orléans is a great and illustrious one; it is the throne of 7 August that demeans it.' The marriage question was settled through the charitable good offices of the king of Prussia who persuaded the French to accept Helen of Mecklenburg, the daughter of a minor but extremely old princely house, for the French crown prince. Thiers was furious with the Austrians and would have intervened in Spain if the king had not opposed this step, but in any case the attempted rapprochement was followed by definitely cooler relations. France was isolated in Europe when the great Near-Eastern crisis broke out in 1839–40.

France's Near-Eastern policy under the July Monarchy

In 1832 the conference of London had definitively fixed the status of the young independent State of Greece by giving it a king, the French candidate Otto of Bavaria, and viable frontiers from the Gulf of Arta to the Gulf of Volo. Yet the survival of the Ottoman Empire remained an unsolved problem.

Ever since the Treaty of Andrinople, Russia had occupied the principalities of Moldavia and Walachia and its conquests in Asia, which had made the Caspian Sea into a Russian lake, permitted it to press down on Erzeroum, the key to Asia Minor. It appeared to the other powers that if the lock to the Straits should give way under its pressure, Russia would gain access to the Mediterranean, the crucial sector from the strategic and commercial point of view, and thereby attain the hegemony in Europe that had seemed to threaten as far back as 1814.

The powers had therefore taken a favourable view toward Sultan Mahmud's efforts to reorganise his empire. But the religious character of a regime founded on inequality between Turks and raïas severely hampered any modernisation of the existing structures. Mahmud's powerlessness was made strikingly obvious by comparison with the effective regime that was created by his vassal Mahomet Ali, the pasha of Egypt.

Mahomet Ali and the resurgence of the Near-Eastern problem

Mahomet Ali, an Albanian soldier of fortune, had become pasha of Egypt in 1806. He had broken his opposition. Having made all of the country's resources the property of the State, he had undertaken its modernisation with the help of western technicians, among whom the French contingent far outweighed all others (Napoleonic soldiers who had stayed there and converted to Islam, retired officers on half pay, business-men from Marseille, Saint-Simonians). The French General Boyer directed the training of the Egyptian army, in which Colonel Sève (Suleiman pasha) was head of the chiefs of staff; as successor to Navarin, the engineer de Cerizi had built, from the bottom up, all the installations needed for the creation of a modern fleet; the horticulturist Jumel had developed the long-fibre cotton that still bears his name; Linant de Bellefonds construc-ted the first great dams; Lambert bey directed a polytechnical school; and the physician Clot bey was inspector of the sanitation department. French public opinion was therefore most enthusiastic about Mahomet Ali, a 'continuator of Bonaparte' and held an exaggerated idea of his power.

Mahomet Ali planned to use the modern achievements of Egypt for conquest. Having gained control over a part of the Sudan and Arabia with its holy cities, he wanted to take over Syria; when the pasha of Acre opposed his plans, Mahomet Ali invaded his territory in 1832.

The sultan's troops tried in vain to stop him: on 21 December 1832 they were defeated at Konieh in Asia Minor by Ibrahim, Mahomet Ali's adopted son, and the grand vizier Rechid was taken prisoner. Constan-tinople seemed threatened.

The advance of Mahomet Ali revived the Near-Eastern issue in its international aspect: the Russians did not wish to see 'a strong and vic-torious neighbour succeed a weak and defeated one'; France offered its mediation and hoped to restore some kind of equilibrium in the Near East.

But while the French ambassador, Admiral Roussin, was engaged – and eventually succeeded – in the difficult task of persuading the sultan to invest Mahomet Ali with Syria and the district of Adana, the Russians had landed troops on the Asian side of the Bosphorus and forced the Sublime Porte to sign the Treaty of Unkiar-Skelessi (1833).

This treaty established a defensive alliance between Russia and the Ottoman Empire. One secret article, which soon became known to the other powers, specified the terms of mutual assistance in the following terms: in case of an attack by a third power the czar would furnish armed support to the sultan, whereas if Russia were involved in a war the sultan would limit his support to closing the Straits to enemy ships, thereby making an attack from the Black Sea impossible. Even the sultan was aware that this treaty was designed to make the Ottoman Empire a Russian protectorate.

Austria and Prussia were so involved with the situation in Germany that they recognised the czar's position in the Turkish Empire at the meeting of Munchengrätz. At that moment Palmerston was more concerned about a possible Russian takeover of Constantinople than about the conquest of the Empire by the pasha. But he assumed that the treaty would remain a dead letter as long as no one attacked the Ottoman Empire. He therefore preferred to wait. In the course of the following years, however, his policy evolved toward the preservation of an Ottoman Empire that would be, if possible, regenerated by internal reforms, for the Ottoman Empire was becoming a market of considerable importance for English commerce at a time when tariff barriers were thrown up everywhere in Europe. Moreover the problem of a trade route from England to India via the isthmus of Suez or southern Syria was becoming acute and Palmerston was concerned about the power of the pasha and French influence over him. The Near-Eastern crisis thus broke out in a context in which the relations between France and England – in the Near East and elsewhere – tended to be characterised by underhanded dealings rather than by an Entente Cordiale.

The actual crisis was precipitated by Sultan Mahmud, possibly with the encouragement of the British ambassador Ponsonby. The extent of Mahomet Ali's possessions and his intention to declare his independence clearly posed a threat to the Ottoman Empire, which stood to lose the better part of its Asian territory, in particular the holy cities from which the sultan derived his religious prestige; moreover, Ibrahim's presence in Syria created a perpetual state of alert in Constantinople and entailed heavy military expenditures. As far as the sultan was concerned, a defeat would be better than the *status quo*, for England would intervene to save the Empire, and as a last resort the Treaty of Unkiar-Skelessi would probably come into play. And indeed, the debacle took place almost immediately: on 24 June at Nezib, Ibrahim wiped out the Turkish army. The sultan died six days later without having learned of this disaster, and on 4 July the Turkish fleet left for Alexandria, where it was incorporated into the Egyptian forces.

Soult, the French Minister of Foreign Affairs, called for a congress of the major powers; Palmerston and Metternich could not refuse, and on 27 July the ambassadors warned the Porte not to deal with Mahomet Ali directly. The fear of seeing the Russians at Constantinople had prompted France to act with such haste. But Palmerston was still hoping that the majority of the powers would compel Mahomet Ali to abandon Syria, even though Soult refused to envisage any coercive action at Alexandria.

This difference of opinion prompted the czar, who had declined the invitation to the congress, to take a renewed interest in the Near-Eastern question. He was sure that by renouncing the advantages accruing to him under the Treaty of Unkiar-Skelessi and by offering England his help against the pasha, he would be able to break the Franco-British Entente. His expectation proved correct after two missions to London undertaken by his envoy Brunnow.

But if Palmerston was easily tempted by the Russian offers, he had to reckon with the francophilia or the russophobia of certain of his colleagues in the cabinet. He tried to satisfy France by offering to let the pasha keep southern Syria. Against all prudence, this offer was refused by France. Consequently, at the end of 1839, Palmerston informed the French government that the other powers were quite capable of enforcing a settlement to this conflict without the participation of France.

The failure of Thiers's policy

The disagreement became aggravated when Soult was replaced by Thiers on 1 March 1840. Disregarding the warnings of Guizot who at that time served as French ambassador to London and was therefore well informed about the discussions within the British cabinet, Thiers embarked upon a dangerous course of action by causing the international conversations to drag on while attempting to bring about a direct agreement between the sultan and the pasha. This endeavour failed, but Palmerston was well aware of these negotiations.

That is why he was able to persuade his reluctant colleagues in the cabinet to sign the accord with Russia. A treaty of which France was not informed and which it was not asked to join was signed in London on 15 July; the signatories were Russia, Prussia, England, and Austria. The four powers pledged themselves to uphold the integrity of the Ottoman Empire and the suzerainty of the sultan. They decided that the pasha of Egypt should be presented with three successive summonses to cease and desist at ten-day intervals. If he heeded the first he would be given Egypt as a hereditary fief and the **pashalic** of Acre for his lifetime; if he heeded the second, he would be given Egypt only; and on the third occasion his fate would be left to the discretion of the sultan. On the very day of the treaty, Palmerston ordered the British fleet to disrupt communications between Syria and Egypt.

When it became known in Paris, this treaty with its intentionally insulting wording gave rise to an extraordinary outburst of chauvinist feelings. It was perceived as the resurrection of the alliance of Chaumont. From the duc d'Orléans to the republicans, everyone was ready to go to war. They would carry the tricolour all over Europe, they would call on all peoples to rise up against the princes. There were fantasies about campaigns on the Rhine and in Italy. Actually, the German people responded to this war fever with a patriotic fever of their own: far from wishing to be liberated by French troops, they countered the French provocations with patriotic songs, such as Becker's *Wacht am Rhein* and *Deutschland über Alles*.

As for Thiers, he mobilised the troops, readied the arsenals and arms depots, and ordered the building of fortifications around Paris. In fact he was bluffing, and while he succeeded in worrying Metternich, he did not cause Palmerston to lose his composure. Thiers thought – and this was a strange error of judgment – that the English would not be in a position to make the pasha yield as long as the latter remained on the defensive. He was soon disabused: the English fleet bombarded Beirut without encountering any resistance, and when a Turkish corps was sent ashore, Ibrahim had to retreat to Egypt.

The pasha had ignored the deadlines of the ultimatum, but neither Austria nor most of the English ministers wanted to push France to extremes by having him deposed, knowing that a note of 8 October had stated that his deposition would constitute a *casus belli*. Forced to give up all of his conquests, Mahomet Ali was therefore recognised as the hereditary pasha of Egypt.

Meanwhile in France, Thiers had wanted to insert a bellicose statement into the speech from the throne for the convocation of the Chambers on 28 October 1841. Louis-Philippe did not permit it. His prime minister resigned; throughout this crisis he had pandered to patriotic feelings, leaving the king to face unpopularity and muster the courage to work for peace. In the Soult government that succeeded the Thiers government (29 October 1840) the portfolio of Foreign Affairs was given to Guizot. He faced the formidable task of restoring an isolated and humiliated France to its former position in Europe.

Palmerston for his part had been primarily interested in defending British interests and in 'teaching a lesson' to France, whose advances in the Mediterranean were rather disturbing to him. When the czar proposed an alliance that could have assumed the character of a crusade against the country of the July revolution, he refused to comply.

Moreover, Palmerston considered France's participation indispensable for the enforcement of the new status of the Straits. Once the fate of Mahomet Ali was settled, the five-power agreement known as the Convention of the Straits could be signed (13 July 1841). The crucial clause provided for the closing of the Bosphorus and the Dardanelles to all warships in peacetime. This meant that while Russia gave up the possibility of gaining access to the Mediterranean from its privileged position in Constantinople, it would remain secure in the Black Sea. Its position as a buffer State gave the Ottoman Empire a new lease on life. As for Egypt, it would henceforth devote its efforts to its own development. France soon resumed its important role there.

In short, no fundamental change seemed to have occurred, but the psychology of peoples is also a political force. The fact is that France was shocked by this crisis and experienced a renewed burst of hatred for the treaties of 1815 and 'foreign powers'. Any conciliatory gesture in the government's policy was seen as weakness or indeed treason. Unjustly, in this instance, the July Monarchy was discredited.

Guizot's foreign policy (1840–8)

In defiance of public opinion, Guizot attempted to restore the Entente Cordiale. In August 1841 the election victory of the Tories brought the formation of a Peel government and the return to the Foreign Office of Aberdeen, an understanding, conciliatory, and peace-loving man. His friendly personal relations with Guizot were complemented by family ties between the two royal families: Victoria had married Albert of Saxe-Coburg, the nephew of Leopold, himself the son-in-law of Louis-Philippe; moreover, two of Louis-Philippe's children had also married into that family. Victoria's visit to the château of Eu in September 1843 broke the other crowned heads' ostracism of the July monarch. Louis-Philippe was to visit Windsor in October 1844, and in 1848 Victoria paid him another visit. Yet behind this façade of intimate family relations many disagreements in the policies of the two countries continued to exist.

It is well known that the English attached great importance to their customs policies. While Peel favoured free trade, the French were strengthening their protectionist system. As a counter-measure to the *Zollverein*, Guizot wanted to establish a Franco-Belgian customs union. Aberdeen protested, invoking the neutral status of Belgium; and since Guizot also encountered opposition from the French manufacturers, he could conclude no more than an agreement limited to free trade for Belgian linen and French wine.

Another issue on which England with its more lofty views was unwilling to compromise was the repression of the slave trade. Sponsored by England, an international agreement permitting the inspection of ships had been drawn up. In December 1841 Guizot had signed this agreement on behalf of the French government, but the Chamber refused to ratify it. After prolonged negotiations, a more limited bilateral agreement was finally passed in 1845, but it proved rather ineffective. Nor did an Anglo-French naval expedition against the Argentine dictator Rosas lead to lasting collaboration.

On the other hand, the preceding year had been marked by several incidents that could have put an end to the Entente if the ministers (on both sides) had not kept cool heads. The first of these incidents was the Pritchard affair (see below) which on both sides of the Channel provoked an extraordinary wave of hatred in the parliaments, in the press, and in public opinion.

In itself, the Moroccan affair was more serious, since it involved an invasion of Morocco in order to chastise the sultan for his support of Abd-el-Kader. But the immediate withdrawal of the French troops as soon as reparations were obtained justified Aberdeen's equanimity.

Throughout this period the foreign ministers of the two countries were constantly called upon to settle disputes between French and English individuals, from admirals or missionaries in the Pacific to diplomats in foreign courts. This was the case at Athens, where Piscatory had ties to the 'kilt' party and its chief, Rumeliotes Colettis, while Lyons sided with the 'dress-coat' party; it was also the case at Madrid, where Bresson, in opposition to Lord Bulwer, supported General Navarez, who had replaced Espartero in 1843.

As far as Guizot was concerned, the Entente with England did not preclude other alliances. Given the circumstances of the time, his policies were bound to be more concerned with the entire western Mediterranean, where France had a foothold on both shores. A close relationship existed with Maria Christina, the regent of Spain, and Guizot attempted to bring about a rapprochement between her and the court of Naples, which was infeudated to Austria and had long supported Don Carlos. Having persuaded Naples to recognise the Spanish regime, Guizot thought about a marriage alliance between the two courts in keeping with the old Bourbon policy of family alliances that had been revived by the Restoration. It is not really surprising to see such a policy pursued by this liberal, who was in fact profoundly traditionalist. He therefore considered the marriages of the young queen of Spain and her sister, the Infanta Luisa Fernanda, as particularly important issues.

In 1845 Guizot persuaded Aberdeen not to place a Saxe-Coburg as prince-consort in Spain. It was agreed that the young queen would marry a Bourbon prince of the Neapolitan branch and that, as soon as she had a child, her younger sister would be married to the duc de Montpensier, Louis-Philippe's youngest son. On condition that the two marriages not be simultaneous, Aberdeen accepted.

Then, in July 1846, Palmerston came back to the Foreign Office. He revived the idea of a Coburg candidacy. Guizot decided to steal a march on him by bringing about the double marriage in one fell swoop. Announced in August, Isabella's marriage to her cousin, the duke of Cadiz, and her sister's marriage to Montpensier were celebrated on 10 October.

Palmerston reacted as if a crime had been committed, flooding the courts of Europe with memoranda demonstrating that France had violated the Treaty of Utrecht, attempting to discredit Louis-Philippe by arranging for the publication of compromising texts from his past as an exile, and affronting Guizot whenever possible.

At that point Guizot was trying to improve France's relations with Austria and the continental powers. Not only did he refrain from protesting when Metternich decided to occupy the Republic of Crakow, he also followed the old chancellor's example in supporting the cause of the Catholic Swiss cantons of the *Sonderbund* in their short-lived attempt at secession. In Italy, where liberal and nationalist groups were rebelling against the influence of Austria, France abstained from encouraging these movements. Yet on the eve of 1848 France remained, in fact, isolated in Europe, and its interests were shifting increasingly toward the Mediterranean and distant lands.

The French takeover of Algeria

The Algerian experiment

The French conquest of Algeria, an event that was to have far-reaching consequences for France's Mediterranean and African policies, did not come about as the result of a preconceived plan.

In 1830 the 'Regency of Algiers' was part of the Ottoman Empire. A narrowly defined aristocracy of janissaries (about 15,000) elected the dey of Algiers, who thereupon received his investiture from the sultan. This was the only tie by which Algeria was connected to the Empire. The dey levied taxes and ensured order, but his direct authority was limited to the city and its suburbs. The rest of the territory was divided into three beylics: Tittery (Medea), western Algeria (Oran), and eastern Algeria (Constantine). The total population consisted of diverse elements: fellahin engaged in the growing of trees and in agriculture in the mountains who often still spoke the old kabyle language; semi-nomadic tribes who combined agriculture with animal husbandry; Koulouglis, the offspring of marriages between Turkish soldiers and native women; Moors, an urban bourgeoisie that was organised into guilds and often included descendants of 'Andalous' displaced by the Spanish *reconquista*; and Jews, a minority which, though constantly threatened, had nonetheless furnished an elite characterised by its openness to the outside world and its economic power.

The Regency did not face the West as a hermetically closed Islamic world. With the decline of piracy, economic relations were established with the Italian States, with Spain (which had held Oran until 1794), and with France, which had obtained coral-fishing concessions at La Calle and Bône. Marseille in particular maintained a lively trade with the Regency through the Jewish colonies of its own port or those of Algiers and Livorno.

One specific episode of this trade, involving a shipment of grain under the Directory, was at the root of the dispute between France and the dey. The sellers, two Jewish merchants of Livorno, Bacri and Busnach, had succeeded – thanks to the complicity of Talleyrand, who was to profit from the deal – in having the sum owed them recognised as a debt to the French State; they had also tied its payment to the reimbursement of a debt they themselves owed the dey Hussein. When it came to the liquidation, however, they managed to cheat the dey out of the sums they owed him, whereupon the latter accused the French consul Deval, a shady character, of complicity and insisted that he be recalled. On 29 April 1827, the dey lost his temper in the course of a conversation in Turkish with the consul and struck him with his fly-whisk. Upon receiving Deval's report, the Villèle government had no choice but to demand reparation. This reparation took the form of an ineffective blockade. The Martignac government's efforts to settle the problem by negotiation ended in a second affront when the French vessel *La Provence* was fired on by the batteries of Algiers.

At that point Polignac became Minister of Foreign Affairs and decided that a direct intervention would be undertaken (31 January 1830), not by sea, since Algiers had never been taken in this manner, but by land. Boutin, a colonel sent on a secret mission under the Empire, showed that this was feasible, and his plan was followed. Within a few weeks a fleet of 675 ships, 103 of them belonging to the navy, was assembled at Toulon, where the expeditionary force commanded by Bourmont was embarked. Despite considerable concern, Admiral Duperré was able to impose an even pace on this fleet made up of ships of the line, lightly armed corvettes, barges, and a few steamships. The landing took place on 14 June at Sidi-Ferruch, 17 kilometres west of Algiers. The defending camp of Staoueli was taken on 19 June, on 4 July Fort l'Empereur, Algiers' defence to the south, was bombarded, and on the next day the dey capitulated and went into exile. Bourmont ordered the occupation of a few points along the coast but promised the inhabitants to respect their religion and their property. Polignac himself had not yet come to a firm decision as to what would be done with the presumably conquered territory.

In fact, the expedition had been launched for two reasons: on the one hand it was a legitimist undertaking designed to enhance the prestige of a government under fire from the liberal opposition; on the other hand it was a Marseillais undertaking, since the commercial circles of the great port, even the liberal elements, frustrated by the difficulties encountered in rebuilding the old Levantine trade, were looking for new outlets. The first goal was not achieved, but the second one certainly was.

A restrained occupation

The first act of the July government was to replace Bourmont with Clauzel, a politically safe choice. An officer who had distinguished himself in the Empire's campaigns in Spain and Portugal, Clauzel had also served at Saint-Domingue and attempted to run an estate in the United States. Brilliant and business-minded, he wanted to combine conquest and colonisation and was gripped by the fever of speculation spawned by this undertaking. People were buying properties near Algiers from Arabs who did not wish to live with the Christians, habou properties, inalienable religious foundations and, in the absence of a land register, non-existing land. Clauzel wanted to establish a plantation economy and considered entrusting the eastern and western beylics to Tunisian princes. Owing to disagreements with the minister, he resigned after six months and successfully stood for deputy in order to defend his ideas. Within the government ideas about what to do ranged from military occupation to relinquishment. Coming in the midst of the confusion and the ups and downs of the Belgian involvement, Algiers was no more than a troublesome side-show. The men who replaced Clauzel therefore dealt with it as best they could on a day-to-day basis. The administration increasingly subjected the newly arrived Europeans to arbitrary procedures, and the needs and the mentality of the natives were not even recognised until 1833, when the first bureau of Arabic affairs was founded and placed under the direction of Captain de Lamoricière.

At that same time Paris also attempted to formulate its objectives. A parliamentary investigative committee prepared the findings of a blue-ribbon committee headed by the duc Decazes, which met until the summer of 1834. Testimony from different quarters was heard and members of the committee were sent to Algeria. The result of this investigation was the promulgation of the ordinances of 1834: in naming the occupied territory 'French Possessions in North Africa', these ordinances put an end to the possibility of relinquishing them; the reason given was the importance attached to this conquest by French public opinion. In addition it was decided that Algeria would be ruled by ordinances rather than by laws, that a resident governor-general responsible to the Minister of War would administer the colony, and that he would be advised by a board of directors composed of high-ranking military and civilian officials. The occupation of the territory would be limited to Algiers, Bône, Oran, Bougie, and French settlements would be limited to the first two of these towns.

Already large numbers of European settlers had arrived in the Mitidja and the Sahel. They were large proprietors, often legitimists, referred to as 'settlers in yellow gloves', men like de Vialar or de Tonnac who exploited large estates by means of native sharecroppers. There were also small-scale settlers attracted by a fierce desire for land, who fought heroic battles against the unhealthy climate of the plains (as in the Boufaric area, where they stubbornly clung to their tiny plots despite horrendous mortality rates) and against Hadjout attacks. The system of restricted occupation led the officers of the corps of engineers to develop a concept not unlike that of the great Chinese wall: the *continuous obstacle* was to be a very long ditch surrounding the entire Mitidja; bordered by a tall hedge, it was to be dotted with towers where a few men would be stationed. This project was not even completed when the first structures had already fallen into disrepair and the towers were abandoned. The only guarantee for this policy of restricted occupation was therefore an agreement with the great native vassals, and it was this policy that was followed, albeit intermittently, in western Algeria. The commanding generals of Oran, Desmichels in 1834 and Bugeaud in 1837, put their trust in a young chief, Abd-el-Kader, who planned to unify the old beylic of Oran and even furnished arms against rebellious tribes, some of whom, like the Douairs and the Smelas, sought an alliance with France. The Treaty of Tafna, signed by Bugeaud, recognised Abd-el-Kader's sovereignty over the old Tittery and thereby gave him the right to surround the Sahel, Blida, and the Mitidja. Bugeaud, who at that time was opposed to the conquest and settlement of Algeria, thus entrusted the policing of the interior to a prince who in the Arabic text of the treaty was not even qualified as a French vassal.

When Clauzel regained the governorship, however, he launched a different French policy in eastern Algeria and attempted to overthrow Ahmed, the Kouloughli bey of Constantine. The expedition of November 1836, poorly prepared and carried out under severe weather conditions on the high plateau, ended in a failure for which Clauzel's successor, Damrémont, had to seek revenge the following year lest the French power be completely discredited. He did seize Constantine at the price of very heavy casualties, but lost his life in the venture.

General Vallée, an artillery commander who had come to take part in the siege, was asked to remain as governor. Secretive and authoritarian, and rather disliked by his subordinates, he was a man of integrity and an enlightened administrator. He consolidated the areas of European settlement into camps, undertook public works, and generally tried to organise an official colonisation rather than the anarchic settlement that was taking place. He planned to give the Europeans a civilian administration. First he organised the province of Constantine: the triangle Bône–Constantine–Stora, which ensured the principal city's access to the sea, was administered directly, while the rest of the former beylic was divided among the native chiefs who paid tribute. Nonetheless there was an obvious lack of balance among the French possessions: from this eastern establishment, Algiers could only be reached by sea, and to the west, beyond the Sahel and the Mitidja, the French held only a few isolated points on the coast. The Treaty of Tafna placed them 'in a precarious position, deprived of any guarantees and enclosed within badly designed limits'.

Vallée wanted to make the point that he did not accept this situation: in 1839 the duc d'Orléans on a State visit returned from Constantine to Algiers by land, crossing the Iron Gates Pass in the Biban Mountains (28 October). Challenged in this manner, Abd-el-Kader opted for war: his cavalry ravaged the area around Algiers, ruining agricultural improvements that had been made over several years and massacring settlers. Vallée was unable to devise plans for the kind of counter-attack that was necessary in view of his adversary's mobility. In December 1840, he was replaced by Bugeaud.

Bugeaud and Abd-el-Kader (1840–7)

> One man personifies in himself all the forces with which Algeria opposes us; he increases a hundredfold the difficulties of the soil and the climate, the energy of individuals, and the agonising power of religious fanaticism. Indeed, he towers so high above his compatriots that we will be unable to do anything as long as this man is not brought down . . . This man is Abd-el-Kader.

With these words Veuillot in *Les Français en Algérie* (1843) characterised France's great adversary.

Abd-el-Kader's power had religious roots. His father Mahi-ed-Din, who claimed to be a descendant of the Prophet, had established himself west of Mascara in a guetna, a place for pilgrimages and religious meetings near a Koranic School. Mahi-ed-Din had a widespread reputation for holiness and religious learning. In 1832 he had been chosen as leader of the Holy War, but had come to grief before Oran. In November the tribes renewed their alliance and placed themselves under the command of the 24-year-old Abd-el-Kader, who took the religious title of emir.

Abd-el-Kader combined the prestige of an educated man, an excellent rider, and a Mecca pilgrim with great personal qualities; he possessed elegance and piety, austerity and charm, bravery and generosity, a sense of justice and the ability to dissimulate. He embarked upon a remarkable effort to unify Islamic Algeria.

In 1840 he succeeded in forming a federation extending over two-thirds of the Algerian territory by placing the tribes under the authority of a hierarchy of new powers, the caidats, aghaliks, and khalifaliks. Eight khalifas served as direct lieutenants of the emir; they were either his kinsmen, notable marabouts [priests], or members of great local families. To be sure, force was necessary to impose this system on the anarchic tribes. It was more solid in the province of Oran than in that of Algiers, where the khalifas and the aghas often conducted parallel negotiations with the French. The contingents of irregulars furnished to Abd-el-Kader by the tribes constituted his main strength, but their discipline in the field often left something to be desired. In addition, the tribes also paid him a tax of produce and livestock.

Thanks to these resources, Abd-el-Kader had a small army (10,000 men at most) at his disposal; he set up silos and weapons and munitions factories in the towns of the Tell (Tlemcen, Mascara, Miliana) or in the newer towns of the south, where they were out of reach of the French. (Among these places were Saida and Tagdempt; the latter was called his capital and he minted money there.) But the emir himself rarely resided there; he was constantly travelling through his kingdom with his *smala*, which included his family, his faithful, and his treasures. His mobility was his main weapon against the French, for he knew that he could not face them in a pitched battle and therefore hoped to discourage them by surprise attacks and the complicity of the entire country.

Not many historical figures have been judged as contradictorily as Bugeaud, Abd-el-Kader's adversary. A scion of the lesser nobility of Périgord, engaged as a volunteer in 1804, then an officer risen through the ranks, he had distinguished himself in the guerilla operations in Spain. The Restoration – despite his declarations of loyalty – dismissed him. Having made a rich marriage, he became the apostle of agricultural improvement in Périgord, attempting to set an example on his own estate and organising the first agricultural fairs. The July Monarchy took him back into the army, and Bugeaud served as the duchesse de Berry's prison warden at Blaye before he was sent to Algeria.

His harshness and brutality went hand in hand with concern for the troops' well-being, and a desire to protect the defenceless natives. Deeply hostile to freedom of the press, he nonetheless exposed his convictions with the verve of a great **polemicist** and total contempt for the facts. In trying to understand this contradictory personality, it is not easy to separate out this blend of garrulous *bonhomie* and secretive cunning. Having become a general and deputy from Dordogne, he spent half his time in the Chamber, where the Soult–Guizot government was constantly worried about this troublesome supporter, and the other half in Algeria, where he conducted himself in the style of a proconsul. Under these circumstances the government did not dare haggle over the means he requested. Eventually he had more than 100,000 men under his command, a force none of his predecessors would have dreamt of requesting.

From the military point of view, it was Bugeaud's merit to have found a way to counteract the Arab conduct of the war. Above all, this was a matter of making the French soldier as mobile as the Arab by lightening his garments and foregoing heavy material; in order to accomplish this, it was necessary to organise a veritable gridwork of supply stations, and the French superiority in siege warfare permitted them to integrate most of the emir's towns into this gridwork. As for the role of the 'mobile columns', it was essentially a matter of carrying out *razzias*. Any tribe that had given help to the enemy was raided, its village was set on fire, its harvest destroyed, and its cattle seized. Mercy could be obtained only through total submission.

This war resembled a 'gigantic game of tag', in which the enemy soon came to play the part of the hunted quarry. Few episodes stand out against a whole background of violence, although some of them, in particular the smoking out of defiant tribes in grottoes, gave rise to public protest.

In 1843 the duc d'Aumale with 500 horsemen captured Abd-el-Kader's *smala* in a brilliant raid in southern Algeria, and in 1844 Abd-el-Kader went to Morocco to solicit help. At the same time the prince de Joinville bombarded Tangiers and Mogador, while Bugeaud – going beyond the government's orders – defeated the Moroccan army west of Isly. When Abd-el-Kader was expelled from Morocco, peace was concluded with the sherif Empire. In 1845 a popular uprising against the conqueror, led by local prophets and marabouts, threatened to undo these achievements, but was soon put down. Abd-el-Kader, whose desperate efforts to constitute new bases in the Rif were thwarted by the sultan, surrendered to Lamoricière (December 1847).

By that time Bugeaud, having become a marshal and duc d'Isly, was no longer the governor-general. In the matter of colonisation, he had been obsessed by the idea of creating villages cultivated by soldiers on active duty or soldiers who had completed their military service. When the government felt that it no longer needed the marshal's services, it submitted his plans for military colonisation, which it considered unrealisable, to the Chambers. Their rejection prompted Bugeaud to resign, and he was replaced by the duc d'Aumale as governor-general.

Algeria at the end of the July Monarchy

At that time the Algerian situation was symptomatic of the indecision and the weakness of the regime. In 1847 Tocqueville, who had stated earlier that the Algerian affair was conducted 'in a haphazard manner', read two reports to the Chamber in which he outlined his thinking. Noting at the outset that 'today the peaceful domination and the rapid colonisation of Algeria are unquestionably France's two most important interests in the world', he added: 'Nothing so far indicates the presence of a single and forceful idea, a firm and consistent plan.' Tocqueville then went on to denounce the unwieldiness of the administrative apparatus whose different cogs worked at cross purposes. He might have added that except for a few brilliant civil servants the administration was either mediocre or venal.

The arbitrariness of the military authorities made itself felt everywhere; it was often inspired by hatred for the 'civilians'. Yet the military gave proof of a definite interest for the Arabs, provided of course that they were duly defeated and subjected. Bugeaud had preserved Abd-el-Kader's organisation below the level of general officers commanding the sub-divisions, but had entrusted the leadership to prominent local families and moreover divided the territory into smaller circumscriptions. He intended to interest the tribes in furthering the agricultural colonisation of Algeria and claimed that in this respect his policy would 'offer the best guarantees'. He was opposed to the expulsion (which certain Europeans demanded) or any form of confinement of the tribes.

Meanwhile a rapidly growing European population was pouring into the former Regency. On 1 January 1847 the count was 47,000 Frenchmen and 62,000 other nationals (half of them from Spain). But there were only 15,000 rural settlers, and more than half of the immigrants remained in the cities of Algiers and Oran. Algiers assumed the character of a new city, a half-military and half-civilian society of speculators, hucksters of all races, and adventurers. It had become an episcopal see whose incumbent, the truculent Mgr Dupuch, was constantly at odds with Bugeaud.

Yet rural settlers were the decisive factor for the future. The anarchic phase of the colonisation was over; henceforth the candidates were screened by the State, which also delivered concessions to land. Ordinances passed in 1844 and 1846 had annexed 200,000 hectares to the State domain, 168,000 of them in the Algiers region. These were the properties of the beylic, habou properties, lands confiscated after the massacres of 1839 or taken from owners unable to produce titles and the like. The project director in the Ministry of the Interior, Guyot, was particularly interested in creating villages at the edge of the Sahel and furnished help or commercial services to newcomers who decided to settle in this area. In competition with Guyot, Colonel Marengo and his military convicts built houses and carried out initial clearings. The problem of the colonisation of Algeria fascinated public opinion and a profusion of pamphlets promoting philanthropic, Saint-Simonian, Fourierist, and capitalist ideas was published. As for the crops that were raised, common sense began to prevail: instead of indigo or cotton, cereals, tobacco, vines, and mulberry trees were planted.

The conquest had forged a professional army that was deeply attached to its independence and had little respect for either legality or military science. Lurking behind a minority of remarkable leaders, many of them old 'Algeria hands' like Lamoricière, Duvivier, Cavaignac, or Bedeau, the strong men of 2 December were already emerging.

France and the Pacific

The opening of the Pacific to white people's commerce, civilisation, and colonisation was one of the major developments of the first half of the nineteenth century. In the previous century France had played an important role in the discovery of the Austral regions, and the renascent navy of the Restoration renewed the tradition of the great explorers. The expeditions led by Freycinet, Duperrey, the younger Bougainville, Dumont d'Urville, Tromelin, and Laplace 'placed the Pacific on the map of the human sciences'.

However, it was in the years around 1830 that trade with the littorals of that ocean assumed a new importance. On its eastern shores, the July Monarchy recognised the new States of Latin America and attempted to establish French commerce alongside that of the English. These efforts were not uniformly successful, but Valparaiso became an important base for French sailing ships.

In the West, the French consul-general at Manila, Adolphe Barrot, was charged with rebuilding France's Far-Eastern trade, which had shrunk to almost nothing in 1830.

His reports prompted the government to make a futile attempt to occupy the Bay of Tourane and the small island of Basilan south of the Philippines. In China, Lagrenée's mission conducted immediately after the opium war was well received by the representatives of the emperor: the treaty of Wampoah gave French trade the same advantages that were enjoyed by England, and in addition granted protection to French Catholic missionaries. France also hoped to establish settlers in New Zealand, but this project failed and the British took over in 1845.

Above all, France felt the need to create bases for its navy and to establish control over the whaling ships that were moving from the depleted fishing grounds of the South Atlantic to the Pacific, where cetaceans were still plentiful. France was also interested in maintaining the Catholic missions in the Pacific that Pope Gregory XVI had entrusted to two French orders, the Picpus Fathers in the eastern and the Marists in the western Pacific. The first of these missions was constituted as an apostolic vicariate whose bishop resided in the Gambier Islands (beginning in 1836), and the second had a bishop in New Zealand, although its activities were actually centred in the Wallis and Futuna Islands. This is why in 1842 the Marquesas Islands were subjected to French protection by Admiral Dupetit-Thouars; the islands of Wallis and Futuna (1842), and the Gambier Islands (1844) were also made to 'request' French protection. France officially declined to play this role because it did not wish to jeopardise its relations with England, but French influence remained dominant in this area.

These Catholic missions often came into conflict with the English Protestant missions which, sustained by the London Missionary Society, were solidly entrenched. Tahiti, for example, had become the headquarters of the Methodist ministers. One of them, Pritchard, the influential adviser of Queen Pomaré, had obtained the expulsion of two Catholic missionaries who had come to the island, and Dupetit-Thouars had demanded reparations. In 1839 Palmerston had refused Pritchard's request to establish a British protectorate. In September 1842, Dupetit-Thouars, taking advantage of Pritchard's absence and assuming that the Methodist minister was about to make another request, persuaded the Tahitians to accept a French protectorate, which he transformed into an annexation pure and simple after unrest had broken out in November 1843. At that point Pritchard, who had stirred up this unrest, was expelled. His expulsion led to a Franco-British confrontation, but in the end it was agreed that the protectorate should be restored. Guizot aroused the indignation of the opposition when he granted Pritchard an indemnity for lost property.

The annexation of bases was thus a rather short phase, since both Guizot and Aberdeen refrained from making acquisitions that would create conflicts between the two countries (for example, in the Hawaiian Islands). Nonetheless it marks the resurgence of French influence in a remote part of the world from which France had been almost excluded.

8

The beginning of industrialisation

Long before the July Monarchy, a few segments of French society had
become acquainted with industrial and especially commercial capitalism;
long after the fall of Louis-Philippe the largest segment of the population
would continue to make its living from agriculture or artisanal work. Yet
it was during the reign of Louis-Philippe that the inception of the 'industrial revolution' took place, even though the term revolution seems rather
unsuitable, since the transformations of the French economy took place
more slowly than in other countries. This slow pace fostered the discrepancy between the economic or social reality and the attitudes and outlook
of the country at large. Economic growth, from which the holders of
capital and the workers did not benefit to the same extent, absorbed all
the attention; only a small minority sought, often by conflicting means,
to break out of the pervasive moral conformism of a period that was less
interested than the Restoration in intellectual creativity and the continual
development of new ideologies.

The coexistence of several economic systems

    The old economic system
        Before 1848, the majority of the French people continued to live
under this system. It was characterised by the preponderance of agricultural practices designed to produce local food supplies; yields were often
low and farmers engaged in mixed farming for their own consumption.
Industrial activity was characterised by the production of consumer goods.
The most dispersed and the most artisanal of all industrial sectors was the
building industry, but for the most part the textile industry (in particular
wool and linen) and also small-scale metallurgy retained their artisanal
character. Lacking good technical equipment, these industries valued the
quality and the skill of the worker. Regional and even local industries were
isolated or existed side by side, owing to insufficient means of communication. This population began to experience declining birth rates (below
30 per 1,000 inhabitants after 1829), while death rates declined slightly,

168

albeit with appreciable fluctuations from year to year. Higher death rates ensued from cholera (28.5 deaths per 1,000 inhabitants in 1828) and from bad harvests. Population growth was constant though irregular, especially in the period 1841–6, which marked the most prosperous years of the reign.

This primarily agricultural part of France was located essentially west and south of a line stretching *grosso modo* between Caen, Le Mans, Saint-Etienne, and Grenoble. Its main traits will be described in part 2. Not that this stable France did not undergo changes, but it needed time to assimilate them. In most cases it was indirectly affected by innovations it had not sought. The modernisation of transportation and of industry, for example, began to disrupt the precarious equilibrium that had been achieved, and in many departments this development ruined the rural industries that provided supplementary resources.

The growth of the French population, slow though it was (32.5 million in 1831; 35.4 million in 1846) in conjunction with the development of an agrarian individualism that sharpened the small farmer's land hunger, resulted in the extension of the arable land and greater productivity. The surfaces planted in wheat increased by almost 20 per cent during the July Monarchy, and surfaces devoted to the potato increased by nearly 50 per cent.

The new economic system

This system was dominated by capitalist industrialisation, even though the investment capital was still, for the most part, family owned and came from the enterprises themselves. The changeover from the old-style industry to modern industrial capitalism was usually brought about by the evolution of family enterprises that had started either as modest artisanal operations or small commercial ventures; some enterprises were headed by men of rural background who had left their native villages in their youth. One even finds former officers of the Empire who had gone into business. Certain entrepreneurs under the July Monarchy had started out as workers or artisans; Auguste Mille (1782–1844) for example used the first steam engine in a spinning mill at Lyon. Such cases of wage-earner rising into management, however, became increasingly rare after 1840, and a few individual cases are not sufficient to modify the general pattern of family management.

The dynamic progress of industry was marked by technological advances that made use of the skill and the experience of artisans but also applied new scientific discoveries. This was the case particularly in the chemical industry, whose progress was related to new processes in the production of soda and linked to the names of well-known scientists, such as Gay-Lussac who directed the workshops of the Saint-Gobain company at Chauny, or Frédérick Kuhlman who as early as 1825 had founded an enterprise that would become a major industry in the department of Nord on the eve of 1848. Close relations were formed between the main research institutions (the Faculty of Science at Paris, the Ecole Polytechnique, the Académie des Sciences) and industry. Marriage alliances reinforced the ties among the business community, the high administration, and the scholars whose scientific discoveries were quickly put to use by industry. Thénard (who had just received the title of baron), for example, was the son-in-law of the industrialist Humblot-Conté, a deputy and eventually Peer of France, and also the father-in-law of the engineer Darcy (brother of a prefect) who eventually became one of the great capitalists of the Second Empire.

Industrial progress was also related to the use of coal and its closer association with metallurgy. The production of soft coal almost doubled under the July Monarchy, increasing from 1,490,000 tons in 1834 to 4,210,000 tons in 1845. But consumption increased even more rapidly, so that imports rose almost three-fold (two out of every seven million tons were imported). Despite the protectionism of the period, import tariffs were lowered in 1836, a step that facilitated the arrival of English and Belgian coal. The number of steam engines used in industry rose from 625 at the end of 1830 to 4,853 in 1847, and the power of these machines increased even more rapidly. Railways (still in the early stage), steam-ships, gas lighting that came into use in the cities, and home heating all contributed to an increased consumption of soft coal. Owing to the high cost of transportation, however, this pattern of increased consumption was localised near the areas of production or near the major ports of arrival. In 1837 the price of coal mined in the Saint-Etienne region was more than five times higher in Paris than at the pithead. This fact also accounts for the dispersion of mining sites, for even relatively small deposits were exploited.

Wood remained an important source of industrial fuel for a large part of France. Ironmasters therefore owned large tracts of forest, especially since a certain number of nobles, small or large landowners, were involved in metallurgy. Cast iron continued to be produced by means of wood but became proportionally less and less important, even though Catalan forges were still being built. In 1846 there were only 106 coke-fuelled blast furnaces, compared to 304 charcoal furnaces, yet the coke furnaces already processed two-thirds of all the iron.

Between 1835 and 1840 French metallurgy, stimulated by the develop-ment of new industries, railway construction and shipbuilding, and the development of new agricultural implements, made great strides. The production of cast iron increased from 197,000 tons in 1824 to 439,000 in 1845. Only the tariff barrier shielded French metallurgy from English competition, but even so it was faced with many difficulties and frequent deficits were not apt to attract capital to this sector. The heavy-metal industry was hampered most severely by the scarcity or the high price of coal, but the metal-construction and machine-building industries were stronger in the Paris region, in Alsace, and in central France. Industrial activities occupied three times less labour than agriculture, and this figure even includes the building trade, the sector which, along with the textile industry, employed the largest labour force.

The textile industry had been France's major industrial sector prior to the industrial expansion that affected a wide variety of geographical areas. Yet its evolution was slower than that of its English counterpart. In France the transformation of the textile industry played a less predominant role in the process of industrialisation as a whole, and the rural textile industry (especially weaving) survived for a long time. The number of workers employed in cotton spinning in factories surpassed that of cottage workers (in town and country) only in 1835, although it is true that the latter category rapidly declined thereafter. Another special feature of the French situation, finally, is the fact that the cotton industry, though representing the most dynamic sector, was not as predominant as in England in relation to the other sectors of the textile industry. The French woollen industry was more dynamic; wool imports rose four-fold between 1830 and 1845, while the value of the exported wool cloths more than doubled. In a better position to face English competition, the woollen industry often took the lead in developing technical innovations, such as Godard's mechanical comb at Amiens and later Josué Heilman's comb in Haute-Alsace. Technical advances improved the quality of the French woollens, and France produced a wide variety of wool cloth. Sedan, Aubusson, Elbeuf, and Reims produced high-quality goods, and Roubaix was also expanding rapidly. By contrast, the mills engaged in the production of coarse woollens in southern France, Dauphiné, and Berry began to suffer from the competition of the northern mills, so that the southern manufacturers increasingly limited their production to ordinary cloth and to army supplies. This is one aspect of the de-industrialisation of southern France to which Maurice Lévy-Leboyer has drawn attention.

The old linen industry, dispersed throughout western and northwestern France, felt the effects of the severe depression that affected the linen industry throughout western Europe. Very rural in character and almost completely unmechanised, it was hard put to withstand the competition of the northern mills, which had mechanised after 1830 by copying the English. The silk industry, whose character and problems we will study in connection with the Lyon region, worked for export and specialised more and more in the production of inexpensive goods. Yet in general French production was more interested in quality than in low prices, for reasons that are both psychological and economic in nature. This holds true in the case of silk and wool as well as cotton.

The cotton industry offers the principal examples of industrial modernisation outlined in our chapters on the regions of France. Already production had become relatively concentrated, at least in geographical terms, and progress was much more rapid in eastern than in western France. Between 1814 and 1834, for example, the number of spinning mills at Mulhouse had risen ten-fold, while increasing only three-fold at Rouen, which nonetheless was still France's largest cotton manufacturing centre in 1846. The marked growth in production after 1815 was punctuated by serious setbacks in 1827, 1837–9, and 1847, which resulted in the proletarianisation of the workers (whose lifestyle has been well described by Villermé) but also in a stepped-up modernisation of the industry. During the first half of the nineteenth century, the cotton industry appears to have functioned as the leading sector for industry with a production growth rate almost twice as high as the annual growth rate of France's total industrial production.

Many other industries were also developed; some of the older ones, such as the paper, glass, crystal, and porcelain industries, were rejuvenated, while new ones, such as the manufacture of gas lamps and chemicals, came into being. Public opinion was often uneasy about these innovations, which upset the stability of the social system and the equilibrium of the economy.

This economic expansion owed its momentum to liberalism, which stimulated industrial activity and the desire for power. Yet as money became the supreme value, this desire for power turned against liberalism and produced a competitive attitude that reinforced – in the course of periodical crises – the power of the richest and most capable segments of society.

Modern agriculture

To what extent did advances in agriculture contribute to the development of the new economic system? Practiced only by a small minority of landowners or farmers, a modern, more capitalist, speculative, and market-oriented type of agriculture developed during this period.

New crops and new breeding techniques for livestock were introduced by educated notables, some of them legitimists who took an increased interest in their estates after 1830. Comte Jouffroy-Gonsans, for example, modernised his estate at La Brenne in Indre by bringing in farmers and new ploughs from Flanders. Newly founded agricultural societies, agricultural fairs, prizes and exhibitions contributed to popularising new techniques. One of the most notable innovations was the increase in the weight of livestock due to selective cross-breeding. The constant diminution of the fallow, the draining of marshes, and the stabilisation of sand dunes brought about an expansion in certain sectors of French agriculture.

This evolution was also related to new techniques made possible by

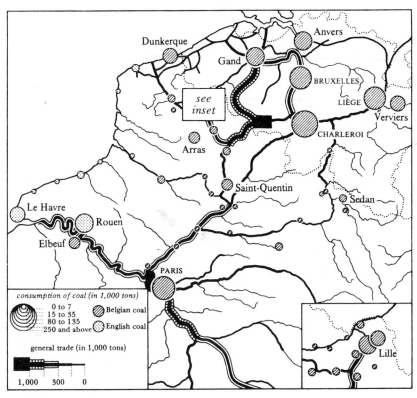

4   Trade routes in northwestern France, *c.* 1840

Source: J. Vial, *L'Industrialisation de la sidérurgie française, 1814–1864* (Paris, 1967)

industrial advances. More modern agricultural implements were promoted, among others, by Matthieu de Dombasle, who as early as 1818 had constructed a threshing-machine, and whose name was long linked to an improved model of plough. Although artificial fertilisers made their appearance at that time, they were not used widely enough to have a major economic impact.

Altogether, however, these advances were still very slow before 1840; initially only the wealthiest landowners benefited from them. Possessing both capital and knowledge, these men used their economic power to reinforce their social power. In dealing with the peasants of their area, they used the introduction of new techniques to reinforce the existing paternalism. These agricultural capitalists had closer ties of solidarity with the leading business circles than with the world of the peasant.

Industrial and financial capitalism

Despite the dispersion of the industrial establishments, French industry was already beginning to experience a two-fold trend toward concentration.

On the one hand, this was a matter of geographical concentration, for existing industries attracted new ones. This was the case at Lyon, but also in Paris, in the northern departments, in Upper Alsace and the lower Seine. These were often the regions that attracted the first railways (the department of Nord, and the regions of Mulhouse and Rouen). This development accentuated the imbalance among regions; the poorest departments became even poorer, and in the richer ones social tension increased because only a small group of industrial entrepreneurs benefited from this accumulation of wealth.

On the other hand, economic concentration also took place. Sometimes this process occurred horizontally, especially in the mining industry exemplified by the Compagnie d'Anzin in the department of Nord and, most strikingly, by the *Compagnie générale des mines de la Loire*, as well as in the crystal industry, where a few major companies soon came to hold a quasi-monopoly. Sometimes the concentration took a vertical form, as in the case of the Paulin-Talabot Company which, with backing from the Rothschilds, acquired interests in the coal basin of La Grand' Combe, in the Alès-Beaucaire railway, and in the engineering works of La Ciotat. Another case is that of the Koechlin family, which acquired interests in the cotton spinneries and the engineering works of Mulhouse. This concentration gave rise to the formation of important groups in which financiers or bankers, industrialists, engineers, politicians, and newspaper-owners worked closely together. Such formations were prompted above all by the railway construction at the end of the reign, and it was for this reason that the regime was particularly prone to collusion between the business world and the politicians. Not that there was anything new about this, but the parliamentary regime in conjunction with the property qualifications for participation in political life was conducive to such collusion.

The bankers played a preponderant role in the July Monarchy. Never perhaps did the Rothschild family wield as great an influence: 'I go to see the king whenever I want . . . he completely trusts me, listens to me, and takes into account what I tell him', wrote James de Rothschild in December 1840.

The influential banking community was composed of a few old houses, which often held interests in other industrial or commercial ventures; its clientèle consisted of a few wealthy families. The leading figures in the milieu were often Protestants, and their shared religion made for solidarity in a large segment of the capitalist financial institutions, which never withheld their political sympathies from Louis-Philippe. Several of these families were of Swiss origin or had spent time in Switzerland; among them were the Mallet and the Delessert families who also had interests in beet-sugar refineries and in insurance companies, as well as the Hottinguer, Odier, and Verne families who were allied by marriage or otherwise related to some of the major French manufacturing families.

Loans to the State, which were plentiful throughout the monarchy of limited suffrage, represented one of the most lucrative activities of the banking community, for the banks were indispensable as a source of funds and therefore able (by agreements and a quasi-monopoly) to charge very high interest rates. Investment in French or foreign public funds, however, tied up capital that might have been put to more productive use. The great financial institutions controlled almost the entire banking system through their management of the Banque de France. This institution played an important role by issuing bank notes, which were as yet rather uncommon (they were issued only in large denominations) and above all by setting the discount rate and thereby determining the conditions of short-term commercial credit for all of France. The Banque de France, whose governor was appointed by the king, was administered by a board of regents and auditors recruited for the most part from the world of high finance. Its stable social structure and its close ties to the government made the Banque de France more accessible to the concerns of the administration than to those of industrial enterprises. The majority of the regents was more preoccupied with security and profits (dividends, after all, had to be paid to stockholders) than with the economy as a whole.

Efforts to modernise the banking system with a view to mobilising available capital and developing credit facilities were made outside the Banque de France by Jacques Laffitte, but the new lending institutions were slow to take firm root. The means to bring people's savings into the economy remained traditional and continued to be in the hands of notaries, tax-collectors, and usurers. At the Paris stock exchange, the number of stocks traded rose from 38 in 1830 to 260 in 1841 and even higher in subsequent years. Yet the 'woollen sock' in which the peasant or the *petit bourgeois* kept the pieces of gold or silver he had saved remained an obstacle to economic growth. Despite France's resources, therefore, the prevailing distrustful attitude toward credit (which after 1842 gave way to overconfidence) made it necessary to import foreign capital to further the country's industrialisation. This society in transition was characterised by the prevalence of financial capitalism (often international in nature) over industrial capitalism, by the rift between a few centres that had already reached the stage of industrialisation and the majority of the country that still lived under the economic system of the Ancien Regime, and by heightened social tensions arising from the unequal distribution of the benefits of technological advances spawned by economic liberalism. All of these factors prompted a questioning of the accepted patterns of thought and unsettled the existing structure of society.

The growth of utopian socialism and the weakness of the workers' movement

The dynamic development of the liberal economy was offset by the aggravation of social inequality, and indeed by the pauperisation of the workers, although one should not entirely dismiss certain self-serving assertions of contemporaries who painted too favourable a picture of the old order of things. This is especially true for legitimists like Villeneuve-Bargemont.

Unlike the more dispersed and hidden misery of the peasants, the workers' misery that was openly displayed at Lille, Mulhouse, Rouen, or Nantes was a phenomenon of great historical significance, for it sowed in the workers' hearts the seeds of agitation and revolt and brought a first, albeit very isolated awareness of pauperism (a social fact) as distinct from poverty (an individual reality).

The ruling classes' wish to reduce the social question to a moral question gave rise to an opposing current of thought that Marx was later to label 'utopian socialism'. First formulated during the Restoration, socialist ideas were sharpened and diversified in the wake of technical and industrial advances and under the impact of a series of crises and strikes and the misery that ensued from them. The utopian character of these ideas had to do with their abstractness, which made them rather inaccessible to the popular masses, and also with their failure to propose an immediate and rational solution to a seemingly hopeless situation. It was precisely this lack of contact with reality, this conviction that it was useless to propose reforms or improvements to the existing system, that prompted the French socialists to formulate their sweeping theories calling for the building of a radically new society.

A shared feature of all socialist thinking was the critique of the liberal economy, but some of its theoreticians took their inspiration from the materialist philosophy of the eighteenth century, others from evangelical Christianity, and still others from the extremist offshoots of the French Revolution, notably Babouvism. They also differed in their assessment of the role of the State and on whether the economy should be primarily geared toward production or toward consumption.

The Saint-Simonians

The Saint-Simonians continued to propound the doctrine of Saint-Simon which we outlined earlier; under the leadership of Prosper Enfantin, the 'pope' of the new 'religion', they formed a socialist community at Ménilmontant. This was a short-lived experiment, for it was declared illegal and its members were prosecuted and imprisoned for several months. After the Ménilmontant experiment, the Saint-Simonians broke up into several branches; most of them became integrated into the capitalist economy and even furthered it by their synthetic vision of technical progress (a vision held, for example, by Michel Chevalier, who became the editor-in-chief of the semi-official *Journal des débats*) or by their interest in communication and credit (Prosper Enfantin, Talabot, the Péreires). Nonetheless a few Saint-Simonians continued in the socialist path and tried to establish contact with the popular masses by means of missions in the provinces. These 'missionaries' combined economic and social analysis with highly Romantic dreams of the future and with an emphasis on the rehabilitation of sensuality that was too non-conformist not to affront public opinion. Their influence was essentially confined to a very limited number of bourgeois youths who seized upon these ideas as a means to distinguish themselves from their elders by scandalising the monotony of conventional society. The Saint-Simonians developed the idea of State ownership of the means of production and exchange; they also popularised the ideas of association and organisation, although these ideas were understood differently than their authors had intended.

Most importantly, their preoccupations were taken up and passed on by other theoreticians, some of whom, like Pierre Leroux, had actually gone through a Saint-Simonian phase, while others, like Fourier, had been opposed to Saint-Simonianism all along.

The Fourierists

As we have seen earlier, Fourier had used a whole new vocabulary replete with neologisms and an unbridled imagination to express a new psychological concept of man with a view to making the satisfaction of the passions and agreeable work the basis of society. His ideas were subsequently popularised in a less original but more intelligible form by the so-called 'membership school' (*école sociétaire*) and above all by Victor Considérant who wrote *La Destinée sociale* (1835), *Exposition abrégée du système phalanstérien* (five editions between 1845 and 1848), and edited the newspaper *La Démocratie pacifique*. The pamphlets of the *Petite Bibliothèque phalanstérienne* published under such titles as *Anarchie industrielle, L'Organisation du travail, Le Livret c'est le servage* often gave rise to social demands presented by the democratic clubs in 1848. Fourierism exerted a more immediate influence primarily because its brand of socialism – unlike Saint-Simonianism – stressed consumption more than production. Moreover, it emphasised the idea of attractive work at a time when work was becoming more and more disagreeable owing to mechanisation and the acceleration of the pace of work. Fourierism criticised city life and pictured its phalansteries (ideal communities) as villages, thereby reviving the illusion that the return to a mythical golden age was possible. The organisation of work it proposed was characterised by an extreme form of division of labour and was the first to include the idea of a guaranteed minimum subsistence for everyone in a kind of anticipation of the 'guaranteed minimum wage'. Finally, it expressed the need for a certain amount of leisure by viewing economic progress exclusively in terms of providing the means to satisfy the human passions, precisely at the time when industrial development was ruining the traditional festivals without permitting the elaboration of a new popular culture.

Proudhon

At the end of the July Monarchy, French socialism was marked above all by the powerful and contradictory personality of Pierre-Joseph Proudhon (1809–64). Karl Marx, with whom he had exchanged polemics ever since 1846, nonetheless wrote of him: 'In France Proudhon marked an important stage in popular thought; he was one of those who helped the working class to become conscious of itself.'

The son of a cooper of Franche-Comté and a cook of peasant origins, Proudhon was a man of the people, and this was rare among the first socialist theoreticians. Starting out as a typesetter and working briefly as a master-printer at Besançon, he received a fellowship from the Academy of that town which permitted him to study political economy on his own. In 1840 he laid down his thinking in a first paper, *Qu'est-ce que la propriété? ou recherche sur le principe du droit et du gouvernement* [What is property? or, a study concerning the principle of law and government]. Soon he was launched on a career of pamphleteering and social protest in the wake of the scandal provoked by his phrase: 'God is evil, property is theft.' Working as a shipping clerk at Lyon, he often went to Paris, finally moving there in October 1847, shortly after publishing *Le Système des contradictions économiques ou philosophie de la misère* [The system of economic contradictions or the philosophy of misery]. Before 1848 his thinking was dominated by a negative dialectic directed against capitalist profit-making (though he did not demand the abolition of private property), against the State, which he denounced for the relations of power and subjection it imposed on the people for the benefit of the propertied classes, and against religion, which he criticised (inspired by the German philosophers) as a source of alienation and as the theoretical basis of social inequality. This triple critique of hierarchy and authority of every kind led him to an anarchism that set him apart from the other socialists. Hostile to political and especially parliamentary activity, he believed only in a social revolution coming from 'the initiative of the masses'. He denounced the disparity between capital and work, between the reliance on machinery and the degradation of the workers, and between the growth of production and popular misery. His plea was for an as yet confused idea of justice as the foundation of an egalitarian and anarchist society resting on spontaneous and purposeful organisation.

Louis Blanc, Pierre Leroux, Philippe Buchez

By the end of the July Monarchy, however, democratic socialism had found its leader in a man dissimilar to Proudhon in every respect. He was Louis Blanc (1811–82), a *déclassé* bourgeois, a republican journalist, and an editor for *La Réforme*, who had expressed his ideas in 1839–40 in *L'Organisation du travail*. Taking his inspiration from the revolutionary tradition, which he grafted onto his own analysis of the economic evolution and the difficulties of the life of the working class, and sharply critical of the principle of competition underlying the liberal regime that he saw as the source of crises and war, he felt that the first step toward the reform of society had to be the reform of the State by means of universal suffrage. These ideas were not new, but Louis Blanc gave them greater resonance because he was a gifted orator and writer who knew how to communicate with the masses and never lost sight of the immediate situation. He was therefore popular among the workers of Paris on the eve of 1848.

Some of the Saint-Simonians had evolved toward a more democratic form of socialism; this was the case of Pierre Leroux (1797–1871) who in 1842 directed the *Revue indépendante* founded by George Sand and later the *Revue sociale*. His social and aesthetic ideas were informed by deeply religious thinking. A democrat, he harked back to Rousseau, but went beyond the demand for purely political equality (nonetheless demanding 'the vote for everyone') and wanted to 'organise the social environment in order to permit the free development of individuality'. A pacifist who wished for a united Europe, he was the social thinker who exerted the greatest influence on the Romantic writers of his time, above all George Sand, but also Victor Hugo and indirectly even Baudelaire.

Christian socialism (a 'splinter group' at the time) associated the evangelical idea of brotherhood with the idea of social justice. One of its spokesmen was Philippe Buchez, a former Carbonaro and former Saint-Simonian whose thinking revolved about the idea of progress. Denouncing the 'abuse of the notion of property and that of the notion of liberty', he wished to place 'the instruments of work into the hands of associations' and inspired the founding of *L'Atelier*, one of the first workers' newspapers that began to appear in 1840. Buchez stood for a democratic socialism resting on an idea of *autogestion* [management by labour] and 'worker emancipation'.

Cabet, Blanqui

Before 1848, the difference between communism and socialism was not so much a matter of ideology as of the ways in which ideas were propagated. Engels recalls in a (later) preface to the *Manifesto of the Communist Party* that in 1847 'those of the workers who, convinced of the inadequacy of ordinary political upheavals, called for a fundamental transformation of society referred to themselves as communists' and then proceeds to cite, in particular, the doctrine of Cabet. Starting out as a radical democrat, Cabet was put on trial for violating the press laws, whereupon he went into exile to London. There he converted to communist ideas, which he exposed in his *Voyage en Icarie*. This book, written in the form of a didactic novel, was published in 1842 after his return to France. It describes an ideal communist society founded on the pursuit of happiness in communal life; his system attaches greater importance to fraternity and equality than to liberty; indeed, individual liberty is practically discarded in the interest of the common good. Cabet was in step with the industrial era when he placed his trust in new technological inventions (the Icarian worker is above all a machine-operator). The State, a centralised, democratic State (with universal suffrage) is the sole property owner, assigns work to every individual, distributes the consumer goods and, through education, forms a public spirit conforming to the community.

While borrowing the peaceful character of its propaganda from the Gospel (Cabet speaks of Christ as a proletarian), Cabet's doctrine with its emphasis on equality was appealing to the as yet unfocused aspirations of the workers. Pierre Leroux spoke of the 'fascination [Cabet] produced within the working class by holding out the promise of material happiness to the most disinherited classes of the big cities'. Aided by the failure of Blanquism in 1839, and also by the simplicity of his system (once the initial principle is accepted), Cabet did not appeal to revolutionary passions. His ideas, in conjunction with those of Fourierism (whatever the contradictions that separated them), contributed to the non-violent character of the February revolution. Martin Nadaud in his *Mémoires de Léonard* reports that the lectures in which Cabet explained his egalitarian ideas were frequented by the 'elite of the Parisian workers, men who were deeply attached to the Republic and devoted to the study of social problems'.

Cabet never ceased to participate in the radical opposition; in his *Histoire populaire de la Révolution française de 1789 à 1830* (the chronological span is significant), he expressed his admiration for Robespierre and the Constitution of 1793, which he incorporated into his system.

The tradition of the Revolution was also claimed by the heirs of the

Babouvists; however, this group postulated that social change would have to be achieved by the violent conquest of power. Its principal leader was Auguste Blanqui. The son of a member of the Convention and a participant in the revolution of 1830 and the uprisings of 1839, he spent most of the July Monarchy in prison. Even at that early date he joined together the ideas of revolution, republic, and socialism and developed the notions of dictatorship of the proletariat and class struggle.

The recourse to violence and secret societies (like Théodore Dezami's group with 200 members at most) had little appeal for socialist opinion, which preferred a humanitarian and utilitarian approach.

This diversity of socialist doctrines, and indeed the contradictions among them, can be accounted for by the fact that they were ideologies and not a movement, certainly not a popular movement. Their ideas, whether humanitarian or utilitarian, could only become accessible to the workers (and a tiny minority in any case) through the mediation of petty bourgeois and intellectuals, most of whom were *déclassés*.

The birth of the workers' movement

The slow awakening of the working classes was not, in its early stages, the direct result of economic progress. The workers of the nascent industries had not yet become conscious of the force they represented by virtue of their members and their collective work. Frequently of rural origin, they found themselves suddenly transplanted into the big city, where they were victimised not only by their employers but also by landlords, innkeepers, foremen, and by working and living conditions. All of these circumstances contributed to keeping them in a state of dependence, anxiety, and degradation from which they sometimes tried to break out by individual acts of delinquency and, on rare occasions, by violent, disorganised, and ephemeral collective movements. By contrast, the older trades (typesetting or carpentry) were much better organised. Journeymen's associations, a surviving form of organisation, still existed in some of the trades least affected by the industrial revolution; although tolerated by the public authorities, they were in decline. Moreover, rivalries between the different trades tended to obscure the antagonism between social classes.

Mutual aid societies (especially prevalent in Lyon, Bordeaux, Lille, and Paris) were often scarcely camouflaged forms of journeymen's associations. The societies governed themselves, elected their delegates, and collected dues that enabled them to help their members in case of illness or disability, but they were often poorly managed. These associations were primarily developed by artisans and miners. The typesetters were also among the first to organise. In some cases the mutual aid societies were imbued with religious traditions. Some of them, however, presented the more modern features of defensive societies of resistance and amounted to early forms of labour unions, which at that time were outlawed in France by the Code. Among such organisations were the gilders' and the copper-smelters' and -moulders' union in Paris, the associations of braidmakers in Saint-Etienne, of silkworkers in Lyon, and of typesetters in Nantes, as well as the typographers' society in Paris. These societies were viewed with suspicion by the authorities, especially by the municipal governments which often held them responsible for the outbreak of strikes. Studies of strikes under the July Monarchy have shown, however, that strikes almost always erupted spontaneously (a fact that often contributed to their failure) and that they were usually provoked by the introduction of machinery, by reductions in wages (which often took the form of a lengthening of the work day or more elaborate specifications for piece-work), or by some other immediate cause of discontent. But when workers or artisans were imprisoned, they came in contact with republican and communist agitators; and in this manner the revolutionary tradition that was still alive in large segments of the Parisian population received new impetus. The workers' movement had a slow start in France. Held back by the country's individualist legislation, it was stimulated not so much by economic causes (for the transformations of industry were neither sudden nor all-pervasive) as by a modification of the workers' mentality brought about by the concerted efforts of artisans and elements coming from the bourgeoisie, certain physicians, for example. This change in mentality was to a large extent caused by the refusal of the ruling group to recognise any limits to the liberty of the employer class.

Intellectual and artistic life

Brought into being by a bourgeoisie intent upon power and profit, the developing industrial society had little use for art and literary creation or misused them by exploiting them to extol hard work and individual initiative. As a result, the artist and the bourgeois became increasingly hostile to each other during the July Monarchy, and even though some artists like Hugo or Musset were integrated into the highest ranks of society, many others were reduced to straitened circumstances or outright poverty.

Liberalism, the ideology of the dominant bourgeoisie, was based on rationalism and the advancement of the individual.

Education

The implementation of the Guizot law was carried out slowly and with varying results from region to region. It is true that the number of pupils in primary school doubled during the July Monarchy, but a gulf was opening within the field of education. Economic transformations changed the nature of work and accelerated a decline in the quality of apprenticeship. A gradual proletarianisation of work took place in the more modern industrial sectors such as the textile industry, metallurgy and mining, where the highly skilled work of an engineer or manager became increasingly separate from the manual labour of the proletariat.

Secondary education and the *grandes écoles* recruited their students among the bourgeoisie and the aristocracy and became the only sources of the expertise that kept access to political and social power within the same ruling groups. Since sending a son to a *collège* (usually a boarding school) was costly for a family, growth in the number of students was limited. At the end of the July Monarchy, it was about 100,000, including seminarians. Scholarships were rare (of the order of 3,000) and granted mainly to sons of civil servants.

Despite the centralisation of the University system, the instruction given was by no means the same in all parts of France; most of the 3,500 students who passed the competitive Bachelor's examination every year came from the royal *collèges* of Paris or the major provincial towns and from a few Parisian institutions catering for the sons of the bourgeoisie. In 1840 fewer than one-third of the students at the Collège Stanislas were born in Paris. In 1840 at the Ecole Polytechnique, 147 of the 210 students who passed the examination had studied in Paris, although only 100 of them came from families living in the department of Seine.

A closed world, the University and particularly the secondary schools lived by the cult of classical antiquity and ancient literature. Literary studies, which were the mainstay of this education, systematically ignored almost everything written after the seventeenth century. The debate carried on in public opinion and in the parliament between the supporters of the University and the partisans of an ecclesiastical school system had nothing whatever to do with a renewed conflict between ancients and moderns; on both sides it was a matter of defending a tradition. Yet it is true that the University system sought to reconcile the values of Greco-Roman antiquity with those of the Judaeo-Christian tradition by adopting an eclectic approach combining the teaching of philosophy and religion, considered to be the two sources of ethics.

Few in numbers and imprisoned in a rigid discipline, the professors – whose devotion and erudition no one would deny – did not teach the young people whom they educated to think. Rather, they were rhetoricians and sophists charged with the transmission of a cultural heritage better suited to a ruling class living on its incomes than to the needs of a society undergoing a major mutation.

The academies

The academies, which counted Catholics and liberals among their members, contributed greatly to the official ideology and to the style of a regime that was at once pompous and bourgeois. Ever since the re-constitution of the *Académie des sciences morales et politiques* in 1832, the *Institut royal* consisted of five academies placed under the patronage of the king and administered under the authority of the Minister of Public Education. Owing in part to their recruitment by co-option and the longevity of several of their members, these academies usually espoused traditional ideas and traditional tastes; the academicians, whether they were writers, artists, or scholars, had become notables, but their reputation was more a matter of social or political notability than of artistic creativity. In 1840 the *Académie française* included eight Peers of France, seven depu-ties, three former deputies and four former Peers of France of the Restora-tion (among them the vicomte de Bonald). Since every regime had sent some of its supporters to the *Académie*, the most contradictory literary and political opinions, albeit softened with the passing of time, could be found there existing side by side. In addition to old republicans like Nepomucène, Lemercier, or Tissot (who had served as deputy during the Directory and compromised himself in the Babouvist movement), the *Académie française* included almost a dozen prominent partisans of the Restoration (among them Frayssinous and Chateaubriand), and the July Monarchy witnessed the election of its outstanding prime ministers (Thiers, Guizot, Molé). Particularly favourable to journalists (De Jouy, and later Saint-Marc Girardin) and political writers (Royer-Collard, Alexis de Tocqueville), the *Académie française* eventually, though not without misgivings, opened its doors to Victor Hugo, Sainte-Beuve, and Alfred de Vigny. A much warmer welcome had been extended to Scribe.

The *Académie des sciences*, by contrast, brought together most of the great French scholars of the time; it also exhibited a much more critical attitude toward the regime, and its two perpetual secretaries, Flourens and Arago, were radicals who headed a whole group of progressive-minded scientists that was accused by the *Revue des deux mondes* of regimenting the world of learning. The *Académie des sciences morales et politiques* was the most politicised (9 Peers, 6 deputies, and 3 former deputies in 1840, out of a total of 30 members), the most official (21 high civil servants) and the wealthiest of the academies.

The theatre

The theatre also reflected the official culture. The classic tragedies still enjoyed the public's favour, whereas the Romantic drama gave rise to differences of opinion and outright conflict (*Hernani, Les Burgraves*) and only appealed to a small segment of the public. The bourgeoisie and the highest circles of Orleanist society enjoyed comedy, which was scorned by the Romantics. Eugène Scribe knew how to flatter the public and to keep its attention by his plays and opera librettos. *Robert le Diable, La Juive*, and *Les Huguenots* were among the most popular theatrical performances of the period. These spectacular productions were matched by the ballet performances that became popular at the time; Adam's *Gisèle* is the prototype of this kind of entertainment to this day. Special mention must be made of Alexandre Dumas; the same bourgeoisie that so passionately enjoyed his novels also ensured the success of the plays he drew from them, such as *La Tour de Nesle, Les Trois Mousquetaires*, or *Le Chevalier de maison rouge*. Sporadic flashes of enthusiasm for liberal causes did not prevent Dumas from giving the hero's role more often to the nobleman than to the bourgeois. In his flamboyance, exuberance, vanity, and truculence, Alexandre Dumas himself was a remarkable character.

A somewhat critical attitude toward the mentality of the businessman was well received by the public, and *Robert Macaire*, first played by the great actor Frédérick Lemaître, became a social type in which everyone recognised his neighbour rather than himself.

The press and public opinion

Intellectual and social conformism was both fostered and challenged by the press. The press experienced considerable growth during the July Monarchy, which in part owed its birth to the work of journalists. Despite the restrictions placed on the freedom of the press, the number of newspapers published increased not only in Paris (where there were some 20 dailies and close to 230 newspapers or periodicals in 1845) but also in the provinces (about 520 periodical papers were published in 1845, among them 245 political papers, often appearing two or three times a week). Almost every *chef-lieu d'arrondissement* had at least one newspaper carrying official announcements and advertisements.

The circulation of the Parisian dailies almost quadrupled between 1830 and the fall of Louis-Philippe; at least half of each edition was shipped to the provinces. This was also the beginning of the large-circulation newspaper. This trend was initiated by Emile de Girardin who in 1836 launched *La Presse*, a newspaper that could be sold at a much lower price because it was financed by advertisements (the subscription cost 40 rather than 80 francs). The same formula was used even more successfully by the dynastic left, whose paper *Le Siècle*, launched with backing from the banker Laffitte, had the highest circulation of all, close to 40,000 copies in 1847. Experiencing fluctuations and even difficult times, these newspapers, which continued to be printed by artisanal techniques, became major enterprises whose impact was felt by business and at the stock exchange. One former

Principal dispositions concerning the periodical press

Law	Regulations	Administrative procedures	Punishable offences	Enforcement
Law of 21 October 1814 (a temporary law whose provisions remained essentially intact until 1819, except during the Hundred Days)	Prior authorisation	Censorship for writings of fewer than 20 pages (with specific exceptions) until the law of 18 February 1817	All forms of attack against the established order and power, including the spreading of alarming news	Control by the police. Trial in criminal court. In certain cases, special courts (laws of 20 and 27 December 1815)
'De Serre' law of 17 and 26 May and 9 July 1819	Simple declaration; posting of bond required	No censorship	Offences not specific to the press: outrages against morality, decency, religion; insults to the king; libel, slander	Trial in assize court (jury)
Law of 31 March 1820 (provisional)	Prior authorisation	Censorship	Offences not specific to the press (as above)	Possibility of administrative suspension
Laws of 28 July 1821 and 25 March 1822	Prior authorisation	Censorship restored but reserved for 'serious cases'	Introduces concept of 'harmful opinions' which makes it possible to repress the 'outlook' of a paper	Possibility of administrative suspension. Trial in criminal court
Law of 18 July 1828	Declaration and bond	No censorship	Return to legislation of 1819	Trial in criminal court
Ordinance of 25 July 1830	Prior authorisation	Censorship	–	Administrative confiscation
Laws of 8 October and 10 December 1830	Declaration and bond	Abolition of censorship	Offences not specific to the press	Trial by jury

Principal dispositions concerning the periodical press (cont.)

Law	Regulations	Administrative procedures	Punishable offences	Enforcement
Law of 9 September 1835	Declaration and bond	Censorship of drawings	Insults to the king, attacks on his person in discussing acts of the government, incitement to change the regime, expression of republican sentiments, attacks upon property	Trial by jury and in some cases by the House of Peers

The principal Parisian periodicals (1815–48)

Archives philosophiques politiques et littéraires, 1817–18

L'Atelier, founded 1840
L'Avenir, 1830–1
Le Bon Sens, 1832–9
Le Censeur, later *Le Censeur européen*, 1814–20 (intermittently)
Le Charivari, founded 1832
Le Constitutionnel, founded 1815, sometimes disguised under other titles, for example *Le Journal du Commerce*, 1817–19
Le Courrier, 1819–20
Le Courrier français, founded 1820
La Démocratie pacifique, founded 1843
Le Drapeau blanc, 1819–27 and 1829–30

L'Etoile, 1820–7
La France, 1834–47
Le Globe, 1824–32
Le Journal des débats
Journal général de la France, 1814–19
Le National, founded 1830
La Patrie, founded 1841
La Presse, founded 1836
La Quotidienne, 1815–47
La Réforme, founded 1843
Le Siècle, founded 1836
La Tribune des départements, 1829–36
L'Union monarchique, founded in 1847
L'Univers, founded 1833

A more complete list with indications about the political tendencies of each journal can be found in C. Ledré, *La Presse à l'assaut de la monarchie* (Paris, 1960), pp. 251–9. For substantial notes about all the French journals see the classic work of E. Hatin, *Bibliographie historique et critique de la presse périodique française* (Paris, 1866).

Saint-Simonian, Charles Duveyrier, founded a *Société générale des annonces*, a clearing-house for all the advertising of the four major Parisian newspapers, *La Presse*, *Le Siècle*, the *Constitutionnel* and the *Journal des débats*. This last paper charged higher prices for advertisements because of its wealthier readership and also obtained considerable subsidies from the secret funds of the government. This was also the time when the first French information agency was founded by Charles Havas.

The political polemics carried on by these newspapers should not blind us to the homogeneity of almost the entire press with respect to content: news of the stock market was reported by the Péreire brothers, one writing for the *National* and the other for the *Journal des débats*; and the serial novels of Alexandre Dumas and Eugène Suë appeared in the *Constitutionnel* as well as in the *Journal des débats*. This was especially true with respect to social content, even though certain legitimist organs did broach the problem of pauperism as a way of criticising the Orleanist bourgeoisie. After 1842 *La Réforme* also began to feature editorials about social issues, but then the circulation of this publication was quite limited, amounting to no more than 1,810 copies.

The preoccupations of the press and the image it conveyed of its era reflected the aspirations and the interests (however divergent) of the bourgeoisie. Economic issues and questions of tariff were approached from the point of view of the manager and the producer, and discussions of education usually concerned secondary education. But above all it was politics that absorbed the attention of the press and made for its diversity. The widening of the representative regime had led to more frequent elections, and these furnished the principal subject-matter of the news and political commentary. Under these circumstances the newspapers, which by reporting the news and shaping public opinion contributed to the strengthening of social cohesion, were also in a position to undermine power and authority. In fact, some of the ruling politicians (Guizot, and Charles X before him) made the serious mistake of underestimating the power of the press. Not that the press determined the opinion of the notables, who influenced the newspapers more than they were influenced by them; but they certainly did shape the opinions of the petty bourgeoisie. And even though this group did not have the political right to vote, Guizot was wrong not to pay attention to the hostility with which he was viewed by the vast majority of the Parisian press.

Yet although the press was controlled – indeed usually owned – by notables, its development eventually undermined the social system based on the preponderance of these very notables. Little by little, their direct, personal authority was replaced, at least in Paris and in some of the major cities, by that elusive and complex collective power called public opinion; and while that power was as yet constituted only by a minority within the nation, it was in the hands of society's most dynamic element, the urban dwellers.

The July Monarchy witnessed the diversification of the press with the founding of a variety of revues, among which the *Revue des deux mondes* quickly took the lead, attaining a subscription rate of 2,000 in 1843. Women's magazines played an important role in publicising and renewing fashions, and specialised publications disseminated the latest developments in such fields as agriculture, medicine, and religion. Newspaper publishing remained an artisanal undertaking, but it was already a means of expression for an urban and industrialised society; and it was precisely for that reason that the Parisian papers, despite the development of a regional press, retained their dominant position.

Romanticism and its evolution

The very existence of Romanticism, its evolution and its contradictory aspects made for a contrast between the world of art and the bourgeoisie. It was as if the triumph of the bourgeoisie had given rise to an intellectual and aesthetic reaction against it. An abiding traditionalist attitude was equally opposed to rationalism and to the spirit of revolution. The royalism of the Restoration had spawned the first Romanticism; in a kind of reversal the legitimism of the July Monarchy was in turn influenced by Romanticism. Alfred de Vigny and of course Chateaubriand were still the most illustrious exponents of this right-wing Romanticism, but in spreading to the provinces its impact modified the behaviour of some of the legitimists by diverting their attention away from action. Finding their own sentiments expressed in literature, they were encouraged in their refusal to accept the present and in their (verbal) revolt against the established system. Having failed to be of effective help to the duchesse de Berry, the young legitimists turned the prisoner of Blaye into a literary theme. Anti-bourgeois in character – and it is above all in this sense that Balzac, whose thinking was often close to that of the legitimists, was a Romantic – Romanticism under the July Monarchy was conducive to a movement toward the left among those who had been disappointed by liberalism (which tended to go along with existing situations) and especially liberals-turned-conservative. In this new form Romanticism became less lyrical and individualist and more social and realistic; the *mal du siècle* gave way to a loss of confidence in society.

A new revolutionary Romanticism, the kind that was later described by Victor Hugo in *Les Misérables* and depicted by Delacroix in his painting *La Liberté guidant le peuple* appeared after 1830. Democratic, patriotic, and leaning toward socialism, it inspired Lamennais at the time of *Paroles d'un croyant* (1834) as well as Alphonse Esquiros's *Chant d'un prisonnier* and Jules Michelet's work.

Their refusal to accept the existing world made it tempting for young intellectuals to retreat to dreams and to reject a social situation in which they were reduced to an unproductive existence unless they submitted to the norms and values of the dominant society. This was the complaint of

Gérard de Nerval: 'The frantic chase after positions and honours that took place at that time kept us away from the spheres where we might have worked.' It was also the attitude of Théophile Gauthier in the early stages of his career when he wrote *Jeune France* (1930) and *Mademoiselle de Maupin*, where one can read: 'Nothing matters to anything.'

Dreaming sometimes led to utopianism, which is another way of rejecting the present. We have seen certain aspects of utopianism when we examined the socialist thought of the period, but there were others. Utopian thinking is, after all, both the literary transformation of reality and an individual need or conversion; it is the suspension of history when its evolution offers no hope for change. In this sense it is subversive.

Intellectual subversion was practised by no more than a tiny minority living or formed in Paris. A bohemian lifestyle was one aspect of intellectual subversion; it has been described by Henri Murger for a somewhat later period (1851). Certain of the adherents to this lifestyle planted the first signposts along the road that was to lead, much later, to surrealism. Among them were Petrus Borel, author of *Champavert, contes immoraux* (1833) and Aloysius Bertrand, a precursor of the so-called 'littérature sauvage'.

A whole literature of protest and critical analysis came into being at that time; this was a different matter from the 'social conscience' of certain English authors of approximately the same period. Both Balzac and Stendhal gave expression to a critical attitude toward the bourgeoisie, the former in psychological and the latter in sociological terms. At a lower level, Louis Reybaud, a rather more sceptical author who was nonetheless much appreciated by his contemporaries inaugurated a self-critical attitude to which the bourgeoisie did not object in his *Jérôme Paturot à la recherche d'une position sociale* (1832). Literature thus became an outlet for ideas that the official society refused to put into practice.

Romanticism and feminism blossomed into a humanitarian ideal in the bucolic and at the same time socialist-inspired novels of George Sand and in the revolutionary evangelism of Flora Tristan. The emancipation of women and the rehabilitation of sensual pleasure, demands that had been voiced by the Saint-Simonian and Fourierist theoreticians, were taken up once again by the second generation of Romantics. In this as in other areas, the Romantic movement broke with the conformism of bourgeois morality, which refused to deal with these problems at the very time when the number of *demi-mondaines* and kept mistresses was steadily increasing. Romanticism thus established itself as the anti-value to the bourgeoisie of the July Monarchy. 'Romanticism', wrote Baudelaire in 1846, 'means modern art; it means intimacy, spirituality, colour, and yearning for the infinite.'

9

The crisis at the end of the regime

The July regime collapsed within a few hours in February 1848 with a speed that surprised contemporaries. Yet even before February it had become obvious to a growing number of observers that the situation could not continue. At the end of November 1847, the socialist Considérant, councillor-general of the department of Seine and by no means a revolutionary, had declared at a banquet at Montargis: 'We need a reform to ward off the storms of the future.' And everyone remembers the prophetic words spoken by Tocqueville before the Chamber on 27 January 1848: 'There is abroad in the country the kind of premonition that sometimes heralds revolution and sometimes produces it.'

Not that the regime was threatened by any specific dangers. It was much more the refusal of the controlling groups to participate than revolutionary pressure that precipitated the demise of the July Monarchy, which had withstood much stronger jolts than that of February 1848. At the deepest level, France was in the throes of a triple crisis – a crisis of consciousness, an economic crisis, and a structural crisis of a society and an economy painfully struggling to make the transition to an industrial society – but on the surface these factors were compounded by a number of developments of a different order. Among them were the breakdown of the alliance with England, which led the regime to make common cause with the counter-revolutionary powers, a step that was interpreted by a large part of French public opinion as a repudiation of its origins; an aging sovereign and an over-self-confident prime minister; bad harvests; and scandals that compromised some of the regime's dignitaries. It was this conjunction of underlying causes and surface events that sparked the revolutionary outbreak of February 1848.

The economic and financial crisis

France's prosperity was not as complete as the conservative press claimed it was in mid-1846; conversely, the situation was not everywhere as dismal at the end of 1846 and in 1847 as it was depicted by many newspapers.

There were pockets – sometimes encompassing entire regions – that were not affected by either the depression or the prosperity because the market was not yet functioning on a national scale. Since France in 1846 was still chiefly a rural country, the economy was still subject to the vagaries of the weather; but, while it is true that the crisis originated in the agricultural sector, the resulting difficulties in the other economic sectors subsequently developed their own momentum.

The bad harvests of 1846

Caused either by a drought during the summer or on the contrary by heavy July rains in Normandy, bad harvests created a situation that was all the more serious as certain regions had already experienced a bad cereal harvest in 1845. The agricultural crisis had a number of different aspects; most critical was the shortage of cereals, for bread was still the mainstay of the popular diet. Poor harvests prompted a disproportionate rise in the price of grain, since speculation and hoarding in anticipation of further shortages slanted the market. In the region of Caen the price of a hecto-litre of wheat rose from 22 francs in May 1846 to 46 francs in May 1847. Rye, the poor man's cereal, rose in Sarthe from 14.9 francs per hectolitre in July 1846 to 42 francs in the spring of 1847. In their starkness these figures reveal the distress the corresponding rise in the price of bread must have caused; they also tell us something about regional and even local disparities. Yet in certain departments the harvest, mediocre though it was, was not bad enough to threaten the people's food supply; it was specula-tion and the sale of grain to other departments that inflated prices and provoked the anger of the local inhabitants. This is what happened in the Mayenne region, where on the road between Laval and Sablé people had seen on a single day of January 1847 no fewer than 92 wagons carrying wheat out of the region. Awareness of the crisis (at a time when informa-tion was very unevenly disseminated) contributed to its spreading.

The potato, another substitute staple, had already been in short supply after the harvest of 1845, nor did the potato harvest improve until after 1848. There was also a crisis in livestock breeding brought about by a fall in prices. The meagre harvests in forage crops (especially in Normandy and Burgundy) forced the stock-farmers to sell their animals; moreover, the increase in cattle herds brought about by the planting of new artificial meadows had led to overproduction and to competition between these new cattle-raising areas (in Poitou and Maine) that began to fatten their young calves for the market, and the traditional beef-cattle areas like the pays d'Auge. However this was a time of crisis when meat consumption declined.

The agricultural crisis obliged the government and the local authorities to intervene, for agrarian disturbances could not be resolved by repressive measures alone. Initially the authorities and the press had tried to minimise the crisis; thus the *Moniteur industriel* stated in an editorial on 4 October 1846: 'It is not lack of grain that troubles us today or will trouble us tomorrow, the trouble is fear.' Yet rising bread prices in conjunction with the threat of widespread unemployment owing to the business recession soon became a matter of some concern in the towns; this was the case at Rouen, Nantes, and Troyes, where on 16 December the prefect of Aube called for the re-establishment of the National Guard: 'In a populous town where because of high grain prices close to 20,000 workers may fall upon very hard times this winter, it is possible that the government may need the help of the National Guard to maintain order.'

Disturbances related to food shortages took various forms. Most frequently they consisted of gatherings of people in rural areas for the purpose of blocking the circulation of grain; brokers were prevented from carrying off the grain they had bought in the market-place, their wagons were unloaded, and in these cases looting frequently ensued. These incidents were especially frequent in western France, in the Loire country, and in Indre. But markets were also disrupted in regions where the crisis was not so severe; such scenes occurred at Castelsarrasin and Moissac throughout the month of February 1847. At Sainte-Foy in Gironde, masked men threatened to kill rich landowners if they sent their grain to market.

Another form of disturbance was the forcing of sales by means of intimidation, which was frequently seen in western France; in Seine-Inférieure the local authorities did not wish to intervene, although they sometimes distributed grain at a lower price. In some towns the municipal governments regulated the price of bread by subsidising the bakers. In some cases, finally, the incidents turned into rioting, especially in the towns. Bakeries were looted in Nord, at Lille (12 May 1847) and in the faubourg Saint-Antoine in Paris. On 31 July at Lisieux, the town that had elected Guizot, a group of unemployed textile workers looted the house of a baker and drove back the National Guard. In Haut-Rhin disorders occurred at Mulhouse, Sainte-Marie-aux-Mines, and Thann. The most serious peasant riot took place at Buzançais, where a wealthy landowner was murdered by the peasants. Newspaper reports about agrarian disturbances fuelled a constantly growing fear of disorder. Bands of beggars roamed the countryside, especially in areas known for their wealth; at night they would gather at the local farms. These bands were not made up only of the traditional vagabonds, they also included unemployed workers and unoccupied day-labourers. A 'Great Fear' swept the countryside even before the February revolution. The repression was severe. Three of the rioters of Buzançais were condemned to death and several others were sent to penal colonies; 17 rioters of Lisieux were sentenced to prison terms of between two and seven years. Troops were dispatched from Tours to Mayenne, from Paris and Tours to Le Mans, Angers, and Châtellerault.

Some of the notables endeavoured to bring in supplies of grain. At Lille the Provident Society (*Société de Prévoyance*) established in March 1847 by the refiner Kolb Bernard and the spinning mill owner Scrive distributed relief in collaboration with the municipal welfare agency, and the charitable efforts made at Lille attracted bands of Belgian beggars who were fleeing the dismal conditions in Flanders. At Grenoble – an area that was, to be sure, much less affected by the crisis – mutual aid societies were able to import grain from Marseille. At Toulouse, Montauban, and Bordeaux, bread coupons were distributed to the destitute.

The harvest of 1847 was satisfactory, but this fact did not relieve the crisis situation that had spread to other sectors of the economy. In fact, even in agriculture improved supplies had a negative impact on all those who out of fear or as a speculative measure had held back too much grain, so that business failures, especially among the wholesale merchants of Marseille, further aggravated the situation.

Impact of the crisis on industrial activity

Inevitably, the crisis had an effect on industry; the population was so impoverished that it had to spend most of its resources on increasingly expensive foodstuffs. Textiles, the most widely distributed branch of industry, were affected most severely by the slump in sales at a time when the cost of raw materials (wool and especially cotton) remained high.

In addition, however, the transformations we discussed in the preceding chapter had already created problems for the industries of several departments even before the onset of the agricultural crisis. In the region of Toulouse a difficult situation existed before the agricultural crisis, and business failures had become increasingly frequent in 1844 and 1845. The textile mills of Castres and Mazamet had cut back their work force and their wages as early as 1845. The building industry had been in a recession since 1844 and unemployment among its workers increased in 1846 and 1847. In the region of Lille the precarious balance created by the industry's effort at modernisation was shattered as soon as the agricultural crisis reduced the sales of textiles; at Roubaix the number of unemployed workers reached 4,800 in February 1847 and 8,000 in May, out of a work force of 13,000.

In Calvados the number of business failures among the manufacturers doubled between 1846 (already a bad year) and 1847, putting large numbers of workers out of work. Factories closed down everywhere, and those that continued to operate cut back their work force and their wages. In November of 1847, the prefect of Rouen estimated that these wage reductions amounted to about 30 per cent; at that date some 1,600 unemployed workers were still working in the town's charitable workshop, despite a slight improvement of the economic situation. By 1847, depending on the conditions in the local economy, the crisis either continued or abated with the decline in food prices. In other sectors (metallurgy and railway construction) industrial activity was paralysed by the crisis of the stock market and by speculation.

The financial crisis

The financial (and especially monetary) crisis was more complex. The poor harvests of 1846 had necessitated grain imports and, as a result, created an outflow of gold, especially to Russia. But there was one additional factor that made the crisis beginning in 1846 more than an ordinary depression in the business cycle, namely, the fact that in 1845 the new railway craze had flooded the stock market with shares sold on margin. Then, as early as June–July 1846, certain railway shares began to decline in value, and investors lost confidence even before the agricultural crisis compounded the situation by limiting the amount of funds available to cover stock issues. By the end of 1846, the effects of the different crises (in agriculture, industry, and finance) became cumulative and led to a further deterioration of the commercial and monetary situation. The Banque de France began to be alarmed at the depletion of its gold reserves (65 million francs were withdrawn in the month of October alone). The decision on 24 January 1847 to raise the discount rate to 5 per cent was both a clear sign of the crisis situation and an attempt to deal with it.

In several regions the economic conditions further deteriorated when banking houses whose apprehensive or impoverished clients came to withdraw their deposits were forced to suspend payments or declare bankruptcy because they lacked sufficient funds to make these disbursements. Such bankruptcies occurred at Lisieux, Montpellier, and Le Havre.

The financial difficulties of the railway companies either led to bankruptcy and the total cessation of construction (in the case of the Bordeaux–Sète and the Lyon–Avignon lines) or to a reduction in the scope of this work (as in the case of the Strasbourg company). By the end of 1847, altogether 700,000 workers in railway construction or the metallurgical enterprises that were indirectly affected by the same crisis were laid off. By contrast, coal mining, the sector in which industrial capital had most recently been concentrated, continued to expand.

The crisis of 1847 had the aspect of a crisis of capitalism itself, for it reached beyond national frontiers and was exacerbated under the impact of the acute crisis experienced by England (which had purchased large quantities of French railway stock) and Belgium. The apparent recovery at the end of 1847 only superficially covered up the dangers that lay ahead. The full scope of these difficulties was revealed by the February revolution which brought so many economic disasters in its wake that it was blamed for everything that went wrong.

The social effects of the crisis

The distress of agriculture and the working class gave rise to unrest that in turn exacerbated the crisis; and the social agitation of which we spoke earlier led to an increase in delinquency that greatly alarmed the population. In mountainous areas, the agitation was directed against the forestry administration.

The crisis severely affected the life of the local populations, and its demographic consequences are evident. Mortality rates increased throughout France, reaching a level of 239 deaths per 10,000 inhabitants (compared to 220 in 1844), while birth rates were in decline. However, marked regional differences continued to exist. In 1847 at Strasbourg, the number of deaths exceeded that of births, and this was also the case at Lille, where 29,000 of the town's 76,000 inhabitants were on welfare. The same ratio of births/deaths also obtained in Basses-Alpes, Haute-Garonne, and Tarn-et-Garonne.

The crisis also spawned social unrest. In several towns (Tourcoing, Lisieux, Mulhouse, and others) workers and unemployed labourers held the employers responsible. Strikes broke out with increasing frequency in 1847, especially in the building and the textile industries. Amiens experienced strikes in May, Roanne in July; and in Haut-Rhin, at Lillebonne, Darnétal and in Seine-Inférieure, at Elbeuf, strikes occurred in October.

Another symptom was the fact that in 1847 the savings banks, for the first time since their creation, registered more withdrawals than deposits. The tax yield (especially from indirect taxes) diminished and the public treasury's deficit increased; the deficit of 258 million francs was the highest since 1815.

Yet the State had been obliged to grant subsidies to local welfare agencies or municipalities. Those municipalities that had opened charitable workshops or become involved in grain purchases were in serious financial difficulties; yet their efforts often failed to appease popular discontent. At Montauban, for example, the inmates of the beggars' workshop revolted against their supervisor on 1 February 1847.

To all of this must be added the psychological tension spawned by insecurity. Fear of social upheaval was rampant among property owners large and small (for strong feelings about property are not tied to the extent of property owned) and rekindled at the slightest sign of disturbance. That same fear also silenced disagreements that had hitherto seemed fundamental.

Business, finally, was paralysed for a long time by a pervasive lack of confidence that retarded its recovery despite the good harvests of 1847.

Contemporary views of the crisis

The crisis appeared to be over by the end of 1847. The return of the discount rate to 4 per cent decided upon by the board of the Banque de France on 27 December seemed to be the official confirmation of its end.

Once the storm had abated, it was time to explain what had happened. The moral and political crisis that will be analysed presently certainly played a part in the assessment made by public opinion; responsibility for the economic crisis was bound to be attributed to the government which, by taking credit for the earlier prosperity, had opened the way to the view that individuals could be responsible for economic developments.

Business leaders also discerned other causes compounding the bad harvests. Stating that the severity and the persistence of the crisis were to a considerable extent due to a shortage of credit, the newspaper *La Presse* declared on 25 July 1847: 'Our financial system compares to economic science as the housewife's spinning wheel compares to the machines of a spinning mill or as delivery by messenger compares to the transportation of goods by railway.' Investments in railways and appeals for funds by the railway companies were incriminated. The large number of stockholders, even small ones, was said to have made the stock market too sensitive, since every sign of decline in the market revived old memories of the Law system or the *assignats*.

The crisis made the task of the governing circles very difficult and also complicated all social relations, for those who had a grievance (the ruined stockholders or the bankrupt merchant, the starving peasant or the unemployed worker, the arrested vagabond or the impoverished bourgeois) needed somebody to hold responsible for their misfortune. As the case might be, this could be the grain hoarder or the administrator of the railway company, the mayor, the municipal guard, the head of a manufacturing company, the banker who had refused to grant an extension for a loan, the notary who had taken advantage of the situation to buy a piece of land cheaply, and above all the king and his ministers under whose government these trials were suffered. Public opinion became more critical when the ruling classes seemed to offer more grounds for criticism.

The moral and ideological crisis of the ruling groups

Breakdown of authority and fear of social upheaval

Faced with economic difficulties and social unrest, the notables of several regions had already exposed their fear of social upheaval, an attitude that considerably impaired their prestige. In January 1847 the prefect of Loir-et-Cher indicated that near the department of Indre 'the wealthy inhabitants of the countryside are leaving their residences and taking refuge in town'.

More than ever, the business world of trade and finance was suspected of wrongdoing; indignation about *agiotage* and speculation was especially rampant among the *petite bourgeoisie* of shopkeepers and small stockholders. The administrators of the railway companies were attacked by several newspapers; in the *Mystères de la Bourse* of 14 January 1847 for example, they were characterised as 'totally unqualified men whose only merit in the eyes of the uneducated public consists of having made scandalous amounts of money'. Municipal governments complained of insufficient help from the central government. In the large towns the National Guard was loath to become involved in repressing unrest, and the lower and even the middle bourgeoisie no longer trusted a government that did nothing to stop ruin and disorder. Yet many notables were deeply concerned about the widespread misery precipitated by the crisis. As we have seen, some mayors or notables paid out of their own pockets for the importation of wheat for the population of their town or village. Others were willing to wait for their rents. But aside from the fact that they were insufficient, these measures were sometimes misunderstood; it is obvious that the social distrust that became so all-encompassing after the February revolution was already a factor in the agricultural crisis and in the agrarian and working-class agitation of late 1846 and 1847. As baron de Barante stated in a letter of 27 February 1847: 'The lower classes have become rather impatient. A ferment of communism has been added to their apprehension or their discontent.' It is interesting to note that he expressed this concern even before a large number of scandals came to light in 1847.

The moral deficiencies of the ruling groups

To some extent, these deficiencies reflected the upheaval in the traditional hierarchy of values precipitated by the industrial revolution and by the uncontrolled and unequal growth in wealth, especially since these developments were compounded by the disorders following in the wake of the economic crisis. But first and foremost, the charges were of a political nature. Corrupt election procedures, which were both practiced and denounced at the time of the 1846 elections, discredited the representative regime. Yet corruption in this area was less flagrant than in England and the United States. A series of scandals made headlines in 1846 and 1847. But corruption was not limited to the ruling groups, for the Ministry of Justice in its annual reports established a connection between a rise in offences and crimes and the financial and economic crisis; 6,685 criminal cases had been tried in assize courts in 1845, and by 1847 this number had risen to 8,104.

Two cases were principally responsible for spreading the impression that the ruling groups were immoral. In the course of criminal proceedings against a mining company in which General Cubières, a Peer of France and former cabinet minister, held interests, the general was accused of having bought the cooperation of Teste, another Peer of France who at the time served as Minister of Public Works. In July 1847 Teste, who attempted to commit suicide, was condemned to three years in prison by the Court of Peers; in addition both he and Cubières were sentenced to loss of civil rights and high fines. Shortly thereafter, on 18 August, it became known that another Peer of France, the duc de Choiseul-Praslin (who eventually committed suicide in prison) had murdered his wife, a daughter of Marshal Sébastiani. Other cases also struck public opinion; at Toulon a suspicious fire broke out just in time to obliterate traces of mismanagement. In the budget for Algeria, the Chamber discovered more and more irregularities. A Peer of France, comte Bresson, who served as ambassador to Naples committed suicide on 2 November 1847, another attempted to kill his children in a fit of madness. News stories involving sex and money in France's great families were treated in epic detail in the *Gazette des tribunaux*; the public avidly followed the case of the widow of the prominent ironmaster Aubertot de Coulanges who demanded that the will of her daughter leaving her fortune to her husband, the legitimist deputy Combarel de Leyval, be declared invalid for reason of insanity. There were other acts which, though not punishable under the law, contributed to the discredit of high society; nepotism for example was rampant in public office and in the magistracy. The image of the ruling classes presented in certain of Balzac's novels such as *Splendeur et misère des courtisanes* or *Le Cousin Pons* (1847) and in the serial novels of Eugène Suë or Alexandre Dumas, all of which were denounced as immoral by the contemporaries, was overdrawn, to be sure; yet certain of its traits did not contradict what could be observed every day.

These weaknesses severely impaired the notables' prestige, especially in the eyes of the newspaper-reading *petite bourgeoisie*. But they also gave rise to concern within the ruling groups themselves. The fact that these men began to doubt the legitimacy of their power amounted to a first indication of their abdication.

Guizot himself wrote to Mme Laure de Gasparin on 18 September 1847: '... no one judges the moral state of our time more severely than I do, and no one is more convinced than I am that our affliction goes deep'. In addition to this crisis of behaviour, however, there was also a crisis of mentality.

The decline of the liberal ideology

Liberalism emerged doubly impaired, both incomplete and inadequate, from the crisis that weighed on France at the end of the July Monarchy. It was incomplete in the sense that liberty did not exist in all areas. In economics, the most specific area of liberalism, demands for free trade had grown more urgent during the crisis, which had made it necessary to open the markets (temporarily) to foreign grain. It was also in economics that the programme of liberalism was most inadequate. The economic crisis had revealed the need for State intervention in economic life. The free interplay of individual initiatives no longer seemed sufficient to ensure prosperity. Ideas of State intervention were gaining ground, both among those who wished to use the existing structures (and this was the attitude adopted by high-ranking officials such as baron Charles Dupin and by economists like Dupont-White) and among those who were questioning both the social system and the political regime. Louis Blanc or the Fourierists promoted the notions of organisation of work and the 'right to work' among some segments of public opinion.

Liberalism also proved inadequate in politics; in fact, it was one of the weaknesses of the dynastic opposition that its programme was essentially negative and only called for the overthrow of the government.

The bourgeois youth, students in *collèges* and law schools, turned their backs on the official liberalism, which they saw only as the appropriation of the hard-won liberties by a small, wealthy minority. They were moved to enthusiasm by Michelet and by Lamartine's *Histoire des Girondins* and carried the apology of liberty to its extreme conclusions: liberty for all, equality.

The political crisis

Every revolution is political, but every economic crisis does not spawn a revolution. Social discontent can be channelled into political action only if it is politicised, if, starting out as an attack on those who hold power (the king, the ministers), it reaches the existing institutions through them.

Decline of respect for the monarchy

The king's and his sons' meddling in political and especially diplomatic matters resulted in a very marked decline in the prestige of the dynasty. Despite the widespread anglophobia of French public opinion, many people felt that breaking the Entente Cordiale in order to marry one of the king's sons, the duc de Montesquieu, to a Spanish infanta was more beneficial to the dynasty than it was to the nation. Despite the September laws, criticism of the king, his deviousness and his (real or imagined) avarice appeared more and more frequently in legitimist or radical newspapers. It is true that certain legitimists had rallied to the Guizot government to further their own careers, but this did not mean that their attitude toward Louis-Philippe had fundamentally changed. On the other hand, the favours they received to reward them for their defection was demoralising to the oldest supporters of the July regime.

Nonetheless it did not occur to the voting minority to question the monarchical form of the State. Indeed, it was in order to ensure its continuity that the dynastic opposition embarked upon its banquet campaign.

The banquet campaign

This campaign started out as the result of a parliamentary stalemate. The government forces' success in the elections of 1846 had crushed all hopes of breaking the government's majority without enlarging the electorate; and indeed the new Chamber of Deputies, in its vote of 26 March 1847, rejected the bill for electoral reform introduced by Duvergier de Hauranne (by a margin of 252 to 154), also rejecting (219 to 170) the bill for parliamentary reform introduced by Rémusat in April of the same year. The first bill, which proposed to reduce the tax qualification for voting to 100 francs and to make the right to vote contingent on certain 'capacities' would have given the vote to two categories supposedly favourable to the dynastic opposition; the second, which multiplied the incompatibilities between government service and membership in the Chambers, was directly aimed at a certain number of deputies of the majority. In effect, it asked a majority to vote for its own demise.

It was as a means of involving public opinion in this matter of parliamentary reform in hopes that it would exert pressure on the government that the dynastic opposition initiated a campaign of banquets punctuated by toasts and calls for reform. This appeal to the country, beyond the Chamber, whose representative character was thereby contested, challenged the validity of the entire political structure and did not have the support of all the members of the opposition; neither Thiers, nor Dufaure, nor Rémusat wanted to become involved in it.

The campaign began with the banquet held at the Château-Rouge in Paris, which was attended by 1,200 persons on 9 July 1847; other banquets were held in the provinces. The themes developed in the toasts concerned the electoral reform but also a reform of political morality in general. Glasses were raised to 'political integrity' and to 'the end of corruption'. The social problems spawned by the recent economic crisis were often evoked: 'to the abolition of poverty through work' (at Valenciennes), 'to the improvement of the lot of the working classes', 'to the working class'. Among other themes sounded were national independence and the problems of foreign policy.

These banquets were usually presided over by a notable, a deputy or former deputy, or a councillor-general. At Arras, a retired colonel presided; at Rouen, it was the barrister Sénard; at Strasbourg, the president of the barristers' association, Liechtenberger, who was also a member of the town council; and at Saint-Quentin, the mayor. The first banquets had nothing revolutionary about them; a (mandatory) toast 'to the king of the French' was always the first to be proposed. But gradually the movement became radicalised, especially after the banquet of Lille, where Ledru-Rollin, having ousted Odilon Barrot, called for universal suffrage on 7 November. Speaking at Chalon-sur-Saône on 19 December, the radical deputy raised a toast 'to the unity of the French Revolution, to the indivisibility of the Constituent Assembly, the Legislative Assembly, and the Convention'. The banquets of Dijon and Autun were more concerned with criticising the economic and social policies of the regime. These banquets were attended by a few local notables, country bumpkins, and shopkeepers in their Sunday best at whom Flaubert gently poked fun; they cheered for certain members of the dynastic opposition or radicals who a few weeks or months later were to come to power in their towns. Some fifty of such banquets, held in twenty-eight departments, especially in northern France, in the region of Paris and in the Saône and Rhône regions, were financed by about 22,000 subscribers. Even considering that the number of those who actually heard the speeches was three or four times as high, it is clear that the campaign failed to arouse public opinion in the way its promoters had hoped. On the pretext that it would not do to yield to threats, Guizot refused to make any concessions for the time being; the king's speech from the throne of late December 1847 denounced the 'hostile or blind passions' in a clear allusion to the reformist banquets. An amendment introduced by a conservative deputy, Sallandrouze, expressing the hope that the government would initiate 'wise and moderate parliamentary reforms' was rejected by Guizot on 12 February, and also was defeated by 222 votes in the Chamber (189 voted in favour).

Driven to the wall, the opposition countered by reviving the idea of another banquet in Paris, to be held in a crowded neighbourhood, the XIIe *arrondissement*. Eventually, however, Odilon Barrot and his friends, afraid of an outbreak of popular violence that they would be unable to control, decided to hold their banquet on 22 February, a Tuesday rather than a Sunday, near the Champs-Elysées. Anxiety was growing among the conservatives, among the king's sons (especially Joinville), and even among the deputies of the dynastic opposition who were willing to accept any compromise that would permit them to save face in the eyes of the rank and file.

But by now the chiefs of the dynastic opposition could no longer hold back the radicals, who called upon the National Guard and the students to march from the Madeleine to the Champs-Elysées. As a result, the government ruled out any future compromise. In speaking to Duvergier de Hauranne on the evening of 21 February, Odilon Barrot acknowledged: 'The chariot is launched; whatever we do, tomorrow the people will be in the streets.'

The demise of the July regime

It is too easy for historians to present the concatenation of facts as a rigorous mechanism; after all, they know the outcome. There is no such thing as a political revolution without revolutionary events, and it must certainly be kept in mind that these events do not contain their explanation in themselves but must be understood in the context of the mental and social structures in which they unfold. Yet it is also true that the study of structures in itself does not reveal the meaning of the historical evolution either; the event must be seen both as the driving force of history and the manifestation of structural change. Demonstrators gathered on 22 February even though the unauthorised banquet had been cancelled. On 23 February, a few barricades were erected in several sections of Paris; in the most conservative neighbourhoods, the National Guard refused to be appeased as long as the inhabitants continued to support Guizot. In the afternoon the king decided to ask the cabinet to resign and offered the prime ministership to Molé, a move that was received with disappointment in the lower-class neighbourhoods of Paris. A few hours later, Molé had to hand over the reins to Thiers amidst growing confusion in the ranks of the army and as columns of demonstrators assembled in many parts of Paris. That evening, the situation was greatly aggravated by a fortuitous incident, the burst of gunfire on the boulevard des Capucins, in front of the Foreign Ministry, where some 50 demonstrators who had gathered to revile Guizot were killed by the government troops. Following this incident, the riot turned into a revolution. Henceforth, neither the National Guard nor even the soldiers would dare to stand in the way of the uprising.

The fall of the regime was above all the fall of the king. The aging Louis-Philippe (he was almost 75 years old) who with the death of his sister Madame Adélaïde had lost a level-headed adviser and who, after all, had come to the throne through a revolution, was not in a position to fight against a revolution. In February 1848 he lost control over the events; he decided too late to get rid of Guizot, thereby weakening the power of the government at a time when he needed it most. Neither Molé, who was not the man to handle a difficult situation, nor Thiers, nor Odilon Barrot, who had been in the opposition for too long to be prepared on short notice to take over the direction of the government, were willing or able to act.

Rioting continued throughout the day of 24 February, and when the sound of gunfire came closer to the Tuileries, Louis-Philippe hurriedly signed an act of abdication in favour of his grandson the comte de Paris and rushed off in a hackney coach across the place de la Concorde toward Saint-Cloud and from there to England.

Because of Louis-Philippe's prolonged and stubborn refusal to acknowledge reality and his excessive confidence in his own political sense, and later because of his utter dejection and his abdication, the July regime was swept away with him.

The Chamber also was swept away. Even though the government party had a large majority, the conservatives were upset that Guizot had been asked to resign. When the king's abdication was announced, confusion broke out in the Chamber; the majority, being more faithful to the government than to the dynasty and more interested in its own security than in maintaining a regime that was falling apart, left it to members of the opposition like Odilon Barrot to make some bids in favour of a regency of the duchesse d'Orléans who had come before the Chamber with her two young sons. Groups of insurgents and National Guardsmen made their way into the Chamber, and as the president and most of the deputies were fleeing, Dupont de l'Eure took over the presidency and read – and Ledru-Rollin subsequently reread – a list of names to be included in a provisional government. The July regime foundered in Paris. 'Against a moral uprising, it was no use attacking or defending ourselves', Louis-Philippe was to declare later in a statement that justified not only his own abdication but also the failure to stand by the July regime on the part of those who had supported it and benefited from it. This double abdication – permanent on the part of the king and temporary on the part of the ruling bourgeoisie – cannot be understood solely as a function of the events of the February days; the events must be related to the different aspects of the crisis (analysed in the preceding pages) and to the deterioration of congested political and social structures which also aroused the combative spirit of the lower classes and helped to unite the *petite bourgeoisie* and the people of the cities against the supremacy of the notables.

PART 2

The life of the nation

Introduction

Having presented in the first part of this volume France's general evolution between 1815 and 1848 in its political, economic, social, cultural, and ideological aspects, we will devote its second part to a regional study of France during this same era of the monarchy of limited suffrage.

The life of the regions will confirm and illustrate the major features of the nation's evolution that we have described earlier, but it will also show the extreme diversity of a country which in the absence of modern communications was yet to be unified. Since space does not permit us to attempt a complete description of the various regions, we have endeavoured to highlight the most significant aspects.

Delineating the socio-geographical units is a delicate and indeed timely problem: it seems to us that, except for western France and despite the essentially rural character of nineteenth-century France, the least arbitrary units are those that were created by the cities and their influence.

For this reason we have devoted the last chapter of this volume to an analysis of the conditions in Paris, which in some ways was both the antithesis and the synthesis of the provinces.

Finally, we will also present a general conclusion to both parts of this book.

10

Western France

The geographical individuality of western France is immediately percept-
ible, even though it is composed of an array of complex parts that are not
always contained within the same boundaries and moreover assume a
variety of shadings. Among the characteristics of western France are its
changeable skies and its oceanic climate, the presence of the ancient mountain range and of the *bocage* [mixed woodland and pasture land], the
pattern of scattered settlements, and the predominance of large noble or
bourgeois properties. Yet western France also evokes the two great ethnic
duchies of Brittany and Normandy, the Vendée whose originality had been
brought to light by the Revolution, and the border areas of Anjou and
Maine with their stark contrasts.

Nineteenth-century liberals saw this area as a whole in terms of an
isolated bloc of archaic rural life ruled by nobles and priests. Yet in the
preceding century, isolation had not prevented commercial activities
originating in some of the major ports from spreading to the rural countryside, nor had it prevented the establishment in almost all parts of western
France of a linen and hemp industry that supplemented the resources of
an unequally endowed agriculture. But after 1815 it was unclear if it
would be possible to revive or reconvert this economy tied to overseas
commerce, now that the blockade had ended.

There is no doubt that the majority of the population of western France
was happy to see the collapse of the imperial regime. And yet, contrary to
the opinion shared by many historians, few rural regions elsewhere had
greeted the movement of 1789 with as much enthusiasm. It was only two
years later that it began its long revolt against the central power, against
conscription, and against the anti-religious laws. Peasants as well as
artisans soon found themselves in the same camp with the nobles who,
however, were by no means always patriarchal landlords. The nobility's
hold over some of these rural areas, where the feudal dues had been
relatively light, seems to have owed more to the anti-revolutionary struggle
than to the traditions of the Ancien Regime. However that may be, the
dominant feature of political life in this area was the latent conflict

between rural and urban dwellers. Napoleon assuaged and moderated this conflict, but such success as he obtained was not to last. He was unable to eradicate the old hatred, kept alive by the memory of massacres, torture, and murder, between the 'whites' who mustered the rural proletariat as well as the châtelain, and the 'blues' who dominated even in tiny market towns and whose opinions were shaped by the bourgeois, some of them buyers of nationalised property, others former members of revolutionary clubs, and still others simply people shocked by the siege-mentality of their past. The 'whites' would have been glad to seize the occasion of the king's second return to deal once and for all with the *'patauds'* ['fat-cats'] who had openly expressed their joy at Napoleon's return from Elba and had embraced the federation movement with an enthusiasm that it did not arouse elsewhere, thereby exacerbating the existing antagonism.

Brittany

The particularity of Brittany

In 1853, the geographer Malte-Brun was scandalised that other geographers still spoke of Brittany rather than of the five departments into which it was divided under the law. Naive grumbling, perhaps, but similar misgivings were expressed by some of the prefects, especially under the July Monarchy: administrators serving in Brittany felt that they had no support; equally distrustful of the masses and of the notables, they acquired the mentality of colonial governors. As for the Romantic travellers, their bewilderment was obvious, especially after they crossed the linguistic frontier. One is surprised to see the lack of tolerance of such writers as Michelet, Hugo, Merimée, or Flaubert; perhaps all of them felt rather like Balzac who, speaking of Brittany in relation to France, likened it to a 'frozen piece of coal that would lie dark and black amidst a brilliant fire'. Stendhal actually thought about a remedy and suggested that this barbarian land should be civilised by bringing in Alsatian settlers.

Yet at that time very few regions had as flourishing a peasant civilisation as Brittany. Shaped by a long tradition that had become an amalgam of many diverse elements in the course of the ages, this civilisation was still very much alive in the nineteenth century. However cautious one must be in treating this matter, there is no question that it transmitted a very old Celtic stock of customs and mental representations, though without losing its inventiveness in the decorative arts and especially in the areas of dance and poetry. The local workshops of popular sculptors who went from church to church to repair the damages wrought by the Revolution testified to a rich and lively imagination. Cabinet-makers also furnished their rural clientèle with cupboards and sideboards whose traditional local motifs inspired them to invent an unending variety of fanciful decorations.

The isolation of the farms, which usually formed small hamlets scattered throughout the *bocage*, was the outstanding feature of this region. Nowhere else did the fields form such citadels, their high slopes planted with tall trees and bristling with live hedges. The market town where the church was located was scarcely more than another hamlet. Yet the *plou*, the parish, was a living cell. The community it constituted was stronger than any other in the *bocage* country, and the authority of the parish priest who, of peasant origin himself, served as preacher, arbiter of morality, and exorcist to the community remained virtually unchallenged. Sometimes the whole community would work together during the harvest season, and mutual support in the countryside often combined work and celebration: when it was time to prepare a new surface where the grain would be threshed, everyone brought water and clay and walked his horses over the ground, and when the task was accomplished joined in ritual dances, gavottes or jabadaos, to the sound of the bagpipe and the bombard.

But there were ties of solidarity that extended beyond the *plou*, foremost among them solidarity with the clan. People felt themselves to be Glazic (from the region of Quimper), for example, or Bigouden (more to the southwest), distinguished by a different mentality and particular ethnic traits that were no doubt due to a long practice of endogamy. All the travellers recognised the Breton man with his round hat over shoulder-length hair and with his pleated *bragou braz* breeches (in fact they were wrong, for these breeches were by no means worn everywhere in Brittany). A trained eye could tell from the items and the embroidery of a man's costume and by the dresses, blouses, and bonnets worn by a woman to which clan the wearer belonged, and even his or her age and social rank. There was an admirable variety of these costumes, which actually changed with the fashion, a fact of which the ambulant tailors who went from farm to farm and worked in their customers' homes were well aware. Innumerable fairs and *pardons*, where large crowds gathered under the patronage of a renowned saint, brought several cantons and several clans in contact with each other. After the mass and the procession, booths, open-air drinking and athletic contests (the '*soule*' – a ball-game – and Breton wrestling) recalled ancient Greece. But these Breton Olympiads rarely failed to give rise to a public disturbance: two clans or two parishes would rush at each other amidst fierce battle cries and some of the combatants would be left dead or wounded on the field.

Popular culture also manifested itself in the survival of an old literature ranging from mystery plays to canticles, from love songs to the expression of popular grievances. Bards – partly poets and partly beggars – continued to sing them throughout the countryside. In addition, however, the great European current of cultural nationalism also reached Brittany, and in its wake some intellectuals began to devote their lives to the study and the glorification of Breton traditions. A modest civil servant, Le Gonidec, published a *Dictionnaire de la langue celto-bretonne* (1821) and a grammar, concluding from the study of the various dialects that that of Léon was the purest and using it as the basis of the written language. After him, Hersart de Villemarqué (1815–95) published his collection of popular songs under the title *Barzag Breiz* (1838). In doing so, Villemarqué – actually a forger – gave a decisive stimulus to literary creation in Breton language. Nonetheless, the poet Auguste Brizieux (1806–58) published his principal works in French. The first of these, *Marie*, a collection of poems inspired by his childhood memories, appeared in 1840. Brittany thus made an early and original contribution to the reawakening of regional traditions.

Life in the countryside

The size of rural farms in Brittany rarely exceeded 25 hectares; moreover, they were often worked by several families related by ties of blood or friendship. However, large landed estates decidedly outnumbered the small farms and the land was still predominantly owned by the nobility. A comparison of the number of property taxpayers in the different departments of Brittany shows marked differences in the pattern of landholding: in Loire-Inférieure and Côtes du Nord, the number of property owners had risen steeply, by 19 and 16 per cent, respectively, while the national average rose by only 8 per cent. In Morbihan and Finistère, by contrast, this rise was only slight, and in Ille-et-Vilaine the number of landowners actually decreased by about 4 per cent.

The legal status of the farms was variable: sharecropping was relatively rare, except in the vineyards around Nantes, where the *bail à complant* stipulated that the fruits be divided between the owner of the land and the vintner, although the latter was guaranteed his tenure in perpetuity. Renewable rent contracts were widespread. In Lower Brittany one also finds a form of land tenure that was practically unknown elsewhere, the *domaine congéable*. Although the Revolution had wanted to abolish this system as 'feudal', it was subsequently recognised as legal. It consisted of sharing the ownership between the landlord who owned the soil and the tenant who owned the 'edifices and surfaces', that is, the buildings, trees, and hedges (except very large trees on the property), and even the grass. The tenant who, incidentally, had the right to rent out what he owned, could not be evicted by the landlord unless the latter purchased the tenant's share of the property. This system ensured the security of the peasants, but the imposition of restrictive clauses concerning any new buildings or any improvement of the property by the tenant severely hampered agricultural progress.

However that may be, throughout the first half of the nineteenth century agriculture continued to be based, as it had been in the past, on the equal division of the land between enclosed fields planted with cereals and the gorse-studded heath (where once in a long while some meagre crops were raised on a burnt patch). It is true that in the course of the years the enclosed fields had gained ground over the heath and that their size had been expanded as much as possible as part of a more intensive agriculture. Yet the heath continued to be indispensable: gorse was a source of fodder and bedding for the livestock, and it was also used as a supplementary fertiliser, which is why it was left to decay in sunken lanes. Unfortunately, the heath was often in poor condition; the hills of the Argoat region had the aspect of an almost totally barren grazing ground, where a few sickly sheep roamed through the windswept, wolf-infested wilderness.

In Morbihan and Finistère, whose interior was particularly poor, the heath occupied more than 40 per cent of the soil; in the other departments it took up about 20 per cent. As for the cereals, which were often cultivated under a biennial system of crop rotation, wheat was only grown on the good land of the Rennes basin, near the coast, or close to roads or rivers that made it possible to improve the soil. Elsewhere, rye, oats, and buckwheat were the principal crops.

The farmhouse was a low dwelling built, depending on the region, of granite, schist, or daub and thatched with straw. Men and beasts were living under the same roof, although the first efforts were being made to separate them more rigorously; Finistère even had stables apart from the house. However, the farmyard, where the liquid manure pit and the drinking pond were in close proximity and where sheaves were dried in the wind for lack of a barn, remained archaic, as did the farm tools (in certain cantons the ploughs still had wooden blades and mould-boards).

In the human dwellings the hearth, which was used both for heating and cooking, provided more light for the interior than the narrow window. The diet of the inhabitants was frugal indeed, consisting of porridge of oats or rye served with a piece of butter, buckwheat pancakes, fresh or sour milk, and a little fat pork. However, meat did appear on the tables of the Breton peasants in early winter when some of the livestock had to be sacrificed, and Brittany was one of the regions with the highest meat consumption. Salt- and fresh-water fish, from cod to salmon, also made for a healthy diet. Cider and, in the Nantes region, white wine, increasingly replaced water, which had contributed to the spread of epidemics. The consumption of alcohol was rising, and the drunkenness of the Bretons was a common topic of conversation in the nineteenth century; only the Norman Flaubert found them sober.

There is no question that the agricultural economy of this area, which was not as self-enclosed as is often believed, provided the peasants with some cash, despite the rise in rents. Wheat (in those areas where it was possible to cultivate it) and especially livestock were good sources of income. Consider for example that in 1838 Finistère, with its 40,000 to 50,000 farms, had 100,000 cows, 33,000 oxen, 40,000 calves, and 73,000 horses.

Yet this affluence was not solid, for it was only enjoyed by the large tenant farmers, a privileged group. The large population of day-labourers and farmhands received very low wages and lived in sordid hovels. Yet they were not as miserable as the beggars who travelled the roads or swelled the ranks of the indigent in the small towns. Pauperism appears to have been increasing and some of the economic crises uprooted entire villages from their cantons: in *Les Derniers Bretons* Emile Souvestre has left us a moving description of the invasion of Léon by the starving inhabitants of Cornouaille in 1816. His story makes the point that Brittany was made up of a number of very different areas. Even from the physiological point of view, there was nothing in common between the solid mariners and the robust girls of the northern coast and the rachitic individuals of certain cantons in the interior. Generally speaking, the essential contrast was between the Armor and the Argoat regions.

While it is true that a richer agriculture existed in the countryside around Rennes and Nantes, especially in the latter area, where vegetable fields, vineyards, and meadows were cultivated along the banks or on the islands of the Loire, it is a fact that the agricultural development of Brittany was most successful in those cantons that benefited from the alluvions, the climate, or the fertilisers provided by the sea. At the time the best example for the advances made by the coastal areas was no doubt Léon: the grain-producing region of Roskoff and Saint-Pol also sent vegetables to all the western ports of France, to England and the Netherlands and after 1830 to Paris as well. In this area the value of the hectare of land rose from 1,500 francs in 1820 to 3,500 francs in 1845. Plougastel was already specialising in the cultivation of melons and strawberries, while Pont-Aven specialised in fruit trees. Léon was still the leading agricultural producer during the July Monarchy, when it began to use artificial feed for livestock. The potato also assumed added importance with the growth in numbers of its satellite, the pig.

Nonetheless, imbalances persisted in the life of the Breton countryside. The wars of the Revolution and the Empire had closed overseas markets to Breton linens, and this decline in the African and Central American trade was compounded by the ever-growing competition of the much cheaper cotton. At the beginning of the July Monarchy, to be sure, Brittany still accounted for one-eighth of the French linen and hemp production. Evening gatherings were still spent spinning, and many rope-makers still plied their trade. But for all that the decline was inexorable and drove the poorest segments of the rural population from the country-side.

To some extent this was due to the fact that, in relation to the resources of its land, Brittany was overpopulated, having grown from a population of 2,200,000 at the beginning of the century to 2,794,000 in 1846. During the monarchy of limited suffrage, this growth was about equal to that of France as a whole, for while the birth rate remained high, the death rate had not yet begun to decline. But Brittany had started out at an unusually high level, and by 1846 the population density reached 81 inhabitants per square kilometre, while the average density for France was 67.

And indeed, it was precisely around 1846 that the solution to this over-population of Brittany began to take shape; emigration, which had originally affected mostly the Rennes area, now became a mass pheno-menon. It was, of course, a regrettable solution, but it can be largely explained by the insufficiency of other possibilities. The fact is that the rural economy of the eighteenth century, based as it was on the association of farming and cottage industry, was unable to convert to a new system.

Industry, transportation, and fishing

Were the other industrial activities able to compensate for the decline of the textile industry by absorbing the surplus rural population? The annual statistics call attention to the presence of a wide variety of mineral deposits and mention granite, porphyry, and slate quarries as well as iron, zinc, pewter, and silver-bearing lead mines. Large numbers of forges and blast furnaces are also referred to. However, these deposits were mediocre, and there was a shortage of fuel since most of the forests had already been cut down and since the coal seams were so meagre that mining had stopped everywhere before 1848. The metal industry of Brittany's interior consisted only of modest enterprises that survived thanks to protective tariffs or to the early stages of railroad construction and went out of business as soon as the province emerged from its isolation. The mining of silver-bearing lead at Poullaouen and Huelgoat, the most important of such mines in France, was exceptional in appearance only.

The only industries that had a future were those located along the coast. These were the shipyards of the major ports, the foundries of Hennebont that were to expand greatly in the future, and the foundries and rolling mills of Indret. Created in 1774 on an island in the Loire downstream from Nantes by the English manufacturer Wilkinson in connection with a cannon foundry, this enterprise began to build steam engines for ships in 1827; subsequently, steam engines became the only speciality of the *Société de la Basse Indre* which took over the enterprise in 1839. Thus the coastal area of Brittany, whose agriculture was richer than that of the interior, also became its most important industrial region.

It is true that it was also the only region where trade in bulky food-stuffs was possible. Here is a particularly telling example of the military imperatives that had guided government policies. In the north and the south, the roads of the eighteenth-century intendants, conceived for the defence of the coasts, passed through the little towns located at the mouths of the estuaries but ran toward Brest and Audierne without touching the agricultural centres. Napoleon had made plans for a network of canals that was completed only under the July Monarchy, the Blavet canal between Nantes and Brest, and the Ille-et-Rance canal. These canals were intended primarily to afford protection against the British fleet and their practical importance was never more than secondary. In eight departments, among them Ille-et-Vilaine and Loire-Inférieure, the building of a strategic network of roads that would make it possible to control the *chouan* country in the wake of the duchesse de Berry's caper was authorised by a law of 27 June 1833, but the construction of an interior road between Rennes and Brest was not decided upon until 1837. In fact, it was only by the middle of the century that Brittany was attached to the general network of transportation. That is why coastal shipping remained vitally important, why very small ports were well-frequented, and why a high percentage of the tonnage built at Nantes consisted of small coastal vessels. Passengers also travelled by steamboat.

Fishing also had been reactivated in 1814. Deep-sea fishing was concentrated on the northern coast, where cod fishing boats regularly went from the ports of the gulf of Saint-Malo and the bay of Saint-Brieuc to the fishing grounds off Newfoundland (whaling had become an unusual activity, but was still practised by the Dobrée company of Nantes). Elsewhere coastal fishing for sardines in the Atlantic, which encroached upon the English channel more than it does today, was the principal speculative venture; between Le Conquet and Le Croisic, 15,000 families made their living from it. For the most part, the sardines were packed in barrels and in this form sold by the 'packers' of Le Croisic, Douarnenez, and Concarneau to wholesalers in Nantes, La Rochelle, Bordeaux, Bayonne, and Sète. As early as 1834, Nantes began to use Appert's method of preserving fish in tin cans. Twenty-five years later, almost all the ports of southern Brittany had fish frying and tinning plants, a monopoly they were to preserve for close to half a century. Other fishing activities, such as the gathering of the flat oysters that had already made the reputation of Cancale or the trapping of lobsters near the reefs, were of lesser importance.

By the end of our period, each summer brought visitors to such seaside resorts as Saint-Quay-Portrieux or Le Croisic.

The towns. The region of Nantes

Brittany was not as predominantly rural a region as one might suppose. In 1836 the percentage of the rural population did not reach 68 per cent in any of its departments. This figure was substantially higher in all the departments of western France except Seine-Inférieure. To some extent this view of the situation is the result of imperfect statistics. Yet it is a fact that Armorica was dotted with numerous small towns, not only at the mouths of the estuaries but in the interior as well. They were inhabited by middle bourgeois, large numbers of merchants and artisans, and by poor people who harried the traveller with their begging for alms. The mentality of these small towns was very different from that of the rural world, and the inhabitants were kept informed about political matters by means of the *diligence*. The townspeople had given up the traditional costume and knew French, even in Lower Brittany. It is noteworthy that the 'blues' constituted an active party in such places as Guingamp or Pontivy.

Rennes was still a modest capital with fewer than 40,000 inhabitants; it was an administrative town where the main source of excitement was the turbulence of the students in law or medicine who opposed the Bourbon regime. The port of Lorient had not yet recovered from the failure of the *Compagnie des Indes* and only slowly emerged from the doldrums during the Restoration years. As for Brest, it was a kind of colony implanted in western Brittany and lived a life of its own, totally controlled by the navy, which ran the arsenal, the shipyards, and the military prison. Two populations symbiotically lived together at Brest: the Bretons who furnished most of the work force of the arsenal and the outsiders who constituted most of the bourgeoisie and the business community. Numbering close to 10,000 persons, the military personnel and the crews of the navy accounted for almost a quarter of the total population. Gradually overshadowed by Toulon as a result of France's new Mediterranean policy, Brest was almost like a foreign body enclosed in the province. Its bourgeoisie was ardently liberal, and the religious mission organised in 1819 gave rise to such anticlerical virulence that it had to be called off.

The most important city was still Nantes, which throughout our period was the sixth or seventh largest town of France and the country's fourth largest port. Reaching 94,000 inhabitants in 1846 and located at the mouth of the Loire estuary in a site where the river was easily crossed, Nantes benefited from a double advantage, that is, from the intersection of a land route with a sea route on the one hand and its location at the junction of river shipping and Atlantic shipping on the other. Ever since the eighteenth century, the Graslon section near the quai de la Fosse had been the centre of the overseas shipping trade; but in addition Nantes also occupied some of the islands of the 'seven-armed river, bound with a chain of bridges', among them the wealthy residential quarter of the île Feydeau and the slums in the interior of Gloriette island; other islands were occupied by flour mills, sugar refineries, and cotton mills. Made idle by the blockade under the Empire, Nantes had lost the market of Saint-Domingue, and moreover the slave trade could henceforth be conducted only as a clandestine activity. Not before 1830 did the port's shipping recover its volume of 1790.

With respect to the traditional colonial trade, Nantes' relations with île Bourbon did not make up for the relative decline of the trade with the West Indies (in 1828, the port received 31 ships from Guadeloupe, 28 from Martinique, and 28 from Bourbon). On the other hand, trade with foreign countries was developing; imports of coal from England (which reached 63,735 tons in 1847), of iron ore and iron, wood and fertiliser were registered alongside of imports of sugar, coffee, rice, and cotton. Exports consisted essentially of manufactured goods, while salt (from the region of Le Croisic) and wine played a major role in coastal shipping. Yet as early as during the Restoration years, the difficulties in rebuilding the city's commerce had led investors to place their capital in industrial ventures. In 1828 the industry of Nantes and its surrounding area included 25 cotton spinneries, 31 cloth mills, 12 shipyards, 17 marine forges, 9 copper or iron foundries, 13 refineries, and 5 tinning plants.

If the city's population was politically divided (on 29 July 1830, the liberals did not wait to hear about the outcome of the Parisian revolution to instigate an uprising of their own), its commercial middle class under the July Monarchy unanimously supported the city's struggle to prevent the government from giving favourable treatment to beet-sugar (after a great deal of effort, fiscal equality between beet and cane sugar was obtained in 1843) and the struggle to keep the ports of the Seine from receiving special concessions for the import of coal. In the same manner, Nantes also tried to take some of the new transatlantic shipping lines away from Le Havre. Strenuous efforts to achieve these goals were made by the mayor of Nantes, Ferdinand Favre, and by its two deputies, Dubois and especially Billault, a solicitor and son-in-law of the shipping magnate Dobrée who by the end of the regime had established himself as one of the great debaters in the Chamber.

The acquisitiveness of the bourgeoisie was not the only characteristic of Nantes. The city's large working-class population, constantly at the edge of destitution, lived in attic rooms or dismal cellars and spilled over into wretched suburbs. As early as 1828, there were more than 16,000 workers, with the textile workers in a particularly precarious condition; wages showed a decreasing trend and the crisis of 1846–7 was to be devastating (15,000 to 20,000 persons became totally dependent on public or private charity).

On the eve of 1848, then, Nantes was an active city whose timely efforts to bring about the conversion of some of its economic activities was hampered by extremely serious geographical and social problems that endangered its recovery.

Nantes' relations with the interior made considerable use of the Loire: the traditional 'pine bottoms' (*sapinières*) brought foodstuffs from Roanne and were sold plank by plank after they had reached Nantes. Then, as early as 1822, the steamboat made its appearance in the estuary; soon a passenger service to Angers was established, and by 1825 merchandise could be sent to Paris by water. Roads also made it possible to organise a rapid passenger service by *diligence* (in 1830 the trip to Paris took 48 hours via Le Mans, 54 hours via the levée of the Loire) and passenger services for Rennes, Bordeaux, and Quimper also became available. The hauling of merchandise, of course, was much slower: normal deliveries reached Paris in 16 days, special delivery took 7 days. There was one major problem, however, that darkened the city's outlook for the future. This was the silting up of the estuary, which made it necessary to lighten cargoes of heavy foodstuffs at Paimbeuf and to have part of the cargo carried to Nantes in barges. By 1838 this problem drew the city's attention to the site of Saint-Nazaire; tentative plans were made to connect it to the port by a canal, but since the railway was coming – it had already reached Le Mans and the Touraine – all other solutions were put off until later.

Normandy

For the Parisians, Normandy was much closer and more familiar than Brittany. To be sure, Normandy had its own way of life, but in many respects the inhabitants of the two provinces shared a similar mentality: the practice of witchcraft and the veneration of healing saints took the same form in both provinces. Moreover, the common people of both Normandy and Brittany shared a sympathy for the *chouannerie* [counter-revolutionary activity] which, in addition to spawning a string of acts of brigandage, had turned into a kind of passive resistance under the Empire, although the 'blues' in the Norman towns did not react as strongly as those of Brittany. Yet Normandy was not set apart from the visitor by the screen of a coherent peasant culture. It was simply picturesque, with its peasants in their smocks and cotton caps, its women in their lace head-dresses who were often shown in popular engravings, and its Gothic monuments that had been popularised by the Romantic sensibility.

From Paris, it did not take long to reach the Norman towns: in 15 hours one could go to Evreux by *diligence*, and the mail-coach took 23 hours to Cherbourg. As for Rouen, Jouy, the 'hermit of the chaussée d'Antin' waxed enthusiastic in 1824 about all the 'vehicles that at all hours of the day and night leave Rouen for Paris and Paris for Rouen. The connections are so good that this great city seems to have become a suburb of the capital. Today it scarcely takes more time to go to Rouen than it used to take to go to Versailles or Saint-Germain.' Actually, by taking the most direct route, that of the plateau, one could reach Rouen in 12 hours.

It should be pointed out that such rapid transportation was available only on very special routes. The Empire had left the secondary roads in pitiful condition, and they were repaired only at the end of the Restoration. And it was even later, under the July Monarchy, that the Norman countryside was gradually connected to the French road system as a whole. Jouy's statement should be contrasted with a letter written nine years later by Tocqueville at his château in the Saire valley east of Cherbourg:

> Never in many centuries has a vehicle entered the courtyard of the château. The reason is simple. There is no road passable enough to bring it here. For six leagues in every direction there are only muddy paths that will just about do for a man on horseback or on foot. No mail is delivered here, and a newspaper is an unknown thing in our area.

Nonetheless, Normandy as a whole had the aspect of an active and prosperous region. Jules Janin noted in 1844 that even though it occupied one-seventeenth of France's territory, Normandy held one-twelfth of its population and produced one-ninth of its revenue, paying 103 million francs in taxes.

A comparison with Brittany provides a clear picture of Normandy's relative wealth. The same agricultural statistics of 1836 that estimated that 40 per cent of the arable land in two Breton departments was occupied by heath, moors, and fallow indicated a proportion of only 2 to 3 per cent of such lands in all of Normandy except Manche.

There were other contrasts between the two provinces as well, foremost among them a difference in their respective demographic evolution. At the beginning of the Restoration, Normandy had all the characteristics of a densely populated region whose population was growing rapidly: by 1831, its population had grown to 2,582,000 inhabitants, which spelled a density of 92 inhabitants per square kilometre. However, this growth began to slow down shortly after that date, and the *arrondissement* of Coutances as well as certain cantons of Calvados already began to lose population; by 1846, Eure showed a net population decrease since 1841. Then, between 1846 and 1851, only Seine-Inférieure registered a slight increase in population, while the province as a whole lost more than 17,000 inhabitants. The population of Brittany, which had 163,000 fewer inhabitants in 1821 and 31,000 fewer in 1841, exceeded that of its neighbour by 67,000 in 1846 and 130,000 in 1851. Normandy still had 95 per cent of the population of its neighbour on 86 per cent of its surface, but its resources were better. The people of Normandy contributed to the formation of the Parisian population earlier than those of Brittany.

The economic evolution of the two provinces was also different. Nineteenth-century Brittany, unable to convert its artisanal activities, had become a more exclusively agricultural area than it had been in the eighteenth century. Normandy, by contrast, experienced a renaissance, and its evolution followed the ups and downs of the industrial revolution.

Nor was local life the same. Because of Normandy's greater diversity, there was no pronounced contrast between the coastal areas and the interior. The coast of Normandy was indeed an active area that sent the products of its coastal fishing to Paris: aside from shipments of mackerel and herring, flatfish, crayfish, and oysters from Courseulles, Granville, or Saint-Vaast were greatly appreciated delicacies on the tables of the capital; in addition, spring vegetables were raised on the western coast of the Cotentin as well as in the Saire valley, among them the cauliflower that became a veritable fad in Paris in 1845. Yet, unlike in Brittany, the richer area was not delimited by the use of marine fertilisers; rather, the succulent meadows and fields of the interior stretched all the way to the cliffs and beaches.

The centre of the province was a contrasting scene of small plains rich in brooks and rivers, greenery and trees like the pays d'Auge, and limestone plateaux like the plain of Caen, while the south and the west, marked by the Massif armoricain, here interspersed with patches of *bocage*, constituted a more austere, more archaic, and less industrial environment. In short, the essential contrast was between western and eastern Normandy. Thanks to the royal highway of the Seine and the influence of Rouen – which was incomparably more widespread than that of Nantes, its Breton counterpart – the latter area provided stimulation for part of the province. Faced with the successive challenges of a rapidly developing economy, Normandy used the Lower Seine as a reservoir of men, capital, and ideas that enabled it to meet this challenge.

The Norman countryside

The census of 1836 found a percentage of rural dwellers higher than the national average (74.8 per cent) in four Norman departments (78.8 to 88 per cent), but only 66 per cent rural dwellers in the department of Seine-Inférieure. The outstanding feature of the demographic evolution over the next few years was the rapid urbanisation of the department of Orne (matched by that of the departments of Maine) where, by 1851, 30.3 per cent of the total population lived in towns, compared to 17.8 per cent in 1836. In the province as a whole, however, rural dwellers still predominated.

Like the landscape itself, human dwellings varied from region to region. One finds substantial villages with solid limestone houses in Eure, farm buildings grouped about a courtyard in the Vexin, daub and half-timbered buildings surrounded by a rectangular ditch scattered among the apple trees in the poorest areas of the pays de Caux, and so forth. Despite this variety, certain problems existed everywhere: straw-thatched roofs, for example, were still predominant, but slate was gaining ground under the impetus of the fire insurance companies.

The cultivated land also had only one common characteristic, namely, its division into small pieces. In a different context, M. Vidalenc has noted that the land was not necessarily owned by those who exploited it. Generally speaking, large noble or bourgeois properties remained important throughout our period, and it seems that the nobility was trying, as it did in other provinces, to recover what it had lost during the Revolution. In any case, the great landowners often, though to varying degrees, took an interest in agricultural improvements and participated in local learned societies – such as the Norman Association that was interested in both archaeology and agriculture – thereby actively furthering an evolution that propelled Normandy toward a high-yield agriculture.

Nonetheless, middling property owners subsisted almost everywhere. More importantly, very small pieces of property – especially in the valleys – were owned by workers or artisans who supplemented their wages by cultivating a patch of vegetables or flax. Liberal economists have always admired this system, claiming that it was an incentive to saving and hard work for the labouring classes. The fact is that it did little more than make the grain shortages less murderous and slow down – albeit at the price of increased hardship – the exodus from the countryside when due to the general evolution the local cottage industry fell by the wayside. However that may be, the rural farm was often quite large. Held either in its entirety or in part under a money-lease, it employed domestic servants who had been hired at the country fair in addition to day-labourers; direct exploitation by the owners of more modest properties was by and large confined to the department of Manche.

Cereal production remained an important speculative venture. It was of course most lucrative by far in the limestone areas where wheat was the basic crop. The traditional crop rotation, wheat/barley or oats/fallow, was still solidly entrenched in the plains of Eure. In the Vexin and in the pays de Caux, however, the fallow disappeared almost completely toward the middle of the century, and occupied no more than one-twelfth or one-sixteenth of the land by 1820. The triennial system of crop rotation was changed to a sexennial system in the pays de Caux, where wheat was grown in the first and the fourth year, followed the first time by oats and clover, the second time by colza and flax, and the third time by fodder beets and potatoes. On the ancient massif, where the practice of biennial crop rotation continued, the basic cereals were the traditional rye and buckwheat, since the peasants were faithful to their triple fare of buckwheat cakes, fat pork, and soup with lard. This is another instance of the time-lag between the more routine-bound department of Orne and the department of Manche, which increasingly specialised in animal husbandry.

In addition to cereals, Normandy continued to raise crops connected with its industrial pursuits, which made for unique agricultural cycles.

Flax, which had been very widespread in Normandy – as throughout western France – in the eighteenth century, was now restricted to the few cantons where the humid climate was particularly favourable to this crop; the teasel that replaced it for a time became obsolete with the introduction of metal carding-brushes. Colza, by contrast, a crop that had been widely cultivated since the Empire and had overcome a slump at the beginning of the Restoration, yielded good profits until the middle of the century. Used both in cloth-making and as a lighting fuel, its cultivation would receive a decisive blow only when it was superseded by petroleum.

Vineyards, which could be found almost everywhere in the old days, were declining rapidly, except to some extent in the Seine valley. This may not have been altogether unfortunate. In 1835, Jules Simon, having tasted a country wine from the area of Caen, gave his impression: 'If you pour together every kind of verjuice and every kind of vinegar, you will be unable to match the diabolical taste that made my eyes water.' On the other hand, the first twenty years of the century witnessed the rapid proliferation of apple trees whose fruit provided both the everyday beverage and high-quality cider like that of the valley of the Auge. Throughout Normandy the increased use of cider also went hand in hand with the making of hard liquor, and although it is impossible to calculate the volume of domestic production, it is known that this liquor was supplied to the last of the clandestine slave ships that sailed from Honfleur and Le Havre to the African coast.

Animal husbandry played an increasingly important role in the agricultural economy. This was true even on the limestone plateaux. In the early years of the Restoration, general de Polignac and other wealthy landowners had purchased large flocks of Merino sheep, which their tenant farmers pastured on the fallow fields; these flocks produced a high-quality wool for the cloth industries of Elbeuf and Louviers. After 1820, however, the revival of large-scale sheep-rearing in Spain made this speculative activity less lucrative, even before the exotic wools arrived on the French market. The Norman stockbreeders therefore began to cross their sheep with English Dishley rams in hopes of breeding an animal that would produce both meat and carding-wool. These experiments largely failed. Experimentation also marked the history of the Norman horse in that period. Decimated by the Empire, the old races of the eighteenth century had died out; around 1830, the Perche region succeeded in breeding the strong draught horse appropriate for the heavy short-distance hauling of the early railroad age.

Cattle-raising remained the essential speculative activity. Young animals or lean oxen from Maine, Poitou, or Berry were brought to Normandy for fattening. The well-established reputation for cattle-fattening of the pays d'Auge was spectacularly confirmed by the famous fattened ox of 1846

(2.46 metres around the neck!). Herds of fattened cattle, their ranks swelled by new contingents as they went along, slowly moved from the department of Manche toward the markets of Poissy and Sceaux. Equally important were the dairy products. Churned and salted butter from all the farms within a wide radius was collected at Isigny, from where it was shipped by water to the capital and, after 1845, to England. At the market of Gournay in the Bray region, 40,000 kilograms of butter and 80,000 eggs were traded every Tuesday; during the following night forty or fifty carts took most of these products to Paris. The Norman cheeses (Camembert became famous at this time) were also exported far from their place of origin. While some areas in the Norman *bocage* remained archaic and provided so meagre a livelihood for their inhabitants that some of them emigrated as tinkers, old-clothes peddlers, or mole-hunters, much of the agriculture in other areas had become commercialised.

Industry and commerce

Normandy was also an old industrial region undergoing a major mutation. Its metal industry had been important at the end of the eighteenth century when the province, along with Franche-Comté and Champagne, was one of the three great iron-making centres of France. At that time the blast furnaces and forges were owned exclusively by the nobility and a few abbeys; owing to the presence of iron ore and large tracts of forests, they were located for the most part in the region of the Ouche, in the Perche, and in the Bocage. This type of metallurgy was completely transformed between 1815 and 1848. Many enterprises changed hands, and new establishments were founded. Yet the traditional iron-making techniques (smelting over a wood-fuelled fire and the use of water-driven forging hammers) were still solidly entrenched until the middle of the century. The outstanding development was the rise of a new group of enterprises along the upper Risle; while the individual mills were modest in size, they were grouped together under the direction of one company, such as the Palyart Company which, with its 16 forges, was the tenth largest enterprise in France. The Norman holdings of comte de Roy, finance minister under the Restoration, were among the largest in France and combined forestry with metallurgy.

Alongside these traditional enterprises, however, English-style forges also came into being. Founded with English capital and sometimes directed by English personnel, they imported their coal and their scrap iron from the British Isles. Owing to their need for constant supplies of heavy raw materials, they were concentrated in the lower Seine region, essentially in the triangle formed by Le Havre, Rouen, and Pont-Audemer. These plants were large, integrated production units, and their business volume was very much larger than that of the traditional enterprises. In fact, the York Company with two plants did better in this respect than the Palyart Company with sixteen. In addition to the iron industry, the copper foundries of Normandy – among them France's most high-powered copper foundries at Romilly-sur-Andelle – also made use of ore imported from eastern Europe. Even the shortage of coal (which persisted even though the only Norman mine, that of Littry, was at its peak of production around 1840) was no obstacle to the emergence of a modern metal industry in addition to the old one.

The output of this basic metal industry was used by a secondary metal industry, which became extremely diversified and specialised: needles and nails were produced at Rugles and Laigle, cutlery at Mortain, kettles at Villedieu-les-Pôeles, bells at Sourdeval, metal utensils at Tinchebray, etc. Almost everywhere this work was done in small workshops and even at home by a work force that remained largely rural.

To a greater extent than metallurgy, the textile industry assumed a dominant role in certain regions. However, and for the same reasons as in Brittany, the importance of linen had declined. Hand-spinning on the spinning-wheel was still done to some extent on the farms, and the patient work of the lacemakers which, owing to the demands of fashion, had spread throughout the province in the eighteenth century, was now by and large confined to Bayeux and the countryside around Bray. Spinning mills furnished the threads for the traditional looms that continued to be used for the weaving of linen cloth; and it was only in 1840 that the Jacquard loom was used in Normandy in the manufacturing of drill. The manufacture of woollen cloth, by contrast, underwent a remarkable expansion from the very beginning of the Restoration. Elbeuf, which had strictly confined itself to making cloth for uniforms during the Empire, once again went in for novelty materials in 1825. In the fifteen years before 1842, Elbeuf increased the number of its textile mills from 60 to 125; these mills operated 3,000 looms (one-third of them in the countryside) and employed 17,000 workers (2,500 of them children); the value of Elbeuf's production represented over half of the value of the entire French woollen-cloth industry. Louviers, for its part, had 40 cloth mills and 500 looms and employed a work force of 6,000. Even though Elbeuf and Louviers shared many interests, they began to compete for the railway line at the end of the July Monarchy; in the end, neither town was successful. The raw wool they processed came from the Beauce and from Brie and Picardy, as well as from Spain and Germany. Their woollen cloths were exported to Switzerland, Spain, Italy, and Mexico.

Even in the eighteenth century, Rouen was famous for its '*rouenneries*', that is, its imitation '*indiennes*' [printed cottons]. During the Revolution and the Empire, the use of mule-jennies, which eliminated hand-spinning, was introduced in many places. After 1815, these machines could be found in the valleys near Rouen, where they could be powered by water. In 1840 there were 40 spinneries along the banks of the Robec and Aubette rivers, and 127 along the Clères river and its tributaries. The 317,000 spindles counted in 1837 furnished work for the shuttles of 52,650 weavers scattered over a much larger area stretching from Neubourg to Picardy, although their greatest density was concentrated in the square formed by Fécamp, Bolbec, Yvetot and Tôtes, where every village had a hundred or more weavers. Every week, carters went back and forth between these villages and the merchant–manufacturers of Rouen, and the weaver practically never left his loom, except during the harvest season. Working under less unhealthy conditions than the woollen-weaver who spent his life in a dank cellar, he was poorly paid by comparison with the spinning-worker and the linen-weaver. After the reign of Louis XVIII, he was already threatened by the stepped-up mechanisation of the looms in the cotton industry: the first mechanical loom appeared at Fécamp in 1825, and by 1834 there were 600 mechanised looms in the department of Seine-Inférieure. In the coastal zone hand looms were no longer used when work resumed after the crisis of 1839, and elsewhere their days were numbered.

It would be tedious to enumerate the other industries of Normandy. Some of those that no longer exist today were in decline, among them the salt works of the bay of Mont Saint-Michel, paper mills, and glass works.

Since communications were slow in this pre-railway era, the relative commercialisation of agriculture and industry resulted in the creation of many new fairs and markets, where trading was brisk. Officially set up for the sale of livestock (Guibray, near Falaise, Lessay, Le Neubourg), they were often the setting for all kinds of other transactions; at Lessay for example, a whole temporary tent city, complete with outdoor cook shops, was erected for the three days of the fair. With a few exceptions (among them Valognes, the aristocratic Norman Versailles), the towns were active trading centres, and most of them also had an industrial life of their own.

A special case is that of Cherbourg, which owed its advancement to its role as a naval base and to its shipyards. Caen, whose progress was modest (37,200 inhabitants in 1821, 44,000 in 1846), remained a bourgeois university and administrative town. Meanwhile, its port was silting up, and the canal that was to link it with the sea, although authorised in 1837, was not to be finished until 1857. Plans for a canal between the Orne and the Loire rivers were cancelled in 1841.

At that time priority was given to the building of the railway network whose star-shaped design reproduced that of the eighteenth-century royal roads. Under this plan, Rouen was the first city to be served. The Paris–Rouen line was opened in 1843 and extended to Le Havre, over the objections of the Rouennais, in 1847.

Le Havre, which had completely lost its military aspect, had indeed become the commercial rival of Rouen by monopolising the warehousing of coffee under the Restoration and by becoming the point of departure for steamship lines sailing for Holland, Germany, and England. Once the railway was built, the first transatlantic shipping line for New York settled at Le Havre. But if Rouen lost the business of the ocean liners, it kept that of the coastal vessels plying a very large area extending from Saint Petersburg to Naples. In the years 1840–2, just before the railway came into its own, the annual volume of shipping in the port of Rouen exceeded 337,000 tons. In addition to serving as the centre of a regional network of food supply, Rouen was the point of departure for an important river navigation toward the capital. Thanks to the improvement of its facilities in 1835, its port was able to accommodate barges with a draught of 1.80 metres, some of them displacing 600 tons. Eight hundred ships flitted through its waters, and every day a regular steamer service linked Rouen with Maisons-Laffitte in 22 hours. Yet the sea-port was in jeopardy, for deep-sea vessels of 300 tons drawing 3 metres of water could only sail up the estuary by keeping within a hazardous channel marked out with the remnants of shipwrecks, a situation that made it necessary to hire the services of a pilot at Quilleboeuf or to unload part of the cargo at Le Havre, where light barges performed a shuttle service to Rouen. These conditions were incompatible with the development of steamship navigation; and moreover Rouen would soon be faced with the competition of railroad lines to northern Europe.

In 1848 Rouen was still a major importer of primary products and foodstuffs, among them coal from England or northern France, Russian lumber, Spanish and Italian wool, American cotton and linen, wine from Bordeaux, salted and smoked fish from Holland, and colonial commodities such as rice, sugar, tobacco, and spices. Exports were much less extensive, consisting essentially of cotton cloth (one-fourth of the French production), cereals, butter and fish from Normandy, and articles of Paris.

Rouen was the fifth largest city of France with 87,000 inhabitants in 1831, and almost 100,000 in 1848. The old nobility of the parlement had lost its influence. Henceforth, the city's leadership was in the hands of a wealthy and down-to-earth bourgeoisie whose main interest was industry and trade.

The border areas of the Massif armoricain

Regional contrasts

The old provinces of Maine, Anjou, and Poitou consisted of several natural regions, each with its own personality. Yet here, too, there was a well-defined contrast between east and west.

The west was marked by the strong contours of the Massif amoricain, by a dense *bocage*, and by a scattered pattern of settlement. The east had a less uniform character; south of the Loire and beyond the right bank of the Layou, one entered Anjou with its plateaux of long fields unenclosed by hedges, with its wide and cheerful valleys, and settlements clustered together in substantial market towns, although further north the scene shifted back to *bocages* and isolated farms coexisting with villages inhabited by artisans, heath, and forests. Yet this indistinct zone was traversed by a political dividing line so sharply drawn that it could separate the townships of one and the same canton: on either side of this dividing line, townships were united, from the Revolution to our own time, by their common allegiance or on the contrary their common hostility to the Church and by their common allegiance to the right or the left, respectively. One only has to evoke these present-day political reflexes to give an inkling of the strong feelings of hatred between opposing groups at a time when the veterans of the Vendée and the republican armies or their direct descendants were still alive.

In the western part of this region a more homogeneous and self-enclosed rural civilisation had refused to buckle under to the growing power of the towns after 1790. By contrast, the peasants and artisans of the eastern part, a more docile breed that was relatively accustomed to outside influence, had gone along as the nation evolved in the direction of Jacobinism. In this manner a population that appears united if one studies its demands in 1789 was rent asunder by divergent movements culminating in an absolute break, in war and its ensuing massacres.

The Restoration propagated a distorted image of this past: the western parts of these provinces, it was said, representing the faithful old France, had risen up against the revolutionary brigandage on behalf of God and its king (and it should be added that the adversaries of the Restoration regime adopted the negative version of this account: backward peasants, in their inability to understand the emancipatory glories of the Revolution, blindly allowed themselves to be led by nobles and priests). It was a creative myth. In fact, the Bourbon government showed little gratitude when it did not grant villages burnt or ruined during the Revolution the same indemnities that were given to former émigrés who had lost their properties and limited its efforts to distributing a few pensions, sending some members of the royal family to visit the area (the duchesse de Berry for example made a visit in 1828), and to erecting commemorative monuments in the Vendée and Brittany. The local nobility, by contrast, often did try to live up to the image of its ancestors as benefactors of their vassals. Many nobles took a kind and sometimes effective interest in the life of this faithful people especially, it should be said, after 1830, when 'Philippe' had shut them off from the court and from public office. M. de Falloux in his Angevin town of Iré spent his own fortune developing better breeding techniques for livestock and increased agricultural yields and in founding schools and hospitals. Many of his fellows involved themselves in similar activities.

Nor was this a matter of trying to bring an economically backward 'chouan' country up to the level of a more favoured and richer 'patriot' country, for the life of the country people remained frugal indeed, both in the eastern and the western part of this region. The peasant of Maine usually lived in a dark hovel, baked a coarse bread every week, drank a sour cider, and filled up with soup. The peasant of Anjou was not housed much better, but his bread was often made of wheat, and he had vegetables, onions, broad beans, and cabbage to go with it. Together with dairy products, vegetables formed the mainstay of the diet in the Vendée. However, the potato was slow to be accepted for human consumption. Another common feature was the hierarchy of peasant holdings, ranging from *métairies* (in fact this term also applied to farms with a team of oxen to pull the plough, since there were practically no *métairies* in the proper sense [i.e. sharecropping farms], except in lower Maine and in Poitou) to *bordages* and *closeries* of 10–20 hectares and patches of dry soil in the hands of very small owners. The condition of farmhands was as dismal as ever.

Variations in the quality of the soil also made for disparities. In the old massif, for example, there was some very poor land that was cultivated only intermittently. Rye and buckwheat were better suited to siliceous soil than wheat, although wheat did very well on adjacent clayey soils. East of the massif, between the Huisne valley and the val d'Anjou, the gravelly and sandy soil was covered with wasteland and heath. This area was kept alive by the work of its artisans; it also had a floating population that worked in the forest as charcoal-burners, sabot-makers, etc. and sometimes lived by theft or odd jobs beyond the margins of the law and the rules of morality of the traditional rural world and with complete disregard for civil status and religion. Toward 1840 townships and great landowners took the initiative in planting fir trees on this meagre land.

By contrast, the Angevin valleys, those of the Loire, the Loir, the Authion, and the Layon, developed a specialised, commercial agriculture whose products could be distributed by means of the rivers. In this area the lands of the great Ancien Regime abbeys had been bought up piecemeal by little people who profited from the bourgeois' preference for large *métairies*. Here the work of the shovel took the place of ploughing and swarms of gardeners and vintners went to work on the land. Above Angers, tree nurseries alternated with orchards whose fruit was sold fresh or dried and with vineyards already concentrated in the areas known for their wine today: Layon, Bourgueil, and Saumur. The latter wine was made into Champagne and exported to Belgium and Holland.

As in other regions of western France, textile enterprises had spread throughout Anjou and Maine during the eighteenth century; since many of them produced linen, the eventual crisis had the same effects as in Brittany. Despite the attempts of the industrialists of Laval to create a cotton industry and despite Cholet's conversion to a specialised production of handkerchiefs made of a blend of cotton and linen, these efforts were unsuccessful in the long run. Lower Maine, for example, once again became an almost exclusively agricultural area.

The evolution of upper Maine took a different course. Here the manu-facture of woollens and bolting-cloth had declined so much that by 1815 only a few vestiges of these industries were left; their decline also entailed a reduction in sheep-raising. However, the department of Sarthe and some parts of the department of Maine-et-Loire found an excellent substitute in hemp. Used for making the coarse cloth worn by many peasants and sold to the cordage- and sail-makers of Angers, hemp was intensively cultivated throughout the area on tiny plots, and by the middle of the century endeavours to increase its production had become the foremost concern of the richest cantons. Hemp was still spun by hand on the farms (the first mechanised spinnery of Angers dates from 1842) and hemp-weaving was the most important activity in such little towns as Fresnay, Mamers, La Ferté-Bernard, Château-du-Loir, etc. Wealthy merchant–manufacturers sold the finished products far and wide: in 1814, at the height of the international crisis, Cohin of La Ferté-Bernard obtained a huge contract for canvas and duffel-bags from the War Department, and in 1842 Angers had a monopoly on sailcloth for all the ports except Toulon. More than Le Mans, whose prosperity was to start only with the railroad, Angers at that time was an active centre of trade in other respects as well.

Nonetheless, the essential industrial activities remained dispersed. Very few of those that flourished at that time, such as wood-fuelled smelting or ceramic and marble works, survived beyond the Second Empire.

Meanwhile a new activity of major importance came into being. Start-ing in 1809, the discovery of numerous small anthracite deposits led to the creation of lime kilns in Maine and Anjou, and the addition of lime made it possible to raise wheat on the soil of the old massif. The lime producers of Maine enjoyed an excellent reputation during the July Monarchy, when new roads enabled them to expand their operations.

In fact it was the development of the road system that permitted this region to take the first modest steps toward the activity that would eventually be its true vocation, namely, animal husbandry. To be sure, young animals were already being sent to Normandy, and beef cattle was also being sent to the Parisian markets. But in lower Maine and in the Vendée this trade was hampered by the poor condition of the roadways. Fortunately, the July Monarchy made decisive improvements in road construction and maintenance. While the law of 1836 concerning local roadways had not yet produced the intended results, the government hastened to build the strategic roads planned in response to the disturbances of 1832, and soon these roads criss-crossed the Bocage. Not without some bitterness the agronomist Leclerc-Thouin, a 'blue' from Anjou, pointed out in 1834 that this policy favoured the *chouan* country which, when all was said and done, received more from the detested July Monarchy than from the legitimate kings.

'*The last hurrah of the Vendée*'

The disturbances that occurred in western France in 1832 in connection with the attempted *coup* of the duchesse de Berry remained the central issue of the area's political life under the monarchy of limited suffrage.

The story of the duchess's wild adventure has been told many times: arriving on the coast of Provence aboard the steamer *Carlo Alberto* on 29 April, she had to leave Provence when the military uprising of Marseille was put down on the following day. Having reached the Vendée on 17 May, she lived there disguised as a peasant woman or peasant man, moving from hideout to hideout and receiving the principal leaders of the Carlist movement in the dark of night. Eventually (9 June) she took refuge at Nantes, where she was arrested on 6 November. Transferred to the fortress of Blaye, with Bugeaud as her jailer, she gave birth to a daughter. The sentimental legitimist disquisitions about the 'heroic queen' and about the treason of the Jew Deutz, a 'new Judas' who betrayed his benefactress, were countered by ribald innuendoes about the 'virtue' of the duchess and the implications of that virtue for the legitimacy of Chambord spread by the Orleanists, who heaped ridicule on the naive *gentilshommes* who, before the birth of the baby, were ready to smite Madame's 'slanderers'. All of this served to mask the very real fear felt by the new regime and the seriousness of the situation. Moreover, the unrest of western France coincided only in part with the duchess's odyssey. If the *chouans* had not made a move before 14 August 1830, the day when Charles X sailed from Cherbourg, it was because these people did not suddenly erupt on the occasion of one 'day' but, rather, took their time mulling over their grievances. Yet by September and October, the authorities of the new regime began to sense throughout western France the latent hostility of the country: members of municipal councils went on strike, conscripts failed to report, and police were harassed. While waiting for instructions that were slow in coming, the conspirators organised bands, set up weapons' deposits, and signed up unemployed policemen or Swiss guards. But Charles X failed to do anything, and it was only in 1832 that the duchesse de Berry, by now living in Italy, engaged the help of Bourmont to organise

– on paper – the ten army corps that would support the insurrection of Provence.

This dilatoriness allowed the government to seize documents, to set up a system of espionage, and to consolidate its strength. By the time the duchess arrived, the more reasonable of the Carlist leaders saw clearly that the time to act – if indeed there had ever been such a time – had passed. Nonetheless the duchess decided to launch the insurrection on 23 May, and when it was called off at the last minute, some of the bands that had not received the counter-order in time were left unprotected. One of them in particular lost about one hundred men in a battle against the government troops near Bouëre, south of Château-Gontier. A second uprising planned for 4 June and put off until 12 June with similar inconsistency was more localised south of the Loire and provoked the bloody episodes of Le Chêne and La Penissière. Even thereafter, sporadic outbreaks continued until 1833.

Unlike during the Revolution, the peasant were incited to revolt by the nobles or by the sons of ringleaders of the heyday of the *chouannerie*. The support of the peasantry was generally less than great, and many were enlisted under duress; nonetheless the tacit complicity of the peasants cannot be doubted, and their visceral hatred of Paris and of the 'blues' continued to play a role. Furthermore, the preventive measures taken by the government gave rise to bitter resentment throughout the *chouan* country: searches of châteaux and convents, arbitrary arrests, the quartering of garrison troops in the houses of suspects, and the exactions of the soldiery reawakened burning memories. Yet this was no longer the great tragedy of 1793, and the situation had its comical aspects as well: the police forbade the wearing of the white robes of the children of Mary, the question whether the lily was the emblem of purity or of legitimacy was discussed at great length, police constables were sent to mass to make sure that during the *salve fac regem* the cantor had duly included the word *Philippum*, and so forth.

Religious and political life

Considering that the escapade of the duchesse de Berry showed that the peasant masses of western France still preserved, albeit in an attenuated form, certain *chouan* leanings capable of making a bourgeois government uneasy, and that these bourgeois often encountered nothing but hostility on the part of the masses, one does wonder about the role of the clergy and the nobility.

The clergy, issued in large part from the peasantry, exerted a profound influence in the countryside. The Sunday gathering around the priest was the only occasion for which the parishioners left their isolated hamlets. That is why the Catholic revival that took place everywhere in France was particularly successful in these areas. The theses of M. Langlois for the diocese of Vannes and of abbé Faugeras for that of Nantes have shown us the successful endeavours of local vicars to strengthen the clerical institutions and to improve the discipline of the clergy. Very soon in the first case and during the July Monarchy in the second, these dioceses had enough religious vocations to fill all the vacancies that a generation without new priests had left in the local parishes. In this endeavour the Church was more interested in restoring the past than in innovation and resolutely placed major emphasis on fostering a popular and traditional Christianity. Superstitious practices were tolerated as long as assiduous attendance at mass and respect for the authority of the priest were not affected by them. Vigorous efforts were also made to instruct the young generation and to increase the number of Christian primary schools. The creation of a new theology or mystique more in keeping with the times, on the other hand, aroused suspicion on the part of the hierarchy and most of the priests, and there is a striking contrast between the failure of Felicité de Lamennais who tried to make Malestroit a centre of spiritual renewal and the success of his brother Jean-Marie who founded the Order of the Christian Schools. Generally speaking, it should be pointed out that the traditional cliché according to which the clergy's thinking did not clearly distinguish between God and the legitimate king is not altogether accurate. It is true of course that on the whole the clergy had 'Carlist' leanings; it is also true that its more fanatical members were virulently opposed to the government of 1830; nonetheless the great mass of the churchmen, and especially the bishops, seem to have made every effort not to compromise the Church and the Concordat [of 1801] in the shipwreck of the elder branch of the house of Bourbon. The 'petite Eglise' [non-adherents to the Concordat], having hoped in vain that the restored monarchy would reject the Concordat, became more radical in its impotence.

As for the nobility, it certainly was much less careful to separate its Catholicism from its legitimism. In 1815 it had spontaneously adopted the ultra line and had trouble understanding that there were other options. These nobles felt that it was up to them to decide who represented western France in the Chamber of Deputies, and many of them served in the Chambers of the Restoration. Leaving aside the case of the 'Incredible Chamber', if one counts the number of deputies from western France belonging to the right-wing opposition against the Richelieu–Decazes government, it turns out that 70 per cent of these men were nobles. Was this still the case at the end of the Restoration? When the vote of no confidence against the Polignac government passed with 221 against 181 votes in March 1830, 47 per cent of the western deputies had voted for the motion of no confidence. But if one does not count the deputies chosen on the department level and only looks at those elected on the level of the *arrondissement* by voters paying 300 francs or more in taxes, one realises that 64 per cent of these men were among the 221.

To what extent did the lowering of the tax qualification for voting to 200 francs after 1830 strengthen the power of liberalism associated with the bourgeoisie? It should be noted from the outset that the legitimism of western France was almost identical with the influence of the great noble landowners whose influence remained considerable and even increased as agriculture became more prosperous (in Brittany, 36 per cent of those who paid more than 1,000 francs in taxes in 1840 were nobles). Taking the form of a muted hostility against the regime, this legitimism was not interested in seizing power. Less than a political party and more than simple social conformism, it was a somewhat disillusioned fidelity to the past, and the tone of *Hermine*, the legitimist newspaper of Nantes, remained moderate. The meetings among 'Carlists' were enough to give Philippe's 'henchmen' nightmares; but even when large numbers of legitimists took themselves off to London in 1843 to greet the comte de Chambord, their political impact was insignificant. Individually, some of the legitimist notables of western France developed an at least ambiguous attitude toward the ruling circles. Three electoral colleges of Brittany had indeed sent great legitimist landowners to the Chamber, but only one of them, La Rochejaquelein, was actively engaged in the opposition, although he eventually rallied to the Second Empire. Elsewhere, the legitimists formed a voting block that gave its support, not without bargaining, to a candidate of the government party. In some electoral colleges the 'blues' triumphed by electing members of the liberal opposition to the Chamber: Fontenay-le-Comte was represented by Chambolle, an editor with *Le Siècle*; the Vendée sent its most left-wing delegation of the century during the July Monarchy; and Le Mans elected first the elder Garnier-Pagès and then Ledru-Rollin (although in the latter case the influence of the mayor of Le Mans, Trouvé-Chauvel, a very powerful figure in the financial world, was the decisive factor). There were few 'political circumscriptions' (Tocqueville), meaning that candidates were usually elected for opportunistic reasons, because they were thought to be in a position to defend the interests of the region, regardless of their personal political inclinations. This was quite obvious at Rouen, Nantes, and Elbeuf and became rather scandalous in the case of Cherbourg at the time when its deputy, Quénault, shamelessly delivered the favours he had obtained for his supporters, or in the case of Louviers, which elected Charles Laffitte to four consecutive terms in exchange for his promise to bring a railway to town. For the most part, however, the deputies were landowners, magistrates, military men, and bearers of locally respected names.

11

The Mediterranean south

The Mediterranean region did not have a common historical tradition, and the presence of many towns made for multiple centres of influence; at the same time this situation gave rise to antagonisms and strongly differentiated regional identities. Yet from Toulouse to Toulon, from Perpignan to Avignon or Aix, there was a society based on clientage that had not yet resolved the conflicts of the revolutionary era and by the same token perpetuated their memory. Indeed, the opposition sometimes dated back to even earlier times. Languedoc, Provence, and the Comtat Venaissin were ultra strongholds during the Restoration, which was their way of refusing to accept modern centralisation. This opposition to the centralised State whose power was embodied by Paris still existed during the July Monarchy, when it found expression in the persistence of a strongly legitimist public opinion and, in certain places and at certain times, in the coalition of diametrically opposed factions against the ruling 'juste milieu'.

Not that the life of the departments of southern France was all tranquillity and stability; rather, tradition and innovation at times collided and at other times converged. A whole cluster of factors contributed to a climate of effervescence: mild weather conditions that allowed people to participate in public life in the squares, avenues, and promenades of the towns; the proximity of the Italian States to the east and of Spain to the southwest at a time when both of these countries were in the throes of revolutionary or counter-revolutionary upheavals; the new importance of the Mediterranean littoral resulting from France's installation in Algeria after 1830; and, with respect to economic activities, the transhumance of large herds of sheep and the seasonal migration of grape- and olive-pickers.

Between the time of the white flag of 1815 and that of the red flag of 1848, these departments experienced a more rapid evolution in their political than in their economic life. The passions of the people proved more tenacious than their desire for profit. Liberal individualism, an attitude that is able to make allowances for the contingencies of the present, had yet to come into its own, and power and tradition still carried more prestige than money.

The traditions

It is no coincidence that the foremost theoretician of traditionalism in France, Louis de Bonald, was a man of the Midi, where the individual was embedded in the family, the religious community, and in all the forms of sociability to which Maurice Agulhon has recently drawn attention in his analysis of the social life of Provence. The effect of tradition was not limited to mentalities and political opinions; they pervaded all areas of life, including the language of southern France, the *langue d'oc*.

From the ultras to the legitimists

The dominant tradition at the beginning of the monarchy of limited suffrage was fidelity to the monarchy and to religion. By the end of the Empire, many royalists and Catholics had already been openly hostile to Napoleon, and their attitude influenced not only the wholesale merchants of Marseille or the notables of Toulouse but the fishermen and common people of Provence and Languedoc as well. In 1815 there was considerable resistance to the Hundred Days.

In these southern departments, far from Paris, rumour had greatly exaggerated the 'revolutionary' character of the Hundred Days. This fear of revolution was to persist, and it explains why in 1830 the supporters of Charles X failed to act, even though they were in the majority.

Royalist sentiments were at least as strong in the towns as among the rural population, although they differed from town to town. The great landlords who rented out their properties and divided their time between the towns and their estates were, along with the clergy, the natural and traditional intermediaries.

The clergy continued to exercise its social influence in a region where religious sentiment found expression in outward, collective displays. Even at Toulon, a working-class city that was unusual in many respects, religious traditions remained deeply embedded. Initiated by the Concordat, the reconstruction of the French Church continued with the revival of the old religious confraternities. New congregations made their appearance, among them the Oblates of the Immaculate Virgin Mary founded at Marseille by Eugène de Mazenod. Public displays of religious sentiment, such as missions, processions, public preaching, and expiatory ceremonies, all of which by definition had a counter-revolutionary aspect, proliferated in the Midi. Some of the bishops who had been appointed during the Napoleonic era found themselves in a rather awkward position; this was the case at Avignon and Aix.

Catholic charities were developing, and the brothers of the Christian Schools began to have a major impact on primary education. Being practically the only form of public welfare, the Church's charities greatly enhanced its influence. This local influence of the clergy was further strengthened by the close ties between throne and altar that characterised the Restoration. When the liberal and for the most part anticlerical bourgeoisie came to power in 1830, the Catholic clergy and the legitimists formed a close alliance that lasted for several years and had different effects in different departments. Deprived of official support, the clergy unquestionably lost some of its prestige and was challenged by a part of the population in the towns and even in the countryside. Yet its influence over the lower classes remained extensive, especially since the priest shared the hostility toward a government that relied on the support of the Parisian bourgeoisie. Another pillar of royalism was the aristocratic element, which often coincided with the class of great landowners; it was this group that under the Restoration furnished the deputies, especially in the Incredible Chamber, and the personnel of the high administration and the magistracy.

Yet its influence was quite uneven. It was most powerful in the region of Toulouse, which had the highest concentration of aristocratic estates. The wealthy noble landowners who spent the winter in their townhouses near the cathedral of Toulouse drew their incomes from their estates. There were many châteaux in the region where Villèle owned the château of Morvilles; the Hautpoul, Rességuier, de Nouailhan, de Limairac families also divided their time between their châteaux and Toulouse. During the July Monarchy, 18 of the 30 greatest fortunes in the department of Haute-Garonne, fortunes whose owners paid more than 3,000 francs in taxes, still belonged to nobles. This situation was even more pronounced in the department of Ariège, where all seven of the men who paid more than 3,000 francs in taxes in the *arrondissements* of Foix and Pamiers were noble.

In these families the Restoration had surely kindled the hope that the developments of the revolutionary era could be undone. Carriages complete with lackeys holding on to the back dashed through the streets of Toulouse, where they passed sedan chairs in which pious dowagers were carried to mass. Comte de Comminges reported that 'customs still had a kind of feudal colouring'; his father resided at the château of Saint-Lary, and 'the peasants were greatly attached to him, even though he treated them like black slaves. Woe to anyone who failed to doff his cap when he spoke to him, a blow of the cane would soon send the offending headgear flying.'

In other departments, especially in Tarn-et-Garonne and in Hérault, the landed aristocracy furnished the leadership of the royalist movement; these nobles were descended from the robe nobility of the parlement and from the nobility of the sword.

The influence of the great landed proprietors was also manifest in

Vaucluse, an area of large estates usually cut up into small farms. Some of these landowners, among them the Forbin-Janson family, introduced new agricultural techniques or new crops into the area, thereby adding an extra dimension to their influence. In the *arrondissement* of Arles in Bouches-du-Rhône as well, the aristocracy wielded great power, and the royalist fervour of this *arrondissement* earned it the telling label of 'Provençal Vendée'. The erstwhile seigneur (or his descendants) often became the mayor of the township, as in the case of the marquis de Barbentane or the marquis d'Albertas. Aix more than Marseille remained an aristocratic town that preserved a clearcut separation between the nobility and the bourgeoisie. In the department of Var, many noble families had kept their land, especially the forests. Almost everywhere this solid entrenchment on the land was the underlying reason for the nobility's power over at least some of the countryside, especially during the Restoration, when in addition to its economic power it began to exercise administrative or municipal functions. The exploitation of noble estates by stewards, share-croppers, or foremen made for a closer relationship between the landlord or 'master' and the farmer.

Having suffered the blow of Charles X's downfall in 1830, the ultras of the Midi turned into intransigent legitimists. Owing to the tactlessness of their local adversaries who now came to power – the prefect Thomas was a case in point – they were able to win over most of the population of the area, to the extent that it was Catholic. During the July Monarchy it was therefore the conflict between religious confessions (in places where significant Protestant communities existed side by side with the Catholic population) that was the impetus for popular support of legitimism in Gard and Haute-Garonne, in Tarn and a part of Hérault, in Aveyron and Lozère. But the duchesse de Berry failed to distinguish between sympathy and commitment, so that her adventure ended in disaster in April of 1832. She had counted entirely too much on a popular uprising of the urban masses.

Yet the royalist (ultra and later legitimist) tradition of southern France did have the support of the urban classes. A part of the bourgeoisie was devoted to it, especially at Marseille, whose Chamber of Commerce had sent a three-man delegation to the king as early as 1814. In a report dated 31 January 1818, the prefect had praised the city's business community, stating that it was respected 'because of a probity that it had preserved throughout the ages . . . and because of its services to the State that have been recognised by our kings'. The new merchants, those that had gone into banking or manufacturing, also shared this attachment to the Bourbons; the two groups were united in their hatred for Napoleon, and the economic difficulties they had experienced under his rule were not unrelated to their feelings. Even after the July Monarchy a segment of the bourgeoisie of Marseille (both in the business community and among professional men) preserved its legitimist sentiments, which were expressed in the election of the lawyer Berryer. A royalist bourgeoisie also existed at Toulouse, Nîmes, Montpellier, and Montauban.

In these towns the popular classes also preserved their royalist sentiments. This was especially true at Marseille, where the authorities of the Restoration permitted the development of workers' associations reminiscent of the old guilds, brotherhoods, or mutual aid societies. In 1816, for example, a dockworkers' mutual aid society directed by six elected 'priors' secured a monopoly over all the work on the quays. For a long time, the artisans as well continued to be sympathetic to the Bourbons, partly in obedience to the clergy, partly out of deference for the authorities or the notabilities, and later, after 1830, out of hostility against the July regime. This was not so much a matter of joining a cause after careful consideration as of conforming to the rules of conduct in a society based on clientage and patronage.

After 1830, the legitimists began to make a greater effort to disseminate and perpetuate their ideas in the press. Their originally often rather dull newspapers had ceased publishing at the fall of Charles X; now new, better-produced and more dynamic ones were launched. At Marseille, the *Gazette du Midi* began to appear as early as January 1831; Toulouse had the *Gazette du Languedoc*, Montpellier, the *Mélanges occitaniques*, founded in 1830, and from 1843 the *Echo du Midi*, Nîmes had the *Gazette du Bas-Languedoc*, Avignon, the *Messager*, and in 1843 even Draguignan published its own local legitimist paper, the *Gazette du peuple*. As a result, the legitimists were able to preserve an unusually strong political representation in the department of Bouches-du-Rhône; at one point two of the three deputies from Marseille were legitimists, and Tarascon elected a legitimist deputy as early as 1834. In Tarn also two of the three deputies were legitimists. In other departments the proportions were two out of six in Hérault, two out of five in Gard, two out of three in Ariège in 1839, and two out of three in Toulouse. Southern France furnished leaders for rival factions within legitimism, among them Berryer of Marseille and abbé de Genoude, who was elected in Toulouse in 1846.

The liberal core groups

After 1815, former Jacobins as well as liberals kept quiet and sometimes even went into exile because they feared local persecution. The bishop of Avignon, a former constitutional priest, was forced to retire, and the archbishop of Aix resigned from his see. For a long time there was no place and no hope for liberals in these areas. The lawyer Manuel went to the Vendée, where he was elected deputy; Thiers and Mignet left Aix, and Romiguières moved from Toulouse to Paris. It was not before the elections of 1827 that a liberal opinion emerged with the support of a segment of the business and professional community whose views were expressed in the *Sémaphore* of Marseille or the *France méridionale* of Toulouse.

While it is true that Narbonne, Béziers (in the person of Viennet) and Marseille (in the person of the lawyer Thomas) had elected liberals in 1828 or 1829, the reaction that took place under the Polignac government found a great deal of support in southern France. At Marseille the new prefect, marquis d'Arbau-Jouques, went to war against the *Sémaphore*, and the ultras profited from the enthusiasm sparked by the expedition against Algiers to reconquer Thomas's seat in June 1830. One of the main components of the liberals' resentment against the royalist ultras was the fact that before 1830 the latter had used the advantages of power for their own benefit; as Rémusat wrote in his *Mémoires* – and his observation can be extended beyond the region of Toulouse – this was 'a region where respect for the law, the vigorous pursuit of justice, devotion to the public good, sincerity, and clear thinking are rarely found under any circumstances'.

The July revolution, which took the populations of southern France by surprise, sparked a certain excitement in the liberal youth and was mainly greeted as an opportunity for revenge by those segments of the population who had suffered under the reign of Charles X. In the absence of disorders, and also because of the passivity of the supporters of the older branch of the Bourbons, much of the bourgeoisie rallied to Louis-Philippe, even though its attitude was more conservative than liberal. In 1830 the liberals represented the tradition of the 'blues' or indeed the Girondins; this was quite obvious in the departments of Gard and Hérault, where the most prominent liberals had inherited nationalised property or came from families that had furnished administrators under the Convention or the Directory and then under Louis-Philippe. It was in these departments (Gard, Hérault, Tarn-et-Garonne), which had a long-standing history of religious and social conflict between Protestant employers and Catholic workers and artisans, that the Protestants were most eager to show open support for the July regime. Yet Protestant support also existed in places where they only formed a very small minority. Cases in point are the Rabaud, Leenhardt, and Fraissinet families of Marseille as well as the banking family Courtois and the foundry owner Mather of Toulouse.

Another nucleus of liberalism was freemasonry. The looting and the threats suffered by the lodges of southern France in 1815 had accentuated their liberal and even anticlerical tendencies. Under the July Monarchy the membership of most of these lodges consisted of *petits bourgeois* or artisans, while the bourgeoisie that had belonged to them during the Restoration sometimes broke away. At Aix-en-Provence the lodge of the *Amis de la bienfaisance* had counted Manuel among its members, as well as a number of Jewish merchants like Crémieux, Bedarride, and Lisbonne.

After 1830, the members of the lodges often held municipal office, as for example Bernard, a wealthy pharmacist who was mayor of Béziers or Doumet, the mayor of Sète, a former squadron commander. Although a part of the business community continued to be legitimist after 1830, many of the Orleanist leaders in southern France were businessmen: this was the case at Marseille, where the mayor's office was occupied after 1830 by Alexis Rostand, a man who had been elected to the Chamber of Representatives under the Hundred Days and who would serve for many years as president of the departmental general council. It was also the case at Montpellier, where the mayor's office was occupied by well-to-do merchants or manufacturers. Yet the Orleanist leadership of the Midi lacked self-confidence; in 1831 the departments of Gard, Hérault, and Bouches-du-Rhône suspended the application of the new law calling for the election [rather than appointment] of municipal councils because they were afraid that it would lead to the election of legitimists. Municipal governments frequently experienced crises at Marseille, Montpellier, and Toulouse, which had ten mayors during the reign of Louis-Philippe. The slender margin of Orleanist opinion among the notables was compounded by a pervasive cliquishness; ensuing either from separate religious opinions or confessions or from membership in different occupational groups, this lack of unity within the ruling society was bound to weaken the local authorities. After 1830 the liberals counted on support from the central power, which is why their liberalism gave way to conservatism, opportunism, and place-seeking. It is no coincidence that *La Curée*, the satirical poem to which the invasion of public employment by the old liberals of the Restoration gave rise at the beginning of the July regime, should have been written by two poets from Marseille, Barthélémy and Méry, despite their involvement in the Three Glorious Days. In the southern departments the nomination of Orleanist candidates by the *collèges* of the *arrondissements* was often the result of pressure from the administration, which had transformed certain circumscriptions into rotten boroughs or fiefs; this was particularly evident in Vaucluse and Aude. In many cases the most important positions were firmly in the hands of the clients of a few liberal notables who sought revenge for the ordeals they had suffered under the White Terror. But of course it was impossible to satisfy all demands, and so the liberals of the Midi became divided after 1830, thereby further reducing the options of the government and fostering the persistence of a liberal opposition that gradually became radicalised. In the Midi adherence to the new dynasty was not so much a matter of ideological choice as of concern for family, professional, or local interests. The conservative and government-supporting element relied on the central power for extra advantages from the State and in particular for the material development of the region; but the fact is that placing realistic goals above passion was not in keeping with the spirit of the region. Eventually the maintenance of order and peace was to entail economic mutations that would inevitably upset the structures and mentalities of the traditional society.

The power of tradition was centred above all on the family.· While kinship relations in the widest sense were the over-riding concern throughout the Midi, with the clan and its clients assuming the widest scope in Corsica, continuity and the cult of the past pervaded all areas of life and had the entire sympathy of the country people and the artisans. There was a whole popular mythology that closely associated the cult of the dead and the cult of the saints, religious rituals and rituals of everyday life. Water, which was difficult to keep in the limestone regions of the Mediterranean littoral, was often treated with reverence and easily credited with healing powers, as it was at Sainte-Baume or at the grotto of Saint-Cer; Saint Agricol, who brings rain, was venerated in many places. The vitality of local customs is also evident in the persistence of a folk art that found expression in rustic furniture as well as in popular songs. Rigorously rejecting any abrupt break with the past, this tradition had definite counter-revolutionary overtones during the Restoration, but it also rebelled against inevitable economic change and gave rise to systematic resistance against the present. The Mediterranean south had few natural sympathies for liberalism, and the fact that liberalism had the support of the central power during the July Monarchy eventually drove the Mediterranean populations toward the democratic movement, although the economic evolution of the region also contributed to this shift.

The economic and social evolution

Whether born of local circumstances or of outside influences, the economic innovations of the time were promoted by the ruling classes – it could not be otherwise in so hierarchical a society. The administration was a factor of modernisation. During the Restoration era there were prefects who were both political moderates and sponsors of economic progress; such men were Siméon in Var, Christophe de Villeneuve-Bargemont at Marseille, and Charles de Rémusat's father at Toulouse. The July Monarchy only rarely permitted the kind of productive continuity that was achieved by the prefect Delacoste who served at Marseille from 1836 to 1848; once the power of the administration was weakened, the evolution took a more spontaneous course in the free interplay of individual initiative and collective constraints.

The populations

In the first half of the nineteenth century all the Mediterranean departments, except Aude, experienced an increase in population greater than that of France as a whole. This increase resulted above all from an increase in the populations of the towns, and it should be kept in mind that these departments (again, with the exception of Aude) had started out with a higher percentage of urban dwellers than France as a whole, and that the largest towns, which showed the greatest increase, continued to attract population. Marseille, which had about 110,000 inhabitants at the beginning of the Restoration – fewer than in 1801 – grew rapidly during the Restoration (145,000 in 1831) and then again after 1840 (183,182 in 1846). Whereas the principal centres of the old city were the port, the Cannebière and the rue d'Aix, the new city extended from the porte d'Aix to the place Castellane, and along the cours Julien to the allées de Meilhan. Construction continued apace with the increase in population, and the building industry in turn brought in a labour force from outside the city. Mortality was still high; indeed it was very high at the beginning of the July Monarchy when the cholera epidemic affected Marseille later than the rest of France, and especially in 1835, when the death of several thousand persons caused many people to flee the city in panic. The subsequent growth of the city resulted almost exclusively from immigration of people from the Alps, from Italy, and from Corsica.

Toulon also experienced rapid growth; its growth rate was among the highest for France as a whole. Counting 20,500 inhabitants in 1801, it had 62,000 in 1846. This growth was related to the development of the military port and the arsenal, which employed more than 5,000 men and attracted immigrants (not counting the special category of convicts).

Toulouse experienced considerable growth and became the fifth largest city of France in 1846 with 94,000 inhabitants. Yet it had very little industry and its principal activities were of an administrative and commercial nature. Its traditional role as a regional metropolis made it an attractive residence for the wealthy landed proprietors who spent the revenues from the land in the city, and a large student population spread its influence throughout the region. Thus, its active population was relatively small, while what we would now call the tertiary sector was quite large. Under these circumstances the supply of labour exceeded the demand, a fact that is indicated by the presence of large numbers of domestic servants.

All the other major towns experienced a growth in population, albeit not always of the same kind and at the same rate. Moreover, the rural population of the Midi, much larger than that of the rest of France, included the inhabitants of the many small towns which, although they were in some ways beginning to decline, were nonetheless marked by a strongly urban mentality. Their local patriotism ('*esprit de clocher*') often compounded the new problems arising from the evolution of the economy with long-standing local rivalries; rural markets like those of the small towns of Vaucluse gave this department an urban population of 48 per cent of the total (compared to 24 per cent for France as a whole), even though there was not a single major agglomeration. In upper Languedoc and in the westernmost part of the Midi, the population was more predominantly rural. Many small towns of this region (Castres, Mazamet, Lavaur, Foix and Tarascon in Ariège) had some industry operating in the traditional artisanal manner that was increasingly threatened by the evolution of the economy, a situation that sometimes formed a stark contrast with the agricultural prosperity of these departments.

The development of agriculture

In 1836 the rural populations still predominated in all the departments of the Midi except in Bouches-du-Rhône, and cereal production was the mainstay of agriculture. This was the case in upper Languedoc, in Vaucluse, and in Provence, where large landed estates were more prevalent than in the rest of France. Nobles or wealthy commoners, many of whom had been ousted from administrative or political office after 1830, turned to the management of their estates, introduced innovations and disseminated them in their cantons. These large estates were managed either directly or by sharecroppers (*métayers*). Nonetheless, the fragmentation of the land – further accentuated by peasant acquisitions in Gard and in the region of Tarascon and the sale of land to city-dwellers in Haute-Garonne – made for a large number of small owners.

In some areas, for example in Vaucluse, both large estates and many day-labourers who also owned a little land existed in the same region. The production of cereals was the most important consideration in the system of crop rotation practiced in the plains (where wheat was the principal cereal) as well as in the mountainous areas (where more rye was grown). Wheat remained the dominant crop in the plains of Hérault and the Orb valley, and much of the new land gained by the draining of the marshes of the lower Rhône was planted in wheat. Cereals occupied most of the surface in the mixed farming practiced almost everywhere. In addition to cereals, legumes and maize were raised in the west, while much of the Comtat and Provence engaged in market gardening, which often produced low yields. Some regions began to cut back their wheat production around 1840; in Provence this change was prompted by the large-scale imports of Russian wheat and in lower Languedoc it was due to the planting of new vineyards.

Among the other elements of the traditional agriculture that experienced a relative decline were the olive trees of the Mediterranean region and sheep-raising. Olive, fig, and mulberry trees were planted in rows around the fields or interspersed among the vines. However, the olive trees fell victim to the severe winters of 1820 and 1830, and then, in 1828, to the worms that gave a reddish tint to the oil; in addition, the production of olive oil was also threatened by the competition of oleaginous grains. As for sheep-raising, the practice of transhumance had been the source of contact but also conflict between shepherds and farmers for many generations; now agriculture evolved in such a way that the flocks were driven from the farmland of the plains.

Several rather speculative crops related to certain industrial activities were developed by archaic methods. Among them were products used in tanning, such as sumac, a small bush that was raised in Vaucluse between 1820 and 1828, and teasels. Madder [a red dye] was a good source of income for the small peasants of Vaucluse and Provence for a few years after 1815. Mulberry trees and silkworms were cultivated more intensively in Gard and Vaucluse and brought welcome supplementary income, especially to modest landowners. Agricultural progress was promoted by agricultural societies and such publications as the *Annales provençales d'agriculture*, the *Journal de la société d'agriculture de Toulouse*, the *Guide du propriétaire*, or the *Cours d'agriculture* published by Adrien de Gasparin, the founder of the *Société agricole* of Orange who served as prefect and later minister during the July Monarchy.

The expansion of agriculture was linked to technical advances, such as the extension of irrigation. For the most part, such major improvements were made by large landowners and represent the first involvement of large-scale capitalism in agriculture; under the July Monarchy several financing partnerships, led by Talabot, joined together to form the *Compagnie générale de desséchement* [Land Reclamation Company] which contributed to the development of the eastern Camargue.

Of particular importance was the introduction of rice-growing in the Camargue. The reclamation of the Crau and of the marshes of Arles was also begun under the July Monarchy. By the end of the period, almost 70 estates of more than 1,000 hectares in the Camargue, using the most advanced techniques available at the time for draining and irrigation, were developing fodder crops and new meadows.

The Mediterranean south was not yet producing more wine than any other region of France. In 1828 only 12 per cent of the French harvest came from the departments of Hérault, Gard, Aude, and Pyrénées-Orientales, and the vine had by no means monopolised the landscape. However, in lower Languedoc this was the time when vineyards were beginning to replace mixed farming. Wine exports by the port of Sète increased from 119,554 hectolitres in 1818 to 328,424 hectolitres in 1844.

The extension of surfaces planted in vines was particularly marked in Hérault, where vineyards took over much of the *costières*, the hillsides and the old terraces by the sea. The development of new vineyards made it possible for the populations of the large villages to stay on the land. Eventually the vine spread to the plain in Aude or near Frontignan and Lunel, around Montpellier, and finally in the region of Saint-Gilles. New vineyards appeared in Var and Vaucluse. Upper Languedoc also had considerable acreages of vineyards (10 per cent of the surface in Tarn-et-Garonne, 7.2 per cent in Haute-Garonne) that essentially produced wine for home consumption, but the region of Gaillac (Tarn) had begun to produce a better quality of wine that was sold commercially. New varieties of grapes were introduced, and new hybrids were developed by Bouschet and Bernard. More and more wine was produced for the market; but if high wine prices under the Restoration yielded a much better income than cereal production, this situation was not to last, and the wine industry experienced a severe slump in sales between 1840 and 1843.

The agricultural landscape of the Mediterranean south, then, was extremely varied and testified to great contrasts in resources and forms of farming. Whether archaic or modernised, the agriculture of the region was bound to be affected whenever the economic conditions were modified by changing commercial activities.

Commerce and its relations with Algeria

More than elsewhere, industrial activity was a function of the evolution of commerce. Poor roads, for example, ensured the survival of a local artisanal production, as in the case of some of the textile industries of Languedoc or the wood-fuelled forges of Ariège that were protected by their isolation from the competition of more modern technology (and, incidentally, often owned by noble landowners who were primarily seigneurs rather than investors). On the other hand, industrial activity sometimes also responded to the needs of a more commercialised agriculture, as in the case of the cork-workers who manufactured bottle corks in the Massif des Maures.

Trade within the region still moved extremely slowly. Every day Toulouse, located at the intersection of many roads, saw the arrival or departure of more than 60 *diligences* and gave work to 40 coach-building enterprises; yet in 1825 it took eight to ten hours to reach Castres (75 km) and twenty-six hours to reach Perpignan; one could go from Toulouse to Carcassonne and from there to Nîmes in thirty-eight hours, and even in 1840, twenty-seven hours was the best time one could make between Toulouse and Marseille.

Because the Mediterranean rivers were prone to violent flooding, the bridges were often swept away or were extremely expensive to build. The bridge at Avignon was completed in 1819 but broke apart in September 1821 and again in 1830, so that it was decided to replace it with a suspension bridge in 1840. The six new bridges over the Durance were either damaged or destroyed by the flooding of 1840.

Railway construction was discussed very early but remained in the planning stage until 1848. The first line to be built in the region linked Alès and La Grand' Combe with Beaucaire; its construction was directly related to the exploitation and the marketing of coal from the mines of La Grande Combe. In July 1839, a railway line made the connection between Nîmes and Beaucaire, and by 1840 there were altogether 89 kilometres of railway. The production of the coal mines of Alès, which had increased from 20,000 tons in 1815 to 45,000 tons in 1835, amounted to 415,000 tons by 1845. The local business circles were not ready for these construction projects; as a result, they lost out to business interests from outside the region. The Alès–Beaucaire railway was financed by Talabot, and the business community of Montpellier lost its bid for the Montpellier–Sète railway to a company headed by a Belgian investor, the duc de Mecklembourg. Large-scale trade was carried out by sea in the rapidly expanding port of Sète (still spelt Cette at the time), at Toulon, and especially at Marseille.

Shipping was becoming an increasingly important activity for Marseille. The growth of its port was stimulated by the considerable increase in the volume of shipping brought about by the French expansion in Algeria and by a rise in industrial production. Increased production was achieved by some of the older enterprises that had modernised, such as the soap factories that were beginning to use palm oil; these factories in turn were a stimulus to the production of soda. Oil-works still processed the regional olive harvests but also made use of oleaginous grains, and after 1842, the Régis brothers imported peanuts from Gambia. Candle-making (during the Restoration there were five workshops in Bouches-du-Rhône) and later the production of stearin were also developed at Marseille. Cane-sugar refineries were closely associated with foreign trade (the most important of these refineries belonged to marquis de Forbin-Janson). Flour-mills, some of them operating by steam after 1840, produced the raw material for the production of semolina and pasta products. The development of such industrial and commercial activities in turn stimulated the building trades, and with them the production of cement near Arles.

In the years around 1840 the port of Marseille, decayed but undergoing modernisation with the building of the port of Joliette, was frequented by 3,800 ships annually. It received 78 per cent of all French imports of fats and sulphur as well as 71 per cent of the foreign cereals imported from Egypt and the Black Sea, and 45 per cent of the imported leather. In 1846 Marseille was leading France's foreign trade with 18 per cent of all the import duties collected. The law of 1845, which raised the import duties on sesame, reduced the import of oleaginous grains, but thanks to the efforts of Marseille's mayor and deputy Reynard, the import duty on peanuts was not raised. Imports of coal and also the opening of the Beaucaire–Alès railway line in 1840 and its extension to La Grand' Combe in 1841 reduced the price of coal in Marseille and permitted its increased industrial use.

The metal industry connected with the shipyards of La Ciotat and La Seyne was stimulated by the building of locomotives or iron steamships. In 1847 the first copper-ore processing plant was opened in Marseille.

Nonetheless, much of this industry remained traditional, even at Marseille and Toulon, and the use of steam engines was still rare on the eve of 1848. Scattered activities were a developing tanning industry in Var (whereas tanning was in decline at Marseille) and in Hérault. Elsewhere a traditional textile industry continued to be the mainstay of such places as Castres, Mazamet, Bédarieux, Lodève, or Ganges.

Southern France was slow to mobilise its capital; in 1825 the prefect of Toulouse was unable to persuade the local investors to pool their resources. Retailers or middlemen were reluctant to have recourse to banks or to credit. The founding of the Bank of Toulouse in 1828 had little effect on business. Marseille was suffering from a chronic shortage of specie for financing its operations; following a number of unsuccessful projects, the narrowly adopted ordinance of 27 September 1835 finally created the Banque de Marseille. This bank was severely affected by the recession of 1839, but it withstood the crisis, as it did in 1846, and proved beneficial to the transaction of business. At Montpellier, which already had several major banking houses, among them that of Zoé Granier, the city's deputy and mayor, in addition to the banking house of Reynaud of Sète, a branch of the Banque de France was established in 1838 with the backing of members of the Chamber of Commerce. This branch worked mainly with the wine and brandy trade (notably Reynaud) and with the textile firms (in particular the silk manufactures of Ganges). No doubt it also became involved in the Algerian trade, since it was a merchant of Montpellier by the name of Lichtenstein, who also served as the Prussian consul, who in 1845 was asked by the merchants of Algiers to arrange for a branch office in their city.

The growth of large-scale capitalism was particularly evident in the wine trade and in salt production (which had recently become Lichtenstein's quasi-monopoly). Local fairs continued to play a vital role in the interior trade; in 1845 a regent of the Banque de France could write about the fair of Beaucaire: 'People will come from all the neighbouring departments to make their annual purchases of all kinds of merchandise.'

Marseille, Sète and Toulon traded with Algeria; in 1840, 403 ships sailed for Algeria from Marseille alone. Business firms benefited from this trade, but local industries were also stimulated by it. Shoes were manufactured at Toulon, and cloth for the Algerian army was produced at Lodève as well as by the cloth factories of Castres and Mazamet which, moreover, enjoyed the support of Marshal Soult, the Minister of War and the all-powerful protector of the department of Tarn. As a result, public opinion in southern France unanimously clamoured for continued conquest in Algeria – albeit for a variety of reasons, since the Orleanist notables were mainly interested in increased economic opportunities, while the legitimists were emotionally involved. At Toulon a newspaper took the telling title of *Sentinelle de la marine et de l'Algérie*. Actually, the economic development of southern France varied from department to department and even within these departments; this situation accentuated the social disparities that played a role in the birth of the democratic movement (this will be discussed later). The Mediterranean south was one of the few regions that favoured free trade at the end of the July Monarchy – with some exceptions, to be sure. The drapers, especially those of Bordeaux, remained protectionist, and most of the legitimists did not like the free trade movement, which they saw as a manifestation of anglophilia. While the recession of 1847 did have an impact, notably with the decline of wine prices, southern France and Marseille were relatively well protected against economic crises before the February revolution.

Opposition to the July regime and the democratic movement

The very fact that towns where the 'whites' had won overwhelming victories in 1815 should have cast large percentages of votes for the 'reds' of 1848 or 1849 presupposes that a latent evolution had taken place during the monarchy of limited suffrage.

The opposition groups

As we saw earlier, Louis-Philippe's monarchy was sustained in the southern departments only by a minority that had cast its lot with the central power. To be sure, the indifferent masses and the opportunists of Toulouse, Avignon, Toulon, and most of the other towns went along with it; but the regime made the mistake of confusing the ordinary citizen's habit of accepting successive regimes with enthusiastic assent and indeed with the active support it received from the National Guard.

Opposition during the early 1830s was mainly a matter of deep hostility for Louis-Philippe, grounded in strong legitimist feelings and disseminated by newspapers, placards, and cartoons. By taking measures designed to stop the legitimists' subversive activities and by exaggerating their impact, the government unintentionally played into their hands, for the very fact that they were feared gave them power, which was always respected in the Midi.

The anniversary of Louis XVI's death on 21 January 1831 was celebrated with solemn church services. In one incident at Toulouse, for example, young people who had attended mass tore posters announcing the singing of the *Marseillaise* from the walls of a theatre, thereby arousing the indignation of liberal students and members of the National Guard. Secret councils, journeys, and communications, and supposedly clandestine meetings, established close ties among the legitimists and kept up their hopes. The supporters of Charles X had formed an organisation in Haute-Garonne and the neighbouring departments, as well as in Hérault, Gard, Vaucluse, and Bouches-du-Rhône, but they obviously misjudged if not their number, then at least their will to fight: when the duchesse de Berry disembarked, the supporters – who had spent too much time waiting – were bogged down in petty quarrelling. The planned uprising miscarried on 30 April 1832 in Marseille; at dawn only 60 supporters appeared at the place where 2,000 were supposed to assemble, and in the other towns that were waiting for a signal, no uprising was even attempted. However, the duchesse de Berry and her entourage could not possibly have travelled through Provence and Languedoc, pursued by all the Orleanist authorities after their initial surprise, without the widespread support of the inhabitants of these regions. Since they had not actually engaged in fighting, the legitimist organisations of the south were not persecuted as severely as those of the west; however, the most serious blow to their cause, more serious even than the subsequent revelations about the duchesse de Berry, was the dereliction of the Carlist leaders, which led to many defections among the legitimist rank and file.

In the wake of this affair a somewhat paradoxical agreement was reached in many towns between the extreme wings of the two oppositions to the new monarchy. Yet the democratic movement had initially, in the immediate aftermath of the July revolution, taken the form of open hostility toward everything that recalled the elder branch of the Bourbons, toward their supporters and in particular toward the Catholic clergy, which was accused of continued sympathy for the Restoration regime. Democratic opinion was propagated by a few short-lived newspapers; at Marseille the *Peuple souverain* (which printed an edition of 650 copies) was forced, its title notwithstanding, to suspend publication for a long time for lack of readers. Republican associations originally found members in the major towns only. At Marseille, a patriotic association consisting of a few bourgeois was founded by Demosthène Olivier in October 1832. At the other end of the region, republican ideas began to spread in the Pyrénées-Orientales under the influence of the *savant* Arago: the *Société des droits de l'homme* counted more than 300 militants at Perpignan, but branches were also founded at Estagel, Rivesaltes, Collioure and in some ten other communes. Altogether, they assembled more than 2,500 republicans. At Toulouse, republican ideas were reawakened in the years after 1830 through the cultivation of Bonapartist sentiments; Saint Napoleon's day (15 August), for example, was celebrated with banquets. Here the *Société des droits de l'homme* recruited its members mainly among the *petite bourgeoisie* of the National Guard and among the students of the medical school and the school of veterinary medicine, but also among the workers of the faubourgs Saint-Etienne and Saint-Cyprien; by 1834, it had more than 2,000 members. A left-wing periodical, *L'Emancipation*, was founded at the end of 1836; upon becoming a daily in 1838, this paper adopted the motto *Dieu et la Loi, Réforme et Progrès* [God and the Law, Reform and Progress]. In the region between Marseille and Toulouse the principal centres of republicanism were in the Vaunage region (Gard), at Calvisson, Sommières, Clarensac, and Montpellier, where the republicans were also in evidence when the Saint-Simonians passed through the city in March of 1833. The Saint-Simonians' entry into Marseille on 16 March 1833 'followed by several hundred men of the lower classes singing the *Marseillaise* and the *Carmagnole*' explains why in a later report the Saint-Simonians were called the 'travelling salesmen of the Republic'. This double influence [of the *Société des droits de l'homme* and Saint-Simonianism] also made itself felt among the officers of Perpignan, at Toulon where it was represented by an administrator of the Navy, Blache, and by Jean Aicard (the father of the poet) and at Castelnaudary in Aude.

Saint-Simonianism, which had taken hold in Languedoc before 1830, began to spread throughout the south after that date, usually among groups that subsequently adopted democratic ideas. As early as 1833, the success of the Saint-Simonians among the workers of Marseille was an indication that some segments of the 'people' were evolving toward republicanism; on 14 July 1833 the anniversary of the storming of the Bastille was celebrated by 250 workers. Medallions bearing the image of Robespierre or Marat and red caps were in fashion among some of the workers in the shoemaking and carpentry trades who had been won over by the *Société des droits de l'homme*, which counted 700 members divided into 36 sections in Marseille. From there the society spread to Aix, Tarascon, Avignon, and especially to the department of Var. At Draguignan, Brignoles, and Le Luc, republican groups were formed, and the vivid oratory of Flora Tristan delivered at Toulon in 1844 led to the formation of a republican club. All in all, this type of opposition took many different forms. Turmoil in the streets triggered by charivaris at the homes of authority figures of the regime or disturbances in theatres usually did not amount to more than youthful unruliness, especially on the part of the students of Toulouse and Montpellier.

Sometimes the movement participated in public opinion campaigns on the national level, as for example between 1838 and 1841, when demands for electoral reforms were voiced by petitions and banquets. This first reformist campaign of southern France was greatly helped by the efforts of Arago in the region of Perpignan and by those of Joly, another radical deputy, in the Toulouse area. In October 1840 meetings followed by banquets calling for electoral reforms were held at Marseille and Toulouse, at Montpellier, Perpignan, Carcassone, and Callas in Var.

One must not of course exaggerate the influence of the republicans of the south; the voicing of popular discontent stemmed mainly from the deteriorating condition of the labouring class and from the difficult situation faced by small property owners. Yet it is true that the legitimists and the left-wing opposition alike made it their business to sharpen the focus of this diffuse discontent or to defend those whose demands or protests had been squelched. Although strikes were never comparable in scope to those of other regions, labour coalitions did spring up. Some of these had already existed during the Restoration, among them the bakers' association formed at Marseille in July 1823 and the masons' association formed at Toulon in May 1826, but at that time the authorities had paid little attention to them. The artisanal nature of the small enterprises had made for close ties between the owner and the workers working side by side. Under the July Monarchy labour unrest became more frequent. In February 1838 the carpenters of the arsenal of Toulon went on strike, even though they were considered to be very docile workers. In May 1845 the first major strike, involving 2,510 workers (half of the work force), broke out at the arsenal. This is one of the few instances of a modern type of strike. During the monarchy of limited suffrage, workers' coalitions in southern France were for the most part formed in the traditional trades (among shoemakers, tanners, tailors, and coopers) and at the construction sites of major public work projects (by the stonecutters working on the Alès railway in September 1839 or by the navvies working on the canal of Marseille near Aix). In the textile industry, finally, many of the archaic factories were unable to compete in an expanding market; in this sector strikes were prompted by wage reductions, by the workers' hostility to new machines, which they suspected of depriving them of work, and in general by the wretched conditions of the working class, aggravated by each successive crisis. Already in November 1828, new carding and weaving machines had been smashed by textile-workers in Aude. In February 1839, a strike broke out in the factory of Lodève. The comings and goings of a seasonal labour force for the grain and especially the grape harvests also gave rise to popular unrest, fights, and even delinquent behaviour. Repression was generally swift and severe, as was the repression of strikes. Violence also occurred in clashes between the journeymen of the different trades: in May 1839 for example, on the feast day of Saint Honoré – the patron saint of the bakers – several persons were killed in a fight between the bakers and the carpenters of Toulouse.

Another form of opposition, aimed more directly against the State, developed with respect to taxation on the occasion of a rather ambiguous modification of the tax base and the taking of the census of 1841. A great deal of anti-fiscal agitation took place in many regions of France, especially in the Midi. This agitation assumed the most serious scope at Toulouse, where on 9 July 1841 the first census-taking operations, misinterpreted by rumours carefully planted by the left-wing opposition, and especially by the legitimists, led to the gathering of crowds and the building of barricades in the streets, which in turn provoked cavalry charges, injuries, and arrests. On 13 July one demonstrator was killed; the prefect Mahul and the solicitor-general were assaulted and fled the city, and calm was not restored for some time. Some municipal councils, among them those of Toulouse and Montpellier, declared the new forms of census-taking illegal. Hostility against the fiscal powers was also aroused by the excise tax on beverages.

Although popular protests did not necessarily translate democratic aspirations, the collective expression of discontent and especially the voicing of demands did promote the development of democratic behaviour. That this was the case is shown clearly by the municipal elections (the only ones in which a popular element was able to vote) at the end of the July Monarchy. In southern France the growth of the democratic movement – which was to burst into full bloom during the Second Republic – was fostered by two very different developments.

From Carlism to the Republic

Southern France moved from legitimism to republican ideas as a result of the alliance between Carlists and republicans that had been concluded in several of its cities. In 1834 legitimists and men of the Movement had formed a coalition that won a majority in the city council of Marseille. It is symptomatic that in the towns where an alliance between Carlists and republicans was formed (if only temporarily), the number of legitimists elected decreased with each municipal election. In the city council of Marseille, for example, they declined from 17 (out of 41) in 1834 to 8 in 1837 and then to 5. There is no doubt that many of the legitimists viewed this rapprochement – which did not take place everywhere – with grave misgivings and preferred to shift their allegiance to the July Monarchy, especially as the regime was becoming more and more conservative.

It is a telling fact for the evolution of the popular classes that some of the lower-class legitimists turned to the democratic movement because of the increasing inaction of their original party, especially since at the same time the denunciation – notably in the press – of the scandals or simply the profit-making among the ruling classes gave rise to considerable discontent and vivid jealousies, particularly with respect to parvenus. On the other hand, the artisans' long-standing tendency to form occupational groups contributed to the popularity of the traditional associations that kept up their contacts with the royalist notables and the clergy. Indeed, certain segments of the popular classes of the Midi maintained these contacts long after 1848. Yet it was precisely because a lagging economy and a pervasive spiritual conservatism had prevented these populations from coming in contact with the individualism of bourgeois liberalism that radical ideas and ardent adherence to any idea that combined notions of political and social reform could so easily take hold among them. Moreover, the guilds were so tradition-bound that new workers or rapidly developing occupational groups could not be fully integrated into this system, a situation that contributed to the success of the *Société de l'union* of southern France, which seems to have been founded at Toulon in 1830. This movement represented the desire of young artisans to break out of the traditional journeymen's associations, even though the latter were not necessarily in agreement with the legitimists' political traditionalism.

Democratic opinions also developed among the disappointed liberals who had initially supported the July Monarchy and who had come to believe that the defence of liberty demanded more equality, at least in the realm of politics. Particularly strong in the region of Toulouse and in Aude, this egalitarian attitude was often reinforced by the Napoleonic legend, which was still very much alive among some segments of the public in these departments – unlike in Provence, where it had very little influence. The stability of the central government, translated on the local level into the monopolising of power, influence, and favours from the administration by the same families or factions, contributed to widespread discontent. The fact that the government relied more and more on rallied legitimists to ensure the election of its candidates in the elections of 1846, in which the government party often did very well indeed, goaded the democratic left into action. Especially in Languedoc and Roussillon, many of its members became involved in the banquet campaign of 1847 that afforded the local populations a first impression of the men who a few months later became the local cadres of the Second Republic in its first stages.

Despite its improved showing in the elections, the July Monarchy had never taken firm root in the Midi. Local antagonisms facilitated the task of the administration, which had the responsibility for arbitrating and, in the final analysis, making the decisions in all new problems: long-standing rivalries between Arles and Tarascon, or between Montpellier and Nîmes, for example, were further aggravated by the projected railway. Yet the extreme parties (legitimists and radicals) did form coalitions to fight the central government and everything they considered to be part of the domination of the north. But this common opposition did not by any means prevent local antagonisms and passions from erupting on the occasion of the Léotade case that was tried before the Toulouse tribunal in early February 1848. A brother of the Doctrine Chrétienne, brother Léotade, was accused of having raped and murdered a 14-year-old girl. Given the circumstances of that moment, this criminal case assumed sociological and political significance and unleashed a storm of anticlerical passion.

The Mediterranean and Languedocian south felt the need to express passions more than ideas. The preacher in the pulpit, the artist in the theatre, the political orator at a reformist banquet, and the lawyer in the courtroom all sought to stir their public (and they often had the same public) by turning day-to-day occurrences into a spectacle in which the audience took part. Public affairs played as important a role in the cities as they did in the small villages of the Midi; at times interest in such matters was kept up by a local occurrence, at other times it was stimulated by some national event.

12

The southwest

Some of these departments looked toward the ocean, often with nostalgia for the eighteenth century and for the prosperity brought by the trade with the West Indies. Yet these were predominantly rural regions, where agriculture had actually progressed due to the decline of artisanal activities and the reduction of commercial activities that had ensued from the shift in the pattern of international trade.

How, then, shall we define the southwest? A region without historical unity, it included areas with strongly marked traditions such as the Basque country and Béarn, which were quite different from the others. Lacking linguistic and administrative unity, this region may have drawn a very relative unity from the existence of a regional metropolis, Bordeaux. But the influence of Bordeaux varied considerably in strength and character, depending on the place and the local activities. The Charente, some of the Limousin, the Landes, Périgord, the Agenais, and the western part of the Pyrenees, as well as the department of Gers (which in many respects was pointed more toward Toulouse) – altogether nine or ten departments may be said to represent the southwest at that time.

The originality of the southwest in the first half of the nineteenth century was related both to the persistence of an old-style economy characterised by the predominance of agricultural and commercial activities and to the peculiarities of a regional temperament. But was this regional temperament a political phenomenon? It was not so much rooted in that famous 'Girondism' which seems to be more myth than reality as in an adaptation to the constitutional monarchy and a propensity for the *'juste milieu'* that was a (conformist) form of liberalism. Still, one wonders whether this attitude was the cause or the result of the lesser development experienced by the departments of the southwest south of Poitiers. All in all, the southwest under the monarchy of limited suffrage can be defined by contrast with the neighbouring regions, for it was distinguished from western France, which extended as far as the Vendée, and also from Languedoc, by a different kind of political behaviour that corresponded at least in part to different social structures.

254

The pervasive individualism of the region – not a theoretical postulate but an actual experience – marked by greater concern for liberty than for equality, was as hostile to constraints as to disturbances; and a greater tolerance, for example in the relations among Catholics, Protestants, and Jews, went hand in hand with distrust for everything that came from Paris and was too brazenly new.

Diversity and inadequacies of the rural world

In all of these departments, the preponderance of the rural population was greater than the average for France as a whole, amounting to 90 per cent in Dordogne and Charente in 1836, 89 per cent in Landes, 77 per cent in Gironde (despite the presence of the metropolitan area of Bordeaux, the only large city in the region). After a spurt of growth that affected all parts of the region during the Restoration, the population – even in such low density areas as the Landes, where there were 30 inhabitants per square kilometre in 1831 – had reached a saturation point in relation to the available resources, either because there had been a marked increase in sparsely populated departments like Landes or Hautes-Pyrénées, or because the population had reached a plateau and remained stationary and even began to decline, as was the case in Gers and Lot-et-Garonne. These few generalisations, however, should not be permitted to obscure the great diversity of the land.

Even the main wine-producing areas continued to practice mixed farming. In Charente and Charente-Inférieure, brandy exports doubled under the Restoration, bringing prosperity to the *arrondissements* of Cognac and Angoulême and to large numbers of small owner–occupiers who converted more and more land into vineyards. Large wine-producing estates, by contrast, still existed in Gironde, the department which, along with Charente-Inférieure, had the most extensive vineyards in 1840. The vine was also an important resource in Gers, where Armagnac was produced, in Lot-et-Garonne, in the Dordogne, and in the regions of Bergerac and Montbazillac.

In most of these regions cereals were the principal crop; in Gironde, the area devoted to wheat increased from 61,000 hectares in 1825 to 69,000 hectares in 1835, and wheat production (after some initial fluctuations) rose by 30 per cent during the same period. In Lot-et-Garonne the surface planted in wheat increased by 40 per cent and production increased by 50 per cent after having actually doubled in 1830. In Landes and Basses-Pyrénées, maize prevailed over wheat. A special zone was that of the coastal dwellers: in Saintonge, the most populated stretch of the coast, salt marshes were exploited by small operators, but this activity began to decline after 1830 when it was unable to compete with the salt mines of eastern France and the salt-works of the Mediterranean south. The native flat oysters on the other hand, which were beginning to be harvested on the Seudre, were no longer simply gathered; commercial oyster beds were developed in the region of Saintes and Marennes, whereas mussels still contributed only locally to the wealth of the Bay of Aiguillon. As for fishing, it was generally speaking in decline during this period: fewer and fewer fishing expeditions to Newfoundland left La Rochelle, and it was only toward the end of the period that the tinning of sardines in oil, a technique that had been developed at Nantes, was practiced in Charente-Inférieure.

There were three distinct forest areas in the southwest. Forests played an important role in the Pyrenees, where they were often owned by the townships. In the Landes forests were actually being expanded, since it became necessary to plant young pines in order to contain the marshes and ponds that threatened to encroach upon the cultivated land. Pine forests formed the basis of an entire artisanal and domestic industry, since workers tapped the trees for resin and potters manufactured the receptacles for it. But the resin-workers did not receive their share of the profits to be made from the rise in the price of resin or turpentine for which there was an increasing demand; in February 1836 at Lespéron they rioted for better pay. Under the July Monarchy the production of charcoal in the Landes led to the development of a metal industry that exploited the iron ore to be found in the soil of that region. Bertrand Geoffroy had come from the Ardennes in 1831 and brought modern metallurgy to the area, despite local attempts to thwart his undertaking. The *Société des hauts fourneaux, forges et laminoirs de l'Adour*, which he financed with Belgian capital, was the first to use the steam engine in its factory at Abesse. In Périgord and in the transition zone to the Massif central, the forestry interest encountered opposition mainly from the stock-breeders, for the tillers of the soil were much more concerned about the transhumance of large herds of animals between Auvergne and the lowlands of the Garonne. In the Landes, baron Poyféré de Cère came to the defence of the shepherds who watched over their flocks perched on stilts. Sheep-raising had survived from an older economy, and cattle-raising had yet to come into its own in the first half of the nineteenth century.

Among the developing sources of wealth, mention must be made of fruit trees, especially in Lot-et-Garonne. Plums from Agen were exported far and wide, and the cultivation of tobacco expanded in the departments of Lot and Lot-et-Garonne. Hemp production, by contrast, was in decline, although a few cord factories continued to work for the navy at Marmande and Tonneins.

Farming and the distribution of property

Sharecropping (*métayage*) was most prevalent in Aquitaine, except in wine-producing regions, where direct management and large domains existed side by side. Working conditions were extremely diverse; wherever there was a surplus of population, the share of the *métayer* tended to decrease in favour of the landlord, as was the case in Gers. In other regions the decline of working opportunities in the artisanal crafts inflated the agricultural labour force, which had to accept low wages; this could be observed in Lot-et-Garonne and in the Dordogne. In hard times the sharecropper of Landes lived exclusively on the products of his garden plot. Sharecropping perpetuated the old techniques and the practice of mixed farming for domestic food production. In this manner, the structure of land tenure contributed to economic underdevelopment in a region that did not experience periods of dire misery, but was also cut off from development of the capitalist type.

Small property and direct management were prevalent in Dordogne and along the Isle and Dordogne rivers, in Charente, and in Béarn. In the departments located in the Pyrenees, the land was extremely fragmented; in the canton of Monein, for example, 2,591 of the 10,581 inhabitants were landowners, owning a total of 25,000 plots of land. In many rural communes virtually every family owned at least a small plot. The owners of extensive noble estates, though definitely in the minority, commanded the respect of the local populations. Under the Restoration the landed aristocracy dominated the rural areas of Aquitaine and the Pyrenees.

The deterioration of the countryside and the exodus to the city

In several regions the conditions of peasant life deteriorated under the monarchy of limited suffrage. First and perhaps foremost, this deterioration was nothing more than the persistence of a long-standing situation, but the real or supposed improvement of other regions and the growing lure of the cities made chronic misery more difficult to bear. The decline of the rural artisanal trades contributed to the degradation of the countryside; thus the rural textile industry of the region of Nay was badly hurt by the slump in exports to Spain. The division or sale of communal property was another factor. In the department of Landes, the prefect's office urged the departmental council and the communes to sell their communal wastelands. The local landowners, however, worried that they might lose the right to pasture their sheep on this land; others were opposed to auctioning off the commons because it would bring in 'outsiders, and even companies which, by way of speculation, would buy up large tracts of heath', as a wealthy ironmaster, Lareillet, expressed it in 1836. The sale of the commons, the draining of marshes, and the clearing of the heath often aggravated the social cleavage between a few wealthy, educated and dynamic landowners and the majority of the peasants whose condition remained as precarious as ever. A few years later this condition was depicted by Eugène Roy whose novel *Jacquou le Croquant* was modelled on the countryside of Périgord in 1830. Overpopulated in relation to their resources, most of the rural areas of the southwest reached their highest population density at the time of the census of 1846, that is, before they were affected by the railway revolution that further aggravated their economic and demographic imbalance. The fragmentation of the land and the practice of mixed farming for domestic consumption had scarcely prepared the southwest for a more advanced commercialised agriculture and for facing the competition that was brought by the railway in the third quarter of the nineteenth century.

Urban centres and commercial activities

The southwest had only one large city, Bordeaux. Its preponderance was unchallenged, but connections with Béarn, not to mention the Agenais, were so slow that its influence did not reach very far under the monarchy of limited suffrage. Owing to the underdevelopment of industry in this area, most of Bordeaux' trade was concerned with agricultural products, a situation that reinforced the symbiosis between the city and its hinterland.

Bordeaux and the towns of the southwest

It was thus the region that was responsible for the growth of Bordeaux which attracted the populations that were forced to leave lands that could no longer feed them. Only in 1840 did Bordeaux regain its population of 1789. The splendour of their city at the end of the Ancien Regime was a memory dear to the hearts of the Bordelais of the first half of the nineteenth century; and yet in 1846, Bordeaux with its 121,520 inhabitants was still the fourth largest city of France. In order to accommodate the often unstable populations arriving from the hinterland, Bordeaux expanded, building new neighbourhoods to the north, beyond the Chartrons quarter where the upper bourgeoisie connected with the wine trade lived on broad avenues; to the northwest, where the Saint-Seurin quarter was developed without as yet reaching Caudéran, which became the most populous suburb; and to the west, where the Saint-Bruno quarter benefited from the construction of a tobacco factory that had been in the planning since 1811. The trade in colonial produce was concentrated in the Saint-Pierre quarter and in the rue de la Rousselle. The demographic situation of Bordeaux was marked by high mortality due to the unhealthy proximity of marshes, and by a high birth rate that was

5 Bordeaux under the July Monarchy
  Drawing by Pierrughes

accentuated by the fact that the city offered a refuge to unwed mothers. In 1831 almost two-thirds of the population was born at Bordeaux, but this percentage subsequently declined.

The demolition of the Château Trompette, begun in 1789 and resumed in 1816, created an open space for the future Quinconces park. The dominant consideration in the improvement of the city was the river. The construction of the stone bridge initiated by Napoleon was resumed in 1816, and when it was opened to traffic on 1 May 1822, it did not interfere with navigation. After all, Bordeaux was above all a port, even if the modernisation of its facilities took a long time; and although the first steamship, the *Garonne*, made its appearance on the Bordeaux–Langon run in 1818, barges continued to be pulled along the tow paths for a long time to come. The building of new facilities for the port proceeded slowly, and it was only in 1828 that the first hand-operated cranes appeared. Shipyards were established at Bordeaux and Lormont. As a business town, Bordeaux had several institutions that facilitated its commercial operations, among them a bonded warehouse created in 1822 and the Banque de Bordeaux founded in 1818 on the initiative of Balguerie-Stuttenberg, Daniel Guestin, Paul Portal, and W. Johnston. Among the 160 original stockholders were 131 merchants but only two industrialists, one printer–publisher and one shipbuilder – a constellation that perfectly reflected the city's business structure. Yet the traditional activities were insufficient to give employment to the newly arrived population. In this manner Bordeaux was at least spared the practice of putting young children to work, and even female labour was used less than elsewhere. There were only twenty-three enterprises employing more than twenty workers, and in 1840 the largest one was Johnston's ceramic factory, recently taken over by Vieillard. Thoroughly bourgeois (both upper and lower) in character, educated, tolerant, and proud of its theatre, Bordeaux had an active intellectual life, especially during the Restoration, when Madame Nairac's salon was flourishing, as well as a vigorous popular literature in Gascon, exemplified by Meste Verdié. Bordeaux was an agreeable surprise to visitors, among them Stendhal and Victor Hugo. Having spent some time there, Hugo wrote in 1843: 'Bordeaux is an interesting, original, perhaps unique city. Take Versailles and add Antwerp to it, and you have Bordeaux.'

No other town in the southwest was even comparable to Bordeaux, and communications were still too slow to give rise to competition between Bordeaux and Toulouse. For the same reason, Pau was also able to preserve its special character. Yet Pau was only a small provincial capital (it reached a population of 24,000 inhabitants only in 1946). In part, Pau owed its vitality to its renowned climate and especially to the proximity of thermal waters, particularly those of Eaux-Bonnes, which attracted wealthy foreigners. For this reason the capital of Béarn was extremely interested in the question of transportation, as is indicated by its choice of André Manescau, a lawyer but also the owner of a coach line, as mayor in 1843. Tourism fostered a fashionable social life, and horse racing was a definite incentive for the stud farms of Hautes- and Basses-Pyrénées as well as for the wealthy English families who spent the winter season at Pau.

Trade was the life-blood of the towns of the southwest; in the case of Bayonne and La Rochelle, it was maritime trade. At that time Rochefort was an important shipbuilding centre; in the 1830s ships measuring more than 60 metres in length were built in its largest dry-dock, and in addition to the navy arsenal a small commercial port was developed after 1840. These ports, however, were not equipped to accommodate larger tonnages, and there was no region-wide activity that would have provided an incentive for improving their port facilities. Coastal shipping connected with inland river navigation was their main activity, while other towns of the region, like Agen, were stagnating because of the decline in industrial activity. Angoulême presents the example of a small town (20,085 inhabitants in 1841) that profited from the brandy trade, which earned it the establishment of a branch of the Banque de France. Under the July Monarchy a dynamic prefect, Larréguy, formerly a banker and wholesale merchant in Paris and Le Havre, headed the department from 1832 to 1842; he contributed to the economic progress of the area and had a better working relationship with the liberal notables – such as the president of the departmental general council, the deputy Albert – than with the conservative members of the government party; yet in the end the latter faction succeeded in having him removed. Industrial activities in the southwest were mainly carried out by small enterprises and by artisans. That is why journeymens' associations, especially in Bordeaux, continued to be of major importance, as one can see from the testimony of Agricol Perdiguier. Discontent at the deterioration of the workers' condition was most pronounced in the urban areas. In 1831 the sawyers and stonecutters instigated strikes at Bordeaux, while shoemakers and weavers of Agen circulated petitions protesting the competition of prison workshops in January 1832. In 1836 the tailors who tried to organise their trade in several regions of France found a favourable response in Bordeaux and La Rochelle.

Commercial difficulties of the region

The return to peace had enabled Bordeaux to resume its maritime trade. The initiative was taken by the great merchants and ship-outfitters, among whom Balguerie-Stuttenberg particularly distinguished himself; yet hopes of regaining the commercial prosperity of the eighteenth century were crushed both by strictly regional circumstances (the insufficiency of the hinterland and the lack of a regional industry paradoxically brought about by improved communications) and by the configuration of international economic factors.

The means of communications, roads, rivers, and canals, were adequate for local transactions; and the practice of mixed farming and rural crafts had taught the peasants to produce almost everything they needed. Under these circumstances anything that threatened the existing commercial balance was bound to create conflict and uneasiness. The construction of a bridge over the Dordogne at Cubzac, for example, gave rise to conflict between the Bordelais and the Libournais and provoked demonstrations in the streets of Bordeaux: the Bordelais saw new bridges as part of their programme of improved roads, while the Libournais feared that a bridge supported by very large pilings would impede the river navigation that was a major source of prosperity for the Dordogne valley. On the middle Garonne, never-ending disputes took place between the boatmen and artisans who made their living from river navigation and the farmers. A general plan for the development of the Garonne drawn up in 1830 was implemented between 1835 and 1840; the construction of a lateral canal was begun in 1838, but the intensive work carried out until 1845 in the region of Agen was slowed down by the new enthusiasm for the railway. Although the first steamship travelling between Bordeaux and Langon was launched as early as 1818, the Garonne was the last of the major French rivers to be taken over by steamship navigation. Much of the local trade made use of coastal shipping, which at the beginning of the Restoration accounted for 45 per cent of the tonnage entering the port of Bordeaux and provided a considerable share of their work for the frades connected with the port.

Railway construction was short-lived in this region. The concession for the Bordeaux–La Teste line along the bay of Arcachon had been obtained in 1837. Completed in 1841, it had caused nothing but trouble: the design of the route (an error of 10 metres in the grading of the roadbed, despite the rather flat conformation of the terrain), the siting of the railway station, and the rules for using the track had divided Bordeaux into rival camps and neighbourhoods. The failure of a group of Bordelais led by Duffour-Dubergier and the deputy Wustenberg to obtain the concession for the Paris–Bordeaux line further aggravated these misgivings. The bourgeoisie of Bordeaux preferred to invest its capital in the construction of bridges or houses or to use them in traditional commercial activities.

The southwest bypassed by the major international trade routes

The shift in the old shipping patterns took place very slowly. Trade with the German and Russian ports already began to develop under the Restoration, but at that point beams, cask-wood, hemp, and even iron were brought in by English, Dutch, or German ships, which took back cargoes of wine, brandy, and plums. English ships also brought coal: 100 of the 120 English ships that docked at Bordeaux in 1840, and 80 of the 85 that docked at La Rochelle, were colliers. The arsenal of Rochefort also received coal from England. But there was no coal nearby, and so this commodity was expensive and therefore scarce in the southwest. Trade with the West Indies, the kingpin of Bordeaux's commerce, was theatened; and while Bordeaux was still first among the French ports that traded with the Islands during the Restoration, it was increasingly faced with the competition of Le Havre, which had the advantage of the Parisian market. Moreover, three-fourths of the return cargoes from Martinique and Guadeloupe in the years around 1818 consisted of sugar, and in the following years cane-sugar faced increasingly strong competition from beet-sugar produced in France. The idle hope of restoring the commercial relations with Haiti (the former Saint-Domingue, many of whose settlers had taken refuge in Bordeaux), the pursuit of illusions concerning Latin America, and the decline of the trade with Spain, a country whose economic life had been badly shaken both by the loss of its transatlantic colonies and by internal anarchy – all of these factors complicated and reduced the commercial activities of the southwestern ports of Bordeaux and La Rochelle. The formerly flourishing textile industry of the middle Garonne perished for lack of outlets. In 1821 the wholesale merchant Balguerie had confidently written to the department of commerce: 'The vast South American continent offers considerable opportunities to compensate our commerce and our fleet for all our colonial losses, if we know how to take advantage of it.' As it happened, the refusal of the Restoration governments to recognise the new American States ruled out the commercial treaties that had been demanded by the Chamber of Commerce of Bordeaux. Trade with La Plata, Brazil, and Mexico was far outdistanced by the British trade, and the export of wine to the United States was mainly carried out by American ships. Exports to La Plata, moreover, were adversely affected by a relative shift in taste from Bordeaux wine to the wines of Languedoc and Provence. Neither Balguerie-Stuttenberg's short-lived attempts in the 1820s to find trading partners in the Indian Ocean and in Indochina, nor the African trade that had been initiated as early as 1828 by the firm of Prom and Maurel with the establishment of several branch offices in Senegal could fill the gap.

Bordeaux was also handicapped by the heavy expenses entailed by its location on a river. The ports of the southwest were increasingly bypassed by the major shipping lines operating out of the port of London. The transoceanic trade favoured Le Havre, which was located closer to France's highly industrial zones and profited from a much more populated hinterland. In addition, Bordeaux was also overtaken by Marseille, which benefited from the conquest of Algeria and from the renewed vigour of trade in the Mediterranean. Challenged by an unfortunate combination of economic factors and unable to take part in an industrialisation for which it was scarcely equipped, the southwest – following the lead of Bordeaux – believed that it could meet the challenge by espousing a free-trade policy.

The free-trade policy

The southwest had been disappointed when the Restoration re-instated a protectionist policy, a policy that remained essentially unchanged under the July Monarchy. Duchatel, a deputy from Charente, was one of the few ministers to favour – unsuccessfully as it turned out – a more liberal trade policy. Bordeaux showed considerable originality in its views on commercial policy, which ran counter to the protectionist attitude shared by most of France. This economic liberalism was by no means unmitigated, however, for on occasion the business community of Bordeaux did not hesitate to seek special privileges or even monopolies, for example, a shipping monopoly on all relations with Senegal or, on the contrary, injunctions (against the competition of beet-sugar). The tariff wars among the European States, the disappointing results of the African trade, and the difficulties in re-establishing commercial relations with the West Indies eventually confirmed the view of the Bordelais that it was necessary to revise France's commercial policy. The fact that a major nineteenth-century current of opinion was born outside of Paris was unusual indeed, although it is true that when a free-trade policy was instituted some fifteen years later, it was done by the will of the prince (Napoleon III in 1860) rather than in accordance with the will of the majority. The free-trade movement had found a first theoretician in the journalist Fonfrède, who began writing as early as at the time of the Restoration. Motions calling for the attenuation of the protectionist system had been passed in 1842 by the general councils of Gironde and Gers (1841), Charente, Charente-Inférieure, Hautes- and Basses-Pyrénées. The failure of the plan to establish a Franco-Belgian customs union and the example of Cobden's campaign in England convinced the Bordelais of the need to act and to create bonds of solidarity among the different interests affected by the retention of protectionism. This broader solidarity was first established on the regional level. Landowners and merchants agreed to work together in order to further their wine-growing interests and the commercial activities connected with the trade in colonial produce and wine. Yet a critical attitude toward protectionism was by no means general in the southwest; Bugeaud for example was adamantly opposed to free trade in his capacity as cattle-farmer and deputy of Dordogne. It was at Bordeaux that an Association for the Freedom of Trade was founded on 23 February 1846. A subscription that raised 60,000 francs, contributed in the space of a few days by 524 subscribers, gave the association the means to engage in action and propaganda; its president was the mayor of Bordeaux, Duffour-Dubergier. This association included legitimists, members of the government party and also members of the dynastic opposition, among them the economist Frédéric Bastiat. Overriding political differences of opinion and personal antagonisms, the free-trade movement provided an ideological foundation for the defence of local interests and a motivating idea on which to base an opportunistic attitude; at the same time it was also a response to the underdevelopment of the southwest.

Political moderation and the 'juste milieu'

The major factor in the disaffection of the southwest, and especially of the city of Bordeaux, for the Napoleonic regime was the economic decline of the region brought about by the restriction of maritime trade during the Napoleonic wars. At the beginning of the Restoration the departments of the Atlantic south were the first to recognise the Bourbons; they also came through the contrasting periods of the first Restoration, the Hundred Days, and especially the beginning of the second Restoration without experiencing major upheavals.

'The faithful city'

These two facts are especially surprising in view of some of the royalist leaders' strong sympathies for a 'duchy of Aquitaine' that would have been largely autonomous under the authority of the duc and especially the duchesse d'Angoulême. On 12 March 1814 comte Lynch, the mayor of Bordeaux, had handed over his city to the English, whose first detachment was acclaimed by the population, and had ordered the raising of the white flag to receive the duc d'Angoulême. The example of Bordeaux had hastened the spread of disaffection for the Napoleonic regime throughout the southwest, where the National Guards defected in droves. Yet a few months later, in March 1815, the arrival of General Clausel on behalf of Napoleon was enough to make the duchesse d'Angoulême (who had been unable to incite the troops to resistance) leave for Spain. The fact that the population of Bordeaux had no desire to resist did not mean that it was favourable to Napoleon. When the news of the defeat of Waterloo came, only the garrison troops remained loyal to Napoleon. Regaining all his popularity, the duc d'Angoulême dissuaded the Spanish from entering France and ruled all of southern France on behalf of his uncle, Louis XVIII. The events of 12 March 1814 and the coolness toward Napoleon during the Hundred Days had earned Bordeaux its reputation as 'the faithful city'; in 1820 its name was given to the new heir to the throne, the posthumous son of the duc de Berry. The new prefect of Bordeaux, comte de Tournon – though suspect to the city's ultras because he had served as prefect of Rome under the Empire – was nonetheless able to arrange for the departure of the troops that remained faithful to Napoleon from the Château Trompette without a popular incident and also to expedite Clausel's passage to America. Yet he could not prevent the trial, condemnation, and execution of the Faucher brothers, two former republicans of La Réole who had been officers of the imperial army. This was the most serious act committed during the White Terror in the region. Tournon, who wrote on 2 September 1816: 'I certainly do not intend to go along with the reactionary spirit that exists in this region', ousted comte de Lynch from the mayor's office of Bordeaux, which was entrusted to vicomte de Gourgne, a former émigré and member of the *Chevaliers de la foi.*

The southwest, along with the rest of France, contributed greatly to the ultra majority of the Incredible Chamber; but while the entire delegation of Gers, Hautes- and Basses-Pyrénées, and – with one exception – Dordogne, consisted of noblemen, the bourgeoisie had a large majority among the deputies from Charente-Inférieure, Lot-et-Garonne, and Gironde.

At the beginning of the Restoration, the southwest felt that its interests were well looked after. Bordeaux gave the Chamber of Deputies its presidents, first Laîné (who subsequently became Minister of the Interior) and then Ravez; above all, it seemed that the Admiralty, being controlled by baron Portal, the scion of a prominent merchant family of Bordeaux, was bound to gratify the wishes of the Bordelais who hoped for the resumption of the colonial activities that had made the prosperity of the city and the region in the eighteenth century.

The Aquitaine liberalism

If the southwest had furnished the most moderate of the ultras in the persons of Ravez and Peyronnet, it also soon brought forth liberal leaders. Among them were Decazes, an opportunist rather than a true liberal, and more influential at Libourne and in the rest of the department than at Bordeaux, later Laffitte of Bayonne and General Lamarque, whose power base was in the Landes, and finally Martignac, who began his career as a lawyer of Bordeaux and deputy from Lot-et-Garonne. The population remained deeply attached to Charles X and the members of the royal family, an attitude that was fostered more by the clergy than by a nobility that was devoted, to be sure, but had little influence in the region. When liberal ideas resurfaced at Bordeaux during the Decazes era, they were based on feelings of disappointment arising from the return to protectionism in 1822; in Charente and Charente-Inférieure, they fell in with Bonapartist sentiments that in this region, unlike in Gironde, were still alive.

The electorate, having submitted for many years to the influence of the ultras and pressure from the administration, modified its attitude in the elections of 1827, except in the department of Hautes-Pyrénées, which continued to support the government party. A majority of constitutional monarchists asserted itself in all parts of the region and eventually appeared among the signatories of the address of the 221.

On the eve of 1830, it was especially at Bordeaux that the untimely attitudes of the prefect, vicomte de Curzay, who dismissed large numbers of civil servants and insultingly referred to the Bordelais as 'grocers', aroused popular resentment. As a result Bordeaux was one of the few provincial cities to experience a revolutionary *journée* in 1830. On 30 July, even before the outcome of the Parisian events was known, a group of demonstrators, exasperated by the seizure of the presses of two liberal newspapers, sacked the printing house of Bordeaux's ultra newspaper, the *Défenseur de la monarchie de la Charte*; when it became clear that the Parisian revolution had succeeded, workers, sailors, and young shop assistants marched to the prefecture, assaulted the prefect, and threatened to throw him into the river; and he was saved only by some young liberals like Galos, who spirited him away to his father's house. Having been thwarted in this manner, the rioters then turned on the excise tax station, and for a few days merchandise entered the city without being taxed. This was the most serious incident to take place in the region.

The passivity of the partisans of the older branch of the Bourbons contributed greatly to the appeasement of the situation. In the southwest the legitimists did not receive as much support from the clergy as they did elsewhere, partly because the prelates had rallied to the new regime and partly because the influence of the clergy was no longer very strong. In many cases mayors who had been too closely identified with Charles X's regime resigned even before they were dismissed. The new authorities were chosen from among the notables of Bordeaux: the former councillor of the prefecture, Barenne – who had resigned a few days earlier to express his disapproval of the new ordinances – became prefect, and the new mayor, marquis de Bryas, was a former member of the city council who had been ousted by the Polignac government.

The republicans wielded little influence outside of certain neighbourhoods of Bordeaux, La Réole, and a very small number of local pockets. Yet in the aftermath of 1830 the Movement, that is, those who favoured an evolution toward more democracy within the framework of the July Monarchy, had some influential spokesmen in such men as Laffitte, a native of Bayonne, General Lamarque in Landes, and the engineer Billaudel in Bordeaux.

The economic difficulties of which we spoke earlier spawned some disturbances that no one could use for political ends. It is true that by the end of 1833 the Bordeaux *Société des droits de l'homme* had a certain following among the city's stevedores, dockhands, and coopers, but the labour unrest of April 1834 amounted to little more than one or two demonstrations of young people who made a lot of noise but were quickly dispersed. At the beginning of the July Monarchy neither the social nor the political agitation of the southwest was very dangerous. The bourgeoisie was pleased to see the broadening of the electorate. In the absence of a protest movement that would have threatened the social and political order, political issues lost their ideological character, while a shared distrust of Paris created sympathy for decentralisation. The liberalism of the southwest was more concerned with administrative or economic freedom than with political liberty, which seemed to be adequately secured under the July Monarchy. Liberalism was understood in several different ways, all of which made allowances for existing local situations. While Fonfrède or Bastiat constructed theoretical models of free trade, the liberal policies that were sought by the southwest were a matter, first and foremost, of defending the acquired interests of a bourgeoisie that dominated a society in which the lines between classes were fluid. More than elsewhere, this liberalism evolved in a conservative rather than democratic direction because it was more attached to liberty than to equality.

Conservative liberalism

The southwest seemed predestined for Orleanism, a more sober version of 'Girondism'; it is perhaps symbolic that in this region Orleanism found its principal spokesman in Henri Fonfrède, son of the Girondin Boyer-Fonfrède, a regicide who had himself ended under the guillotine in 1793. The very notion of *juste milieu* that served to designate the followers of Louis-Philippe was taken from the tradition of Montesquieu.

The legitimists could count on the support of the great aristocratic landowners who backed such newspapers as *La Guienne*, founded in September 1831, *Le Périgord*, and *Le Mémorial agenais*, but they were never able to win over the voting citizens, except in the *arrondissement* of Lombez, department of Gers. The one legitimist elected by the *arrondissement* of Blaye in 1837, E. de la Grange, a cousin of Lamartine, rallied to the regime when he had taken his seat in the legislature, and the conservative bent of the legitimists of the southwest caused many of them to rally to the July regime, thereby weakening the legitimist party in Gironde, Dordogne, and the two Charentes.

There was indeed a legitimist notability, but it consisted of notables who lacked a political clientèle, and the influence they may have wielded over the rural and even urban population (in the Saint-Michel and Sainte-Croix quarters of Bordeaux for example) was not translated into legal political action. Yet all other action was disquieting to the legitimist leadership, whether it took the form of noisy demonstrations, as at the time of the controversy over the duchesse de Berry, or of agitation against the census of 1841, which was particularly lively at Bordeaux.

Conversely, the Movement itself, represented by the dynastic left more than by the republicans, soon lost the standing it had enjoyed at the beginning of Louis-Philippe's reign. The electorate of the southwest was increasingly inclined to vote for the partisans of the July Monarchy. The region furnished a number of high dignitaries to the regime, among them the duc Decazes and several other ministers, Duchatel, elected from Jonzac, Dufaure, deputy from Saintes, Lacave-Laplagne from Gers, Dumont from Lot-et-Garonne, and Marshal Bugeaud, the governor-general of Algeria and deputy from Exideuil in Dordogne. As it became clear that the July regime was solidly entrenched and that it had the ability to deal with difficult situations, the majority of the notables rallied to it, not so much as a matter of conviction as by way of realism and opportunism. In this manner several deputies of the Movement went over to the government party. One example is Laurence, the deputy of Mont-de-Marsan, a former protégé of General Lamarque. Having made the switch to conservative ideas, he was promoted to director of African affairs, councillor of State, and director-general of direct taxation; eventually it was he who distributed the government's favours in the department of Landes. The prelates, especially Mgr de Cheverus, the first cardinal to be appointed during the July Monarchy, and later Mgr Donnet at Bordeaux, did not wish to be too closely allied with the legitimists. On the other hand, the ranks of the latter included Protestants (members of the Journu family, merchants at Bordeaux) and members of the business and professional community.

Conversely, the electorate adapted to the situation and was most likely to choose a candidate for his (real or perceived) effectiveness. In 1837 Bordeaux even elected Thiers, protectionist though he was. In 1841 the Bordelais would have liked to replace their arch-conservative deputy Wustenberg, who was made a Peer of France, with their mayor Duffour-Dubergier; but the mayor refused, declaring, 'having the choice between a deputyship and the administration of Bordeaux, I prefer the latter as a matter of taste and sentiment', whereupon Bordeaux chose the candidate he proposed, the economist Blanqui, a stranger to the department. Blanqui's candidacy at Bordeaux and his election in the third round reflects the electorate's desire for an effective deputy and its determination to succeed in the campaign for free trade that had already been introduced in the parliament.

In most of the cantons political life continued to be limited to municipal issues, and political opinions were often the result of personality clashes. Thus the conservative mayor of Exideuil, Dr Chavoix, became a member of the radical opposition when he had a disagreement with Marshal Bugeaud. Yet the effect of the law of 22 March 1831 calling for the election of municipal officers was not as drastic in the southwest as in other regions; participation in municipal elections soon fell to a very low level, so that municipal affairs remained in the hands of the wealthiest land-owners. The difficulty of finding a municipal councillor willing to carry out the function of mayor was a factor of stability. The growing importance of financial questions and, particularly in this region, the problems connected with managing communal properties almost naturally called for the intervention of the prefectoral administration and had the effect of promoting centralisation. The manner in which Guizot's policy man-aged the nation's material interests had the approval of the opinion-makers of the southwest.

In the elections of 1846, the conservatives throughout this region did very much better than in the country as a whole. In Charente, Gers, Landes, Hautes- and Basses-Pyrénées, only candidates of the government party were elected; in Gironde, seven out of nine belonged to that party. The conservative system worked almost perfectly in the southwest. Administrative centralisation was not very effective, and while it was certainly criticised, it was tempered by the notables' influence over the local administration.

13

Lyon and the region of Lyon

The diverse and contradictory character of Lyon was shaped by its relations with a whole region. The city's importance was not, as in the case of other regional metropolises, a matter of historical tradition; to a great extent it was to its economy that Lyon owed the network of influences that established its more or less exclusive predominance throughout the region.

Lyon and its sphere of influence

Lyon as a regional metropolis

Limited at the beginning of our period, Lyon's sphere of influence grew with the development of commercial exchanges and was enhanced by other towns such as Grenoble or Saint-Etienne, which sometimes also played an original and dynamic role. From the eastern rim of the Massif central to the highest peaks of the Alps, from southern Burgundy to the gates of the Comtat Venaissin, it comprised regions that differed greatly in their traditions, economies, and opinions; regular contact with Lyon was the only trait that the rich agricultural lands of the Bresse or the Rhône valley and the poor, mixed-farming regions of Lower Dauphiné or the Massif central had in common.

The population of Lyon

Lyon was a melting-pot for all kinds of different people who were attracted by the city. Not that Lyon experienced exceptional growth during the first half of the nineteenth century; Marseille and Paris grew even more rapidly.

Lyon grew by fits and starts, particularly under the Empire and at the beginning of the Restoration; in 1821 the city proper had 149,000 inhabitants. However, the census of 1831 revealed a decrease in population, which had fallen to 133,715 inhabitants. From then on, there was a constant increase until 1846 (when the figure reached 177,976 inhabitants). While this increase was to some extent the result of a rise in the birth rate,

La Croix — Rousse

Vaise

fort de la tête d'Or

Les Broteaux

Quai Saint-Clair

Pont Morand

Quai de Retz

Pont Lafayette

pl. des Terreaux

Hôtel de Ville

Fourvière

Saint-Just

pl. des Jacobins

rue Mercière

rue Royale

Préfecture

Quai de l'Arsenal

place Bellecour

Pont de la Guillotière

pl. du Pont

La Guillotière

Quai de la Quarantine

Hôp. Militaire

Quai de la Charité

Arsenal

fort de la Vitriolerie

Saône

Gare

Rhône

6 Lyon in 1847

■ built-up zone

□ non-built-up zone in 1847

it was primarily caused by immigration, both at Lyon and in the rest of the department of Rhône. The death rate was higher than in France as a whole, reaching a high of 30 per 1,000 in 1834, a year of misery, strikes, and unrest. Even though Lyon was spared during the cholera epidemic of 1832, typhoid, malaria, and smallpox were endemic threats.

For the most part, the newcomers were mountain people from Auvergne, from the Velay and the Forez; some of the people from Creuze migrated to Lyon by the Limoges–Lyon highway. In addition, the stream of immigrants was fed by the Jura and by the region of the Alps, by the Dauphiné and especially by Savoy (not a French territory at the time), which sent young girls (as it had done since the eighteenth century) and, more recently, boys. Other colonies of foreigners, especially Swiss and Rhinelanders, were also found at Lyon; this situation contributed to sensitising public opinion to events that were taking place in neighbouring states.

The more rapid growth of the outlying communes can be explained in part by the excise tax levied by Lyon, which made foodstuffs and construction more costly in the city; this disadvantage did not exist at La Croix-Rousse or at La Guillotière, which grew from 7,000 inhabitants in 1815 to 35,000 in 1846. The extremely rapid growth of the department of Rhône (from 299,390 inhabitants in 1801 to 545,635 in 1846) testifies to the scope of its economic development. This demographic growth had a profound impact, not only on society – several of the notables of Lyon had arrived from their native villages with few belongings or were born abroad – and on economic life, but also on the very conditions of life in the city.

The urban setting

After 1815 Lyon, situated at the confluent of two rivers and at the junction of several trade routes, experienced an expansion contingent on the development of its economic activities and the massive arrival of immigrants that was both the result and the cause of that development.

The city's topography reflected both its history and its development. The centre of all activity and of commerce was located between the place des Terreaux and the place Bellecour; Michelet has described this 'teeming ant heap nestled among rocks and rivers, crowded into dark streets that slope downward in the rain and the eternal fog'. The more airy rue Centrale was opened only toward the end of the July Monarchy, connecting the prefecture with the place Bellecour which, together with the Saint-Martin d'Ainay parish, formed the aristocratic section of town. However, the nobility of Bellecour was either descended from petty nobles, most of whom had come from the Forez, or from merchants and silk manufacturers who had become large landowners and were ennobled by honorific positions, such as membership on hospital boards, or by the purchase of an office. Although the trappings of nobility carried little prestige in Lyon, this group was determined to stand apart. Under the Restoration this aristocracy, isolated and living on the income from its landed properties, wielded little influence but did furnish the most violent ultras. They were the heirs of those ultras who, together with the *Compagnons de Jéhu* or the *Compagnons du Soleil*, had cherished dreams of a White Terror as early as in the days of the Directory. In 1815 all five of the deputies of the department of Rhône were ultras (four of them nobles), but already by 1818, the number of ultras had fallen to less than one-fourth of those who could vote.

By contrast, the wealthiest merchants or *fabricants* who had settled near the place des Terreaux or the quai de Retz and the quai Saint-Clair on the left bank of the Rhône formed, from the time of the Restoration, a notability in keeping with Lyon's activity. A bourgeoisie that had only recently gained access to wealth, this group had in some measure taken the place of the old families who had left manufacturing or who had fallen victim to the repression of the Montagnard Convention.

To the west, the city had long been spreading along the left bank of the Saône between the river and the hills of Fourvière, the site of many convents and religious schools. Near the quai de la Quarantaine and the quai Saint-Georges, crowded neighbourhoods had sprung up; and upstream the old quarters of Saint-Jean and Saint-Paul, where the archbishop's palace stood, were dominated by the clergy and the legal profession. More to the south, the confluent of the Saône and the Rhône delimited the peninsula for which Perrache (for whom the area was later named) had conceived vast though unrealised plans back in 1776; in 1832 most of the surface still consisted of wasteland, and it was primarily the decision of 1845 to locate the railway station at Perrache that subsequently led to the industrial development of this area.

Without giving up their autonomy, three towns were closely associated with Lyon: to the northwest, on the right bank of the Saône, Vaize, a peaceful market town inhabited by landowners and market gardeners, benefited from the expansion of trade by river and road; also upstream, but located between the rivers and nestled against the hillside, La Croix-Rousse was increasingly populated by silk-weavers (*canuts*). On the right bank of the Rhône, Les Brotteaux and especially La Guillotière – the latter located in a still partially marshy zone – owed their development in large part to the extension of commercial relations, in which the bridge at La Guillotière played a vital role. Factories – particularly factories that produced vitriol and other unhealthy substances that could not very well be placed within the narrow confines of a city built like Lyon – as well as silk-weavers' shops had been established at La Guillotière, but they were threatened by floods, especially by the flood of 1840, which destroyed 200 houses in the working-class neighbourhood.

Lyon as a centre of attraction and communication

As a centre of consumption, the metropolitan area of Lyon was a determining factor in the rural production of the neighbouring departments that contributed to its food supply. Fowl from the Bresse, game from the forests of Ain, fish from the lakes of the Dombes, cereals and cattle from Saône-et-Loire and Isère, meat from the Charolais, wine from the Beaujolais and southern Drôme, and vegetables from Lower Dauphiné, all were consumed in the city. Lyon was surrounded by villages that served as relay stations for this trade. Some of the notables of Lyon owned estates in the Dombes or west of the city; they were nobles who often served as mayors of their communes during the Restoration, as well as merchants, *fabricants*, and legal practitioners, especially in the *arrondissement* of Villefranche.

As an intersection of major trade routes, Lyon was above all the city of the Rhône and Saône, but the proximity of the great fluvial axis also accounts for the increased growth of Vienne, Valence, and Chalon-sur-Saône under the July Monarchy, the era when river navigation made great strides under the impact of the steam engine. Road construction in the Alps during the Napoleonic era (especially that of the Mont-Cenis road) and the shift in the flow of trade brought about by the blockade had been a source of prosperity for many new haulage contractors. The two highways from Paris ended at the suburb of Vaize, which could be reached by coach in four or five days. The road through the Bourbonnais, via Nevers, although somewhat shorter, passed through more mountainous territory and was traditionally reputed to be unsafe; and the road through Burgundy, via Auxerre, reached the Saône at Chalon. Two other roads passed through La Guillotière. One of them led to the Italian States (and by 1846 it still took 15 hours to reach Chambéry, 40 to reach Turin) and the other, running along the left bank of the Rhône, reached Marseille in three days without crossing the river again before Pont-Saint-Esprit. By the end of the July Monarchy, travelling time between Lyon and Paris had been reduced to 40 hours by combining road travel and steamship navigation on the Saône.

Yet the transport of merchandise remained very slow; barges took 60 hours to sail upstream from Lyon to Chalon, and the convoys of 15 to 18 carts that travelled between Lyon and Marseille in six to ten days damaged the roads by digging deep ruts.

The waterways benefited from the preference of commerce for water transportation. Under the Restoration, the river fleets used a large labour force, supplemented by towing-crews for the trip upstream; in crossing Lyon, which did not have continuous quays, horses were replaced by gangs of men called '*modères*'; they needed a full day to cover the 4 kilometres for which the Saône ran through Lyon. Large numbers of artisans and trades made their living from this river navigation: the boatyards at Seyssel, Condrieu, or Chalon, at Auxonne or Gray, and the cordage factories at Vienne as well as the boatmen and also the peasants who furnished the horses used for towing the boats upstream. As part of its plan to complete the existing network of canals, the Restoration made a major effort to enlarge the scope of navigation on the Saône and the Rhône. Thus the canal de Bourgogne between the Seine (at Laroche) and the Saône (at Saint-Jean-de-Losne) was completed in 1832, and the canal Monsieur (between the Rhône and the Rhine), which had been navigable between Besançon and Saint-Jean-de-Losne since 1826, was completed in 1834. By 1826, 238,000 tons of coal were shipped on the small canal de Givors.

Towing demanded large numbers of horses, but this kind of operation could be carried out by family enterprises, which stood to make large gains from it. At every halting-place, wagoners and boatmen gathered in the many taverns, thereby contributing to the wealth the valley derived from the transportation trade, which also stimulated the demand for horses bred in Ain and Isère and for fodder. The unreliable, indeed dangerous character of this trade accounts for the fact that with the return to peace in 1815, the major currents of trade between north and south sought to find more rapid and safer means of communication. The fear of being outdone, not only by maritime transportation but also by the highway from Rotterdam to Milan by way of the Rhine and Switzerland, prompted the business community of Lyon to look for improvements in its transportation system.

Lyon as a centre of activity and decision-making

The city was the seat of public administrative agencies directed from Paris as part of the centralisation that had been maintained by the Bourbons. The department of Rhône experienced a great turnover of prefects and spelled the end of many careers (especially under the July Monarchy), even though the Restoration prefect was well-nigh all-powerful. In the early stages this power came close to arbitrary rule with comte de Chabrol de Croussol, the prefect who so compromised himself in ultra intrigues that he had to resign his post at Lyon in 1817. Under the July Monarchy Jayr, who served as prefect from 1839 to 1847, owed his success and his long tenure both to his marriage to a daughter of Lyon and to his active interest in the improvement of navigation and his support for railway construction.

The authority of the central State at Lyon was backed by sizeable military forces. From the time of the Restoration the presence of troops was not so much a matter of strategic considerations as of keeping control over a dangerous city that had become suspect as a result of its liberal agitation following the incidents of 1817 and its labour unrest at the beginning of the July Monarchy. In the early days of the Restoration half of the municipal council consisted of present or former wholesale merchants. On the eve of 1830, when the city government was once again in the hands of the ultras, the municipal council of thirty-six still included eighteen merchants, nine landowners, six magistrates, one lawyer, and the city's receiver-general; but now fourteen of its members were nobles or pseudo-nobles. Under the July Monarchy Lyon had a succession of mayors representing the most conservative milieux, such as Martin (between 1835 and 1840), or the bourgeoisie of merchants and *fabricants* in the person of Dr Terme.

The political and intellectual influence of Lyon

This influence was spread above all by the city's press and by its learned societies. In addition, it should be noted that a certain number of Lyonnais became deputies or members of the general councils of neighbouring departments (Ain, Loire, and Ardèche). The case of Camille Jordan, who was elected as a constitutional monarchist in Ain before becoming deputy from Rhône was not an isolated one. After 1819 several newspapers represented the various tendencies of public opinion: the ultra periodical, *Gazette universelle de Lyon*, though initially quite prosperous, had to suspend publication in 1828, while the *Précurseur* became the newspaper of the liberals in 1826. It was under the July Monarchy, however, that Lyon had the broadest spectrum of newspapers, ranging from one of the first workers' newspapers to be published in France, the *Echo de la Fabrique*, to the legitimist publication. The most widely read paper, the *Courrier de Lyon* (3,500 subscribers in 1833), was circulated in Ain, Isère, Drôme, Ardèche, Haute-Loire, Puy-de-Dôme, Saône-et-Loire, and Jura – an area that provides a fairly accurate delineation of Lyon's influence.

Lyon was also a centre of intellectual life because of its schools, in particular its religious schools. The Brothers of the Christian Doctrine (whose mother house was at Lyon) and many other religious congregations played a predominant role in primary education. The bourgeoisie of Lyon was extremely interested in the development of primary education, and by 1835, 73 per cent of Lyon's children attended school (80 per cent of the boys and 66 per cent of the girls).

Under the July Monarchy Lyon became a university town with the creation of a Faculty of Science in 1836 and a Faculty of Letters in 1838. It also had a famous old school of veterinary medicine and a school of design. Several learned societies were attended by members of the bourgeoisie and high society. Salon life, by contrast, hardly existed at all; at most one can cite the salon of Mme Yemeniz, the daughter of a family of place Bellecour and wife of a Greek merchant who had established himself in the silk trade.

The impact of Catholicism, finally, was a major aspect of Lyon's influence, even in the absence of the city's archbishop, cardinal Fesch, who was exiled for twenty years. For Lyon remained a centre of religious fervour; religious missions in March of 1818 had easily revived old traditions that had never quite died out, especially among certain segments of the lower classes. In *L'Hermite de province*, Jouy noted the prestige enjoyed by Notre-Dame de Fourvière: 'The peasants who come to Lyon to bring their milk and their fruit never leave town without paying their respects to the Madonna.'

Lyon's Catholic establishment was extremely interested in missions, which it supported by assigning priests (106 between 1816 and 1839, and 13 bishops) and giving moral and financial support to the efforts of the *Oeuvre de la Propagation de la Foi*, a society founded in 1820 by Pauline Jaricot, the daughter of a wealthy silk merchant. In this region the success of ultramontane ideas was linked to the close relations between the clergy and the Catholic laity which, perhaps more than elsewhere, played an active role, and to the work of the archbishopric, directed after 1840 by Mgr de Bonald, the son of the philosopher. Lyon became one of the cradles of social Catholicism with Frédéric Ozanam, the founder of the Saint-Vincent-de-Paul conferences who, although he began his activities in Paris, had close ties with Lyon where he had been educated and where he taught for some time.

Another aspect of Lyon's Catholicism was its influence over a segment of the working class: the Saint-François-Xavier society, whose members paid a small annual fee that entitled them to relief payments, especially in case of illness, had a membership of 6,000 workers in 1848. Communal workshops called 'providences' or 'refuges' took care of orphans or unattached young girls. These workshops aroused the hostility of those workers with whom they competed. Better organised and more conscious of their condition, these workers were the first to claim that justice rather than charity was the basis of social relations. Lyon thus witnessed both the first manifestations of social Catholicism and the first socialist critique directed against it.

Industrial and commercial centres of the region

Lyon was the only city with more than 50,000 inhabitants in the approximately ten departments over which its influence extended, yet this influence depended on a loose network of urban centres punctuated by a few towns whose importance was either of long standing and based on the presence of administrative agencies (such as Grenoble) or new and based on economic assets (such as Saint-Etienne).

migrations and residence
commercial relations

7   The connections of the Périer family
      Migrations and residence
      Commercial relations
Note: The departments shown were represented in the Chamber at some point during the nineteenth century by a member of the Périer family.
Source: Pierre Barral, *Les Périer dans l'Isère au XIXᵉ siècle* (Paris, 1964)

Grenoble

An administrative town that declined during the first half of the nineteenth century (its population decreased from 26th place among French towns in 1832 to 33rd place in 1846), Grenoble nonetheless remained an important political and intellectual centre. The election of the erstwhile abbé Grégoire in 1819 aroused more strong feelings in French political life than any other provincial election in the era of limited suffrage. Grenoble's Faculty of Law and its royal law court had given it a liberal tradition that harked back to Vizille. The few prominent families that dominated the most important fields of activity in Dauphiné had become united, in many cases by a network of marriage alliances, a fact that in turn reinforced the cohesion of a bourgeoisie that gradually shifted from liberalism – the dominant attitude under the Restoration – to the defence of law and order. The Périer family – indeed one should call it a dynasty – although it had dispersed its members to Paris and to other departments, definitely occupied the top of Grenoble's society in the first half of the nineteenth century.

Grenoble was still a fortified frontier town, a situation that was in part responsible for its restricted development and for the continued existence of its narrow streets, for any extension of the centre had to be authorised by the Ministry of War and in any case was confined within the new rampart (the Haxo rampart) begun in 1832. Upon becoming mayor in 1835, the deputy military intendant, Berriat, rehabilitated the centre of town; the bridges were repaired, quays were built along the banks of the Isère, and the sanitary conditions were improved by draconian measures against the infestation of stray dogs, some of which had rabies. But since many of these measures were costly, they led to repeated crises in the municipal government. A new mayor, Taulier, a professor of law, also came into conflict with the prefect, who saw symptoms of agitation everywhere. Taulier wrote on 3 September 1846: 'The people of Grenoble are above all interested in keeping order. They enjoy a good discussion and they want to keep track of what the public authorities are doing, but they are always willing to stay within the bounds of legality.' The economic notabilities (following the lead of the Périer family) had gone along with the authoritarian prefect Pellenc since 1830, but the other notables, judges, engineers, officers, and lawyers, had adopted a more liberal stance.

At the end of the July Monarchy almost a third of Grenoble society consisted of a *petite bourgeoisie* of artisans and shopkeepers. The working class in the narrow sense of the term was small; barely half of this group were wage-earners, while the other half consisted of domestic servants, who were still employed in large numbers. Shopkeepers and wholesale merchants played the most important economic role. All in all, inherited wealth remained preponderant, and both landed property and movable assets were in the hands of the same families. The countryside in the vicinity of the town belonged to a few large landowners.

Saint-Etienne

The very rapid growth of this town was a function of industrial development. The growth of this simple sub-prefecture from 19,102 inhabitants in 1820 to 49,612 in 1846, one of the outstanding instances of rapid growth in all of France, resulted from an influx of immigrants from the nearby mountains at the time of industrial expansion. Saint-Etienne's industry grew out of the traditional ribbon-making, hardware, and gun-smithing operations, supplemented later by the development of coal mining and metallurgy as well as by the impact of the railways. For generations, the industrial activities of Saint-Etienne had been dependent on capital from Lyon, but now the town was becoming emancipated, thanks to the establishment of a branch office of the Banque de France (which became the most successful of all its provincial branch offices). In 1840 the deputy governor of the Banque de France, impressed by the growth of the town and the numerous construction projects in the suburbs, drew attention to the heavy speculation in the region's coal deposits, pointing out that the local industry was becoming more and more dependent on outside capital. Yet the city government remained in the hands of the local ribbon manufacturers and silk merchants. Personal rivalries rather than ideological disagreements concealed the fundamental conflict between the local industrialists and the attempts of a large-scale financial capitalism (backed by the **Delahante** family of Lyon) to gain a foothold. Saint-Etienne thus furnishes the example of a situation in which the basic character of a society of notables was challenged by the most advanced forms of economic activity. Simply unable to resolve these conflicts, the local bourgeoisie was primarily interested in maintaining order, particularly in view of the town's increasingly large working-class population.

In all other places, relations between town and country were much closer, since the administrative centres were often also market towns. This was the case at Chalon (12,220 inhabitants), Valence, and Mâcon (which barely reached 11,000 inhabitants under the July Monarchy), Bourg, or Lons-le-Saunier. Administrative centralisation and the development of the economy encouraged close relations between Lyon and these small towns, which served as intermediaries between the regional metropolis and the rural populations.

The rural populations

In all the departments surrounding Lyon, with the exception of Rhône (50 per cent rural population in 1836) and Loire (66 per cent), more than three-fourths of the population was rural in 1836; in Ain this figure was even 94 per cent, and in Saône-et-Loire it was 86 per cent.

But there were major differences among these rural societies. A study of the great notables undertaken by the prefects in 1821 showed that large noble estates were still a dominant feature from Drôme to Saône-et-Loire and from Isère to Nièvre, but it also showed that these properties were owned by only a few dozen persons. The great noble estates were located primarily in the mountains and the plateaux of the Lyonnais and the Forez, and often worked by sharecroppers holding small farms. In the rural cantons of Rhône, especially in the eastern part, the amount of noble property remained considerable: half of those who paid more than 1,000 francs in 1829 were nobles, particularly in the Beaujolais region, where the peasants continued to call their noble landlord their seigneur. Even in a department where the influence of the nobility was as inconsequential as in Isère, this group continued to account for a high proportion of the large landowners, namely 39 per cent of those who paid more than 1,000 francs under the July Monarchy. However, these large estates tended to become fragmented in the course of this period.

There were many small owners in these departments; sometimes one finds that one-half or one-third of a village's territory was owned by a few large proprietors, while the rest of the land was divided among very large numbers of small owners, many of whom were also day-labourers or lease-holders on a great estate: this situation existed in the Crésivaudan or in the Alpine lowlands near Donzère. Small owners were particularly numerous in wine-growing areas, for example, in most of the department of Saône-et-Loire; in 1833 a survey of 485 communes showed that this last department comprised 685,000 hectares divided into more than one million plots belonging to 125,950 owners. Of the population of Saône-et-Loire, 27 per cent owned some land; this proportion was even higher in Ain (where 38 per cent of the inhabitants owned land in 1843), in Drôme (29 per cent), and in Isère (30 per cent). In the last two departments the number of landowners had grown by about 50 per cent over the previous two decades.

Although their agricultural resources varied greatly, all of these agrarian societies were affected by one major element of disturbance, studied by Philippe Vigier for the Alpine region, but to be found elsewhere as well. This was the practice of usurious lending and the abuse of mortgage loans, which in hard times transferred some of the peasant property to their creditors, be they notaries or other bourgeois.

The economic evolution

In the period 1815 to 1848 the region of Lyon experienced a considerable intensification of its commercial relations. Indeed, it appears that in this region industrialisation received more impetus from the development of commercial and financial capitalism than from the extension of the manufacturing system.

The Lyon 'Fabrique' [silk trade]
Preserving its artisanal structures even after its reconstruction under the Restoration, silk-making remained the dominant component of the city's economic activity. Silk-making involved a great variety of operations. The cultivation of silkworms and mulberry trees had developed in Drôme, Isère, Ardèche, and Vaucluse; in Isère for example the number of mulberry trees increased from 454,000 in 1820 to one million in 1847.

Nonetheless, the Lyon merchants also bought raw silk from Italy and had successfully lobbied for the ordinance of 29 June 1833, which reduced the import duties on foreign silk, although even then the Lyon silk trade was not assured of regular supplies; bad harvests (not to mention speculation) periodically caused prices to rise at Aubenas and Beaucaire as well as at Bergamo.

The spinning and throwing operations were rapidly industrialised in Drôme, Ardèche, and Vaucluse; and even in Gard the decline in the number of spinning mills resulted in large measure from concentration. This modernisation was carried out either by the spinners and throwers themselves or by the *fabricants* and merchants of Lyon; the Arlès-Dufour firm, for example, operated a throwing mill at Clérieux in Drôme and a spinning mill at Beaucaire. The weaving of the silk was done by the *canuts* or silk weavers in small workshops; a workshop owner who worked at his home and owned his looms (from two to six) was not really a master artisan, since he depended on a wholesale merchant who furnished his materials and sold his finished goods, paying him a certain sum per item. The price was set by this wholesale merchant, who was called the *fabricant*. Under the July Monarchy some 500 commercial houses, whose total annual turnover exceeded 115 million francs, formed the so-called *Fabrique*.

The owner of the workshop housed the four or five workers or journey-men who worked with him. But because of the very great variety in the quality of the workmanship and also in the prices paid for the finished goods, there were considerable differences in the wages and the conditions of the silk weavers. The owners of workshops who created the fashion of flowered tissues were concentrated in Lyon itself; since they designed complicated patterns that were difficult to imitate, they were not afraid of competition. Skilled workers were hard to find and therefore expensive; the head of a workshop that produced the best grade' of finished tissues could earn as much as 8 francs a day (according to Villermé). Other silk weavers working in the narrow and insanitary streets of Lyon itself, especially in the Saint-Georges quarter on the left bank of the Saône, earned only 2 or 3 francs, weaving the plain or patterned cloths for which there was a wider market, although they had to compete against goods from Switzerland (especially Zurich) or the Rhineland. The use of the Jacquard loom created the demand for spacious and healthier workshops; as a result, multi-storied houses were built at La Croix-Rousse.

The working days were long, often 15 hours. Villermé who observed the *canuts* in 1835–6 considered them to be more hardworking and sober than the other workers of Lyon; they were better paid but also under threat of being laid off, owing to the precarious character of their luxury produc-tion. In 1835 it was estimated that there were 8,000 workshop-owners and 30,000 journeymen and apprentices in Lyon and its suburbs. The subsequent shift to the neighbouring countryside was instigated by the Lyon *Fabrique*, which sought to disperse the silk-weaving operations in the hope that the lower wages paid to rural weavers would enable it to face British competition. At the time of the crisis of 1825–6, 2,000 looms were already operating in the rural cantons of Lyon or at Villeurbanne. However, the major shift took place after the labour unrest of 1831; in 1833, out of a total of 40,000 looms, 17,000 were operating in Lyon, 9,000 in the three communes of La Croix-Rousse, La Guillotière, and Vaise, and more than 5,000 in the rural areas of the department of Rhône, while almost 9,000 looms were distributed throughout the neighbouring departments of Saône-et-Loire, Loire, Ain, Drôme, and Isère. Factories employing a large work force were rare; practically the only case cited is the factory of La Sauvagère on the banks of the Saône near Lyon, founded by a merchant of Frankfurt, Berna, who employed some 500 workers. At the end of the July Monarchy, 80,000 of the inhabitants of the greater Lyon area made their living from silk.

The *fabricants* or wholesale merchants played an essential role not only in the silk and silk-cloth trade but also as local bankers. These two activities were closely linked, since large amounts of money changed hands when the raw silk was purchased in June; in October, when wine and brandy were sold; and again in January, when the proceeds from the sale of finished silk goods came in. Selling three-quarters of its silk cloth abroad, Lyon was more exposed to the effects of foreign problems than any other city in the interior of France. In the years around 1830, the market of the United States alone absorbed a third of Lyon's exports; it is therefore understandable that Lyon's Chamber of Commerce stated on 26 November 1835: 'An American crisis is more fatal to us than a French one.'

Older industries and industrial transformations

The older industries had for the most part preserved their artisanal structure. In Dauphiné, industrial activity had been slowed down during the revolutionary and Napoleonic era; communications remained precarious and the choice of Mont-Cenis rather than the col du Genèvre for a main highway had disadvantaged Grenoble. In 1815 the pig iron from Allevard was still exported only on the backs of mules. The traditional metallurgy of Dauphiné, which furnished pig iron and steel to Saint-Etienne and Thiers, continued to operate its wood-fuelled furnaces at Belledonne. In the department of Loire, industrial activity was limited to the northern cantons around Roanne and to the southern cantons; at Saint-Etienne, the manufacturing of ribbons, hardware, and guns had long made use of water power and the special properties of the local water for soaking and tanning.

At Lyon itself, many different artisanal activities were carried out; some of its enterprises, like the 70 dyeing workshops, were connected with silk-making, while others, like the printing and gilding trades, had existed for centuries.

At Grenoble, the traditional glovemaking trade was somewhat changed after 1838 by the introduction of a mechanical leather-cutting device; in addition to the dressed skins from Dauphiné, it was beginning to use skins from the tanneries of Drôme and Ardèche and even imports from the Italian States.

Other older activities were also stimulated by new developments. In 1839 the chemical industry still had an artisanal character at Lyon, where chemicals were produced by eighteen factories. However, it was in this period that Lyon acquired the major chemical industry that was to become one of the most important sources of the region's wealth. Claude Perret moved a small soda factory from Les Brotteaux to Perrache, transforming it from an artisanal operation into a modest industrial enterprise. This factory produced acids, sulphates, and bleach and manufactured its own apparatus; moreover, Perret bought a vitriol plant at La Guillotière, invested in prospecting for copper and in salt works in the Camargue as well as in other enterprises that will be mentioned later.

The most important stimulus to the region's industrial development was furnished by the metal industry and by the introduction of mineral coal. A whole new metal industry developed at Lyon as local firms became involved in the construction of steam engines, steamboats and railway equipment in association with the nearby factories of the Loire basin that furnished the necessary coal, iron, and ore. The Perrache yards of the Saint-Etienne Railway Company were founded at Lyon by the Seguin brothers in 1827; in 1844 a former engineer of the Saint-Gobain Company, Alphonse Clément-Desorme, created railway equipment plants and forges at Oullins; and finally in 1847 the yards for the construction of the Paris–Lyon railway were located at La Buire. Shipyards for river navigation, which had initially been carried out by ships made in England, developed at La Vaise on the Saône and in the Boucle quarter of Lyon.

The region's most important metallurgical enterprises, however, were located outside the department of Rhône. The Creusot works in Saône-et-Loire had experienced difficulties since 1815. Then, in 1835, the enterprise was bought by the Schneider brothers. Quickly restored to a sound position, the Creusot plant produced the first locomotive for the Paris–Versailles line in 1838 and the first steamboat in 1839. Its expansion was reflected in the growth of the town of Le Creusot, which increased from 2,700 inhabitants in 1836 to 5,850 in 1845.

Although increased coal production was one of the major features of this economic modernisation, older enterprises also continued to function. The great increase in output was related to the concentration of the mining operations. Begun at Rive de Giers in 1837, this concentration progressed by stages, eventually leading to the formation of the *Compagnie des mines de la Loire* in 1840. In economic terms, increased coal production had been a stimulus to the improvement of transportation (by canal and railway), which in turn reactivated the exploitation of coal mines through the cumulative effect of technological advances. The capitalist character of this modernisation is mirrored in the development of the limited company; Lyon in particular became an important centre of financing. Yet the investors of Lyon were to occupy only a secondary position in the *Compagnie des mines de la Loire*, which operated on a national rather than merely a regional scale.

The modernisation of commerce

In the region of Lyon capital investment played a greater role in commercial and financial transaction than in the development of industry. That is why the issue of circulation, whether it related to the transfer of capital or to the transportation of merchandise and passengers, played such an important role in the achievement of economic transformations.

Banks and credit

In 1830 Lyon was still the principal relay station of the entire trade between north and south, and its storage and transit facilities involved considerable monetary transactions. In those years many insurance companies, water transportation, and gas-lighting firms were founded at Lyon.

Lyon's banking activities were closely tied to the *Fabrique*. Around 1840, for example, the Guérin bank had 137 foreign customers, for the most part in Italy (30 in Turin, 25 in Milan), but also in London (9), Frankfurt, Leipzig, Zurich, and Antwerp. It also had 140 customers in France, especially in the region but also in Paris, Montpellier, and even Bordeaux.

In 1835 a departmental bank was founded for the purpose of stabilising the discount rate, which fluctuated greatly with the needs of the *Fabrique*. The receiver-general Delahante was appointed president of this bank, and its administrators included the most important bankers and merchants of Lyon, among them Bontoux, Laurent Dugas, Guérin, Morin-Pons.

The first attempts to create a commercial credit institution failed when a *Caisse de commerce* at Lyon declared bankruptcy in 1838. However, the Lyon *Omnium*, set up in the same year, represented a veritable holding company with which the city's principal financiers were associated.

Steamshipping

Steamshipping was stimulated by the increased volume of trade and also by the competition of another continental trade route which, by way of the Rhine and Switzerland, threatened to divert some of the traffic away from the Rhône valley. The local authorities took an active interest in the development of steamshipping along the Rhône–Saône corridor at a very early date; the first steamboat appeared on the Saône as early as March 1827. To be sure, this new form of navigation was hampered by all kinds of difficulties; among other things it was not easy to find good crews, since steamboats were viewed with hostility by the traditional shipping trade. Yet steamshipping soon prevailed, first over transportation by the Lyon–Chalon road and then over the towed barges. Especially between 1839 and 1845, many new shipping companies sprang up along the Rhône. Keen competition among companies led to constant technical improvement, but since these operations demanded increasingly large capital outlays, few of them could remain in the hands of one family. The trip upstream from Arles to Lyon that had taken one month by rowing-boat or horse-drawn barge could be made in 60 hours by steamboat, and after 1843 in 35 hours.

Traffic along the river continued to bring an important transit trade to Lyon; it also brought wealth to smaller towns along the way. Thus the lawyer Grosson responded to a survey question in 1833: 'Located along the main highway, Montélimar and its territory has 29 inns . . . On any given day, it lodges 800 draft horses, 230 waggoners and drivers of carts, stage coaches, and public conveyances, as well as 120 travellers.' At the time, Montélimar was a little town of 6,300 inhabitants. In 1845 the annual volume of merchandise passing through Lyon was estimated at 700,000 tons, 500,000 tons of which arrived by water. At the very time when steamshipping seemed to have become firmly established, it was faced with new competition, that of the railway.

Railway projects and the first railways

The building of the first French railways was closely related to coal mining. In 1823 the government granted – over the protests of transport enterprises and local landowners – the concession for a railway between Saint-Etienne and Andrézieux on the Loire. It was 18 kilometres long, and became the first French railway line. Another spur, built in 1830 between Epinac and Pont-d'Ouche (on the canal de Bourgogne) on the initiative of Jacob Blum, the director of the mines of Epinac, was also related to the extraction of coal. The concession for the building of the railway between Saint-Etienne and Lyon (56 km) was granted to the Seguin brothers in 1826 and the line was completed in 1832. Although the number of passengers grew rapidly, from 171,000 in 1834 to more than 500,000 in 1844, this railway was mainly used for the transport of coal. Yet it did not bring down the price of coal in Lyon, a fact that gave rise to much polemic in the city, both about the prices charged by the railway and the benefit of railways in general. Opposition to the railway came from the postmasters and from the leading families in the river-shipping trade, who succeeded in mobilising some of Lyon's public opinion for their cause. So persuasive were their arguments that Lyon's integration into the great railway network was held up for many years.

Lyon showed little initiative in the protracted discussions concerning the building of the line between Paris and the Mediterranean. Barillon, one of the few defenders of railway construction on the municipal council, complained in January 1842 about the lack of interest in this matter shown by Lyon. Following the approval of the law of 26 July 1826 fixing the itinerary of the Paris–Lyon line by the Chamber, the concession was granted to the representatives of four different companies that had finally agreed on the terms of a joint bid. Five of the thirty-five members of the first administrative board of this company were Lyonnais, but the company fell victim to the crisis of 1848.

Even under the July Monarchy Lyon's commerce was still mainly engaged in transit shipping and dominated by the river transportation that kept the city in isolation and separated its neighbourhoods from each other. Although the railway revolution had had a major impact only in the mining areas of the Loire, by 1848 the whole region was deeply involved in discussions about itineraries, the siting of railway stations, the formation of companies, and speculation in railway stock. The rivalries, suspicions, and accusations spawned by these discussions tended to tarnish the authority of the notables and gave a new twist to the issue of power and leadership in the context of antagonisms that had both ideological and social connotations.

Social movements and political life

After 1815 the social effects of the economic evolution had produced acute crises, confined for the most part to urban areas, where they spawned fierce antagonisms. To some extent, however, the political configuration of the time was also conducive to tension.

The conflict between ultras and liberals

The enthusiasm with which Grenoble, Lyon, and Bourg had greeted Napoleon on his return from Elba, the spontaneous formation of federations during the Hundred Days, and the Austrian occupation, brief though it was, had once again divided public opinion at the time of the second Restoration. But at least the ultra reaction in the region of Lyon was less excessive than in the Midi. Yet this region too was dominated by the ultras, who benefited from the support of the deputies of the Incredible Chamber and from the connivance of the public authorities and the special courts. Large segments of the popular classes and of the *petite bourgeoisie*, however, preserved their Bonapartist sentiments, which is why as early as 14 November 1815 the military governor of Lyon called a meeting of the prefects of Rhône, Isère, Loire, Ain, and Saône-et-Loire in order to prepare 'all the means for preserving order, communication, and security that might become necessary'. Such concerted action was an unusual step; at the same time it reveals certain similarities in the behaviour of these different departments. The prefect of Lyon noted on 18 January 1816: 'The twenty reports I have received both from the department of Rhône and the neighbouring departments have made it clear to me that the same symptoms of popular unrest have been observed throughout the region.' The members of the federations of 1815 were tracked down everywhere and mayors were dismissed in large numbers.

It was at Grenoble that exasperation with these measures among Bonapartists and liberals spawned the first (aborted) conspiracy against the Bourbons. J.-P. Didier, the former dean of the Law school and a few former civil servants and officers had envisaged a surprise takeover of the administrative centre of the department of Rhône, to be carried out during the night of 20–21 January 1816, but this coup never occurred. Didier then hoped to take over Grenoble instead, counting especially on the support of the Piedmontese soldiers and former officers of the Napoleonic army who had nowhere to go. He was also able to involve some of the peasants of the cantons of Vizille, La Mure, and Bourgdoisans in his plot. The taking of Grenoble had been set for the evening of 4 May 1816 and was supposed to be followed by a general uprising against the Bourbons. But General Donnadieu, whose allegiance to the ultras was strengthened by his need to obliterate the memory of his role in the massacres of Vendean peasants during the Revolution, happened to learn of the plot and gave the alert. The insurgents, more than 500 men, were quickly dispersed by government troops during the night of 4–5 May. One hundred and fifty of them were arrested and fourteen were condemned to death. They were executed in their villages as a warning to the local populations.

Didier fled to Savoy, but he was betrayed, brought back to Grenoble, and executed on 10 June 1816. This affair – the background to which is unclear to this day – spawned a new wave of repression; yet Bonapartist agitation, carefully watched by a host of police spies, continued. The belated condemnation and the execution at Lyon on 23 July 1816 of General Mouton-Duvernet, designed to intimidate the Bonapartists and the liberals, only served to deepen the gulf between the population and the ultras.

Infuriated by the dissolution of the Incredible Chamber, the ultras of Lyon relied on a military police force set up by generals devoted to their cause without the consent of the lieutenant of police to back up their authority. It was in this climate that a subsistence crisis, coming on the heels of two bad harvests, brought misery in the winter of 1816–17. When popular protest movements sprang up, the adversaries of the Bourbon regime attempted to exploit this discontent, which was clearly more social than political in nature. Most of the Lyonnais learned of the disturbance that took place in their city on 8 June 1817 only from the proclamation of the lieutenant-general, Canuel, who announced on the following day that an alleged Bonapartist plot had been foiled. The unrest subsequently spread to eleven neighbouring communes, especially Ambérieu and Saint-Denis-Laval, where it was led by a captain on half pay by the name of Oudin. More than 200 persons were arrested at Lyon or in the country-side, many of them on simple suspicion. The special court, travelling to the local communes, condemned 79 of the suspects (11 were executed in the countryside), but the ringleaders could not be found. The lieutenant of police Charrier-Sainneville, who had been absent from Lyon on the day of the disturbance, easily found out that what had been presented as the conspiracy of 8 June had been instigated by *agents provocateurs* with the support of the military authorities. The central government assigned him to a new post, along with the prefect Chabrol (who nonetheless was pro-moted to Under-Secretary of State for the Interior) and General Canuel. Colonel Fabvier and Sainneville, both of whom had published a white paper highly critical of the manoeuvres of the ultras, were condemned to fines by the royal court of Lyon; a subscription opened by the liberals of Lyon easily raised the sums needed, since 12,000 persons contributed, proof that the liberal movement was solidly entrenched in the region of Lyon. In 1819, a committee of liberals successfully supported the candi-dacy of Tircuy de Corcelle, whom they preferred even to Jars, a former mayor of the Hundred Days, because Corcelle was considered more hostile to the Bourbons. The most outstanding success of the liberals, however, was the election of the former member of the Convention, abbé Grégoire, at Grenoble.

The political life of Lyon became more lively when greater liberty was granted by the Decazes government. Freedom of the press initially benefited the ultras, who launched the *Gazette de Lyon* in 1819, while the constitutional royalists only founded their organ, the *Journal de Lyon et du Midi*, later renamed the *Précurseur*, in March 1821. At that point, after the death of the duc de Berry, the entire region was dominated by the ultra reaction. And while the application of the law of the double vote did not prevent the re-election of Corcelle in 1820, the two new deputies nomin-ated by the electoral college of Rhône, the merchant Pavy and Colonel Chambost, were ultras. Actually, the voting bourgeoisie remained liberal in its attitudes, but since it consisted mainly of peaceful businessmen, it had little taste for violent resistance to reactionary measures. There was an obvious contrast between Lyon, which gave a polite reception to the duc d'Angoulême in 1820, and Grenoble, which treated him quite badly.

When Villèle came to power a new prefect, comte de Tournon, was appointed and charged with bringing the city under control. His intervention in the elections of May 1822 resulted in the defeat of Corcelle, which provoked a tumultuous protest on 10 May. In its aftermath a few young people, most of them Sardinians and Swiss, were arrested. Animosity against the Bourbons and sympathy for Napoleon became more and more widespread among the popular classes of Lyon; however strictly they were prohibited, Bonapartist emblems, tricolour cockades, and seditious songs turned up again and again.

By 1824, however, public opinion seemed once again to be dominated by the ultras, and Lyon's prosperity had returned. Several years passed before the bourgeoisie of Lyon were prepared for a more moderate, perhaps, but more effective opposition, which resulted in the success of the liberals in the elections of 1827. The liberals won in the electoral colleges of the *arrondissements* of Isère, Rhône, and Saône-et-Loire, but not in the departmental colleges, which were dominated by the great landowners who nominated candidates of the government party.

In September 1829 the bourgeoisie of Lyon gave a triumphal welcome to La Fayette and made no secret of its hostility toward the authoritarian measures of Charles X and Polignac. On the eve of the revolution of 1830, there was a good deal of political unrest, compounded by social protest movements, such as the strike of the carpenters in June. As soon as the ordinances were announced, a resistance movement was organised on 29 July under the leadership of Dr Mornand. On the following day the liberal leaders held a meeting in the offices of the *Précurseur*; having tried in vain to come to a compromise with the prefect, they formed a vigilante committee that distributed arms to the liberal rank and file and established contact with the liberals of Bourg, Vienne, Mâcon, Valence, and Annonay. On 31 July barricades were set up on the place des Terreaux, and the prefect, comte de Brosses, had to yield since the government troops could not be trusted, whereupon the committee assumed authority. The workers had acted only on behalf of the bourgeoisie.

The supporters of the older branch of the Bourbons did not disappear from Lyon in 1830; they represented most of the voters who abstained in the parliamentary elections of 1831 (29 per cent of the eligible voters). But the conflict between traditionalists and liberals was toned down at the beginning of the July Monarchy in the face of the social antagonisms (these will be analysed later). Moreover, Lyon's Catholic establishment refused to stay within the political confines of legitimism, and the fact that the Catholic Church rallied to the July regime caused some of the legitimist notables not, perhaps, to rally to the new regime but at least to assume some administrative duties in cooperation with their fellow notables. In this manner Laurent Dugas, a prominent merchant, accepted the presidency of the Chamber of Commerce in 1840. Yet it was precisely the religious issue that reanimated the conflict between legitimists and Orleanists at the end of the July Monarchy. The ultramontanism that came into its own with Cardinal de Bonald who fully supported the activities of Father Maillard, the provincial of the Jesuits, generated both aid to the Swiss Catholics and a movement for freedom of education fostered by a new newspaper, the *Gazette de Lyon*. Yet in the capital of Rhône, this conflict was more ideological than political, for the most momentous antagonisms were of a different nature.

By contrast, more active legitimist groups existed in the *arrondissement* of Villefranche and in Haute-Loire, at Riom in Puy-de-Dôme and at Moulins in Allier. Considerable numbers of young nobles, having resigned from the administration or the army, had retired to their ancestral properties in these areas. The nobility accounted for 42 per cent of those who paid more than 1,000 francs in taxes in the department of Allier, especially in its northern part. Yet this 'Vendée of the Bourbonnais' had little contact with Lyon, unlike the legitimists of the department of Loire who dominated the Forez region by controlling the elections in the *arrondissements* of Feurs and Saint-Chamond without engaging in systematic opposition.

Henceforth the conflict between the aristocracy and the bourgeoisie ceased to be the most important social issue in the region of Lyon.

Social conflicts

The revolt of the silk-workers

In the years after 1815 the economy of Lyon, dominated by the silk trade and based on a luxury industry that was highly sensitive to international fluctuations, underwent a period of adaptation for which the price was often paid by the working class. The shrinking of the American market in 1816 provoked widespread unemployment whose deplorable effects were further compounded by a series of bad harvests. However, the scope of the local charitable institutions and the rather generous relief distributed by the public authorities somewhat mitigated the misery of the working class during the crisis of 1816–19. On 29 December 1817, the *conseil des prud'hommes* [industrial relations tribunal] succeeded in having a municipal ordinance passed that re-established a pay scale of 1811. Amounting to what today would be called a collective contract, this ordinance fixed the price to be paid for finished velvet. During the Restoration Lyon experienced a few strikes, but they were mainly limited to workers in the millinery trade and to bakers' apprentices and – at least in the beginning – the sanctions against them were not too severe. A new economic crisis in the years around 1825 was all the more disturbing to the *Fabrique* of Lyon as there was increasing concern about the competition of silk manufactured in Zurich and in England. The problem was that, given the shortage of skilled workers, labour was relatively expensive at Lyon.

Social unrest and the silk-workers' revolt of 1831

The profound transformations of Lyon's economy between 1827 and 1832 compounded the existing social tensions; a reduction in the standard of living, even more than actual poverty, produced a situation in which conflict was endemic. The agitation spawned by the revolution of 1830 was bound to attune the workers to the nascent socialist ideologies or to republican ideas; moreover the revolution marked the beginning of a new commercial crisis, further aggravated by foreign policy difficulties and the cholera epidemic. Faced with decreasing sales, the *fabricants* adopted a harsher attitude. The workers were not demanding work but higher wages. The silk-workers of Lyon were accustomed to having their wages fixed by the municipal authorities; mutual aid societies had been formed as early as 1826. In October 1831, these societies endeavoured to organise the workshop owners in order to obtain a fixed wage scale for their work. On 18 October a central committee of workshop owners presented the prefect **Bouvier-Dumolar** with a petition couched in very moderate terms, asking for the establishment of a minimum wage scale. On 25 October the prefect called on a joint committee of *fabricants* and workshop owners to establish this wage scale. On that same day, some 6,000 workshop owners and workers staged a quiet and orderly march through the streets of Lyon in support of this demand. Motivated by fear, many *fabricants* decided to sign the new wage scale on 26 October.

About 100 *fabricants*, however, refused to recognise it and did not raise their wages. As a result, handwritten placards were posted and groups were formed for the purpose of preventing silk-workers from working for employers who did not apply the new wage scale. Lacombe – a workshop owner and former free corps captain during the Hundred Days – assumed the leadership of this movement, while the workshop owners began to lose control of the journeymen workers who had formed their own organisation. On 21 October the workers of La Croix-Rousse, directed by Lacombe, threw up barricades in order to keep the police and the National Guard out of their neighbourhood; the first gunfire was exchanged and several men were killed. At this point, however, some members of the National Guard who were themselves workshop owners joined the workers. Disagreements within the authorities facilitated the spread of the uprising. By 22 November the insurrection had spread to all the working-class neighbourhoods of Lyon, to La Croix-Rousse and La Guillotière. When almost 900 footsoldiers made common cause with the insurgents, General Roguet retired the troops from the city during the night of 22–3 November and the authorities abandoned the City Hall.

Still, the negotiations continued; the workers had adopted as their emblem a black flag and as their motto: 'To live by working or to die fighting.' The prefect, Bouvier-Dumolart, had made an appeal to Lacombe, who succeeded in preventing any looting. Meanwhile, certain republican agitators like Rosset or Dervieux attempted to channel the silk-worker's anger into political action, but the workers refused to participate in any such action. Taking advantage of the confused state of affairs in the offices of City Hall, the prefect, aided by the deputy mayor Boisset, regained control over the situation on 24 November by setting up a Council of Sixteen made up of moderate silk-workers. While this was happening, the troops sent to restore order entered Lyon without encountering resistance, except near the quai Saint-Clair. Lyon was placed under the dictatorship of Marshal Soult, the prefect was suspended, the minimum wage was abolished, the National Guard was disbanded, and a garrison of more than 10,000 men was established.

The news of the events of Lyon caused a certain excitement at Tarare, Saint-Etienne, Rive de Gier, Montbrison, Roanne, and even Grenoble. While the movement had arisen out of essentially social demands, its suppression would provoke a backlash of sympathy for a more political, republican opposition.

Republican agitation and the riots of April 1834

The republican propaganda diffused throughout eastern France by clubs in close cooperation with the press soon found its principal centre in Lyon. A local branch of the *Association pour la liberté de la presse* was radicalised in 1833 by a new recruit, César Bertholon, the son of a wealthy merchant, who pushed for a merger with the local branches of the *Société des droits de l'homme*. This society, which used the premises of the *Précurseur*, was directed by a committee constituted in 1833 and consisting of Bertholon and Eugène Baune, a former Carbonaro who had just published a pamphlet entitled *Essai sur le moyen de faire cesser la détresse de la Fabrique de Lyon* [Essay on the Means of Putting an End to the Distress of the *Fabrique* of Lyon]. Anselme Petetin's *Précurseur*, though openly republican since 1832, nonetheless remained a paper for the bourgeoisie and was therefore soon overtaken by the *Glaneuse*, a considerably more left-wing paper. The workers also had a newspaper influenced by republican ideas in the *Echo de la Fabrique* founded in 1831 by Marius Chastaing. The disagreements between the authoritarian prefect Gasparin and the more liberal mayor Prunelle afforded the republicans many propaganda opportunities. By 1832 radical ideas had spread beyond Lyon and found expression in such newspapers as the *Patriote de Saône* of Chalon, the *Patriote de la Côte-d'Or* of Dijon, the *Dauphinois* of Grenoble, and the *Sentinelle du Jura* of Lons-le-Saunier. In 1834 a reduction in the plush-workers' wages prompted a work stoppage of most of the silk-workers. Many *fabricants* hoped to use this incident to resolve a long-standing crisis situation, but the republicans themselves advocated a resumption of work, which indeed took place on 22 February. This setback had aggravated the workers' discontent. Some disturbances occurred on 5 April, the day when sentence was pronounced in the case of 'mutualists' [i.e. members of the mutual aid societies discussed above] indicted for their participation in the last coalition; one mutualist was killed and a procession of 8,000 workers marched to his funeral.

Between 9 and 12 April, the reopening of the mutualists' trials in conjunction with the agitation aroused by several bills concerning the right of association and the outlawing of public proclamations led to rioting under the slogan: 'Associations, Resistance, and Courage.' The insurgents were led by the heads of the local branches of the *Société des droits de l'homme* and Charles Lagrange, a 30-year-old clerk, directed the uprising of the central city. By 8 April groups of insurgents had assembled on the place Saint-Jean, the place de la Prefecture, and the place des Terreaux, and on the next day the Saint-Georges, Saint-Paul, and Saint-Just quarters fell into the hands of the insurgents who issued orders of the day dated 22 Germinal Year XLII of the Republic. On 11 April groups of insurgents disarmed the National Guards of rural communes in order to obtain guns.

The Minister of the Interior, Thiers, had given orders to let the movement develop, the better to crush it afterward. The number of insurgents seems to have reached almost 6,000 and to have included only a small minority of silk-workers and mutualists. Having set up their headquarters in the church of the Cordeliers, the republican leaders were hoping for a general uprising throughout France. However, on 12 April General de Fleury overpowered the suburb of Vaise, and by the following evening the army was in full control of the city. The government troops suffered 129 fatalities and close to 300 wounded; among the civilian population, 192 persons were killed and more than 500 wounded. The events of Lyon precipitated disorders in several other towns, among them Saint-Etienne (led by Caussidière), Arbois, Grenoble, Chalon, Marseille, and Clermont-Ferrand; in all of these places order was restored more rapidly. A suspect and dangerous city, Lyon was henceforth carefully watched and surrounded with fortifications. Yet the opposition between the city's social groups did not subside, for it resulted from a growing disparity of wealth: of the 13,752 persons who died between 1845 and 1847, 10,724 had nothing to bequeath, while the 18 wealthiest ones left 45 million francs.

The clandestine diffusion of republican ideas

After 1834 the workers were so discouraged that they dropped out of the republican movement and no longer engaged in political activities of any kind.

The diffusion of new social ideas had begun in 1831 when the Saint-

Simonian movement had sent a number of propagandists to Lyon, among them Laurent de l'Ardèche, Jean Reynaud, and Pierre Roux, who was received by Arles-Dufour. The Fourierist campaign of 1832 does not seem to have struck a responsive cord among the Lyonnais (perhaps because Fourier had spent more than ten years in their city). The Saint-Simonian and the Fourierist influences did not clash, but rather complemented each other in the minds of the workers to whom they brought the notions of association, minimum wages, and education. A phalansterian group was formed in 1837 on the initiative of Romano (who died in 1847), and this group exerted a certain influence over the workers of Lyon, while another Fourierist group consisted mainly of bourgeois, physicians, and lawyers; both had the support of the masonic lodge, whose members included Romano and Joseph Reynier, a cloth-worker.

Lyon was also the site of an important Babouvist movement, as we learn from the *Souvenirs d'un prolétaire* by Joseph Benoit, its principal founder. Finally, there was also an Icarian movement at Lyon; the influence of Cabet was particularly marked in the articles of Auguste Morlon published in the *Tribune lyonnaise* and in that paper's polemics against the *Censeur*. A rift thus developed between the republican bourgeoisie and the republican or socialist workers.

The split between the voting citizens and the population at large

The region of Lyon did nothing to bring about the fall of the July regime. Yet the revolution of 1848 produced a more lasting jolt here than in other regions of France. This apparent contradiction can only be understood if one analyses, even briefly, the manner in which the July Monarchy had blocked the political system to the point that its collapse was bound to throw the entire social system into disarray.

Suffrage was still extremely limited in the region after 1830; in the departments of Ain, Jura, Haute-Loire, and Ardèche, fewer than five out of 1,000 inhabitants were entitled to vote. As a result, many electoral *arrondissements* had a very small number of registered voters: 169 at Nantua, 150 at Sainte-Claude. In several cases these men used pressure and influence to constitute veritable electoral fiefs and a French version of the 'rotten borough'. In October 1839 the prefect of Ardèche wrote in connection with the election for general council: 'Voters of different persuasions concur in favouring the candidate whose position, influence, or ability promise to give the canton the most useful representative.' Whether by necessity or by the choice of the electorate, it appears that in this region, more than elsewhere, the voting regime was used for the benefit of private interests or at least to further the interests of the restricted group constituted by the wealthiest social category. This was even the case at Lyon, the only large city to be represented only by deputies of the government party at the end of the July Monarchy. The disturbances of 1831–4 had left a deep mark on the bourgeoisie of Lyon; the liberal deputies quickly went over to the government side, for they saw every political change as a potential source of disorder.

The liberal or radical opposition was firmly entrenched in several departments. On the eve of 1848 the four deputies of Drôme were members of the opposition, as were five out of the seven of Saône-et-Loire and two of Isère. Yet the influence of these deputies was rather limited, since the prefectoral administration and the magistracy often preferred to co-operate with the more conservative elements rather than with the deputies, and moreover their opposition was rarely uncompromising. A reformist banquet presided over by Alcock, councillor at the royal law court and a former deputy, was held on 23 November 1847 at the Rotunda of Les Brotteaux. It attracted more than 1,600 but many of the workers considered that, given the narrow scope of the demands, this banquet was too moderate an affair. Reformist banquets were also organised at Autun and Chalon-sur-Saône, at Saint-Marcellin, Vienne, and Grenoble; in Drôme opponents of the dynastic, radical, and even legitimist parties spoke at the reformist banquets of Montélimar, Valence, and Roanne.

The last election of the July regime, in which a conservative was elected to the general council by the fourth canton of Lyon on 24 February 1848, makes it quite clear that the voting citizens were completely out of touch with the population of Lyon.

14

The mountains of central France

The Massif central, France's 'water-tower', was the source of migrations that contributed to the growth of many cities, such as Lyon, Montpellier, Bordeaux, and especially Paris. Subject to a variety of contradictory influences, this diverse region played a very special role, for it isolated the Mediterranean south and separated eastern from western France south of the Loire by fostering the relations between north and south that favoured Paris. Shunned by an economy based on competition that drained it of a part of its youth, it was the mainstay of the government majorities in the Chamber; it was the region *par excellence* of rotten boroughs, since it expected more from the favours of the central government than from the meagre resources produced by its own hard labour.

Difficult and isolated living conditions in the plateaux and mountains
Covering large stretches of the region, especially the more humid western part of the massifs, forests reinforced its wild character. The people's ways were rough; as in other mountainous departments, crimes against persons were more prevalent than attacks on property, especially in Haute-Loire, Lozère, Corrèze, and **Creuse**. The terror aroused by tales of travellers robbed and killed at the inn of Peyrebille was compounded by rumours about such things as the 'dread beast' of the Gévaudan. There was no lack of refractories, and in 1823 the prefect of Puy-de-Dôme mentioned desertion as one of the scourges of the region.

Practised in all parts of the region, animal husbandry also contributed to its isolation. The transhumance of the herds determined the rhythm of rural life in the Cézallier, Cantal, and Aubrac regions. A few landowners, such as Tissandier d'Escors, the first president of the agricultural fair of Salers in 1845, practised selective breeding for the improvement of the cattle breeds, thereby initiating the spread of the Salers cattle. Even more wild, though blessed with a somewhat milder climate, the Grands Causses [high plateaux] southwest of the Massif central were suited for little more than the very extensive raising of sheep, especially ewes whose milk was sold at Roquefort, where cheese production was considerably expanded.

Forests and pasture lands were often owned by the commune; usurpations or sales reduced their scope, despite the prefects' efforts to preserve them.

Wherever it was possible to grow anything, the peasants lived mainly on what they produced. Farmers in the summer, they were part-time artisans in the winter, unless they migrated for the season. In many cantons the harvests produced by archaic methods were insufficient to feed a family, yet the least amount of money earned made the peasants think of buying more land rather than of improving the land they had. Money leaseholds had become more prevalent, but in the mountains sharecropping was still widespread. On certain lands fees comparable to the old seigneurial fees were still collected at the time of the Restoration. As for the crops produced, the potato was added to rye and buckwheat, but the new crop did not reach Haute-Auvergne until about 1830.

This isolation perpetuated ignorance and age-old obsessions. The 1834 *Annuaire de la Corrèze* notes: 'In the rural villages one finds very few persons able to read and write or speak the French language.' In Haute-Loire the report of an inspection tour made in 1836 describes 'the poverty that has bred not diligence but resignation, and a sustained fear of seeing any change in customs and habits that has more to do with forms of piety than with religion'. Even in Puy-de-Dôme – after all, one of the more prosperous areas – the inspector of primary education noted in his report of September 1836, 'the profound indifference to education on the part of the rural population'. Under these conditions, the members of the legal profession (notaries or solicitors) and sometimes the physicians became the representatives of the local councils almost as a matter of course, regardless of whether they were legitimists, liberals, or conservatives. Legal practitioners and physicians accounted for almost half of the general council of Cantal in 1840, and more than one-third in Haute-Loire and Corrèze. The prefects had little choice in appointing mayors, especially when the municipal councils were chosen by election. When it came to appointing a mayor for a mountain village under the July Monarchy, the prefect did not worry too much about a man's political opinions as long as he had a minimum of wealth and education. Administrative pressure, on the other hand, was easily brought to bear. As one example of stability among many others, Dr Marsal was mayor of Massiac in Cantal from 1831 to 1857: changes of regime obviously had little effect on him.

Plains and towns

The Massif central did have its islands of rich soil: limestone deposits formed a prosperous and densely populated area, with densities of more than 90 persons per square kilometre in certain cantons at the beginning of the Restoration. In these areas much of the land was owned by the bourgeoisie, which had increased its holdings through the purchase of nationalised property to such an extent that in the commune of Saint-Agoulin, for example, the peasants owned a smaller proportion of the land in 1829 than in 1789. The many estates that belonged to aristocratic families, like the Chabrol, were cut up into small farms. Population growth had brought a rise in rents, so that the farmers sought to increase their production. This was especially true for vineyards; new vineyards were planted in the pays des Buttes and in the cantons of Clermont and Pont-du-Château. During the Restoration as much as 60 per cent of the village territory was planted in vines at Chamalières or Beaumont, while 40 per cent of the land was used in this manner at Aubières. The vintners of the last two communes were much given to violent protest, rioting against the excise tax on beverages in August 1831, and participating in the anti-fiscal riots at Clermont-Ferrand in August 1841, when the mayor's house was sacked.

Another source of change and prosperity for the Limagne [area of limestone deposits] was the sugar-beet. A few sugar factories had been established at the end of the Empire but had failed. A new start was made after 1829. By 1831 the future duc de Morny settled at Clermont-Ferrand where he bought a sugar factory to which he devoted part of his time while beginning his political career as a deputy of the government party.

The natural environment and the local wealth of the Grande Limagne created favourable conditions for commercial activities and the presence of towns. Riom had made every effort to keep its royal law court and saw itself as the heir to the old parlement; throughout much of the July Monarchy, it was represented by a legitimist deputy, the former prefect of Seine, Chabrol de Volvic. A sharp division still separated the commercial and liberal bourgeoisie of the towns from the aristocracy. The persistence of this state of affairs made the bourgeoisie rather touchy and gave rise after 1831 to considerable distrust of the great families on the part of the smaller proprietors. Since at that point the latter formed an important part of the electorate, they chose as their deputies liberals who were opposed to any rapprochement with the men of the Restoration.

Situated at the centre of the only department of the region that had more than 500,000 inhabitants (601,000 in 1846), Clermont was a town whose growth was rather slow (34,000 inhabitants in 1846). As the commercial centre of Auvergne, it exerted a major influence over the neighbouring departments through its fairs, its newspapers, and through the relations with Paris that were kept up by a constant stream of emigrants.

Limoges, located in a less populated and poorer department, experienced a more rapid development, doubling its population in the first half of the nineteenth century. In 1846 its population exceeded 38,000, having gained almost 10,000 over the last five years. This rapid growth was the result of migration from the department itself and from the neighbouring departments and can be accounted for by the development of industrial activity (paper- and porcelain-making). Although these were traditional activities, they had benefited from the crisis of the Parisian handicrafts and from the initiatives of the merchant–manufacturer Alluaud. After 1840 Limoges made its mark on the porcelain market with twenty-four porcelain works and 5,000 workers within its zone of influence. The establishment of the American manufacturer Haviland in 1842 opened the American market to Limoges porcelain. The commercial bourgeoisie had played a preponderant role at Limoges even before the revolution of 1830; indeed there were fewer representatives of the economic professions in the town council after the elections of 1831 than under Charles X. Some of these men – among them the members of the Pétiniaud family, one of the porcelain dynasties that furnished a legitimist deputy, and the printer Alluaud – remained faithful to the older branch of the Bourbons. When this bourgeoisie had become wealthy, it purchased large landed estates in the region.

Aurillac was a small town of 10,000 inhabitants under the July Monarchy, the *chef-lieu* of an extremely poor department that year after year furnished a large contingent of emigrants. But Aurillac was located at the centre of a basin that made it look rich by comparison, for it had a prosperous cheese trade and its twelve annual fairs, especially the Saint-Géraud fair on 13 October, brought people, merchandise, and money to the town.

Brive, which took pride in being the capital of the lower Limousin, was situated at the crossroads of a plain devoted to cereal and wine production and cultivated by small owners who did not want to divide up their land and therefore sent their younger sons to work in town. This was one of the factors in the growth of Brive. The township barely counted 9,600 inhabitants. The building of a large bridge over the Corrèze as part of the Paris–Toulouse highway was completed in 1833; this example once again demonstrates the relationship between modernisation and patterns of circulation.

Shifts in the pattern of population and communication

Despite its high birth rate, the region of the Massif central experienced little demographic growth, since many of its inhabitants went to live elsewhere. This current of emigration followed the major valleys and swelled the population of other regions, as described in various other chapters. In *La Vie de Léonard*, Martin Nadaud has described the life of a mason from Creuse who left his birthplace at the age of thirteen or fourteen. In Creuse the number of migrants had doubled, reaching 30,000 in 1846. Most of them were peasants rather than artisans with a fixed residence, and more came from areas of small properties than from large estates, which seemed better able to retain their population. Several characteristic occupations were beginning to emerge: the migrants became sawyers, peddlers, and cloth-sellers – and this group was usually suspected of begging or, worse, accused of every foul deed by the prefect, the police, and the clergy – and wine- or coal-dealers in the towns, especially in Paris, where the image of the *bougnat* soon became a stereotype. Most of the time these migrations were temporary or even seasonal; and while they did affect the cohesion of the family, they also gave a special role to the old during the temporary absence of the younger men. The migrants brought back what money they had earned and on their return contributed to driving up the price of land and to its increasing fragmentation.

Here too the contacts with the rest of France and the relations with the State were maintained by the notables. Some of these notables did not live on their properties full time, but family origin and periodic visits were sufficient to preserve the people's attachment for the bearers of well-known names, as in the case of **Prosper de Barante, Peer of France and president** of the general council of Puy-de-Dôme throughout the better part of the July Monarchy. Others made their influence felt in Paris and from Paris, as in the case of the Councillor of State Dessauret, Director of Religious Affairs, member of the general council and deputy from Saint-Flour. Still others – and this was the most frequent situation – were minor local notables who exercised an administrative or municipal function, as in the case of Girot-Pouzol, the son of a deputy of the revolutionary era, who had been a member of the liberal opposition at Issoire under the Restoration and became sub-prefect in 1830, remaining in that post throughout the July regime.

This double weight of the local notables and the central administration was not without its drawbacks. It is true that under the Restoration Auvergne furnished an outstanding member of the opposition in the person of comte de Montlosier, but as a rule the departments of the Massif central regularly sent to Paris deputies of the government party, and the men who elected them often resembled the voters of Ambert about whom the solicitor-general wrote on 24 July 1846: 'Political preoccupations are practically non-existent in this *arrondissement*; material interests are the main focus of all hopes and all attention; the election of a deputy is little more than a matter of personality and local influence.'

The development of communications was furthered not so much by local aspirations as by specific initiatives on the part of the administration. A local witness wrote in 1836: 'Cantal has no country roads and will not build any unless coerced by the administration. The localism of this area is narrow, ignorant, apathetic, and ill-tempered.' The most serious incidences of social unrest were perpetrated by peasants upset by the bad harvests of 1816–20 who rioted at Argental, Ussel, and Eymoutiers, and later protested against taxes. One of the first strikes in the region affected the porcelain works at Limoges in September 1833, and one of the first strikes in Creuse broke out among the navvies working on a departmental road near Aubusson in June of 1840.

Modifications in the traditional structures were bound to produce social imbalances as the new liberal economy sacrificed the poorest for the benefit of the wealthiest members of society. As early as 20 December 1825, the mayor of Ardes complained to the sub-prefect of Issoire about the exodus of his fellow-citizens: 'It is precisely the opening of new roads, the most important source of public prosperity, that has totally wiped out the commerce of Ardes, for Besse and Murat are today prospering at its expense.' The consequences of the bankruptcy of two Clermont banks in May 1842 were particularly serious because, according to the deputy-governor of the Banque de France who made a special visit to Clermont on this occasion, it 'was a heavy blow not so much to business . . . as to the small investors, artisans and domestic servants who had placed their savings in these two banking houses. This event has caused a sensation and has made all other bankers suspect . . . even the depositors of savings banks have become alarmed.'

Liberal and even democratic ideas were found among the bourgeoisie. At Clermont, Trélat had founded a republican newspaper called the *Patriote* in 1839. This publication was short-lived, but it did serve to bring together a small group of republicans that was still active in 1848. A reformist banquet held on 23 August 1847 near Clermont and presided over by Antoine Couthon, the son of the *conventionnel* Couthon, even indicates the survival of Jacobin sympathies.

In these departments the political regime was never of interest to more than a small minority of the population. It was not until the revolution of 1848 that the inhabitants of these regions, where the traditions of Catholicism, the family, and the monarchy had become weakened over the years (although they were very much alive in certain cantons), became involved in an active and sometimes turbulent political life. The July Monarchy had simply not taken root among these populations, and the regime had made the error of interpreting the self-interested and half-hearted support of the voting bourgeoisie and the political indifference of the peasants as allegiance.

15

Eastern France

1814 did not have the same significance for eastern France as it did for the country as a whole. The return to tradition that this date implied lost much of its meaning in regions that had entered the national community at a late date: Franche-Comté had become French in 1678, Lorraine only in 1766, and in Alsace, most of which had been incorporated into the kingdom of France under Louis XIV, the republic of Mulhouse had lost its independence as late as 1798. Moreover, in 1789 these three provinces were still markedly different from the rest of France because foreign enclaves within their territory created a positively medieval tangle of local privileges and liberties and a customs frontier that separated these 'reputedly foreign' provinces from the rest of France and created economic ties with Germany and Switzerland. The Revolution had made these populations feel that they were part of France. The operation had succeeded because it was accompanied by the abolition of feudal rights and because these regions soon became the key provinces of an empire that dominated central Europe. Money was to be made from passing armies, from legitimate trade or from smuggling, and many men made their careers in the French army.

The massive invasion of enemy armies and a defeat that brought greater hardship than elsewhere in France marked the year 1814. In 1815 a second invasion inaugurated a military occupation that was to last until 1819 (40,000 men were stationed in Alsace alone). In addition, the treaties truncated Alsace and Lorraine by several cantons and, even more important, established the first clearcut military and customs frontier. At the same time, the end of the British blockade reopened France's Atlantic and Mediterranean seaboards to commerce, thereby dealing a harsh blow to the trade centres of eastern France.

These regions' status as frontier provinces had other consequences as well, since many of the towns that were classified as fortified places had lived in a symbiotic relationship with the army. The patriotism of such towns was nurtured by the memory of the Empire and by a contempt for the present. Since loyalty to the Bourbon monarchy was rather weak by comparison, public opinion soon returned to its old reflexes in favour of local independence, while the ruling classes wavered between unenthusiastic acceptance of the various regimes and opposition inspired by republican principles.

This attitude was particularly marked in Alsace.

Alsace

The special character of the population

The Alsatians formed a compact block of 800,000 inhabitants in 1814, 914,000 in 1830, and 1,067,000 in 1846. At that date a population density of 124 inhabitants per square kilometre made Bas-Rhin and Haut-Rhin the fifth and sixth most populated departments of France, since the population density for France as a whole was only 67 inhabitants per square kilometre. This growth of the population by one-third in 32 years had not occurred at a steady pace: rather slow at the beginning of the Restoration, it had peaked between 1820 and 1830 and declined somewhat thereafter.

Benefiting from a high birth rate, Alsace had also made a remarkably successful effort to promote vaccination. In addition, it was the terminus of many roads that brought outsiders from every direction: workers from Lorraine, Baden, Franche-Comté, or Switzerland who were attracted by the industries of Haut-Rhin, as well as political refugees, ranging from civil servants of the Napoleonic Empire who retreated to their adopted country and German liberals fleeing their country's absolutist repression to defeated Polish insurgents. Alsace easily absorbed all these different elements. Yet, like the other regions along the Rhine, it fed a stream of emigrants to southern Russia and the United States. The bulk of this stream of emigrants consisted of a rural proletariat whose condition had further deteriorated as a result of the reduction of communal rights over the land and increased repression of poaching and stealing of wood. Every crisis brought a temporary surge in the number of departures.

Except in the region of Belfort and Cernay and in the upper stretches of the Bruche valley, the Alsatians spoke one of several German dialects; the centralising efforts of the Revolution and the Empire had proved unable to dislodge this 'Germanic idiom'. The upper classes of the towns did know French, but it was virtually unknown in the countryside. Like the previous regimes, the Restoration and the July Monarchy sought to establish French as the first language in these areas, but the attempt of the Restoration to send instructions to the rural mayors in French ended only in dismal failure. Meanwhile, judges, tax-collectors, and even sub-prefects often did not know German. This situation was the source of innumerable problems. In the law courts, for example, the proceedings were conducted in French and the jurors made their decision on the basis of a few indications that were translated to them – and this of course was grounds for annulment by the Court of Appeals. One of the most insistent demands of Alsatian particularism was therefore the recruitment of local civil servants and the dismissal of those who had arrived 'by the mail coach'.

It was only after the Guizot law was passed in 1833 that a serious effort was made to teach French in the primary schools. Until then the Catholic, Protestant, and private schools of Alsace, where school attendance was higher than elsewhere in France, had taught in German; and despite the existence of the teachers' college of Strasbourg, France's only such institution until 1821, very few teachers were capable of imparting the rudiments of French.

The Alsatian population was divided with respect to religious affiliation. About three-fifths were Catholic. In addition, about 183,000 Lutherans were counted in the 1820s, especially in Bas-Rhin (where there were 154,000 Lutherans, although the city of Strasbourg was divided almost equally between Catholics and Protestants), as well as 40,000 Calvinists who formed a compact group of 7,000 persons – out of a population of 9,000 – at Mulhouse, but were dispersed in small congregations elsewhere. Finally, there were 14,000 Jews in Alsace, half of them living in the *arrondissement* of Altkirch, while the rest belonged to more than 200 congregations that had often settled in very small towns. These differences in affiliation were a constant source of tension in the villages. The *simultaneum* system, under which both Catholics and Protestants used the church if there was only one in the village, gave rise to all kinds of reciprocal chicanery among lower-class people, but even the upper classes did not trust anyone who belonged to a different group. As for the Jews, their legal status had become that of French citizens, but this fact had practical implications for only a few individuals, men like Colonel Cerfberr, who was elected deputy from Wissembourg under the July Monarchy; and moreover the synagogues were divided over the question whether the Jews should mix with the goyim. In actual fact, most of the Jews continued to live separate lives. The peasants hated them because they were reputed to be usurers (and this reputation was reinforced by the fact that some of them lent their names to Christian capitalists), and spread epidemics by travelling from place to place as peddlers and old-clothes merchants. Until 1848, inclusively, practically every crisis prompted some outbreak of anti-semitism in Alsace.

The towns of Alsace

The old and closely-knit network of towns remained a driving force in the economic and political life of the region. The Alsatian nobility, being of recent origin, and either without firm local roots or uprooted by the Revolution, played a very minor role. The bourgeoisie, by contrast, a varied and enterprising group led by rich and influential families, who had a clear understanding of the needs of the province, formed an effective ruling class. It included professional men, important merchants, bankers, and the manufacturers who were so powerful in Alsace that they have been called a 'fabricantocracy'.

The many extremely particularist small towns were reminiscent of the era of the imperial free cities. Each one of them had its own set of convictions, which might be conservative and clerical or, on the contrary, quasi-'republican'. The inhabitants were split into factions, each of which sought to use municipal power for its own ends, and there is little doubt that the mayors of the Restoration era perpetuated a long tradition of abuse of power and compromise of principles. Furthermore, the rivalry among towns could be very harsh indeed: a long-drawn-out conflict over the possession of the sub-prefecture pitted Sélestat against Benfeld and Barr, Wissembourg against Haguenau. The variety of these towns was the result of their geographic structure and their history, which determined their function or functions. Wissembourg or Neuf-Brisach were military towns; Sainte-Marie-aux-Mines used the waterfalls coming down from the mountains for industrial purposes; Ribauvillè, because of its proximity to vineyards and forests, was a marketing centre for wine and wood as well as an industrial centre; Belfort, a fortified place with six access routes, was also a major centre of transportation, and so forth. All of these towns were quasi-rural in character, since country people came to work there every day, and gardeners and vintners actually lived there. Three of them, however, played a very special role: Colmar, Mulhouse, and Strasbourg.

Colmar, the administrative seat of the department of Haut-Rhin, remained a modest-sized town of about 15,000 inhabitants, most of them Catholics. Its old ramparts had been made into terraced gardens and a public promenade. Its well-paved streets were still narrow and darkened by the overhanging upper storeys of the houses. In the most aristocratic sections of the rue des Bleds were the homes of the magistrates of the Court of Appeals, the successor to the 'sovereign council', and of many of the town's lawyers. The revolution of 1830 produced a kind of 'musical-chairs game' between these two groups. Prominent families of lawyers, often bearing French names even though they were fixed in Alsace since the Ancien Regime, dominated the local society. Even modest families owned a garden plot outside the town, planted in vines and complete with a hut called a '*gloriette*'. Despite its calm provincial character, Colmar continued to function as a major agricultural market, especially for wine; the completion of the Rhine–Rhône canal (1834) and of the Strasbourg–Basel railway (1842) enhanced and diversified its function as a transit centre. In addition, the suburb of Logelbach was the site of textile mills, among them the famous printed cotton works of J. M. Haussmann, to which a spinnery had been added in 1822.

The annexation to France resolutely propelled Mulhouse toward the future, wrenching it out of a past as a modest town of the Helvetic type in which full citizenship was granted sparingly. Its population increased from 9,300 inhabitants in 1815 to 13,000 in 1827, to 17,000 in 1836, and 29,000 in 1847. This invasion by proletarian and for the most part Catholic hordes, who had come from all the poorest regions from the Jura and the Vosges to the Tyrol, did not cause the bourgeoisie to lose control over the town and its hinterland. Initially formed by a fusion of German and Swiss with indigenous elements, this bourgeoisie had, by the time of the monarchy of limited suffrage, become a closed caste whose members were related by intermarriage. Passing differences of opinion might occasionally trouble these patriarchal clans (Koechlin, Dolfus, Schlumberger, Mieg, etc.), yet they were fundamentally united by their shared religious faith. Rarely was the relation between Calvinism and capitalism as close as it was at Mulhouse. A deep faith in progress, often intensified by membership in a masonic lodge, was the driving force behind the boldness of these industrialists who worked together in the Chamber of Commerce and its ambitious creation, the *Société industrielle de Mulhouse*, founded in 1825 for the purpose of 'advancing industry from its present empiric state to the rank of a true science'. The prominent manufacturers of cotton cloth, the most important product of Mulhouse, made use of every technical innovation that could improve their product. This policy enabled them to compensate for their location far from the markets where they bought their raw materials or sold their finished goods. The future industrialist was often educated in Swiss schools of the Pestalozzi type and sometimes also studied chemistry in Paris, whereupon he learned his trade by spending long periods of apprenticeship away from home in Normandy, England, or Russia, before going to work in the paternal enterprise.

This openmindedness went hand in hand with a paternalistic attitude: the employers of Haut-Rhin created primary or technical schools, founded the first savings banks for the workers, and set up mutual help and retirement societies; they also tried to deal with the crucial problem, especially in overpopulated Mulhouse, of housing for the workers. The 'barrack houses' built under the July Monarchy proved rather unsatisfactory, but in 1853 the first French workers' garden city was built at Mulhouse.

Despite its unusual features, this employer class was sincerely attached to France, whose language was spoken in many of the households. Yet its patriotism, which might well have Bonapartist overtones, went hand in hand with an extremely liberal attitude. This liberalism was suspect to the Restoration government, which appointed an outsider as mayor of Mulhouse. Yet this suspicion scarcely impaired the predominant influence of the Mulhouse manufacturers throughout Haute-Alsace. In 1845 the department had 167 cotton-cloth mills, only 26 of which were located at Mulhouse (34 were at Sainte-Marie-aux-Mines); yet all of them were tied to the town by family alliances, by financial arrangements, and by their use of the Chamber of Commerce and the stock exchange. The large contingent of rural weavers never played the predominant role they played, as we have seen, in Normandy, because the foremost Alsatian speciality was printing on cotton, a delicate operation that could only be performed in a factory setting. The shift to the production of high-quality cloth led the Alsatian industrialists to create separate spinning mills in order to produce the fine threads that still had to be imported in the early years of the Restoration. In the course of the July Monarchy, hand looms were replaced by mechanical looms. In fact, the scope of the cotton manufacturers' involvements reached even beyond the integration of all the operations of cotton making, from spinning to the printing of cotton cloth, since they pointed the metal industry of Belfort toward the construction of looms for the cotton industry, while the cotton manufacturer Koechlin took the initiative in the building of the first major French railway, the Strasbourg–Basel line, which opened in 1842.

A history of steadily increasing production reveals this constant effort at adapting to new developments: cotton from the Levant or the Antilles was used until 1823, at which time it was replaced by the long-staple Egyptian cotton, which in turn was supplanted by American cotton around 1840. Great progress was also made in marketing: although some of the cotton was still sold at the great fairs, the Mulhouse exchange began, by the end of the Restoration, to act as a clearing-house for all transactions involving raw materials and semi-finished goods. As for the markets, they were expanding rapidly: in addition to the French market, Alsatian cotton goods gradually recovered their European markets (Spain, the Netherlands, Italy, Germany) and, more importantly, conquered such extra-European markets as Persia, Mexico, South America, the United States, India, and so forth. By 1839 the leading factories exported half of their output, which had risen considerably since the beginning of the Restoration. Using more than one-fifth of all the imported cotton and equipped with 683,000 spindles and 6,000 mechanical looms, the region of Mulhouse was the third largest cotton producer after Normandy and the region of Troyes. The variety of markets called for a variety of products, ranging from rather coarse-patterned Turkish towelling to fine muslin shawls. Different events (war in Spain, the Zollverein, Franco-Mexican tension, etc.) slowed down the expansion by the end of the July Monarchy.

Haute-Alsace had other industries as well: paper mills in the region of Munster, tanneries, blast furnaces and forges, among others those of Oberbrück belonging to the famous liberal Voyer d'Argenson who, when he had to flee France in 1822, had studied their modernisation during his stay in England. All in all, however, it was under the predominant influence of the bourgeoisie of Mulhouse that Haute-Alsace became an unusually advanced industrial region; the importance of Mulhouse was recognised by the opening in 1846 – at the same time as at Strasbourg – of a branch of the Banque de France.

Basse-Alsace, for its part, was not lacking in industry either. Already in the eighteenth century, the exploitation of the iron ore deposits at Niederbronn and the blast furnaces and forges that used the ore had placed their owner Frédéric de Dietrich, the famous mayor of Strasbourg, in the position of a veritable iron king. Under the Restoration his widow succeeded in reviving this enterprise in the form of a limited company among whose stockholders one finds such men as Scipion Périer and Renaud de Bussière. It employed some 900 workers and 350 woodcutters. Also prospering under the Empire were the gun factory at Mutzig and the bayonet factory at Klingenthal. Initially employing a core of workers from Solingen, the latter enterprise had only 16 foreign workers in a work force of 600 by the beginning of the Restoration. When this 'royal manufactory' was transferred to Châtellerault in 1830, its directors, the Coulaux brothers, founded a sickle and scythe factory in its place. It should also be noted that the famous bitumen and petroleum deposits of Pechelbronn were already being exploited.

Nonetheless, Basse-Alsace was first and foremost an agricultural region, which did not receive the same stimulus from Strasbourg as Haute-Alsace received from Mulhouse. Strasbourg had a completely different and much more complex function, being a military town as well as the 'natural transfer station for merchandise in transit from Italy and Switzerland, Holland and Hamburg, or for foodstuffs coming from the interior of France', and a major cultural and academic centre where French and German culture intermingled.

The ninth largest town of France, its population remained stable under the Restoration (50,000 inhabitants) but increased by more than 20,000 persons under the July Monarchy. The year 1815 had made Strasbourg a frontier city rather than the gateway to Germany; this was a crisis from which it does not seem to have fully recovered until after 1830.

The site on which the city was built remained as marshy and unhealthy as ever, for it was crossed by several arms of the Ill, by the Bruche, and by a number of canals. Its walls, pierced by seven gates, were still intact and its inhabitants were tightly packed into its 3,600 houses. At the time of the Restoration the narrow, dark, and poorly paved streets were lit by oil lanterns, but only in winter. Yet the French eighteenth century, lacking the funds to remodel all of the city, had inserted some noble vistas and palaces of great elegance into the tangled lanes of the old German town. This effort was completed under the Restoration with the building of the Orangery and the new theatre. The July Monarchy subsequently embarked upon a programme of sanitary improvements: the mayors Turkheim (1830–5) and especially Schützenberger (1837–48) built quays along the Ill, covered the Tanners' Ditch which gave off a terrible stench along the promenade de Broglie, replaced a group of small butchers' shops located behind the Aubette by a covered meat market, built a grain market, and introduced pavements and gas lighting.

The centre of Strasbourg's activity was its port, which was also enclosed by walls. It occupied a naturally advantageous position at the point where navigation on the Rhine became difficult, so that shipping was obliged to turn into the Ill. Cargoes were unloaded at the port of Strasbourg and sent west and south by overland routes. However, the customs legislation enacted at the beginning of the Restoration strictly regulated the storage and transit of foreign goods and set up protective tariffs, in particular against the entry of cattle from Germany, all of which convinced the Strasbourgeois that the central government favoured the ports and the stockmen of western France.

Nevertheless, Strasbourg maintained a wide variety of industries, and even gardeners and boatmen continued to ply their trades. Looms were clattering in the neighbourhood around the cathedral, while small iron-works, goldsmithing and clockmaking existed elsewhere. Strasbourg had a comfortable bourgeoisie: in addition to the old families who kept up the patrician ways of the past, a great many parvenus had joined its ranks during the Empire, when 'half the city engaged in smuggling' during the blockade, and moved into the old townhouses of the quays Saint-Thomas and Saint-Nicholas. A typical representative of this newly rich class was Jean-Georges Humann, who at the time of his death was Louis-Philippe's finance minister. Having started out in the grocery and transport business and almost certainly having done his share of smuggling, he became a great tycoon who involved himself in such varied ventures as the canal between the Rhône and the Rhine, steamshipping on the Rhine, and the mines and forges of Decazeville and Audincourt.

A banking and commercial centre as well as a judicial town, with its influential Bar whose star was the impassioned republican orator Liechten-berger, Strasbourg was also the seat of a major university. This was the only provincial university to have, like Paris, all five faculties of Theology, Letters, Science, Medicine, and Law. The Faculty of Theology was divided into a Catholic and a Protestant section, the latter established in 1821. The influence of Strasbourg's Faculty of Theology was a primary factor in the development of Alsatian Protestantism, both Lutheran and Calvinist, which experienced a 'great awakening' at this time. As for the bishop of Strasbourg, his diocese encompassed all of Alsace, and the future priests were trained at the theological seminary of Strasbourg. In addition, the town also had a military establishment. Barracks, magazines, and the arsenal were grouped together in the citadel quarter on the east bank of the Ill. A large garrison of footsoldiers, artillerymen, and pontoneers was kept in the city, and its commanding general was a personality to be reckoned with. Despite occasional rivalry, he collaborated with the prefect in maintaining order. The army, incidentally, had close contacts with the population through the retired soldiers on half pay who lived in Strasbourg in greater numbers than anywhere else, except in Paris. Finally, Strasbourg had given asylum to many refugees, especially from Germany. The German colony was distinguished by the presence of Goerres.

Alsatian sociability welded these different elements into a lively and at times boisterous city. There were Catholic and Protestant salons, the most famous among them being the very international salon of comtesse Levetzov, whose daughter Ulrike was the last passion of Goethe in his old age. Merchants, lawyers, and professors met in casinos to read and discuss the latest news. Some sixty breweries, whose owners sold their product on the premises, were filled every night with lively crowds. Strasbourg was deeply stirred by international events, whether it be the arrival of defeated Polish insurgents in 1831 or the meeting of German liberals at the Hambach festival in 1832. Statues of Kleber and Gutenberg were inaugurated amidst popular enthusiasm. Strasbourg's most widely read and most long-lasting newspaper, successor to the *Strassburgische Zeitung* of 1789, was the staunchly liberal bilingual *Courrier du Rhin*. Uncompliant and given to charivaris and demonstrations in which radical bourgeois, students, artisans, and retired military men marched under the aegis of popular societies, Strasbourg nonetheless remained a patriotic and liberal town. The flag-waving eagerness with which the National Guard was resuscitated immediately after the revolution of 1830 and the refusal of that same Guard to buckle under to authorities in whose election it had not had a hand is indicative of this double attitude.

That same attitude also marked the work of the poets who, like Ehrenfried Stoebel, wrote in German about their love for France, despite the literary influences that came to them from across the Rhine. Characteristically Romantic attempts were made to use the local dialect as a literary language. In the same spirit scholars examined the local past: the archaeologist Geoffroy Schweighoeuser and Philip de Golbery published the *Antiquités d'Alsace*, while Kentzinger, who had been mayor of Strasbourg throughout the Restoration, brought out a collection of *Documents historiques tirés des Archives de Strasbourg*.

Such a city was no paradise for the prefects. Neither the Restoration prefects, who appear to have been mediocre, nor an eminent administrator like Choppin d'Arnouville (1830–7), achieved success in this difficult post.

However, the levelheadedness of baron Sers who succeeded d'Arnouville and his sustained defence of his constituents' material interests, earned this Protestant from Bordeaux the confidence of the local notables.

The peasants and workers of Alsace

The land of Alsace was structured in the same manner as that of the other eastern provinces, featuring a three-fold system of crop rotation on long open fields, old communal practices of free pasture on communal land and areas set aside for pasturing communal livestock, as well as clustered settlements. The Alsatian village, on the other hand, resembled that of Germany, with its two-storey, half-timbered daub houses covered with extremely steep thatch or tile roofs, decorated with carved porches and balconies. The gables faced the street, while one of the sides opened onto a courtyard flanked by the barn or the stable. One-storey houses were found only on the slopes of the vineyard country of the lower Vosges.

Travellers were less impressed by the pleasant appearance of the Alsatian villages than by the rare sight, at a time when fallow and uncultivated fields were still widespread, of 'land that never rested'. While this was certainly true for the alluvial plateaux of Basse-Alsace, there were many exceptions to this rule in the marshy swamps and on the gravelly or rocky terraces of the Sundgau. By and large, however, rural Alsace was indisputably ahead of the rest of France in its adoption of the agricultural revolution. In the northern sections the old triennial crop rotation had long ago been largely replaced by a biennial rotation that made it possible to produce wheat every other year. In the course of our period, complex systems of rotation over six or nine years were developed, testifying to the variety and the progressive commercialisation of production. The crops produced included wheat, maize, fodder plants or plants for industrial use (madder, tobacco), oleaginous plants (colza, poppies), textile plants (hemp), and field-grown vegetables, such as cabbage for sauerkraut. By 1815 potatoes, together with bread, had become the basis of the inhabitants' diet; it also enabled farmers to fatten their pigs in the stable rather than send them into the woods to forage for acorns, thereby increasing the number of pigs produced from 5,500 in 1798 to 60,000 in 1857. Cultivation gradually encroached on the commons, which were no longer needed, as artificial forage plants made it possible to keep livestock in the stable. Rural communities therefore divided up their communal lands, either by giving each inhabitant a proportional share of it to cultivate or by leasing it out. Although this change was fiercely resisted by a rural proletariat whose very existence was threatened by the decreasing size of the communal herd, it eventually became irreversible.

Yet despite the practice of raising livestock in the stable, and despite the extension of irrigated meadows, the large livestock remained mediocre in quality. No efforts were made to improve the breeds, and there were more horses than were needed for the work in the fields. Above all, the fragmentation of the fields was pushed to extremes.

To be sure, Alsace did have a few large estates owned by aristocratic families or Lutheran foundations. But the sale of nationalised property had brought a great deal of land into the hands of peasants. The Alsatian bourgeoisie, unlike its counterparts elsewhere, had bought such property only for the purpose of making a profit on its resale rather than in order to exploit it. The property owned by the villagers was often extremely small, amounting to no more than 5 hectares; a proprietor of 30 hectares was a '*coq de village*'. What is unusual in the French context of that time is the fact that these small owners adopted methods of intensive farming that deliberately broke with the time-honoured routine. No doubt the influence of the prefect Lezay-Marnesia, the famous 'prefect of the peasants', who died in an accident during the first Restoration, had been a stimulus to this innovative attitude; in fact his influence continued to make itself felt through one of his creations, the *Société des sciences, agriculture et arts du Bas-Rhin*, which still flourished during the Second Empire.

One must be careful, of course, not to paint an idealised picture of the free peasant of Alsace. Not only did he have to work very hard, his land hunger had often caused him to become indebted to a usurer. Poor harvests, which could easily occur in this climate, or a plague of mice might aggravate his situation and sometimes ruin him altogether. The situation of the vintners, who owned the tiniest plots of all, was even worse, for the entire period was marked by a crisis of the Alsatian wine trade. The tariff policy that prohibited the import of livestock from Baden and Switzerland prompted these countries to retaliate with measures against French wine, and moreover heavy excise taxes curbed consumption within France.

Briefly stated, by 1750 the traditional agrarian system was no longer adequate to the task of feeding a greatly increased population. The improvements that made it possible to break out of its constraints and to increase agricultural yields gave new vitality to the province. But by 1850 the pressure of a population that had tripled in just one hundred years produced another crisis, not perhaps of subsistence but of employment. The proliferation of rural artisans in the first half of the nineteenth century is symptomatic of the overpopulation of these rural areas. Whenever a few factories closed down, a whole group within the population was reduced to begging. The series of bad years that began in 1845 would produce an unprecedented wave of emigration.

In actual fact, Alsace can hardly be described as a 'rural democracy' as Vidal de la Blache has claimed. On the contrary, it was an area where a rural proletariat went to work for the largest landlords, who paid preposterously low wages. Part of this proletariat entered the working class, which soon accounted for about one-tenth of the entire French working class. But whether these workers worked at home or in a factory setting, the law of supply and demand kept their wages extremely low. In the cotton industry, moreover, women and children supplied the bulk of the work force (in 1847 a statistic for Mulhouse indicates that 13,000 of the 60,000 wage earners were children).

On the whole, there may have been a slight increase in the wages of factory workers over the period 1815–48. Yet the slightest seasonal or generalised slump produced unemployment that threatened the very life of these workers. This situation accounts for the charitable endeavours of the Mulhouse employers and at the same time underscores their strictly palliative character.

Political life in Alsace

Nonetheless the Alsatian masses were peaceful, and the relations between the workers and their employers rarely assumed an acrimonious character. Except at Strasbourg, the working masses took little interest in politics, even if they regretted the demise of the Empire. Several incidents, however, were symptomatic of their most pressing economic grievances: the beef revolt at Strasbourg (25 September 1831) that forced the customs officials to let cattle from across the Rhine enter duty-free; the wine revolt at Colmar (25–6 October 1833) during which the crowd publicly consumed large quantities of wine after having refused to pay the excise tax; and the 'bakers' holiday' at Mulhouse (26 June 1847) that brought a workers' riot against the high price of bread. There were other grounds for discontent as well, one of the most acute being the tobacco monopoly which, although established in 1810, was implemented only after the end of the allied occupation and was detrimental to the interests of farmers and manufacturers.

Political and religious issues were always liable to take a particularist turn in Alsace. The White Terror, for instance, turned into a severe purge among the clergy: Napoleon had appointed Mgr Saurine as bishop of Strasbourg, an ultramontane diocese, and Saurine had brought in a number of former constitutional priests who were out of favour elsewhere. Saurine having died in 1813, the vicars-general used the events of 1815 to get rid of 'Saurine's coat-tail riders'.

Discipline was restored by the ultramontane bishop Thanin, a friend of the Jesuit and Redemptorist Orders. He in turn was succeeded by an elderly prelate from Brittany, the Gallicanist Le Pappe de Trevern (1826–42). His administration was troubled by the Bautain affair. Bautain, a disciple of Cousin, had been a professor at the Faculty of Letters of Strasbourg at the age of 21, had converted to Catholicism and been ordained a priest in 1828. Influenced by German philosophy, he sought to renew the foundations of metaphysics, since he doubted that man could be led to faith by reason alone. Following the example of Lamennais at Malestroit, he gathered a small group of disciples at Molsheim, among them two converted Jews, Ratisbonne and Level, the future cardinal de Bonnechose, and Father Gratry. Having encouraged him at first, Le Pappe de Trevern eventually became alarmed at the irrationality of his doctrine and condemned it. The case was taken to Rome, where Bautain was not censured, but he nevertheless left the diocese for Jouilly. The theological school of Alsace which had formed at Mainz around Mgr Colmar had won the day. After Le Pappe de Trevern one of its adepts, Mgr Roess, would govern the diocese of Strasbourg for many years.

In the political arena the liberalism of the voting bourgeoisie was evident throughout the Restoration. In the Incredible Chamber only one of the thirteen Alsatian deputies voted with the ultras, and only one was a member of that party in 1830. Despite the efforts of the prefects in the period 1824–9, the department of Haut-Rhin sent 21 constitutional monarchists to the Chamber, out of a total of 29. In Bas-Rhin, 22 of 33 were constitutional monarchists. Electing Humann, Turkheim, and Jacques Koechlin, Alsace was also proud to be represented by such opposition leaders as Voyer d'Argenson and Benjamin Constant, who was enthusiastically received whenever he passed through Strasbourg.

Indeed, the revolutionary opposition also felt that it could count on Alsace. On 30 December 1821 a conspiracy organised by the Carbonari called for an uprising of the garrisons of Belfort and Neuf-Brisach, where-upon popular support would permit the triumvirate La Fayette/Voyer d'Argenson/Koechlin to seize power in Colmar. The plot was discovered and failed; but its instigators were able to protect themselves. In June of the following year a full-scale provocative police action was carried out for the purpose of flushing out the partisans of the Emperor in Haute-Alsace, with troops and officers from Colmar marching through the countryside shouting 'Vive l'Empereur!' This operation yielded little more than the arrest and subsequent execution of Lieutenant-Colonel Caron.

Yet in 1828 Charles X was well received in Alsace. The hostility of many liberals for the Bourbons might have been softened if the regime had adopted a liberal policy, as indeed many people hoped in the early stages of Martignac's prime ministership. This hope proved to be an illusion, and Alsace rejoiced at the king's fall. But before long severe disagreements sprang up between the party of resistance and the party of Movement. In Bas-Rhin Humann became the leader of the resistance. The partisans of the Movement party frequently turned to the republicans for support. The opposition parties usually won without much difficulty in the municipal elections of Strasbourg, but the delegation of Bas-Rhin in the Chamber included six members of the government party. Haut-Rhin was more resistant to government pressure and preserved two liberals in its delegation of five.

At this time the Humann clan, despite the recent loss of its head, dominated the political arena of Bas-Rhin, a department 'about to become the fief of one family that has chosen Prefect Sers as its captain' (*Le National*). And indeed, the prefect had just married his daughter to a member of the clan; moreover, the younger Humann, his brothers-in-law Saglio and Renouard de Bussière, and his cousin Lemasson had been elected to the Chamber of Deputies. Another family network existed in Haut-Rhin, where Nicolas Koechlin was the leader of the liberal opposition, while his cousin André Koechlin was head of the conservative party. The latter had just been defeated in the election by another cousin, Emile Dolfus. At any rate, the predominance of the great manufacturers was uncontested.

In Alsace, whose firm attachment to the ideas of the Revolution was beyond doubt, the regime of narrowly limited suffrage prepared the way for the rule of a new aristocracy.

Lorraine

Population and resources

The four departments into which Lorraine was divided (Vosges, Moselle, Meurthe, Meuse) had a total of 1,406,000 inhabitants at the time of the 1821 census, and 1,648,000 in 1846. These figures represent densities per square kilometre of 64.1 and 69.3 at these two dates. The population growth of Lorraine had not proceeded at an even pace: slow at the beginning of the Restoration, it accelerated in the last ten years of that regime, only to slow down again under the July Monarchy, to the point of ceasing almost altogether after 1841. In 1846 the population density of Lorraine was slightly higher than the French average, but distinctly lower than that of Alsace.

These averages conceal disparities that are brought to light by individual departmental statistics: speaking only of the densities per square kilometre, in 1821 and 1846 that of the department of Vosges rose from 58.8 to 73.3, Moselle from 70.1 to 83.4, Meurthe from 62.4 to 73.4, and Meuse from 46.7 to 52.3. The low density and the slow growth of Meuse are striking indeed, and the high density of Vosges – higher by 19 per cent· than that of Moselle – and its rapid growth are also surprising.

After all, the department of Vosges had a very slender resource base. The cultivated land was associated with a pattern of isolated dwellings or tiny hamlets and was subject to the traditional problems of agriculture in mountainous areas: eroded soil constantly had to be carried back to the high fields by the basketful, and the ground had to be hoed by hand. Most of the fields were actually fallows that were periodically cleared by burning, seeded for two years in a row, and then permitted to rest for another six or seven years. The poor yields of the mixed crops that were raised – some wheat, but primarily rye and potatoes (which had taken hold quite early) – would have been insufficient without the products of the livestock that grazed on the mountain pastures during the summer months. An essential supplementary resource, however, was work in the woods, given the constantly growing demand for wood in the nearby industrial regions. Lumber was transported by *schlittage*, a technique by which tree trunks felled high on the mountainside were loaded onto sleds that coasted down on specially prepared tracks. Various industries had sprung up in these mountains: saw mills, furniture factories, paper mills, as well as a small-scale metal industry that used the energy of the waterfalls. A minor textile industry at first engaged in the spinning of hemp for local consumption, but became increasingly involved in the production of cotton cloth in small factories connected with the conglomerate of southern Alsace whose influence extended to the western slope of the Vosges. In spite of all these activities, the area suffered from an overpopulation that brought poverty and degeneracy in its wake.

The other regions of Lorraine were almost textbook examples of the agrarian structure known as the open field system. The fields had the shape of long, unenclosed strips, and the village territory as a whole was divided into three growing areas (*soles*) on which wheat, spring grains, and fallow regularly succeeded each other. Each of the farms, many of which were very small, was composed of fields dispersed over the three growing areas. All ploughing and harvesting took place, as it had done under the Ancien Regime, simultaneously, and even the grapes of the vineyards located on the sunswept slopes were picked at the same time. After the harvest, the arable land was given over to the communal herd in keeping with the old customary right of free pasture. Despite legislation, calling for the division of communal property, that was passed under the Revolution and the Empire, most villages still owned considerable amounts of communal land, and the inhabitants' right to wood from the communal forest remained important.

The village, located at the centre of the village territory, was often quite small, but all of the inhabitants lived there. Their houses were lined up along both sides of a street that might be more than 40 metres wide. In front of every house a strip of ground called the 'parge' served to keep a manure heap and a stack of firewood and to store the plough. The front of the house, which was built of stone, contained the human dwelling, a bedroom and a kitchen separated by an entrance hall and the 'warming-room' (*poêle*) that was a necessity in this harsh climate. Under the same roof, but directly accessible from the fields, were the stable and the barn. Everyone was entitled to use the communal wash-house, the public drinking-trough, and the wine press.

In many cases the village of Lorraine had the aspect of a democracy of small farmers, each of whom owned some 10–15 hectares of land. The abolition of feudal dues and the sale of nationalised property had been a great boon to them, but now they faced a different threat, namely the fragmentation of their farms through division among their heirs, especially in the context of a high birth rate. Below these independent farmers, moreover, there was also a plethora of day-labourers, especially at the beginning of our period, who eked out a meagre living thanks to a tiny plot of land and to the benefits provided by the commune. The land hunger of the peasants of Lorraine was so great that many of them went into debt to satisfy it. Actually, this self-contained society, 'whose predominant interest was ownership rather than improvement' knew only one way to increase the arable land, and that was by clearing the forest. These efforts, however, could not go very far, since trees were precious to industry in this first half of the nineteenth century and therefore protected by the State.

All in all, one should not exaggerate the predominance of small peasant property. Estates of more than 60 hectares occupied 12 per cent of the arable land, and these properties were owned by the nobility and especially by the bourgeoisie. The mainstay of the wealth of the upper bourgeoisie, which was then concentrated at Metz, was still the land. In most cases the owners were absentee landlords who simply collected their revenues from their stewards. Yet there were some exceptions, such as Emile Bouchotte, nephew of the Jacobin minister and future mayor of Metz, who in 1822 began to farm an estate of 400 hectares where he introduced a new sequence of crop rotation, and above all Matthieu de Dombasle, who at the same time founded an experimental school of agriculture at Roville. Dombasle was particularly interested in breeding better livestock and in promoting the use of feed plants. He also taught agricultural bookkeeping and later developed the light wheel-less plough that still bears his name. Although he eventually had followers all over France, his influence never played more than a limited role in the agriculture of Lorraine.

Agriculture continued to be predominantly concentrated on the production of cereals for local consumption only: the department of Meurthe was the only one to export grain. In addition to wheat, rye, and oats – and in some places the latter was produced in greater quantities than wheat – new crops were also developed, among them colza and hops, which became more plentiful as beer became more popular. In 1815 wine was the most important commercially produced agricultural commodity. Vines were planted over 36,000 hectares, and although the harvests, owing to the climate, were extremely variable from year to year, certain red or grey wines of the Toulois region and certain white Moselle wines enjoyed an excellent reputation. As in the traditional agriculture, one of the essential functions of the livestock was the production of fertiliser for the land, yet now as in the past this technique was insufficient. Moreover, the livestock was of rather poor quality, and if the greatly increased number of pigs made it possible to export some salt-pork products, the horses were small, and only the best could be used by the light cavalry, while sheep existed in enormous numbers: some 700 to 800,000 sheep were kept in Lorraine, but they were breeds that could not be improved by cross-breeding with Merinos or by the use of English rams.

The industries of Lorraine

Agriculture, then, was Lorraine's most important activity at that time. Yet it was interspersed almost everywhere with traditional industries that were just beginning to show signs of a major economic mutation.

Whereas the flourishing hemp industry of the eighteenth century was declining rapidly, the production of coarse linen held its own. This cloth was either woven in the villages of the region of Montmédy, Verdun, and Briey, or produced in mills like baron de Seillière's factory at Pierrepont, where 800 workers were engaged in the production of cloth, mostly for the army. Another traditional industry, embroidery, experienced a brief expansion in response to the incentives of the versatile financier Chedaux of Metz, but shrunk down to the region of Lunéville and Mirecourt under the July Monarchy. Millinery, for the most part a cottage industry, was widespread in the German part of the department of Moselle, which specialised in straw hats after 1830.

A special feature of the region were the industries that took their raw materials from the forest or from the soil. These were, on the one hand, paper-making and its complementary activity, printing, which often specialised in almanacs and mass-produced the famous pictures known as *images d'Epinal* that were created by Pellerin in 1790; and on the other hand glass-making: aside from ordinary glassware, the glass industry of Lorraine began to produce the renowned crystals of Baccara and Saint-Louis. In addition, Lorraine also produced pottery, the most outstanding pottery works being those of Sarreguemines which had been reorganised by the Bavarian entrepreneur Utzschneider under the Restoration and employed some 400 workers by 1847.

The early nineteenth century was also the time when the foundations of the province's future prosperity began to emerge: salt, iron, and coal. The frontiers drawn in 1815 deprived the salt works that exploited the saline springs of some of the markets they had acquired under the Empire and also made it more difficult to use coal from the nearby Saar for the production of salt. Then, in 1827, rock-salt deposits were discovered, initially at Vie-sur-Seille. The full-scale mining of these deposits was hampered, however, by the government's salt monopoly, which the State did not give up until 1840. Toward the end of the July Monarchy a number of newly-founded industrial societies took over the exploitation of the saline springs and the salt mines (by 1847 some 40,000 tons of salt were produced in Lorraine) and began to develop the manufacturing of soda. The future belonged to the chemical industry.

The extremely dispersed metallurgy of the old economy also subsisted in the densely forested areas of Lorraine. If Meurthe had only a few forges, Meuse had some forty such establishments, while Vosges and Moselle had about thirty each. The blast furnaces of Meuse (which increased from ten in 1804 to twenty-eight in 1833 and thirty-six in 1840) used the same ore as those of neighbouring Haute-Marne, a major iron producer at the time. The forges of Vosges bought more of their pig iron from the producers of Franche-Comté. The metal industry was split into two parts by the Moselle river; modest establishments were located on the eastern bank close to Alsace, while the forges and blast furnaces of the western part used local ores that produced an excellent grade of iron. However, these ores were being depleted, but the industries hesitated to use the thick outcroppings of minette that were found in the valleys of the Orne and the Fensch, since the pig iron they produced was brittle. All of this metallurgy was fuelled by charcoal, and the State had been obliged to curtail the cutting of trees in the forests by strict regulations. A few enterprises tried to use coal from the Saar for the refining of iron.

These experiments had been made before 1815, mainly by François de Wendel. Descended from a long line of ironmasters, Wendel had emigrated during the Revolution. Following his return under the Empire he was able to repurchase the forges of Hayange formerly owned by his family and sold as nationalised property, and those of Moyeuvre in 1811. To these forges he added rolling mills and ensured his supply of coal by buying the La Quinte mine in the region of Trier. The treaties of 1815 caused him to lose this acquisition, and moreover, Saarbrücken became part of Prussia. After an additional period of study and training in England, he decided in 1817 to reconvert his enterprises. By 1822 the forges of Hayange were definitively equipped to be fuelled by coke, puddling was introduced, and in 1825 it was decided to mine minette on a large scale. At this point Wendel died, but his work was continued by his widow, his son-in-law de Gargan, and his son Charles. In 1846 the Hayange works used 23,600 tons of minette and also mined it for other enterprises. By then the firm, a major contractor for the army and the railways, had five coke-fuelled and one wood-fuelled coke furnaces, four sheet-iron rollers, one power hammer, nine convection furnaces, sixteen puddling furnaces, a network of carts for transporting the ore within the plant, etc. Hayange and Moyeuvre were the most modern metallurgy plants in France and employed a permanent work force of 2,000. That is why the metallurgy of Lorraine continued to expand even when the crisis of 1844 shut down the wood-fuelled furnaces: in 1847 it had more than doubled its output of 1834, producing 71,000 tons of iron (47,500 in Moselle alone) or 12 per cent of the total French production.

In order to free the metal industry of Lorraine from its dependence on the coal of the Saar, an association of several companies (Wendel, Hainguerlo, d'Hausen) tried to find the extension of this coalfield in French territory. In 1847 drilling revealed a deposit at Petite-Roselle in the heart of the Warndt forest, which had just been purchased by Charles de Wendel.

In 1848 Lorraine had not yet been completely transformed, but the outlines of a major industrial region were already beginning to emerge.

Metz and Nancy

Both of these towns were proud of their past, one as an old free city of the Holy Roman Empire, the other as the capital of the duchy of Lorraine. Both had preserved their eighteenth-century grandeur, somewhat austere in Metz and sumptuously elegant in Nancy.

A stopover and transit station during the Napoleonic Empire, Metz was France's tenth largest town in 1815, with 42,000 inhabitants. It did not grow much until the middle of the century, whereas Nancy increased from barely 30,000 inhabitants to 40,000 in 1848.

Metz still had the aspect of a military town enclosed within its fortifications that gave access through narrow gates. It had a garrison of 10,000 men, footsoldiers, the corps of engineers, and the artillery with its renowned school of artillery instruction. After 1817 the only reminder of Nancy's military past were its ramparts; it had become a university town with a Faculty of Letters, a Faculty of Science, a medical school, and a school of forestry. Both Metz and Nancy were administrative and judicial centres. Their highly segregated upper classes consisted of a nobility – brought to the area, in many cases, by one of its member's military career – great bourgeois landowners, magistrates, and wholesale merchants. Metz was initially the more active of the two, thanks to the trade of its port on the Moselle on which coal was shipped from the Saar, thanks also to its roads to Paris, which could be reached by mail coach in 24 hours and by stagecoach in 30 hours. Nancy only came into its own as a centre of communication at the end of the period; connected with Metz by a regular steamship service in 1841, it was also located along the Strasbourg–Paris railway whose last stretch was completed in 1852 and along the canal between the Marne and the Rhine that opened in 1853.

Public opinion in Lorraine

Absorbed by their harsh life, deeply attached to their traditional celebrations, and speaking a Romance or, in the eastern part of the department of Moselle, Germanic dialect, the peasants of Lorraine seemed to live strictly within the horizon of their village. This was by no means the case, however, for they did not object to serving in the revolutionary or imperial armies to which Lorraine gave many generals and seemed to have forgotten their province's past. In 1814 they accepted the Bourbons with resignation, but in the following year Napoleon's return was greeted with enthusiasm. Although the traditional rivalry between Metz and Nancy prevented the formation of an eastern Federation, Meurthe led all other departments in the number of votes by which the Additional Act was approved in the plebiscite. After Waterloo, Metz refused to capitulate and engaged in lengthy quibbling before accepting the white flag, while the peasants harassed the allied troops. A Jacobin patriotism seemed to pervade the province, and the masses remained intuitively attached to the tricolour flag. The royalist reaction remained moderate and did not give rise to clerical chicanery as it did in Alsace.

The electorate, consisting in 1830 of 2,000 voters in Meurthe, 2,400 in Moselle, 1,400 in Vosges, and 1,400 in Meuse, was definitely moderate and oscillated as it saw fit between compliance with the wishes of the central power and a liberal tendency. In 1815 the ultras had won the elections, albeit with candidates who were free of sectarianism. The most notable among them was François de Wendel, president of the general council of Moselle, who in 1824 had a disagreement with Villèle because he backed – against the wishes of the administration – the candidacy of his friend de Serre. Except in Moselle, the success of the right was short-lived. For the most part, Lorraine sent to the Chamber large landowners, officers, liberal magistrates, or ironmasters; in addition it manifested its opposition by electing former deputies of the Hundred Days, such as General Grenier, Rolland, and Etienne. In 1830 the latter, as deputy from Meuse, read before the Chamber the famous report of the committee of 221 calling for a vote of no confidence against the Polignac government. The subsequent elections were won in the departments of Lorraine by the anti-government forces, and although these deputies remained within the dynastic opposition, republican-oriented newspapers like Dornès' *Courrier de la Moselle* began to spring up at that time.

The revolution of 1830 was followed by a resurgence of revolutionary and patriotic fervour that was particularly evident in the zeal of the National Guard. Metz was the birthplace of a National Association for the Defence of the Territory. The bishop of Nancy, Mgr de Forbin-Janson, having written an untimely pastoral letter in favour of the Polignac government, was forced to flee, and the seminaries of Metz and Nancy were closed; the magistracy of Metz was purged on orders of the new mayor, Bouchotte. But this was not to last. By 1834 – despite an attempt to form a conspiracy of low-ranking officers at Lunéville in which the quartermaster Clément Thomas, a future victim of the Commune, compromised himself – everything was calm once again. Everywhere but in the department of Vosges, whose deputy Gauguier agitated in the Chamber for a rule concerning parliamentary incompatibilities, the centre-right prevailed; and it should be added that in 1846 thirteen of the department's twenty-one deputies held government offices!

Franche-Comté

Economic life

The mountainous areas of the Jura were as difficult to reach as ever. Transportation costs curtailed the exploitation of the Jura's pine forests. The mountain people tried to be as self-sufficient as possible by cultivating rye and oats and living on a meagre diet of 'mixed' bread, lentils, '*seret*', the residual whey of their cheese production, a little salt pork and smoke-cured meat, not forgetting the berries gathered in the forest. The raising of cattle was their principal resource, but the animals were puny: during the four months without snow the herds were entrusted to herdsmen who drove them to pastures high up in the mountains, milked the cows, and protected them from the wolves; throughout the rest of the year each owner had to keep his cattle in the stable. However, the summer pastures were overgrazed, the hay meadows were of poor quality, and there was not enough straw for the stables. Yet in the first half of the nineteenth century cheese-making became the principal activity, first of the central Jura and then of the mountain chain, a development that was greatly helped when cheese-making cooperatives came into general use. Wheels of cheese packed in pine barrels were sent to Lyon, Paris, Marseille, and Bordeaux, and its good keeping quality made it especially desirable as a food staple for sailing ships. It was transported and sold by wagoners living in the mountains for whom this was a supplementary activity during the enforced idleness of the winter months. Others tried to work as hemp-combers or peddled their basketry.

Lower down on the slopes the harsh and poor soil of the plateaux was planted in secondary cereals and then left fallow for long periods of time. Nine-tenths of the farmers of Doubs owned some property, but their holdings were so small and so dispersed that large noble estates were being reconstituted at their expense.

Great care was lavished on the cultivation of orchards and especially vineyards on the edge of the plateau. Vineyards divided into tiny holdings occupied 30,000 hectares in the Jura in the early 1820s. Work in these vineyards was backbreaking, for the vintners had to carry baskets of topsoil and manure up the mountain on their backs, and the retaining walls required constant upkeep. Yet the owners could only drink the fruit of their labour on very special occasions, for the sale of wine was their only source of income.

In the gently rolling plains, the soil was much richer than on the plateaux and produced increasing quantities of wheat, hemp, maize, and potatoes. Communal rights of pasturage were being curtailed in many places, and the cultivated fields were interspersed with meadows, oak forests and ponds, where carp and pike were raised. But even in this richer and more densely populated area the peasants lived on a frugal diet of bread, maize gruel, and soup with fatback; and here too their dwellings were dingy hovels.

Although agriculture was the essential activity in all parts of Franche-Comté, industry also could be found everywhere. Before the Revolution, 80 working blast furnaces or forges were counted, all of which used the easily mined iron deposits of the region of Gray and Vesoul and the wood of the local forests. Yet even then the metal industry was experiencing difficulties, but these were temporarily alleviated when the Napoleonic wars stimulated demand. In 1815 there was reason to believe that protective tariffs, in conjunction with technical advances that would reduce the consumption of wood, would ensure the future. At that time most of the area's pig iron was produced in Haute-Saône and most of the iron was produced in Jura, but then a concentration of the capitalist type occurred: the metal industry of Franche-Comté came under the control of Marshal Moncey, while that of Burgundy was controlled by Marmont. Nonetheless, it became obvious after 1830 that the scattered production-units of this metal industry, which produced high-quality iron by almost artisanal means in isolated small towns, were headed for a crisis.

Other activities were developing, however. In the early years of the century waterfalls, especially in the region of Montbéliard, were harnessed for industrial use, particularly in the production of cotton cloth. At this point the first steps toward the establishment of a very diversified metal-processing industry were taken by two families of bold innovators, the Japys and the Peugeots.

Frédéric Japy (1749–1812), the son of a farrier, had brought the manufacturing of watch-mechanisms to Franche-Comté, later adding clockworks to his line. His five sons succeeded him, and when the Allies set fire to the Japy factory at Beaucourt, they already had enough credit to rebuild. Soon they fanned out all over the region of Montbéliard (La Feschotte, Badevel, La Roche-sous-Chataillon, etc.), manufacturing clocks, locks, saddles and harnesses, screws, scythes, and household articles. Also in 1810, two Peugeot brothers, the sons of a dyer, converted a mill into a specialised steel foundry for the making of springs and saws, while their younger brothers operated a spinning mill. In 1833 the family sold its spindle manufactory at Audincourt to the Japy brothers and founded the workshops of Terre Blanche near Valentigney, where tools, household utensils, coffee mills, etc. were manufactured. In 1842 a split within the family resulted in the creation of the workshop at Pont-de-Roide.

Meanwhile the small towns in the mountains also had their industries. In the middle of the century Morez was famous for its clockworks, while Saint-Claude produced wooden lathe-work and exported pipes all over Europe. The market towns in the vicinity of the grain- and wine-producing areas had less industrial activity: while Salines extracted some 140,000 *quintaux* of salt from its sources in 1835, Arbois, Poligny, and even Lons-le-Saulnier continued to be inhabited by vintners, artisans, and shopkeepers.

The opening of the canal between the Rhône and the Rhine and also the efforts to improve the mountain roads had important consequences for the region: some of the wine producers, already in difficulty as a result of the closing of the Swiss market in 1815, were ruined by the arrival of wine from the Midi. On the other hand, improved communication enhanced the economic impact of certain urban centres, especially Besançon, the old provincial capital.

Besançon had missed out on the advantages that accrued to other towns of eastern France under the Empire, and its population remained at its 1789 level of 30,000 throughout the Restoration. By 1846, however, it had risen to 40,000. It was only as a result of improved communications that this administrative and military town became a centre of trade and banking whose importance was confirmed by the establishment of a branch of the Banque de France in 1846.

Intellectual and political life

Balzac has described the town of Besançon with its narrow streets and its old houses, but its real inhabitants were surely better than the nonentities depicted in *Albert Savarus*. They were magistrates of the Court of Appeals, for the most part scions of the parliamentary nobility, professors of the university or the lycée, cultivated clergymen, in fact a whole public that frequented the library, the art exhibits and, above all, the active *Académie des Sciences, Belles Lettres et Arts*.

This academy aroused the wrath of Proudhon when, having granted him a fellowship, it refused to accept the dedication of *Qu'est-ce-que la propriété*, whereupon the irascible author replaced the dedication with a vengeful appraisal concerning the intelligence of the assembled academicians. Still, they had enough intelligence not to withdraw the fellowship. In fact the members of the academy of Besançon stayed in contact with their fellow citizens who had moved to Paris, men like the historian Droz, the philosopher Jouffroy, and Nodier. Recruited among the nobility and the bourgeoisie alike, these men took great interest in the intellectual issues of their time. Hostile to the philosophy of the eighteenth century and divided in their attitude toward Romanticism, they were attached to spiritual religion and to tradition. Yet there were few regions of France that would have bestowed the title of 'grand elector' on an intellectual without property qualifications, like Weiss of Pontarlier.

The Catholic revival in Franche-Comté was also marked by unusual intensity, for the young clerics had intellectual aspirations that were often lacking elsewhere. For a time they were profoundly influenced by Lamennais. Goschler, who was sent from Strasbourg to combat this influence through his teaching at the seminary, was defeated by his students' hostility. It was a Franc-Comtois, Gerbet, who founded the *Mémorial catholique* and tried to keep Lamennais within the Church. Eventually the clergy of Franche-Comté broke away from Lamennais and, under the influence of abbé Gousset, turned to the moral theology of Saint Alphonse de Ligori.

Unfortunately, this interest in ideas did not go hand in hand with political tolerance. At the beginning of the Restoration Franche-Comté experienced a fervent surge of legitimism and clericalism, marked by a series of memorable missions. The reaction was inevitable: in 1830 the cardinal-archbishop, Mgr de Rohan, was physically abused and several priests had to flee.

While most of the popular protests that took place in Franche-Comté under the monarchy of limited suffrage were apolitical in nature (protest of the vintners against the excise tax, 'potato revolt' at Lons in 1840) the rebellion of Arbois was different. In 1830 this little town of wine producers had risen up in spontaneous protest, and in 1831 the protesters had formed the Republican Association of Jura, composed for the most part of 'labouring men'. Upon learning of the uprising of Lyon in 1834, this group incited the citizens of Arbois to proclaim the Republic.

Rebelliousness was particularly marked in the department of Jura. In 1827 the voters had sent to the Chamber of Deputies an extremely vocal opponent of the government: this was Cordier of Lons-le-Saulnier, an engineer of the Ponts et Chaussées who asserted his republican tendencies in the aftermath of 1830. Under the July Monarchy the most notable of the department's deputies was Demesmay of Pontarlier, who was moderate in his opposition to Guizot but fiercely opposed to the salt tax. The legitimist opposition did little more than publish a newspaper at Besançon, the *Gazette de Franche-Comté*, followed in 1846 by the *Union franc-comtoise*. Muiron, a follower of Fourier, published the governmental *Impartial*, while the *Patriote franc-comtois* expressed the ideas of the Movement. At Lons also, the *Sentinelle du Jura*, a '*juste-milieu*' paper, contrasted with the *Patriote jurassien*.

Sometimes unruly, and always independent of mind, the people of Franche-Comté by and large preserved an attitude of prudence and moderation.

Whereas the dominant feature of western France was a tradition-bound peasantry that disliked and distrusted the cities, eastern France was characterised by the impact of regional metropolises or smaller urban centres on the life of the region as a whole. An active liberal, and above all patriotic bourgeoisie that was just becoming conscious of its common purpose, especially through membership in masonic lodges, played a decisive economic and political role. In short, the July Monarchy only slowed down the revolution that led this bourgeoisie to republican ideas.

16

Northern France

The special character of northern France under the July Monarchy was the result of its dynamic economic development, both in agriculture and in industry. The six departments of Nord, Aisne, Ardennes, Oise, Somme, and Pas-de-Calais were ranked among the seventeen most industrialised departments in *La France Statistique* published by Alfred Legoyt in 1843; their location within the zone of Europe that experienced the most thorough economic modernisation caused this aspect to overshadow the other areas of their day-to-day activities.

Economic development

The demographic evolution
Population growth between 1821 and 1846 was very high in the department of Nord (especially between 1836 and 1846), high in Aisne and Pas-de-Calais, somewhat lower in Somme and Ardennes, and low in Oise.

The region's high population density (except in Ardennes and Oise) was due to the conjunction of agricultural work and an artisanal cottage industry that was subsequently replaced by a developing modern industry; and it is this latter factor that accounts for a density of 193 inhabitants per square kilometre that already obtained in Nord in 1843, at a time when the first two factors were still almost exclusively responsible for the population density of Pas-de-Calais (104) and Somme (91). Recall that the population density for France as a whole was 63.5.

Nord was the most populated department of France, surpassed only by the department of Seine in 1836. Although the north was both agricultural and industrial, 61 per cent of its population was still rural. The proportion of rural dwellers – also in 1836 – was 77.7 per cent in Pas-de-Calais, 84.1 in Somme, 86.3 in Ardennes, 88.2 in Aisne, and 90.7 in Oise.

Already there was a certain competition for labour between agriculture and industry. But whereas immigrants from Belgium came to the department of Nord, Pas-de-Calais and Somme increasingly lost population from the beginning of the July Monarchy, due to the spread of pastureland, which reduced the need for agricultural workers. This incipient depopulation was limited to a few localities in rural Picardy.

Despite the draining of the Moers marshes and of the valley of the Authie (undertaken between 1809 and 1827), extensive marshes still existed near the coast of Flanders and in Artois. It was from the coast that the cholera epidemic entered northern France in 1832, but its most devastating effect was experienced at Lille, in the populous quarters of Saint-Sauveur and Saint-André.

Rural society

The basic unit was the commune. However, the number of communes was excessive: 903 in Pas-de-Calais, 838 in Aisne, 814 in Somme, and 700 in Oise. Under these circumstances, there was bound to be a shortage of local cadres, and the management of communal affairs often fell to the few large landowners still to be found in the area. Large properties were rare because much of the land had been broken up into myriads of small plots; in the departments of Nord and Aisne more than half of the nationalised property had been acquired by peasants. Under the monarchy of limited suffrage many small owners had to work for the larger ones in order to make ends meet. The decline of the rural crafts that had traditionally absorbed some of the excess population of the countryside was particularly hard on the agricultural workers.

Actually, northern France was made up of several different agricultural areas and the dominant type of farm or estate varied from region to region. A pattern of scattered settlements was found in the Ardennes and in the Thiérache, small garden plots predominated in the valleys of Picardy, and property was dispersed and divided into smallholdings in Pas-de-Calais and Flanders. By contrast, money leaseholds were the predominant practice in Somme, in the Cambrésis and in the region of Douai, where the tenant farmer dictated his terms to the owner, and in Oise. Large estates were found in Somme, Aisne, and Oise. The landed aristocracy also played a leading role in the *arrondissement* of Saint-Pol, in Pas-de-Calais, and in the *arrondissement* of Hazebrouk, of which the prefect of Nord had this to say in 1837: 'This very wealthy, very densely populated, and completely rural *arrondissement* is in several respects the most backward one of this department. The clergy has been extremely influential there, and the friends of the fallen dynasty are probably more numerous there than elsewhere.'

A dynamic agriculture was practiced everywhere. Increased consumption due to the growth of the towns stimulated production; market gardening became particularly intensive in the Somme valley near Amiens. To the east the poorer soils of the Thiérache and the Ardennes were used to develop the production of livestock. In Nord and in Pas-de-

Calais fallow fields were increasingly replaced by artificial meadows. Cereals were grown throughout the region: in Nord almost one-fifth of the arable land was devoted to wheat in 1836.

The most innovative stimulus to agriculture was the cultivation of beet-sugar. In order to raise it, small farmers cleared new lands in Aisne, Somme (between 1821 and 1833), in Artois (mainly after 1830) and in Nord. However, the law of 1837 that placed the first tax on beet-sugar and the decision of 1839 to work toward equal treatment for both beet- and cane-sugar were of grave concern to the French beet-sugar farmers. As a result, this crop became concentrated in northern France; the departments of Nord, Somme, and Aisne, and the *arrondissement* of Compiègne in Oise accounted for 48 per cent of the soil devoted to beet-sugar in all of France and for 59 per cent of the production. In 1840 more than three-fourths of all the beet-sugar factories (301 out of 389) were located in these four departments. The perpetual competition with cane-sugar stimulated the producers and manufacturers to search for new production and pro-cessing techniques and to make use of the latest discoveries in chemistry and agronomy. Many of the factories belonged to the owners of beet-producing estates. The last operation, refining, was a purely industrial activity. In 1840 the department of Nord had seven refineries. The other industrial crops experienced a less spectacular expansion; indeed flax production in the Lys valley declined to the point of reducing domestic artisanal activity.

Industrial activity

Industrial development was the result of an old tradition and new conditions. Under the stimulus of competition, industry made important but uneven efforts to mechanise.

Textiles were the oldest and the most widespread branch of industry. Small workshops continued to operate with varying degrees of success; lace-making in Artois, linen-weaving in the Lys valley, and the small drapery manufactures of Abbeville were in decline. In the region of Amiens close to 40,000 workers worked in cotton- or wool-processing, notably producing velvet for some 150 merchants and *fabricants*. In the region of Saint-Quentin cotton-processing was the most important activity, employing more than 75,000 workers who for the most part worked in small workshops, even in the villages. In the region of Sedan and in the Ardennes innovation was set in motion by the cloth industry, which had adopted the factory system as early as the First Empire. The place of the influential Ternaux family, who dominated this branch under the Restoration, was taken under the July Monarchy by Cunin-Gridaine, an extremely successful parvenu who was minister in several governments and whose factory combined spinning, weaving, and finishing operations, employing 500 workers. The *Fabrique* [see chap. 13] of Sedan gave work to some 12,000 workers around 1834.

The factory system was particularly well developed in the department of Nord, although rural and artisanal industries, such as domestic lace-making, embroidery on tulle, wool-weaving at Avesne and Le Cateau and spinning in the valley of the Lys also survived. The development of the factories went hand in hand with mechanisation; in 1827 the department of Nord had only 69 steam-powered machines; by 1844 it had 570 such machines, 281 of them in the *arrondissement* of Lille alone. The wool-processing industry of Lille fell to the competition from Roubaix and Tourcoing, since the raw wool trade of these towns attracted new weaving and spinning enterprises. Roubaix emerged from the cotton crisis of 1827 as the outstanding wool metropolis. The linen industry was still the most important activity of Lille at the end of the Restoration; the employers were the sons of former masters in the spinners' or net-makers' guilds or of merchants like the Agache or Scrive families. The linen industry employed two-thirds of the textile workers of Lille at the end of the Restoration. Mechanisation had been initiated only in 1823, when a Belgian machine-builder sold the first machines to the Droulers and Agache spinneries. The number of linen spinneries in Lille rose from two in 1824 to twenty in 1829. After a period of relative stagnation, the surviving enterprises experienced a new period of rapid expansion after 1840. The resulting demise of the artisanal industry spelled the ruin of the spinneries at Armentières, Valenciennes, and Hazebrouk.

By 1845 the cotton industry consisted of 32 spinneries at Lille and 6 in the suburbs. This development was the work of profit-minded but dynamic pioneers. Technical advances brought a decrease in production costs; between 1834 and 1845 the production of cotton thread increased by 50 per cent, even though the number of workers decreased. During the July Monarchy the cotton spinneries of northern France became more and more concentrated, particularly in Lille and its hinterland.

This growth of the textile industry contributed to an increased demand for goods produced by the metal industry and for coal. As one of the principal centres of metallurgy, the Ardennes made use of important technical innovations, thanks largely to Jean-Nicolas Gendarme, who had brought the English puddling furnace to France. An artisanal type of metallurgy continued to exist in the Sambre region (gunsmithing at Maubeuge) and in the Vimeu (locksmithing). Almost non-existent in northern France, iron-smelting was making a slow start under the July Monarchy; in 1845 the department of Nord barely accounted for two per cent of France's steel production. A few other metallurgical establishments were scattered throughout the region, the most important being the

Halette works at Arras, which built engines for steamships and, beginning in 1844, locomotives. Barely in existence at the end of the July Monarchy, the metal industry of northern France was to experience rapid growth under the stimulus of railway construction.

Mining, essentially coal mining, was an old industry in the department of Nord. Among the administrators of the Anzin coal company were Casimir Périer and the prince d'Aremberg, and later Thiers, who had contacts in the business community of northern France through his father-in-law, the receiver-general Dosne. The Anzin company employed some 4,500 workers in 1830 and extracted some 390,000 tons of coal. Its concession extended over half of the coal basin and in 1844 Anzin entered into a price-fixing agreement with the Ouche and the Azincourt companies. New mining operations were started near Denain in 1831 and in the Escarcelles basin near Douai in 1847. The recently discovered deposits of Pas-de-Calais were not yet being exploited.

Commerce and transportation

The geographical space of the inhabitants of northern France expanded with the development of new means of transportation. But this development was extremely uneven, and the most western part of the area had practically no roads at all. Connections with Paris, given their strategic importance, were well organised, albeit slow. At the beginning of the Restoration, Paris could be reached from Lille in 40 hours; it took 30 hours to bring merchandise from Paris to Amiens by rapid transportation. A town like Cambrai was fairly well served by roads that connected it with Arras and even Paris, but connections with the communes of its own *arrondissement* were very poor indeed. In Flanders the local roads were still not passable in winter.

Canals played a major role. Completed under the Restoration, a network of canals connected northern France with the region of Paris, doubling the volume of trade between the two regions and greatly reducing transportation time. As a result, coal became cheaper in Paris. In 1825, 1,540 of the 1,725 barges that used the Saint-Quentin canal were carrying coal.

This excellent system of water transportation may account for the (relatively) late beginning of the railroad. The first lines were planned only after the passing of the law of 1842, and the building of the Paris–Lille railway was made contingent on the French government's agreement to build the necessary spur that would connect it with the Brussels–Lille line. A campaign launched by the *National* against the Rothschilds, who were making plans for the building of the Paris–Lille line, and conflicts between towns that expected to benefit from being situated along the track – Boulogne against Calais, Amiens against Saint-Quentin – prolonged the negotiations until 1845, at which date the Compagnie du Nord was founded as a joint venture of the Rothschilds, Laffitte, Hottinguer, and Baring. On 15 February 1846 the first train connected Paris with Amiens in 4 hours and 40 minutes (instead of 17 hours by road), and the Amiens–Abbeville section opened on 15 March 1847. Despite the disaster of Fampoux, one of the first railway accidents that killed 20 persons in July 1846, railway communication developed rapidly thereafter.

Banking and credit

During the first half of the nineteenth century northern France experienced a discrepancy between the rapid progress of industrial production and the slow development of a banking system. The need for credit was especially great in the agricultural sector, where the large-scale production of cereals and sugar demanded capital investments. In the family enterprises of the textile industry the reinvestment of profits seems to have been the rule.

Banking became important at Lille only under the July Monarchy, when the Banque de Lille was founded by royal ordinance on 29 June 1836, but even then this institution was hampered by the population's abiding distrust of banknotes. A branch office of the Banque de France was opened at Saint-Quentin. Plans were also made for another branch office at Valenciennes, where banking services were especially helpful to the sugar and metal interests; it appears that in 1846 Valenciennes was considered a better location than Arras. Another banking centre was Boulogne, thanks to the Adam banking house, founded before the Revolution. Investments by outsiders were limited to those of a few insurance companies like *Le Nord*. Frédéric Kuhlman, an Alsatian chemist who in 1825 had founded a manufactury of chemical products near Lille, borrowed his first capital from several finisher–dyers of Lille and Roubaix. The fact that he invested some of his earnings in real estate shows that landed property was still the safest means of upward social mobility and also that the relationship between town and country remained close.

Towns and urban societies

The towns of northern France had traditionally dominated the open countryside.

Religious and family life

Although the clergy played only a subordinate role in the town of Lille, religious influences were a major factor in the life of the region. The situation of the Catholic Church was complex. The incumbent archbishop of Cambrai was Mgr Belmas, a former constitutional priest and a Gallican, who had been appointed in 1802; under the July Monarchy he was one of the first bishops to speak of social problems in his Lenten Message. The bishop of Arras, by contrast, Mgr de la Tour d'Auvergne-Lauraguais, had close relations with the aristocratic circles of his diocese. As for the diocese of Amiens, it was a hotbed of ultramontanism, and its *collège* of Saint-Acheul had been directed by the Jesuits since 1814. The enduring vitality of religion had accounted for the ease with which the dioceses of Cambrai and Arras could be reconstructed, for at the beginning of the Restoration these two dioceses (unlike Oise and especially Aisne) had very few parishes without a priest. Religious sentiment had remained strong among the lower classes of Lille, which was one of the reasons for the importance of mutual aid societies (Villeneuve-Bargemont counted 113 such associations in 1828, many of them bearing the name of a saint). A prefectoral report of May 1831 said: 'The clergy has influence and credit, and it would be as impolitic as it would be dangerous to adopt a policy that would interfere with the religious practices of practically the entire citizenry.' To be expected under the Restoration, the importance of religious charities was still mentioned under the July Monarchy: 'There is a Spanish and monastic tradition here. Large donations are being made, and the charity of the inhabitants is inexhaustible.' Religious influence was very strong in primary education, thanks to the brothers of the Christian Schools, but also in the religious *collèges* for the bourgeoisie: '. . . because of the mother, who often makes the decision as to where her son will be educated', wrote the prefect of Lille in 1844. The sacking of the *collèges* of Acheul in July 1830 and its closing obviously had done little to change peoples' attitudes.

The importance of family life was expressed in various ways, and the publication of many bourgeois genealogies makes it possible not only to follow the evolution of these families but also to take the measure of their durability and vitality. The important role of religion in family life is attested to by the religious vocations found in every generation of such families as the Mottes, originally from Tourcoing, and the Bernards of Lille. In addition to giving support to religious congregations, this bourgeoisie began in 1835 to participate in the activities of the Saint-Vincent-de-Paul Society, which had rapidly taken hold at Dunkerque, Roubaix, Douai, Bailleul, Armentières, and Lille, where its president was Kolb-Bernard. It was at this time that the Catholic employer class of northern France assumed its distinctive physiognomy. Marriage alliances contributed to the strengthening of social cohesion within the group. These families had come to form a milieu that would gather strength and exert ever greater authority over the rest of the population with each succeeding generation.

Bourgeoisie and proletariat

The bourgeois tradition of putting the family first had its counterpart in the still vigorous tradition of putting municipal concerns first. Many administrators expressed themselves in similar terms as the prefect of Nord who complained in October 1841 of the 'encroachments of municipal spirit'. 'It is a fact,' he continued, 'that this spirit, especially in a region where it has long been deeply entrenched, relentlessly endeavours to dominate and even annihilate the spirit of centralisation.'

This municipal spirit was particularly strong among the bourgeoisie of Artois and Flanders. It was not as marked in Picardy, perhaps because aristocratic influences played a greater role there. At Amiens members of the aristocracy who lived near the cathedral and the church of Saint-Rémy continued to keep their distance from the bourgeois world of commerce. A similar separation existed in the little town of Abbeville, whose aristocratic society has been described in the *Souvenirs de jeunesse* of marquis de Belleval. Yet the opposition between aristocracy and bourgeoisie, which persisted in some towns until after 1830, gradually became attenuated, since the extension of the right to vote, moderate though it was, reinforced the ascendancy of the bourgeoisie as a whole, thereby creating shadings and sometimes divergences within that group.

The stability of the bourgeoisie of the northern towns was no doubt related in part to the local roots and the multiple kinship ties of these families. A hierarchy of wealth becomes visible in the structure of the electorate. Let us take the example of Cambrai, a town of 20,000 inhabitants in 1840: in the two cantons concerned (which covered a larger area than the commune), 322 individuals were entitled to vote for deputy, while some 800 could vote only in the municipal elections; out of this total, 41 (35 in Cambrai) paid more than 1,000 francs in taxes. At Arras under the July Monarchy the economic occupations accounted for more than half of the electorate, most of which was in the 500 to 1,000 francs bracket. This group included some 30 coal merchants, an equal number of wholesale merchants, and several oil and sugar manufacturers. This bourgeoisie owned considerable amounts of land and landed property. Although by no means homogeneous in terms of its origins, its activities, or even its mentality, this group did share a common type of behaviour: caution in all things, a family-oriented rather than personal individualism, great confidence in its own abilities, and the deep conviction that the inequality of social conditions is an ineluctable fact of life went hand in hand with a paternalism based on religious belief for some and rational thinking for others. Intent upon distinguishing itself from the aristocracy, which even the most staunchly royalist bourgeois did not seek to imitate, this bourgeoisie of the northern departments felt separated by an even greater distance from the proletariat to which it gave work in different settings.

Nor did the working class represent a homogeneous proletariat. The real and much criticised misery of the population of Lille's Saint-Sauveur quarter must not be allowed to overshadow the harsh conditions endured by a part of the rural population; around 1840 the proportion of unfit conscripts was higher, for example, in the rural canton of Clary where the population engaged in both agriculture and weaving (150 rejections for every hundred able-bodied men) than in the manufacturing cantons of Tourcoing (100 rejections for every hundred able-bodied men). The rural artisans working in linen-processing endured the harshest conditions and the longest working days (as much as 15–16 hours); only strong drink offered an illusory escape from the misery of an existence that steadily deteriorated in the course of the period; furthermore, drinking also compounded the alienation of a population that had yet to develop a social consciousness and was dominated by the local notables. The rural artisans who worked under the putting-out system of Sedan were somewhat better off; Villermé noted – not perhaps without expressing a preconceived notion – 'the weavers of the countryside are, as everywhere, very good workers', but he also stressed the lower incidence of alcoholism and the greater prevalence of schooling in the Ardennes. Around Amiens and Saint-Quentin some of the rural artisans had sunk into the proletariat as a result of their integration into the commercial system.

A second category within the working class consisted of the artisanal workers of the towns, the weavers, loom-operators, pressers, and spinners who worked in their own family workshops or for a master artisan. They were dependent on a merchant for their raw materials and the sale of their finished goods; their apparent freedom brought them few advantages, and it was this group that lived and worked in the most unhealthy places. At Lille, home-workers represented almost 50 per cent of the work force, or more than 10,000 persons in the years around 1830. In 1828 more than 3,600 inhabitants lived in cellars. The courtyards in the rue des Etaques in the Saint-Sauveur quarter have become sadly famous through Villermé's descriptions; the female lacemakers, working from the age of six, were suffering from rickets, and half of them ended up with a hunchback. At Saint-Quentin the weavers worked 'in cellar or basement rooms with little or no fresh air, where the temperature is low but unchanging'. Also according to Villermé, the working-class neighbourhoods of Amiens, located in the lower part of the town, consisted of 'narrow streets whose dilapidated, often wooden houses had humid, ill-lit, ill-closed and unhealthy rooms'.

The condition of the factory workers also varied from place to place. Having inspected the putting-out system (*fabrique*) of Sedan in 1836, Villermé reported – citing the workers he had interviewed – 'Those who work in a factory are usually better off than the weavers who work in their own homes.' Villermé accounted for the absence of agricultural day-labourers in this area with his finding that 'all those who must make their living with their hands alone prefer to hire them out to a manufacturer'. This does not mean that the condition of the factory workers was objectively better than that of the agricultural labourers, only that it was imagined to be better. Villermé indicates that in the various textile towns, at Lille, Amiens, and Sedan, sanitary conditions and, on the whole, wages were better in the factories than in the artisans' workshops. On the other hand, factory work had two major drawbacks, one being job insecurity and the other the often extremely poor housing conditions in the worst part of town or, if the worker lived in the suburbs, the necessity of travelling long distances twice a day. At the end of the Restoration one of every six inhabitants received some form of public poor relief in the department of Nord; in 1828 Lille had 31,664 certified indigents out of a population of 70,000. Potatoes and bread formed the basic diet of the workers, who rarely ate meat, and then only meat of questionable quality. The only escape was the *cabaret*, where they drank beer or gin, much of it adulterated. Villermé therefore frequently dwelt upon the evil of intemperance. A different but telling testimony comes from one of the prominent spinning mill owners, Th. Barrois. Barrois denied that corruption and dissolute behaviour were spreading among the factory workers, stating that 'work leaves them only enough time to rest their bodies, not to do evil'. For the ruling classes, uneasiness about the workers' misery mainly took the form of moral disapproval (denunciations of 'libertinage', counting of illegitimate children) or of concern for public tranquillity. The charity recommended by the Catholic Church (an attitude that was discredited after 1830) and the fear that excessive misery might lead to rioting prompted the local authorities to intervene in times of acute crisis, notably between 1826 and 1832, then in 1837 and 1839 and above all in 1846–7.

Nonetheless, despite its wretched condition, the labouring population of northern France was submissive. In the textile mills their dependence upon the owner was complete; the wage scale was set by him alone. The owners even dictated the terms of remuneration, which varied from town to town. At Lille the pay for piecework was not changed in times of crisis but kept low in times of prosperity, while at Roubaix it was subject to considerable fluctuation. The low standard of living in the countryside and in the nearby Belgian provinces, together with the widespread use of child labour in the textile industry (14,000 in the department of Nord, 6,700 in Ardennes, 5,900 in Aisne around 1840) maintained a steady supply of cheap labour. Conflicts were rare, but in 1837 arbitrary wage-cuts by employers who used earlier advances to tie their workers' hands did provoke some agitation, notably at Armentières. However, the workers were more likely to react by individual acts; the incidence of theft, for example, rose sharply at every crisis.

Mutual aid societies represented the only positive effort at establishing some cohesion within the working class; but the fear of the Chamber of Commerce of Lille that such societies might foster social unrest proved completely unfounded. At Lille there were about one hundred societies with a total membership of more than 5,000 workers, largely in the textile industry. Social agitation in the urban areas was usually triggered by the high price of bread, which led to disturbances at Bailleul in December 1830, at Douai in June 1831, and at Lille in May 1845. Except for some strikes in the textile industry in 1830 and other strikes in September 1839, during which the army dispersed some 700 to 800 demonstrators at Lille, major disturbances did not occur until the crisis of 1846–7, when bands of beggars roamed the streets from Tourcoing to Lille and, above all, when the miners of Anzin and Denain staged their strike in July 1846. In northern France social antagonism was not as rife in the textile industry, the predominant activity, as in the mines. The various brands of utopian socialism had few followers; and while the often-noted apathy of the labouring populations had many different causes, municipal particularism certainly contributed to this situation by fostering an *esprit de clocher* and even a competitive attitude toward other localities that was detrimental to the development of a class consciousness within the proletariat.

Urban settings and urban life

The functions of the northern towns were very diverse. They might be a religious metropolis like Cambrai, industrial centres like Sedan, Valenciennes, Roubaix, and Saint-Quentin, judicial centres like Douai, and administrative towns like Arras and Charleville. Some of them, especially Lille and Amiens, combined most of these functions, which is why we will consider them in greater detail. It should be pointed out that voting on the level of the *arrondissement* extended the influence of the smaller towns, many of which were the administrative seat of an electoral district, especially after 1830. In addition, the local press contributed to the predominance of the mentalities and the interests of the urban dwellers, a dynamic minority in a region that was experiencing rapid but uneven growth.

Lille was still a fortress in 1815; it was cut off by marshes to the west, while the rural outskirts extended into the plain to the east and to the north. In the northern and western parts of town, from the main square to the rue Royale, were the handsome dwellings of the aristocracy and the bourgeoisie; the richest and most peaceful parishes were the western ones of Sainte-Madeleine and Sainte-Catherine, and that of Saint-Etienne in the centre. The eastern parishes of Saint-Maurice and Saint-Sauveur were the most insalubrious ones; under the July Monarchy some rehabilitation was undertaken in the Saint-Sauveur neighbourhood in connection with the opening of the rue Wicar between 1835 and 1838, no doubt in response to the ravages wrought by the cholera epidemic of 1832. For Lille, as we have seen in discussing the often wretched condition of the working class, was an unhealthy place; dampness, increased dirtiness due to overcrowding, and the stagnant waters of the canals contributed to its unsanitary conditions. The suburbs were better located, and excursions to Wazemmes were popular outings for the Lillois. Fives, a western suburb, was still only a village in 1821; its growth was brought about by the building of the railway, for since the military corps of engineers refused to permit the piercing of Lille's ramparts, the railway station was located at Fives in 1845. Despite its rather unprepossessing setting, Lille occupied the position of a regional capital. It had close to 70,000 inhabitants in 1830. The prefect of Nord wrote in 1831: 'The town of Lille necessarily wields great influence over public opinion. It is still the capital of Flanders.' The great landed proprietors had dominated the town under the Restoration. After 1830 their place was taken by a largely anticlerical bourgeoisie.

Without being an intellectual centre, Lille owed much of its influence to its opinion-makers. As a reaction against the power of the traditionalist and clerical milieux, the masonic lodges of Lille had become increasingly active during the Restoration. After 1830 complaints about the 'invasion of public employment by the freemasons' were voiced in the department of Nord; when questioned about this matter by the minister, the sub-prefect of Cambrai replied that 'although there are others, it is probably true that most of the civil servants do belong to the lodge, for the simple reason that in this town it is well-nigh impossible to find a liberal devoted to the new order of society who is not a freemason'.

The local press was both a sign and a means of this influence; under the Restoration, newspaper publishing was still rather undeveloped at Lille. However, the founding of the *Echo du Nord* by the Leleux printing company in 1819 provided an organ for the liberal and anticlerical bourgeoisie. The press of Lille assumed increasing importance under the July Monarchy with the founding of a legitimist paper, the *Gazette de Flandres et d'Artois* (circulation 4,000 at the end of the reign) and the publication of the *Echo du Nord* (circulation 6,000, among the highest for a provincial newspaper), the organ of the lower and middling bourgeoisie that supported the deputies and the majority in the municipal council. Conservative papers never succeeded for very long. Several of them were published in succession, among them *Le Nord* and, beginning in 1843, the *Journal de Lille*, which had few readers even though it enjoyed the support of the prefect. By contrast, the *Messager du Nord*, founded by a group of democrats of Lille in May 1845, expanded very rapidly.

Nonetheless, between 1834 and 1848 the dominant element of Lille under the July Monarchy was the bourgeois business community; the mayor, Bigo-Danel, was the owner of a major spinning mill and paid 3,420 francs in taxes, and twenty-nine of the thirty-seven members of the town council were wholesale merchants, textile entrepreneurs, or businessmen who made it a point to be on good terms with those local deputies who opposed the government in the Chamber. This attitude caused the prefect to write in 1844: 'Opposition here is not an opinion, it is a way of life.' For all of their disagreements on religious, political, and social issues, the inhabitants of Lille were in complete agreement when it came to defending protectionism, a subject to which we will return. Their stance fed into a regional consensus which, by stressing the defence of economic interests, contributed to the persistence of regional antagonisms that concealed, or at least attenuated, social antagonisms.

The town of Amiens, its prestigious cathedral notwithstanding, was less susceptible to traditionalist ideas, even at the time of the Restoration. The rapid succession of prefects under the two regimes (seven in the first 10 years of the July Monarchy, among them the liberal economist Dunoyer between 1832 and 1837) had strengthened the influence of the municipal council. A town of artisanal cotton- and wool-workers, Amiens – whose fortified walls were dismantled in 1822 – experienced a renewed spurt of activity under the Restoration. Along with the commercial notability, some of whose members were devoted royalists under the Restoration, the royal law court played an important role in Amiens society. Following the resignation of several councillors in 1830, the court became the major focus of social life under the July Monarchy, when the tone was set more by the magistrates and professional men than by the bourgeois business community with its conservative attitude in political (hence its leanings toward the government party) and economic matters. The mayor, Dr Lemerchier, was a member of the local academy as well as president of the Industrial Association of Amiens; in 1840 the municipal council included sixteen wholesale merchants or textile entrepreneurs, seven landed pro-prietors, six magistrates or lawyers, and two physicians. The liberalism of Amiens under the monarchy of limited suffrage – both in its pro- and its anti-government aspects – went hand in hand with a steady rise in the power of the bourgeoisie, which in 1830 ousted the local aristocracy without, as yet, being challenged by the popular class.

Regional particularism and the support of the State

The economic, social, and historical characteristics of this region we have presented at the beginning of this chapter account for the diversity of its political attitudes. Yet there were times when northern France, despite the absence of a fundamental political unity, shared a common fate as a consequence of circumstances arising from its geographical location.

Fidelity to the Bourbons and the Charter

Napoleon's wars had brought war and its depredations to the departments of northern France. In 1814 Amiens was occupied by the Prussians for three weeks. Dunkerque, which had been badly hurt by the wars of the Empire, greeted the fall of Napoleon with cries of 'Vive le Roi!; Vivent les Bourbons!; Vivent les Alliés!' At the beginning of the Hundred Days Louis XVIII had considered making Lille the seat of his government, knowing that he had the sympathy of the population; in the end, however, the population did not feel strongly enough to fight a garrison of 6,000 anti-Bourbon soldiers. Still, the royalists kept up their numbers in Nord and Pas-de-Calais, though not in Ardennes. The return of the Bourbons met with popular approval, but did not give rise to passionate acts of vengeance as it did in the Midi. While the ultras, for the most part represented by nobles, dominated as they did everywhere, a few constitutional monarchists were also elected, among them baron de Brigode in Nord and Gaudin, duc de Gaëte – a former minister of Napoleon and future governor of the Banque de France – in Aisne. After 1816 some of the deputies elected in this region, such as Harlé of Pas-de-Calais and General Foy of Aisne, were among the first outspoken liberals. The growth of liberalism was most marked in Picardy, where it was fostered by the magistrates.

The people remained deeply attached to the monarchy. Intense emotion was aroused outside of bourgeois circles by the assassination of the duc de Berry, who had been warmly greeted at Lille in August of 1815. Charles X's visit to the northern departments in 1827 was celebrated with great festivities at Dunkerque, at Lille, where he was acclaimed on 9 September 1827, and at Amiens.

Yet in that same year the elections would show that constitutional ideas had made massive inroads in Aisne, Oise, Pas-de-Calais, and Somme; in these departments all but two of the electoral colleges of the *arrondissements* elected constitutional or even liberal deputies who would vote for the famous address of the 221. Only the department of Nord and the departmental electoral colleges (made up of the wealthiest taxpayers) elected a majority of ultra and governmental deputies.

The liberal evolution of northern France

The fact that in 1815 the northern departments had suffered more from the violence inflicted by war and the occupying powers than from internal conflicts may account for the overriding concern for legality and the preoccupation with international issues (notably the Belgian question in 1830) that characterised their subsequent political evolution. Partial elections confirmed this trend within the electorate. The liberal bourgeoisie was increasingly turning against the Church, the clergy, and what was called the 'Congrégation'. In 1830 Amiens, which had just re-elected Caumartin with 365 votes against 127 for the government's candidate Daveluy, had a revolutionary 'day' on 29 July. The occasion was marked by some shouting at the house of Mayor Daveluy, who retired and handed over the municipal government to a committee of the town council, and above all by the sacking of the Jesuit *collège* of Acheul in the suburb of Noyon.

Lille also had its July revolution. The printing-presses of the *Echo du Nord* were seized, but the policemen were won over by a group of liberals led by a former officer of the Empire; the troops of the line refused to intervene to restore order; on the following day the workers took to the streets demanding bread and work, and on 31 July some bakeries and butchers' shops were looted. A liberal deputy from Aisne, Mechin, thereafter served as prefect from 1830 to 1839, and the town hall of Lille came under the control of the textile bourgeoisie.

The liberal bourgeoisie was intent, above all, on dislodging the legitimist aristocracy from its pre-eminent position. For this group had indeed preserved some of its power and received a great deal of support from the Catholic clergy, which continued to wield considerable influence in the lower-class milieux and even in the business world. In the department of Nord as many as three deputies and eight councillors-general might be legitimists; Somme had two legitimist deputies. However, theirs was a legitimism that went along with the representative system. In December 1836 the prefect of Lille wrote: 'The [legitimist] nobility regularly makes morning calls at the prefecture, but abstains from attending evening gatherings, thereby wishing to reconcile the exigencies of polite behaviour and its rather friendly attitude toward the prefect with a reserve that it feels called upon to practice in view of the circumstances and its own antecedents.' In Pas-de-Calais and Somme legitimism had a more aristo-cratic character, which is in part why the bourgeoisie of these departments became more and more Orleanist, and indeed more favourable toward the central government from which it derived support.

Northern France had little use for the republican ideas that were pub-lished by some of the press in the early years of the July Monarchy. On the other hand, the Orleanists were divided into two major factions, those who favoured movement and those who favoured resistance. Yet the bourgeois of the region, whether conservatives or supporters of the dynastic left (which, as we shall see, made great strides), were moderates. Their opinions were shaped by personal or realistic considerations much more than by ideological choices, and family and business relations played a considerable part in their political attitudes. No doubt the mayor of Boulogne, Adam, a banker and the local correspondent of the Rothschilds, had something to do with the election of the Parisian banker François Delessert as deputy from his *arrondissement*. The energetic measures taken by Adam and the sub-prefect were responsible for the rapid failure of Louis-Napoleon's attempted *coup* on 6 August 1840: 'Everywhere the National Guard arrested fugitives and handed them over to the authorities', noted the prefect in his report. The opposition in northern France made sure that the outward forms of legality were preserved.

The contradictions of a liberal bourgeoisie

At the end of the July Monarchy the entire delegation of Aisne consisted of members of the opposition; Somme had a majority of opponents; Oise and Nord had a strong minority of opposition deputies; since 1839 Lille had given two deputies to the dynastic opposition, while the third was a legitimist, Vicomte de Villeneuve-Bargemont, who had been prefect under the Restoration. Only the departments of Pas-de-Calais and Ardennes regularly elected a decisive majority of government supporters.

However, the dynastic opposition that expressed its ideas in the *Echo du Nord* had the support of a lower and middling bourgeoisie whose economic and social ideology was very similar to that of the conservative employer class. This employer class of northern France was unanimous in pressuring the State to defend it against foreign, and specifically British, competition. The widespread anglophobia of this region went hand in hand with protectionist sentiments. The latter had prompted the manufacturers of Nord to send their workers into the streets in 1834 to demonstrate against a government survey at a time when the government was suspected of planning a reduction in the tariff. On this point there was complete solidarity among all classes. In 1841 Dr Lestiboudois, a deputy of the dynastic left, presented a lengthy report legitimising the opposition of the department of Nord to any reduction of the customs duties on the importation of cattle. The dynastic opposition found support among the wealthy bourgeoisie, especially its parliamentary leader Odilon Barrot. Yet much of the bourgeoisie remained conservative and loyal to the government. Sometimes it elected deputies of the government party as a means of counterbalancing the still powerful influence of the great landed nobility; sometimes the conservative deputies were notables whose families had represented the region and served the State for generations (the deputy Harlé was the son of a former ironmaster and deputy of the Restoration, and his brother-in-law Léon d'Herlincourt who succeeded him as deputy was the grandson of a councillor in the Supreme Court of Artois); while others (Cunin-Gridaine of Ardennes and Mimerel at Roubaix) were important manufacturers.

Regardless of whether they supported the opposition or the government, the bourgeois circles of northern France favoured protective tariffs; yet at the same time they were strictly opposed to any intervention of the State in social relations. The law for the protection of child labour in the factories alone was enough to give rise to widespread disaffection at Lille, Roubaix, Sedan, Amiens, and Saint-Quentin. The wealthy business community in the IIIe *arrondissement* of Lille was defeated in the elections of 1846 by an alliance between the liberal and anticlerical elements of the lower and middling bourgeoisie and the great Catholic and legitimist landowners. But then the dynastic opposition itself was overtaken by a more radical opposition at the time of the banquet campaign. Following the banquet at Lille on 7 November 1847, which was attended by close to 900 persons, Odilon Barrot was ousted by Ledru-Rollin, whose call for universal suffrage equally disturbed the liberals, legitimists, and conservatives of the department. Social democratic ideas had recently found a vehicle in the *Messager du Nord* founded by Bianchi; this son of a Tuscan liberal had brought a meridional vivacity to the propagation of a cause that might have awakened the as-yet apathetic proletariat of the department. His propaganda efforts were deeply troubling to almost all of the bourgeoisie. Radical ideas were also presented by Charles Delescluze's *Impartial* at Valenciennes and by the *Progrès du Pas-de-Calais* at Arras. Yet such popular protests as occurred in the region – in the *arrondissement* of Avesne, at Tourcoing, Cambrai, and Lille, where some bakeries were looted on 12 May 1847 – were hunger riots without political connotations.

While northern France did not experience the same unrest as southern and western France, or social upheavals similar to those of Lyon, the region was dissatisfied and troubled on the eve of the revolution of 1848. In 1841 a mayor of Lille noted: 'Unlike the manufacturers and merchants who realise large profits, the working classes are making little progress toward a better life.' He added that the government must regulate the working conditions, for 'if this problem is not solved in a rational, legal, and peaceful manner, there may be another solution that could well compromise the entire social order'. The gulf was widening between a still rather heterogeneous proletariat and an employer class that accumulated wealth and influence but left the management of municipal affairs and political representation to the members of the lower and middling bourgeoisie. Industrial and banking capitalism, which increasingly controlled the economy and shaped the social life of the community, still had only an imperfect hold over political power. The personal power of the notables was beginning to be replaced by the domination accruing to the employer class in the pursuit of its function. In northern France social unease (fear would be too strong a word at this point) did exist before the February revolution; the notables, though divided on many issues, were willing to put aside their disagreements in order to preserve their hold over a rural or working-class population that was still unorganised and submissive.

17

The region of Paris

Bordered by the western provinces, the regions of eastern and northern France, and the Massif central, the Paris basin is a large region of considerable diversity: the climatic conditions vary markedly, and the conformation of the land makes for a contrast between gently indented plateaux and alluvial plains. Above all, great differences in soil offer uneven possibilities for farming. In the nineteenth century the essential contrast was between the northern part, an area whose plateaux are covered with soil suitable for large-scale cereal production that had long been open to innovation, and the south with its deposits of sand and siderolithic clay, its heath, ponds, sparse settlements, and a routine-bound peasantry. Popular speech had always distinguished between the 'good' regions of ancient reputation, like the Valois, the Beauce, and the Brie region, and the arid Champagne, the scrub-covered Hurepoix, the desolate Gâtines, and the marshy Brenne. Actually, there was no clear-cut dividing line between the large-scale agriculture of the north and the small farming of the south; shifting boundaries of enclaves had advanced and retreated throughout history. Isolation and the need to be as self-sufficient as possible still accentuated local contrasts at the beginning of the nineteenth century. The people of the poor cantons were doomed to misery, as we can see from the minutes of the military draft boards. Virtually the entire south of the Paris basin was plagued by endemic fevers; the highest degree of degeneracy was reached in the Sologne, where 'the human race seems to have deteriorated', and where the faces of those adults who had escaped the ravages of a terrifying infant mortality were always 'haggard and emaciated'.

Development of communications and population density

At the time of the monarchy of limited suffrage these small regions were connected – at an uneven pace but in a decisive manner – to the general network of communications, although the consequences of this development were not yet entirely clear by 1848. Here is one example to illustrate

346

the difficulties that still faced the traveller in the very heart of the Paris basin at the beginning of our period. In 1817 the young Montalivet travelled from Paris to the provincial château of Lagrange at Saint-Bouize in the Sancerrois, that is, a distance of 200 kilometres. He left Paris early in the morning by mail coach, spending the night at Montargis; on the next day the coach arrived at Pouilly too late to take the ferry, the only means of crossing the Loire, 700 metres wide at this point. The crossing was made on the morning of the third day: 'Eight or ten men were needed to push the mail coach onto the barge, to hold the horses, and to work the poles from the shoulder . . . three dreadful hours, after which one disembarks on a sand flat.' Thereafter the coach continued toward Saint-Bouize on barely marked paths crossed by bogs, constantly in danger of breaking a wheel. In the 1820s, slowness and high personnel costs inconvenienced the traveller; these inconveniences were even worse and lasted even longer for the transport of merchandise.

That is why, until the railway age, the waterways carried a lively traffic that contrasted with the sluggishness of rural life. A modest river like the Orge transported barges loaded with wheat from the Beauce. Most of the 600 mills that worked for the capital were located along small rivers. The convergence of several waterways around Paris was vitally important in supplying the capital: the Oise canal ensured the connection with the north which, above all, furnished coal (1,300 of the 1,800 barges that moved toward Paris on the Saint-Quentin canal in 1820 were loaded with coal). Upstream from Paris the Seine carried merchandise and passengers: in 1828, some 200,000 passengers travelled from Paris to Corbeil, Melun, and Montereau. The Marne also was an active river; on the eve of 1848 Saint Dizier had 700 boatmen engaged in the transport of wood and iron. However, navigation on the Seine was beset with a number of difficulties: upstream from Paris it was reliable only during six months of the year, and every year traffic came to a complete standstill during two months; downstream it described a number of loops, which made it unsuitable for sailing ships. The Loire was an even more active waterway and enjoys a rather better reputation among certain historians, but one wonders whether this reputation is deserved. It is true that the Loire was plied by sailing ships between Orléans and Nantes. But downstream from Orléans the run between Roanne and Orléans usually had to be made with lowered sails, and even then it was uncertain or dangerous: 'Merchandise sent to Nantes from the Mediterranean and the Midi moves toward its destination by following the tortuous course of the Loire, always in danger of being held up by one of the dry spells that are so frequent in this region or of encountering one of the swift and dangerous floods whose disastrous effects are only too well known.' However, steamshipping provided a new lease on life for navigation on the Loire and several companies were bidding for the Nevers–Orléans and Orléans–Nantes lines. In 1843 the inauguration of the railway brought the activity of Orléans as a river port to an ephemeral peak: in a single week, 197 barges drew alongside its quays.

By the eve of the revolution of 1848 profound changes had taken place. The railway from Paris had reached Lille, Compiègne, Abbeville, Le Havre, Versailles, Orléans, Tours, Vierzon, Bourges, and Châteauroux (indeed an inhabitant of the latter town would have been able to take the train all the way to Stettin, via Paris, Brussels, and Berlin!). The Versailles–Chartres, Paris–Strasbourg, and Paris–Lyon lines were under construction. The new traffic facilities provided an incentive to regional bodies to build secondary roads to the new railway stations, and encouraged local towns to participate in the implementation of the programme of local road construction enacted in 1836 with a view to connecting every commune of France with a regional network of roads. These activities should not make us forget the efforts of the Restoration and the July Monarchy with respect to France's waterways. These included the improvement of the navigability of the Seine and the Oise, the completion of the Ourcq canal and the opening of the Saint-Denis canal in 1823, the construction of the lateral canal to the Marne (opened in 1848), which was later continued by the canal between the Marne and the Rhine, the resumption of work on the canal de Bourgogne, which opened in 1832, and the digging of the lateral canal to the Loire (1832). A major achievement was the building of the canal du Berry whose three branches, converging at Fontblisse, 20 kilometres east of Saint-Amand, flowed toward Montluçon, Bourges, and Vierzon, respectively; by joining the Cher, this canal continued toward Noyon, where that river became navigable, and Marseille-les-Aubigny, where it connected with the lateral canal to the Loire. These canals helped to bring certain regions out of their isolation and facilitated the capital's relations with northern, eastern, southern, and central France.

No secondary metropolis in the Paris basin was able to counterbalance the growing influence of the capital. Only one of these towns was among the twenty-five largest of France, namely, Reims, which occupied fifteenth place in 1831 with 36,000 inhabitants and nineteenth in 1846 with 44,000. With very few exceptions, the other towns were administrative and judicial centres that also served as markets for the trade between complementary regions; their facilities had attracted a few, usually mediocre, industries.

Moreover, excepting the areas in the immediate vicinity of Paris, the population density of the Paris basin was markedly lower than the national average. In 1846 five departments of the Paris basin – Indre, Loir-et-Cher, Cher, Haute-Marne, and Aube – came immediately after the five least populated departments of France. Population density was particularly low in Champagne, where the three departments of Marne,

Haute-Marne, and Aube had a density of approximately 43 inhabitants per square kilometre (national average: 67). A slightly higher density was found to the southwest of this zone: Côte-d'Or, Nièvre, Loiret, and Yonne exceeded 45 inhabitants per square kilometre (with only Yonne reaching 50). Beyond this area, along the middle stretches of the Loire, densities fell to their lowest levels; in the departments of Indre, Loir-et-Cher, and Cher the average density was only about 40 inhabitants per square kilometre. Slightly higher figures were found in Vienne (45) and Indre-et-Loire (51).

This demographic depression did not follow the same pattern in Champagne and in the middle Loire: between 1801 and 1831 the population growth of Champagne was markedly below the national average while that of the middle Loire was markedly higher.

As for the Paris region in the narrow sense, its densities were above average: in Seine-et-Oise, which had remained a primarily agricultural department, it was 84 inhabitants per square kilometre, in Oise it was 69. If these departments marked the transition to northern France, Seine-et-Marne with its orientation toward Champagne barely reached 60 inhabitants per square kilometre. Yet between 1800 and 1825 the surplus of births over deaths produced a strong spurt of growth. The pull of Paris subsequently reduced the impact of this increase. After 1850 the population of Seine-et-Marne was swelled by immigrants who wished to live closer to Paris.

The diversity of the plateaux

South of the Loire, *bocages* alternated with stretches of unenclosed, irregularly-shaped fields. These were not the only features this area shared with western and southern France: here too one finds a pattern of dispersed settlements, biennial crop rotation, and great estates cut up into modest-sized *métairies*. Rural farms were still widely worked by families, except that *communautés taisibles* [patterns of undeclared co-ownership] remained prevalent in Berry and in the Nivernais. Most notably, the cultivated lands had the aspect of islands amidst the 'barrens' ('*brandes*'), gorse-covered heathland given over to sheep, and the forests. The practice of burn-beating and the custom of using the plants of the heath as fertiliser reduced the scope of the communal right of free pasture. Groups of homeless poor people sometimes squatted on a piece of the barrens, and woodcutters and charcoal-burners, much feared by the sedentary population, worked in the forests, which were also the haunt of boars and wolves. Even the limestone plateaux were not fully cultivated. In the Sologne, cultivated fields accounted for less than 20 per cent of the surface. To be sure, some progress was made. In Indre, wheat occupied 59,500 hectares by 1840, compared to 48,100 in 1803; the surface devoted to rye had decreased from 52,600 to 20,600 hectares, and yields had improved. Still, artificial meadows remained insignificant, and the potato was spreading very slowly. The number of sheep in the department reached 274,000 head in 1840, an increase of 30,000 since 1803.

These minor improvements did little to change the traditional economy, but the great landowners did found active agricultural societies for the purpose of studying ways to improve their crops and wrest new land from a harsh environment. The pattern of the Ancien Regime remained unchanged when high grain prices caused by scarcity gave rise to outbursts of popular discontent in the market squares. On such occasions attempts would be made to loot the storehouses and to prevent the grain from leaving the region. Grain riots took place in March 1840 at Aubigny, then at Lignières and Châteaumeillant, where troops had to be used against the rioters. In 1847 grain riots broke out again at Busençais, Lignières and Châteauroux; this time some of the leaders were condemned to death. Meanwhile the great landowners of the Sologne were preparing the conquest of land that would take place under the Second Empire, while in Berry such families as the Charlemagne, de Vogué, and Muret de Bord (who planted extensive pine forests) obtained remarkable results, especially in the breeding of improved livestock. Yet in 1866 Léonce de Lavergne still noted that the provinces of the centre were among the poorest regions of France.

Archaic conditions were also the outstanding feature of the Morvan, the region beyond the Loire of which the famous lawyer and politician Dupin has left us a very vivid description at the end of the July Monarchy. In this land of *bocages* and dispersed settlements, which had no industry and almost no crafts, every peasant family baked its own bread, whittled its own wooden shoes, made its tools, and had only its carts built by an itinerant craftsman. Locally produced wool and flax (the latter grown in a more carefully manured plot) furnished the raw material for their traditional clothing. Agricultural workers were paid in kind: in exchange for their work-days they were given a small plot of land to cultivate. Wheat was almost impossible to raise on the granitic soil, and the peasants continued to grow rye, buckwheat, oats, and rape, while their gardens furnished beans, turnips, and cabbage. The one new crop was the potato, which had been substituted for the chestnut at a relatively early date. The people of the Morvan thus lived mainly on soup and gruel flavoured by a little pork. Actually, conditions were better suited to animal husbandry, since the profusion of streams could be used to irrigate artificial meadows, but beef and geese were fattened for the market only. In fact these animals were raised without much concern for hygiene; the stables were low and dirty, and the fowl spent the night on a perch in the bedroom. Another source of income was the raising of '*petits-Paris*', infants brought from the capital. Under the Second Empire a physician of the Morvan, Dr Monot, was to reveal the scandalous aspects of this practice, citing hapless babies succumbing to starvation or filth, encouragement given to unwed mothers, husbands exhibiting the mentality of a pimp. Even under the July Monarchy, however, the most important commercial commodity remained wood. Having cut down their trees themselves, the owners sold the trunks that bore their mark, which were floated down the rivers as far as Clamecy, where they were gathered into rafts to be shipped to the Parisian market.

Further north, the plateaux of lower Burgundy had a completely different character: here the agrarian structure was a classic open field system, with gardens and vineyards surrounding the village. The Revolution had modified rather than overthrown the pattern of landownership: the nobility now owned 14 rather than 16 per cent of the soil, though most of it was forest; the share of the bourgeoisie had increased from 16 to 24 per cent, and the peasantry owned the rest. Most prevalent were medium-sized holdings; some of the smallest owners, especially vintners, had to supplement their resources by working the harvest in the Beauce. The most important commodity continued to be cereal, especially wheat, which was raised by traditional practices, including that of having the land fertilised by the communal livestock after the harvest. This region was experiencing increasing demographic pressure, yet it was not possible to increase the arable land, since the commons consisted of forests which were an essential resource for the village community. What was needed were higher yields, which meant more manure, which in turn meant more livestock; but this could only be achieved with the help of fodder produced on artificial meadows that would be closed to free pasturing. Yet free pasture was essential to an agricultural proletariat that could not survive without owning a few of the communal herd's animals.

One attempt to solve this quandary was the expansion of vineyard land. Ever since the eighteenth century, some of the region's wines, such as its Chablis, were appreciated in England and also shipped as far as Marseille. The declining wine production of the northern part of the region of Paris and the uncertain character of its harvests provided a market for the ordinary wines of the Tonnerois, which were shipped to Paris, Normandy, and Flanders. In order to meet this demand, new vineyards were planted on the plateaux. However, these light and mediocre wines were taxed as highly as the better *crus*, with the result that the margin of profit was simply too small. The only solution, then, was emigration, a course of action that had already been common in the eighteenth century, despite the greater prosperity of that time, which has been described in the work of Restif de la Bretonne. J. B. Moreau's calculations indicate that people left Coulanges-sur-Yonne at an accelerating rate: the rate of departure for this locality rose from 0.56 per cent in the first twenty-five years of the century to 1.5 per cent in the following twenty-five years. Nor did Paris absorb all of these emigrants, for some of them settled in the valleys to which the new means of communication had brought new opportunities and where major public works created a demand for labour.

Further south, the department of Côte-d'Or, perhaps because its population pressure was less severe, remained an exporter of wheat, which was shipped by the Saône toward Lyon and southern France. Some of the great landowners (Marmont, Heudelet) created on their estates complex cycles of crop rotation in which there was room for ground cover and artificial fodder, but their efforts remained isolated. In vain did the prefects use the example of these estates as a model for the transformation of the old economy and to give a major role in this endeavour to the agricultural societies. Unlike on the other side of the Loire, the obstacle here was not nature, but human behaviour: a whole rural proletariat obstinately defended the practice of simultaneous harvesting (which was actually abolished under the law), its right to free firewood and the use of the forest (despite the forestry code), free communal pasture, and all the communal rights of the old customary law. In *Les Paysans* Balzac has described with great insight the peasants' struggle against the law and against the rich. To be sure, some progress was made: wheat gained ground over rye, sometimes passing through a phase of mixing the two crops, and major advances were made in the field of animal husbandry: in the Auxois new techniques for the fattening of beef cattle were developed, while the improvement of sheep, first orientated to the production of better wool by means of cross-breeding with Merino rams, shifted toward improved meat production when the price of wool began to decline. Unlike the large-scale agriculture of the region of Paris, however, most of the Côte-d'Or remained within the bounds of traditional agriculture.

Champagne as a whole practiced a triennial system of crop rotation. Small properties were the dominant pattern, but the quality of the soils was so variable that it is difficult to analyse the agricultural problems of this region. Good farmlands in Haute-Marne might export wheat, but elsewhere the 'badlands' of Champagne produced only meagre harvests of rye and buckwheat. Owing to the exploitation of the vast forests for the use of the metal industry, reforestation early became a major problem. When the prefect Bourgeois de Jessaint – whose administrative career was so long that this schoolfriend of Napoleon's at Brienne ended up as a prefect under Louis-Philippe – ordered the planting of Austrian pines, alders, and beeches, he only enlarged upon the programme initiated by the intendant Rouillé d'Orfeuil. Jessaint also took steps to improve the quality of the local wool for the cloth industry by importing Merino sheep and raising a model flock on his own estate. By 1828 half of Champagne's sheep consisted of Merinos and mixed breeds that produced an extra fine grade of wool. Subsequent efforts to reconvert these sheep into meat producers did not have the same success.

By contrast, some areas of the Paris region (Soissonnais, France, Valois, western Brie, Beauce) were the very models of a high-yield, largely commercialised agriculture.

Here small properties (less than 5 hectares) accounted for only about one-tenth of the soil, while large estates of more than 100 hectares occupied more than half the surface. This pattern of large estates, attested to by the presence of many châteaux – which, incidentally, were still being built in the first half of the nineteenth century – had long existed in this area and had not been overthrown by the Revolution. The nobility of the Ancien Regime (Condé at Chantilly, La Fayette at Rozay-en-Brie, Bertier de Sauvigny at Morsang, etc.) was solidly entrenched; other great estates were owned by the nobility of Napoleon's Empire, by marshals (Davout at Savigny-sur-Orge), bankers (Laffitte at Maisons-Laffitte), financiers, and Parisian notaries. These properties tended to become larger and larger; they were divided into substantial farms that might reach a size of 200 hectares, unlike those of the Loire region. Characterised by large estates, large farms, and large, trapeze-shaped fields measuring from 10 to 50 hectares, this open field system was very different from that of the eastern section. On these exposed plateaux, notes G. Dupeux, 'only one-tenth of the land escaped the plough. No meadows, no vineyards; on this rich soil, the ploughman is king.' Aside from the production of cereals, essentially wheat, the most important venture was sheep-raising by means of artificial fodder. Some of the large farms had two flocks, one for wool and the other for meat production, which were kept in spacious pens. Sugar-beet, which would subsequently become a major crop, was as yet found only in a few places. However, this was the time when free communal pasture and the fallow disappeared (by 1840 the latter occupied only one-sixth to one-tenth of the land), when imported fertiliser (from the dried night soil of Paris to peat ashes and later guano) and improved farm implements (new ploughs, among them the one-way plough and the first threshing and sowing machines [*c.* 1834]) came into use.

As a result of this agricultural revolution, the farm became an enterprise with a hierarchy of personnel (carters, ploughmen, shepherds, etc.); at the same time, the reduced need for labour created considerable unemployment. Poorer regions had fewer beggars or wretchedly poor proletarians than these rich agricultural areas of the region of Paris.

Valleys, market-gardening, major wine production

Thus, not all of the plateaux that form the underlying structure of the Paris basin had embarked upon the agricultural revolution when the railway age was about to begin. Other factors due to a wide variety of circumstances (such as contrasts between valleys and their surrounding slopes and the plateaux, the influence of the capital on the suburbs, and the world-wide reputation of certain wines) further accentuated the disparities among local areas.

The valleys of the Paris basin were poorly suited to large-scale agriculture. Here rural property was divided into tiny plots, both on the alluvial farmland and on the slopes that lent themselves to the planting of vineyards and orchards. Old villages were often located half-way up the slope, following the line of springs and wells. Large properties did, of course, exist in a few places; in the Val de Loire of the Nivernais, some large landowners began to raise sugar-beet around 1825. By and large, however, very small properties were the dominant pattern, which in these densely populated valleys made for a society that differed markedly from that of the peasantry of the plateaux. Made up of vintners, gardeners, different kinds of artisans, coopers, and sailors who lived there or returned regularly, this milieu was more open to urban influences. In some cases the traditional mixed farming continued to be practiced, as in the isolated peninsula of Saint-Germain-en Laye, tucked away between the river bend and the forest. Very often, however, wine was the most important commercial product: in the region of Paris, vineyards bordered the slopes along the Seine between Bonnières and Saint-Cloud and, on the other bank, from Meulan to the confluent with the Oise, following that river beyond Isle Adam to the river bend at Argenteuil. South of Paris, vineyards were found on the slopes of Montlhéry and Palaiseau, and from Saint-Cloud they reached as far as Versailles by way of Meudon, Sèvres, and Chaville. Yet after 1820 this great wine-producing region began to decline in the face of competition from more southerly wine producers, and wine began to yield to other commodities needed by the capital.

In the Loire valley, the planting of new vineyards followed the waterways used for inland shipping. The availability of transportation also resulted in the production of specialised crops in the alluvial plain. Those of the valley around Tours were already famous in the sixteenth century and were regularly sold in the Antilles in the eighteenth century. Over the centuries, all of the valley's wasteland had been brought under cultivation, usually by backbreaking labour. Here lived the peasants described by Paul-Lois Courier, toiling to extract the maximum yield from the small plot they had wrested from the commons or acquired when nationalised properties were put on sale. By the first half of the nineteenth century the valley was deeply marked by man: hemp or vegetables were grown in the valley, the slopes were covered with orchards of peach and plum trees, and on the hilltops, capped with windmills, vineyards alternated with lucerne fields. Plums were sent all the way to foreign countries, and other commodities, such as pears and dried apples, vegetable seeds, and even licorice, a speciality of Bourgueil, were sold commercially. Yet this prosperity hardly spilled over into the everyday life of the people, for the micro-owners of the overcrowded valley lived frugally indeed and only tasted their wine on special occasions.

By contrast, there was one group of small peasants who did enjoy exceptional prosperity in the France of that time, namely, the market-gardeners of the Parisian suburbs. Their contiguous plots, which were becoming increasingly independent of the quality of the soil, formed a square of 5 or 6,000 square metres enclosed by walls to protect them from the wind and from marauders. A well furnished water and, following the invention of a rotary pump in 1836, the hard work of drawing water was performed by horses. Buying night soil and manure from the city, these market-gardeners were able, thanks to the use of cold-frames and cloches, to produce five or six harvests per year. At the beginning of the century some of them still carried their produce to the central market or to individual shops in Paris in baskets carried on their backs or by pack-horse. But as new construction pushed the gardening zone further and further away from the city limits, the use of the cart became mandatory; however, such travel was facilitated by a particularly dense network of roads. Although every sector had its own renowned speciality (beans from the plateaux of Villejuif or Colombes, asparagus from Argenteuil, straw-berries from Montreuil or Fontenay-aux-Roses, etc.), most of them raised almost the entire gamut of produce, except some new specialities, like cultivated mushrooms. The market-gardeners of the suburbs had a virtual monopoly of the Parisian market, since the development of the railway had not yet reached the stage where it could bring in competition from the south. The prosperity of the market-gardeners was at its peak in the middle of the century.

Markets of much larger scope were sought by the producers of two great wines, Champagne and Burgundy.

In the eighteenth century Champagne was already a wine-exporting region. While the red and grey varieties accounted for most of these exports, the red wines of the Reims mountains as well as the white wine of Scillery and the sparkling wine of Ay already enjoyed a certain reputation. The export of red wine continued throughout our period, for even though the land frontier with Holland had been closed to French wines in 1823, they sold so well in Holland that selling them via Reims, Dunkerque, and Ostende was justified. But the major feature of the period is the rising popularity of sparkling wine.

Witnessing the pillage of her cellars by allied officers in 1814, the daughter of Reims' Mayor Ponsardin, the shrewd widow Cliquot, made the prophetic statement: 'They are drinking, they will pay.' And indeed, it does seem that the allied occupation served to spread the international reputation of sparkling wine. Concurrently with the increase in demand, it also reached its point of perfection. Although Dom Perignon had invented the techniques of making wine into Champagne in the seventeenth century, and although the use of the cork stopper had become more widespread in the eighteenth, the mixing and dosage of different wines was brought to the point of perfection in our period, chiefly owing to the work of the pharmacist François. It is true that progress yet remained to be made with respect to bottling, for in 1830 and 1833, 33 and 25 per cent, respectively, of the stocks deposited in the cellars of the Moët winery exploded in their bottles. But a series of inventions made between 1827 and 1844 – the corking, wiring, drawing, and dosing machines – resulted in considerable savings of labour costs.

In 1832 vineyards covered 20,000 hectares of the hilly area (*côte*) of Champagne; most of them were owned by small proprietors, but already some of this land was being bought up by commercial producers. That year production rose to 480,000 hl, including 60,000 hl of sparkling white wine, 120,000 hl of red wine for export, and 300,000 hl of red wine for French consumption. The great Champagne firms of Reims and Epernay – Veuve Cliquot, Mumm, Moët, Lanson, Roederer, and others – were firmly established. The figures for the year 1844–5 published by the Chamber of Commerce of Reims indicate that of the 6,635,652 bottles of sparkling wine shipped, 2,255,438 were sold in France, 4,380,214 abroad. After Germany, Champagne had conquered Russia and the United States: 'The golden stream of Champagne has been diverted from its bed, but it is still a beneficent river.'

The Côte-d'Or was a region that specialised in wine production. The surface devoted to vineyards had grown by 20 per cent in the period 1804 to 1830, and covered 26,467 hectares at the latter date. The actual *Côte*, stretching northward from Beaune to Nuits-Saint-Georges and Dijon, was the only area to produce the precious Pinot grapes. On the lower slopes or in the flatlands, more recently planted vineyards produced the Gamay grape, which yields a less distinguished wine. Great estates owned by local or 'outside' capitalists (such as the son of the banker Ouvrard at Clos-Vougeot) were the dominant pattern on the *Côte*.

Although the quality of the great Burgundies was recognised – they were considered the best of the French wines – their producers were severely hurt by the price slump of the period 1817–51. The international customs agreements appear to have been particularly detrimental to exports to Germany, Switzerland, and the Netherlands. The rigid pattern of demand caused prices to rise steeply in years of scanty harvests and to collapse whenever the harvest was abundant. The exceptional circumstances that permitted the Champagne trade to flourish amidst this general stagnation did not obtain in the market for the great Burgundies.

The industries of the Paris basin

Agriculture was the dominant activity of the Paris basin, and such crafts or industries as did exist often worked only for a local clientèle. However, some of the towns engaged in specialised productions either as a matter of tradition (Romorantin had been making cloth since the Middle Ages) or under the aegis of the State (Châtellerault was awarded the Klingenthal manufacture of side-arms in 1819 and the Maubeuge manufacture of guns in 1830). Some industries, for example those of the Loire country, had developed in connection with commercial activities: Orléans, a transshipment centre of the Parisian trade, had cotton spinneries, cloth factories, bleacheries, file factories, vinegar- and chocolate-works, etc., but none of these varied though modest activities had a wider impact on the region.

In Champagne, by contrast, a multi-faceted textile industry clustered around the centres of Reims and Troyes.

The major centre of cloth-making was Reims, which had the largest spinning mills for carded wool and also engaged in the processing of combed wool. Its specialities were flannels, 'merinos' and 'schalls'; at the time of the July Monarchy, novelty cloths for summer and winter were added. In 1847 its 238 establishments employed 5,300 persons, men, women, and children. Side by side with major factories like those of Jobert, Lucas, or de Crutelle – the latter had begun to use the water power of the Vesle river in 1837 and increased the number of hydraulic looms in his mill to more than 100 seven years later – existed a whole raft of more modest establishments; moreover, much of the weaving continued to be done by peasant workers whose wages began to decline sharply after 1840 owing to the increasing competition from machines. In 1833 an industrial society was formed at Reims for the purpose of promoting technical progress. This society fostered closer cooperation among the wool merchants, spinners, and weaving entrepreneurs.

To an even greater extent than Reims, Troyes gave work to the countryside, even though the town itself had sixteen cotton spinneries employing 1,900 workers and several loom construction works in 1846. Ever since the severe crisis that had befallen the cloth-weaving industry under the Ancien Regime, a relatively minor local speciality, the making of knitted goods, had become the leading activity. Troyes manufactured stocking caps, hosiery, vests, and underwear, and although it had fewer outlets than the industry of Reims, the solid quality of its goods had conquered the national market. Its influence had stimulated the activity of certain secondary trade centres, such as Romilly and Arcis, which were just beginning to shake off its tutelage. Of the 10,812 looms counted in the department of Aube, only 867 were operating at Troyes. Practically all the rest were scattered throughout the countryside, and every week the peasant artisans would carry their goods to town in a basket on their backs or the backs of mules. It should be mentioned that the different kinds of looms (circular, chain-operated, etc.) were repeatedly improved in the course of the period 1800–50. This rural industry enabled the countryside to absorb its increased population density, but wages were very low and the competition of mechanical looms after 1840 brought dreadful poverty.

Another industry, metallurgy, permeated a wide zone of the eastern and southern part of the Paris basin (Haute-Marne, Aube, Côte-d'Or, Nièvre, Allier, Cher, Indre). This industry had changed little since the previous century: blast furnaces operated near open iron mines and close to the forests, forges were located along a stream or by a dammed-up lake whose falling water could be used to drive the hammers. Small groups of establishments were scattered through the region in keeping with these geographic imperatives. The blast furnaces and forges of Berry formed five groups (in the regions of Vierzon in the north, Grossouvre in the east, the Tronçais forest in the south, Bourges in the centre, and Luçay in the west), while the forges of the Nivernais, located on both sides of the axis formed by the Loire, principally occupied the valleys of the Nièvre, the Ixeure, and the Aubois. The establishments of Haute-Marne were mainly concentrated in the valleys of the Marne, the Blaise, and the Rognon. Most of these operations were very small indeed (this was the case in Haute-Marne, which in 1835 had 52 blast furnaces and 104 forges that produced sheet iron, files, and awls), the only exception being the Guérigny foundry in Nièvre, which worked for the State, and the copper foundry at Imphy.

In 1821 the Boigue family, Parisian iron merchants who had become rich under the Empire, commissioned the construction of a major English-style forge at Fourchambault. Conceived by Dufaud, a graduate of the Polytechnique who hired skilled English puddling and laminating workers, the new establishment had a productive capacity of 6,000 tons of iron, a remarkable figure, considering that the Nivernais as a whole only produced 5,000 at the time. By 1848 the Boigue works produced 16,600 tons of iron and absorbed some of the pig iron producers of Berry.

In Burgundy, the main impulse came from Marshal de Marmont, who had inherited a forge at Sainte-Colombe-sur-Seine. Given to bold and fanciful schemes, he planned to manage his forge himself and to transform it. He let himself be persuaded that it was possible to combine refining by means of wood fuel, puddling, and laminating operations. The costs incurred soon exceeded his expectations and he was obliged to associate with his neighbours, a step that did not save him from personal bankruptcy in 1827. Yet the trend toward conglomerates was set in the Châtillonnais. In another development, one of the most remarkable ironmasters of the time, Rambourg, had added to his blast furnaces in the forest of Tronçais a new coal-fuelled establishment at Commentry. In 1845 his children decided to merge with the Burgundian conglomerate. This was the origin of the powerful metallurgy group of Châtillon-Commentry which used both wood and coal fuel for production. The conglomerate directly managed thirty-seven blast furnaces, fifty-six open-hearth forges, four English forges, and three wire mills. In addition it also leased thirteen blast furnaces, twenty-six forges, and four wire mills to unaffiliated manufacturers in the Marne and Seine valleys. The group controlled the entire iron industry from the southern part of Haute-Marne to the northern part of Côte-d'Or.

Elsewhere individual enterprises subsisted, and the prospect of increased demand for railway tracks even gave rise to the construction of new wood-fuelled blast furnaces. However, older enterprises had difficulties in keeping up with the large companies that produced in massive quantities and could withstand the frequent slumps of the middle of the century.

Considering that the dynamic activity of Paris transformed its agricultural suburbs, one wonders whether it also generated an industrial zone.

The physical growth of the city had, of course, brought a great need for new quarries, plaster works, and brick-making establishments. It was also an abundant and cheap source of refuse (bones, skins, rags, scrap iron) and moreover constituted an attractive market for various food industries. But all of these enterprises were strictly oriented toward the needs of Paris. Even the immediate northern suburbs, despite their excellent network of canals, roads, bridges and, beginning in 1846, railways that gave them easy access to northern and eastern France and to Le Havre, remained largely rural. Saint-Denis, aside from a rather antiquated laminated lead mill, had only one major chemical plant, La Villette had some food industries, and La Chapelle had some machine works, located beyond the fortifications. Without being completely absent, major industry took root only slowly. As J. P. Brunet noted: 'Between 1821 and 1846 the northern suburbs acquired the essential part of their economic infrastructure, and yet the major industries did not settle in the area until 1855–60.' In the southern suburbs, where industry was not completely absent either, it formed small pockets: Gentilly, immediately adjacent to Paris, had some wool-washing establishments and bleacheries connected with the textile industries of the capital and also some tanneries; Ivry and Choisy had mainly chemical industries. In short, it can be stated that while some major enterprises did settle in the northern and especially in the southern suburbs of Paris after 1840, this development was but a weak foreshadow-

ing of the spurt of industrial growth that was to take place under the
Second Empire.

From collective mentalities to political opinions

This extensive region of the Paris basin, whose unification by the modern
means of communication was not yet completed, did not have a uniform
way of thinking and acting. Although it is often difficult to pin down the
convictions and the passions of the largely illiterate masses who have left
little direct evidence, recent studies have brought to light marked differences in attitude from one small area to the next.

Yet a few general traits are attested to by concordant testimonies. The
first is the indifference of the masses to politics in the narrow sense. Under
the Restoration they were made aware of political issues through the
mediation of their attitude toward religion. At that time the problem that
occupied – or was made to occupy – their collective consciousness was that
of a return to Catholicism. The fact is that by the end of the Revolution
large sections of the Paris basin had been engulfed by religious indifference;
and the clergy appointed by the Consulate and the Empire often did not
have the numerical strength and the qualifications to remedy this situation. The violent but brief effort at 'dechristianisation' undertaken by the
Revolution had uncovered a more long-standing problem. Even more
disastrous than the fact that some dioceses were governed by unworthy
bishops in the eighteenth century was the diffusion of zealous Jansenist
piety in the same period. In reading Royer-Collard's unforgettable
description of the biblical exaltation and the moral austerity that pervaded
the parish of Sompuis in Champagne where he lived as a child, one realises
that an attitude that can steep a few elect souls in piety and animate a
small community is even more likely to discourage the mass of the faithful.
And indeed we know that several dioceses of the Paris basin, among them
those of Sens and Orléans, had come under the spell of this Jansenist
rigour, which banned sinners from the sacraments, preached an intract-
able morality, and in fact paved the way for widespread disaffection. The
religious revival that accompanied the Restoration entrusted many
parishes to the 'young conscripts of the militant Church'; but their zeal
was powerless against an apathy that had existed for generations, and
their relative isolation accounts for their inept attempts to align the altar
with the throne and to rely on the support of a nobility that had returned
to religion. Anathematising the atheist Revolution and sometimes refusing
absolution to those who had acquired Church property – and this did not
have to happen often before the owners of such property became thoroughly alarmed – they succeeded in discrediting both the Church and the
restored monarchy. Missionaries brought in to rectify the situation did not

necessarily arouse violent reactions, but their efforts seem to have failed virtually everywhere. A certain popular consensus that created the pre-conditions for a Catholic renewal in western and eastern France did not exist in the Paris basin.

The opposition between town and country may have been less vivid in this region than in western France; nonetheless, the towns were centres of liberal or revolutionary propaganda. After all, urban merchants and artisans were in contact with the outside world, news was brought in by the passing postchaise, former revolutionaries and retired soldiers on half pay who hankered after the past had settled in towns, and newspapers, usually those of the opposition, were discussed in the *cabaret*. To be sure, the authorities condemned the anti-religious brochures and the anti-government almanacs that were carried deep into the countryside by peddlers, but in any case this kind of propaganda was less effective than the influence of day-to-day contacts in a small town. The valleys also were thoroughfares by which new ideas penetrated into the countryside. Thus, the religious surveys of the diocese of Versailles distinguished the 'good' regions, that is, the Beauce, the centre of the Vexin, parts of the plateau of France, and the plain of Montmorency, from the river valleys south of Paris, that is, the Juine, Essonne, and Orge valleys and the Seine valley south of Meulan. Having been 'dechristianised' earlier than the plateaux, the valleys were also more open to new ideas. Paul-Louis Courier's vint-ners were people of the Loire and Cher valleys, very much like the men of Luynes whom he defended in 1816, when they were arbitrarily imprisoned for what they had said. The influence of the boatmen of the Yonne made Auxerre a centre of republicanism under the July Monarchy, while the boatmen of the Marne spread the socialist ideas they brought from Paris throughout Champagne on the eve of the revolution of 1848.

The decline of Christian faith was matched by a deterioration of morals that was noted over and over in the surveys of the Church and in the reports of the Restoration prefects (increase of drunkenness, 'it is hard to find a girl who approaches the altar in a state of purity', and so forth). Yet under the July Monarchy the people still had a certain attachment to a 'customary' religion and filled the churches on the high holidays, even though the number of *pascalisants* [people who partake of the sacraments at least at Easter] was almost nil. Even in as dechristianised a region as Yonne, the villagers might demand that their reticent priest say a special mass (which they did not attend), preceded by the ringing of the bells, on Saint Philip's day. This was a way of teasing the clergy, but a report also notes: 'To make their holiday complete, they want to hear the church bells in the morning.' Perhaps they would have preferred bells without priests to priests without bells. Yet despite sudden and sporadic incidents of violence (the sacking of seminaries and priests' residences following the

July days) they could not have managed all that easily without these priests, whom they often distrusted; although their faith had broken down, the old superstitions were as strong in the Beauce as they were in the Bourbonnais, and the priest was needed to baptise a child, just in case, to lead a pilgrimage to the shrine of a specialised saint, or to conduct a procession to bring rain.

The reactions of these uncouth rural or urban people were viewed with suspicion by the cultivated classes, even if popular and bourgeois forces seemed to work toward the same goal. It is well known that during the Three Glorious Days in Paris the deputies were embarrassed by their allies. What happened at Versailles on 30 July was a comical version of this same attitude: upon hearing of the events in Paris, a group of lower-class people looted a military magazine, seized the horses, and offered its help to the mayor and the bourgeois and liberal-minded National Guard. Desperately trying to find a way to get rid of these unwelcome auxiliaries, the Guard decided to wear them out by endless marching and disarmed them while they were sleeping. On the other hand, these same liberal bourgeois felt sorry for the royal guards. The nobles of the Saint-Louis quarter and the bourgeois of the Notre-Dame quarter did not speak to each other at the prefects' receptions; yet, paradoxically, the very struggle that pitted them against each other in their bid for power brought them closer together at the first stirring of the lower classes.

Such episodes, to be sure, were exceptional, and the normal political contests were carried out within the narrow confines of the voting class. As elsewhere, the ruling classes of the region of Paris had been glad to see the return of the Bourbons. This was the case even in Champagne, a region where a bourgeoisie of buyers of nationalised property, Brumairians, and newly rich parvenus of the Empire had played a preponderant role. In 1814, when these bourgeois, headed by the prefect, rapidly changed course, the widow Cliquot justified their attitude in high-sounding terms: 'Purified by a series of misfortunes and hardships, we have once again become worthy of being governed by our ancient house of France.' Of course this initial enthusiasm was followed by many ups and downs later. Rather than follow the fluctuation of public attitudes in this entire region, let us assess the situation after the fall of Villèle. Recall that the Chamber elected in 1827, having brought down the Villèle government, voted in 1829 for the famous address of the 221 that challenged the Polignac government and marked the point of departure of the revolution of 1830. In analysing the voting records of the deputies of the 17 departments* (not including Seine) that form the region under discussion here, one

---

* Aisne, Allier, Aube, Cher, Côte-d'Or, Eure-et-Loir, Haute-Marne, Indre, Indre-et-Loire, Loir-et-Cher, Loiret, Marne, Nièvre, Oise, Seine-et-Marne, Seine-et-Oise, Yonne.

realises that the government party preserved its majority among the deputies elected by the departmental *collèges* (22 against 10), but that all the deputies elected by the colleges of the *arrondissements* (42) voted for the address, with the exception of one deputy from Yonne, Jacquinot de Pamplune, attorney-general at the royal tribunal in Paris. In the delegations of Seine-et-Oise and Seine-et-Marne (as in that of Seine) not one of the deputies, whether elected by the department or by the *arrondissement*, failed to vote with the opposition; among those who cast their ballot one finds the names of the liberal nobility, famous since 1789: La Fayette, Lameth, Le Peletier.

In these departments near Paris, the prefects had little influence over the elections. In 1827 this was brought home to Hervé de Tocqueville, prefect of Versailles (and father of the celebrated writer), who was well connected and well liked in his department, since three of his cousins sat in the general council. Having decided to let the liberals win in the *collèges* of the *arrondissements*, he tried to have Villèle supporters elected by the departmental *collège*. One of his candidates was elected, but only after he had promised, just before the balloting, that he would join the opposition.

Altogether, 69 per cent of the deputies of these 17 departments voted for the address of the 221, whereas this figure for the Chamber as a whole was 55 per cent. By 1829 only the wealthy landowners who formed a majority in the departmental *collèges* remained unconditionally loyal to the king; even at Reims, whose outstanding industrial character we have noted, the departmental *collège* of sixty-five electors paying at least 841 francs in taxes included only twenty-one merchants and industrial entrepreneurs, but thirty-one landowners, five civil servants, one notary, and one physician, all of whom undoubtedly also owned property.

The lowering of the property qualifications under the July Monarchy and to some extent the economic evolution itself caused the structure of the electoral colleges to become more complex. Let us report the findings of G. Dupeux's analysis of the department of Loir-et-Cher.

In 1847 the electorate of this department could be represented by a sharply pointed pyramid. The 1847 electors at the base paid only one-fourth of the taxes collected, while 54 very large landowners at the top paid 2,000 each; among them were 23 of the 113 nobles inscribed on the electoral lists (Vibraye, Chalais-Périgord, Saumery, Salaberry, etc.). The total number of eligibles who paid over 500 francs in taxes was 447, and in this group landed proprietors had a decided majority over bourgeois and manufacturers. The 1,400 other eligibles (paying between 200 and 500 francs) were absentee landlords (about 400), professional men (94 notaries, 10 solicitors, 30 barristers, 50 physicians, etc.), members of the economic occupations (100 millers, 50 innkeepers, 100 shopkeepers, 50 artisans). In this department, which took in part of the Beauce, part of the Sologne, and part of the Val de Loire, and yet was not completely lacking in industry, the political predominance of the large landed proprietors remained very marked; the rank and file of the voters followed the instructions of the notables. Although the great legitimist landowners were no longer represented in the Chamber after 1830 (when they had Sala-bery), they still sat in the general councils, thanks to an electorate that was more democratic than the one we have just analysed. The members of the conservative and liberal bourgeoisie wanted to make sure that they exercised their share of political power; but some of them chose to let themselves be represented by a kind of proxy. The barrister Durand, representing Romorantin in the Chamber, fulfilled this function for the liberals.

A brief survey of the outcome of the elections of 1846 for the group of departments whose election results we have analysed for 1827 yields several apparently contradictory facts. To begin with, these departments did not share one single major current of public opinion. The democratic propa-ganda promoted by a few notables did little more than banish them from polite society, as George Sand and her friend the lawyer Michel de Bourges found out in Berry. The local press, usually consisting of an organ of the opposition and a paper controlled by the government, was for the most part bogged down in petty polemics and personality issues. Nonethe-less, the elections sometimes did give rise to genuine conflicts between political ideas. In Yonne, for example, the two northern circumscriptions of Auxerre and Joigny, where influences from the capital played a major role, took strong positions for or against the rather Bonapartist liberalism of Larabit and the quasi-republican ideas of the pamphleteer Cornemin. At Reims the government supporter Chaix d'Est Ange, standing for re-election, was opposed by the liberal journalist Faucher: Faucher won, thanks to the support of Bishop Gousset's newspaper the *Champagne Catholique*, which demanded freedom of education; Chaix d'Est Ange had failed to support this issue in the Chamber. Elsewhere the electorate con-tinued to place its trust in a man or a clan. The best example for this attitude is the La Fayette family: the general had died in 1834, but members of his family still remained at the château of Les Granges near Rozay-en-Brie, which was perceived as a high place of liberalism. Their prestige was undisputed, even in distant electoral districts, so that even in Seine-et-Marne Georges and Oscar, son and grandson of the hero of two continents, were sent to the Chamber by the towns of Coulommiers and Meaux.

Yet in many electoral districts the voters sought to defend their interests by electing civil servants, especially councillors of State, permanent secretaries in the ministries, judges, and engineers of the Ponts et Chaussées. In these departments the percentage of civil servants elected was 36 per cent, somewhat lower than the national average of 40 per cent. Although few of the elected deputies directly represented economic interests, Yonne, Haute-Marne, Nièvre, and Cher were competently served by the ironmasters they had elected, Châteauroux was represented by the cloth manufacturer Muret de Bort, Corbeil by a wholesale grain merchant, and Senlis by a transport entrepreneur.

Finally, these elections disclosed the relative political originality of the Paris basin. While France as a whole elected 29 government supporters and 168 members of the opposition, this region sent – even counting the undecided deputies as Guizot supporters – 44 governmental and 36 opposition deputies to the Chamber. After adding the 3 governmental and 11 opposition deputies elected by Paris, one finds that the delegation as a whole was split exactly in half: 47 deputies for and 47 against the government. It is thus clear that the political trends of the capital reached the voting bourgeoisie of the Paris basin. But before they could form a national political consciousness, these trends had to confront local interests and local practices; this was but the political aspect of the mixture of attraction and revulsion exerted in these years of transition by the growing influence of the great capital.

18

Paris

Paris around 1815

In 1815 Paris was still enclosed by the barrier of the Farmers-General. Broken only by the river entrances of La Rapée and the Invalides, this was a simple wooden customs barrier, 3.3 metres high and pierced by 52 toll-gates. Some of these 'toll-stations' housed collectors' offices designed by Ledoux, who had had visions of making them the 'Prophylaea of Paris'. Following the path of this barrier in present-day Paris, one finds that on the Right Bank it went from the Trocadéro to Bercy by way of avenue Kléber, the place de l'Etoile, the boulevards de Courcelle, Clichy, Rochechouart, la Chapelle, la Villette, Belleville, Ménilmontant, Charonne, Picpus, and Reuilly; on the Left Bank from boulevard de Grenelle to boulevard de l'Hôpital by way of boulevards Garibaldi, de Vaugirard, Edgar-Quinet, Raspail, Saint-Jacques, d'Italie, altogether covering a distance of 24 kilometres on both banks. The surface enclosed within this perimeter was only 3,440 hectares, a third of present-day Paris; it would remain almost unchanged until the incorporation of the suburban communes in 1860.

Beginning in 1823 the Restoration had the customs barrier torn down, but the July Monarchy decided to build new fortifications for the city. A law of 1841 gave Paris a continuous city wall that also took in the outlying communes of Auteuil, Passy, Batignolles, Montmartre, La Chapelle, La Villette, Belleville, Charonne, Bercy, Vaugirard, and Grenelle. Built between 1841 and 1845, this 36-kilometre wall was punctuated by 94 bastions; in addition, 17 detached forts defended the approaches. Here was the protection against a potential invader that had been so cruelly lacking at the end of the Empire, asserted Thiers and Guizot, for once in agreement on this point, while the men of the opposition insinuated that it was being built as a threat to the Parisians.

However that may be, the city did not have a homogeneous urban texture. To begin with, there was an imbalance between the Right Bank with its half million inhabitants and the Left Bank with slightly more than

8 Paris in 1828
Paris History Library

367

200,000. Above all, the historical growth of the city by concentric circles had left its marks, creating a contrast between a densely populated centre and a periphery characterised by discontinuous patches of settlement. Taking in both banks, the central core stopped in the north at the line of the Grands Boulevards; on the Left Bank it did not reach beyond a line extending from La Bourbe (Port Royal) to the boulevard des Invalides.

In the heart of the city subsisted the île de la Cité, the île Saint-Louis, and the île Louvier, the latter connected to the rue du Petit-Musc by a bridge, while the two others were united by the pont Saint-Louis built in 1803. The Cité contained Notre-Dame Cathedral and, in the eastern part, the archbishop's palace, sacked during a riot in 1831, the Palais de Justice, and many churches. Napoleon had also established the police headquarters there and had ordered the clearing of the square facing the cathedral. The île de la Cité still had its medieval hovels with their pointed roofs and its labyrinth of narrow streets evoked by Eugène Suë in *Les Mystères de Paris*: 'The mud-coloured houses, pierced by a few windows with worm-eaten frames almost touched each other at the top because the streets were so narrow. Dark and filthy alleyways led to even darker and filthier stairways that were so steep that one could barely climb them by holding on to a rope attached to the humid walls by iron hooks.'

The area between the police headquarters and the Palais de Justice was full of disreputable *cabarets* and 'doss-houses', and no bourgeois would have ventured there at night. Nearby, ill-reputed neighbourhoods had sprung up in places where modern police regulations would not tolerate them: upon leaving the île de la Cité by the Pont Neuf, which was occupied by old-clothes dealers and food vendors, and after skirting the Louvre, one would come upon the Carousel quarter, wedged between the two palaces of the Louvre and the Tuileries, a maze of narrow streets passing among old townhouses, demolition sites, the shacks of bird-sellers, and waste ground, where mountebanks, dog-clippers and tooth-pullers plied their trades. Queen Marie-Amélie later complained that she could not leave the Tuileries without being greeted by uncouth remarks. Yet north of the [Tuileries] garden the rue de Rivoli, which had been cut through during the Empire, led, beginning at its intersection with the rue Saint-Honoré near the Madeleine church, to a renovated neighbourhood, although the entire area, including the church, remained one vast building site. Toward the west, the Palais Royal had preserved some of its elegance, with its galleries of fine objects, its famous restaurants, Very and the Frères Provençaux, and such cafés as the café Foy; but even here there were dives, prostitutes, and a motley crowd that easily absorbed 'all the irregulars of Paris'.

The northern sections of Paris were as rich in contrasts as ever: some of the more airy streets, the rue de Richelieu or the rue Croix-des-Petits-

Champs, were lined with individual townhouses, with a courtyard in front and a garden at the back, shops selling luxury goods (elegant shops often opened not onto the street itself but onto a passage; this had become quite the rage, no doubt because it allowed pedestrians to stroll unmolested by vehicles or mud; the first such passage, the passage des Panoramas, was opened in 1800 (by 1840 there were about 100), and renowned restaurants, such as the *Rocher de Cancale* in the rue Montorgueil, close to les Halles. Yet at the present-day rue de l'Opéra one came upon the butte des Moulins, a neighbourhood of sordid streets where, as Balzac tells us, unclean trades existed side by side with modest dress shops and the haunts of prostitutes. The Emperor's plan to renovate the neighbourhood of les Halles had not come to fruition, and Napoleon's contribution was limited to a new iron cupola for the grain market and the building of the marché des Prouvaires. Many of the transactions were still carried out on the old site of the cemetery of the Innocents, which the market-gardeners could reach by narrow streets. Only the wider rues Saint-Denis and Saint-Martin connected Paris with the northern suburbs, and it was not until the Second Empire that these streets reached the place du Châtelet, which had been carved out of the old medieval fortress. Wedged between les Halles and the Seine were, to cite Balzac again, 'the very entrails of the city'. It was a teeming place exhibiting an infinite variety of heterogeneous merchandise, mixing noisome odours and pretty sights, herring and muslin, silk and honey, butter and tulle. On the banks of the Seine in front of the Hôtel de Ville, the place de Grève, not bordered by any quay until 1831, was inundated by the waters of the Seine whenever the river overflowed.

The Marais quarter, traversed by the rue Saint-Antoine – for a long time the widest street in Paris – was no longer the aristocratic neighbourhood it had been in the past. Already by the eighteenth century, some of the resident families had moved to the faubourg Saint-Germain and the Revolution had accelerated this exodus. Bourgeois families did not have to pay too much for these townhouses near the place des Vosges.

Toward the east and beyond the Bastille, where the plaster elephant, Gavroche's hiding place in *Les Misérables*, was slowly decaying, crumbling away under the teeth of the rats because hard times had made it impossible to build the definitive bronze monument, was the faubourg Saint-Antoine. Finally recovering from the revolutionary turmoil, it had returned to the cabinet-making for which it had been famous since the seventeenth century, and also to copper-smithing. Beyond the barrière du Trône lay the private cemetery of Picpus where since 1801 great families had assembled the remains of those among them who had fallen victim to the Revolution. But Picpus was already in the zone of suburban market-gardening.

Under the Restoration the ring of the Grands Boulevards became the most animated part of Paris, for unlike in the old city where the streets had no pavements and where coaches were constantly in danger of striking a milestone, the boulevards provided enough room for carriages at full tilt as well as tree-lined lateral promenades appointed with benches and chairs. To the east, many theatres opened in the popular boulevard du Temple, which came to be called the 'boulevard of crime' owing to the success of the romantic melodramas. The more aristocratic boulevard des Italiens was a favourite haunt of dandys who frequented cafés and re-nowned restaurants, such as the Café Anglais, the Café de Paris, the Maison dorée, or Tortoni's.

Beyond the boulevards the pattern of continuous settlement took the form of tentacles or isolated clusters along the access routes to the capital. In the city's north-eastern section, for example, the former pattern was found along the streets of the faubourg Saint-Denis and the faubourg Saint-Martin and also along the main street of La-Grange-aux-Belles, even though the air of this area, depending on the direction of the wind, often reeked of the foul smell of the charnel house of Mountfaucon, an enormous deposit of animal carcasses and refuse. Clusters of dwellings varied greatly in character, as is exemplified by the two neighbouring ones of the Chaussée d'Antin and Petite Pologne: the Chaussée d'Antin quarter, whose construction had been begun during the reign of Louis XVI, had become the favourite dwelling-place of the bankers of the Directory and the Consulate and now attracted high society and established artists. By contrast, Petite Pologne, wedged between the rue de la Pépinière and the rue du Rocher, was a filthy jumble of hovels and shacks, the wretched abode of rag-pickers, scrap-collectors, and immigrants.

Taken as a whole, the peripheral sections of the Right Bank of Paris formed a varied landscape of marshes, wasteland, fields (harvesting took place in the plain of Monceau) and goat, sheep, and even cow pastures that reached the Seine south of the Champs-Elysées. Old houses of 'cow-keepers' and millers were still in place, interspersed among large and deserted monastic properties enclosed within their walls. The most extensive of these was the Saint-Lazare property between the faubourg Poissonière and the faubourg Saint-Denis, complete with several walled-in parks, including the parc Monceau that was returned to the Orléans family in 1815. Here also were several old eighteenth-century 'follies' converted to public use, like the Tivoli garden which enjoyed great popularity when Ruggieri staged his magnificent fireworks, the folie Blanjon, turned into an amusement park, and the folie Marbeuf, a public dance hall.

During the eighteenth century the rue Saint-Honoré had been extended beyond the present avenue Marigny with magnificent mansions (among them the Elysée, the former home of Mme de Pompadour). The gardens of these mansions abutted the north side of the present Champs-Elysées, then called the avenue de Neuilly, the meeting-place of fashionable carriages and cavaliers on horseback on their way to the Etoile, where the Arc de Triomphe was being built. Yet the nearby Carré Marigny was the domain of boatmen, the allée des Veuves (today avenue Montaigne) was not safe, and in the deserted streets between the Champs-Elysées and the Seine one could find harmless *guinguettes* but also underground *cabarets* where respectable people would not venture.

The Left Bank presented similar contrasts. In order to connect it more effectively with the Right Bank, Napoleon had created three new bridges (pont d'Iéna, pont des Arts, and pont d'Austerlitz) in addition to the seven existing ones. However, the south end of the pont Saint-Michel led only to the tortuous maze formed by the rue de la Harpe, the rue de la Huchette, and the rue Saint-André-des Arts, the latter meeting the rue Dauphine, an outlet of the Pont-Neuf, at the crowded intersection of Buci. The Latin Quarter, populated by students and people living on modest annuities, did not extend much beyond the slopes of the montagne Sainte-Geneviève. Some of the less crowded parts of the Left Bank, among them the impasse des Feuillantines where Victor Hugo spent his childhood, included gardens like the Luxembourg, which was much larger than it is today but closed to all but the owners of adjacent properties who had the key to it. Further south, the boulevard Montparnasse had dance halls frequented by students and seamstresses, such as the Chaumière, the Moulin de Beurre, and later the Closerie des Lilas. This was the starting-point of the rue d'Enfer where Mme de Chateaubriand had founded the Infirmary Marie-Thérèse and where the great writer lived, not far from the *doctrinaire* Royer-Collard. Further east, between the faubourg Saint-Jacques and the banks of the Seine, where the wine market and numerous small landings for passenger boats, wine, and wood-carriers shared the territory with the Jardin des Plantes, began the wretched faubourg Saint-Marceau with its poor lodgings, an urban environment that has been unforgettably described by Victor Hugo in *Les Misérables*. Toward the south, the houses gradually thinned out, the streets turned into paths, and the Bièvre meandered through the Champ de l'Alouette where washer-women came to do their laundry. Further downstream, near the pont des Gobelins, this was no longer possible, since the water was polluted by the dyes discharged by the manufactures.

In the western part of the Left Bank, between the rue de Seine, the Invalides, and the rue de Vaugirard, lay the faubourg Saint-Germain. Its rich eighteenth-century mansions had suffered from the Revolution, but many of them were once again occupied by the old nobility. In addition, some of the deputies of the departments, who liked the proximity of the

Palais-Bourbon, and many upper-echelon civil servants who wished to be close to their ministries, also lived there. This section was not as wealthy as the fashionable new neighbourhoods on the Right Bank, but its prestige was unchanged. The plaine de Grenelle beyond the Invalides continued to be used for manoeuvres and military parades.

Paris, then, experienced little change between the Ancien Regime and the Second Republic. Foreign visitors were amazed by its contrasts. Its palaces, its monuments and its many churches were firmly wedged into neighbourhoods where houses with gables, houses with turrets, shacks with flat or protruding fronts, houses of stone, brick, wood, or daub lined the streets. Running down the middle of each of these streets, a stream (like the stream of the rue du Bac so nostalgically remembered by Madame de Staël in exile!) that had to be crossed with the help of a burly Savoyard in case of heavy rain, carried off the sewage. A few poor oil lamps only lit these streets on moonless nights. 'The Auvergnat' kept the bourgeois supplied with Seine water, for the springs did not give enough water; sewers were few, and in many places the dust-carts that were to keep the streets clean were unable to pass. The cholera of 1832, which caused the most murderous ravages among the poor classes, focused public attention on the insanitary conditions of a city plunged into an almost perpetual fog, where 'the atmosphere of the streets spews cruel miasmas into stifling back shops . . . The forty thousand* houses of this great city stand ankle-deep in sewage . . . Half of Paris sleeps among the putrid exhalations of courtyards, streets, and slaughterhouses.' Yet the same Balzac, with his keen sense of the contradictions of the Paris of his day, proudly proclaimed: 'Is not Paris a sublime ship carrying a cargo of intelligence? . . . Its crew is immense . . . cabin boys or street urchins laughing in the rigging; a heavy ballast of bourgeois; workers and sailors blackened with tar; happy passengers travel in its cabins, and elegant midshipmen smoke their cigars leaning against the railing; the soldiers on its main deck, innovative or ambitious men, are ready to land on every shore . . .'

The population of Paris in the first half of the nineteenth century

The relative stability of the urban setting was in stark contrast with the rapid growth of the population attested by the following figures:

1801	547,000 inhabitants	
1811	623,000 inhabitants	
1817	714,000 inhabitants	
1831	786,000 inhabitants	(861,000 with the immediate suburbs)
1836	866,000 inhabitants	(969,000 with the immediate suburbs)
1841	936,000 inhabitants	(1,060,000 with the immediate suburbs)
1846	1,054,000 inhabitants	(1,227,000 with the immediate suburbs)

* In fact, scarcely 29,000.

These figures show that the population of 1801 grew by almost 93 per cent over the next forty-five years. The rate of growth would be even higher, at least toward the end of this period, if one added the figures for the immediate suburbs to those of the capital itself: between 1831 and 1842 the growth rate would be 26.5 per cent, instead of 20.0 per cent for the capital alone. This phenomenon of rapid growth followed a period of population loss during the revolutionary era.

The excess of births over deaths is insufficient to account for this situation: during the period 1831–46, this natural increase amounted to 36,000 persons out of a total increase of 268,000. By subtracting the first figure from the second, one obtains the net gain from migration, which was greater than the loss of population due to migration to the provinces. For it must be remembered that emigration from Paris, principally consisting of infants sent to be nursed in the country and retired persons who wished to spend the remainder of their days in the provinces, was by no means negligible. Louis Chevalier, who has studied the age distribution in the capital, has estimated that it amounted to about 30,000 persons in five years. Assuming that this calculation is correct, the actual rate of immigration would be 20,000 arrivals per year between 1831 and 1836, 16,000 between 1836 and 1841, and 25,000 between 1841 and 1846.

It is true of course that shifts in population fluctuated under the impact of political circumstances. The census figures for 1817 are inflated by the return of the discharged soldiers, while those for 1832 are marked by the departure of Parisians who had been frightened by the revolution. But neither the cholera of 1832, which exacted a toll of more than 44,000 victims, nor the constant disturbances of the first years of the July Monarchy could slow down the flow of immigrants. It took the economic crisis of 1846–7 and the revolution of 1848 to produce in 1851 a population figure slightly lower than that of 1846; but even this was only a temporary plateau in a pattern of growth that continued into the second half of the century.

Although this great current of immigration did include some bourgeois elements, it consisted mainly of proletarians who swelled the ranks of the capital's lower-class population. Many of the newcomers came from the area north of the Loire, above all from the departments closest to the capital, but also from northern France, Champagne, Burgundy, and parts of Lorraine. To the west, not many came from beyond Normandy. South of the Loire, most of the influx came from Auvergne, particularly the department of Cantal, where emigration became a mass phenomenon, originating in the seasonal migration of construction workers who spent the summer working in Paris. Over the years, the proportion of those who permanently settled in Paris became steadily higher. Unlike the individual immigrants from northern and eastern France, many of whom came from urban areas, the Auvergnats moved directly from their native villages to the capital. Furthermore, foreigners from Germany, Belgium, and Switzerland were also attracted by the lure of Paris. Higher wages than in the provinces, at least until the middle of the century, and above all a labour market of such scope and variety that serious unemployment seemed to be out of the question were among the essential reasons for this flow of immigrants.

The result was a replenishment of Paris's ethnic groups, although to some extent this development seems to have continued a trend already present in the eighteenth century. Samples taken in various parts of Paris indicate that at the end of the Ancien Regime many of the inhabitants were not native Parisians and already reveal the predominance of people from Ile-de-France and the eastern provinces. At any rate, the typical Parisian of the Romantic era was of less than average height, blond, and blue-eyed.

The newcomers preserved their provincial solidarities, and in certain respects Paris seemed to be made up of juxtaposed population groups who knew little about each other. The Burgundians who controlled the transit facilities of Bercy and the wine trade formed a tightly-knit community at Bercy itself: 'the Auvergnat water-carriers go to the *musette* [bagpipe dance] . . . never to the French dance hall . . . they keep to themselves like the Hebrews of Babylon'. Brutal village quarrels were sometimes fought out in the middle of Paris, and ties of loyalty to journeymen's associations, going back to their members' travels through France, could give rise to violent fighting.

In short, a whole population of youthful elements, many of them coming out of the unpolished, aggressive society of eastern France, had virtually no contact with the old Parisians. Camping out in furnished rooms or cohabiting, since they had rejected the old collective morality that had traditionally curbed young people's instincts in the provinces, they were packed into the old overcrowded neighbourhoods near the Hôtel de Ville, les Halles, the rue Saint-Denis, or the faubourgs Saint-Jacques and Saint-Merceau. In these places the crowding was such that the Arcis quarter had one inhabitant per 7 square metres and the neighbourhood of the market (despite the space occupied by les Halles itself), one inhabitant per 8 square metres. This crowding of people into sordid hovels was in itself a 'pathogenic factor', for, as soon as there was an economic slump, some of these uprooted young people slid into the 'dangerous classes' that lived on the fringes of the law; as soon as there was any political excitement it turned into rioting that was threatening not only to the government but to all property owners. The term 'Barbarians' naturally flowed into the pens of intellectuals, even those given to the charitable attitude of a Frédéric Ozanam. Most importantly, these young people inspired the bourgeois National Guard of Paris with a hostility that foreshadowed the June days of 1848.

The urban policy of the Restoration and the July Monarchy

Until 1834 the administration of Paris continued to be governed by the laws of the Consulate; two prefects, the prefect of police and the prefect of Seine, were charged, respectively, with maintaining order and managing the city's affairs, although in practice conflicts of competence between them were not unusual. The 24-member general council of the department, which was chosen by the authorities among the notables, assisted them in certain matters concerning both the city and the department. The city was divided into 12 *arrondissements*, each with its own mayor, a figurehead without any effective power; the *arrondissements* in turn were divided into four quarters (corresponding to the sections of the Revolution). The law of 20 April 1834 created an elected municipal council or, more precisely, formed a municipal council out of those members of the departmental council who had been elected by the city proper (3 per *arrondissement* or 36, out of a total of 48). This municipal council was elected by an electorate in which the regular voting citizens were reinforced by a rather small group of '*capacités*' (members of the Institute, professors at the Collège de France, doctors of medicine, etc.). Essentially, power remained in the hands of the prefect of Seine, but the debate about the budget by an elected body and the very calibre of its members (Arago, Laffitte, Périer, Ganneron, etc.) gave Rambuteau, a Burgundian who served in this capacity at the end of the July Monarchy (1833–48) rather less elbow-room than his predecessor, the Auvergnat Chabrol de Volvic (1812–30) had enjoyed at the time of the Restoration.

But then Chabrol had faced a different set of problems. The last years of the Empire had exhausted the city's resources, and it was necessary to borrow in order to meet the expenses of the allied occupation. Chabrol handled this disastrous situation in the best possible manner. A former pupil of the Polytechnique, he also had the merit of continuing the public works programme of the Napoleonic era. Although he abandoned the grandiose projects that as yet existed only on paper, he found a way in difficult times to carry through various projects, from the Madeleine to the slaughterhouse and the Halle aux vins. Chabrol was very much aware of the economic stimulus provided by major public works which 'give to large numbers of inhabitants the facilities they need and moreover serve to reactivate the circulation without which a large population cannot live with any degree of ease'. He was also aware of the need for a policy of monument-building, 'which will profit the entire country, for the multitudes of foreigners who are attracted to France by our arts will leave some of their wealth with us'. He would have liked to clear large sections of the old city by commissioning the entire public works programme to a private investment company, but had to settle for more modest accomplishments, among them the systematic development of pavements and quays and the linking of the Seine and the Ourcq canal by the Saint-Martin canal. Being an authoritarian administrator, he repeatedly tried to avoid paying indemnities for expropriated properties, claiming that buildings that had to be realigned following the widening of a street increased in value; but the Restoration governments had too much respect for property and the forms of legality to follow his reasoning.

Under Chabrol's administration, investment groups were formed for the purpose of creating new neighbourhoods in the empty spaces that still existed between the circle of boulevards and the outlying sections. The prefect favoured such projects but set certain requirements for these developments: streets had to be at least 10 metres wide and bordered by pavements, paving and lighting had to be installed by the developers. The building fever that gripped Paris between 1824 and 1827 caused wages in the building industry to soar and attracted large numbers of construction workers from the provinces. Among the investors involved in these different ventures were bankers, like Laffitte, architects – one of whom, Constantine, overextended himself to the point of bankruptcy – but also the duc de Bassano, Dosne (Thiers' father-in-law), and madame Hamelin, the erstwhile *merveilleuse*. This was the origin of a number of new Parisian neighbourhoods: the Europe quarter, traversed in 1835 by the Saint-Germain railway line to the gare Saint-Lazare, the Poissonière quarter near which the gare du Nord was located in 1846, the Beaujon quarter, which absorbed the amusement park that had gone bankrupt in 1825, the Saint-Georges quarter that continued toward Clichy, the Chaussée d'Antin quarter, the François I quarter near the ill-reputed allée des Veuves, where Colonel de Brack had a Renaissance house, transported stone by stone all the way from Moret and reconstructed for Mlle Mars as a gesture of love and publicity. The construction of new neighbourhoods took more time than the speculators had expected. By 1848 these new urban settlements, with the exception of the Saint-Georges quarter, which had the active backing of Dosne – perhaps because it was contiguous with an already well-established neighbourhood and perhaps because Thiers was able to provide some extra official help for it – still consisted only of isolated houses. The new housing policy, incidentally, accentuated a social segregation that was already under way and would come into its own in Haussmann's Paris: the rich moved from the city's central and eastern sections to the more luxurious neighbourhoods in the northern and western parts, where they were not exposed to the smoke and the foul odours that the prevailing winds carried to the Marais or the faubourg Saint-Antoine.

Comte de Rambuteau was not without kindness (he took a great interest in the care provided by the hospitals and their management) and subtlety. If we can believe his memoirs, he planned to give the Parisians 'water, air, and shade'. As far as water is concerned, he worked for the increased use of artesian wells, the installation of public fountains, and the bringing of water to individual houses, without increasing the amounts of water available in Paris. As for air, he seems to have concentrated on combating bad smells by reorganising the refuse-collection services and by having the refuse taken to the forest of Bondy rather than to Montfaucon, by building convex streets in order to eliminate the central stream with its odour of 'rotten cabbage', and by building seven or eight kilometres of cemented gutters every year. And for shade, he was an inveterate planter of trees. In other matters he continued the work of Chabrol. Chabrol had introduced gas-lighting; his successor increased the 63 lamps of 1830 to 8,600 in 1848. Rambuteau clearly understood certain major problems: he saw the importance of the suburban villages, which he connected by lateral roads; he realised that it was necessary to reorganise the central market and therefore approved the plans submitted by Baltard that were finally implemented under the Second Empire, and he attempted to clear that area by building the street that today bears his name. But Rambuteau was a 'budget man'. He failed to see the need for a major public works programme financed by credit. As far as he was concerned, improvements for the capital had to be paid for with moneys saved through tight management. That is why there is something petty about his accomplishments: for example, he continued the building of the rue Soufflot, which was already under way, by making it narrower. And the very rue Rambuteau of which he was so proud was only thirteen metres wide!

Aside from any official action, the Parisians aspired to greater mobility. People who had never left their neighbourhood except in extraordinary circumstances were becoming increasingly rare. In 1820 the transport company Laffitte et Caillard had the idea of connecting Paris with the suburbs by a service of light carriages running on a regular schedule. In 1828 the first omnibus, the *Madeleine-Bastille*, made its appearance; its extraordinary vogue caused a whole raft of rival companies to operate public conveyances under such names as *Ecossaises*, *Dames blanches*, *Hirondelles*, *Favorites*, etc. The following years brought the building of the first railway stations; the gare Saint-Lazare, opened in 1837, was conceived only as a temporary installation; the plan was to continue the railway line to the place de la Madeleine, and perhaps even to use the church as the permanent station. In 1840 it was decided to locate the gare du Nord on a part of the old Saint-Lazare property, close to the major thoroughfare in the flat area between the butte Montmartre and the butte Chaumont. The goods yard and the repair shops were placed beyond the city limits.

The building of monuments continued. Napoleon had considered monuments important to the formation of a civic spirit and had used them in connection with patriotic festivals. The Restoration initially followed his example: a chapel of atonement commemorated the cemetery where Louis XVI and Marie-Antoinette were buried, a Henri IV, cast out of the bronze from two statues of the Emperor, was placed on the Pont-Neuf, Bosio's Louis XIV decorated the place des Victoires, and of course many streets were renamed. But soon it became rather awkward to organise popular festivals in a Paris whose loyalism was not exactly strong. The July Monarchy made some attempts to return to earlier traditions. The Viennese writer Grillparzer has left a most vivid description of the celebration of Saint Philip's day, which was used as a pretext for great patriotic spectacles performed outdoors, free and open to the public, on the Champs-Elysées. The Thiers government held a solemn inauguration of the July column on the place de la Bastille, and when the remains of the victims of the Three Glorious Days were conveyed there, they were escorted by an immense procession to the strains of a funeral march executed by several hundred instrumentalists and singers. The music had been commissioned by Rémusat from 'a clever man whom some of his friends call a genius' (this happened to be Berlioz's *Symphonie funèbre et triomphale*!). The return of Napoleon's ashes was the occasion of a solemn celebration. In 1836 the Arc de Triomphe was finally inaugurated and restored to its original purpose. At the same time the place de la Concorde was also completed. Louis-Philippe felt that in this instance it would be wisest to forego any commemoration that might give rise to controversy. The obelisk sent by Mahomet Ali had arrived just in time to serve as an apolitical statement.

From the artistic point of view, the programme of monument-building carried out in the capital between 1815 and 1848 was not altogether insignificant. The Arc de Triomphe, for example, is a stately crowning adornment to an admirable perspective. Yet it is striking that this period (which, in the years before Haussmann destroyed many fine works left by earlier centuries, to the great indignation of Chateaubriand and Victor Hugo) was unable to find its own style: Vignon's Madeleine, which finally opened in 1842, and Brongniart's Bourse [stock exchange], completed in 1826 are marked by a heavy and composite classicism. The neo-Romanesque churches of Notre-Dame de Lorette (Lebas) or Saint-Vincent-de-Paul (Hittorf) are simply banal. The monumental fountains of Visconti (the Bishops' fountain of the place Saint-Sulpice and the French Rivers in the square Louvois) are academic. At the end of the period, the neo-Gothic style came into fashion: Viollet-le-Duc restored Notre-Dame, and in 1841 the German architect Gau began building the uninspired church of Sainte-Clothilde.

Parisian society

On the basis of her critical and comparative analysis of the sources that contain information about the material conditions of the Parisians, Adeline Daumard has been able to chart the property structure of Paris in 1820 and 1847 and to draw up a pyramid that is extremely revealing of the hierarchy of social conditions.

This pyramid 'rests on a wide basis of poverty'. Including those who made no declaration at all, 79.1 per cent of the deceased in 1820 and 80.6 per cent in 1847 left less than 500 francs at their death; 4.1 per cent left between 500 and 2,000 francs in each of the years considered. The number of Parisians buried at collective expense (81 per cent between 1821 and 1826 and 73 per cent between 1829 and 1848) or in a mass grave (78.6 per cent) confirms the impression that large segments of the population were close to indigence. One might wish to correct these figures somewhat by pointing out that on the average the poor died younger than the well-to-do. Another indication are the rents paid for housing: in 1817, 76.9 per cent of the renters paid less than 400 francs, while 52.5 per cent paid less than 150 francs (at the time, rents below 150 francs were used as the index of indigence and inability to pay taxes). Generally speaking, one can conclude that the lower class accounted for 75 to 80 per cent of the total population.

This class was made up of various elements: large numbers of domestic servants (almost 165,000 according to the statistics for 1841); a sizeable group of military men (7 per cent of the deceased were qualified as military men in 1831); many artisans working alone or with one or two journeymen; and shopkeepers who eked out a meagre living, barely able to meet the payments on the loans they had contracted. The most compact group were the wage labourers.

Given the availability of labour, capital, and convenient means of transportation, it would have been surprising if Paris had failed to become an industrial centre. Already under Napoleon – notwithstanding the Emperor's statement that the capital should be 'neither a great factory nor a vast counting house, but a city of palaces, a universal museum' – the industrial development of Paris had made remarkable strides, notably in the area of cotton spinning. The crisis at the end of the Napoleonic era, marked by the collapse of the Richard-Lenoir company, revealed certain inherent weaknesses in this sector. The food-related activities, on the other hand, were more solid and predominated throughout the first half of the nineteenth century. It is estimated that 50,000 persons were employed by the various markets and slaughterhouses in 1848. With few exceptions (for example the manufacture of fans), the Parisian industries worked primarily for Paris.

A major source of employment was the building industry. In the prosperous years of the Restoration construction workers (masons, carpenters, painters, roofers, plumbers, etc.) accounted for at least two-thirds of the permanent or seasonal immigrants to the capital. Even during a recession as acute as that of 1847, the Parisian building trades employed 41,600 workers or 12 per cent of the total labour force in more than 4,000 enterprises. The ratio between the number of workers and the number of enterprises, incidentally, indicates that, with the exception of a few construction companies, most of the building trade consisted of extremely small operations. This pattern was found in many other sectors as well, for example in the food industry, where 25,000 workers were employed by more than 3,600 enterprises, and in cabinet- and furniture-making, which continued to be an important activity that still employed over 10 per cent of the labour force in 1848. The rapidly developing chemical industries were more concentrated. Yet the new enterprises that sprang up along the Ourcq canal, at Pantin or Aubervilliers, the famous Javel works or Delessert's equally famous sugar refinery, do not tell the whole story. Side by side with these major enterprises, mostly located in the suburbs, there existed in Paris itself a host of artisanal operations engaged in the manufacture of laundry soap, perfumes, pharmaceuticals, and cosmetics. The cotton spinneries, for their part, had steadily declined from 67 in 1821 to 12 in 1847; significantly, those that subsisted were of modest size. The wool spinneries (16) were also in difficulty. One notes that the weaving trade as well tended to move to the provinces. (However, 11 per cent of the work force was still employed in the textile industry in 1847.) The middle years of the July Monarchy brought the emergence of the Parisian glass and especially metal industries that were destined to play such an important role; a whole raft of small machine shops had trained the skilled work force needed by the first major machine construction works (Beslay and, above all, Derosne et Cail, which employed several hundred workers). In 1843 the department of Seine already occupied eighth place among the French departments in the field of iron processing, seventh in steel processing. At the same date, the department was second, after Nord, in the number of steam engines (649), and third (after Nord and Loire) in the amount of steam generated by these machines.

Nonetheless, it is true that some types of industry were considered, and rightly so, specifically Parisian, namely, printing, engraving, the manufacture of fancy sweets – which were beginning to conquer foreign markets – and above all the production of the so-called 'articles of Paris'. These included handmade objects of gold, silver, and bronze, fancy trays and boards, and finely crafted goods of every kind, from hand-painted porcelain to religious articles produced in tiny workshops or by artisans who worked for an entrepreneur by themselves in their own homes. One wonders whether these trades employed 'old Parisians'. However that may be, they gave to the Parisian working class an elite whose taste for independence and good workmanship was to survive the industrial revolution.

Having analysed large numbers of death inventories, Adeline Daumard has attempted to establish a threshold between the bourgeoisie and the lower classes. She considers that the bourgeoisie accounted for 16.2 per cent of the population in 1820 and 14.6 per cent in 1847. Within the bourgeois classes, differences in wealth permit us to distinguish among the following groups: those who had fortunes between 2,000 and 20,000 francs represented 8.4 per cent of the total population in 1820 and 6.9 per cent in 1847; fortunes above 500,000 francs represented 0.3 per cent in 1820 and 0.8 per cent in 1847. These figures indicate that under the monarchy of limited suffrage the middle classes of Paris decreased somewhat, with those on the lower end of the scale joining the proletariat, while those on the upper end joined the wealthiest classes.

This classification by income level does not, of course, provide a rigid criterion; family tradition and occupational category played an essential role. There were newly rich shopkeepers (Balzac shows several characteristic examples), retired military men on half pay or poor lawyers who, by virtue of their connections, belonged to a higher social milieu, despite the importance of money. As for the *rentiers* or bond-holders, they were found at every level of society. Large numbers of former domestic servants and retired artisans lived on modest annuities, and the emotional plea on their behalf by the archbishop of Paris in the House of Peers tipped the scales against Villèle's conversion of the public bonds. It should be noted that there was considerable social mobility, and that one could show many examples of men of modest background who rose to great heights, sometimes returning to obscurity even more rapidly.

Artisans and shopkeepers formed the backbone of the lower bourgeoisie. Many of the smaller artisans had started out as workers; journeymen furniture-makers sometimes sold furniture they had made with wood bought on credit, thereby hoping to achieve a definitive change in status. The shopkeepers, who appear to have been extremely numerous despite the competition of the fancy-goods' shops that appeared during the Restoration under such names as '*Les Vêpres Siciliennes*', '*La Fille mal gardée*', or '*Le petit Saint-Thomas*', were frequently newcomers from the provinces, in some cases peddlers who invested their savings in a shop in Paris, but more often simple peasants. In addition, a hardworking shopkeeper's assistant could hope to rise into the employer class by marrying the boss's daughter.

The middling bourgeoisie, whose solidarities were often of a strictly professional character or based on neighbourhood relations, comprised a number of different groups: merchants, who in most cases were not yet appreciably different from industrial entrepreneurs, architects, physicians, other professionals (the ranks of the notaries and solicitors were constantly swelled by newcomers from the provinces) and middle- or upper-level civil servants.

The very rich included the old aristocracy, an amphibious class that occupied its Parisian mansions only in the winter and spent the summer at its châteaux in the provinces, which were often the main focus of their interests and their affections, at least under the July Monarchy. Also in this category were the wealthy owners of urban property and land, many of whom adopted a similar lifestyle in order to make the world forget the revolutionary origin of their wealth; bankers whose fortunes were grounded in multiple ventures, railways and property, industry and government bonds. Despite the meteoric rise of the Rothschilds and the daring of a Péreire, the Jewish banking community still occupied a secondary position, while the Protestant banking houses, many of them originally from Geneva (Delessert, Hottinguer, etc.) played an outstanding role. And no one in the Parisian bourgeoisie was more popular than the amazing business tycoon Jacques Laffitte, the very image of the self-made man of that day, possessed of a keen sense of his own time, but also given to a moralising liberalism and to conceited speech-making.

Paris did not escape the social segregation that pervaded the society of that time, as the patterns of recreation show better than anything else. On Sunday the worker went to drink the cheap wine of Suresnes in the taverns on the other side of the toll barrier, watched dog- or cock-fights at the barrière du combat, and participated in the famous *descente de la Courtille* on Mardi Gras. The shopkeeper shunned such vulgar pleasures and took his family to pick cherries at Montmorency or braved the risks of a donkey ride or a canoe trip on the Seine. Salons, fancy balls, and especially the opera attracted the upper classes. There were a few places, however, for example the boulevard theatres, where the different classes intermingled.

The political behaviour of the Parisians

It was only in 1820 and 1828 that the Restoration inscribed the tax-paying voters of Paris on the electoral lists separately from those of the suburbs. At the first date there were 8,459 Parisian voters, or 11 per cent of the population, and on the second their number had shrunk to 8,154 as a result of Villèle's tax reduction. The lowering of the tax qualification from 300 to 200 francs after the revolution of 1830 increased the electorate by 36 per cent, and this new electorate would grow by another 33 per cent until 1844, the year when a reform of the *patente* [licence fee paid by business and professional men] eliminated 2,000 voters from the lists. The lists of 1842 included 18,138 names, representing 19.4 per cent of the inhabitants, or 22.2 per cent if one counts those who were registered in the provinces. This was the highest proportion of voters in all of France.

How representative was this electorate of the population of the capital as a whole or of its elites? It can be observed that as early as 1828 a majority of the voters was subject to the *patente*, even if 77 per cent of them paid property taxes as well. If the *patente* had not been included in the tax qualification, as one of the famous ordinances of July 1830 attempted to do, one-third of the voters would have been stricken from the lists. Under the July Monarchy the lists of 1847 showed the following distribution of the capital's voters:

Economic occupations	65.1%
Liberal professions	10.1%
Public service	4.5%
Property owners	23.8%

This image of the distribution of wealth in Paris is distorted by a fiscal system that was unable to operate on the basis of real incomes. The fact is that the *patente* was extremely heavy in Paris, with the result that large numbers of businessmen, including those that were not well-to-do (more than two-thirds of the *patente*-paying voters paid between 200 and 500 francs in regular taxes) attained the status of voters. As narrowly defined as it was, the Parisian electorate included 1,555 wine merchants, 649 grocers, 307 butchers, and 300 bakers. On the other hand, the bondholders, most of the professional men, and all of the civil servants were taxed on the goods they purchased rather than on their incomes or salaries. Under this system the representatives of the 'City of Light' in the Chamber of Deputies were elected by 'the shopkeepers', at least under the July Monarchy.

Although in 1815 Paris had sent a delegation of pure royalists to the Incredible Chamber, by 1817 there was already a liberal opposition that took over three of the eight seats. In 1822 the law of the double vote benefited the liberals, both in the electoral *collèges* of the *arrondissements* and in the departmental *collège*. At that time the Parisian delegation was already composed of bankers and industrialists and the leaders of a more or less vocal opposition, men like Laffitte, Casimir Périer, De Laborde, and later Benjamin Constant, Dupont de l'Eure, and Delessert, would become prominent in 1830. The defence of the Charter was a stirring issue in Paris, and although the ultras regained some of their lost ground in the elections of 1824, November 1827 marked the triumph of the liberals. Some of the important notables were elected in two places; in such cases most of them opted for the provinces and ceded their Parisian seat to men of lesser stature.

Under the July Monarchy the Parisian bourgeoisie first hesitated between resistance and movement; eventually the constant threats to the established order seem to have caused it to lean more toward resistance. Yet beginning in 1842, at the very time when the provinces rallied to the Guizot government, Paris unequivocally went over to the opposition. On the eve of 1848 the Paris delegation ranged from moderate members of the opposition, like the banker Ganneron, all the way to radicals like Hippolyte Carnot and Marie.

The evolution of the National Guard, another embodiment of the Parisian bourgeoisie, took a parallel course. In 1814 the Guard had favourably received the king and uncomplainingly done onerous police duty during the occupation. But the government, knowing neither how to organise nor how to mollify it, eliminated the lower-class elements, which it considered unreliable, but failed to retain the well-to-do elements. Service in the Guard – which could be costly if it was done in uniform – consisted of tedious guard and patrol duty. Disenchantment soon gave way to outright disobedience: in 1823 the refusal of Sergeant Mercier, a braidmaker of the rue aux Fers, to remove the deputy Manuel from the Chamber, earned him an hour of glory. The National Guardsmen felt strongly that one of their essential prerogatives was the right to demonstrate their enthusiasm for or disapproval of the government's policies whenever they passed in review. This return to the consensus of Merovingian times caused a disagreement between the 'shopkeepers' and the heir to the third French dynasty: in April 1827, when certain legions of the National Guard had shouted: 'Down with the ministers,' and 'Down with the Jesuits!' during a review, Charles X dissolved the National Guard altogether. This fact unquestionably gave the liberals of Paris a larger margin of victory in November of that year.

Immediately after the revolution of 1830, the reconstituted National Guard of Paris played a leading role in the formation of that armed federation which, under the command of La Fayette, covered the entire country. After La Fayette's departure, when most of the provincial units were too discouraged to continue their activities, the Parisian Guard played an active role in suppressing rebellions. Commanded by the popular Lobau, entitled to elect its own officers, and full of zeal for the king, it seemed to be the soul of the new regime. But as soon as the regime was no longer threatened, boredom set in, and moreover there were calls for reform that would give every member of the Guard the right to vote. After 1840 the great reviews of the early years were no longer held. Called up in 1848, the National Guard exhibited an attitude that contributed to the old king's decision to abdicate.

Paris as a metropolis

The lure of Paris reached far beyond the frontiers of France, and the city was touted throughout Europe as a citadel of luxury and pleasure, a place of jewels and furnishings, elegant carriages and attire, art exhibits, gala evenings at the opera, and lovely women, too; its gay bohemian milieu had already made the reputation of Marie Duplessis, the model for the *Dame aux camélias*, and other actresses and singers of more talent than virtue, from Rachel to Fanny Elsser. But Paris was also a place for intellectual encounters, with its French and foreign salons, where the ancient art of conversation had one last flowering, reminiscent of the eighteenth century, among an elite passionately devoted to the things of the mind. This was also the era of the first clubs. Aristocratic men met in their *cercles*, and in addition to the *cercle de l'Univers* and the *cercle général du Commerce*, an Englishman, Lord Seymour, founded the Jockey Club. In this France of the notables, where most ministerial portfolios were held by men from the provinces, and where provincial capitals still carried a great deal of weight, Paris nonetheless played a unique role.

Its importance was related to the increased centralisation of the administration. The number of civil servants in Paris (25,000 under the Empire according to M. Tulard) grew under the July Monarchy, as did the scope of their concerns. Many of the deputies from the provinces spent their time soliciting favours from the various bureau chiefs on behalf of their constituents who, given the fact that only the propertied could vote, tended to form a homogeneous group. Tocqueville tells us that in modern nations civil servants increasingly take the place of an aristocracy.

In the economic realm, Paris came to set the course of the nation's business. Provincial industrialists secured their supplies and their markets through Parisian agents, who had taken over the functions formerly fulfilled by the great commercial fairs. The large enterprises of this era of industrial development had no choice but to have recourse to Parisian banks, for Paris was an unequalled money market. The Banque de France, which played an increasingly vital role in the country's economic growth, was directed by members of the Parisian banking community. The successful efforts of the *Ponts et Chaussées* administration to endow France with a star-shaped network of railways patterned after Louis XV's network of roads marked its abiding centralising tendency and gave definitive priority to exchanges between Paris and the provinces by attracting labour to the capital and making Paris the trans-shipment centre for the entire country.

In fact, the provincial notables implicitly acknowledged the superiority of Paris: the *collèges* Louis-le-Grand and Stanislas received pupils from western and southern France, and provincial families began to take a keen interest in sending a talented son to the Polytechnique, the very symbol of high social status. The notables themselves gradually lost their purely provincial character: 140 of the 445 provincial deputies in the Chamber of 1842 exercised a government function in Paris. As for the aristocracy, it was equally divided between Paris and the provinces ever since the Revolution had decimated the great families of the capital. At all levels of society, Paris lived on the substance of the provinces, assimilated their people, and tended to be admired by them as the very centre of culture, wealth, and power.

Conclusion

The evolution of France between 1815 and 1848 varied greatly according to region and class. Yet the outstanding difference between France and the rest of continental Europe lay in the fact that the attainments of the revolutionary era had created conditions in which aspirations toward liberty were satisfied to a greater extent than in other countries. Postulated, granted or repressed, public and indivitual liberties were the foundation of French public law; and while it is true that the concept of liberty itself had very different meanings in the different ideological camps, 'liberal', which had been synonymous with 'revolutionary' at the beginning of the Restoration, had virtually come to mean 'conservative' by the eve of 1848.

It was one of the positive aspects of liberalism that it fostered aspirations toward liberty. Under the Restoration and the July Monarchy France gave shelter to foreigners who fled from the oppression of their homelands, Italians like Mazzini, Polish freedom-fighters after 1831, and Germans (including, briefly, Karl Marx). But liberal aspirations always went beyond what governments were willing to concede. France was therefore perceived as a haven of liberty for foreign travellers, who realised that the powers of the State were limited and that the very foundation of the State, representative government, eventually followed by the extension of the electoral regime to local government, contributed to this liberty. Until the enactment of England's electoral reform in 1832, suffrage was more extensive in France than in any other European country. Political liberties went hand in hand with an equality that remained largely theoretical, inasmuch as it was a matter of civil rights only. Equality was a boon mainly to the bourgeoisie, which had better opportunities for participation in public life than anywhere else; in this respect the French bourgeoisie was better off than even the English aristocracy. Even before the end of the Restoration, the struggle for predominance between the aristocracy and the bourgeoisie was won by the latter, although this group too was composed largely of landowners. After 1830, this conflict continued only in a few departments of the west and the south. The gradual emergence of the parliamentary regime thus coincided with the ascendancy of the bourgeoisie and the rise of liberalism. But in coming into its own, liberalism changed its meaning, and the very fact that it became the ideology of those who held power spawned opposing ideologies. Nonetheless, the close interrelation among bourgeoisie, parliamentary regime, and liberalism laid the groundwork for the economic transformations that enabled France to join the industrial age: for this much we must give credit to the monarchy of limited suffrage; nor should we forget that the regime was almost completely successful in preserving peace in an era whose record in social and spiritual matters was by no means without blemish. Preserving the peace was not achieved, as has sometimes been said, by overly cautious policies on the part of Villèle or Guizot; after all, it was accompanied by the expansion of France's political and economic interests in Europe, the Mediterranean, the Near East, and even to the shores and islands of the Pacific.

The monarchical system of limited suffrage that ruled France between 1815 and 1848 was a transitional regime in a three-fold sense. From the institutional point of view, it accustomed public opinion to the representative regime. To be sure, the adoption of universal suffrage in 1848 wrought a profound change in French political life, since the very concept of the vote was overturned when voting became a right rather than a public function. Yet although the system of property qualifications was abruptly abolished, it left traces, not in the electoral process itself (although it did familiarise the French with the system of direct suffrage and although the July Monarchy's practice of the *scrutin d'arrondissement* [voting on the level of the *arrondissement*] became an important part of the electoral process under the Third and the Fifth Republic), but in the functioning of the parliamentary system. After 1830 the system of property qualifications gradually evolved into a parliamentary regime, but it exerted an abiding influence, in large measure because of the notables' distrust of the two subsequent regimes.

The monarchy of limited suffrage rallied the French politicians to bicameralism as well as to the preponderance of the elected Chamber (which was later elected by direct voting); for more than a century it also defined the traits needed by the successful French politician, who had to know how to speak at the tribune and to manage his influential constituents' interests in the various ministerial offices. The moral preaching of a Guizot, coupled with the unsavoury compromises that often characterised electoral or parliamentary coalitions at the end of Louis-Philippe's reign, already foreshadowed the close relationship between politics and business that would be found so often under the regime of universal suffrage, particularly on the level of the *arrondissement*. In large part, the system of property qualifications was in a position to slant the parliamentary system toward the interests of the bourgeoisie because of the growing power of public opinion and the press, which expressed the ideas of the wealthy and the educated and even propagated them among some segments of the popular classes. The system of property qualifications gave rise to the politics of the notables, who would survive the end of limited suffrage.

The notables represented the ruling class of a society in transition between the more rigid hierarchy of a society of orders in which an aristocracy of birth predominated and the more anonymous domination of the great capitalist, whose resources and prestige were derived from profit in a society where economic relations and an industrial economy were paramount. It is certainly true that several types of notables existed side by side in France under the monarchy of limited suffrage; yet the dissimilarities between a Breton aristocrat like the comte d'Andigné and a leading industrialist of Mulhouse like Koechlin, great as they seem to be at first sight, should not obscure the fact that they wielded analogous forms of power over their peasants and their workers, respectively. In both cases economic, social, and political power was concentrated in the hands of the same man. Both wielded a power that was at once personal, long established in the geographical area, and willingly accepted by those over whom it was exerted. Indeed, this last characteristic is the most original feature of the period; it can be said that the power of the notables was perfectly suited to a society in which all social relations were of an interpersonal nature. The notable's power was based on more than ability to apply pressure (which was provided by his wealth), on powerful allies (which were likely to be at the disposal of one who belonged to a well-established family and a network of kinship), or on institutions (which, in a regime of property qualifications, by definition privileged the wealthy by giving them a monopoly of political power); it was also based on a concensus shared by most of the population and carefully nurtured by the notables themselves, who promoted or controlled a whole system of norms, values, and symbols that characterised the basic identity of French society. Only a minority remained free of this social and mental conformism, especially in Paris and in some of the big cities that produced the two antitheses of the notable, the revolutionary and the parvenu; but then the former had often come from the milieu of the notables, while the latter sought to become part of it. The notable defined by his assets (ownership), his family (he was the son or the protégé of a notable), and his competence (reading and knowledge) was well suited for leadership in a changing society whose horizons were expanding. Economic relations, as much as people's mentalities, began at least to expand beyond the parish, the commune, or the *arrondissement*. The emergence of a national economy and nation-wide currents of public opinion brought a new need for intermediaries. It was the notable who played this role, mediating between the

State and the population, Paris or other cities and the countryside. An intermediary as well between tradition (by virtue of his family background) and the future, he understood his and his contemporaries' time. Yet this role of intermediary was gradually modified by the economic evolution; industrial development and especially the new railways brought ever greater concentration of economic power. For every industrialist or manager of a new company who extended his influence over a whole department, many a notable experienced the decline of his influence at the end of the July Monarchy; most of the time, however, the notable's position was preserved, thanks to the persistent economic rivalries between localities and social interests. This 'local spirit' – a favourite expression of the time – was in keeping with a predominantly rural society and with the domination of the notables.

New economic issues also unsettled the organisation of society. The rule of the notables coincided with a weakening of the State, since historical reasons had prompted the regime that followed the authoritarian rule of Napoleon to attenuate the intrusion of the representatives of the State, while ideological reasons caused liberalism to insist on the curbing of the State's powers, especially after 1830. Notables in local government, industrialists in their factories, and great landowners on their estates were all-powerful, and the government, unwilling to interfere with this power, adjusted its role accordingly. Subjected to opposing pressures, the State tried to solve every problem by compromise, relied on precedent and custom, and avoided innovation wherever possible. Yet technological and economic changes forced it to face new situations; the State was called upon to act and arbitrate in such matters as railway construction, expropriations for public purposes, the formation of limited companies, and health hazards, often involving factories. The pressures brought to bear on the State were becoming increasingly stronger, and those who sought to control or use it for their own ends sought to strengthen it; in doing so, they threatened to break the traditional local dominance of the notables. The notables' power base was in the provinces, but now the fate of the departments was increasingly decided from Paris. The historical and demographic role of Paris, which had engendered the centralised State in the first place, now also perpetuated its growth. The development of the representative regime further strengthened the influence of Paris, for here was the seat of the Chambers and of the government, here public opinion was moulded, expressed in newspapers and formed in the schools, here major business transactions were negotiated. Yet Paris, with its stark contrasts in social conditions, rejected the hierarchy and the consensus that held the world of the notables together; twice – in 1830 and again in 1848 – the capital broke out of the political frame of reference that informed the power of the notables, but in the long run it was unable to impose a new democratic order on the rest of France.

Finally, the monarchy of limited suffrage represented a period of ideological transition in its attempt to establish a *juste milieu* (the expression will always remain attached to it) between order and freedom. As the successor to the despotic rule of Napoleon, the Restoration had awakened the desire for liberties more than it had granted them, with the result that it was overthrown by the aspirations that had been created in this manner. Order, on the other hand, was most important to those who most fully enjoyed the existing liberties. Since they alone were in a position to express a political opinion, it is not surprising that most of them were satisfied. In the course of its evolution, liberalism became more and more similar to the traditionalist attitude it had so violently opposed in the past, and this rapprochement provoked a split among the liberals and caused some of them to demand liberties for all (peoples and individuals), thereby contributing to the rise of a nation-wide democratic movement. Arising from the same disenchantment, the socialist critique of liberalism was until 1848 considered utopian by most segments of the population. A middle ground between traditionalism with its idealised image of the past and socialism with its dreams of the future, liberalism in the years after 1830 was above all an ideology designed to justify the existing situation.

Under the label of eclecticism, the July Monarchy evolved a philosophy that sought to combine spiritualism and rationalism, for liberalism, which did not carry its liberal aspirations far enough to consider democracy an option, was also unwilling to let its anticlericalism turn into free-thinking and materialism.

From the political, economic, and ideological point of view, then, the era of the monarchy of limited suffrage was a period of transition that benefited mainly the group referred to at the time as the middle classes, in other words, the bourgeoisie. But this rise of the bourgeoisie, which led to its undisputed preponderance after 1830, had as its counterpart a growing dissension within the bourgeoisie itself (which at the time faced few threats from the other classes) and an individualism that reduced its sense of social and even national responsibility.

The regime of limited suffrage, which in other countries like Belgium or England existed longer than in France, was suited to a particular type of political regime as well as to a particular type of society. In France it disappeared at a time when it seemed to be more firmly entrenched than ever, considering that political evolution of any kind had long been blocked by the restrictive and rigid concept of government held by France's ruling classes. Yet limited suffrage did serve to establish a solidarity between the bourgeoisie and the parliamentary system that would survive this period.

In 1848 the State was not strong enough to withstand the popular onslaught, but the notables survived its demise all the more easily as they did not exhaust themselves in the defence of the very regime that had enabled them to consolidate their preponderance.

Bibliography

Reference works:
For a more complete bibliography, see the following bibliographical works:
1. P. Caron and H. Stein, *Répertoire bibliographique de l'histoire de France*, Nendeln, 1977
2. *Bibliographie annuelle de l'histoire de France*, Paris, 1956–
More detailed bibliographical indications can be found in two works that were frequently used by the authors:
3. J. Vidalenc, *La Société française de 1815 à 1848*, I, *Le Peuple des campagnes*, Paris, 1970; II, *Le Peuple des villes et des bourgs*, Paris, 1973
4. A. J. Tudesq, *Les Grands Notables en France 1840–1849*, 2 vols., Paris, 1964
and in the
5. *Tables analytiques des publications de la Société d'histoire de la révolution de 1848* L. Dubief (ed.), La Roche-sur-Yon, 1957

Sources

The annual reports of the departments and the local communities in the series LC of the catalogue for French history in the Bibliothèque Nationale and, particularly
6. *Almanach royal 1816-1930*, Paris. After 1831 titled *Almanach royal et national*, Paris
Works of contemporary authors
7. Ch. Dupin, *Forces productives et commerciales de la France*, 2 vols., Paris, 1827
8. E. de Jouy, *L'Hermite en province*, Paris, 1818–22
9. V. A. Malte-Brun, *La France illustrée; géographie, histoire, administration et statistique*, 2 vols., Paris, 1853
10. *Statistique générale de la France*, 1st series, Paris, Imprimerie royale, 1840–4
11. A. de Villeneuve-Bargemont, *Economie politique chrétienne*, 3 vols., Paris, 1834
12. M. Villermé, *Tableau physique et moral des ouvriers employés dans les manufactures de coton, de laine et de soie*, Paris, 1840
The works of Balzac and Stendhal (especially the *Mémoires d'un touriste*) are indispensable sources.
   The following list presents only the most outstanding testimony left by contemporary authors (*mémoires*, correspondence, diaries).
13. Baron de Barante, *Souvenirs*, 8 vols., Paris, 1890–1901
14. Ch. Beslay, *Mes souvenirs*, Paris, 1873
15. J.-C., comte Beugnot, *Mémoires*, 2 vols., Paris, 1866
16. V., duc de Broglie, *Souvenirs*, 4 vols., 1886
17. Comtesse de Boigne, *Récits d'une tante*, 5 vols., Paris, 1921–3

18. F.-R., vicomte de Chateaubriand, *Mémoires d'outre-tombe* (M. Levaillant, ed.), 3rd edn, 2 vols., Paris, 1957
19. Count Ferrand, *Mémoires* . . . , Paris, 1897
20. Baron A. F. Frenilly, *Souvenirs* . . . (*1768–1828*), Paris, 1808
21. F. Guizot, *Mémoires pour servir à l'histoire de mon temps*, 7 vols., Paris, 1858–67
22. Baron C. d'Haussez, *Mémoires* . . . , 2 vols., Paris, 1896–7
23. Marshal McDonald, *Souvenirs* . . . , Paris, 1892
24. A. de Marmont (Marshal), *Mémoires*, 9 vols., Paris, 1857
25. P. Mérimée, *Correspondance générale*, I–V, Paris, 1941–7
26. Count L. M. Molé, *Le Comte Molé . . . sa vie, ses mémoires*, 6 vols., Paris, 1922–30
27. Count de Montalivet, *Fragments et souvenirs*, 2 vols. (I. *1810–32*. II. *1836–48*), Paris, 1899–1900
28. E. D. Pasquier, *Histoire de mon temps*, 6 vols., Paris, 1893–5
29. L. Passy, *Le Marquis de Blosseville, Souvenirs*, Evreux, 1898
30. Ch. de Rémusat, *Mémoires de ma vie*, I–IV, Paris, 1958–62
31. A., duc de Richelieu, *Lettres . . . au marquis d'Osmond (1816–1818)*, Paris, 1939
32. Sainte-Beuve, *Correspondance*, I–VIII, Paris and Toulouse, 1935–59
33. Baron Sers, *Souvenirs d'un préfet de la monarchie*, Paris, 1906
34. A. de Tocqueville, *Oeuvres complètes* (III. *Ecrits et discours; politiques*. VIII. *Correspondance Tocqueville–Beaumont*. XI. *Correspondance Tocqueville–Ampère et Tocqueville–Royer-Collard*), J.-P. Mayer (general ed.), Paris, 1951
35. J., comte de Villèle, *Mémoires et correspondance*, 5 vols., Paris, 1888–90
36. Baron E. de Vitrolles, *Mémoires*, 3 vols., Paris, 1884. Reprinted 1950–2 in 2 vols.

Basic Studies

a. Political history and institutions

37. D. Bagge, *Les Idées politiques en France sous la Restauration*, Paris, 1952
38. Barthélemy, *L'Introduction du régime parlementaire en France, sous Louis XVIII et Charles X*, Paris, 1904
39. P. Bastid, *Benjamin Constant et sa doctrine*, 2 vols., Paris, 1966
40. E. Beau de Lomenie, *La Carrière politique de Chateaubriand*, 2 vols., Paris, 1929
41. Cl. Bellanger, J. Godechot *et al.* (general eds.), *Histoire générale de la presse française*, II, Paris, 1969
42. G. de Bertier de Sauvigny, *La Restauration*, Paris, 1963
43. — *La Révolution de 1830 en France*, Paris, 1970
44. — *Un type d'ultraroyaliste; le comte Bertier de Sauvigny et l'énigme de la Congrégation*, Paris, 1948
45. P. Bruguière, *La Première Restauration et son budget*, Paris, 1969
46. S. Charlety, *La Restauration*, Paris, 1921
47. — *La Monarchie de Juillet*, Paris, 1921 (vols. IV and V of the *Histoire de France contemporaine*, Ernest Lavisse (general ed.))
48. M. Deslandres, *Histoire constitutionnelle de la France*, II, Paris, 1932
49. L. Diez del Corral, *El liberalismo doctrinal*, Madrid, 1945
50. P. Duvergier de Hauranne, *Histoire du gouvernement parlementaire en France 1814–1848*, 10 vols., Paris, 1857–71
51. *Etudes sur les mouvements nationaux et liberaux de 1830*, Société d'histoire moderne, Paris, 1932
52. Eymard, *La Politique financière de la Restauration*, Paris, 1924

53. J. Fouques-Duparc, *Le Troisième Richelieu, libérateur du territoire en 1815*, Paris, 1940
54. J. Fourcassié, *Villèle*, Paris, 1954
55. J.-P. Garnier, *Charles X, le roi, le proscrit*, Paris, 1967
56. L. Girard, *Etudes comparées des mouvements révolutionnaires en France de 1830, 1848 et 1870–71*, mimeograph, Paris, 1960
57. — *La Garde nationale 1814–1871*, Paris, 1964
58. — *Le Libéralisme en France de 1814 à 1848, doctrine et mouvement*, mimeograph, Paris, 1966 and 1967
59. P. Guiral, *Le Libéralisme en France de 1815 à 1870*, in *Tendances politiques dans la vie française*, conference, Paris, 1960
60. D. Johnson, *Guizot, Aspects of French History*, London, 1963
61. S. Kent, *Electoral procedure under Louis-Philippe*, New Haven, 1937
62. G. Lacour-Gayet, *Talleyrand*, III, *1815–1838*, Paris, 1931
63. P. de la Gorce, *La Restauration*, 2 vols., (I. *Louis XVIII*. II. *Charles X*), Paris, 1928
64. R. Langeron, *Royer-Collard*, Paris, 1956
65. — *Decazes, ministre du roi*, Paris, 1960
66. Ch. Ledré, *La Presse à l'assaut de la monarchie*, Paris, 1960
67. E. Le Gallo, *Les Cent-Jours*, Paris, 1924
68. J. Lucas-Dubreton, *Louis XVIII*, Paris, 1952
69. L. Madelin, *Fouché 1759–1820*, Paris, 1900
70. S. Mitard, *Les Origines du radicalisme démocratique, l'affaire Ledru-Rollin*, Paris, 1952
71. J.-J. Oechslin, *Le Mouvement ultra royaliste sous la Restauration*, Paris, 1960
72. J. Orieux, *Talleyrand ou le sphinx incompris*, Paris, 1970
73. E. de Perceval, *Un adversaire de Napoléon, le vicomte Lainé*, Paris, 1926
74. G. Perreux, *Au temps des sociétés secrètes. La propagande républicaine au début de la monarchie de Juillet*, Paris, 1931
75. D. H. Pinkney, 'A new look at the French Revolution of 1830', *Review of Politics*, XXIII, 1961, pp. 490–506
76. F. Ponteil, *La Chute de Napoléon Ier et la Crise française de 1814–1815*, Paris, 1943
77. — *Les Institutions de la France de 1814 à 1870*, Paris, 1966
78. Ch. H. Pouthas, *Guizot pendant la Restauration*, Paris, 1923
79. — *Histoire politique de la Restauration*, mimeograph, Paris, 1947
80. R. Rémond, *La Droite en France de 1815 à nos jours*, Paris, 1954
81. D. P. Resnick, *The White Terror and the political reaction after Waterloo*, Cambridge, Mass., 1966
82. P. Simon, *L'Elaboration de la Charte constitutionnelle de 1814*, Paris, 1906
83. A. B. Spitzer, *Old hatreds, young hopes. The French Carbonari against the Bourbon Restoration*, Cambridge. Mass., 1971
84. P. Thureau-Dangin, *Histoire de la monarchie de Juillet 1884–1892*, 7 vols., Paris, 1884–92
85. A. J. Tudesq, *La Démocratie en France depuis 1815*, Paris, 1971
86. J. Vidalenc, *Les Demi-soldes*, Paris, 1955

b. Foreign and colonial policy

87. J. Ancel, *Manuel historique de la question d'Orient*, Paris, 1927
88. R. André, *L'Occupation de la France par les Alliés en 1815*, Paris, 1921
89. G. Bertier de Sauvigny, *Metternich et la France après le congrès de Vienne. I. De*

Napoléon à Decazes, Paris, 1968. II. *Les Grands Congrès*, Paris, 1970. III. *Le règne de Charles X*, Paris, 1972

90. J. Ch. Biaudet, *La Suisse et la monarchie de Juillet (1830–1838)*, Lausanne, 1941
91. Marshal Bugeaud, *Par l'épée et par la charrue. Ecrits et discours*, Paris, 1948
92. A. Bussière, 'Le Maréchal Bugeaud et la colonisation de l'Algérie', *Revue des deux-mondes*, 1853
93. J. Demontès, *La Colonisation militaire sous Bugeaud*, Paris, 1918
94. H. T. Deschamps, *La Belgique devant la France de Juillet*, Paris, 1956
95. E. Driault, *La Question d'Orient*, Paris, 1898
96. E. Driault and M. Lhéritier, *Histoire diplomatique de la Grèce de 1821 à nos jours*, I and II, Paris, 1924
97. Ch. Dupuis, 'La Sainte-Alliance et le Directoire européen de 1815 à 1818', *Revue d'histoire diplomatique*, 1934
98. J.-P. Faivre, *L'Expansion française dans le Pacifique de 1800 à 1842*, Paris, 1953
99. — *Le Contre-Amiral Hamelin et la Marine française*, Paris, 1962
100. E. F. Gautier, *Un siècle de colonisation. Etudes au microscope*, Paris, 1930
101. E. de Guichen, *La Révolution de Juillet et l'Europe*, Paris, 1917
102. — *La Crise d'Orient de 1839 à 1841 et l'Europe*, Paris, 1922
103. R. Guyot, *La Première Entente cordiale*, Paris, 1925
104. M. Huisman, 'Quelques dessous de la conférence de Londres', *Revue d'histoire moderne*, 1934
105. Ch. A. Julien, *Histoire de l'Algérie contemporaine. I. La conquête et les débuts de la colonisation*, Paris, 1964
106. S. Mastellone, *La politica estera del Guizot (1840–1847)*, Florence, 1957
107. H. Nicolson, *The Congress of Vienna. A study in allied unity, 1812–1822*, London, 1946
108. V. A. Nigohosian, *La Libération du territoire après Waterloo (1915–18)*, Paris, 1929
109. H. Pirenne, *Histoire de Belgique*, III, Brussels, 1948
110. J.-J. Pirenne, *La Sainte-Alliance*, 2 vols., Neufchâtel, 1946–9
111. Ch.-H. Pouthas, *Chateaubriand diplomate et ministre*, Livre du centenaire, Paris, 1949
112. — *La Politique étrangère de la France sous la monarchie constitutionnelle*, mimeograph, Paris, 1948
113. — 'La Politique de Thiers pendant la crise de 1840', *Revue historique*, 1938
114. V. J. Puryear, *France and the Levant from the Bourbon Restoration to the Peace of Kutiah*, Berkeley, 1941
115. P. Rain, *L'Europe et la restauration des Bourbons*, Paris, 1908
116. P. Renouvin, *Histoire des relations internationales. V. Le XIXᵉ siècle*, I, Paris, 1954
117. W. S. Robertson, *France and Latin American Independence*, Baltimore, 1939
118. Ch. Schefer, *L'Algérie et l'évolution de la colonisation française*, Paris, 1928
119. J. Stengers, 'Sentiment national, sentiment orangiste et sentiment français à l'aube de notre indépendance', *Revue belge de philologie et d'histoire*, 1950
120. J. T amond and A. Reussner, *Eléments d'histoire maritime et coloniale contemporaine (1815–1914)*, Paris, 1943
121. Ch. Webster, *The foreign policy of Castlereagh, 1815–1922*, London, 1925
122. — *The Congress of Vienna*, London, 1934
123. — *The foreign policy of Palmerston (1830–1841)*, 2 vols., London, 1951

c. Economy and society

124. J.-P. Aguet, *Contribution à l'histoire du mouvement ouvrier français, 1830–47*; les *grèves sous la Monarchie de Juillet*, Geneva, 1954
125. D. Ansart, *Saint-Simon*, Paris, 1969
126. A. Audiganne, *Les Populations ouvrières et les industries de la France dans le mouvement social du XIXe siècle*, Paris, 1854
127. Ch. Ballot, *L'Introduction du machinisme dans l'industrie française*, Paris, 1923
128. J. Bache, M. Audin, *et al.*, *Histoire générale des techniques* (M. Daumas, general ed.). III. *L'Expansion du machinisme*, Paris, 1968
129. F. Bedarida and Cl. Fohlen, *Histoire générale du travail* (L. H. Parias, general ed.). III. *L'Ere des révolutions (1765–1914)*, Paris, 1960
130. G. and H. Bourgin, *Le Régime de l'industrie en France de 1814 à 1830*, 3 vols., Paris, 1912–41
    F. Braudel and E. Labrousse (general eds.), *Histoire économique et sociale de la France*, III, 2 vols., Paris, 1976
131. R. E. Cameron, *La France et le développement économique de l'Europe*, Paris, 1971
132. H. Cavaillès, *La Route française, son histoire, sa fonction. Etude de géographie humaine*, Paris, 1946
133. A. Chabert, *Essai sur les mouvements des prix en France de 1798 à 1820*, Paris, 1943
134. — *Essai sur les mouvements des revenus et de l'activité économique en France de 1798 à 1820*, Paris, 1949
135. L. Chevalier (general ed.), *Le Choléra de 1832*, La Roche-sur-Yon, 1958
    A. Dumard (general ed.), *Les Fortunes françaises au XIXe siècle*, Paris, 1973
136. A. Dauzet, *Le Siècle des chemins de fer en France*, Fontenay-aux-Roses, 1948
137. E. Dolléans, *Proudhon*, Paris, 1948
    — *Histoire du mouvement ouvrier*. I. *1830–1871*. Paris, 1936
    G. Duby and A. Wallon (general eds.), *Histoire de la France rurale*. III. *Apogée et Crise de la civilisation paysanne*, Paris, 1976
138. A. L. Dunham, *La Révolution industrielle en France 1814–1848*, Paris, 1953
139. O. Festy, *Le Mouvement ouvrier au début de la monarchie de Juillet*, Paris, 1908
140. Cl. Fohlen, *Qu'est-ce que la révolution industrielle?*, Paris, 1971
    — *Charbon et Révolution industrielle en France (1815–1850)*, Conference Papers, 'Charbon et sciences humaines', Paris and the Hague, 1966
141. B. Gille, *La Banque et le Crédit en France de 1815 à 1848*, Paris, 1959
142. — *Histoire de la maison Rothschild*. I. *Des origines à 1848*, Paris, 1965
143. — *Recherche sur la formation de la grande entreprise capitaliste 1815–1848*, Paris, 1959
144. P. Gonnet, 'Esquisse de la crise économique en France de 1927 à 1832', *Revue d'histoire économique et sociale*, 1955
145. L. M. Jouffroy, *La Ligue de Paris à la frontière d'Allemagne (1815–1852)*, 3 vols., Paris, 1952
146. E. Labrousse (general ed.), *Aspects de la crise et de la dépression de l'économie française au milieu du XIXe siècle*, La Roche-sur-Yon, 1956
147. P. C. Laurent de Villedeuil, *Bibliographie des chemins de fer*, 1906
148. L. de Lavergne, *Economie rurale de la France*, Paris, 1860
149. M. Leroy, *Histoire des idées sociales en France*. II. *De Babeuf à Tocqueville*. III. *D'Auguste Comte à Proudhon*, Paris, 1950–4
150. M. Lévy-Leboyer, *Les Banques européennes et l'industrialisation internationale dans la première moitié du XIXe siècle*, Paris, 1964

151. — 'La Croissance économique en France au XIXe siècle', *Annales ESC*, July–August 1968

152. J. Marczewski (general ed.), *Histoire quantitative de l'économie française*, Paris, 1961

153. E. Marjolin, 'Troubles provoqués en France par la disette de 1816–1817', *Revue d'histoire moderne*, 1933

154. Ch. Morazé, *La France bourgeoise*, Paris, 1947

155. G. Palmade, *Capitalisme et capitalistes français au XIXe siècle*, Paris, 1961

156. Ch. H. Pouthas, *La Population française pendant la première moitié du XIXe siècle*, Paris, 1956

157. P. L. Reynaud, *J.-B. Say, textes choisis et préface*, Paris, 1953

158. H. Rigaudas-Weiss, *Les Enquêtes ouvrières en France entre 1838 et 1858*, Paris, 1936

159. R. Scherer, *Fourier ou la Contestation globale*, Paris, 1970

160. H. See, *La Vie économique de la France sous la monarchie censitaire 1815–1848*, Paris, 1927

161. J. Vial, *L'Industrialisation de la sidérurgie français 1814–1864*, Paris, 1967

162. J. Vidalenc, 'Notes sur la vigne en France de 1789 à la fin de la Restauration', *Annales de la faculté de Lettres d'Aix*, 1955

d. Cultural and religious issues

163. R. Baschet, *E. J. Delécluze, témoin de son temps (1781–1863)*, Paris, 1942

164. R. Bray, *Chronologie du romantisme (1804–1830)*, Paris, 1932

165. J. Chantavoine and J. Gaudefroy-Demombynes, *Le Romantisme dans la musique européenne*, Paris, 1955

166. A. Dansette, *Histoire religieuse de la France contemporaine*, Paris, 1948

167. P. Delaunay, *D'une révolution à l'autre (1789–1848) ; l'évolution des théories et de la pratique médicale*, Brussels, n.d.

168. S. R. Derre, *Lamennais, ses amis et le mouvement des idées à l'époque romantique*, Paris, 1962

169. P. Droulers, 'Des évêques parlent de la question ouvrière en France avant 1848', *Revue d'action populaire*, April 1961

170. N. Dufourq, *La Musique française*, Paris, 1949

171. J. B. Duroselle, *Les Débuts du catholicisme social en France (1822–1870)*, Paris, 1951

172. H. Focillon, *La Peinture française au XIXe siècle*, Paris, 1928

173. A. Garnier, *Frayssinous. Son rôle dans l'Université sous la Restauration (1822–1828)*, Paris, 1925

174. A. S. George, *The development of French Romanticism; the impact of the industrial revolution on literature*, Syracuse, 1955

175. G. Gerbod, *La Condition universitaire en France au XIXe siècle*, Paris, 1966

176. H. Gouhier, *La Jeunesse d'Auguste Comte et la formation du positivisme*, 3 vols., Paris, 1933–41

177. L. Hautecoeur, *Littérature et peinture*, Paris, 1942

178. — *L'urbanisme à Paris de la Renaissance à la monarchie de Juillet*, Paris, 1957

179. — *Paris, connaissance d'une capitale*, Paris, 1961

180. E. Herriot, *Mme Récamier et ses amis*, Paris, 1904

181. C. A. E. Jensen, *L'évolution du romantisme, l'année 1826*, Paris, 1959

182. P. Labracherie, *La Vie quotidienne de la bohème littéraire au XIXe siècle*, Paris, 1967

183. J. Lucas-Dubreton, *Le Culte de Napoléon*, Paris, 1960
184. Luc-Benoist, *La Sculpture romantique*, Paris, 1928
185. P. Moreau, *Histoire de la littérature française* (J. Calvert, general ed.). VIII. *Le Romantisme*, Paris, 1957
186. F. Picavet, *Les Idéologues*, Paris, 1897
187. L. Réau, *L'Ere romantique. Les arts plastiques*, Paris, 1949
188. D. Robert, *Les Eglises réformées en France*, 1961
189. C. A. Sainte-Beuve, *Tableau historique et critique de la poésie française et du théâtre français au XVIᵉ siècle*, 2 vols., Paris, 1828
190. E. Sevrin, *Les Missions religieuses en France sous la Restauration*, 2 vols., Paris, 1948–59
191. — *Un évêque militant et gallican au XIXᵉ siècle; Mgr Clausel de Montals, évêque de Chartres*, 2 vols., Paris, 1955
192. J. Touchard, *La Gloire de Béranger*, 2 vols., Paris, 1967
193. Ph. Van Thiegem, *Le Romantisme dans la littérature européenne*, Paris, 1969

The Regions

Since 1969 a series of regional histories entitled *L'Univers de la France* is being published at Toulouse under the direction of Philippe Wolff. In the volumes published so far, the nineteenth century occupies only a minor position, except in the works on Alsace and Brittany. However, all these volumes contain valuable bibliographical material. Many histories of French provinces have been published in the Que sais-je? series. Some of these (M. Crubillier and Ch. Juillard, *Histoire de Champagne* and F. D. Dornic, *Histoire du Maine*, and some others) are useful for studying the nineteenth century. But here again, bibliographical material can be found.

a. The western regions

194. Y. Brékilien, *La Vie quotidienne des paysans en Bretagne au XIXᵉ siècle*, Paris, 1966
195. Créveil, *1848 et les révolutions du XIXᵉ siècle* (La Condition ouvrière et la crise de 1847 à Nantes), 1948
     G. Désert, *Une société rurale au XIXᵉ siècle, les paysans du Calvados (1815–1895)*, Lille, 1975
196. M. Faugeras, *Le Diocèse de Nantes sous la monarchie censitaire*, 2 vols., Fontenay-le-Comte, 1964
197. R. de Felice, *La Basse-Normandie*, Paris, 1907
198. G. Frambourg, *Un philanthrope et démocrate nantais; le Dr Guépier*, Nantes, 1964
199. E. Gabory, *Les Bourbons et la Vendée*, Paris, 1923
200. P. Jeulin, *L'Evolution du pont de Nantes*, Paris, 1931
201. Cl. Langlois, *Le Diocèse de Vannes*, unpublished thesis, 1971
202. D. Leclerc-Thouin, *L'Agriculture de l'Ouest de la France particulièrement dans le département de Maine-et-Loire*, Paris, 1843
203. G. Lerat, *Etudes sur les origines, le développement et l'avenir des raffineries nantaises*, Paris, 1911
204. A. Maurois, Ch. Brisson, J. Clarenson, *Elbeuf, Louviers*, Elbeuf, 1951
205. J. Mouchet, 'L'Esprit public dans le Morbihan sous la Restauration', *Annales de Bretagne*, 1938
206. L. Ogès, *L'Agriculture dans le Finistère au milieu du XIXᵉ siècle*, Quimper, 1949
207. G. Richard, *La Métallurgie normande en 1845*, Paris, 1964

208. — *Histoire de la sidérurgie*, Paris, 1964
209. Ch. Robert-Muller, *Pêches et pêcheurs de la Bretagne atlantique*, Paris, 1944
210. J. Sion, *Les Paysans de la Normandie orientale*, Paris, 1909
211. E. Souvestre, *Les Derniers Bretons*, Paris, 1843
212. Abbé J. Y. Tanguy, *Une ville bretonne sous la Révolution, Saint-Pol-de-Léon*, Brest, 1903
213. C. Vallaux, *La Basse-Bretagne . . .* , Paris, 1906
214. J. Vidalenc, *Le Département de l'Eure sous la monarchie constitutionnelle*, Paris, 1952
215. — *L'Industrie dans les départements normands*

b. The Midi

References concerning voters' lists, official annual reports, and the archives of the Banque de France can be found in no. 4 of the present bibliography.

216. M. Agulhon, *The Republic in the Village*, Cambridge, 1983. First published by Plon, Paris, 1970
217. — *Une ville ouvrière au temps du socialisme utopique ; Toulon de 1800 à 1852*, Paris, 1970
218. *Annales du Midi* (Toulouse)
219. A. Armangaud, *Les Populations de l'Est-aquitain au début de l'époque contemporaine*, Paris, 1961
220. M. Blanchard, *Essais historiques sur les premiers chemins de fer du Midi languedocien et de la vallée du Rhône*, Montpellier, 1936
    G. Cholvy, *Religion et société au XIXᵉ siècle, le diocèse de Montpellier (1802–1894)*, Paris, 1972
221. Congrès national des Sociétés savantes, section d'Histoire moderne et contemporaine, Aix-Marseille, 1958
222. — Montpellier, 1961
223. — Nice, 1965
224. P. Droulers, *Action pastorale et problèmes sociaux sous la monarchie de Juillet chez Mgr d'Astras, archevêque de Toulouse*, Paris, 1953
225. R. Dugrand, *Villes et campagnes du Bas-Languedoc*, Paris, 1965
226. *Encyclopédie des Bouches-du-Rhône*, V–XI
227. J. Fourcassié, *Une ville a l'époque romantique ; Toulouse*, Paris, 1953
228. P. Georges, *La région du Bas-Rhône*, Paris, 1935
229. P. Guiral, *Marseille et l'Algérie, 1830–1841*, Paris, 1957
230. W. Joyce, La Vie locale dans le département des Bouches-du-Rhône sous la monarchie censitaire, unpublished thesis, Université d'Aix, 1951
231. J. Leflon, *Eugène de Mazenod, évêque de Marseille*, 3 vols., Paris, 1965
232. A. Pieyre, *Histoire de la ville de Nîmes depuis 1830 jusqu'à nos jours*, 3 vols., Nîmes, 1886–8
233. Ch. Portal, *Le département du Tarn au XIXᵉ siècle*, Albi, 1912
234. *Provence historique*
235. P. Seignour, *La Vie économique de Vaucluse de 1815 à 1848*, Aix, 1957
236. L. J. Thomas, *Montpellier, ville inconnue*, Montpellier, 1930
237. — *Montpellier, ville marchande*, Montpellier, 1936
238. J. Vidalenc (ed.), *Lettres de J. A. M. Thomas, préfet des Bouches-du-Rhône à Adolphe Thiers, 1831–1836*, Gap, 1953

c. Lyon and the region of Lyon

239. J. Arminjon, *La Population du département du Rhône, son évolution depuis le début du XIXe siècle*, Lyon, 1940
240. C. Beaulieu, *Histoire du commerce, de l'industrie et des fabriques de Lyon depuis leur origine jusqu'à nos jours*, Lyon, 1838
    R. Bezucha, 'Aspects du conflit des classes à Lyon, 1831–1834', *Mouvement social*, July–September 1971
241. Congrès des Sociétés savantes de Lyon, 1964
242. H. Dumolard, *La Terreur blanche dans l'Isère, J.-P. Didier et la conspiration de Grenoble*, Grenoble, 1928
243. F. Dutacq, *Histoire politique de Lyon pendant la révolution de 1848*, Paris, 1910
    G. Garrier, *Paysans du Beaujolais et du Lyonnais (1800–1970)*, Grenoble, 1973
244. J. L. Gras, *Histoire des premiers chemins de fer français*, Saint-Etienne, 1924
245. E. Herriot, 'Camille Jordan et la Restauration', *Revue d'Histoire de Lyon*, 1902
246. J. Ibarrola, *Structure sociale et Fortune mobilière et immobilière à Grenoble en 1847*, Paris, 1965
247. M. Laferrère, *Lyon, ville industrielle*, Paris, 1960
248. P. Léon, *La Naissance de la grande industrie en Dauphiné*, Paris, 1954
249. — 'La Région lyonnaise dans l'histoire économique et sociale de la France', *Revue historique*, 1961
250. Capitaine P. Montagne, *Le Comportement politique de l'armée à Lyon sous la monarchie de Juillet et la IIe République*, Paris, 1966
251. E. Pariset, *Histoire de la Fabrique lyonnaise*, Lyon, 1901
252. G. Ribe, *L'Opinion publique et la vie politique à Lyon 1815–1822*, Paris, 1957
253. F. Rivet, *La Navigation à vapeur sur la Saône et le Rhône, 1783–1883*, Paris, 1962
254. J. A. Roy, *Histoire de la famille Schneider et du Creusot de 1836 à 1841*, Paris, 1962
255. F. Rude, *Le Mouvement ouvrier à Lyon de 1827 à 1832*, Paris, 1944
256. L. Trénard, *Lyon, de l'Encyclopédie au préromantisme*, 2 vols., Grenoble, 1958
257. R. Voog, 'Les Problèmes religieux à Lyon pendant la monarchie de Juillet et la IIe Republique d'après les journaux ouvriers', *Cahiers d'Histoire*, 1963

d. Eastern France

258. J. Bapicot, *Arbois*, in the *Notes de géographie urbaine comtoise et montbéliardaise*, compiled by M. Chevalier, Paris, 1954
259. — *La Bourgeoisie alsacienne*, Sociétés savantes d'Alsace et des régions de l'Est, Strasbourg, 1954
260. H. Contamine, *Metz et la Moselle de 1814 à 1870*, 2 vols., Nancy, 1932
261. — *Les Conséquences financières des invasions de 1814 et de 1815 dans les départements de la Moselle et de la Meurthe*, Metz, 1932
262. J. Cousin, *L'Académie des sciences, belles-lettres et arts de Besançon (1752–1952)*, Besançon, 1954
263. S. Daveau, *Les Régions frontalières de la montagne jurassienne, étude de géographie humaine*, Paris, 1956
264. L. Febvre, *La Franche-Comté*, Paris, 1908
265. Cl. Fohlen (general ed.), *Histoire de Besançon*, II, Paris, 1965
266. — *La Décadence des forges franc-comtoises*, in honour of Professor Anthony Bebel, Genève, 1853
267. A. Gibert, *La Porte de Bourgogne et d'Alsace, étude géographique*, Besançon, 1930
    P. Gonnet, *La Société dijonnaise au XIXe siècle (1815–1890)*, Paris, 1974
268. G. Girard, 'La Disette de 1816–17 dans la Meurthe', *Annales de l'Est*, 1955

269. R. Haby, *Les Houillères lorraines et leur région*, Paris, 1965
270. — *Histoire de Lorraine*, Nancy, 1949
271. P. Huot-Pleuroux, *Le Recrutement sacerdotal dans le diocèse de Besançon de 1801 à 1960*, Besançon, 1966
272. G. Juillard, *La Vie rurale dans les plaines de Basse-Alsace*, Paris, 1953
273. M. M. Kahan-Rabecq, *La Classe ouvrière en Alsace pendant la monarchie de Juillet*, Paris, 1939
274. R. Laurent, *L'Agriculture en Côte-d'Or pendant la première moitié du XIXe siècle*, Dijon, 1931
275. — *Les Vignerons de la Côte-d'Or au XIXe siècle*, 2 vols., Dijon, 1957–8
276. R. Lebeau, *La Vie rurale dans les montagnes du Jura méridional, étude de géographie humaine*, Lyon, 1953
277. — *Les Lettres en Alsace*, Sociétés savantes d'Alsace et des régions de l'Est, Strasbourg, 1959
278. P. Leuillot, *L'Alsace au début du XIXe siècle*, 3 vols., Paris, 1959–61. I. *La Vie politique*, 1959. II. *Les Transformations économiques*, 1959. III. *Religion et culture*, 1960
279. — *La Première Restauration et les Cent-Jours en Alsace*, Paris, 1958
280. — *Paysans d'Alsace*, Sociétés savantes d'Alsace et des régions de l'Est, Strasbourg, 1959
281. F. Ponteil, *L'Opposition politique à Strasbourg sous la monarchie de Juillet, 1830–1848*, Paris, 1932
282. — 'La Renaissance catholique à Strasbourg, l'affaire Bautain', *Revue historique*, 1930
283. G. Richard, 'L'Esprit public en Lorraine au début de la Restauration', *Annales de l'Est*, 1933
284. R. Sédillot, *La Maison de Wendel de 1704 à nos jours*, Paris, 1958
285. — *Peugeot, de la crinoline à la 404*, Paris, 1960
286. P. P. Viard, 'La Disette de 1816–1817, particulièrement en Côte-d'Or', *Revue historique*, 1928

e. Northern France

287. R. Blanchard, *La Flandre*, Paris, 1905
288. A. de Calonne d'Avesne, *Histoire de la ville d'Amiens*, 3 vols., Amiens, 1899–1906
289. A. Demangeon, *La plaine picarde*, Paris, 1905
    M. Gillet, *Les Charbonnages du Nord de la France au XIXe siècle*, Paris, 1973
290. A. M. Gossez, *Le Département du Nord sous la IIe République*, Lille, 1904
291. J. Lambert-Dansette, *Quelques familles du patronat textile de Lille–Armentières (1789–1914)*, Lille, 1954
292. A. Lasserre, *La Situation des ouvriers de l'industrie textile dans la région lilloise sous la monarchie de Juillet*, Lausanne, 1952
293. P. Pierrard, *Lille et les Lillois*, Paris, 1967
294. P. Pinchemel, *Structures sociales et dépopulation dans les campagnes picardes de 1836 à 1936*, Paris, 1957
295. *Revue du Nord*

f. The southwest

296. Congrès national des Sociétés savantes, sections d'Histoire moderne et contemporaine, Bordeaux, 1957

297. P. Deffontaines, *Les Hommes et leurs travaux dans les pays de la moyenne Garonne*, Lille, 1932
298. Ch. Filloles, 'La Bourgeoisie landaise sous la monarchie de Juillet', *Bulletin de la Société de Borda*, 1970–1
299. P. Guillaume, *La Population de Bordeaux au XIXᵉ siècle*, Bordeaux, 1970
300. Ch. Higounet (general ed.), *Histoire de Bordeaux*, VI, Bordeaux, 1969
301. P. de Joinville, *Le Réveil économique de Bordeaux sous la Restauration; l'armateur Balguerie-Stuttenberg*, Paris, 1914
302. Abbé Lacouture, *Histoire religieuse et politique des Landes de 1800 à 1870*, Bordeaux, 1940
303. M. C. Larive, *La Vie mondaine à Pau sous la monarchie de Juillet*, Bordeaux, 1970

g. The central mountains

304. J. de Bergues La Garde, *Dictionnaire historique et biographique des hommes célèbres et de tous les illustres de la Corrèze*, Angers, 1871
305. L. Berland, *La Franc-maçonnerie limousine*, 1949
306. G. Bonnefoy, *Histoire de l'administration civile dans la province d'Auvergne*, IV, Paris, 1897
307. M. A. Carron, 'Prélude à l'exode rural en France: les migrations anciennes des travailleurs creusois', *Revue d'histoire économique et sociale*, 1965
308. M. Chaulanges, *L'Histoire vue de l'Auvergne*, III, Clermont-Ferrand, 1959
309. Congrès national des Sociétés savantes de Clermont-Ferrand, 1963
310. A. Corbin, 'Migrations temporaires et société rurale au XIXᵉ siècle, le cas du Limousin', *Revue historique*, October–December 1971
311. M. Deruau, *La Grande Limagne auvergnate et bourbonnaise*, Grenoble, 1951
312. A. Durand, *La Vie rurale dans les massifs volcaniques des Dores, du Cézallier, du Cantal et de l'Aubrac*, Aurillac, 1946
313. C. Grellier, *L'Industrie de la porcelaine en Limousin, ses origines, son évolution*, Paris, 1908
314. M. Nadaud, *Les Mémoires de Léonard (ancien garçon maçon)*, Bourganeuf, 1895

h. The Paris basin and the plains of central France

315. G. Boussinesq and G. Laurent, *Histoire de Reims*, II, Reims, 1933
316. J. P. Brunet, 'L'Industrialisation de la région de Saint-Denis', *Acta geographica*, 1970
317. — *Structure agraire et Economie rurale des plateaux tertiaires entre la Seine et l'Oise*, Caen, 1960
318. G. Charlemagne, *Le Pays d'Ardentes en Berry*, Paris, 1926
319. A. Chatelain, 'Une classe rurale au milieu de XIXᵉ siècle, les ouvriers agricoles de Seine et Oise', *Bulletin de la Société historique et géographique de la région parisienne*, 1955
320. A. Colomés, *Les Ouvriers textiles de la Champagne troyenne*, Bar-le-Duc, 1943
321. L. Desternes and G. Galland, 'La Réaction royaliste en Touraine', *Révolution française*, 1903
322. — 'La Réaction cléricale en Touraine', in *Révolution française*, 1903
323. R. Dion, *Le Val de Loire*, Tours, 1933
324. G. Dupeux, *Aspects de l'histoire politique et sociale du Loir-et-Cher*, Paris, 1962
325. Baron Dupin, *Le Morvan*, Paris, 1844
326. H. Forestier, 'Le Clergé et l'opinion dans l'Yonne sous la monarchie de Juillet', *Bulletin de la Société des sciences historiques de l'Yonne*, 1957–8

327. L. Gallicher, 'Quelques renseignements sur l'état de la production des forges du Berry (janvier 1841)', *Revue archéologique du Berry*, 1898

328. L. Guéneau, 'La Disette de 1816–1817 dans une région de production de blé, la Brie', *Revue d'Histoire moderne*, 1929

329. A. Huges, *Statistique du mouvement de la population de Seine-et-Marne, 1800 à 1896*, Melun, 1897

330. H. Lemoine, 'Le Département de Seine-et-Oise de l'An VII à 1871', *Revue de l'Histoire de Versailles et de Seine-et-Oise*, 1940

331. — 'L'Instruction primaire publique en Seine-et-Oise de 1789 à 1850', *Revue de l'Histoire de Versailles et de Seine-et-Oise*, 1940

332. C. Lévy, 'Les Paysans de l'Yonne vers 1848', *Annales de Bourgogne*, 1951

333. C. Marcilhacy, *Le Diocèse d'Orléans au milieu du XIXᵉ siècle*, Paris, 1969

334. J. P. Moreau, *La Vie rurale dans le sud-est du Bassin parisien entre les vallées de l'Armançon et de la Loire*, Paris, 1958

335. P. Pédelaborde, *L'Agriculture dans les plaines alluviales de la presqu'île de Saint-Germain-en-Laye*, Paris, 1961

336. J. Ricommard, *La Bonneterie à Troyes et dans le département de l'Aube . . .* , Paris, 1934

337. J. P. Rocher, 'Les elections dans l'Yonne sous la monarchie de Juillet', *Bulletin de la Société des sciences historiques et nationales de l'Yonne*, 1958–9

338. G. Thuillier, *Aspects de l'économie nivernaise au XIXᵉ siècle*, Paris, 1966

339. P.-L. de Vaudreuil, *Promenade de Paris à Bagnères-de-Luchon . . . Promenade de Bagnères-de-Luchon à Paris*, Paris, 1820–1

340. J. Bastié, *La Croissance de la banlieue parisienne*, Paris, 1964

341. A. des Cilleuls, *Histoire de l'administration parisienne au XIXᵉ siècle*, 2 vols., Paris, 1900

342. L. Chevalier, *La Formation de la population parisienne au XIXᵉ siècle*, Paris, 1950

343. — *Classes laborieuses, classes dangereuses à Paris pendant la première moitié du XIXᵉ siècle*, Paris, 1958

344. R. Clozier, *La Gare du Nord*, Paris, 1940

345. A. Daumard, *La Bourgeoisie parisienne de 1815 à 1848*, Paris, 1963

346. B. Gille, *Fonctions économiques de Paris, Paris fonction d'une capitale*, Paris, 1962

347. B. Léon, *Paris, histoire de la rue*, Paris, 1947
    G. Massa-Gille, *Histoire des emprunts de la ville de Paris (1814–1875)*, Paris, 1973

348. A. Morizet, *Du vieux Paris au Paris moderne, Haussmann et ses prédécesseurs*, Paris, 1932

349. M. Philipponneau, *La Vie rurale de la banlieue parisienne*, Paris, 1956

350. J. Pronteau, Constructions et aménagement des nouveaux quartiers de Paris (1820–1826)', *Histoire des Entreprises*, 1957, 5–32

SUPPLEMENT

Basic Studies

a. Political history and institutions

J. Cabanis, *Charles X, roi ultra*, Paris, 1972

E. Harpaz (ed.), *Benjamin Constant. Recueil d'articles: Le Mercure, la Minerve, la Renommée*, Geneva, 1972

— (ed.), *Benjamin Constant. Correspondance avec Goyet de la Sarthe, 1818–1822*, Geneva, 1973

J. Merriman (ed.), *1830 in France*, New York, 1975

D. Porch, *Army and revolution. France, 1815–1848*, London, 1974

P. Reboul, *Chateaubriand et le conservateur*, Paris, 1973

b. Foreign and colonial policy

A. Sked (ed.), *Europe's balance of power, 1815–1848*, London, 1979

c. Economy and society

E. Lavasseur, *Histoire des classes ouvrières et de l'industrie en France de 1789–1870*, 2 vols., Paris, 1903–4

d. Cultural and religious issues

D. G. Charlton, *Secular religions in France, 1815–1870*, Oxford, 1963

D. O. Evans, *Social romanticism in France, 1815–1848*, Oxford, 1951

C. Johnson, *Utopian communism in France: Cabet and the Icarians, 1839–1851*, Cornell, 1974

B. Reardon, *Liberalism and tradition. Aspects of Catholic thought in nineteenth-century France*, Cambridge, 1975

The Regions

b. The Midi

B. Fitzpatrick, *Catholic royalism in the department of the Gard, 1814–1852*, Cambridge, 1983

R. Huard (ed.), *Histoire de Nîmes*, Toulouse, 1975

c. Lyon and the region of Lyon

P. Cayez, *Métiers Jacquard et hauts fourneaux. Aux origines de l'industrie lyonnaise*, Lyon, 1978

f. The southwest

P. Mcphee, 'On rural politics in nineteenth-century France: the example of Rodès, 1789–1851', *Comparative Studies in Society and History*, 23, 1981

g. The central mountains

P. M. Jones, 'Political commitment and rural society in the southern Massif central', *European Studies Review*, 10, 1980

Index of names